Psychology and Law

To Maddie, because of everything you are and everything you will be.

Psychology and Law

Research and Practice

Curt R. Bartol

Anne M. Bartol

Los Angeles | London | New Delhi
Singapore | Washington DC

Los Angeles | London | New Delhi
Singapore | Washington DC

FOR INFORMATION:

SAGE Publications, Inc.
2455 Teller Road
Thousand Oaks, California 91320
E-mail: order@sagepub.com

SAGE Publications Ltd.
1 Oliver's Yard
55 City Road
London EC1Y 1SP
United Kingdom

SAGE Publications India Pvt. Ltd.
B 1/I 1 Mohan Cooperative Industrial Area
Mathura Road, New Delhi 110 044
India

SAGE Publications Asia-Pacific Pte. Ltd.
3 Church Street
#10-04 Samsung Hub
Singapore 049483

Printed in the United States of America

A catalog record of this book is available from the Library of Congress.

ISBN 978-1-4522-5891-1

This book is printed on acid-free paper.

Certified Chain of Custody
Promoting Sustainable Forestry
www.sfiprogram.org
SFI-01268

SFI label applies to text stock

Acquisitions Editor: Jerry Westby
Associate Editor: Theresa Accomazzo
Editorial Assistant: MaryAnn Vail
Production Editor: Libby Larson
Copy Editor: Teresa Herlinger
Typesetter: C&M Digitals (P) Ltd.
Proofreader: Scott Oney
Indexer: Sheila Bodell
Cover Designer: Janet Kiesel
Marketing Manager: Shari Countryman

14 15 16 17 18 10 9 8 7 6 5 4 3 2 1

Brief Contents

Detailed Contents

Preface

The relationship between psychology and law can be traced to the turn of the 20th century, when experiments in the psychological laboratory were found to be relevant to the law. Since at least that time, the two fields have been interrelated while retaining their independence. For more than 100 years, the relationship has developed, often gradually and cautiously, but always in a steady direction. Psychology and law today is well established as a mutually advantageous relationship and, for research psychologists, a vibrant field of study. Practicing psychologists find the requests for their services are ever increasing, as will be apparent throughout the book.

There are many observable differences between psychology and law, reflected in their assumptions, goals, and practices. Like all sciences, psychology is exploratory and its knowledge is evolving. Often this means that psychology cannot provide definitive answers to questions the legal system poses. For example, psychologists cannot say who would be the better parent, but they can evaluate parenting plans. They cannot predict with a high degree of certainty whether an individual will or will not be violent, but they can offer some assessment of the probability that a given individual will do harm to himself or others. Psychology also has accumulated a wide store of knowledge in areas such as human memory, cognitions, and decision making, which are relevant to the legal system.

The text, intended as a book for undergraduate and graduate students with serious interests in psychology and law, is based heavily on psychological concepts and research that are relevant to the law. Research on memory and cognition is relevant to eyewitness testimony. Research on group and individual decision making is relevant to the work of judges and juries. Research on the emotional and cognitive development of juveniles is relevant to juvenile responsibility for criminal acts as well as juvenile decision making. Research on risk assessment is relevant to the prevention of violence. These are but a few of many topics to be discussed in the book.

Numerous appellate court cases are cited throughout the book. In the hands of law professors and law students, the cases in this book would be subjected to extensive legal analysis. We use them not for that purpose, but rather as a springboard to cover psychological concepts and issues. The material presented is not simplistic, because psychology itself is not a simplistic science. Nevertheless, we have made the book "reader friendly" and contemporary by using many examples, identifying key concepts, and including discussion questions to accompany the cases and research studies that have been highlighted in boxes. Key concepts are listed at the end of each chapter, bolded when they are first discussed, and defined in a glossary.

The subject matter of the cases chosen relates to psychology, and the decisions themselves have typically led to more psychological research. For example, prior to the landmark *Miranda v. Arizona* case, suspects in police custody were routinely submitted to psychologically coercive interrogation techniques without being advised of their legal rights. The decision by the U.S. Supreme Court, requiring police to warn suspects, placed some limits on this practice but, as many readers undoubtedly know, this was not the last word on the subject. The *Miranda* case, however, eventually led many psychologists to ask, "Do people really understand these *Miranda* warnings?" as well as to design and validate instruments to measure this comprehension.

In addition to conducting research on legally relevant topics, psychologists interact with the law in many contexts. They serve as consultants, clinicians, and experts testifying in court. Professional organizations, most notably the American Psychological Association, submit briefs to appeals courts that summarize the research in given areas, such as research on adolescent decision making or the effects of discrimination.

Many mental health professionals associated with psychology and law conduct psychological assessments that are requested by lawyers and courts or mandated by statutes. For example, psychologists assess risk, they assess parenting plans, they assess children for educational purposes, they assess criminal defendants, they assess emotional suffering in civil suits, and they assess the capacity of individuals to write their wills and make health care decisions. Assessment is woven explicitly or implicitly into virtually every chapter of this book, and a special concluding chapter focuses directly on this topic.

Writing this book has been both challenging and stimulating. At the start of the journey, we anticipated there would be changes in both the law and psychological research—and that did indeed happen. Both fields are dynamic and constantly in flux, despite the fact that each is based on a solid body of theory, research, and—especially in the case of law—precedent. In addition, the news media often provide new information to illustrate concepts in the chapters. We believe the material covered herein is fascinating and hope the reader will as well.

⊠ Acknowledgments

A number of individuals have been with us and have offered support in many ways. Jerry Westby, SAGE publisher, again took on—with his usual competence and professional skills—the many supervisory tasks associated with producing the book. He has been a steady, extremely supportive administrator in all phases of this project, for which we are most grateful. His assistants, Terri Accomazzo and MaryAnn Vail, were very helpful. MaryAnn ably fielded questions, and Terri obtained reviews of early chapters, summarized the reviewer comments, and offered suggestions. We are deeply appreciative of these early reviewers: Barbara Abbott, *New England College;* Julie Allison, *Pittsburg State University;* Eve Brank, *University of Nebraska, Lincoln;* Jonathan Lewis, *University of North Texas, Denton;* Fadia M. Narchet, *University of New Haven;* Judith Rauenzahn, *Kutztown University;* and Elizabeth Swenson, *John Carroll University.* Production editor Brittany Bauhaus was most responsive to any questions we raised. We cannot praise enough the work of copyeditor Teresa Herlinger—or thank her sufficiently. She is professional, efficient, perceptive, tactful, witty, and patient; each of these characteristics has been well-demonstrated as we completed this project. A special thank you to Libby Larson for overseeing the final work on the book.

The usual gang—Gina, Ian, Soraya, Jim, Kai, Maddie, Darya, and Shannon—continues to be there to remind us of what matters most in our lives. As years go by, we realize more and more how much Madelene Gerrish Bartol—now 92—means to both of us. Extended family and friends could all be acknowledged and named, but Mom deserves very special mention.

About the Authors

Curt R. Bartol was a college professor for more than 30 years, teaching both undergraduate and graduate courses, including Biopsychology, Criminal Behavior, Juvenile Delinquency, Introduction to Forensic Psychology, Social Psychology, and Psychology and Law. He earned his PhD in personality/social psychology from Northern Illinois University in 1972. He was instrumental in creating and launching a graduate program in forensic psychology at Castleton State College in Vermont and served as its director for 6 years. As a licensed clinical psychologist, he has been a consulting police psychologist to local, municipal, state, and federal law enforcement agencies for more than 25 years. In addition to *Psychology and Law,* he has cowritten *Introduction to Forensic Psychology* (now in its 3rd ed.), *Criminal Behavior: A Psychosocial Approach* (now in its 10th ed.), *Juvenile Delinquency and Antisocial Behavior: A Developmental Perspective* (3rd ed.), and *Criminal and Behavioral Profiling*. He also coedited, with Anne Bartol, *Current Perspectives in Forensic Psychology and Criminal Justice* (3rd ed.). In addition, he was the editor of SAGE's *Criminal Justice and Behavior: An International Journal* for 17 years.

Anne M. Bartol earned an MA and a PhD in criminal justice from the State University of New York at Albany. She also holds an MA in journalism from the University of Wisconsin–Madison. She taught criminal justice, sociology, and journalism courses over a 20-year college teaching career and has worked as a journalist and a social worker in child and adolescent protective services. In addition to *Psychology and Law,* she has coauthored *Criminal Behavior, Introduction to Forensic Psychology, Criminal and Behavioral Profiling,* and *Juvenile Delinquency.* She has also served as book review editor and managing editor of *Criminal Justice and Behavior.*

Introduction

This book is an invitation to think about common knowledge in a different way. It is common knowledge, for example, that everyone sleeps, we all experience stress, our relationships with others are imperfect, and children are not miniature adults. It is not surprising that psychology—commonly defined as the science of human behavior—has something to say about all of this. Psychologists have studied sleep, stress, healthy and dysfunctional relationships, and child development—and these represent only a minute portion of subjects that make psychology a fascinating enterprise. What we invite the reader to do in this book is appreciate the interaction of psychology and the law with regard to these and other topics. Let us illustrate with two legal cases.

In the early morning hours of May 23, 1987, twenty-three-year-old Toronto resident Kenneth Parks arose from the couch where he had fallen asleep while watching *Saturday Night Live*. He put on his coat and reportedly sleepwalked to his car, got into the vehicle, and drove (apparently while still asleep) 14 miles to the home of his in-laws and broke in. Both were asleep in bed at the time. He stabbed his mother-in-law to death with a kitchen knife and seriously assaulted his father-in-law. Immediately after the incident, Parks drove to a nearby police station. He said the next thing he could recall was being at the police station asking for help and confessing to the killing.

Parks was charged with first-degree murder and attempted murder. At his trial, he presented a defense of automatism, stating that at the time the incidents took place, he was sleepwalking and was not aware of what he was doing. Briefly, **automatism** is defined as behavior performed in a state of mental unconsciousness or dissociation, without full awareness (Black, 1990). Parks had a history of sleepwalking and had been experiencing significant stress in his life, but there was no indication he had ever committed violence, either awake or asleep. In fact, his mother-in-law had called the

6'5" man the "gentle giant." Parks admitted he probably committed the violence but did not have the necessary criminal intent. The trial court heard from two behavioral scientists and three mental health professionals called by the defense. They testified that Parks was sleepwalking at the time the violence occurred, that sleepwalking was a relatively common sleep disorder, and that there was no medical or psychological treatment designed to prevent it. Parks was acquitted of the crimes. In a final ruling on this case, the Supreme Court of Canada (*Regina v. Parks*, 1992) set guidelines for a sleepwalking defense and provided some clarity on issues relating to injurious acts and consciousness during the human sleep cycle.

In the United States, sleepwalking is rarely used as a defense to criminal conduct, but some legal commentators indicate it is only a matter of time before automatism reaches more courts (Melton, Petrila, Poythress, & Slobogin, 2007). Although violent behavior during sleep is relatively rare, it presents troubling implications for the legal system (Weiss et al., 2011). The notion that it is possible to engage in complex injurious or violent behavior while asleep is usually met with skepticism. During the night of January 16, 1997, Scott Falater, a 41-year-old product manager with Motorola, claimed he was sleepwalking when he killed his wife of 20 years. He stabbed her 44 times with a hunting knife, wrapped the bloody knife in his clothes, and hid it and other evidence in the wheel well of the family car. When he returned to a still-alive wife, he dragged her to a swimming pool and held her head underwater until she drowned. Falater did not deny killing her, but stated he did not remember anything about the incident because he was sleeping throughout. Like Park, he had a history of sleepwalking. The prosecutor in the case said the sleepwalking defense was complete nonsense and informed the press he would seek the death penalty if Falater was convicted. It is clear that the prosecutor believed that Falater was malingering, or faking, and was conscious of his actions at the time of the offense. Experts testified for both the defense and prosecution, disagreeing over whether the violence was committed while sleepwalking. According to experts for the prosecution, Falater's actions were too calculated and deliberate for him to be sleepwalking. The jury found him guilty of first-degree murder, and the court sentenced him to life in prison without parole (*Arizona v. Falater*, 1997).

Why do we open this chapter—and this book—with two cases illustrating sleepwalking? This is not a topic that most readers probably associate with psychology, yet neuropsychologists are at the forefront of research in this area. Advances in sleep research have discovered that complex, violent, and potentially injurious acts can, and do, arise during the sleep cycle, without conscious awareness, and therefore, without responsibility (Mahowald & Schenck, 2000). Therefore, cases in which defendants deny responsibility for violent or injurious acts they committed while supposedly asleep appear to be on the increase (Cramer Bornemann, Mahowald, & Schenck, 2006; Mahowald & Schenck, 2000; Weiss et al., 2011). Many of these cases have involved sexual assault and rape. However, the fact that someone injures another while purportedly asleep does not necessarily mean that person will not be held accountable, as we saw in the two cases discussed above. Psychological research may help explain this phenomenon, but the law will decide what to do with that explanation.

These two cases—Parks and Falater—illustrate the fascinating intersection of law and psychology. In each case, respected researchers and behavioral scientists informed the court about sleep and the not-so-common phenomenon of sleepwalking. They also discussed **malingering**, which is the deliberate faking or feigning of a disorder to achieve a particular desired outcome (VandenBos, 2007). In the Falater case, we also saw contrasting opinions from experts testifying for the defense and the prosecution. This is a common feature of the adversarial process that psychologists often find themselves a part of, as we discuss later in the chapter.

Goals and Definitions

This book is about psychological knowledge as it pertains to the law. It is designed to educate students about contemporary psychological research and theories that are relevant to the legal system, particularly but not exclusively as represented by the courts. Research indicates that students—though they may be very interested—know very little about psychology and law (Stark-Wroblewski, Wiggins, & Ryan, 2006). According to Stark-Wroblewski et al., "it appears that students' knowledge of psychology and law related careers is not commensurate with their levels of interest in these areas" (p. 275). One of the major goals of this book is to fill this gap. (For information on activities and careers in psychology and law, see Boxes 1-1 and 1-2.)

Throughout the book, you will find reference to court cases and to pretrial and posttrial proceedings. Occasionally, we will refer to psychology as it relates to the legislative process, such as the framing of bills or the passage of laws. Sleep research, malingering, and expert testimony are only a few of numerous topics that will capture your attention throughout the book.

The field of psychology and law is extremely diverse, and it is expanding and changing rapidly. A substantial portion of the available research in psychology and how it relates to legal issues has been published since the 1980s, so it remains a relatively new field. Furthermore, psychology and law is a vibrant specialty with the potential for considerable additional growth in the future (Heilbrun & Brooks, 2010). This is reflected in the work of a special section of the American Psychological Association (APA), Division 41, the American Psychology-Law Society (AP-LS). Its many activities include conducting a survey of career opportunities in psychology and law, publishing online graduate school information, studying special ethical problems in expert testimony, surveying women's issues in psychology and law, and providing comprehensive information for anyone interested in the field. Students—both undergraduate and graduate—may join the division as Associates-at-Large.

Definitions of Psychology and Law

"Psychology and law" is often used interchangeably with "forensic psychology," but there is a distinction. (*Forensic* originates from the Latin adjective *forensis*, which means of or before a forum or place of assembly—where discussions and debates of law or justice were held in ancient Rome.) In recent years, forensic psychology has been both narrowly and broadly defined (Bartol & Bartol, 2013; DeMatteo, Marczyk, Krauss, & Burl, 2009). Narrowly defined, forensic psychology is restricted to clinical work performed for and presented to the judicial system. As DeMatteo et al. (2009) note, the narrow definition encompasses only clinically based practitioners, such as clinical psychologists, counseling psychologists, school psychologists, or other specialists who testify in or consult with courts. Research psychologists who conduct research and do not consider themselves clinical or practicing psychologists are excluded from the definition. Broadly defined, forensic psychology includes both clinicians and researchers, and it includes activities related directly to the courtroom as well as both activities and situations *before* they reach the courtroom and *after* going through the civil and criminal justice systems. For example, a broad conception of forensic psychology not only includes such professional activities as trial consultation, courtroom testimony, and court-ordered child custody evaluations (all of which would be within the narrow definition), but also includes research on lie detection or eyewitness testimony by a nonclinician. Some (e.g., Bartol & Bartol, 2013; Weiner & Otto, 2014) include topics related to law enforcement (such as the screening and selection of candidates) and corrections (such as clinical services to offenders) within the realm of forensic psychology.

There continues to be debate as to the proper definition of forensic psychology, however. The most recent *Specialty Guidelines for Forensic Psychology* (American Psychological Association, 2013b) describes forensic psychology broadly but also emphasizes that it is practitioner oriented. However, the guidelines do state that practitioners can be researchers as well as clinicians. According to the guidelines,

> *forensic* psychology refers to professional practice by any psychologist working within any subdiscipline of psychology (e.g., clinical, developmental, social, cognitive) when applying the scientific, technical, or specialized knowledge of psychology to the law to assist in addressing legal, contractual, and administrative matters. . . . *Such professional conduct is considered forensic from the time the practitioner reasonably expects to, agrees to, or is legally mandated to provide expertise on an explicitly psycholegal issue.* (p. 7, emphasis added)

These guidelines, revised from a previous edition called *Specialty Guidelines for Psychologists* (Committee on Ethical Guidelines for Forensic Psychologists, 1991), are undoubtedly of great benefit to psychologists providing expertise to the law.

The main topic of this text, psychology and law—which sometimes is referred to as legal psychology—can be regarded as a subdivision of a *broadly defined* forensic psychology, but it is better defined standing alone. Psychology and law is essentially the interaction between two disciplines; it encompasses any and all topics that are of legal interest. As such, psychology and law is nearly infinite in scope, limited only by the creativity of scholars and practitioners in disparate fields. As we will note shortly, other mental health and behavioral science professionals play prominent roles in the law as well, often in collaboration with psychologists. Separating psychology and law from forensic psychology allows us to avoid definitional and territorial dilemmas and to explore interesting areas pertaining to the relationship between psychology and the legal system in greater depth.

◪ Psychology and Law: Three Approaches

Over 30 years ago, Craig Haney (1980) suggested a perceptive approach to the psychology and law relationship, which we adopt and integrate throughout this text. He believed it useful to distinguish three relationships: (1) **psychology *in* the law**, (2) **psychology *and* the law**, and (3) **psychology *of* the law**. These three relationships are important in identifying the various roles that most psychologists take when working with the legal system.

It is important to emphasize that, though this text focuses on the professional roles of psychologists, other professionals may be equally important. They include psychiatrists, social workers, certified special educators, and psychiatric nurses, to name but a few. As we will mention in chapters ahead, these professionals work both individually and in teams to conduct research, consult with the legal system, and operate clinics offering services in legal contexts.

These cooperative efforts across disciplines have resulted in some blurring of the professional lines and, fortunately, less animosity between professionals than was displayed in the past. Although each profession maintains its separate identity and associations, we see increasingly more collaboration in both work settings and publications. In this spirit, for example, academic journals publish interdisciplinary articles, often coauthored by professionals from different disciplines. One current handbook for professionals (Drogin, Dattilio, Sadoff, & Gutheil, 2011) consists of multiple chapters, each of which is written by a psychologist and a psychiatrist. Therefore, while we cite in particular the work of psychologists, we acknowledge the important contributions of other professionals as well. Often we refer to clinicians and mental health practitioners, rather than to psychologists, to emphasize the interdisciplinary nature of the expertise available to the law.

BOX 1-1 WORK SETTINGS OF PSYCHOLOGISTS WHO PARTICIPATE IN PSYCHOLOGY AND LAW ACTIVITIES

Based on recent statistics (Griffin, 2011), independent practice is the primary work setting of psychologists involved in psychology and law activities (43%). These are usually clinically trained, such as clinical psychologists, counseling psychologists, or school psychologists. Some clinically trained practitioners prefer to call themselves forensic psychologists, and in some states they are certified as such. In fact, in some jurisdictions, certification is a minimum requirement for testifying on such matters as the defendant's competency to stand trial or sanity, topics to be discussed in Chapter 4. Those psychologists in independent practice also conduct risk assessments, perform child custody evaluations in family law proceedings, and assess disability claims, among other activities.

Another 25% of psychologists in psychology and law indicate they work in university or other academic settings. Most likely, they engage in teaching and research endeavors but also offer consulting services. Twelve percent of those psychologists involved in psychology and law activities said they worked in a hospital or other human service setting. Ten percent surveyed identified governmental settings, which probably involve state-sponsored psychological clinics, Homeland Security agencies, correctional facilities, and state and local police agencies. Almost 99% of the surveyed psychologists indicated they have a doctorate degree. Some have both a doctorate in psychology and a law degree.

Career opportunities in psychology and law are promising, but another recent survey (Buck et al., 2012) indicates there are gender disparities, as there are in many professions. Although women are at least as likely as men to obtain advanced degrees in this field, and although they readily obtain entry-level positions in both academic and nonacademic spheres, they often do not rise as rapidly in the ranks, despite their competence or level of productivity. This tendency to not progress as rapidly as men is referred to in the literature as the "leaky pipeline" effect. The survey by Buck et al.—an anonymous survey of 738 female members of the American Psychology-Law Society (AP-LS)—indicated that gender disparities were particularly evident in academe. However, respondents in all settings expressed concerns over balancing work and life obligations. The results of the survey highlight the critical importance of recognizing the contributions of all members of professional associations and providing career assistance and mentoring to reduce disparities within professions.

Psychology in the Law

Of the three relationships described by Haney, the psychology *in* the law relationship is the most common. In this situation, attorneys and judges utilize psychologists and their knowledge and experience to help in the resolution of cases. Most of the psychologists involved in this relationship are counseling, clinical, or forensic psychologists with some legal training and experience. Let's take, for example, the family court system, which is technically a subset of civil law and is covered in Chapter 9. Family courts today are widely considered overwhelmed, due to large volumes of cases often associated with both economic crises and natural disasters. The family law courts handle a large variety of cases, including but not limited to child custody requests, domestic violence restraining orders, divorce matters, care of the elderly, requests for child and spousal support, child neglect, and delinquency proceedings. Traditionally, the role of psychologists in the family court system has been relatively limited and clearly defined (Juhas, 2011). However, in light of the shifting needs and extended duties of the family court in recent years, the roles of psychologists have also expanded significantly (Juhas, 2011). It is noteworthy that psychologists are the most preferred experts in cases involving child custody (Bow, Gottlieb, & Gould-Saltman, 2011).

As illustrated above, then, the psychology *in* the law relationship is typically a clinical and consulting one. In both criminal and civil contexts, psychologists conduct various assessments whose results are communicated to judges and lawyers or even advise lawyers on strategies for interviewing witnesses or selecting jurors. Numerous handbooks and articles are available to assist mental health practitioners in conducting this clinical work (e.g., Grisso, 2003; Heilbrun, Grisso, Goldstein, & Laduke, 2013; Melton et al., 2007; Weiner & Otto, 2014). In addition, the American Psychological Association (APA) provides guidelines to advise clinicians. Among the most recent are the above-cited *Specialty Guidelines for Forensic Psychology* (APA, 2013), *Guidelines for Assessment of and Intervention With Persons With Disabilities* (APA, 2011), and the *Guidelines for Child Custody Evaluations in Family Law Proceedings* (APA, 2010b). These and additional guidelines will be referred to in later chapters. Finally, all psychologists who belong to the APA are expected to act consistently with the standards in the document *Ethical Principles of Psychologists and Code of Conduct* (EPPCC; APA, 2002). Guidelines are advisory in nature, whereas standards hold greater force. For example, a psychologist who violates the EPPCC may face censure by the APA and even be barred from membership.

Psychology and the Law

In this relationship, psychology remains a separate discipline, analyzing and examining various components of the law and the court processes from a psychological perspective. Psychology *and* the law represents a relationship where psychologists conduct basic and applied research into the most challenging issues faced by the legal system. With the execution of well-designed studies and the thoughtful formulation of theory to tie the results of these experiments together, psychology can develop an impressive body of psychological knowledge relevant and helpful to the law. The sleep research mentioned at the beginning of this chapter is one example. Another is the research on eyewitness testimony and lineup identifications. Mistakes in identifying criminal suspects have—far too many times—implicated innocent people (Dror & Bucht, 2012). Research by psychologist Elizabeth Loftus and others has cogently demonstrated why these mistakes happen and has suggested ways to avoid them. Professor Loftus's research is covered in Chapter 5. Psychologist Saul Kassin and his colleagues have conducted considerable research on confessions and discovered that many confessions—even to serious crimes—are less reliable than previously assumed. Psychologists Thomas Grisso, Allison Redlich, Kirk Heilbrun, Mark Cunningham, and Richard Rogers, among others, have studied issues relating to mentally disordered offenders, comprehension of one's rights, inmates on death row, and malingering. A majority of these research psychologists in the psychology *and* the law relationship are social psychologists, cognitive psychologists, neuropsychologists, community psychologists, and—more generally—human experimental psychologists. The following are additional examples of questions research psychologists try to answer:

- Can decision making by jurors really be unaffected by information they are told to disregard?
- Are some people better at detecting lies than others?
- How reliable and valid is criminal profiling?
- Does human memory work well under stressful and traumatic circumstances?
- Do mentally disordered individuals have the ability to make decisions in their own best interest?
- Can hypnosis uncover long-lost memories?
- Under what conditions do false confessions to a crime occur?
- Can courts find untainted jurors in the age of the Internet?

In the psychology *and* law relationship, psychology tries to answer questions like these and communicate them to those working within the legal system. The communication may take the form of courtroom testimony or research briefs filed with courts of appeal (to be discussed in Chapter 2). Psychological research also finds its way into judicial conferences; bar association meetings; and newsletters, journals, and books accessed by the legal community. In this sense, the relationship is truly interdisciplinary and independent. Even if the legal system chooses not to change its policies and procedures in the direction of the scientific evidence, the body of psychological knowledge remains intact.

We make no pretense that the legal system will change, even with knowledge of sound psychological principles, research, and theory. Law's practices are built upon a foundation of long traditions and conservative attitudes toward innovations. The legal system in most societies does not wish to be a weathervane, shifting with every new idea or untested theory that comes along. Understandably, it does not alter its practices unless there is a cogent reason for doing so. However, it is precisely the mutually independent psychology *and* law relationship that holds promise for significant improvements in both disciplines. An incisive comment by John Conley (2000) illustrates the nature of the relationship well:

> Just as lawyers-in-training must be taught to appreciate the culture of social science, so social scientists must develop a greater appreciation of the culture and traditions of law. Irrational as some of these traditions may seem, they are ancient and deeply ingrained. (p. 287)

Further below, we will cover key differences between psychology and law.

Psychology of the Law

The third relationship, psychology *of* the law, represents a more abstract approach to law as a determinant of behavior. It tries to understand the way that law seeks to control behavior as well as how people react to and interact with the law. The following questions underscore this focus.

- How does law affect society, and how does society affect laws?
- How successful are laws and the consequences for their violation in controlling and altering human behavior?
- Why are some laws embraced or tolerated and others resisted?

Psychology *of* the law poses and grapples with questions such as these. Social psychologists, political psychologists, and psychologists working on policy issues within government agencies tend to be among the vanguard in this relationship.

A significant contribution in the psychology of the law area is the book *Crimes of Obedience* (Kelman & Hamilton, 1989), which identifies social psychological factors that operate in individuals who commit crimes or other illegal actions at the direction of those in authority. These phenomena were pertinent as long ago as the Vietnam War (e.g., in the notorious My Lai massacre), and as recently as Abu Ghraib prison, where some military personnel abused and degraded detainees. The topic is also highly relevant to corporate crime, such as when someone in a management position participates in fraudulent practices at the direction of a chief financial officer. Another good example of scholarship in psychology *of* the law is Tyler's (1990) *Why People Obey the Law*, an incisive examination of psychological principles associated with legal behavior. Like Kelman and Hamilton, Tyler tries to understand both why individuals defy the law and why they conform to it.

In sum, Haney (1980) proposed an excellent framework for thinking about the relationship between psychology and law. The present book includes material relevant to each of the above three relationships, although it focuses on the first two. It is not a "how to" book, but it often describes how psychologists do their work, including what tests or measures they employ. It does not train you in how to testify in court, prepare a profile of a serial murderer, or provide an opinion about which of two parents should be given custody of a minor child. Students of psychology know that extensive education is required before anyone acquires expertise to engage in these activities (see Box 1-2 for career path possibilities in psychology and law).

BOX 1-2 EDUCATION AND TRAINING IN PSYCHOLOGY AND LAW

The American Psychology-Law Society's (AP-LS) *Guide to Graduate Programs in Forensic and Legal Psychology* (available at http://ap-ls.org/education/GraduatePrograms.php) lists more than two dozen doctoral programs (in both the United States and Canada) that offer clinical training in psychology and law (see also Packer & Borum, 2013). There are also 15 doctorate programs that offer nonclinical training in psychology and law (Packer & Borum, 2013). The clinical training programs usually require a 1- or 2-year internship in a clinical or forensic setting.

As of this writing, seven programs allow students to pursue a degree in law (JD, or Doctor of Jurisprudence) while simultaneously or sequentially completing the requirements for a doctoral degree in psychology (PhD or PsyD). The first law and psychology graduate program was developed at the University of Nebraska (Lincoln) in 1974 and remained for many years the largest and most diverse program in the field, offering both clinical and nonclinical training. Prospective students in a majority of the psychology and law graduate programs must be admitted to both the law school and the department of psychology.

Although there are several doctoral programs that prepare students for specialties in psychology and law, there are many other paths that may be taken to gain entry into this field. For example, doctoral programs in clinical, school, or counseling psychology may provide an excellent opportunity to gain entry into forensic practice, especially if the program has courses in psychology and law as well as internships in forensic settings. A significant number of colleges and universities do offer these courses and internships (DeMatteo et al., 2009). Postdoctoral experiences in psychology and law settings will help immeasurably in developing a professional career in the area. For those students interested in research involving psychology and law issues, doctoral programs in social, cognitive, developmental, experimental, community, neuro-, or organizational psychology are very good choices. Programs are continually changing in focus, research interests, and degrees offered, so interested students should consult specific colleges and universities for updated information.

There are now more than 24 masters programs that identify themselves as providing specialized training in psychology and law (http://ap-ls.org/education/Masters.php). The master's degree by itself does not result in a license to practice psychology, since most states require a doctoral degree to be able use the title "psychologist" (Packer & Borum, 2013).

However, it can lead to a number of career opportunities, including those in forensic settings (see Zaitchik, Berman, Whitworth, & Palatania, 2007). The master's degree in psychology and law might also prepare students to enter and complete training in a doctoral program.

Another excellent source for information on graduate study in psychology and law is the *Guide to Graduate Programs in Forensic and Legal Psychology 2010–2011* (http://ap-ls.org/education/Guide to Graduate Programs in Forensic and Legal Psychology 4-9-12.pdf). The guide is full of helpful information, including tables detailing requirements for admission; available grants, stipends, assistantships, and internships; and the average time to complete each of the programs.

Although this is not a how-to book, it does require the reader's basic understanding of the philosophy and methods of the behavioral sciences, because we will discuss many research studies applicable to the legal process. Despite the rapid growth of research in psychology and law, there is still a great need for well-designed and well-executed studies directed at the many legal assumptions about human behavior. There is an even stronger need for psychological theories that encompass and explain the results of this research.

Ways of Knowing and the Methods of Science

It is helpful to set the stage for a discussion of psychological research by touching a bit more on the philosophy of science. The work of American philosopher Charles Peirce is instructive. Peirce outlined four general ways through which humans develop beliefs and knowledge about their world (Kerlinger, 1973). First, there is the **method of tenacity**, where people hold firmly to their beliefs about others because they "know" them to be true and correct, simply because they have always believed and known them to be true and correct. These beliefs are tightly embraced, even in the face of contradictory evidence: "I know I'm right, regardless of what others say or the evidence indicates."

The second way of knowing and developing beliefs is the **method of authority**. Here, people believe something because individuals and institutions in authority proclaim it to be so. If the courts over the years have said it is so, it is so. If a well-recognized and respected legal scholar makes an argument in favor of or against a proposition, that scholar's name is cited as authoritative evidence for the proposition's soundness or unsoundness. Education is partly based on this method of knowing, with authority originating from teachers, scholars, experts, and the great masters they cite. Elementary school children often quote the authority of their teacher as indisputable evidence in support of an argument; college students may assert, "It says so in the book." Tyler's (1990) research on why people obey the law, however, suggests that this expressed allegiance to authority will not necessarily translate to action unless people believe in the *legitimacy* of the authoritative source.

The **a priori method** is a third way of obtaining knowledge. Evidence is believed correct because "it only stands to reason" and is a product of logical deduction. The a priori method is the dominant approach to knowledge in the legal process. The legal system is replete with formal rules that govern the admissibility of evidence and are intended to present information in a logical, orderly fashion. The legal system also relies heavily—although not exclusively—on precedent, or the principles of law that have already been developed in past cases. The method of authority, then, is also crucial to law. Primary sources such as court decisions, statutes, constitutions, and administrative regulations are consulted by attorneys as they prepare their cases and by judges as they render their decisions. To a lesser extent, law is also derived from secondary sources, such as law reviews, legal treatises, social science journals, books, and other reference works. Basically, however, legal knowledge is derived after consultation with previous authority and a subsequent process of deduction.

The fourth way of obtaining knowledge is the **method of science**, which is the testing of a statement or set of statements through observations and systematic research. On the basis of this systematic study, statements about natural events or processes are revised, reconstructed, or discarded. Science is an enterprise under constant change, modification, and expansion rather than an absolute, unalterable fact-laden system. Science teaches us that there are few certainties in the natural world and that we should base our decisions and expectations on "the best of our knowledge" at any particular time in history. The science of behavior, of course, is full of enormous challenges. As forensic psychologist Diane Follingstad (2010) astutely stated in her acceptance speech at the American Psychology-Law Association convention in Vancouver, British Columbia, "The study of human lives is difficult to do well, and even when done well, our research is only too often, only suggestive. This is our cross to bear" (p. HC 16).

Peirce's four methods of knowing provide a rough framework for determining the source of one's knowledge, and they will be useful guides throughout the remainder of the book. With the possible exception of the method of tenacity, each method has its place in the accumulation of knowledge, as long as we recognize which method we are using to obtain our knowledge and also understand the limitations of each. Authoritative sources and reasoning both are valuable contributors to our beliefs and opinions. The method of science provides us with additional information about the "soundness" of our authoritative and logical knowledge, and it promotes a critical and cautious stylistic way of thinking about our beliefs.

Scientific knowledge, because it is based on systematic observations, hypothesis testing, experiments, and testable statements, places itself permanently at risk of being falsified or shown to be incorrect. The knowledge is constantly updated to account for observations and experiments, and scientists try to make predictions beyond their present experience. Ultimately, scientific knowledge seeks the underlying order of things. The method of science is a testable, self-corrective approach to knowledge that offers one of the most powerful sources available for the understanding of human behavior.

⊠ Courts and the Method of Science

Courts often turn to scientific experts in numerous fields for help in understanding complex matters that are beyond the knowledge of the average layperson. The ballistics expert, the blood spatter analyst, the cancer researcher, the marine biologist, the child developmentalist, the sleep researcher, and the clinical psychologist are all examples. Expert testimony is defined as

> opinion evidence of some person who possesses special skill or knowledge in some science, profession or business which is not common to the average man and which is possessed by the expert by reason of his special study or experiences. (Black, 1990, p. 578)

Before admitting such expert testimony into a court proceeding, a judge must be satisfied that an expert has the proper credentials and that the expert's knowledge is sound. In addition, the court must be convinced that the expert testimony is supported by sound science. However, as noted by Jane Goodman-Delahunty (1997), "The introduction of expert testimony in legal proceedings, particularly testimony regarding social and behavioral scientific evidence, has rarely been accomplished without controversy" (p. 122).

Throughout the text, we will encounter many cases in which expert testimony was introduced, as it was in the sleep disorder cases covered briefly early in the chapter. We are of course most interested in experts on psychological issues. Not everyone claiming expertise can testify, nor is every topic deemed to require expert testimony. Put another way, expert testimony will not necessarily be admitted into a court proceeding. For example, in all courts a minimum academic degree is expected, and in some, the person offering to testify must hold specific certifications. However, in addition to the qualifications of the individual, the topic on which she or he seeks to testify must also be assessed. In some courts, testimony on psychological profiling, hypnosis, or various "syndromes" has not been accepted. Below, we review the legal tests that are applied in determining whether expert testimony should be allowed.

The *Frye* Standard

Before 1993, the most frequently cited case on the admissibility of scientific evidence was *Frye v. United States,* decided by the U.S. Court of Appeals of the District of

Columbia in 1923. In that case, the trial court was asked to admit polygraph evidence that supported James Alphonzo Frye's contention that he was not guilty of robbery and murder. The 19-year-old Frye had taken and passed a "systolic blood pressure deception test" administered by lawyer-psychologist William Marston, who was by far the most influential American psychologist associated with the legal system during this time. He held three degrees from Harvard, a bachelor's degree, a law degree, and a PhD in psychology. Moreover, he was the first psychologist to receive a faculty appointment as professor of legal psychology at American University. James Frye's attorney had asked that Marston be allowed to testify to the results of his polygraph examination, but the trial court denied the request. The attorney then asked if Marston could conduct the test in the jury's presence. That request was also denied. When Frye's attorney appealed, the Court of Appeals upheld the decision of the lower court. Quoting from the brief submitted by Frye's lawyer, the appeals court agreed that,

> When the question involved does not lie within the range of common experience or common knowledge, but requires special experience or special knowledge, then the opinions of witnesses skilled in that particular science, art, or trade to which the question relates are admissible in evidence. (p. 1014)

However, the court also said,

> Just when a scientific principle or discovery crosses the line between the experimental and demonstrable stages is difficult to define. Somewhere in this twilight zone the evidential force of the principle must be recognized, and while courts will go a long way in admitting expert testimony deduced from a well-recognized scientific principle or discovery, the thing from which the deduction is made must be sufficiently established to have gained general acceptance in the particular field in which it belongs. (p. 1014)

Then the appeals court continued:

> We think the systolic blood pressure deception test has not yet gained such standing and scientific recognition among physiological and psychological authorities as would justify the courts in admitting expert testimony deduced from the discovery, development, and experiments thus far made. (p. 1014)

In short, *Frye* made "general acceptance" of scientific knowledge the standard or test for admitting expert scientific testimony into federal courts. If the knowledge was not recognized and accepted by the scientific community at large—and the systolic blood pressure test administered by Marston was not—it should *not* be admitted as scientific evidence. Eventually, as the polygraph was developed in more sophisticated fashion, it became more acceptable as evidence in courts, though it is not universally accepted and is usually admitted into court only at the defendant's request (Iacono & Patrick, 2006).

For the greater part of the 20th century, the *Frye* "general acceptance" test was widely applied by federal courts, and many state courts accepted the same standard. In 1975, however, Congress adopted a slightly different standard in its Federal Rules of Evidence (FRE), the rules that govern the admissibility of evidence at trials in federal district courts. Many states adopt evidence rules that are patterned on federal rules (Black, 1990). Specifically, Rule 702 referred to the reliability of the evidence rather than its general acceptance (see Box 1-3). Even after these rules were passed, state and federal courts continued applying a variety of standards for admitting expert evidence (including the *Frye* standard) and with varying rigor (Shuman & Sales, 1999). It is not surprising, then, that the U.S. Supreme Court attempted to clarify the issue.

[handwritten margin note: reliability v. general acceptance]

The *Daubert* Standard

In 1993, the U. S. Supreme Court, in what is now considered a far-reaching, landmark case (*Daubert v. Merrell Dow Pharmaceuticals, Inc.*), issued a decision that primarily supported the federal rules of evidence, but also gave approval to *Frye*'s "general acceptance" approach.

BOX 1-3 TWO FEDERAL RULES OF EVIDENCE REGARDING TESTIMONY

Article VII: Opinions and Expert Testimony

Rule 701: Opinion Testimony by Lay Witnesses

If the witness is not testifying as an expert, the witness's testimony in the form of opinions or inferences is limited to those opinions or inferences which are (a) rationally based on the perception of the witness, and (b) helpful to clear understanding of the witness' testimony or the determination of a fact in issue, and (c) not based on scientific, technical, or other specialized knowledge within the scope of Rule 702.

Rule 702: Testimony by Experts

If scientific, technical, or other specialized knowledge will assist the trier of fact to understand the evidence or to determine a fact in issue, a witness qualified as an expert by knowledge, skill, experience, training, or education, may testify thereto in the form of an opinion or otherwise, if (1) the testimony is based upon sufficient facts or data, (2) the testimony is the product of reliable principles and methods, and (3) the witness has applied the principles and methods reliably to the facts of the case.

In the *Daubert* case, two minor children and their parents sued Merrell Dow Pharmaceuticals, Inc., arguing that the children's serious birth defects were caused by their mothers's ingestion of Bendectin, a prescription anti-nausea drug manufactured by the company. Merrell Dow submitted expert evidence that the drug had not been shown to be a risk factor for human birth defects. The plaintiffs obtained the testimony of eight experts who had conducted new studies and reanalyzed previous research. The federal district court and a federal appeals court both rejected the new evidence, ruling that it did not meet the *Frye* standard of "general acceptability." The U.S. Supreme Court, however, unanimously ruled that "general acceptability" was too austere and should no longer be the sole criterion in federal trials. The Court asserted that

> [t]he merits of the *Frye* test have been much debated, and scholarship on its proper scope and application is legion. Petitioners' primary attack, however, is not on the content but on the continuing authority of the rule. They contend that the *Frye* test was superseded by the adoption of the Federal Rules of Evidence. We agree. (*Daubert v. Merrell Dow Pharmaceuticals,* 1993, pp. 586–587)

Therefore, in *Daubert*, the Court emphasized that the traditional *Frye* standard had been replaced by the Federal Rules of Evidence in federal courts. The Court did not say that general acceptance was not relevant, however; rather, it could be one of several factors to take into account in deciding whether evidence should be admitted. A majority of the Court also made it clear that trial judges should screen any and all scientific testimony or evidence for (1) relevancy, (2) legal sufficiency, and (3) reliability. All three elements are important in deciding on the acceptability of the scientific evidence presented by the experts (see Table 1-1). Some critics observed that by making federal judges scientific gatekeepers, the Court charged these judges with deciding the merits of evidence about which they had little training. We will summarize briefly each of the elements and discuss problems that can face the trial judge in applying them.

Relevancy refers to the expectation that the scientific findings must be directly pertinent to the specific case being presented. When the relationships between the scientific evidence and the facts of the case are not adequately demonstrated, the evidence is not admissible. Goodman-Delahunty (1997) provides a good example in which the defendant was charged with the statutory rape of his daughter. This is a sex crime in which there is no force, but the victim is too young to give consent under the law. The defense tried to show—through expert testimony—that the defendant did *not* belong in a category that characterized 40% of incest abusers. Individuals in this group, a large minority of incest abusers, were fixated pedophiles (child molesters).

The defense sought to show that because the defendant did not exhibit the characteristics of a fixated pedophile, he was unlikely to have committed the crimes charged against him. The court pointed out that the defendant was never changed with being a fixated pedophile, and unless the defense could show a link between nonproclivity for pedophilia and nonproclivity for incest abuse, the relevance of the testimony was lacking. (p. 130)

The *Daubert* criterion of *legal sufficiency* refers to the expectation that the expert evidence be probative rather than prejudicial. In other words, the scientific evidence must provide proof or evidence specific to the issues of the case, rather than misleading, prejudicing, or confusing the jury. If the impact of the evidence is more prejudicial than probative, the court may exclude the expert testimony. For example, "some courts merely preclude the expert from mentioning the term 'rape trauma syndrome' while favoring the more neutral term 'posttraumatic stress disorder,' because the former tends to give the impression that rape had occurred, which is prejudicial" (Goodman-Delahunty, 1997, p. 130). Still, some lawyers have argued that expert testimony is prejudicial by its very nature because an expert may be perceived by jurors to possess some sort of deep knowledge and skill considerably beyond the layperson (Goodman-Delahunty, 1997).

The third criterion articulated by *Daubert* refers to *reliability*. Here, the Court specified four factors that federal trial judges should consider: (1) whether the scientific theory or technique can be and has been tested, (2) the error rate of the particular scientific technique, (3) whether the theory or technique has been subjected to peer review and publication, and (4) general acceptance of the theory or technique within the scientific community. (Note that this last is essentially the standard set in the *Frye* case.) An absence or weakness in one of the four factors would not necessarily exclude the evidence, however.

The first of these factors refers to whether a scientific theory is formulated in such a way as to be capable of being tested and *falsified* by a researcher, often referred to as

Table 1-1	Factors for Trial Judges to Take Into Account in Deciding Whether to Admit Scientific Evidence in Accordance With the *Daubert* Case
Factor	**Questions to Ask**
Relevancy	Does the evidence pertain directly to the case?
Legal Sufficiency	Does the evidence have probative value?
	Does its probative value outweigh its possible prejudicial impact?
Reliability	Can the evidence be tested, and has it been tested?
	If tested, what is the error rate?
	Is the technique/method/test peer reviewed and published?
	Is the technique/method/test accepted by the scientific community?

falsifiability. This point is an important one in the world of science, but it is also somewhat difficult to understand. For example, in *Daubert*, Chief Justice Rehnquist, dissenting in part with the majority decision, wrote, "I defer to no one in my confidence in federal judges; but I am at a loss to know what is meant when it is said that the scientific status of a theory depends on its 'falsifiability,' and I suspect some of them will be, too" (p. 600).

In his classic work, *The Logic of Scientific Discovery*, the philosopher of science Karl Popper (1968) (referred to by the Justices in *Daubert*) asserted that a truly scientific statement not only is capable of being verified or shown to be correct for the time being, but also is capable of being *falsified* or shown to be *incorrect*. In fact, Popper argued that one crucial criterion of a scientific statement is its constant vulnerability to being refuted by common experience or special experience. That is, the terms in any scientific statement or theory must be so precise, clear, and unambiguous that anyone planning to test the statement clearly understands what it is saying and can test it and potentially show the statement to be incorrect. "A theory which is not refutable by any conceivable event is nonscientific," Popper (1962, p. 26) affirms. According to Popper (1962, 1968), the prudent scientist must ask whether it is conceivable to set up conditions where the statements accounting for the observed phenomena could be shown to be incorrect. If such conceivable conditions cannot be proposed, the statement or theory is not scientific. A truly scientific statement, then, is constantly at risk of being shown incorrect in accounting for observations and experience.

The Supreme Court's second reliability factor refers to the question, is there a known or potential error associated with the scientific evidence? This implies that federal courts should determine the acceptable level for an error rate. However, the Court did not define error rate, nor did it provide guidance by indicating what the acceptable level might be. Moreover, precisely how should these considerations be applied to the evidence presented in a case?

The third reliability factor that the *Daubert* Court recommended refers to the question, have the findings been subjected to **peer review** and publication? In other words, has the evidence been reviewed by other experts (peers) in the field and met with their approval? Most professional and scholarly journals and periodicals in science (including the social and behavioral sciences) require that each manuscript undergo a rigorous evaluation by peers before being acceptable for publication. If the majority of these peer reviewers believe the manuscript falls short of the scientific requirement of solid methodology, analysis, conclusions, or contributions to the literature, the manuscript is likely to be rejected by the journal editor. Therefore, if research is published, the courts can assume that the evidence has at least received some approval from the scientific community.

The fourth factor refers to the question, is the technique or methodology at issue generally accepted by the scientific community? Therefore, the *Frye* standard did not disappear. Instead, the **general acceptance standard** was imbedded into questions asked by federal courts in deciding whether scientific evidence should be admitted. In other words, is the technique or methodology generally accepted by a majority of the researchers in that particular field? Interestingly, this general acceptance hurdle often remains a major one for scientific evidence. As we will see in later chapters, expert testimony on some psychological tests, methods, and syndromes is often rejected primarily because judges believe they lack acceptance in the field. On the other hand, other courts have moved away from general acceptance and toward a closer examination of the scientific foundations of evidence (Ogloff & Douglas, 2013).

Supreme Court Decisions After *Daubert*

The *Daubert* rule was reaffirmed and extended by the U.S. Supreme Court in *General Elec. Co. v. Joiner* (1997) and *Kumho Tire Co., Ltd. v. Carmichael* (1999). Together, these three cases represent what is called "the *Daubert* trilogy," and they also represent the Supreme Court's *landmark* rulings on admissibility of expert testimony.

The *Joiner* case centered on identifying the cause of lung cancer diagnosed in Robert Joiner, an electrician who alleged that his exposure to electrical transformer chemicals (PCBs, dioxin, and furans) promoted his lung cancer. The case was a complex one and shifted from state to federal courts, with many pretrial proceedings in both jurisdictions. Relevant to our discussion is Joiner's wish to call researchers who were ready to testify that these chemicals could promote cancer and likely did so in Joiner's case, even though he was a smoker and had a family history of lung cancer. The trial court did not admit the testimony, saying the experts failed to demonstrate a relationship between the chemicals and the cancer in Joiner's case. Joiner appealed that decision, and the federal appeals court (11th Circuit) ruled in his favor. The three corporations affected by the suit (General Electric, Westinghouse Electric, and Monsanto) appealed that decision to the U.S. Supreme Court, saying that the trial court had been correct in not admitting the testimony of the scientists.

The U.S. Supreme Court unanimously supported the decision of the trial court to exclude the expert testimony. Two of Joiner's four experts were not willing to link increases in lung cancer to exposure to PCBs. The other two, who were more willing to do that, had conducted studies that the trial judge thought were not directly related to the case or that included exposure to other contaminants, in addition to PCBs. The Supreme Court decided that the district court judge had carefully reviewed the evidence and had not abused his discretion by refusing to admit the expert testimony. As a result of that decision, it is clear that to be admissible, experts must adequately explain their scientific conclusions to trial judges (Blanck & Berven, 1999). The unanimous decision also demonstrates the reluctance of the Supreme Court to second-guess decisions at the trial level, particularly if presiding judges have carefully performed their roles as finders of fact. We will see additional illustrations of this in other landmark cases.

The *Kumho* case involved testimony of an engineer concerning the role a defective tire played in causing an auto accident. The engineer's testimony had been classified as "technical" rather than traditionally "scientific." Basically, the question raised by *Kumho* is extremely relevant to psychology, because it relates to the admissibility of expert opinion based on *clinical* experience and observation rather than science that is normally conducted under controlled laboratory conditions (Blanck & Berven, 1999). As discussed earlier in the chapter, both clinicians and research psychologists participate in the relationship with law. The Supreme Court concluded that the admissibility rules articulated by *Daubert* extended to clinical and technical knowledge. Therefore, the *Kumho* conclusion means that federal trial courts should apply the **Daubert standard** to what was traditionally considered "nonscientific" testimony from experts. This would include the clinical testimony of psychologists and other mental health workers. As Otto and Heilbrun (2002) note, it is now clear that clinicians as well as researchers are scientists for the purpose of providing expert testimony. Indeed, since the *Daubert* trilogy cases, the methods used by clinicians—such as the instruments they administer in assessing individuals—are often scrutinized by trial courts in deciding whether to allow expert testimony.

In addition, treatment approaches may also be challenged if they are not supported by empirical research. This has led to a major focus in the literature and in the psychological profession on **evidence-based practice**. An evidence-based treatment or practice is one that has been tried and tested, with favorable results overall. "Whatever clinical value unvalidated psychological assessment or treatment techniques may or may not have in the consultation room, *Daubert* makes plain that testimony employing such techniques has no place on the witness stand" (Faigman & Monahan, 2009, p. 23). Commentators note that the trilogy of cases has influenced the practice of law as well as the practice of psychology and other sciences. Attorneys are more proactive in selecting their experts and preparing for trial, and judges are more likely to exclude evidence now than before *Daubert* (McAuliff & Groscup, 2009).

Some states decided to apply the *Daubert* scientific standard soon after the Supreme Court issued the ruling. However, approximately 14 states continue to apply the *Frye* or similar test for the acceptability of scientific evidence in the courtroom (Hunt, 2010). That is, rather than conducting an elaborate review of relevance, error rate, falsifiability, and other aspects of the complex *Daubert* case, they focus primarily on whether the science has general acceptance among peers.

It has been 20 years since the *Daubert* case was decided by the Supreme Court. Over this time period, both civil and criminal courts have dealt with scientific evidence and have measured it according to the guidelines issued in that opinion. There is even an online "*Daubert* tracker" that allows people to follow relevant cases. Scholars in both psychology and law will likely continue to cite and study this case well into the future.

Psychology and the Law: A Challenging Alliance

The above section on the admissibility of expert testimony illustrates the occasionally tenuous relationship between psychology (and other sciences) and the courts, representing but one component of the legal system. As will be seen throughout the text, psychologists confront numerous situations that may test their patience with the law as a whole. This is particularly likely to occur in the relationship of psychology *in* the law, where clinicians may encounter challenges to their scientific methods or be pressed to provide opinions that they believe to be beyond the scope of their role or even their knowledge. We will show in later chapters, for example, that it is not unusual for psychologists to be asked, "Was this defendant insane?" or "Is this person dangerous?" Insanity is a legal determination, not a clinical one, and dangerousness cannot be absolutely predicted. Therefore, a psychologist will be more apt to say that an insanity defense can be supported or that there is a significant likelihood that someone will harm others if not detained. Even these statements are not universally condoned without some qualification, however.

As another example, psychologists are sometimes asked which parent should be given custody of minor children in divorce proceedings. Psychologists can assess parenting plans, but many believe they should not provide a recommendation to a judge making a custody decision, although both professional standards and guidelines allow them to do so if they wish. In sum, psychology cannot provide absolute truths or easy answers. Instead, it has many partial, often tentative answers embedded in probabilities.

Even in the psychology *and* law relationship there are pitfalls. Recall that it is in this relationship that we find more researchers than clinicians, although it is important to emphasize that many psychologists are both. The clinician may conduct research, and the researcher may agree to a lawyer's request to testify about her work. Research psychology is largely nomothetic as opposed to idiographic in scope. The **idiographic approach** emphasizes the intensive study of one individual. The **nomothetic approach** focuses on the search for general principles, relationships, and patterns by combining data from many individuals. Therefore, research psychologists—like clinicians—are generally cautious in responding to questioners who would prefer simple, certain answers or solutions to complex issues. Moreover, the principles and theories proposed by psychology are confirmed only through the collection of consistent and supporting data, a process that is not only long and rigorous, but is also punctuated by debate and differing interpretations of the data. "History suggests that the road to a firm research consensus is extraordinarily arduous" (Kuhn, 1970, p. 15).

Psychological theories or "truths" are arrived at primarily through studies that employ methods emphasizing prediction, measurement, and controlled comparisons. As will be seen later in the text, in some areas, research psychologists have amassed a good deal of information that allows them to make statements with confidence. We know, for example, that eyewitness testimony is extremely fallible under certain conditions but should not be totally discounted; we know, also, that as a group, juveniles lack a comprehension of the constitutional rights guaranteed to them, leading many to believe juveniles should not be allowed to waive their rights to a lawyer. On the other hand, research on the effects of divorce on children is still evolving, questions on the validity of psychological profiling abound, and research is mixed on the reliability of some measures intended to assess risk of sex offending. All of these topics will be discussed in the chapters ahead.

Defining and Classifying Law

Law is difficult to define. To paraphrase a wise legal scholar, Judge Learned Hand, the person who has given up trying to define law has attained humility. Crafting a universal definition of law is an elusive enterprise. Few scholars are able to propose a definition that will satisfy everyone else. There is less disagreement when scholars discuss classifications or types of law. For example, law can be classified both by its *content* and by its *origin*.

Content Classifications

The traditional content classifications are two-category distinctions—those between civil and criminal law and between substantive and procedural law, to be discussed below. Increasingly, scholars prefer to use terms that specify content even more clearly, such as education law, media law, mental health law, environmental law, family law, medical law, and public health law.

Civil and Criminal Law

The distinction between civil and criminal law rests primarily on the disputive versus punitive nature of a case. In **civil law,** two or more parties (litigants) approach the legal system seeking resolution of a dispute. The **plaintiff,** the person bringing the case, is hoping for some remedy from the law. Although the remedy may include fines, compensatory damages, and punitive damages, the concept of punishment is not the main purpose of civil law. It is designed to settle disputes, or to "make whole" the person or persons who suffered harm. This is accomplished through such means as monetary awards or **injunctions** (court orders to one party to cease some activity, such as venturing on property).

Criminal law, on the other hand, involves an alleged violation of rules deemed so important that the breaking of them incurs society's formal punishment, which must be imposed by the criminal courts. An important component of criminal law is the need to have the rules stated clearly by Congress when it comes to federal crimes, and state legislatures when it comes to state crimes. Very rarely, crimes are covered in the state or federal constitutions; for example, the U.S. Constitution prohibits treason. To be a crime, an action or failure to act (e.g., failure to file income taxes) must be prohibited (or mandated) in the statutes, and the maximum punishment for violation of that rule must be specified. This does not mean that the person found guilty of violating the law *will* receive that maximum punishment; rather, it is considered fair that people be warned of the possible punishment before committing a crime.

Although it may not seem difficult to discern criminal from civil law, the lines between the two are sometimes blurred. In most states, for example, if a juvenile is charged with violating the criminal law, he or she will most likely be brought to a juvenile or family court, which is considered a civil rather than a criminal setting. Likewise, a mentally disordered individual charged with a criminal offense may be committed to a mental institution through civil proceedings, rather than led through the criminal courts. Over the past two decades, there has been increasing *civil* commitment of dangerous sex offenders after they have completed their criminal sentences. Disputes between private persons or organizations, such as breaches of contract, libel suits, or divorce actions, clearly represent civil law. The government also may be a part of a civil suit, either as plaintiff or defendant (also called respondent). However, when the government fines a corporation for dumping hazardous waste or polluting the waters, the fine may be either a civil or a criminal penalty. In December 2012, the oil corporation BP pled guilty to criminal charges associated with the Deepwater Horizon oil spill in the Gulf of Mexico in 2010. Civil suits against that company continue to this day, although some settlements have been reached. Earlier, the massive cases of Enron Corporation, Anderson Accounting Firm, and WorldCom in 2002 included violations of both criminal and civil laws. Anderson was convicted of obstruction of justice, and Enron was faced with both criminal and civil investigations into its corporate practices. This also happened in the case of Bernard Madoff, who pled guilty in 2009 to numerous federal charges involving securities fraud, money laundering, and perjury over a 20-year period. In the largest fraud case in Wall Street history, Madoff received a 150-year prison sentence.

Civil law cases are often more complex and difficult than criminal law cases, and the legal territory is more likely to be uncharted. The notorious Agent Orange civil case, for example, in which approximately 16,000 families of Vietnam veterans sued Dow Chemical and six other chemical companies for exposing them to the toxic effects of a defoliant made of dioxin, took nearly 20 years to settle in the federal courts. Other high-profile cases were the tobacco litigation proceedings of the 1990s. As noted above, cases arising from the 2010 oil spill continue to be heard. In the Madoff case, his victims—who included individuals, banks, investment firms, and charitable foundations—filed more than 1,000 civil lawsuits.

Substantive and Procedural Law

Another way of classifying law by content, besides civil and criminal, is to divide it into substantive and procedural categories. Substantive law defines the rights and responsibilities of members of a given society as well as the prohibitions of socially sanctioned behavior. For example, the Bill of Rights in the U.S. Constitution specifies fundamental rights of citizens, such as the right to freedom of speech and the right to be free from unreasonable search and seizure. In landlord–tenant laws, certain duties of both parties are described. Other examples of substantive law include state and federal statutes that define and prohibit fraud, embezzlement, murder, rape, assault, arson, burglary, and other crimes against personal safety and property.

Procedural law outlines the rules for the administration, enforcement, and modification of substantive law in the mediation of disputes. In a sense, procedural law exists for the sake of substantive law. It is intended to give defendants in a criminal case and litigants in a civil case the feeling that they are being fairly dealt with, and that all are given a reasonable chance to present their side of an issue before an impartial tribunal (James, 1965). State laws that tell how to initiate a civil suit or that specify the documents to be filed and the hearings to be held in child custody disputes illustrate procedural law. Other examples are the rules of evidence in criminal courts, such as the type of testimony that may be offered by an expert witness (see Box 1-3). Other excellent examples of procedural law are the Federal Rules of Civil Procedure and Federal Rules of Criminal Procedure, which are periodically revised to reflect the spirit of the times as well as modern technological advances.

Classifying by Origin

Another common method of classifying law is by looking for its sources, such as constitutions, court decisions (case law), statutes, rules of administrative agencies, and treaties. With the exception of treaties, the sources of law exist at both the federal and state (including municipal) levels.

Constitutional Law

The law contained in the U.S. Constitution and the constitutions of individual states comprises constitutional law. It provides the guidelines for the organization of national, state, and local government, and it places limits on the exercise of government power (e.g., through a Bill of Rights). Thus, in two psychology-related U.S. Supreme Court decisions, the Court announced that it was cruel and unusual punishment, in violation of the Constitution, to execute individuals who are intellectually disabled (*Atkins v. Virginia*, 2002) or so severely mentally ill that they could not understand why they were being executed (*Ford v. Wainwright*, 1986). As will become evident in later chapters, though, these decisions are not as clear-cut as they may appear.

The law that emerges from court decisions is sometimes referred to as case law or "judge-made" law. It has developed from common law (local customs formed into general principles) and through precedents set in previous court decisions. Case law may involve the interpretation of a statute. For example, if the legislature of a given state passes a law including a provision that psychiatrists are to conduct evaluations of a defendant's competency to stand trial, a court may be asked to interpret whether the legislature intended *psychiatrist* as a generic term that could also cover psychologists.

The rules and principles outlined in the courts' written decisions become precedent under the doctrine of *stare decisis* (to stand by past decisions) and are perpetuated, unless a later court chips away at or overturns them. As we will note below, precedent is a key element in distinguishing law and psychology. However, *stare decisis* is more a matter of policy than a rigid requirement to be mechanically followed in subsequent cases dealing with similar legal questions. Thus, while lower courts are expected to follow the precedents set by higher or appellate courts, an appeals court need not follow strictly the doctrine established by an earlier appeals court in the same geographical area. They generally do, however, because doing so contributes to efficiency, equality, and the development of the law (Abraham, 1998). As will be noted in Chapter 2, it sometimes happens that federal appeals courts in different parts of the United States have issued very different decisions on similar matters; in these situations, the U.S. Supreme Court may decide to hear a case to resolve the discrepancy.

Statutory Law

Written rules drafted and approved by a federal, state, or local law-making body are known as statutory law. Thus, local ordinances such as parking regulations or noise abatement orders are included in this category. Statutes are what most people mean when they refer to "law." They include a multitude of provisions, such as what services will be provided to the public, what factors entitle a person to initiate a civil suit, what crimes will be considered felonies or misdemeanors, and what are the responsibilities of individual citizens. Congress or state legislatures pass numerous statutes directly relating to psychology. For example, a state legislature may mandate that all law enforcement officers must pass a psychological test before hire or that certain mentally ill individuals must receive ongoing treatment in the community. As other illustrations, Congress enacts statutory law in its periodic passing of health care legislation (e.g., the Affordable Care Act) and crime control legislation that includes provisions relating to bail reform, violence against women, or gun safety.

Administrative Law

Law that is created and enforced by representatives of the numerous administrative and regulatory agencies of national, state, or local governments is known as **administrative law.** Examples of such agencies at the federal level are the Nuclear Regulatory Commission (NRC), the Food and Drug Administration (FDA), the Securities and Exchange Commission (SEC), the Federal Communications Commission (FCC), and the ubiquitous Internal Revenue Service (IRS). These and other agencies have been delegated broad rule-making, investigation, enforcement, and adjudication powers by Congress. In addition, every state assigns agencies to create, administer, and enforce laws such as those pertaining to zoning, public education, and public utilities. Examples of state agencies that relate to psychology are departments of mental health and the various professional licensing boards that oversee the quality of services provided by psychologists, lawyers, physicians, and other professionals.

⬙ Psychology and Law: Some Differences

There are many differences between psychology and law that make the relationship a challenging one. As the late Allen Hess (2006) wrote, "As psychologists and lawyers work together with greater frequency, there are more chances for misunderstandings to occur. It is useful to consider distinctions that can become troublesome if not recognized" (p. 43). Hess then provided a useful chart outlining these differences, several of which we discuss here (see also Table 1-2).

The law often requires quick answers, and psychologists—particularly when conducting assessments for lawyers and courts—are sometimes asked to produce results under less-than-ideal situations, such as interviewing a defendant in a jail setting. The law tends to be idiographic, while psychology tends to be nomothetic. Law is case focused, intent on solving each case, one at a time.

Law is generally conservative, and it builds a body of knowledge slowly, based on precedent. While psychology builds on past research findings, it is not precedence bound. As scientists, psychologists can and often do embark on exploring new research territory, but they cannot expect that the law will embrace their findings immediately or enthusiastically.

The major difference between psychology and law is the adversarial nature of the law and the exploratory and objective nature of psychology. The dominant model used in the American legal system is an adversarial one. It assumes that the best way to arrive at truth is to have proponents of each side of an issue advocate and present evidence most favorable to their position. The contenders confront one another in pretrial proceedings or during the trial, where truth is tested and refined through the "fight" theory of justice (Frank, 1949). It is assumed that justice will prevail once each side has had the

Table 1-2	Some Differences Between Psychology and Law
Psychology	**Law**
Values objectivity	**Values advocacy**
Research based	Adversarial approach
Empirical	**Rational**
Method of science	Method of authority
Nomothetic data	Idiographic or case data
Exploratory	**Expedient**
Seeks falsification	Seeks resolution
Sees knowledge as tentative	**Emphasizes importance of precedent**

opportunity to present its version of the evidence to a neutral decision maker—the judge or the jury. It is assumed, also, that "objective" truth about human behavior cannot be acquired from only one version of the story. Instead, different versions of the truth are sought, which, when put together, allow for judgment within an acceptable margin of error. By contrast, psychology, often directed by theory, arrives at "truth" and scientific knowledge through the accumulation of data derived from well-designed and thoughtful studies. This knowledge does not occur instantly.

The adversarial model presents problems for clinicians and for research psychologists. Not only does it concentrate on just one case at a time, but it also encourages lawyers to dip in and out of the data pool and pick and choose the segment of psychological information they wish to present in support of their position. The lawyer may select only part of an experiment and present the material out of context. Even in cross-examination, the opposing lawyer may be unaware of the real context or of contradictory findings. This procedure allows distortion and misrepresentation of research findings, since the lawyer's main concern is to provide the decision maker with evidence that will be favorable to the lawyer's client. Therefore, by using legal skill—but without having to appreciate the goals of science—lawyers can apply almost any psychological data in the service of their position. The adversarial model relies not necessarily on truth, but on persuasion (Haney, 1980). Adversary proceedings have the advantage of avoiding the dangers of unilateral dogmatism, but we cannot forget that the essential purpose of each advocate is to outwit the opponent and win the case (Marshall, 1972).

Psychologists may agree that the most desirable role for the psychologist who is called as an expert witness is that of the "impartial educator." Many experienced psychologists, however, contend that this role is extremely difficult if not impossible to maintain. For one thing, there are pressures from the attorney who hired the psychologist. For another, even when the psychologist is court-appointed and is acceptable to both sides (as might happen during pretrial proceedings), the presiding judge may press the psychologist to provide simple, "yes" or "no" answers. Often, the psychologist would like to expand on his findings but may be precluded from doing so by the rules of evidence or the objection of one of the attorneys.

It must be emphasized, though, that law needs psychology, along with other sciences. Law is, after all, a basically human enterprise and practice. It should be clear by now that a vast store of knowledge obtained by the sciences is making its way into the legal arena. Moreover, mental health evidence is frequently viewed "as important, if not essential, to addressing certain legal issues (e.g., sanity, emotional damages, parental fitness)" (Edens et al., 2012, p. 259). However, "some judges, attorneys, academics, and jurors view at least some mental health experts—if not the entire field—with a considerable degree of suspicion, if not overt distain and/or hostility" (Edens et al., 2012, p. 260). It can be said that persons associated with both fields are at fault. Skeem, Douglas, and Lilienfeld (2009) reflect this viewpoint in the preface to their book, *Psychological Science in the Courtroom*: "Many legal decisions are still based on inadequate psychological science or, worse, no psychological science at all" (p. ix). Thus, the uneasy alliance continues. Although there will always be an imperfect fit between law and psychology—due to their underlying philosophical and methodological differences—there is reason for optimism as professionals in both fields become better at the work they do and more appreciative of their respective contributions.

SUMMARY AND CONCLUSIONS

Psychology is the science of behavior. This is not a perfect definition, but it is the one commonly subscribed to by many if not most psychologists today. This science makes numerous contributions to the legal system.

Haney (1980) proposed a helpful tripartite relationship between psychology and the law: psychology *in* the law, psychology *and* the law, and psychology *of* the law. Although there is overlap, psychologists engaged in the first relationship are primarily clinical, in the second primarily research based, and in the third primarily philosophical in their approach. These relationships are not mutually exclusive; a given psychologist may operate in all of these realms, although one is likely to predominate.

This book focuses on psychological knowledge as it relates to the legal system—particularly but not exclusively reflected in the work of criminal and civil courts. This chapter has provided illustrations and has alluded to many topics—sleep research, eyewitness testimony, expert testimony, child custody determinations, lie detection, insanity—and numerous other examples are included throughout the book. Because this volume will include references to research, the chapter included material on the philosophy of science and how courts evaluate (or are expected to evaluate) scientific testimony. The U.S. Supreme Court's *Daubert* trilogy of cases and the *Frye* standard were offered as foundations to studying material in later chapters. In deciding whether scientific evidence should be admitted into court, the trial judge considers its relevance, reliability, and legal sufficiency, as well as the credentials of an expert.

The respective fields of law and psychology differ in both philosophy and methodology. Law is not easy to define. It is often conceptualized on the basis of its classifications, its sources, or its content. Law—at least in the adversarial system—is based on advocacy and precedence. It is expedient, case oriented, rational, and geared toward solutions to a problem. Psychology is nomothetic, research based, and exploratory in nature. As in most sciences, firm conclusions are evasive, and theories are constantly being tested. There is always the possibility that a discovery will be falsified. In law, although judgments in individual cases may be reversed, the general principles are retained unless there are compelling reasons to do otherwise. In other words, the law tends to be conservative (Hess, 2006). These fundamental differences may make for a challenging and sometimes uneasy alliance between psychology and law, but it is clear that their interaction has increased and developed in recent years. As will be illustrated throughout the book, this is to the benefit of both fields.

KEY CONCEPTS

A priori method	Falsifiability	Peer review
Administrative law	Forensic psychology	Plaintiff
Automatism	*Frye* standard	Procedural law
Case law	General acceptance standard	Psychology and the law
Civil law		Psychology in the law
Common law	Idiographic approach	Psychology of the law
Constitutional law	Injunctions	*Stare decisis*
Criminal law	Malingering	Statutory law
Daubert standard	Method of authority	Substantive law
Error rate	Method of science	
Evidence-based practice	Method of tenacity	
Expert testimony	Nomothetic approach	

2

Psychology and the Courts

An Overview

We all know what a typical courtroom in the United States looks like, and many of us have been in them as participants or observers. Print news media have long covered criminal trials, but it was not until the broadcast media were given access to courtrooms that this technology allowed us to observe at least some "real" court proceedings from a distance. A recent example is the Florida trial of George Zimmerman, who was charged with second-degree murder in the death of 17-year-old Trayvon Martin and was found not guilty on July 13, 2013. Other examples are the 2013 trial of Jodi Arias, who was convicted of murdering her boyfriend, and the sentencing of Ariel Castro, who pled guilty to 937 counts associated with kidnapping, sexual assault, and holding captive three young woman for nearly a decade. With rapidly developing technology, court proceedings can now occur with participants in different locations. For example, a witness may testify from a prison or even from a hospital bed.

As a matter of law, criminal proceedings should be open to the public, which includes print reporters and other members of media organizations. However, some restrictions do apply. For example, judges do not have to allow access to broadcast and other high-tech media, although when they deny it, sketch artists are permitted. The first images of James Holmes, the man charged in the so-called "Batman" shooting case in an Aurora, Colorado, movie theater, were based on courtroom sketches. In many courthouses today, persons entering must go through electronic scanners, and space limits are observed. Judges also may close off part of a criminal trial to the public and the print media. Many judges, for example, have closed courtrooms during the testimony of child victims of sexual assault. The above are all principles of media law extensively covered in other sources (e.g., Pember & Calvert, 2012).

The courtroom proceedings we see through the eyes of the news media are most likely to be unrepresentative, however. They are typically portions of a sensational criminal trial such as the testimony of a key witness or the sentencing of an individual convicted of a heinous crime. Both the Zimmerman and Arias trials were covered at length, but they did not rival the most noteworthy court-related "media event" of the 20th century, the O.J. Simpson criminal case in which the former professional football player was charged and ultimately found not guilty of murdering his former wife and a friend, Ronald Goldman. In that case, both pretrial and trial proceedings were broadcast to the public, almost in their entirety. Civil trials, compared with criminal trials, get little attention. Even Simpson's civil trial, in which he was found civilly responsible for the death of Ronald Goldman and for the battery of Nicole Brown Simpson, received far less publicity than his criminal trial. Furthermore, the public rarely is informed of pretrial proceedings, which can be extensive and result in the resolution of most cases. Exceptions to this rarity include terrorism-motivated or mass shooting cases. Research demonstrates that about 90% of *criminal* cases are settled between a defendant's first court appearance and the trial stage (Neubauer, 2002). Over three quarters of *civil* cases that reach the courts are settled without going to trial (Abadinsky, 2007).

The entertainment media have also helped increase public familiarity with courts and how they work. Although network "law shows" of old were considered naive and unrealistic, there are now highly regarded network and cable shows that depict law in action in a realistic way. Nonetheless, like even the best of the "hospital shows," their main characters—particularly lawyers—may be flawed, but they are almost invariably intellectually sharp, quick-witted, and impeccably dressed. These shows also have led to a significant increase in law school applications.

Despite growing familiarity with the courtroom and its various proceedings through both news and entertainment media, we are generally less knowledgeable about the structure of courts or the legal questions and standards that judges, lawyers, and jurors must address. Even basic legal distinctions, such as the difference between criminal and civil law, may be foreign to many people. This chapter, therefore, introduces the reader to the court system and discusses the judicial process in both criminal and civil cases. We will cover fundamental concepts and focus on matters relating to courts that are most relevant to psychology. In addition, we will highlight issues that create special challenges to those trying to "span the boundaries" between psychology and law, which in some ways are such disparate disciplines, as we saw in Chapter 1.

⊠ Organization of the Courts

The court system in the United States is a **dual system** consisting of federal and state courts, which are interrelated yet independent of one another. Federal courts deal with matters relating to the U.S. Constitution and a wide variety of federal criminal and civil laws, including administrative laws. In addition, they hear cases involving disputes between citizens of different states, although their power to do this has been shared with state courts in order to lessen the burden on federal courts (Abraham, 1998).

The federal court system has its origins in the U. S. Constitution, which establishes one Supreme Court and "such inferior Courts as the Congress may from time to time ordain and establish" (Article III, Section I). The very first law passed by the Congress of the United States was the Judiciary Act of 1789, which began to create the federal judiciary. Over the years, Congress has tinkered with a variety of courts, adding and deleting them as the country grew and the geography of the nation changed. Today, the federal court system comprises appellate and trial courts. The **appellate courts** consist of one Supreme Court and, at an intermediate level, 13 courts of appeal for the various circuits. The **trial courts** in the federal system represent 94 judicial districts, including one district in each state, the District of Columbia, and Puerto Rico. Three territories of the United States—the Virgin Islands, Guam, and the Northern Mariana Islands—also have district courts. Attached to these district courts are magistrate judge's courts, where much of the preliminary work on criminal and civil cases is done. In addition, the federal system includes a variety of **specialized courts**, such as bankruptcy courts, patent courts, and special district courts. Figure 2-1 provides a simplified view of the federal court structure.

State courts deal with matters concerning the laws of the 50 states. They parallel the structure of federal courts in that there are both trial and appellate courts.

Figure 2-1   Illustration of the Federal Court System

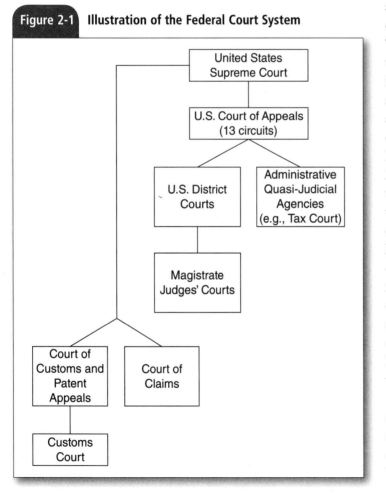

However, there are wide variations in the numbers and levels of courts within each state. Particularly in heavily populated states, a bewildering array of courts can exist. All states have a court of last resort, but some have no intermediate appellate court. If that is the case, decisions at the trial court level are appealed directly to the state's court of last resort. The great majority of states today also have a wide variety of specialized courts (e.g., traffic, small claims, and family courts), and as will be seen shortly, many states are experimenting with other specialized courts, such as drug, mental health, domestic violence, and veterans' courts. Figures 2-2 and 2-3 contrast the court structure in two states, one very simple and the other complex.

The term **jurisdiction** is used to refer to the authority given to a particular court in resolving a dispute. Jurisdiction is best understood as "the geographic area, subject matter, or persons over which a court can exercise authority" (Abadinsky, 1995, p. 144). Occasionally, two or more courts may have the authority to hear a case, which is called **concurrent jurisdiction**. For example, a particular law violation may have the potential of involving both federal and state courts. An employer who refuses to promote a disabled employee may be violating both federal and state statutes. In this situation, the

Figure 2-2 **View of the Court Structure of Virginia**

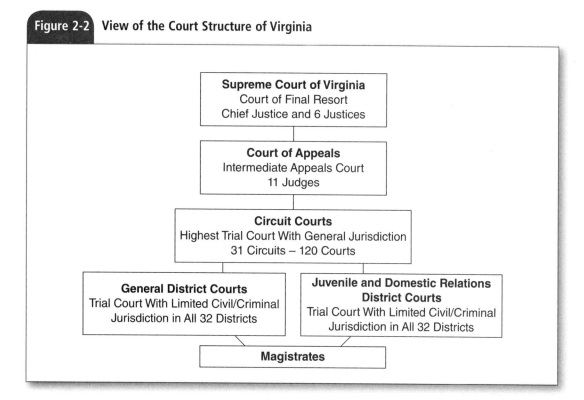

Figure 2-3   Court Structure of Texas

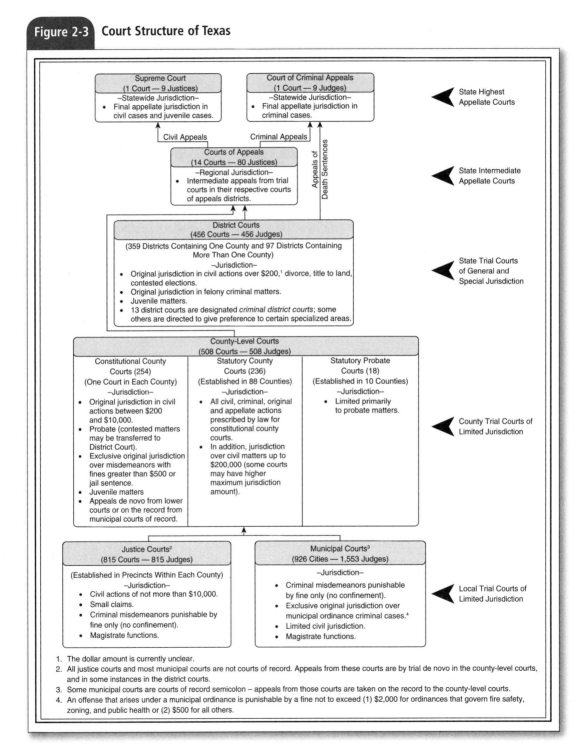

1. The dollar amount is currently unclear.
2. All justice courts and most municipal courts are not courts of record. Appeals from these courts are by trial de novo in the county-level courts, and in some instances in the district courts.
3. Some municipal courts are courts of record semicolon – appeals from those courts are taken on the record to the county-level courts.
4. An offense that arises under a municipal ordinance is punishable by a fine not to exceed (1) $2,000 for ordinances that govern fire safety, zoning, and public health or (2) $500 for all others.

person filing suit (the plaintiff) may have the choice of filing in the federal or state court. Likewise, in the criminal context, one incident can represent an alleged violation of both federal and state law.

Trial courts, compared with appellate courts, are divided into courts of **general jurisdiction** and **limited jurisdiction**. Trial courts are often referred to as the work-horses of the judicial system, because their dockets are filled with a multitude of cases and papers to be processed. Trial courts of general jurisdiction have broad authority to deal with a wide range of issues. Felony trials as well as major trials in civil cases are held in these courts. Courts of limited jurisdiction, by contrast, are the entry-level courts. They typically cannot conduct felony trials, although judges can hold preliminary hearings, issue search warrants, and conduct a variety of pretrial proceedings. In state court systems, courts of limited jurisdiction are referred to as lower courts, municipal courts, or inferior courts. Magistrate judges' courts, attached to U.S. District Courts, are the courts of limited jurisdiction in the federal system.

We will now look more closely at the work of federal and state courts.

Federal Courts

The subject matter jurisdiction of federal courts is set forth in Article III, Section 2 of the U.S. Constitution. Clearly, the federal courts had high demands on their time right from the outset:

> The judicial Power shall extend to all Cases, in Law and Equity, arising under this Constitution, the Laws of the United States, and Treaties made, or which shall be made, under their Authority;—to all Cases affecting Ambassadors, other public Ministers and Consuls;—to all Cases of admiralty and maritime jurisdiction;—to Controversies to which the United States shall be a Party;—to Controversies between two or more States;—between a State and Citizens of another State;—between Citizens of different States;—between Citizens of the same State claiming Lands under Grants of different States, and between a State, or the Citizens thereof, and foreign States, Citizens or Subjects.

Congress over the years has passed a wide array of laws that have had the effect of increasing the work of federal courts, but in some cases limiting it as well. Laws relating to the protection of the environment, employment discrimination, health regulation, crime control, safety in the workplace, and broadcasting are but a few examples of the workload expansion. On the other hand, Congress also has limited the role of the federal courts on some matters. In the Prison Litigation Reform Act (PLRA) of 1996, for example, Congress required that state prisoners exhaust all appeals in state courts before going to the federal courts.

The 94 U.S. District courts—the trial courts—carry most of the workload in the federal system. At the next level up from the trial courts are the appellate courts. The United States is divided into 12 geographically defined jurisdictions or circuits, each with a court of appeals (see Figure 2-1). In addition, there is a federal circuit court of appeals, which has nationwide jurisdiction in a variety of subject matters, such as government contracts. The 13 federal appellate courts comprise between 3 and 15 judges, who meet both in panels of three and, in major cases, as a whole (*en banc*). The primary purpose of the court of appeals is to review decisions made by the federal district courts within its jurisdiction. A court of appeals also reviews cases heard by specialized courts, such as tax courts, and the various federal administrative agencies.

In essence, the work of federal courts today is both varied and overwhelming. A federal judgeship is a prestigious position and, for judges appointed under Article III, it is a lifetime appointment. These federal judges are appointed by the president and confirmed by the Senate. In recent years, however, many federal judgeships have been unfilled. At the beginning of 2013, for example, there were 83 vacancies in federal courts, with 33 nominations pending. On the crucial and influential D.C. Circuit Court of Appeals, 3 of 11 positions were vacant, and a fourth was expected to be vacant shortly. Legal scholars agree that positions are often left vacant because of the failure of the Senate to approve of a sitting president's pending nominations.

While the intermediate appellate courts in the federal system must rule on all cases properly presented to them for review, the highest court in the land, the U.S. Supreme Court, has much more discretion. The Supreme Court consists of nine Justices appointed for life by the president, and again with the advice and consent of the U.S. Senate. One of the nine is designated Chief Justice by the president, and the Court is usually referred to collectively by the name of that individual—for example, the Supreme Court today is referred to as the Roberts Court, after Chief Justice John Roberts. The Supreme Court begins to meet on the first Monday of October each year and usually continues in session until June.

Although what the Court may hear (subject matter jurisdiction) is defined by Congress as well as the Constitution, the Justices are given nearly complete control of their docket by refusing to hear and review specific cases. The cases the Justices select are usually those believed to address important unanswered questions, and they often involve an interpretation of the U.S. Constitution, such as in the Court's recent interpretations of the Second Amendment's right to bear arms, which the Court considered in *District of Columbia v. Heller* (2008) and *McDonald v. City of Chicago* (2010). By a close majority (5–4), the Court in *Heller* struck down D.C.'s ban on handguns and ruled that the Second Amendment's right to bear arms was an individual right given to people in their own homes for protection. That ruling was affirmed and extended to states and municipalities in the Chicago case. The U.S. Supreme Court also emphasized that the right to bear arms was not absolute; government could place reasonable restrictions, such as who could obtain them and where weapons could be prohibited.

The Supreme Court also has issued recent major decisions on other constitutional issues, such as those related to marriage equality (*United States v. Windsor,* 2013), affirmative action (*Fisher v. University of Texas,* 2013), and voting rights (*Shelby County v. Holder,* 2013). The *Windsor* case struck down as unconstitutional Section 3 of the Defense of Marriage Act (DOMA), which defined marriage as a relationship between a man and a woman and had consequently denied same-sex couples the federal benefits available to heterosexual couples. The Voting Rights Act of 1965 was dealt a major blow by the Court, however, when it ruled in the *Shelby* case that states with a history of discriminatory voting practices were no longer required to gain approval from the federal government before making changes in their voting laws. Likewise, affirmative action was not enthusiastically supported by the Court, when a majority sent the *Fisher* case back to Texas courts for a closer look at the formula the University of Texas used to admit students. Each of these cases was watched closely by legal psychologists, and in two—*Windsor* and *Fisher*—the American Psychological Association had filed *amicus curiae* briefs. (Amicus briefs will be discussed shortly.) In 2014, the Court is expected to decide whether it is constitutional for states to declare an outright ban on affirmative action in employment and educational settings.

Petitioners or appellants request review of their cases by filing documents summarizing the facts of the case and the decision of the lower court, and by setting forth their arguments as to why the Court should hear the case. Other interested parties may also file briefs urging the Court to hear a case. If the Justices agree to hear the case, they issue a **writ of certiorari** calling for the record below to be sent up for review. A writ is a written judicial order. In this case, the lower court is ordered to produce the documents needed to review the proceedings.

About 5,000 appeals are filed with the U.S. Supreme Court each year, but a vast majority are denied because the subject matter is either not proper or not of sufficient importance to warrant full Court review. In addition, there is simply not enough time for the Justices to hear all of the cases that come to their attention. Four of the nine Justices must agree to hear a case. The denials of certiorari may or may not include a brief statement explaining why the decision of the lower appellate court must stand. In 2013, the Justices refused to hear a case, *Delling v. Idaho* (2012), that likely would have answered whether states may eliminate the insanity defense from their statutes. We discuss this case in Chapter 4. Interestingly, three of the nine Justices wanted to hear that case and wrote a brief dissent to the denial of certiorari.

State Courts

As described earlier and illustrated in Figures 2-2 and 2-3, state courts follow roughly the same pyramid structure as the federal courts, usually with one highest appellate court, or court of last resort. Some states choose to call their highest court something other than "Supreme Court," however. Massachusetts's court of last resort, for example, is the Supreme Judicial Court. New York's highest court is the New York Court of Appeals, while lower courts in that state are called supreme courts. In some states, including Texas, there are separate courts of last resort for civil and criminal cases. The process and administration of these state courts vary widely from state to state, as do the state laws under which they operate.

State courts have a general, unlimited power to decide almost every type of case, subject only to the limitations of state law. Therefore, state courts, primarily the trial courts, are the place where most of the legal business of American society begins and ends, although it has been asserted that the rate of growth in federal courts is surpassing that in most state courts (Abadinsky, 2007; Abraham, 1998; Posner, 1985).

Specialized Courts: Drug and Mental Health Courts

Toward the end of the 20th century, a trend toward the creation of specialized courts intended for therapeutic purposes became apparent. Sometimes referred to as problem-solving courts, most of them focused on substance abuse and mental health problems. Others dealt exclusively with domestic violence cases, cases involving prostitutes, or cases involving military veterans. Veterans' courts are one of the most recent specialized courts to arrive on the scene (see Box 2-1). We focus here on the two types of specialized courts that have received the most research attention, drug and mental health courts

Drug Courts

The progenitor of treatment-oriented courts was the drug court, pioneered in Miami, Florida, in 1989. A decade later, approximately 500 drug courts operated nationwide. There are now around 2,600 drug courts operating in the United States, including some in federal courts in eight states (National Institute of Justice, 2012).

Although these courts differ in clientele and in procedure, they typically deal with defendants whose substance abuse is believed to be at the root of their offending. By all accounts, this covers a high percentage of individuals, but only a small percentage are eligible for drug courts. Drug courts generally deal with minor, first-time offenders, although some also accept those with violent misdemeanors (e.g., simple assault) or nonviolent felonies (e.g., burglary). It is estimated that 80% of criminal offenders in the United States were arrested for a substance-related offense, were intoxicated at the time of their offense, committed their crime to support a drug habit, or had a serious history of substance abuse (Marlowe et al., 2012).

BOX 2-1 VETERANS' COURTS

Should certain groups of defendants be processed differently from other defendants, in specialized courts dedicated to their treatment? In the late 20th and early 21st centuries, many scholars, researchers, and legal practitioners began to think so. The establishment of drug courts and mental health courts was widely regarded to be a step in the direction of unclogging court dockets and providing much-needed treatment to persons with substance abuse and/or mental health problems who were charged with relatively minor crimes. It is not unusual for these problems to coexist in one person. As noted in the text, recent research on the success of these courts has been positive.

There is less research on one of the newest forms of specialized courts—those intended to help veterans readjust to life in their communities after returning from wars. The first veterans treatment court was established in Buffalo, New York, in 2008, by Judge Robert Russell. Since then, approximately 100 cities in 27 states have set up separate dockets "to deal with an increasing number of veterans whose scrapes are due to substance abuse and mental health issues. More than 100 other courts are planning to start Veterans Treatment Courts soon" (Thomas, 2013, p. 1).

In some jurisdictions, rather than establishing separate courts, the judicial system consolidates hearings for veterans on certain days, and special efforts are made to link them with services in the community. It is not known how many jurisdictions take such approaches (Christy, Clark, Frei, & Rynearson-Moody, 2012).

Research on veterans treatment courts is in its infancy, but it should be noted that these specialized courts appear to overlap the mission of traditional drug and mental health courts. In fact, many are subsumed under the mantle of or otherwise associated with drug courts. Interestingly, some observers have indicated that veterans' courts were formed because veterans had higher functioning than defendants referred to the more traditional mental health courts; others have observed, though, that their problems are more severe than those of non-veterans referred to mental health courts (Thomas, 2013). Many returning veterans are clearly in need of care on a number of fronts. In Chapter 4, we discuss needs of veterans with post-traumatic stress disorder (PTSD), for example.

Is a separate court structure needed to meet the needs of veterans? We might ask the same question about domestic abusers and prostitutes, both groups for which specialized courts have been formed in some communities. Critics of veterans' courts suggest that veterans may receive favorable treatment compared with other defendants who are accused of similar crimes. However, supporters maintain that persons who served their country deserve special treatment. Critics of domestic violence courts suggest that mediation is too often emphasized in these courts and that the victims of domestic abuse are not adequately protected. On the other hand, supporters say domestic violence is too complex an issue to be left to traditional criminal courts. Critics of prostitution courts argue that if prostitution were legalized, there would be no need for such special courts. Supporters say it must not be

(Continued)

(Continued)

legalized, but that these courts are sensitive to the victimization of women and both male and female young offenders.

Reasonable people obviously may have varying opinions on these issues. The question remains, how far beyond drug and mental health courts should we go? At this point, until further research is available, the jury is out on the need for more specialized courts.

Questions for Discussion:

1. What are the advantages and disadvantages of assigning certain groups of defendants to specialized courts?

2. Assuming that specialized courts are a good idea, which groups of defendants should benefit from them?

When a drug court exists in a particular location, certain defendants are identified shortly after arrest as good candidates for the court, and they are diverted from the standard prosecution process. Others may make the usual courtroom appearances, be found guilty or plead guilty, and then be placed under the supervision of the drug court based on a conditional release arrangement. In a recent special journal issue devoted to diverting persons accused of crime from standard prosecution (DeMatteo & Heilbrun, 2012), scholars described many alternative approaches. Typically, though, drug court defendants have been accused of nonviolent offenses and have been long-time users or addicts. They are then offered treatment in the community as an alternative to continued prosecution or, if referred to drug court after conviction, as an alternative to incarceration. The judge overseeing the drug court takes a case-management approach, requiring mandatory drug testing and monitoring the treatment progress. Drug court defendants also are asked to make restitution to their victims when appropriate.

Early research on the success of drug courts produced mixed results, with some studies suggesting a high level of effectiveness (e.g., Belenko, 1998; Goldkamp & Weiland, 1993) and others showing few if any differences between defendants who go through drug courts and those who go through regular criminal courts (e.g., Miethe, Lu, & Reese, 2000). More recent research has been more consistently positive. Marlowe et al. (2012) cited six meta-analyses conducted by independent investigators that concluded that drug courts reduced recidivism by 8 to 26 percentage points. However, there is mixed evidence regarding whether drug courts consistently reduce the drug relapse rate (Heilbrun et al., 2012). Nevertheless, as Heilbrun et al. point out, they are cost-effective, they deliver appropriate services, and they are perceived favorably by those who participate in them. Despite their proven efficacy, though, drug courts sometimes provide services to clients who do not have serious substance abuse problems and may not really need them (DeMatteo, Marlowe, Festinger, & Arabia, 2009). On the other hand, it is believed that drug courts serve less than 10% of the adults arrested each year who would meet their criteria if drug courts were more widely available (Marlowe et al., 2012).

Mental Health Courts

Many communities have established mental health courts, closely akin to the drug court model. These courts are intended to divert mentally disordered individuals away from the traditional criminal court process. Although the first mental health courts were restricted to defendants charged with minor offenses, they gradually expanded to accept defendants charged with felonies, even in some cases violent ones. In an early monograph focusing on four such courts, Goldkamp and Irons-Guynn (2000) summarized the common features of mental health courts. Typically, they are

- Voluntary, requiring the consent of the defendant;
- Available only to individuals with demonstrable mental illness that was likely to contribute to their criminal activity;
- Concerned for public safety;
- Desirous of preventing the jailing of the mentally disordered; and
- Likely to exclude offenders with histories of violence.

Like drug courts, mental health courts differ on a variety of procedures, including the point at which individuals qualify for these services. Some operate on a "preadjudication" model: If the defendant successfully completes the court's requirements (e.g., mental health counseling), the record of arrest will be expunged. Other courts follow a "postadjudication" model, in which defendants are convicted and, in some cases, briefly incarcerated before being supervised in the community under the mental health court model. Although some degree of mental illness is a criterion, having a mental illness will not necessarily qualify a defendant for admission. Moreover, although mental health courts as a rule do not accept defendants charged with serious felonies, there are exceptions.

Over the past decade, there has been a plethora of studies on mental health courts (Heilbrun et al., 2012). Similar to the research on drug courts, this research has been generally positive, finding lower recidivism rates (even for those who participated but did not graduate). In addition, like drug courts, they are cost-effective. The actual services provided by mental health courts remain elusive, though, and require much more research. In a recent study of a large, well-established mental health court, Luskin (2013) found that outpatient mental health treatment was more frequent and varied for participants than for a matched sample of defendants who met criteria for mental health court admission but went through regular court processing instead. However, the mental health court did not provide social services—such as help finding housing or employment—nor did it address the criminological needs of these defendants. **Criminological needs** is the term used for aspects of a person's life that make him or her vulnerable to crime, such as criminal thinking patterns or substance abuse. Luskin concludes that such needs should be addressed if mental health courts are to be effective in the long run.

Some scholars who expressed early concerns about mental health courts noted that these courts must grapple with special problems associated with their voluntary nature, confidentiality, and timeliness (Goldkamp & Irons-Guynn, 2000). They ask, for example, whether a mentally disordered individual truly can comprehend the options offered to him by the mental health court, particularly when the treatment is contingent upon a guilty plea. However, mentally disordered individuals often plead guilty to crimes in traditional criminal courts, where it may be less likely that their mental health needs are recognized. Critics also noted that referral to the mental health court requires the need to obtain personal information that may well be irrelevant to the criminal charge. Finally, while courts may desire early intervention and efficient processing, the mental health professional needs time to conduct a thorough assessment. "To put it simply, it is hard to rush such an assessment and still have it be accurate and complete" (Goldkamp & Irons-Guynn, 2000, p. 3).

To function efficiently and presumably to be effective, mental health courts require the cooperation of the judicial system and mental health professionals. Psychologists, psychiatrists, and clinical social workers are typically involved in the screening and treatment of mental health court clients. However, it is usually the court that decides whether the individual being treated is cooperating and making adequate progress. Critics have noted that lack of available treatment resources could be problematic and that a judge's subjective decision making regarding an individual's mental health is unwarranted (Hasselbrack, 2001). More recent research suggests that the availability of treatment is increasing, but the specific kind of treatment needs further study (Luskin, 2013).

Despite early concerns about both drug and mental health courts, it would seem at this time that both are here to stay. There is, to be sure, some research that questions their effectiveness, particularly on a long-term basis, and changes in procedures are likely warranted in individual courts. The bulk of the research literature, however, has a positive view of these specialized courts, and it is likely that they have a permanent place in the judicial system.

The above overview of court structure, together with the classifications of law discussed in Chapter 1, should give students a foundation for dealing with material throughout the book. In the next section, we will look at the judicial process in more depth, including how the psychologist might participate at various stages.

The Judicial Process

For our purposes, we divide the judicial or court process in both criminal and civil cases into four major stages: (1) pretrial, (2) trial, (3) **disposition**, and (4) appeals. Illustrations of what contemporary psychologists can contribute at each of these stages abound (see Table 2-1 for examples). Because of psychology's intense interest in the judicial process and the many issues that arise as a result, these stages will be discussed in detail, together with some illustrative cases and research studies. Unless otherwise specified, the discussion relates to both civil and criminal cases.

Pretrial Stage

The pretrial process in a *criminal* case begins when a crime is reported and investigated, and evidence begins to accrue. Very early on, police may contact a court officer

Table 2-1 Examples of What May Occur at Four Main Points in the Judicial Process and How Psychologists May Participate

	Actions or Proceedings	Psychologist
Pretrial	Complaints or charges filed Arraignment Defendant sent for evaluations Depositions Plea negotiation Bail decision making Transfer of juveniles to criminal courts	Evaluate criminal defendants Provide evidence in depositions Testify in pretrial hearings Assess risk of dangerousness Consult with lawyers Restore incompetent defendants Assess juveniles
Trial	Jury selection Presentation of evidence Cross-examination Summations Jury deliberation	Consult with attorneys on jury selection Testify as expert witness providing specialized knowledge
Disposition	Verdict Acquittal Finding for plaintiff or respondent Assessment of damages Sentencing	Testify as to mitigating factors Testify as to risk of dangerousness Recommend treatment approaches for a convicted offender
Appeals	Appeal to overturn conviction or reduce sentence Petitions for writ of habeas corpus Reduce damage awards	File amicus curiae briefs

(magistrate or judge) to obtain a warrant to search or to arrest a suspect. The judicial system becomes more involved when police clear a case by arresting a suspect and turning him or her over for prosecution. It should be noted, of course, that there are many instances when a case is dropped or is diverted from standard prosecution, as we saw in our discussion of specialized courts. When a suspect is arrested and held in jail, an **initial appearance** before a court officer must occur, usually within 24 hours, to assure that there are legal grounds to hold the individual. For major federal crimes and for some state violations, **grand juries** directed by the prosecutor weigh evidence, sometimes call witnesses, and decide whether there is sufficient evidence to go forth with prosecution. The **indictment**, is the grand jury's formal accusation against the individual. Essentially, the grand jury is agreeing with the prosecutor's assertions. In the absence of a grand jury, the prosecutor takes an accused person directly before a trial court judge for a **preliminary hearing**, called a probable cause hearing in many jurisdictions. The judge in this court, typically a lower court, hears evidence from the prosecutor and decides whether there is sufficient evidence to proceed with prosecution.

Preliminary hearings are adversarial, allowing the defendant an opportunity to cross-examine any witnesses the prosecutor may call as well as present evidence to refute a finding of probable cause if the defendant so wishes. In January 2013, James E. Holmes—the alleged shooter in the Batman case—sat through 3 days of a preliminary hearing but did not present evidence on his own behalf. Holmes eventually entered a plea of not guilty by reason of insanity. By contrast, in the infamous O.J. Simpson case in 1994, an extensive, publicly broadcast preliminary hearing was held during which Simpson's lawyers called multiple witnesses to the stand. Preliminary hearings can be and are commonly waived, however. Such a waiver is an acknowledgment that the state has sufficient evidence against the defendant. The defendant may be planning to plead guilty, may want to save the time that would be spent on the hearing, or may want to avoid the publicity that could ensue. On the other hand, lawyers for defendants may want to buy time or see what evidence the state has obtained.

The next step is to formally charge the defendant in an open court, a proceeding called the **arraignment**. In some jurisdictions, arraignments occur before preliminary hearings. At the arraignment, the presiding judge asks defendants if they understand the charges, informs them of their right to counsel, and asks them to enter pleas. Dzhokhar Tsarnaev, facing 30 federal charges in the Boston Marathon bombing of April 15, 2013, pleaded not guilty during a 7-minute arraignment in federal court. Tsarnaev and his older brother allegedly planted two bombs along the marathon route. After a 5-day manhunt, which included a shoot-out in which the brother was killed, Tsarnaev was found hiding in a boat in a suburban backyard.

It is not unusual for persons charged with minor offenses and even many felonies to plead guilty at their arraignments and receive an immediate fine or sentence. A considerable amount of research in psychology and law has questioned the competency of some defendants—such as the intellectually disabled, the mentally ill, and juveniles—to plead guilty. We discuss this in Chapter 4. Other possible pleas are *nolo contendere* and not guilty by reason of insanity (NGRI), the plea entered by Holmes. The latter is actually a not guilty plea accompanied by notice that insanity will be used as a defense. In a handful of states, defendants are allowed to plead guilty but mentally ill (GBMI). GBMI is a plea and verdict form that will be discussed along with insanity in Chapter 4. The nolo contendere plea indicates that the defendant will not contest the charges but will also not admit guilt. For purposes of the criminal law, both the guilty and the nolo pleas have the same result—a conviction is entered into the record.

A plea of guilty is a waiver of the fundamental constitutional right against self-incrimination—the right to remain silent. Pleading guilty also waives Sixth Amendment constitutional rights, such as the right to a public trial by a jury of one's peers, the right to confront and cross-examine witnesses, and the right to present witnesses on one's own behalf. Ariel Castro pled guilty in 2013 to 937 criminal counts in a televised hearing shortly before his sentencing. The presiding judge in the case carefully questioned him to be sure that he understood the charges against him and that his lawyers had explained the consequences of his plea. In some cases, guilty pleas can be withdrawn. Moreover, a plea of not guilty at the arraignment can be subsequently changed to guilty at later stages of the process, even up to the moment before a jury renders a verdict.

If the defendant pleads not guilty, the judge must decide on conditions of release (amount of bail, release on recognizance, release to the custody of a third party). An increasingly common approach is denial of bail (**preventive detention**) on the basis that an individual is a high risk for flight or is dangerous to society. In the latter case, psychologists or other mental health professionals may be called in to assess the risk of violence. This bail decision is made after consideration of the nature and circumstances of the offense, the background of the accused, and recommendations from the prosecutor or other relevant individuals. If a bail amount is set and cannot be posted, or if the individual is denied bail, he or she is placed in or returned to jail.

The not guilty plea sets the trial process in motion. The next step is one or more pretrial hearings, during which witnesses, arresting officers, and other parties may present evidence. Numerous decisions may be made during these pretrial hearings. They include whether evidence is admissible, whether a trial should be moved because of extensive pretrial publicity, whether a youth should be transferred to juvenile court, whether a defendant is competent to stand trial, and the aforementioned issue of whether bail should be denied because of the alleged dangerousness of a defendant. The juvenile transfer, competency, and dangerousness issues represent pretrial situations in which practicing psychologists are very often involved.

During the pretrial hearings, and between these and the trial, extensive negotiating and plea bargaining often take place, with the result that criminal cases rarely get to the trial stage. In some jurisdictions, as many as 90% of the defendants charged with crimes plead guilty at arraignment or change to guilty pleas before the trial date (Neubauer, 2002).

The pretrial process in *civil* cases has parallels to the above. When one individual (the plaintiff) sues another (the respondent or defendant), there are no grand jury indictments or formal charges, however. Instead, a complaint outlining the alleged wrong and the desired remedy is filed by the plaintiff; the respondent or defendant then receives a summons and has a time limit in which to respond. As in criminal cases, there may be extensive negotiation between parties before they ever see the inside of a court-room. In addition, there are pretrial conferences with the judge in an attempt to facilitate a settlement. In some jurisdictions, litigants are encouraged or even required to try to settle with the help of a mediator. Unlike in criminal cases, speedy trials are not an issue, and years may elapse before a case comes to trial.

The **discovery process** is an important component of the pretrial process in both criminal and civil cases. This requires each side to make available certain information at its disposal to the other side in the preparation of its case. As an officer of the court and in the interests of justice, a prosecutor in a criminal case is obliged to make known *exculpatory* evidence to the defense. This is evidence that would help the accused, such as the fact that a witness to the crime had identified a different person as the culprit. The defense lawyer does not have to inform the prosecution of incriminatory material, however. This is because, in a criminal case, the burden is on the state to prove that the defendant is guilty beyond a reasonable doubt.

As part of the discovery process, **depositions** may be required. These are proceedings during which potential witnesses, including expert witnesses, are questioned by attorneys for the opposing side, under oath and in the presence of a court reporter, although typically away from the courtroom. Some psychologists have commented that the grilling they receive during a deposition can be more extensive than courtroom cross-examination. Furthermore, because most cases are settled before trial, clinicians are more likely to be called to testify in depositions or in pretrial hearings than in trials. Although the deposition may take place in an informal setting, it is part of the court record, and information obtained may well reappear at the trial. For this reason, Hess (1999) recommended strongly that psychologists not waive their right to review the transcription of the deposition, in the event that clerical errors might be present.

The Role of Psychologists

In the pretrial stage, psychologists often consult with key players in the judicial process, particularly lawyers. The emergence of mental health courts discussed above has created new opportunities for clinicians to assist in the early identification of defendants who are mentally disordered and could benefit from community treatment rather than incarceration. Likewise, community and counseling psychologists specializing in substance abuse may also assess drug court clients. An array of other court-ordered or independent evaluations may be conducted at the pretrial stage as well. Examples are evaluations of a person's competency to stand trial or competency to plead guilty, evaluations of mental state at the time of the offense, or neurological evaluations (as might be required in a civil suit resulting from an automobile accident).

Psychologists who specialize in **trial consultation**—sometimes called litigation consulting—find no shortage of tasks to perform at the pretrial stage, but they encounter many ethical pitfalls (Finkelman, 2010), which we discuss in later chapters. Lawyers planning their trial strategies may begin alerting potential expert witnesses that they will likely be called to testify on a wide range of psychologically relevant issues. It is at the pretrial stage, also, that lawyers may be concerned about the potentially damaging effects of pretrial publicity. Thus, trial consultants are asked to conduct surveys of the community and collect evidence of negative publicity, which would support a motion for a change of venue. Lawyers also may enlist the help of social and behavioral scientists in finding the type of juror who would be most sympathetic to their side. This **"scientific jury selection"** process may include community surveys, focus groups, or even mock trials. Both because the research in this area has not been promising, and because these are time-consuming and expensive undertakings, trial consultants today are more likely to help attorneys prepare witnesses and determine effective strategies for presenting evidence and persuading jurors (Myers & Arena, 2001). We will discuss many of these examples of psychological involvement in more detail in the chapters ahead.

Trial Stage

In both criminal and civil cases, trials follow a similar pattern of stages, beginning with jury selection, unless the verdict will be rendered only by a judge (called a **bench trial** or a **court trial**). The jury selection process is followed by opening arguments, the presentation of evidence and the presentation and cross-examination of witnesses for both sides, summations of cases, the judge's instructions to the jury, jury deliberation, and a verdict. A few important differences between criminal and civil cases should be noted, however. There is no constitutional right to a lawyer in civil cases, for example, whereas lawyers are guaranteed to indigent defendants facing the possibility of at least 1 day's incarceration in criminal cases (*Gideon v. Wainwright*, 1966; *Argersinger v. Hamlin*, 1972; *Alabama v. Shelton*, 2002). Defendants (sometimes called respondents) in civil cases do not have the right to remain silent, as they do in criminal cases. The right to cross-examine witnesses is also more limited in civil cases, whereas it is a fundamental right in criminal trials. The standard of proof also differs. In criminal cases, each element of the crime must be proved **beyond a reasonable doubt**, whereas judges and juries in civil cases must be convinced by a **preponderance of the evidence** or, in some situations, by **clear and convincing**

evidence. Juvenile delinquency proceedings, however, while considered civil in nature, do provide juveniles with the constitutional guarantees provided adults in criminal courts, although juveniles are not constitutionally guaranteed a trial by jury. Table 2-2 provides definitions of the three above standards of proof. The burden of proof is "the obligation of a party to establish by evidence a requisite degree of belief concerning a fact in the mind of the trier of fact or the court" (Black, 1990, p. 196).

The Role of Psychologists

The role of psychologists during the trial stage has received extensive attention. During *voir dire,* which is the process of choosing jurors for a particular trial (discussed in Chapter 3), the social scientist again may serve as a trial consultant, helping the attorney make decisions as to whether a particular proposed juror is acceptable. In this capacity, the psychologist is essentially a member of the trial team. The consultant may suggest voir dire questions to lawyers and make inferences about prospective jurors based on their responses or even on their nonverbal behavior (Strier, 1999).

Psychologists also are active during the trial stage as expert witnesses. They may testify on matters such as criminal responsibility; eyewitness testimony; or the emotional state of a litigant, such as one claiming PTSD. Clinical psychologists report on their evaluations of the individual; research psychologists may be asked to testify about the empirical evidence relating to the disorder. As covered in Chapter 1, evidence offered by expert witnesses is evaluated by trial judges and will not be admitted into court unless the expert holds the necessary credentials and the evidence meets specific scientific criteria.

Disposition Stage

Sentencing

The third major stage of the judicial process is most relevant to criminal cases, since it is the stage at which a judge or jury imposes a sentence or other penalty upon a convicted

Table 2-2 Standards of Proof Applied by Judges and Juries in Trial Courts

Proof Level	Evidence Level
Preponderance of the evidence	Evidence that is of greater weight or is more convincing than the evidence offered in opposition. Evidence that the fact sought to be proved is more probable than not.
Clear and convincing proof	Proof that results in reasonable certainty of the truth. More proof than preponderance of evidence but less than beyond reasonable doubt.
Beyond a reasonable doubt	Fully satisfied, entirely convinced, satisfied to a moral certainty. In criminal law, absolute certainty is not required, but the trier of fact must come very close to being absolutely certain. If there is reasonable doubt, the defendant should not be found guilty.

offender. In the civil process, when a verdict favors the plaintiff, a **judgment** is handed down, specifying the remedy to be borne by the respondent or defendant. The standard civil case does not involve the psychologist once this has occurred. Nevertheless, in deciding upon a remedy, judges and juries certainly consider testimony relating to the psychological harm a plaintiff may have suffered. It should be realized, also, that the juvenile process—which is civil—also may involve a "sentence," which is called a disposition in juvenile courts. Clinical information is often used in this context.

In criminal cases, it is at the disposition stage that a decision is made whether to incarcerate the individual and for how long and, in death penalty cases, whether to impose the ultimate penalty (discussed later in this chapter), an alternative life sentence, or life without possibility of parole. Sentencing includes a hearing at which the victim may speak about the effects of the crime and may even take the opportunity to address the offender directly. One of the victims in the Ariel Castro case told her abductor that her hell was over, but his was just beginning. (Ironically, Castro hung himself in his jail cell not long after his sentencing.) Judges also may provide the offender with an opportunity to make a statement, including a statement to the victim. Castro offered a semi-apology to his victims, but also declared that he was "not a monster." In addition to the victim and offender, other individuals on both sides may address the court during the sentencing hearing.

The Role of Psychologists

Psychologists often enter the disposition stage in the criminal process. They may be consulted by the probation officer preparing a **presentence report**, which is a document submitted to the judge intended to provide helpful sentencing information. The report is submitted after the probation officer has conducted a **presentence investigation (PSI)**. It typically contains background data on the offender, including prior record, as well as a review of the facts of the case and a summary of victim reactions. The judge also may request, or grant an attorney's request for, a psychological evaluation of the offender's amenability to rehabilitation. For example, a judge may sentence an offender convicted of lewd and lascivious behavior to probation with the condition that he participate in a community-based sex offender treatment program, after having heard from psychologists that the offender would be a good candidate for such a program. The PSI also may include the probation officer's sentencing recommendation. Judges seem to agree with the recommendation in 70% to 90% of the cases (Clear & Cole, 2000), but it is not clear whether the probation officer actually influences the judge's decision. As Clear and Cole observe, "it is hard to know whether judges are following the officers' advice or whether the officers' experience has given them the ability to anticipate the sentences that the judges would have chosen anyway" (p. 182).

The competency inquiry that may occur early in the judicial process also can reoccur at sentencing. Thus, psychologists may evaluate a recently convicted offender if there is a question whether he or she has sufficient ability to understand the proceedings. In addition, in the death penalty context, psychological input is often critical. Before the offender can receive the death sentence, the jury weighs aggravating and mitigating factors associated with the crime and the offender. An *aggravating factor* is one that adds to the seriousness of the crime, such as the torture of a murder victim. A *mitigating factor*, such as a developmental disability or a history of child abuse, lessens the culpability of the offender. Some states with the death penalty also require some assessment of risk or prediction of "future dangerousness" of the offender, a standard generally thought to require the input of an examining clinician. As will be seen in later chapters, this is a controversial topic among clinicians today.

Appellate Stage

During the appeals process, as you may recall, a higher court reviews the findings of a lower or trial court on matters of law. This stage involves the filing of the trial transcript and numerous documents on both sides, as well as documents that do not necessarily advocate for one side but are intended to help the appellate court arrive at a decision. The losing party in the trial court files an intention to appeal, which puts the winning party on notice that the case has not ended. The party approaching the appellate court becomes the appellant or petitioner, and the other party becomes the respondent. In criminal cases, the petitioner may appeal the guilty verdict or the sentence, based on any number of decisions made by the judge before and during the trial. The petitioner also may argue that his or her constitutional rights were violated, as when denied the Sixth Amendment right to adequate assistance of counsel. In 2013, a court vacated the 2002 conviction of Michael Skakel, who had been found guilty in the murder of a young girl almost 30 years before, when he was 15 years old. The court said his lawyer had not adequately represented his interests in 2002 and the judge freed him on bond to await a new trial.

In civil cases, the losing party may appeal the jury award or may appeal on the basis of errors that allegedly occurred during the trial. It is important to note, though, that in both criminal and civil cases, the attorney during the trial should have objected for the record, providing the trial court with an opportunity to correct the error as soon as it occurred. Even if errors did occur, however, appellate courts decide "whether or not the error(s) was serious enough to justify a new trial or if it was a 'harmless error' not affecting the outcome of the trial" (Abadinsky, 1995, p. 304).

In any given state, the court of last resort—the highest appellate court in the state—has discretion as to whether to hear a case, as long as there has been opportunity for the appeal to be heard in a lower-level appellate court (intermediate appeals). If there is no intermediate court, the court of last resort must hear the appeal, providing that it has been properly filed and states a legitimate basis for appeal. An offender would not get very far if she were to appeal her 4-year sentence on the basis that prisons are, per se, cruel and unusual punishment. On the other hand, if she received a 30-year sentence for a first-time burglary in which no property was either taken or damaged, she could argue that this sentence was disproportionate to her crime and would have a good basis for an appeal. In criminal cases, offenders have a constitutional right to at least one appeal. Persons unable to afford their own lawyer have a right to free legal representation during this first appeal.

The Role of Psychologists

Psychology may enter the appellate process in two primary ways. First, the very basis of the appeal may be a clinician's own involvement in the pretrial or trial process. For example, a father appealing a custody decision may argue that the one psychologist who interviewed his child did not have the proper credentials as outlined in the statutes. Alternatively, a person convicted of rape might appeal his conviction, arguing that expert testimony by a psychologist on rape trauma syndrome should not have been introduced. A second way in which psychology enters the appellate process is through the filing of amicus curiae (friend of the court) briefs.

An **amicus curiae brief** is a document filed by interested parties other than those directly involved in the case (the appellant and the respondent). They file the brief either because they have specialized information that could be helpful to the appeals court in arriving at its decision or because they could be affected by the outcome of the case. Psychologists often join other concerned social and behavioral scientists in filing these briefs.

Bersoff and Ogden (1991) summarize five purposes of the amicus brief: (1) to supply information not readily available to the parties in the case; (2) to develop arguments that one party has been able to present only in summary form; (3) to make arguments that one party has been unable to make because of lack of resources; (4) to fill a void by making arguments that one party prefers not to make; and (5) to address the broad social implications of a decision (p. 950). Considering psychology's interest in discipline-relevant public policy, it is not surprising that the filing of amicus briefs on behalf of the profession is both vigorous and controversial.

The American Psychological Association has aggressively acted on its responsibility to inform the courts about relevant research evidence by filing amicus curiae briefs (see Table 2-3 for a list of representative briefs recently filed by the APA). At times, the APA's positions have been controversial. A good example of this is several cases involving decision-making abilities of juveniles. On the one hand, the APA has supported the right of juvenile females to obtain abortions without parental involvement (*Hodgson v. Minnesota*, 1990); on the other, the APA has questioned the maturity of juveniles accused of serious crimes, maintaining that juveniles should neither receive the death penalty (*Roper v. Simmons*, 2005) nor be sentenced to life imprisonment without opportunity for parole (*Miller v. Alabama and Jackson v. Hobbs*, 2012). Can juveniles be given the same autonomy as adults in making an abortion decision but not be held as responsible as adults for crimes they have committed? Some critics, including some Supreme Court Justices, have argued that the APA "flip-flopped" in taking a position on these cases (Fischer, Stein, & Heikkinen, 2009). Psychologists involved in writing the briefs, however, see no conflict in the two positions (Steinberg, Cauffman, Woolard, Graham, & Banich, 2009a, 2009b). Among other points, they note that adolescent crime is typically committed spontaneously and is often influenced by other juveniles or committed with criminal adults. In contrast, the decision to abort a fetus is rarely spontaneous, involves considerable thought, and is usually made after consultation with a caring adult. We discuss adolescent development and decision making at several points throughout the book. It is relevant to many topics, including participation in crime, health decisions, waiving constitutional rights, and participating in custody proceedings.

Table 2-3	Examples of Amicus Curiae Briefs Recently Filed by the American Psychological Association in Federal and State Appellate Courts	
Case Name	**Year Brief Was Filed**	**Topic**
United States v. Windsor*	2012	Marriage equality
Fisher v. University of Texas*	2012	Affirmative action
Miller v. Alabama and Jackson v. Hobbs*	2012	Juvenile life without parole, juvenile murderers
Donaldson v. Montana	2011	Domestic partnerships
Michigan v. Kowalski	2011	False confessions
Perry v. New Hampshire*	2011	Eyewitness testimony
Coble v. Texas* (cert. denied)	2011	Testimony on future dangerousness in death penalty case
Graham v. Florida*	2010	Juvenile life without parole
Panetti v. Quarterman*	2007	Level of mental illness required to preclude execution
U.S. v. Fields	2006	Reliability of expert testimony in death penalty cases
Roper v. Simmons*	2004	Juvenile death penalty
Lawrence v. Texas*	2003	Criminalization of sodomy

*Briefs filed with U.S. Supreme Court

Note: A complete list of cases in which the APA filed briefs is available at the APA website: www.apa.org.

Thomas Grisso and Michael Saks (1991) urge psychologists not to be discouraged when judicial decisions either ignore social science evidence or do not comport with it. They assert that the U.S. Supreme Court's expertise in constitutional analysis and the numerous other sources of information available to the Justices must be considered. Grisso and Saks also argue that the Court has not directly *rejected* social science evidence, but rather has often based its decisions on other grounds. They emphasize that it is important for psychology to continue informing the Court about the findings of research in order "to provide a safeguard against judicial use of erroneous presumptions about human behavior. With this as a criterion for judging success, psychology has reason to take heart" (p. 208). Saks (1993), however, further cautions psychologists to be conscious of the melding of advocacy and educational roles. In other words, on some issues they may be very tempted to advocate for one side or the other. Their role, though, should be one of providing objective data to assist the courts in arriving at a decision. In the brief-writing process, he notes, "conflict between the duties of conscientious advocates and conscientious psychologists is likely" (p. 238).

The Psychologist as an Expert Witness

Few areas of psychology and law have attracted more attention than the use of psychologists as expert witnesses in courtroom settings. As described earlier in this chapter as well as in Chapter 1, psychologists and other mental health professionals may be called to testify in pretrial proceedings, during the trial itself, or at the sentencing stage of criminal cases. When their testimony relates to their evaluations of defendants, victims, plaintiffs, or witnesses, it is considered *clinically based*. Alternatively, they may be called to testify because of their *research expertise* on a specific issue, such as the reliability and validity of the polygraph, the effect of divorce on children, or the limitations of eyewitness identification. However, we must be careful not to make too sharp a demarcation between clinical and research skills. When clinicians testify in court proceedings, their testimony should be based on scientific knowledge. As Rotgers and Barrett (1996) have remarked, "The practice of clinical psychology can be conceived of as the art of applying scientific knowledge of human behavior to the analysis of the behavior and psychological states of individuals" (p. 468). Thus, according to the authors, because clinical psychology has adopted the "mantle of science" (p. 468), clinical psychologists should expect to be required to adhere to the same scientific standards of data gathering as other scientific experts.

Expert Certification

In order for an individual to qualify as an expert, courts require that he or she possess specialized knowledge that is "beyond the ken" of the average layperson and that will assist the trier of fact (judge or jury) in understanding technical evidence. In the tobacco litigation cases of the 1990s, for example, medical researchers interpreted complex scientific data to help the courts understand the effects of carcinogens on both smokers and those exposed to secondhand smoke. Obviously, individuals who testify as expert witnesses must first establish their credentials, including the requisite advanced degree, licensing or certification if relevant, and research or practical experience in areas about which they are testifying. Until the mid-20th century, courts were divided over whether psychologists were competent to testify on mental health issues, so the typical expert on issues such as insanity, competency to stand trial, dangerousness, or amenability to treatment was a psychiatrist. In *Jenkins v. United States* (1962), however, the court of appeals for the D.C. Circuit, sitting en banc, acknowledged that psychologists as well as psychiatrists could qualify as expert witnesses. The decision paved the way for psychologists to testify as experts from that point on. In each case, it is left to the discretion of the trial judge to accept or reject an individual's qualifications as an expert, subject to review by appellate courts.

Some research (e.g., Edens et al., 2012; Mossman, 2013) indicates that expert witnesses are perceived or depicted negatively by lawyers and sometimes by appellate judges. Edens et al. found comments disparaging the expert witness in 160 published civil and criminal court cases. For example, lawyers referred to them as "charlatans" or "weasels" and indicated they were practicing junk science or pseudoscience. Because the study was based on published cases, it could not evaluate the impact of these comments on jurors, however.

Legal Standards

The trial court judge also decides whether the evidence is relevant to the case at hand (see Table 1-2 in Chapter 1). Recall that the "general acceptance" rule remains in effect in many states. Moreover, general acceptance is often part of the inquiry even in states that have adopted the *Daubert* standard, whereby courts are expected to evaluate the scientific nature of the evidence.

These standards are well illustrated by referring to a number of "syndromes" that have emerged in the clinical literature in recent years, and that courts have often rejected because they did not have general acceptance in the field or were not scientifically documented. "Profiling" evidence is also viewed suspiciously by many courts. This criticism has been leveled not only at "syndrome" research (Hess, 1999; Otto & Heilbrun, 2002) or profile evidence (George, 2008; Kocsis, 2009), but also at specific tools used in psychological assessment (Edens, Skeem, & Kennealy, 2009; Otto & Heilbrun, 2002), and issues relating to child custody determinations (Bolocofsky, 1989). Most recently, some courts have refused to admit expert testimony on false confessions (e.g., *Michigan v. Kowalski*, 2011) despite the fact that research in this area is growing rapidly.

Psychologists themselves have argued that research evidence in some areas is transferred to the courtroom prematurely, before it has gained general acceptance by the research community. Faigman and Monahan (2009) urge caution in this sphere, reminding psychologists of the need to exercise critical judgment in deciding what has gained general acceptance: "Especially deleterious to self-criticism is that some psychologists measure the success of their work by whether courts accept or reject it" (p. 15).

Once decisions to certify the expert and admit her testimony have been made, there are still more hurdles for the expert witness. As many commentators have remarked, testifying in court is not an exercise for the faint of heart. Even if the expert has successfully vaulted the court's credentials and testimony barriers, she faces the possibility of being subjected to grueling cross-examination or pitted against another expert with conflicting views. Some experts also face concerns about issues revolving around confidentiality and "ultimate opinion" testimony. We will discuss each of these hurdles below, beginning with the problem of confidentiality.

The Confidentiality Issue

The obligation to maintain confidentiality in the patient–therapist relationship is fundamental. If you entrust the most intimate details of your life, such as your fears or bizarre behaviors, to a clinician, you expect that these will not be repeated outside the clinical setting. Nevertheless, the law places limits on that confidentiality. In all states, practitioners are required by law to report evidence of child abuse (and in some cases, elderly or other abuse) encountered in their practice to appropriate parties, which may include law enforcement or social service agencies.

In many states, clinicians have a duty to warn (and sometimes to protect) third parties who may be in danger from a patient who has threatened their lives. This is referred to as the *Tarasoff* requirement, named after a court ruling (*Tarasoff v. Regents of the University of California*, 1974). In this early part of the 21st century, issues involving patient–therapist confidentiality have been discussed in the public forum in a number of noteworthy contexts, but particularly with respect to mass shootings. In both the Virginia Tech and "Batman" theater case, the perpetrators had seen mental health practitioners shortly before their crimes. In the Virginia Tech situation, the shooter had received a court order to obtain treatment. We discuss these cases in later chapters.

In the context of providing testimony in court, psychologists can make few claims to confidentiality. For example, court-requested evaluations, which require practitioners to forward written reports to a range of judicial actors, are not confidential. In these situations, the clinician's client is the court, not the individual being examined. However, psychologists are ethically bound, and in some situations legally bound, to warn the individual of the potential uses of their reports.

If the person [being assessed] is not the client, the psychologist owes no duty of confidentiality to that person; but, because of the requirement of informed consent, must make the fact known to the person being assessed that the information to be obtained is not confidential. (Ogloff, 1999, p. 411)

Likewise, under the *Specialty Guidelines for Forensic Psychology* (APA, 2013b), clinicians are advised to inform the individual of the nature and purpose of an evaluation, as well as who will be receiving a report. They should also ensure that the individual is informed of his or her legal rights. Nonetheless, even if notified of the limits of confidentiality, the individual in reality has little choice in submitting to the evaluation if it is mandated by the court, even if he or she has not requested it. In these situations, the clinician can conduct the evaluation over objections and without consent of the person being evaluated (Guideline 6.03.02).

Ultimate Issue or Ultimate Opinion Testimony

In most jurisdictions, *lay witnesses* can testify only to events that they have actually seen or heard firsthand. Their opinions and inferences are generally not admissible (Schwitzgebel & Schwitzgebel, 1980). An **expert witness,** on the other hand, testifies to facts he or she has observed directly, to tests conducted, and to the relevant research evidence. Moreover, the opinions and inferences of experts are not only admissible but also often sought by the courts. Recall that a main role of experts is to assist triers of fact in matters about which they would not otherwise be knowledgeable.

Currently, there is considerable debate among mental health professionals about the wisdom of offering an opinion on the "ultimate issue." The **ultimate issue** is the final question that must be decided by the court. For example, should the expert provide an opinion about whether the defendant was indeed insane (and therefore not responsible) at the time of his crime? Should the expert recommend which parent should be awarded custody? Should the expert opine that a defendant is competent to be executed? Should the expert recommend that a juvenile's case be transferred to criminal court? It is quite clear that courts frequently request and hope for such opinions (Melton et al., 1997, 2007; Slobogin, 1989). With respect to custody evaluations, "there is at least a clinical lore that judges do not like making custody decisions and would prefer—sometimes in their order for the evaluation—that the evaluator make explicit recommendations" (O'Donohue, Beitz, & Tolle, 2009, p. 298). A study involving judicial personnel in Virginia (Redding, Floyd, & Hawk, 2001) found that judges and prosecutors in particular wanted the expert to provide an opinion on the ultimate issue of whether a defendant was insane at the time of the offense. Defense attorneys were less likely to support this. The researchers noted that the desire among judges and prosecutors to have this opinion was interesting in light of that state's statutory prohibition on such ultimate issue testimony.

Slobogin (1989) has summarized the arguments for and against allowing testimony on the ultimate legal issue before the courts. While acknowledging that judges, lawyers, and juries all want this testimony, he cautions that courts be extremely wary of its use, allowing it only if rigorously tested through the adversarial process. Ultimate issues, he notes, are moral judgments. Although experts are surely capable of making such judgments, this is not their field of expertise. Those who oppose ultimate issue testimony also fear the undue influence of the expert on the fact finder. In other words, a jury or judge may overvalue the expert's opinion. Michael Saks (1990) has said that mental health experts too often see themselves as "temporary monarchs" in the courtroom. "This danger is exacerbated," Slobogin remarks,

> if the willingness of the expert to provide an ultimate conclusion and the eagerness of the fact finder to hear it minimize efforts to examine the basis of the conclusion; the opinion on the ultimate issue may come to assume disproportionate weight relative to the underlying facts in the mind or minds of the fact finder because the facts are not developed, or are not properly emphasized. (p. 261)

Research to date has not supported the undue influence of the expert at the trial stage, however, even on the ultimate question. A review of contemporary jury research, for example, indicates that, though jurors are not immune to an expert's opinion, their decisions are not unduly dictated by it (Nietzel, McCarthy, & Kerr, 1999). While influenced to some extent by the testimony, "the effect is modest and leaves opportunity for both foes and fans of ultimate opinion testimony to find support for their positions" (p. 41). It should be understood, however, that the influence of the expert in *pretrial* proceedings, such as when the judge is making a decision as to whether a defendant is competent to stand trial, is significant (Melton et al., 2007).

S. R. Smith (1989) identifies three possible sources of error in ultimate issue testimony, and finds that these are common occurrences in expert testimony. First, the expert may misunderstand the law and thus reach the wrong conclusion. Some experts, for example, confuse the legal constructs of sanity and competency to stand trial. Second, the expert may apply hidden value judgments rather than scientific principles, such as might occur if a psychologist testified that a mother was not a fit parent on the basis of an assumption that she is unfit because she works nights or does not have a religious affiliation. Third and finally, the expert may arrive at the wrong conclusion in order to produce a desired result. For example, a psychologist might conclude that an individual should be institutionalized, even though he does not meet the criteria for institutionalization. However, those who favor testimony on the ultimate issue (e.g., Rogers & Ewing, 2003) argue that judges often depend on it, and that such testimony can be carefully controlled, particularly by means of effective cross-examination.

Recognizing the lack of consensus on this matter, the American Psychological Association has not taken a stand on whether ultimate issue testimony should be provided, but in recent years there is evidence of a more favorable view to providing opinions, even in child custody cases. For example, the *Guidelines for Child Custody Evaluations in Family Law Proceedings* (APA, 2010b) indicate that "psychologists render a valuable service when they provide competent and impartial opinions with direct relevance to the 'psychological best interests' of the child" (p. 863). Even so, Guideline 13 emphasizes that the field has not reached consensus, so practitioners should remain aware of the arguments on both sides of the issue.

> Psychologists may conclude that this is an inappropriate role for a forensic evaluator or that available data are insufficient for this purpose. If a recommendation is provided, the court will expect it to be supportable on the basis of the evaluations conducted. (p. 866)

Surviving the Witness Stand

"The courtroom is a place best reserved for those who are brave, adventuresome and nimble-witted." This comment (Schwitzgebel & Schwitzgebel, 1980, p. 241) summarizes well the perils inherent in cross-examination and the discomfort likely to be felt by all but the most seasoned expert witness. The professional literature contains ample advice for psychologists who approach the witness stand. Poythress (1979), for example, suggested early on that good preparation for the psychologist intending to be an expert witness should include thorough experiential learning in mock trial situations, observations of experienced expert witnesses, and specific course work or field placements in forensic settings. Others have addressed stylistic as well as substantive effectiveness both on the witness stand and during a wide range of meetings and proceedings that are part of the trial preparation process (e.g., Brodsky, 2004; Melton et al., 2007). In light of the Supreme Court's ruling in the *Daubert* case, scholars also advise prospective experts to be well versed in scientific methodology and ready to address the reliability and validity of their findings, as well as the basis for their observations and conclusions (Skeem et al., 2009).

When two or more experts present opposing testimony, this can be problematic. Such a "battle of the experts" often occurs where the stakes are highest, as in criminal cases that could produce lengthy sentences. Experts often disagree on whether an individual is competent to stand trial or is a continuing danger. Some commentators have remarked that conflicting testimony by two psychologists or two psychiatrists or by one of each confuses the courts and the public and can undermine the credibility of both professions (Yarmey, 1979). Interestingly, studies have found that "opposing experts weakly affect jurors' ultimate verdicts in criminal cases or damage awards in civil cases" (McAuliff & Groscup, 2009, p. 37). These authors go on to say, however, that opposing expert opinions may affect the manner in which jurors evaluate evidence. They also believe that opposing experts can be a safeguard against unreliable expert testimony, mainly via effective cross-examination. In other words, to use a simple example, expert A makes an assertion supported by empirical evidence; expert B makes an opposite assertion, without sufficient supportive evidence. The attorney cross-examining expert B is able to place this expert's deficiencies on full display.

Differences of opinion between and within professions should not necessarily be interpreted as error, misinformation, or bad science, however. The "collision of experts" is partly due to the complexity and ambiguity of the issues about which they are commenting. Problems and inconsistencies may also be due to differences in training and philosophies. Because the science of psychology is tentative, complex, and ever evolving, it is not surprising that two well-qualified, experienced experts sometimes arrive at a different opinion in the same case.

Because psychologists represent the science of behavior, they would be well advised to be highly familiar with the behavioral research literature directly related to the legal issue upon which they will testify. They should also be prepared to substantiate the reliability and validity of any assessment instruments and procedures used in arriving at their conclusions. Writing about "survival on the witness stand," Brodsky (2004) notes that this preparation is essential. When experts are able to defend their specific theories, methods, and conclusions, their testimony becomes much more credible.

Virtually all writers who give advice to the expert witness emphasize the importance of establishing a communicative relationship with the attorney who contacts them early in the legal process.

> Some attorneys stereotypically view psychologists as soft thinkers, lacking in discipline, while psychologists often regard attorneys as narrowly focused, rigid, and inflexible. These stereotypes result from a failure to understand the other's professional needs at the outset of the consultation. (Singer & Nievod, 1987, p. 530)

This is reminiscent of the fundamental differences between psychology and law that were noted in Chapter 1. Singer and Nievod also urge psychologists not to be persuaded to enter the courtroom without advance notice and sufficient preparation time. This occurs with surprising frequency and typifies the relationship of "psychology in the law," also described in Chapter 1. In addition, Singer and Nievod warn that a psychologist's work products, such as interview notes, correspondence, and tape recordings relating to the case, will be made available to attorneys for both sides under the rules of discovery.

> Only wisdom and personal preference can dictate how extensively to maintain case records. There is no one way. If the psychologist takes few notes, an opposing attorney may attempt to characterize these notes as skimpy, careless, or the work of a cursory effort. (p. 538)

SUMMARY AND CONCLUSIONS

This chapter had two main purposes. The first was to provide an overview of court structure and the judicial process. It is important that the reader become familiar with a variety of courts, concepts, terms, and processes in order to understand the material that is to follow in later chapters. The second purpose of the chapter was to give readers an overview of the various ways in which psychologists and other mental health professionals interact with the law and the issues that arise as a result of that interaction.

Among the many changes on the court landscape in recent years has been the emergence of specialized courts. Drug courts and mental health courts, both discussed in the chapter, are good examples of this trend. Whereas early research on the success of these courts was mixed, more recent research finds many positive outcomes. Studies have demonstrated lower recidivism and greater satisfaction with the court process on the part of all participants, including judges and attorneys. Positive effects in the long term are not as easily demonstrated, but this is not to say that they have not occurred. New forms of problem-solving courts—such as domestic violence and veterans treatment courts—have not been adequately evaluated.

The steps in the judicial process were covered in some detail, along with examples of the roles psychologists perform in each. Considerable work is done at the pretrial stage, when psychologists and other scientists may serve as consultants or evaluators. In later chapters, these specific tasks will be covered in more depth. At each stage, however, there is ample opportunity for psychological involvement in both criminal and civil contexts, and their influence can be substantial. One example is amicus curiae briefs that are filed with appellate courts; these typically are extensive documents, which invariably include references to cutting-edge research in psychology. They are often cited in landmark cases of both the U.S. Supreme Court and the highest appellate courts of various states.

The topic of psychologists as expert witnesses was revisited in this chapter, after being introduced briefly in Chapter 1. This chapter focused on the challenges faced by witnesses on the witness stand. When a psychological evaluation is court ordered, for example, the client is the court, not the individual being evaluated. Therefore, there are limits on confidentiality, although the mental health practitioner is expected to inform the examinee of those limits. Another topic of concern to some psychologists is "ultimate issue" opinion testimony. Researchers, clinicians, and scholars all agree that judges often press mental health practitioners to make recommendations about the final legal question.

There is no shortage of advice available to psychologists willing to testify as experts. Professional guidelines, training programs, workshops, monographs, books, and videos are widely available. These materials are also, of course, available to lawyers seeking to challenge an expert's testimony or ruffle the expert on the witness stand.

KEY CONCEPTS

Amicus curiae brief

Appellate courts

Arraignment

Bench trial

Beyond a
reasonable doubt

Clear and convincing
evidence

Concurrent jurisdiction

Court trial

Criminological needs

Depositions

Discovery process

Disposition

Dual system

Expert witness

General jurisdiction

Grand juries

Indictment

Initial appearance

Judgment

Jurisdiction

Limited jurisdiction

Preliminary hearing

Preponderance of the
evidence

Presentence
investigation (PSI)

Presentence report

Preventive detention

Scientific jury selection

Specialized courts

Trial consultation

Trial courts

Ultimate issue

Writ of certiorari

The Investigative Process

Detection of Deception, Interrogations, False Confessions, and the Polygraph

Police had Van Chester Thompkins in custody and were questioning him about a murder. They had advised him of his Miranda rights, but he refused to sign a waiver of those rights when they passed one to him. However, he did not specifically say he did not want to talk to police, and he did not ask for a lawyer.

Thompkins was questioned for about three hours, during which time he remained silent, looked down at the floor, and responded only occasionally to a non-crime-related question.

Finally, police asked, "Do you pray to God to forgive you for shooting that boy?" and he answered "yes."

—Berghuis v. Thompkins, 2010

In 1989, a 29-year-old woman was jogging in Central Park when she was attacked, beaten, and raped. She had no memory of the incident and remained hospitalized for 6 weeks. Five youths, ages 14 to 16, were arrested and charged with the crimes. Police interrogated the youths aggressively, at one point confronting them with incriminating but false information. Each of the five suspects provided a videotaped confession, describing in vivid (but erroneous) detail how the jogger was attacked and the role he himself had played (Kassin & Gudjonsson, 2004). Thirteen years later, DNA evidence was linked to another individual, and the five convictions were vacated.

It's not my job to protect a suspect's rights. It's my job to get a confession.

—Anonymous investigator

The above illustrations set the stage for our discussion of topics that have captured the research attention of many contemporary psychologists who are interested in the relationship between psychology and law. They revolve around police interviewing and interrogation while investigating crime. The difference between an interview and an interrogation is a critical one. Police "interview" witnesses, victims, or anyone who may have knowledge of a crime. They also interview people who could eventually become criminal suspects. When suspicion is cast on an individual, he or she becomes a suspect and is then subject to "interrogation," or more intensive questioning.

Central to the topics in this chapter are the *Miranda* warnings that are intended to protect suspects from using their own words to incriminate themselves. The warnings also tell suspects they have a right to a lawyer, and that if they cannot afford one, a lawyer will be appointed. Any waiver of those rights must be made knowingly, intelligently, and willingly. If suspects speak to police after receiving their warnings, anything they say—including confessing to the crime—can be used against them. There are limits on the tactics police may use in obtaining confessions. For example, confessions cannot be coerced. As we indicate in this chapter, however, coercion is not always easy to establish, and there is no universally required terminology for delivering *Miranda* warnings. In essence, police are allowed considerable latitude in their interrogative approaches.

Legal psychologists and other legal scholars worry that many suspects do not comprehend their constitutional rights and are often subjected to psychological coercion in order for police to obtain a confession (N. E. S. Goldstein, Goldstein, Zelle, & Condie, 2013). Furthermore, psychologists, along with many others, are concerned about the growing evidence of false confessions (N. E. S. Goldstein et al., 2013; Kassin et al., 2010; Leo, 2008; Redlich, Kulish, & Steadman, 2011), such as those made in the Central Park case described at the beginning of the chapter.

The primary purpose of criminal interrogation is to obtain a confession from a suspect or to gain information that will lead to a conviction. Once a confession is obtained, the individual may recant it, arguing that it was obtained illegally or, less often, that it was a false confession. If the case goes to trial and the confession evidence is admitted, this confession is damaging evidence that clearly has a profound impact on jurors. Nevertheless, most convictions are obtained not from an individual's confession but from the weight of other evidence gathered by police. Furthermore, recall that the great majority of cases do not go to trial. It is estimated that only 4% of felony cases do (T. H. Cohen & Reaves, 2006). Therefore, a confession obtained by police is more likely to result in a plea of guilty.

Prior to the 1950s, courts accepted arguments that some methods employing physical restraints, prolonged physical discomfort, beatings, and a wide variety of physical abuses were, not surprisingly, coercive and not to be tolerated. Gradually, courts also began to acknowledge the existence of more subtle forms of **psychological coercion.** A confession is considered psychologically coerced if it "was elicited by brute force; prolonged isolation; deprivation of food or sleep; threats of harm of punishment; promises of immunity or leniency; or, barring exceptional circumstances, without notifying the suspect of his or her constitutional rights" (Kassin, 1997, p. 221).

Legal Background

Most adults—as well as most adolescents—are familiar with the *Miranda* warnings. Familiarity does not equal understanding of the rights associated with the warnings, however. Despite frequent references in the media, research indicates that even college students have false beliefs about their *Miranda* rights (Rogers, Rogstad, et al., 2010). For example, many people think police are not allowed to deceive them or that they can speak "off the record" under certain circumstances without police being able to use that information against them. We will discuss more of these false beliefs shortly.

The Fifth Amendment of the U.S. Constitution gives those accused of crime the right not to incriminate themselves, and courts have repeatedly reminded us that individuals may not be forced to confess or otherwise to provide evidence that may be damaging to their cases. Earlier decisions by the U.S. Supreme Court focused on police brutality. In *Brown v. Mississippi* (1936), for example, the suspect had been beaten by police until he confessed to a crime. In later cases, the Court addressed the psychological coercion that was implicit in the interrogation process (e.g., *Ashcraft v. Tennessee*, 1944; *Spano v. New York*, 1959). In the landmark case *Escobedo v. Illinois* (1964), the Court ruled that a suspect's confession should not have been admitted into court because it was made only after he had repeatedly asked for and been denied counsel. The Court also found that the interrogation methods used by the police had so emotionally upset Escobedo that his capacity for rational judgment was impaired. As a result, his confession did not follow a valid waiver of his constitutional rights. The best way to prevent potential injustice of this sort, the Justices said, was to allow subjects to be interrogated in the presence of their attorneys. Therefore, the Court held that once a police interviewing process shifts from an investigatory to an accusatory focus, the individual must be permitted (but not required) to have counsel present.

In *Miranda v. Arizona* (1966) the U.S. Supreme Court determined that the Fifth Amendment rights against self-incrimination and to a lawyer were so crucial that law enforcement officers must inform suspects of those rights prior to interrogating them. Ernesto Miranda was questioned by police after being arrested for kidnapping and rape. The victim provided a description of her assailant but did not positively identify Miranda in a subsequent lineup. However, during the interrogation, which occurred without a lawyer present, Miranda was told that the victim had identified him, and then he confessed to the crime. Miranda's case was one of four that came before the Supreme Court raising similar issues from different states, but because his was the lead case, his name has been attached to the decision—and to the warnings—ever since (N. E. S. Goldstein et al., 2013). In 2000, following a number of decisions that had seemed to diminish the *Miranda* ruling, the U.S. Supreme Court reaffirmed the central importance of *Miranda* warnings as a well-established procedural requirement in the law (*Dickerson v. United States,* 2000).

In the *Miranda* case, the Supreme Court commented extensively on the pressure tactics of interrogation and made several references to the powerful effects of psychological coercion associated with that process. Acknowledging that beating suspects in order to obtain a confession was a thing of the past, the Justices wrote,

> We stress that the modern practice of in-custody interrogation is psychologically rather than physically oriented. As we have stated before . . . this Court has recognized that coercion can be mental as well as physical, and that the blood of the accused is not the only hallmark of an unconstitutional inquisition. (p. 448)

The Court in *Miranda* felt it was paramount that the accused be notified of (1) the right to remain silent, and (2) the fact that what the accused says can be used against the individual if he or she chooses not to remain silent. Furthermore, suspects must be told (3) of their right to an attorney and (4) that if they cannot afford an attorney, one will be appointed for them. In addition to the above four elements, most jurisdictions also tell the suspect that he or she can stop answering questions at any time and request a lawyer (N. E. S. Goldstein et al., 2013). In addition, many jurisdictions ask suspects if they understand these rights or ask them to sign waivers, such as what occurred in the case cited at the beginning of this chapter (*Berghuis v. Thompkins*, 2010).

Phrasing the *Miranda* Warnings

The Supreme Court in the *Miranda* case did not require a specific wording, but anyone exposed to the entertainment media is probably aware of a typical recitation. The TV drama version may not be so typical, however. Rogers (2008b) reports that surveys across American jurisdictions yielded a surprising 945 distinct warnings. In addition, 122 juvenile warnings were found, along with 121 written in Spanish. Furthermore, written *Miranda* versions vary widely in reading levels, from mid-grade school to college level (Greenfield, Dougherty, Jackson, Podboy, & Zimmermann, 2001). It is unwarranted, therefore, to assume that there is a universal *Miranda* warning or one easily understood by most people. In fact, the Supreme Court has itself ruled that the exact words from the *Miranda* case are not needed (*California v. Prysock*, 1981) and that even ambiguous warnings satisfy the *Miranda* requirement (*Duckworth v. Eagan*, 1989).

The anonymous officer quoted at the beginning of this chapter—the one who indicated it was his job to get a confession—might not do any of the following, unless required to by departmental policy or law. He might not (1) ask if suspects understand the rights; (2) tell suspects that he will stop questioning if the suspect asserts the right to remain silent; (3) tell suspects that a lawyer can be consulted both before and during the interrogation; (4) obtain written waivers; (5) speak slowly and articulate his words; (6) provide warnings in any language other than English; or (7) take particular care in warning juveniles, the intellectually disabled, or the mentally disordered. The officer is likely also to try to deceive suspects into thinking there is more evidence against them than actually exists. As will be seen, this type of deception is perfectly legal, although police report that they do not use this tactic extensively (Kassin, Leo, et al., 2007).

The Custody Aspect

A suspect does not *have* to be informed of his or her rights *at the moment of arrest*. The operative point in time is *before **custodial interrogation***. A line of U.S. Supreme Court and lower court decisions after *Miranda* have interpreted and applied this phrase, specifying more clearly the situations under which the warnings are and are not required. The Court has accepted law enforcement's distinction between an interview and an interrogation, reiterating that the point at which the questioning shifts from an investigatory to an accusatory function is the point at which interrogation begins. Many cases have revolved around the issue of whether a reasonable person would believe that he or she was free to leave; if one is free to leave, one is not in custody (see Box 3-1 for a recent case relating to custody analysis).

BOX 3-1

Case Study. Police Questioning at School: Where Do We Draw the Line?

The point at which a person is "in custody" for purposes of giving *Miranda* warnings has been at issue in many court cases. Courts have determined that if a person was free to leave, he or she was not in custody. In a recent juvenile case, *J.D.B. v. North Carolina* (2011), the Supreme Court ruled that the age of the individual should be taken into account in custody analysis.

J.D.B. was a 13-year-old seventh grader who was taken out of his social studies classroom by a uniformed police officer, led to a conference room, and questioned by police relative to a burglary and theft of a digital camera. In the conference room with J.D.B. were two police officers (one a school resource officer) and two school administrators. The conference room door was shut. J.D.B.'s grandmother, who was his legal guardian, was not contacted. Initially, he was not informed of his *Miranda* rights nor told he was free to leave. Over a 45-minute period, police began with small talk, brought up the burglary and incriminating information they had obtained, and mentioned the possibility of juvenile detention. J.D.B. asked what this meant, and it was explained that he could be held overnight in a juvenile center. The assistant principal encouraged him to do the right thing and tell police what he knew. J.D.B. then confessed that he and a friend were responsible for the burglary. At that point, one of the officers told him he could refuse to answer more questions and was free to leave. When he asked if he understood this, J.D.B. nodded. The Supreme Court later noted that the officer's words did not qualify as a *Miranda* warning—this was irrelevant to the present case, however, because the prosecution claimed he was not in custody during the questioning.

Lower courts agreed with prosecutors and ruled that J.D.B. was not in custody and was free to leave during the questioning. For that reason, *Miranda* warnings were not required, and his confession was valid. The Supreme Court in this case did not say whether the lower courts were correct; rather, the Court majority (5–4) said J.D.B.'s age should have been taken into consideration in determining whether he perceived himself to be free to leave, and it was not. After citing past cases and psychological research on child development, the majority ruled that a child's age properly informs custody analysis. J.D.B.'s case was sent back to the trial court for a redetermination of whether he was in custody at the time of the police questioning.

Questions for Discussion:

1. Was J.D.B. in custody? Would he have been likely to think he was free to leave, before being told so by police?

2. Would this situation have been different if J.D.B. had been a 32-year-old office worker led to a conference room?

3. What should be the role of school resource officers in a situation such as this?

4. If the investigating officer had given J.D.B. adequate *Miranda* warnings at the beginning of the questioning, would this change your answer to any of the above questions?

Since *Miranda v. Arizona*, numerous appellate courts have issued rulings based on that case, including the U.S. Supreme Court itself (see Table 3-1 for a representative but not inclusive list of Supreme Court cases and holdings relating to *Miranda* rules). Some courts, like courts in the J.D.B. case, focused on the custody aspect; others focused on the wording of the warnings or when warnings may not be necessary. In *Berghius v. Thompkins* (2010), the case referred to at the beginning of the chapter, the Court, in a divided 5–4 decision, ruled that suspects must *actively assert* their right to remain silent; refusing to answer relevant questions over a 3-hour period and refusing to sign a waiver of his rights did not qualify as an active assertion on Thompkins's part. He did not specifically state his wish to remain silent. Therefore, responding "yes" to the police officer's question was a valid confession.

In a recent *Miranda*-related case decided by the U.S. Supreme Court, *Salinas v. Texas* (2013), the person had willingly accompanied police to the police station and was not under arrest. He was "interviewed" for an hour, at which point he remained silent when asked an incriminating question. At the trial stage, the prosecutor commented on that silence, implying that it pointed to the defendant's guilt. A five-Justice majority ruled that the prosecutor's comment did not violate his constitutional rights, while the four-Justice minority indicated that Salinas's silence was in effect his indication that he did not wish to incriminate himself, and it should not have been commented upon.

Although we do not dwell on legal issues in these and other *Miranda*-related cases, we will focus on the two psychological issues that are most relevant to police questioning: suspects' understanding or comprehension of *Miranda* warnings and the intractable problem of false confessions. Related to these issues, we discuss the ability of law enforcement officers—or anyone else—to detect deception in other people.

Comprehending *Miranda* Warnings

The *Miranda* warnings have remained an essential component of police procedure—some version of the *Miranda* warnings is routinely administered, sometimes more than once, but as noted above, there is no universal language. In some jurisdictions, warnings and confessions are audiotaped or videotaped, but it is less likely that the entire interrogation process will be so recorded. Warnings also may be delivered orally or in writing. In the case of juveniles, many jurisdictions today require that a parent or guardian be notified before custodial interrogation, and most of these also require their presence. Legal psychologists have noted, however, that parents are not necessarily the best protectors of their children's rights (Grisso, 1981). For example, parents and guardians may urge children to confess without appreciating the implications of a confession, or they

Table 3-1	Representative Supreme Court Cases Relating to Self-Incrimination Following *Miranda v. Arizona*	
Case Name	Year	Holding
Brewer v. Williams	1977	Warnings are required for the *equivalent* of a custodial interrogation—suspect was in police car, officers addressed him but did not question him.
Fare v. Michael C.	1979	Juvenile's request to see his probation officer is not the equivalent of request to see lawyer.
Rhode Island v. Innis	1980	Conversations between officers do not require *Miranda* warnings to suspect being transported.
California v. Prysock	1981	The exact wording used in *Miranda* decision is not required.
Berkemer v. McCarty	1984	Person is not in custody during a routine traffic stop, so *Miranda* warnings are not required.
New York v. Quarles	1984	Warnings not required if public safety is at risk.
Duckworth v. Eagan	1989	Ambiguous warnings still satisfied *Miranda* requirement.
Davis v. United States	1994	After waiver of rights, suspect must make an unambiguously clear statement of wish for lawyer.
Dickerson v. United States	2000	Miranda warning is established law; required before custodial interrogation by both federal and state law enforcement.
Yarborough v. Alvarado	2004	17-year-old interviewed without *Miranda* was free to leave, therefore not in custody.
Berghuis v. Thompkins	2010	Suspects must explicitly assert their right to silence; waiver can be implicit.
Florida v. Powell	2010	Warnings are sufficient as long as they reasonably convey the right to an attorney during interrogation. In this case, the police told suspect he had a right *before answering questions* but did not say he had a right *during interrogation*. The Court said this was sufficient.
J.D.B. v. North Carolina	2011	A youth's age should be taken into account in deciding whether he was in custody for purposes of *Miranda*.
Salinas v. Texas	2013	A person's silence in response to a police question prior to arrest and without *Miranda* warning can be used against him at trial.

may feel it important to teach a lesson. Therefore, some jurisdictions require by statute that a lawyer or a non-lawyer law guardian be present when a juvenile is interrogated. A law guardian is a person appointed by courts to protect the legal interests of persons who are believed not able to protect their own interests.

Despite public familiarity with *Miranda* warnings as a general concept, the public is remarkably uninformed about their significance, even though most people believe they understand them (Rogers, 2011). Early research in this area (e.g., Grisso, 1981) focused on juveniles, finding that even streetwise juveniles thought that anything they told their lawyers could be shared with prosecutors or judges. Over half the juveniles in Grisso's study thought that judges could revoke their constitutional rights once they asserted them. Numerous similar and later studies on juvenile comprehension of *Miranda* rights led some commentators to argue that juveniles should not be allowed to waive *Miranda* (Melton et al., 2007; Viljoen, Zapf, & Roesch, 2007). Interestingly, in a recent national survey of law enforcement officers (Reppucci, Meyer, & Kostelnik, 2010), the officers themselves were aware of developmental differences between youth and adults. However, they did not incorporate this knowledge into their interrogation practices, and they did not treat adolescents very differently from adults when they were questioning them.

Other research on comprehension of *Miranda* has focused on persons with intellectual disabilities or a mental disorder. Even individuals with a mild rather than severe intellectual disability have been found to lack comprehension of a simple version of the *Miranda* warning (O'Connell, Garmoe, & Goldstein, 2005).

As mentioned above, more recent research suggests that false beliefs about *Miranda* rights are not limited to juveniles, the mentally disordered, or those with an intellectual disability. Rogers, Rogstad, et al. (2010) compared the beliefs of pretrial defendants to those of college undergraduates with respect to *Miranda* rights and found "surprisingly similar" results (Rogers, 2011, p. 729). Significant portions of both groups believed that they could give "off-the-record" statements that would not incriminate them and thought police had to "play fair." For example, they thought police could not falsely tell them that an eyewitness had identified them (when they in fact can). In addition, even individuals who have considerable experience with the criminal justice system, measured by frequent arrests, have no better understanding than those less experienced (Rogers, Rogstad, Steadman, & Drogin, 2011).

The Supreme Court has repeatedly stated that waivers of one's constitutional rights—in this case, the right against self-incrimination and the right to a lawyer—must be intelligent, knowing, and voluntary. If a suspect confesses to a crime after providing an invalid waiver, his confession is subject to being suppressed—or not used against him. A confession made after physical beatings is obviously invalid; however, a confession that is psychologically coerced is more difficult to identify. To evaluate the validity of confessions, courts—including the Supreme Court—have used a "totality of the circumstances" approach to decide whether an individual knowingly, willingly, and voluntarily waived her constitutional rights. Thus, courts have looked at such factors as the length of the interrogation, how the warnings were delivered, the age of the suspect, education, intellectual ability, and the suspect's past experience with the criminal justice system.

Assessing *Miranda* Comprehension

The issue of the validity of a specific waiver usually does not arise unless an officer of the court—typically the defense attorney—argues that the waiver was not a valid one. This can occur at the pretrial stage, such as when a defendant is asked to enter a plea; during the trial itself; or, more commonly, after a person has been convicted and seeks to have his conviction overturned. As Rogers (2008b) states, defense attorneys "operate from their own limited knowledge base in deciding when, if ever, to raise issues regarding the invalidity of Miranda waivers" (p. 777). He does not spare psychologists and psychiatrists, either, who he says "rely on methods yielding limited relevant knowledge in evaluating Miranda waivers" (p. 777).

Ideally, mental health practitioners should be asked to assess the competence of a suspect to waive *Miranda* rights at the police station, before interrogation begins. However, this is extremely unlikely to happen in the case of the average suspect. (Exceptions may and can be made in the case of juveniles or persons who are so obviously intellectually or emotionally impaired that interrogators know that a confession would likely be invalidated.) For the most part, though, mental health practitioners are called in to assess *Miranda* comprehension after a suspect has confessed to a crime and the defense attorney tries to invalidate the confession. Clinicians may evaluate a suspect's intelligence, reasoning ability, and reading levels to do this, and they increasingly take into consideration psychological impairments.

Instruments specifically designed to measure *Miranda* comprehension are also available. Most of these were developed by Grisso and his colleagues after extensive study of juvenile comprehension (Grisso, 1998a). They include the Comprehension of Miranda Rights (CMR), Comprehension of Miranda Rights–Recognition (CMR-R), and Comprehension of Miranda–Vocabulary (CMV) and Function of Rights in Interrogation (FRI)—all recently revised (N. E. S. Goldstein, Zelle, & Grisso, 2012). Rogers and his colleagues have also developed an as-yet unpublished Miranda Statements Scale (MSS; Rogers, 2005) and a Miranda Vocabulary Scale (MVS; Rogers, 2006b).

Despite concerns about comprehension of *Miranda* rights and the false beliefs people hold about these constitutional protections, psychologists do not seem to be performing many evaluations in this area. Ryba, Brodsky, and Shlosberg (2007) found that only about one quarter of forensic practitioners in their sample reported that they performed *Miranda* evaluations, and those who did had performed an average of 6.9 over the past year. Commenting on this finding, Rogers (2011) speculated that "roughly 1 in 199 cases with probably impaired Miranda abilities is referred" for evaluation (p. 731).

Detection of Deception

Deception is behavior that is intended to conceal, misrepresent, or distort truth or information for the purpose of misleading others. It is obvious that the ability to detect it is a valuable tool in the investigator's armory. At the police academy, in training manuals, and in on-the-job training, police are taught methods of interviewing and interrogation that are said to be tried and true for successfully dealing with witnesses and victims of crime, persons of interest, and—of course—suspects. The predominant method used for interrogating suspects in the United States is the **Reid method**, first published by Inbau and Reid in 1967. The two latest editions of *Criminal Interrogation and Confessions* were authored by Inbau, Reid, Buckley, and Jayne (2004, 2013). As Redlich and Meissner (2009) assert, "It is important to note, however, that these techniques have never been subject to any scientific evaluation by the authors/users" (p. 131). Although the Reid method is recognized as effective in many respects, it has also been widely criticized for its lack of scientific validity (King & Snook, 2009). Most recently, there has been concern that, while it can produce true confessions, it is vulnerable to producing false confessions, a topic we will cover later in the chapter. Suspects who are actually innocent are at a disadvantage when confronted with this method of interrogation.

Research on Deception

Over the past two decades, research has identified three basic psychological processes that are involved in deception: (1) emotion, (2) attempted behavioral control, and (3) cognitive load (Vrij, 2008; Zhang, Frumkin, Stedman, & Lawson, 2013). These processes are assumed to be revealed through nonverbal and verbal cues provided by the person who is trying to deceive.

Emotion Cues

For a long time, it was believed that emotions were the best indicator of deception. Telling a lie has been most commonly associated with two different types of emotions: guilt and fear (Vrij, Granhag, & Mann, 2010). Traditionally, it was accepted practice to associate nervousness, arousal, and anxiety with deception. For example, excessive leg movements, blinking, foot wiggling, hand wringing, finger tapping, the picking of fingernails, or the fumbling with objects such as paper clips or a pencil were assumed to be manifestations of lying. In recent years, research has consistently demonstrated that these behavioral patterns are not reliable cues for deception. It appears that very, very few people—whether they are professionals or laypersons—are able to detect deception (or honesty) with much accuracy or consistency based on emotion-based cues. The state of the "art" of deception detection in recent years is aptly summarized by van Koppen (2012):

> The cues to deception that have been identified are faint and unreliable, polygraph lie detection [another topic to be covered later in the chapter] is more of a promise than a valid instrument, and the theoretical underpinning of all this is weak. (p. 124)

Nevertheless, people (especially professionals) firmly believe they can correctly identify liars on the basis of nonverbal indicators of emotion. For example, in a survey of police officers, social workers, teachers, and the general public conducted by Vrij, Akehurst, and Knight (2006), it was discovered that a large majority of the participants thought liars acted nervously, such as looking away and making grooming gestures. Overall, the four groups had little faith in other people's ability to deceive them. (See Box 3-2 for a study involving the detection of deception in employment interviews.)

BOX 3-2 RESEARCHERS AT WORK

Detecting Deception in Employment Interviews

"I can get someone to believe anything I want them to believe about me in a job interview." The person quoted is referring to impression management, or the ability of someone being interviewed to lead the interviewer to see positive traits, even though they are not really there. Apparently, effective tactics of self-presentation do influence the decision making of interviewers. If the picture one is presenting to others is an honest one, impression management is not a problem. However, if the person being interviewed is deliberately trying to deceive, it can be.

Research indicates that most job applicants say at least one deceptive thing during a job interview. For example, they may exaggerate their responsibilities in previous jobs, attribute personality characteristics to themselves that they do not really possess, or fake agreement with work attitudes expressed by the interviewer (Reinhard, Scharmach, & Müller, 2013).

How accurate are interviewers at detecting deceptive responses? As noted in the text, nonverbal behaviors (failure to maintain eye contact, leg twitching, etc.) have long been thought to be indicators of deception, and it appears that employment interviewers are not immune from believing these myths.

Reinhard et al. (2013) showed video clips of an alleged job applicant to 138 participants with experience in conducting job interviews and 214 laypersons with no such experience. The experienced interviewers had conducted a mean of 24.45 interviews. Forty-six had conducted 20 or more, and 23 had conducted 100 or more. In the video, the job applicant falsely claimed to have work experience, which qualifies as an extreme case of deception. The researchers speculated that experienced interviewers should at least be able to detect such an extreme falsehood. Overall, though, the participants were barely above chance in their ability to tell truths from lies. Most significantly, the experienced interviewers were no better at the task than the non-experienced participants.

The researchers also found that participants held many of the myths about detecting deception that are prevalent among the general population. Those participants who held correct beliefs about deception detection performed somewhat better, although not markedly so. The researchers concluded that the employment interview was a questionably valid instrument for

(Continued)

(Continued)

selecting from potential job applicants, although "ridding people of their invalid beliefs about indicators of deception should improve their accuracy at detecting deception, to some extent" (Reinhard et al., 2013, p. 477).

Questions for Discussion:

1. Do you agree with the researchers that the employment interview has questionable validity for selecting from potential job applicants?

2. What additional information about the methodology and the results of this experiment would it be helpful to know before assessing its importance?

In general, the research to date suggests that investigators who concentrate only on nonverbal cues are less accurate in identifying deception than those who take speech content and timing into account. Although most police investigators take some aspects of speech into consideration, the overall tendency is to rely on nonverbal behavior patterns. In most cases, investigators do not focus on the words of denial of suspects and prefer to monitor bodily signs to detect deceit. The police manuals—after all—have traditionally emphasized nonverbal cues as crucial in identifying deception.

Interestingly, there are signs of some change in this exclusive focus on emotion and nonverbal indicators. For example, Inbau et al. (2013) have incorporated a smattering of recent psychological research into the most recent edition of *Criminal Interrogation and Confessions*. They write, "The suspect's posture, eye contact, facial expressions, and word choice, as well as response delivery, may each reveal signs of truthfulness or deception" (p. 4). They also include a chapter on **behavior analysis investigation** (BAI), which considers the three channels of communication (verbal behavior, paralinguistic behavior, and nonverbal behavior) in its analysis. As noted by Vrij (2008), the BAI system is taught to hundreds of thousands of law enforcement personnel in the United States. The verbal channel relates to word choice and arrangement of words to send a message. The paralinguistic channel refers to characteristics of speech falling outside the spoken word (e.g., silent pauses, pattern of stuttering). The nonverbal channel refers to such things as posture, arm and leg movements, eye contact, blinking, and facial expressions.

However, so far, the research has failed to support BAI's effectiveness in detecting liars (Kassin, 2012a; Vrij & Granhag, 2012; Vrij, Mann, & Fisher, 2006). While our society is replete with folklore concerning how to discern whether someone is lying, the empirical research cogently demonstrates that the human ability to identify liars from truth tellers is abysmally poor (C. F. Bond & DePaulo, 2006; Vrij et al., 2006). In their review of the research literature, Bond and DePaulo (2006) found that research participants average 54% in correctly classifying truth tellers and liars, which is low given that 50% could be expected by flipping a coin. Ironically, trained individuals are more confident in their ability to detect deception but are less accurate than naive participants (C. F. Bond & DePaulo, 2006; King & Snook, 2009).

Behavior Control Cues

The developing research on this psychological process has generally concentrated on what makes a "good liar." The limited research to date indicates that not only do good liars try to monitor their own behavior; they also monitor the interviewer's reactions to their answers to the questions asked (Burgoon, Blair, & Strom, 2008; Vrij et al., 2010; Zhang et al., 2013). Good liars are aware of the common belief that nonverbal cues may connote deceit and therefore focus on controlling them, such as looking directly at the investigator's eyes, or limiting their own bodily indicators of nervousness. Good liars generally realize, therefore, that they must control their behavior so that they will appear credible, and to be successful they must suppress nervousness effectively while masking any signs of overthinking their responses to questions (Vrij et al., 2010). These observations indicate that one requirement to be a good liar is to also be a good actor. Moreover, "When liars are exposed to negative feedback from the receiver, expressed verbally or nonverbally . . . the liar might realize that his or her performance is lacking credulity and might therefore attempt to make behavioral adjustments over time to diminish suspicions" (Vrij et al., 2010, p. 82). Interestingly, some researchers have observed that deliberate self-regulation of nervous behavior tends to come across as contrived, tense, and overcontrolled (Vrij, 2008; Zhang et al., 2013). On the other hand, liars tend to be more careless about the other forms of self-regulation, such as their own speech patterns.

Cognitive Load

Aldert Vrij and his colleagues (e.g., Vrig & Granhag, 2012; Vrij et al., 2009, 2010) have observed that empirical research finds virtually no support for the belief that nonverbal cues alone can indicate deception. Furthermore, trying to train people to detect deception by focusing on nonverbal cues has not been successful. Vrij and Granhag argue that a procedure that approaches deception detection from two different angles would be more fruitful. Although they fully understand that it is unlikely any single cue will reliably identify deception, they believe that (1) examining the verbal patterns of the suspect and (2) studying the way the interviewer or interrogator handles the question offer considerable promise in detecting deception.

Vrij and Granhag (2007, 2012) maintain that verbal cues are more stable and diagnostic of deception than nonverbal ones. Nonverbal cues are inconsistent, unreliable, and extremely difficult to discern, even by well-trained investigators knowledgeable about up-to-date research. Also, nonverbal cues are highly dependent on the context that elicits them, as well as the cultural background of the person being questioned. It would be wise, therefore, for investigators to pay more attention to speech patterns rather than relying strictly on nonverbal indicators that are so often advocated in police manuals and in police training programs.

Vrij and Granhag (2012) also encourage interviewers to impose **cognitive load** on those they are questioning. In other words, they should try to increase the "work" of answering questions, such as by asking unanticipated questions. More specifically, they argue that the interviewer should create conditions that substantially increase the cognitive difficulty of lying compared with truth telling.

Lying apparently requires extra cognitive effort, as the person being deceptive must actively suppress truthful information and construct and remember false information (Carrión, Keenan, & Sebanz, 2010; Vrij et al., 2008). Liars also often find it very difficult to provide much additional detail for their stories, whereas truth tellers normally do not. Liars usually try to keep their story simple (Granhag & Strömwall, 2002; Strömwall, Harwig, & Granhag, 2006). Therefore, one effective approach to detecting deception is to ask questions that are not anticipated (Lancaster, Vrij, Hope, & Waller, 2013). Asking for more detail makes it more likely that the person not telling the truth will trip up. Another approach to increasing cognitive load would be requesting that the person tell his story in reverse order. These approaches increase cognitive load because they run counter to the normal sequence of telling stories (Vrij & Granhag, 2012). The assumption is that when liars are asked unexpected questions, they are forced to fabricate their answers quickly, which is a difficult task (Vrij et al., 2009). The increased mental demands of dealing with unanticipated questions usually are characterized by longer times to answer and many more pauses than normal (Boltz, Dyer, & Miller, 2010). Increased cognitive load is also often accompanied by an increase in arousal, as the individual is fearful of being detected. Consequently, spontaneous lies to unanticipated questions often contain more clues to deception than planned lies (DePaulo et al., 2003).

The cognitive load approach is intriguing, but van Koppen (2012) points out its practical problems if applied to police interrogations. To learn whether a suspect is deceiving the police, the interrogator(s) must persuade the suspect to talk—and criminal suspects have a right to consult with a lawyer before doing so as well as to have a lawyer present during the interrogation itself. In many cases, the suspect refuses to talk or, if he or she agrees, will say very little. If a lawyer is present, the lawyer will rightfully monitor the interrogation process at every step. Koppen believes that telling the story in reverse order will only be a viable police method with a suspect who (1) is willing to talk, (2) has an alternative story about the crime, and (3) is prepared to give "this weird reverse order experiment" a try (p. 125). He states that the "[i]ntelligent suspect would not comply and the less intelligent are prone to make a false confession" (p. 125).

⬚ The Interrogation Process

In many cases, the interrogation of suspects can be crucial in securing convictions of guilty persons and freeing the innocent (Meissner, Redlich, Bhatt, & Brandon, 2012). In contrast to historical approaches to interrogation that relied heavily on physical torture, modern American interrogations rely largely on psychological manipulation. The primary purpose of interrogation, of course, is to get a suspect to confess. "The police have a very good reason to do so: a confession, even if it is retracted afterwards, is usually accepted as strong evidence in court" (van Koppen, 2012, p. 125). If there is weak evidence against the suspect, interrogation is a method frequently relied upon by law enforcement. The confession becomes a particularly convincing source of evidence once the suspect produces **intimate knowledge** of the crime. Intimate knowledge refers to information about the crime that only the offender and police investigators know. Moreover, "By definition, interrogations are a guilt-presumptive process . . . led by an authority figure who holds a strong a priori belief about the target and who measures success by the ability to extract an admission from that target" (Kassin & Gudjonsson, 2004, p. 41). One police officer emphasized the importance when he stated to van Koppen (2012), "we need confessions because we just do not have the time to go out there and do a proper investigation" (p. 125).

Research on interrogations has primarily focused on the effectiveness of two approaches: the accusatorial approach (primarily used in the United States) and the information-gathering approach (developed in the United Kingdom) (Evans et al., 2013; Meissner et al., 2012). The **accusatorial approach** is utilized when the interrogator thinks the suspect is guilty. Although it is likely that questioners believe in the suspect's guilt in the information-gathering approach as well, the method used is different—the presenting purpose is simply to get the facts. Thus, accusatorial interrogations "are confession-oriented and designed to manipulate suspects' perceptions regarding the consequences of confession and develop themes that encourage confession" (Evans et al., 2013, p. 84). In this approach, the interrogator is usually instructed to maintain control, use psychological manipulation whenever possible, and ask closed, yes/no questions. This method is strongly advocated by Inbau et al. (2013) in their police manual on interviewing and interrogation. "Conceptually, this procedure is designed to get suspects to incriminate themselves by increasing the anxiety associated with denial, plunging them into a state of despair, and minimizing the perceived consequences of confession" (Kassin & Gudjonsson, 2004, p. 43).

The accusatorial approach requires several steps characterized by (1) custody and isolation, (2) confrontation, and (3) minimization. In the **custody and isolation** step, the suspect is detained in a small room and left to experience the stress, uncertainty, and insecurity associated with police custody and interrogation. We have all seen media images of the in-custody suspect, sitting alone in a small room, observed through a one-way mirror, waiting tensely for a detective to enter and begin questioning. The **confrontation** step involves the interrogator accusing the suspect of the crime, expressing certainty in that opinion, citing real or manufactured evidence, and preventing the suspect from denying the accusations. **Minimization** (which may come into play at any time) involves a sympathetic interrogator morally justifying the crime to the suspect or expressing sympathy with the suspect's predicament. The presumption here is that the suspect comes to believe that lenient treatment will be given if he or she confesses.

The **information-gathering approach**, on the other hand, is less confrontational, even though those posing the questions may believe the individual they are questioning is guilty. It is designed for investigators to take a more neutral role by probing the suspect's knowledge and information through open-ended questions and a more informal conversational style. Unlike the accusatorial procedure, the information-gathering approach avoids trickery and deceit as much as possible. In one of the few investigations of the effectiveness of the two approaches, Evans et al. (2013) found that the information-gathering approach yields more relevant and useful information than the accusatorial approach. In addition, some researchers (e.g., Meissner et al., 2012) believe that the information-gathering approach will lead to substantially fewer false confessions.

Confirmation Bias

Confirmation bias is a long-recognized psychological construct that is a natural, inherent feature of human cognition (Kassin, Dror, & Kukucka, 2013). It is "the tendency to gather evidence that confirms preexisting expectations, typically by emphasizing or pursuing supporting evidence while dismissing or failing to seek contradictory evidence" (VandenBos, 2007, p. 215). Put another way, we look for information that will confirm our previously held beliefs, even though we do not do so consciously. However, being aware of this normal feature of human cognition should encourage us to be cautious in the conclusions we draw. According to Baron and Byrne (2000), when confirmation bias occurs, "it places us in a kind of closed cognitive system in which only evidence that confirms our existing views and beliefs gets inside; other information is sometimes noticed but is quickly rejected as false" (p. 8).

In recent years, legal psychologists and other researchers have demonstrated persuasively that confirmation bias can influence interrogators, jurors, judges, eyewitnesses, and experts in a range of forensic domains (Kassin et al., 2013). Not surprisingly, this bias is relevant to the law enforcement strategies we have discussed thus far as well as those we will discuss below. In their roles both as investigators and as humans, police may develop "tunnel vision"—a rigid focus on one suspect. They may try to amass evidence against that suspect and overlook exculpatory evidence (K. A. Findley & Scott, 2006). Police questioning a suspect are likely to aggressively seek to establish guilt and discount evidence to the contrary, particularly if they have a strong belief that the suspect is indeed guilty (Kassin, Goldstein, & Savitsky, 2003).

In the interrogation context, confirmation bias may be helpful in gaining a true confession—the interrogator is persistent, searching for evidence to confirm his or her preexisting views. However, it works to the disadvantage of innocent suspects, even to the point of putting them at risk for making false confessions. Narchet, Meissner, and Russano (2011) demonstrated in an experimental situation that a bias toward guilt on the part of investigators leads them to use more minimization tactics with the suspects they are questioning. That is, when participants strongly presumed the suspect was guilty, they provided face-saving excuses for the suspects, minimized their offenses, or indicated they understood their predicament. This in turn led to an increase in false confessions. Confirmation bias in forensic contexts is a relatively new area of research exploration and requires more study, particularly with actual law enforcement officers, judges, lawyers, and jurors.

HUMINT Interrogation

Interrogations in the human intelligence (HUMINT) context (Evans, Meissner, Brandon, Russano, & Kleiman, 2010) are somewhat distinct from the standard interrogations conducted in police precincts or most federal law enforcement settings. HUMINT interrogation is used primarily in counter-terrorism situations by military and intelligence operations. Although HUMINT interrogations are somewhat outside the main purpose of this chapter, it is important to be able to identify the differences between their tactics and those of other interrogations. Headlines concerning the controversial methods of information gathering in Guantanamo Bay, Iraq, and Afghanistan have stirred debate among mental health professionals, U.S. government officials, and the public (Evans et al., 2010).

While more standard interrogation is designed to secure a confession, **HUMINT interrogation** seeks information relating to an event or organization (Evans et al., 2013). The targets of HUMINT interrogations range from high-value individuals responsible for harmful acts to individuals not directly involved in wrongdoing but potentially possessing knowledge of critical intelligence information (Evans et al., 2013). The techniques used to gather information have included sleep deprivation, shaming, and exposure to cold and loud noises. Teams of psychologists observe the detainees, suggest lines of questioning, and may intervene when tactics are harsh. On the other hand, they also might give the opinion that interrogators can push harder (Grady & Carey, 2013).

The involvement of psychologists in these interrogations has been extensively debated, most particularly since the events of September 11, 2001. The APA Code of Ethics allows consultations in interrogations as long as they do not involve specified coercive procedures. In 2010, in response to concerns about participation in enhanced interrogations, the APA amended its code of ethics to make it clear that psychologists should never violate human rights. Whereas some psychologists argue that *all* such consultation should be prohibited, others believe that their involvement discourages the use of the most flagrantly abusive practices. Psychologists are conducting systematic experimental research in this context with the hope that ethical, evidence-based approaches to interrogation will be implemented (Evans et al., 2013).

✉ The Psychology of False Confessions

Let us begin this section with an important point: It is likely that most suspects who confess to crime really did it. There is no reason to believe otherwise. Put another way, most confessions are probably true confessions. As we learned in the previous section, though, they may not be valid. A coerced confession, for example, is not a valid one for evidence purposes.

However, the fact that most confessions are probably true should not detract from the fact that suspects sometime confess to crimes they did not commit. False confessions may be made to protect another person, to become famous, or to get things over with if one feels he will not be believed. Some people confess because it is implied that admitting to the deeds will result in a lighter sentence. Some people provide false confessions because they are led to believe police have obtained strong evidence against them. Others are worn down by the interrogation process and are led to believe they will be allowed to go home. What may be surprising is that some suspects confess to a crime they did not commit because they come to believe they actually *did* commit it.

Research on false confessions has exploded, particularly since the early 1990s, although psychology research relevant to this topic reaches further back. For example, as observed by Redlich and Meissner (2009) and by Kassin (2008), research on decision making under stress, suggestibility, human development, cognitive functioning, and psychiatric symptoms all help experts understand the phenomenon of false confessions. "In sum, in disputed confession cases there are more than 100 years of psychological science to draw on, including literature from developmental, cognitive, social personality, forensic, and abnormal branches of psychology" (Redlich & Meissner, 2009, p. 138).

Drizin and Leo (2004) documented 125 cases of proven false confessions in the United States, and with more attention given to this problem the number is likely to rise. The Drizin and Leo study underscored the fact that the interrogation tactics and deception detection strategies practiced by American police result in a disturbing number of false confessions, which often lead to wrongful convictions (Evans et al., 2010). Subsequent studies have discovered that the percentage of miscarriages of justice involving false confessions range from 14% to 60% (Leo & Drizin, 2010). A large majority of these false confessions occur with less serious crimes (e.g., property) compared with more serious offenses (e.g., homicide or rape) (Redlich, 2010). Nevertheless, people do falsely confess to serious crimes, as will be seen below. "Innocent individuals inevitably end up in the interrogation room—hence, this motivation to obtain a confession creates a risk for obtaining false confessions by exposing potentially vulnerable individuals to manipulative interrogative techniques" (Evans et al., 2010, p. 217).

Since the mid-1980s, researchers in psychology and law have carefully explored the issue of false confessions more directly (e.g., Kassin, 2012b; Kassin et al., 2010; Kassin & Wrightsman, 1985; Redlich, Kulish, & Steadman, 2011). They have identified types of false confessions and some of the reasons people make them. Research has determined that there is no single cause of false confession (Leo & Drizin, 2010). Some researchers have compared true and false confessions (e.g., Redlich et al., 2011). Others have examined risk factors for making false confessions, stress during interrogation, and police strategies, among many topics. Both researchers and clinicians have been asked to offer expert testimony on false confessions, with varying results. We cover some of the more prominent research and legal trends below.

Types or Categories of False Confessions

Some 30 years ago, psychologists Saul Kassin and Lawrence Wrightsman (1985) identified three types of false confessions: (1) voluntary, (2) coerced-compliant, and (3) coerced-internalized. The first, a voluntary false confession, is a self-incriminating statement made without external pressure from law enforcement. As a historical example, Kassin (1997) observed that when the young son of Charles and Anne Morrow Lindbergh was kidnapped in 1932, at least 200 people approached police and claimed responsibility for the crime. More recently, some individuals came forward claiming to be the Barefoot Bandit, a person who in 2008 and 2009 burglarized homes in several states, sometimes leaving his barefoot prints behind. The real perpetrator was ultimately convicted and sentenced to prison in 2012. Coming forward in this way is not the same as being suspected, interrogated by police, and falsely confessing, which is what we focus upon here.

Unfortunately, the *voluntary* false confession made while under custodial interrogation is the most difficult to study of the three, because this type of false confessor is unlikely to try to retract the confession, compared with the false confessor who was coerced into confessing. For example, the individual who confesses with no police coercion may be mentally disturbed, may wish to protect someone else, or may have little faith in the criminal justice system and believe it would be useless to fight his or her conviction on that basis. In addition, courts are less likely to accept that a confession was given falsely if no coercion was involved (Redlich et al., 2011). Interestingly, research also suggests that, if we consider the universe of both violent and nonviolent offenses, it is likely that there are more voluntary false confessions than coerced ones (Gudjonsson, Sigurdsson, & Einarsson, 2004).

The other two types of false confessions identified by Kassin and Wrightsman (1985) involve pressure from law enforcement officers. Social science research suggests strongly that skillful manipulation and police deception under stressful conditions may lead to false confessions. This is the **coerced-compliant confession**. According to Leo (2008), in documented false confession cases, police exerted strong pressure to encourage suspects to confess. "Police-induced false confessions result from a multistep process and sequence of influence, persuasion, and compliance, and they usually involve psychological coercion" (Leo & Drizin, 2010, p. 12). Police may use a number of tactics, including trying to trip up a suspect on facts about the case, asking leading questions, showing photos of a crime scene or even taking the suspect to the scene, minimizing the degree of harm—as by telling the suspect that he probably really did not mean to do it, extending the interrogation period, or suggesting that they have incriminating evidence that they do not have. Furthermore, as will be seen shortly, truly innocent suspects often weave detailed alibis that can easily be torn apart by an experienced investigator (Kassin, 2012b) and thus lead the suspect to "confess." (As an exercise, try telling in detail where you were, what you were doing, and who you saw exactly a week ago; chances are good that your description will be flawed. Another person who was accompanying you may well have a very different recollection.)

As Kassin (1997) states, the pages of legal history are filled with examples of coerced-compliant confessions. Such confessions may be more likely to be made by suspects with prior records, since police will be more suspicious of them and less likely to believe in their innocence. In other words, a presumption of guilt often pervades the interrogative process. Interrogators also are influenced by the confirmation bias discussed above. Police questioning 16-year-old Jeff Deskovic believed strongly that he was responsible for rape and murder, and they aggressively interrogated him until he provided a false confession. His case is discussed below, in the section on the polygraph. In another example, some of the five defendants in the Central Park jogger case had apparently had prior run-ins with police. They claimed that harsh police interrogation tactics led to their false confessions, although police have denied these charges. A critically acclaimed documentary on this case, *The Central Park Five,* was released in 2012.

Errors Leading to False Confessions

Leo and Drizin (2010) authored a provocative article in which they summarized the types of errors police may make that can contribute to the false confession problem. They are misclassification errors, coercion errors, and contamination errors.

In **misclassification errors**, police mistakenly come to believe an individual is guilty of a crime and thereby "misclassify" the individual as guilty rather than innocent.

Closely aligned with this error is what Leo and Drizin (2010) refer to as "poor and erroneous interrogation training" (p. 13), producing a belief that the interrogators are human lie detectors, experts at detecting deception. The assumption of guilt is intensified by suspects who act nervous and display the nonverbal signs that supposedly indicate they are being deceptive. Unfortunately, innocent suspects often display these nonverbal indicators, too.

Coercion errors are made when interrogators apply psychological tactics to manipulate the innocent suspect, such as by indicating that they have evidence they really do not have. If a suspect is "truly guilty," it is likely that evidence—DNA, eyewitness, surveillance cameras, and so on—is available. Though such evidence may be flawed, including eyewitness evidence, it is reasonable for interrogators to bring it to the attention of the suspect. Without such evidence, however, the interrogator who is already convinced of the suspect's guilt must find other ways to obtain a confession. The suspect may be told there was a witness, or there may be implied threats or promises. The suspect also may be made to feel he or she has little choice other than to confess, such as would be the case for a suspect with a criminal record.

Contamination errors occur after an innocent suspect has "broken down" and admitted to the crime. As Leo and Drizin (2010) emphasize, "A confession is more than an 'I did it' statement" (p. 19). The police must obtain a believable narrative from the suspect detailing how he or she carried out the crime. Guilty suspects should have no difficulty recounting in detail how they planned and committed their offenses and describing such aspects as the scene, the reactions of victims, or even the weather at the time the incident occurred. They also have intimate knowledge of the crime that no one else but the police knows. Innocent suspects, however, need to spin an account without knowing the actual facts or intimate details of the case. Therefore, consciously or not, the interrogating officers may feed information to the suspect that can be woven into his or her admission. The suspect also may have obtained information from media accounts of the crime. "The postadmission narrative is the story that gets wrapped around the admission and thus makes it appear, at least on its face, to be a compelling account of the suspect's guilt" (Leo & Drizin, 2010, p. 20). Remarkably, research on documented false confessions has indicated that the narratives provided by the confessors were rich in detail, suggesting that they were likely helped in fashioning their accounts. In a content analysis of 20 false confessions, Appleby, Hasel, and Kassin (2013) found elaborate detailed information, despite the fact that the confessors were ultimately cleared by DNA or other evidence.

It is important to emphasize that police are not necessarily always at fault in the production of coerced false confessions. These confessions also can be generated in situations where law enforcement is not *directly* involved (McCann, 1998b). Specifically, pressure to confess may emanate from family members, friends, gang members, church officials, and other sources besides police authorities. Gudjonsson (1992) estimates, for example, that as many as 25% of juvenile offenders in detention facilities may have taken the rap to protect an older offender. What's more, in some situations, pressure to confess may originate from some combination of *both* police (custodial) and non-police (noncustodial) sources.

The third type of false confession, the **coerced-internalized confession**, is the most puzzling to comprehend. "Coerced-internalized confessions are those in which an innocent person—anxious, tired, confused, and subjected to highly suggestive methods of interrogation—actually comes to believe that he or she has committed the crime" (Kassin, 1997, p. 226). This may seem preposterous—after all, how could anyone mistakenly believe he or she is responsible for a criminal act? However, in a series of laboratory experiments, Kassin has demonstrated that this is clearly possible.

In one study, Kassin and Kiechel (1996) had students participate in a computer task. Each one was instructed not to press the "ALT" key on the computer keyboard, no matter what. Doing so, they were told, would cause the program to crash and the data to be lost. (It should be noted that—due to its location on the QWERTY keyboard—the ALT key does not lend itself to being accidentally pressed.) After 60 seconds into the actual experiment, the computer was intentionally programmed to crash. This was followed by a highly distressed experimenter accusing the participants of having pressed the forbidden key. All the participants, of course, were truly innocent, and all initially denied the charge. Overall, though, 69% of the 75 participants eventually signed a confession, admitting that they had, in fact, pressed the forbidden key. Furthermore, 28% of the participants seemed to internalize the guilt, and 9% even made up details to support their false beliefs. Kassin and Kiechel concluded that the presentation of false incriminating evidence can induce people to believe they are to blame for something they did not do. This early study was followed by a later study that produced essentially the same results (Perillo & Kassin, 2011). In this study, the researchers also found that innocent suspects were led to confess when bluffed by questioners, such as when presented with false but incriminating information about their guilt.

Like coerced-compliant confessions, coerced-internalized false confessions also may happen with minimum prompting by interrogators. This is likely to occur, for example, in the case of suspects who were intoxicated with alcohol or other drugs and could not specifically recall incidents related to the crime (Evans, Schreiber Compo, & Russano, 2009). Interrogators may play on this, however, by minimizing the suspect's responsibility: "You were strung out, so you probably don't remember exactly what happened."

It also should be recognized that there are certainly individual differences in susceptibility to coercive pressure. As Gudjonsson (1984, 1992) found, some individuals are unknowingly but particularly susceptible to such influences. Accordingly, he developed a test by which suggestibility is measured, the Gudjonsson Suggestibility Scale (GSS). According to researchers who have used and evaluated the scale (e.g., Kassin, 1997; McCann, 1998a), persons who receive high scores are at serious risk of making a false confession, particularly when deceptive information is provided to them by police. Gudjonsson and his associates also have developed a questionnaire designed to assess the reasons suspects provide *true* confessions (Gudjonnson & Sigurdsson, 1999). The questionnaire is intended to be administered to individuals after their cases have been resolved. The reasons fall into six categories: external pressure, internal need, perceived proof, drug intoxication, understanding their legal rights, and resistance (initial reluctance followed by decision to confess). Redlich and Meissner (2009) note that these are the same reasons given by false confessors in explaining why they confessed to something they did not do.

Age, Mental Impairment, and False Confessions

Age and mental impairment (intellectual or emotional) are both correlated with false confessions. Mental impairment is found in a significant minority of cases (Redlich & Meissner, 2009). It is possible that police are less willing to aggressively question individuals with mental impairment, but the significant minority cannot be overlooked. Youth seem particularly vulnerable to making false confessions and are overrepresented in proven false confession cases (Drizin & Leo, 2004). As we discussed in the section on comprehending *Miranda* rights, juveniles are deserving of special attention during the police interview and interrogation process. As also mentioned, police themselves do not seem to address this in their interrogation methods (Reppucci, Meyer, & Kostelnik, 2010). It should be noted that Inbau et al. (2013) do urge caution in the questioning of juveniles and the mentally impaired.

Psychologists have identified many reasons why the mentally impaired are susceptible to making false confessions, although they do not invariably do so. Persons who are mentally ill or impaired may demonstrate cognitive and behavior deficits that can include distorted perceptions, feelings of hopelessness, lack of self-control, need for attention, and submissiveness to others, among many possible symptoms. All of these can lead to a false confession. Gudjonsson, Sigurdsson, Asgeirsdottir, and Sigfusdottir (2006) found that persons who self-reported a false confession scored higher on anxiety, depression, anger, extraversion, and psychoticism than those who did not report making a false confession. Although this is not an indication that these individuals were mentally impaired, it is a relevant factor associated with cognitions and behaviors. In a more recent study, Redlich et al. (2011) focused on those with serious mental illness and found reasons to be concerned about the validity of their confessions to crimes (see Box 3-3).

BOX 3-3 RESEARCHERS AT WORK

False Confessions and the Seriously Mentally Ill

Psychologist Allison Redlich and her colleagues (2011) conducted one of the few available studies focusing on confessions made by individuals with serious mental illness. They compared persons making true and false confessions. Although their sample was small (65 in all, almost evenly divided between the two groups), their results are worthy of note.

The false confessors in their sample had been questioned more times and had perceived significantly more external pressure to confess than the true confessors. A greater proportion of false confessors (one third) compared with true confessors (one fourth) had been questioned at the police station, where police arguably exert more control. There was no difference in the length of police questioning, but the false confessors took longer to confess (having initially denied responsibility), and they perceived the evidence against them as weaker than the true confessors had. However, the false confessors also were more likely to perceive threat with or without an implication that the system would go easier on them if they confessed. Nevertheless, the researchers did not find evidence of egregious interrogations, such as had been found in many proven false confession cases.

Importantly, controlling for the seriousness of the crime, the false confessors who were convicted received more severe sentences than the true confessors who were convicted. The researchers speculated that stricter sentences might have been imposed because the false confessors had initially confessed but then recanted their confessions.

Questions for Discussion:

1. What safeguards should be in place to protect persons with serious mental illness who are suspected of crime during the police interrogation process?

2. Does the description of the above study suggest that police acted inappropriately during the interrogation process?

As a whole, studies suggest that false confessions can be attributed to two main reasons: (1) the nature of the police interrogation process itself; and (2) the vulnerability of certain suspects, such as juveniles and the mentally disordered or impaired. However, false confessions are not limited to these two groups, nor are situational factors (e.g., length of the interrogation, police manipulation, interrogator bias) necessarily to blame.

Interestingly, Kassin (2012b) observes that the mere fact of one's innocence may make a suspect vulnerable to a false confession. Citing recent research (e.g., Moore & Gagnier, 2008; Olson & Charman, 2011), Kassin writes,

> Innocence is a mental state that leads innocent people to waive their *Miranda* rights to silence and to counsel . . . to behave in ways that are open and forthcoming in

their interactions with police . . . to offer up alibis freely, without regard for the fact that police may view minor inaccuracies with suspicion." (p. 433)

Thus, the innocent suspect, eager to clear his name and cooperate with the police, may actually do himself a disservice. Most innocent suspects never "confess," but those who do face challenging obstacles in their search for justice.

In recent years, researchers in this area have recommended that psychologists work with police to minimize the problems inherent in the interrogation process. "Ultimately, the challenge for future research is to begin the development of evidence-based practices that might aid law enforcement in eliciting more diagnostic confession evidence, and thereby provide an alternative to the problematic methods that are currently employed" (Meissner, Hartwig, & Russano, 2010, p. 43). Meissner et al. believe that, though the focus on false confession research is important, legal psychologists should not neglect to recommend strategies that elicit true confessions. One step in that direction is to encourage law enforcement to videotape interrogations in full, thereby providing a database for researchers that would allow the examination of current practices. That done, it may be necessary to train police in alternate interview methods that are more closely aligned with psychological principles.

Admissibility of False Confessions in Court Proceedings

Once an individual has made a false confession, it is difficult to repair the damage. For example, after a confession is in hand, police tend to stop the investigative process, the case is turned over for prosecution, and law enforcement energies are placed on solving other crimes. Therefore, the "true" perpetrator is less likely to be uncovered. Attempts to retract the false confession and have it excluded from court are often unsuccessful. Research with mock jurors as well as studies with lawyers and judges have demonstrated that confessions have a powerful impact on verdicts, even when they are retracted or perceived as coerced (Kassin, 2012b).

It is now apparent that the problem of false confessions is a serious one. In a database of cases in which convicted offenders were cleared by DNA evidence, 25% contained false confessions (Kassin, 2012b). Courts today are well aware that suspects do confess to crimes they did not commit, but this does not mean they will accept that a recanted confession in the case before them should not be admitted in court. Such a retraction is particularly problematic if the confession was given voluntarily, with no indication of police misconduct (Watson, Weiss, & Pouncey, 2010). Legal psychologists, then, often advocate that psychological experts familiar with the research on false confessions be allowed to testify on behalf of criminal defendants. In one U.S. Supreme Court case on this matter (*Crane v. Kentucky*, 1986), the trial judge had refused to allow expert testimony on false confessions; the Court subsequently ruled that it should have been allowed in that particular case. However, in other cases, expert testimony has been rejected (e.g., *State v. Free*, 2002).

False confession evidence was excluded by the trial judge in a case that reached the U.S. Supreme Court (*Boyer v. Louisiana*, 2013). However, Boyer's argument that it should have been allowed was rejected by a Louisiana Appellate Court, and the appeal to the U.S. Supreme Court raised other issues, such as the right to a speedy trial and legal representation for indigents. Although the Court initially granted certiorari, it later dismissed the case, saying certiorari was improvidently granted.

There is some suggestion in the literature that a psychiatric diagnosis of certain personality disorders may predispose individuals to making false confessions (Watson et al., 2010), but this has not been firmly established. Psychologists are less likely to focus on psychiatric diagnoses, asserting instead that the mentally disordered are not the only ones subject to making false confessions.

Redlich and Meissner (2009) have identified five myths and misconceptions about false confessions that often need to be dispelled. They are as follows:

(1) False confessions do not exist or are exceedingly rare;

(2) Only "vulnerable" individuals falsely confess;

(3) The study of police interrogation and false confessions is in its infancy;

(4) Jurors do not "need" expert testimony; and

(5) Police interrogation is a science.

Allowing expert testimony on these matters will both benefit the falsely accused and bring greater credibility to the justice system.

It should be apparent that the false confession is a major topic of research interest for legal psychologists today. Most confessions are true confessions accompanied by incriminating evidence, but it is now clear that false confessions are not rare and may be the product of both situational and individual factors. It is critical that the extensive body of psychological research in this area be communicated to lawyers and judges. Those who support introducing such research evidence stress that, by their nature, false confessions are counterintuitive—how could someone confess to a crime he didn't commit? Because this phenomenon is "beyond the ken" of the typical juror, it is unreasonable to expect jurors to decide on the merits of a false confession claim once such a claim has been made. Therefore, the help of an expert witness is needed.

The Polygraph

If mere observation, even by trained examiners, is not successful at detecting deception, perhaps we should consider an alternative. Enter the polygraph. Often called the "lie detector," the polygraph does not really detect lies or deception, but only the bodily responses that accompany emotions and stress. Presumably, when one tries to deceive, there are telltale physiological reactions that can be measured with sophisticated equipment and detected by a skillful examiner. However, "After almost a century of research, no one has discovered a physiological reaction associated exclusively with lying" (Iacono, 2009, p. 224).

We discuss the polygraph in this chapter because it is an instrument that may be used in tests administered to individuals who are believed to have knowledge of a crime. Although persons of interest to police, including criminal suspects, cannot be forced to take the polygraph, they may be encouraged to do so. It is not unusual for innocent suspects to volunteer to take a polygraph, learn they have failed it, and falsely confess. Damon Thibodeaux, convicted in 1997 and sentenced to death for the murder of his half-cousin, agreed to take a polygraph when initially interviewed by police. He was told he failed the test. An interrogation that lasted for more than 8 hours produced his confession, which included details that were inconsistent with the actual crime. Although he recanted his confession, he was convicted and sentenced to death. A reinvestigation of the case uncovered new evidence, including DNA testing that confirmed he could not have been the perpetrator. Thibodeau was released from prison in 2012, after spending 15 years on death row (http://www.innocenceproject.org).

In a similar case, Jeff Deskovic was 16 years old when, apparently distraught over a classmate's rape and murder, he tried to help police solve the crime. Police, strongly suspecting he was involved, asked him to take a polygraph, which he did with no parent or lawyer present. The examination was spread over three sessions within a 6-hour period, with police questioning him between sessions. He continually denied committing the offense, until police told him the polygraph conclusively established his guilt, when it did not. Police also apparently told him if he confessed he would get psychiatric help, but if he did not, he would go to prison (Leo & Drizin, 2010). Deskovic eventually falsely confessed to killing his classmate. Like Thibodeau, Deskovic was eventually cleared with the help of DNA evidence that was matched to another individual. Deskovic was exonerated, but not before he had spent 16 years in prison. The true perpetrator, who ultimately confessed to the crime, was a convicted murderer in prison for strangling another woman. In Thibodeau's case, the true perpetrator was never found (http://www.innocenceproject.org).

Due to the tenuous scientific status of the polygraph, its results are not admissible in criminal court proceedings unless the defendant wishes to introduce them or has stipulated that they can be used. Even when defendants ask to enter exculpatory polygraph evidence into their trials, the courts may not allow it, as will be seen shortly. However, failing the polygraph at the interview stage is likely to lead to the police interrogation process; failing the polygraph during the accusatory stage is likely to lead to a confession, including in some cases a false confession. Furthermore, police may deceive suspects by implying that they have failed the polygraph, as happened in Thibodeaux's case.

Iacono (2009) is skeptical about the **stipulated polygraph test**. In this situation, a suspect *against whom evidence is questionable* agrees to take the test with the understanding that, if she passes, charges will be dropped. However, if she fails the test and does not wish to plead guilty, evidence of the failed test will be admitted at trial. Such evidence is likely to weigh heavily on jury deliberations. Because innocent people can fail the polygraph, this is obviously an issue worthy of concern.

The Control Question Test

The polygraph is a highly controversial procedure with a long history of development (see Box 3-4). Scientists and practitioners have argued over its merits for many years. Although there are several types of polygraphs, the most widely used method is the **Control Question Test (CQT)** (or **Comparison Question Test**), advocated and strongly supported by the American Polygraph Association. "Almost all practicing polygraph examiners assert that [it] is nearly infallible" (Iacono, 2009, p. 229). Iacono maintains, however, that polygraphers are generally law enforcement personnel rather than psychologists, and that evidence in support of the CQT is flawed: "Scientists at arms' length from the polygraph profession, critically reviewing the same studies on which proponents rely, have consistently and repeatedly found these studies methodologically inadequate and thus inadequate to substantiate such claims" (p. 229, citing a series of critical studies).

The CQT intersperses relevant questions directly pertinent to the crime with general questions (e.g., regarding age or name) and control (or comparison) questions. The latter are questions that may or may not elicit an untruthful response—for example, "Did you ever take anything that didn't belong to you?" When examinees reply "no" to a control question, their physiological response is compared closely with their response on the pertinent questions. It is presumed that the guilty individual will display a marked difference in physiological response.

Although we describe this method simplistically here, supporters of the polygraph would be quick to point out that interpretation of these results must be done by persons who are highly trained in polygraphy. Polygraphy is a technical skill, not a psychological science. It is typically taught at a polygraph school that may or may not be accredited by the American Polygraph Association. Some but not all states require polygraphers to be licensed. Due to its vulnerability to attack in the courtroom, polygraph evidence is rarely introduced by defendants in criminal cases. As noted above, it cannot be introduced as evidence *against* the defendant unless the defendant has entered into a stipulation agreement with the prosecution.

BOX 3-4 RESEARCHERS AT WORK

From Burned Tongues to Brain Imaging: A Brief History of "Lie Detecting" Techniques

Variants of the modern polygraph have been used in the psychological laboratory for nearly a century, and much cruder versions of its components existed as far back as 300 B.C. (Trovillo, 1939). The Bedouins of Arabia required those whose statements conflicted to lick a hot iron; the one whose tongue was not burned was considered truthful (Smith, 1967). The ancient Chinese required people to put rice powder in their mouths and then spit it out (Smith, 1967). If the powder was dry, the individual was lying. The common principle underlying these and other similar methods used throughout history is that the tense, nervous person (the one who is lying) has less saliva (dry mouth and tongue), and thus is more likely to have his or her tongue burned or spit out drier rice powder—or even less able to swallow the "trial slice" of bread, as practiced centuries ago in England.

The Italian physician and anthropologist Cesare Lombroso is credited as the first to use an *instrument* to detect lies in 1881 (Barland, 1988). The device was designed to measure changes in blood volume in the arm, which were recorded on a chart or graph. Various other devices and refinements were largely developed in Europe (see Barland, 1988), but the idea of lie detection caught on rapidly in the United States. In 1917, the lawyer-psychologist William M. Marston developed a form of lie detection technology that gained widespread use in criminal investigation. As a laboratory assistant in psychology at Radcliffe College, Marston discovered a significant positive correlation between systolic blood pressure and lying. The polygraph technique that was developed as a result of this finding was referred to in *United States v. Frye* (1923) discussed in Chapter 1. Recall that the federal court in that case did not believe the technique had achieved general acceptance in the field, the standard it set for the admissibility of scientific evidence.

Barland and Raskin (1973), however, credit the development of the modern polygraph equipment and technique more to John Larson and Leonarde Keeler. In 1920, Larson was asked by the chief of police in Berkeley, California, to develop a "lie detector" to solve a case under investigation. This detector, according to Barland (1988), became "the first true polygraph used for lie-detection purposes" (p. 75). A number of well-publicized successes by Larson and one of his students, Keeler, catapulted the instrument into the limelight. Eventually, Keeler began to teach a 2-week course for police and military examiners, which soon developed into a 6-week course (Barland, 1988; Keeler, 1984). The increasing demand for polygraph examiners resulted in the formation of at least 30 polygraph schools across the United States (Barland, 1988).

Today, a variety of private and government-sponsored polygraphy schools are in operation, almost all of which are accredited by the American Polygraphy Association. The most

(Continued)

(Continued)

prestigious and intensive is the one-semester-long school operated by the Department of Defense. The Department of Defense Academy for Credibility Assessment (formerly called the Department of Defense Polygraphy Institute) trains all polygraphers employed by federal agencies with the exception of the CIA, as well as polygraphers employed by many local and state agencies. It also includes a research arm, staffed primarily by doctoral-level psychologists (Iacono & Patrick, 2014). Other polygraphy schools vary widely in training and rarely include a research component.

Despite the federal government's research arm, independent scientists outside the field are insistent that the polygraph techniques used by the great majority of polygraphers lack scientific validity. Modern versions of the polygraph—which include computerized evaluations, assessment of brain imagery, and sophisticated technology—have not been sufficiently evaluated by independent researchers. For example, in recent years, the use of functional magnetic resonance imaging (fMRI) has been promoted by some as a good method of distinguishing lying from truth telling. However, there are both scientific and ethical reasons to question this approach, despite the fact that some courts are now admitting it along with other types of forensic science evidence (Langleben & Moriarty, 2013).

The typical polygraph examiner in the United States today—there are more than 3,500 (Iacono, 2009)—does not have graduate psychological or research training, and not all polygraph examiners are licensed, nor are they graduates of accredited schools. In addition, the polygraph profession has almost no input or oversight from psychology (Iacono & Patrick, 2014).

Questions for Discussion:

1. What are arguments for and against admitting polygraph evidence into courts?

2. Should criminal defendants be allowed to introduce polygraph evidence that supports their claim of innocence?

3. If modern techniques, such as brain imaging, eventually become capable of distinguishing "truth" telling from "lying," should these techniques be admitted into evidence in criminal courts? In civil courts?

Guilty Knowledge Test

Another polygraph method, the **Guilty Knowledge Test (GKT)**, has received more positive reviews in the research literature. This method (sometimes called the **concealed information test**) was developed by the psychologist and polygraph expert David Lykken (1959, 1998) as the most powerful procedure for determining deception or truthfulness. Although the method is rarely used by professional polygraphers in

North America, it is used extensively in Israel and Japan (MacLaren, 2001). Interestingly, while the CQT is the most frequently used method for investigative interrogation in the United States, the GKT is probably the method most endorsed by researchers (Ben-Shakhar, 2002; Ben-Shakhar, Bar-Hillel, & Lieblich, 1986; Iacono & Patrick, 2014; Kleiner 2002). The empirical evidence does support the GKT over the CQT in many instances. Furthermore, in a survey conducted by Iacono and Lykken (1997), approximately three fourths of the scientists polled believed the GKT was based on scientifically sound theory.

With the GKT, the examiner uses detailed, publicly unknown knowledge about a crime to construct questions that can be answered only by someone who was present at the scene. Therefore, the GKT does not attempt to uncover "lying," but rather, whether a suspect possesses "guilty knowledge" that only the offender would know about the crime. The answers are offered to the subject in a multiple-choice format. For example, in a case where a robber dropped his hat, Lykken (1988) provides an example of a GKT as follows:

1. "The robber in this case dropped something while escaping. If you are that robber, you will know what he dropped. Was it: a weapon? a face mask? a sack of money? his hat? his car keys?"

2. "Where did he drop his hat? Was it: in the bank? on the bank steps? on the sidewalk? in the parking lot? in an alley?"

3. "What color was the hat? Was it: brown? red? black? green? blue?" (p. 121)

Since the GKT assumes that the guilty subject will recognize the significant alternative, consistent physiological reactivity to this "correct" answer would indicate deception, regardless of the verbal content of the subject's answers. Moreover, since the questions are derived from information presumably not reported in the press and not generally known by the public, innocent subjects rarely give peak physiological reactions to "correct" items. One of the strong points of the GKT is its ability to detect *innocent* examinees with high accuracy (Ben-Shakhar & Elaad, 2002). For example, research suggests that the GKT is successful in identifying about 84% of the guilty examinees and 94% of innocent examines (Ben-Shakhar & Furedy, 1990).

The sensitivity of the GKT depends in part on whether the examiner can generate enough items pertaining to the crime scene that a suspect is likely to remember (Lykken, 1988; Ben-Shakhar & Elaad, 2002). However, the GKT is rarely used in applied criminal cases because its practical utility is severely limited (Iacono, 2009; Raskin, 1988). For example, in a majority of criminal cases, very little inside, salient detail about the crime is known, and when details of the crime *are* known, they are often made available to suspects by investigators, the media, and defense attorneys. Most training programs for polygraphers do not include the GKT (Bull, 1988). Iacono (2009) mentions that this is unfortunate because research supports its utility. In recent years, the GKT also has been modernized to the extent that a variant of the test is marketed as brain fingerprinting (Iacono, 2009). After describing in some detail how this version differs from the original GKT, Iacono notes that it, like the GKT, has considerable potential utility.

We should note that polygraphs are administered in many situations in addition to criminal investigation. These include, but are not limited to, counterintelligence and national security screening, civil litigation, personnel screening, internal corporate investigations, and post-conviction assessments. The last category includes situations where the polygraph is used with sex offenders to detect deception in an effort to control recidivism. For instance, in 1998, a survey revealed that 35 states were using polygraph testing for monitoring convicted sex offenders (Consigli, 2002).

Countermeasures

Countermeasures are anything that an examinee might do to "fool" the polygraph and the examiner. Polygraphers maintain that results of the predominant instrument—the CQT—cannot be manipulated. As Iacono (2009) wryly asserts, however, "if a suspect successfully adopted countermeasures, their use would go undetected" (p. 234). Belief that countermeasures will be detected, he observes, is based on "clumsy" attempts by suspects such as tensing their muscles or holding their breath. In addition, information on methods to "fool" the polygraph is widely available on the Internet as well as in scientific journals.

SUMMARY AND CONCLUSIONS

The distinction between an interview and an interrogation is a crucial one. Police interviews are conducted with anyone who may have knowledge of a matter that has been brought to police attention; they are investigatory in nature, and the interviewee may be a person who has some knowledge of an incident, a direct witness or victim of a crime, or a person who may eventually be suspected of committing it. When the questioning process shifts from investigation to accusation, a person becomes a suspect. Criminal suspects who are questioned in custody must first be informed of their right to be protected against self-incrimination and their right to a lawyer as well as the fact that a lawyer will be appointed for them if they cannot afford one. They must be warned that if they choose to answer questions, anything they say can be used against them. This very basic information must be communicated to suspects, but it is not communicated in a universal manner. Moreover, research is clear that many people do not comprehend their *Miranda* rights. The lack of comprehension is especially problematic among the intellectually disabled, the mentally disordered, and juveniles, but it is not limited to these groups. As revealed in the chapter, even college students hold false beliefs about what police can and cannot do during the interrogation process.

The interrogation process pits one or more law enforcement officers who have been trained in interrogation techniques against suspects who may or may not be actually guilty of crime. The detection of deception is critical for these investigators, but this is easier said than done. Proponents of the predominant method of interview and interrogation used by police, the Reid method, maintain that it is highly effective at discerning truth tellers from liars.

Although law enforcement officers believe they are highly effective in using these techniques, the assumptions on which these beliefs are based lack scientific verification. For example, a vast store of scientific research indicates that deception cannot easily be detected, while interrogators and other professionals (including employment interviewers) believe they can detect it. Researchers now urge interrogators to focus on verbal rather than nonverbal cues, but—more important—to seek truth using different methods. Both the information-gathering approach and the cognitive load approach have been advocated.

Confirmation bias is a normal feature of human cognition. When it operates in the interrogation room, it can be to the detriment of finding truth. If interrogators are strong in their beliefs about a suspect—and that suspect happens to be innocent—they will seek more evidence to support their belief and may overlook or discount evidence to the contrary.

Legal psychologists are concerned about the use of psychological coercion during the interrogation process, particularly but not exclusively as it may result in a false confession. While most confessions are true (although not necessarily valid), there is a disconcerting number of proven false confessions. They may be voluntary, coerced-compliant, or internalized. In the last category, people who are innocent actually come to believe in their own guilt. Research on false confessions has exploded over the last two decades, prompted by evidence that numerous suspects have confessed to crimes they did not commit. False confession research is gradually being introduced into criminal court, but some courts do not allow expert testimony on this issue.

The polygraph, an instrument sometimes used by police to detect deception, is extremely controversial among psychologists. Of particular concern is the CQT, the predominant method used by an increasing number of polygraphers—who are generally not psychologists. An alternative method, the GKT, received positive reviews in the research literature. Polygraphy is a technical skill obtained by polygraphers, who are often law enforcement professionals, in polygraphy schools, the most prominent of which is operated by the federal government. Smaller polygraphy schools exist across the United States, not all of which are accredited by the American Polygraphy Association. The polygraph has been subjected to considerable empirical research by independent scientists over the past three decades, and the evidence regarding its accuracy is not impressive. Many have maintained that it does not meet the *Daubert* or *Frye* tests for scientific evidence, a fact that contributes to the judiciary's reluctance to admit polygraph evidence into the courts, particularly criminal courts.

KEY CONCEPTS

Accusatorial approach

Behavior analysis investigation (BAI)

Coerced-compliant confession

Coerced-internalized confession

Coercion errors

Cognitive load

Comparison question test

Concealed information test

Confirmation bias

Confrontation

Contamination errors

Control Question Test (CQT)

Custodial interrogation

Custody and isolation

Forced-compliant confession

Guilty Knowledge Test (GKT)

HUMINT interrogation

Information-gathering approach

Intimate knowledge

Minimization

Misclassification errors

Psychological coercion

Reid method

Stipulated polygraph test

Voluntary false confession

CHAPTER

4

Competencies and Criminal Responsibility

When movie buffs filed into a theater in Aurora, Colorado, in late July 2012 for the midnight showing of a Batman film, they could not foresee the real-life horror they would be experiencing shortly thereafter. Twelve of these fans would not survive. As the soundtrack to *The Dark Knight Rises* was blaring, James E. Holmes allegedly threw tear gas canisters and opened fire in the theater, killing the 12 and wounding 58 others. Some of the patrons were injured while trying to flee the gunman.

Not long after, the world saw images of the 24-year-old Holmes sitting in a courtroom for his initial appearance, wild-eyed and alternately staring straight ahead or looking down. The shaggy hair at the top of his head had been dyed orange, leaving a layer of dark hair below. These were bizarre images, and they cemented Holmes's notoriety. Subsequent court appearances were closed to broadcast media, but sketch artists presented similar depictions, though the layered hair disappeared and Holmes was seen with closely shorn dark hair.

Holmes's lawyers expressed concerns about his mental state but did not at first indicate whether they would pursue an insanity defense. Very little information about the case was released to the public until early January 2013, when Holmes had a 3-day-long preliminary hearing. Victims described the horror in the theater, and police revealed that Holmes had started amassing weapons in early May and had booby-trapped his apartment the day of the shooting. Following this hearing, Holmes's lawyers asked for a delay in his arraignment, saying he was not ready to enter a plea. Finally, in May 2013, Holmes pleaded not guilty by reason of insanity. His case is expected to go to trial in 2014, and prosecutors are seeking the death penalty.

Competency to stand trial and insanity refer to a defendant's mental capacities at two different points in time. Specifically, **competency to stand trial (CST)** is the individual's ability, at the time of the trial preparation and the trial itself, to understand the charges and legal proceedings and to communicate with his or her attorney. Competency to stand trial deals with the present and the foreseeable future. **Insanity**, on the other hand, is the legal term for lack of criminal responsibility *at the time of the crime*, as the result of a mental disorder. Because the word *insanity* is so widely used as a synonym for mental illness, some commentators prefer to use the phrase "legal insanity" to emphasize the important distinction between lack of criminal responsibility and mental illness.

A defendant may be *legally* sane even if he or she has a mental disorder. A defendant also may be legally sane—criminally responsible at the time of the crime—but incompetent at the trial stage. An example is the careless and negligent driver who kills a pedestrian, is charged with vehicular manslaughter, and is so emotionally distraught as a result of the tragedy that he cannot help his attorney in the preparation of a defense. Conversely, a defendant may have lacked criminal responsibility at the time of the crime, but still may be competent at the time of legal proceedings. Indeed, under the law, a criminal trial of an individual claiming insanity as a defense cannot be conducted if the defendant is not competent.

It must be emphasized that both terms—insanity and competency (or fitness) to stand trial—are *legal*, not psychological concepts, although psychological functioning is clearly relevant to both. The court, not the mental health practitioner or clinician, determines who was insane when an offense was committed or who is incompetent. In reality, however, judges rely very heavily on the opinion of the examining clinician when it is provided (Gowensmith, Murrie, & Boccaccini, 2013; Melton, Petrila, Poythress, & Slobogin, 2007), and judges often ask for a recommendation from mental health clinicians. A judge's finding that an individual is incompetent to stand trial (IST) means that the defendant is so cognitively or emotionally impaired that it is unfair to continue the criminal process. At this point, court proceedings are held in abeyance until the defendant becomes competent. This is what happened in the case of Jared Loughner, the man who shot Congresswoman Gabrielle Giffords and killed six others while the congresswoman was meeting with constituents in Arizona in January 2011. Loughner was evaluated and found incompetent on May 25, about 4 months after the shooting. He eventually was ruled competent, pled guilty to 19 charges of murder and attempted murder, and was subsequently sentenced to life without the possibility of parole. By contrast, if Loughner had gone to trial and been found not guilty by reason of insanity, the outcome would be very different. A judge or jury's verdict that a defendant is not guilty by reason of insanity means that the individual cannot be punished, because he or she did not possess the required guilty mind (**mens rea**). However, the person may be (and usually is) institutionalized for treatment of the mental disorder.

Although we focus in this chapter on competency to stand trial along with insanity, we must emphasize that there are many other "competencies" associated with the legal process, both criminal and civil. In the literature, many scholars prefer the term adjudicative competence to reflect this broad sweep. Grisso (1986, p. 2) summarized the competencies or capacities that a criminal suspect, defendant, or offender must possess. They include the capacity

(1) To waive rights to silence and counsel "knowingly, intelligently, and voluntarily," prior to questioning by law enforcement officers (see Chapter 3);

(2) To plead guilty;

(3) To dismiss counsel, or to conduct one's own defense without benefit of counsel;

(4) To stand trial (i.e., to function in the role of defendant in the trial process);

(5) To possess the requisite cognition, affect, and volition for criminal responsibility . . .

(6) To serve a sentence;

(7) To be executed (i.e., to undergo capital punishment). (p. 2)

In addition to the above, Melton et al. (2007) mention the competencies to consent to a search or seizure, to confess, to refuse an insanity defense, to testify, and to be sentenced. Although these latter competencies should be understood as falling within Grisso's list, specifying them separately helps define even more clearly the role of the criminal defendant. Interestingly, in 2013, the U.S. Supreme Court unanimously ruled that competency was *not* required in another context, specifically, some post-conviction proceedings (see Box 4-1).

BOX 4-1

Case Study. Competency Not Required for Post-Conviction Habeas Corpus Proceedings: *Tibbals v. Carter and Ryan v. Gonzales* (2013)

When prisoners have exhausted all of their appeals in state courts, they sometimes file a writ of habeas corpus with the federal courts. Persons held in jails before trial also may file a writ of habeas corpus, although this is far less common. Basically, the individual is arguing that he or she is being detained illegally. Although a variety of writs fall under the name *habeas corpus* ("you have the body"), the most common—the one referenced here—commands someone detaining another to produce the detainee strictly for the purpose of testing the legality of the detention or imprisonment (Black, 1990). Essentially, the court issuing the writ is telling the person or government authority to produce the detainee so legality can be determined. The writ of habeas corpus is not intended to review innocence or guilt.

(Continued)

(Continued)

Sean Carter and Ernest Gonzales were both on death row, Carter in Ohio and Gonzales in Arizona. Gonzales had killed a man and stabbed his wife during a burglary of their home; Carter had raped and murdered his adoptive grandmother. Both men were convicted and sentenced to death, and—in the opinions of medical practitioners—both became mentally ill on death row. Lawyers for both men were challenging the legality of their imprisonment on various grounds, using the habeas corpus route. They argued that, because of their mental conditions, the two death row inmates were unable to assist them in preparing their appeals. Two different federal appellate courts had ruled that Carter and Gonzales had a right to be competent during these habeas corpus proceedings, and that the proceedings must be delayed until their competency was restored.

The U.S. Supreme Court disagreed, in a unanimous decision. Habeas corpus proceedings were not the equivalent of a criminal trial, the Justices said. Furthermore, the right to be competent in criminal proceedings was a due process right, not one inextricably tied to the Sixth Amendment right to a lawyer. The

Court noted that, for habeas corpus proceedings after conviction, attorneys were capable of reviewing the records and identifying legal errors without their clients' assistance. If judges wanted to delay the proceedings, that was in their purview; but they did not have to do so.

It should be noted, though, that if Carter or Gonzales is judged to be incompetent at the time of his execution, he cannot be executed. We discuss competency for execution later in the chapter.

Questions for Discussion:

1. Read the Sixth Amendment to the U.S. Constitution. Does anything in the amendment suggest that Carter and Gonzales needed to be competent at the time of the habeas corpus proceedings?

2. Read the Fourteenth Amendment. Does anything in that amendment suggest that Carter and Gonzales needed to be competent at the time of the habeas corpus proceedings? Why do you think the *lower* courts ruled that they should be?

Competencies arise in the civil context as well. Civil courts, for example, may be concerned about the competence of mentally disordered individuals to refuse medication, the competence of adolescents to make medical decisions, or the competence of older individuals to change their will (called testamentary capacity). Moreover, in a situation that traverses the criminal and the civil, scholars are drawing attention to the competence of sexually violent predators (SVPs) to participate in proceedings seeking to have them committed for psychiatric treatment after the expiration of their prison sentence (Fanniff, Otto, & Petrila, 2010). These and other issues are discussed in later chapters. Here, we focus specifically on mental states of criminal defendants, both as they relate to various competencies and as they relate to the issue of criminal responsibility.

In addition, we discuss the important matter of competence for execution because it relates to the criminal process.

⌧ Competency to Stand Trial

The U.S. Supreme Court has ruled that defendants are competent to stand trial if they have "sufficient present ability to consult with [their] lawyer with a reasonable degree of rational understanding . . . and a rational as well as a factual understanding of the proceedings" (*Dusky v. United States,* 1960, p. 402). Competency requires not only that defendants *understand* what is happening, but also that they be *able to assist* their lawyers in the preparation of their defense. This is sometimes referred to as the *Dusky* "two-pronged standard." In other words, competency to stand trial is the ability to play the role of defendant (Grisso, 1986; Reisner, Piel, & Makey, 2013). As noted above, this role is relevant not only at the trial itself, but also in a variety of pretrial and posttrial proceedings, including plea negotiations, preliminary hearings, evidence suppression hearings, and sentencing. Competency is not necessary during post-conviction habeas corpus proceedings, as described in Box 4-1 (*Tibbals v. Carter and Ryan v. Gonzales,* 2013).

The competency inquiry has been called "the most significant mental health inquiry pursued in the system of criminal law" (Stone, 1975, p. 200). In decisions after *Dusky* (e.g., *Drope v. Missouri,* 1975; *Pate v. Robinson,* 1966), the U.S. Supreme Court has made it clear that the conviction of an incompetent defendant violates due process of law. (See Table 4-1 for a summary of representative U.S. Supreme Court cases relating to competency.) Some jurisdictions require the government to prove the defendant is competent, while others require the defendant to prove incompetency.

Fortunately, since competency is such a significant inquiry, there is a vast store of research literature on this topic. Recently, Pirelli, Gottdiener, and Zapf (2011) published a meta-analysis of 68 studies on competency published between 1967 and 2008. In addition, Fogel, Schiffman, Mumley, Tillbrook, and Grisso (2013) published a comprehensive update of competency research over the period 2001–2010. Fogel et al. found there was increasing research attention given to the competence of juveniles, malingering (faking) incompetence, restoration of competence, and the constructs underlying adjudicative competence over that 10-year period. We discuss much of this recent research later in the chapter,

A mental disorder per se does not make a person incompetent to stand trial. Mental illness or disorder does not equal incompetency. For example, someone with a depressive disorder may be perfectly capable of understanding the proceedings and helping her attorney. On the other hand, another person with the same depressive disorder could be so severely debilitated that he withdraws from the situation and refuses to communicate. As Grisso (1986, p. 95) remarks, however, "psychological symptoms by themselves are

Table 4-1 Representative U.S. Supreme Court Cases Relating to Competency

Case Name	Year	Holding/Significance
Dusky v. United States	1960	Set standard for competency to stand trial used in virtually all jurisdictions today.
Pate v. Robinson	1966	The competency inquiry can be raised at any time during criminal proceedings.
Jackson v. Indiana	1972	Defendants found incompetent to stand trial may *not* be hospitalized indefinitely for purpose of restoring competency.
Ford v. Wainwright	1986	Establishes principle of competency for execution; prohibits execution if someone is so severely mentally ill that he or she cannot appreciate the reason for the punishment.
Medina v. California	1992	States may require defendant to prove incompetency by preponderance of the evidence.
Godinez v. Moran	1993	*Dusky* standard of competency applies to plea bargaining and waiver of lawyer; no separate standard required.
Cooper v. Oklahoma	1996	State may *not* require proof of incompetency by clear and convincing evidence (compare with *Medina*).
Sell v. United States	2003	Defendant charged with nonviolent crime has right to refuse medication intended to restore him to competency; judge may still grant government's wish to administer medication after careful consideration.
Indiana v. Edwards	2008	Incompetent defendant does not have absolute right to represent himself.
Tibbals v. Carter and Ryan v. Gonzales	2013	Competency not required of defendants in post-conviction habeas corpus proceedings.

not synonymous with legal incompetency, [but] they are certainly relevant for pretrial competency determinations" (p. 95). So, whereas the *lack* of a diagnosis does not serve as a bar to incompetency (Cruise & Rogers, 1998), clinical diagnosis does appear to be a significant contributor to the competency recommendations made by evaluators (Cochrane, Grisso, & Frederick, 2001; Colwell & Gianesini, 2011). Moreover, some diagnoses, particularly psychotic disorder, highly increase the likelihood that a defendant will be found incompetent to stand trial (Pirelli et al., 2011).

Symptoms associated with a diagnosis of a mental disorder may also interfere with a person's *competency to plead guilty*. Recall from Chapter 2 that the vast majority (somewhere in the vicinity of 90%) of criminal cases are settled by way of a plea bargain. Scholars have argued that pleading guilty, in light of its consequences, may require sharper functional ability than going through a trial (Halleck, 1980; Poythress & Zapf, 2009).

In pleading guilty, a person waives a number of constitutional rights, including the Fifth Amendment right not to incriminate oneself and the Sixth Amendment right to a fair trial, along with its accompaniments (e.g., impartial jury of peers, the right to confront and cross-examine witnesses). Before accepting a guilty plea, a judge must address the defendant and inquire into the voluntariness of the plea. The judge also must assure that the defendant understands the consequences of waiving his or her constitutional rights, as the presiding judge recently did in the case of Ariel Castro mentioned in the last chapter. In the late 1980s, scholars argued that the failure to monitor guilty pleas more carefully was one of the factors contributing to the influx of mentally disordered persons in jails and prisons (Steadman, McCarty, & Morrissey, 1989). Lately, scholars are raising similar concerns about defendants' waiving of *Miranda* rights, as we saw in Chapter 3 (e.g., Rogers, 2011).

Raising the Competency Issue

Psychologists or other mental health clinicians are most likely to be asked to evaluate a defendant for competency very early in the criminal process. Typically, at the defendant's arraignment or shortly thereafter, a motion is made by either the defense lawyer or the prosecutor to inquire into the defendant's competency. In some situations, such as when the defendant has financial means, defense lawyers may arrange for a competency evaluation rather than wait for a court-ordered one. Presiding judges also have the authority to raise the competency issue themselves. The judge and the attorneys are all "officers of the court" and thus are expected to preserve the integrity of the judicial process. Numerous factors can trigger a competency inquiry. The arresting police officer may have noticed bizarre behavior, for example, or the person may have tried to commit suicide while detained in jail pending arraignment. Research has found that competency evaluations are also precipitated by previous psychiatric hospitalizations as well as psychologically irrelevant factors, including political motives, a defense lawyer's wish to "buy time," and the defendant's homelessness (Nicholson & Kugler, 1991). Most requests for competency evaluation are neither denied by the judge nor challenged by the opposing attorney (Melton et al., 2007; Roesch, Zapf, Golding, & Skeem, 1999).

However, even if a defense attorney suspects that a client has a mental disorder, he or she will not necessarily seek a competency evaluation. (See Box 4-2 for a study relevant to this.) In fact, research suggests that attorneys seek evaluations of approximately half or fewer of the clients about whose competency they have doubts (Hoge, Bonnie, Poythress, & Monahan, 1992; Poythress, Bonnie, Hoge, Monahan, & Oberlander, 1994). Defendants who display inappropriate or bizarre behavior or give strong evidence of cognitive or perceptual difficulties are, of course, more likely to be evaluated (Viljoen & Zapf, 2002).

BOX 4-2 RESEARCHERS AT WORK

Is a Defendant's Primary Language Truly Relevant?

What prompts lawyers to seek competency evaluations for their clients? Behavioral symptoms of a serious mental illness in a defendant is a logical response, but the answer may not be that simple. Some research suggests that other factors may also be at work.

In an interesting study (Varela et al., 2011), researchers looked at the defendant's primary language as one factor that might influence the decision to make a competency referral. Varela and colleagues asked criminal defense attorneys to read vignettes describing a defendant who exhibited signs of mental illness at an initial consultation with an attorney. The hypothetical defendant was a 30-year-old Hispanic male charged with assault following an altercation in a mall. The victim required emergency medical treatment. Depending upon the research condition, the defendant was described as either English or Spanish speaking. The vignettes also described the defendant as having either obvious or ambiguous symptoms of mental illness, but all vignettes included behavior that independent judges found abnormal.

Defense attorneys were significantly more likely to refer English-speaking defendants than Spanish-speaking defendants for competency evaluation; furthermore, they rated the Spanish-speaking defendant as less mentally ill than the English-speaking defendant, although these differences were not as strong.

Varela et al. (2011) could not examine the reasons for their findings, but they offered possible explanations. For example, the attorneys may have "guessed" that the study involved perceptions of bias and may have avoided making a decision that indicated such bias (e.g., requesting a competency evaluation). On the other hand, the attorneys also may have actually *demonstrated* bias by applying an unfortunate and unwarranted immigrant stereotype to the defendant (i.e., connecting immigrants with criminal activity and therefore assuming their guilt). Finally, the researchers suggested that attorneys may have perceived logistical problems, such as a lack of resources for evaluating Spanish-speaking defendants. Regardless of the reasons, Varela et al.'s study raises important questions about fairness in the competency evaluation process for Spanish-speaking defendants.

Questions for Discussion:

1. In addition to primary language, what else might lead a defense lawyer to *not* seek a competency evaluation for her client?

2. What are the advantages and disadvantages of having research participants respond to vignettes such as those used in the above study?

Incidence of Competency to Stand Trial Evaluations

Estimates of the number of defendants evaluated for competency to stand trial each year in the United States range from 50,000 (Skeem, Golding, Cohn, & Berge, 1998) to 60,000 (Bonnie & Grisso, 2000; Colwell & Gianesini, 2011) and are believed to be increasing steadily (Zapf & Roesch, 2006), paralleling rising arrest rates. The great majority, typically in the vicinity of 80%, are found to be competent (Cochran et al., 2001; Pirelli et al., 2011). Although competency is a legal decision to be made by the presiding judges, these judges almost invariably accept the recommendation of the examining clinician. When two or more clinicians disagree about the competency of a defendant, research indicates that the presiding judge is more likely to find the defendant incompetent (Gowensmith, Murrie, & Boccaccini, 2012).

Both misdemeanor and felony defendants may be assessed for competency. It is believed that between 3% and 8% of all felony defendants are assessed for competency (S. K. Hoge et al., 1997; Roesch et al., 1999). Surveys of public defenders suggest that they have competency to stand trial concerns for 10% to 15% of all criminal defendants, including those charged with felonies and misdemeanors (Melton et al., 1997, 2007). However, as mentioned above, defense attorneys as a group seek evaluations for only about half of defendants about whom they have these concerns.

The Competency Evaluation Process

Until the late 1980s, the typical competency evaluation was conducted while the defendant was hospitalized in a mental institution for anywhere from 15 to 90 days (Nicholson & Kugler, 1991). Researchers found that judges and lawyers often distrusted outpatient evaluations, believing they could not adequately assess a defendant's competency (Melton, Weithorn, & Slobogin, 1985). Beginning in the 1990s, competency evaluations were increasingly conducted in outpatient facilities or in jails or courthouses (Roesch et al., 1999). In addition, with the availability of quick screening instruments, prompt evaluations were even more possible. Similar to the court proceedings at a distance referred to in Chapter 2, some evaluations are even conducted via video teleconferencing (Manguno-Mire, Thompson, Bertman-Pate, Burnett, & Thompson, 2007).

Although competency to stand trial and insanity are often interrelated (Golding & Roesch, 1987), they require separate assessments and determinations. Consequently, we will discuss briefly the assessment of competency in this part of the chapter and the assessment of sanity later on. Additional material on assessment can be found in Chapter 12.

Traditionally, psychiatrists and psychologists failed to focus on the limited issue of a defendant's competency to stand trial (Grisso, 1988; Saks, 1990). Instead, they included irrelevant information in their competency reports as well as in their courtroom testimony. One study, for example, found that 47% of competency evaluations also addressed questions of sanity (Warren, Fitch, Dietz, & Rosenfeld, 1991). Roesch et al. (1999) are very critical of this common practice, recommending instead that separate interviews with distinct reports be prepared: "A trier of fact is required to separate these issues, but it is cognitively almost impossible to do so when the reports are combined" (p. 343). Interestingly, in the Jared Loughner case, the judge specified very clearly that the competency evaluation he ordered was to be limited to that issue, not to the question of sanity. It is more likely that judges presiding over such high-profile cases attend to this distinction than judges presiding over more routine cases, however.

At least 12 competency assessment instruments have been developed over the past 40 years (Pirelli et al., 2011). Although the quality of competency evaluations has improved overall, not all signs are positive. A recent study of evaluation reports submitted to judges found that only 25% were of high quality (Robinson & Acklin, 2010). After reviewing various competency assessment instruments, Poythress and Zapf (2009) wrote, "There is scant scientific evidence for the reliability and validity of many of the adjudicative competence measures" (p. 320). They were not saying that the measures were necessarily unreliable, just that their evidence base has not been sufficiently established.

Making the Competency Decision

When an evaluation has been completed, the examiner transmits to the party or parties requesting it a report that typically includes a recommendation as to the defendant's competency. The great majority of competency decisions are made on the basis of one clinician's assessment (Melton et al., 2007) and without direct testimony from that clinician. Furthermore, as mentioned previously, judges rarely disagree with the clinician's recommendation, particularly if the clinician believes the defendant is incompetent. Studies up to the present continue to document that courts on the whole—as many as 95%—agree with clinical recommendations (Pirelli et al., 2011). As noted earlier, when examiners do not agree, the defendant is more likely to be found incompetent to stand trial (Gowensmith et al., 2012). This implies that if there is doubt regarding the defendant's competency, the judge may not want to risk trying an incompetent defendant and may err on the side of caution.

The Incompetent Defendant

Most defendants evaluated for competency are found to be competent. In an early and widely cited study of the minority of defendants who are not, Steadman (1979) described them as a socially marginalized group with less than an average education, few useful job skills, and few family or employment ties. Nicholson and Kugler (1991), who analyzed 30 studies on competency to stand trial conducted over a 20-year period, reported that the strongest correlates of incompetency were not demographic but rather clinical in nature.

Demographic data include factors such as age, gender, employment, and marital status. Clinical data include information about psychological functioning. Specifically, in Nicholson and Kugler's summary, defendants found to be IST (1) performed poorly on tests specifically designed to assess legally relevant functional abilities, (2) were diagnosed as psychotic, and (3) had psychiatric symptoms indicating severe psychopathology. Most recently, in Pirelli et al.'s (2011) meta-analysis of 68 studies published between 1967 and 2008, they found three characteristics most closely associated with a finding of incompetence: (1) a diagnosis with a psychotic disorder, (2) unemployment, and (3) a history of previous psychiatric hospitalization. Fogel et al. (2013) report that two U.S. studies in the past decade found no differences with respect to gender, but one found that incompetent defendants were more likely to be of minority status. As in earlier studies, however, psychotic disorders—such as schizophrenia or delusional disorders—were found significantly more often in incompetent than competent defendants.

Is Crime Charged Significant?

It may surprise readers to learn that the competency issue is sometimes raised in the case of defendants charged with misdemeanors, or minor offenses. The crime charged should be irrelevant, but many lawyers do not want to raise the issue in minor cases that will likely be dismissed or pled out and lead to a fine or short-term probation. When competency evaluations are sought in misdemeanor cases, it is widely believed that this is done to assure that mentally disordered defendants charged with minor crimes are provided with inpatient treatment. Otherwise, they are unlikely to receive appropriate mental health care.

Ideally, the seriousness of the crime with which a person is charged should be irrelevant to the competency decision. Incompetence reflects the person's psychological status and daily ability to function in the role required. Nonetheless, some early research indicated that defendants ruled IST were most often charged with violent crimes, or at least felony offenses (e.g., Roesch & Golding, 1980; Steadman, 1979). Nicholson and Kugler's (1991) examination of 30 studies, however, indicated that the type of offense "likely bears a stronger relation to the decision to refer [for a competency evaluation] than it does to the decision about competency itself" (p. 366). More than half of the competency evaluees had been charged with violent crimes, but less than a third of those ultimately found incompetent were in that category. Likewise, Warren, Rosenfeld, Fitch, and Hawk (1997), in a three-state study, found that defendants charged with serious crimes (e.g., homicide and sex offenses) were twice as likely as other defendants to be found *competent*. Rosenfeld and Ritchie (1998) found a similar relationship between offense severity and the competency determination; persons charged with less serious offenses had significantly higher rates of incompetence. In addition, Pirelli et al. (2011)

found that defendants with current violent criminal charges were 1.25 times more likely to be found competent than those with nonviolent charges. Thus, the recent research and the meta-analysis suggest that defendants with serious charges are less likely to be found incompetent.

In sum, the nature of the crime charged does seem to bear some relation to the competency decision, but other demographic or extralegal variables also have been identified, including the gender of the defendant, race or ethnicity, employment status, or educational or marital status. As noted above, though, none of these variables has been found *consistently* to have a strong relation to the competency decision. On the other hand, psychiatric diagnoses and prior hospitalizations carry considerable weight with the courts. Colwell and Gianesini (2011) report, "the prototypical incompetent defendant may be described as someone with a history of psychiatric symptoms, particularly some psychosis, poor functional abilities and community resources, and poor psycholegal abilities" (p. 298).

Do Diagnoses Matter?

No variables are as closely connected to a finding of incompetency to stand trial as **psychiatric diagnoses** and previous psychiatric hospitalization. In Pirelli et al.'s (2011) review, defendants diagnosed with a psychotic disorder were nearly 8 times more likely to be found incompetent than those without such a diagnosis. (See Table 4-2 for definitions of common mental disorders.) Defendants with previous psychiatric hospitalizations were twice as likely to be found incompetent as those without hospitalization. In a study of federal defendants nationwide, Cochrane et al. (2001) discovered that psychoses, organic disorders (such as dementia and brain damage), and intellectual disability (formerly mental retardation) were frequent diagnoses in incompetent defendants. They concluded, "the main variable that affects psycholegal opinions is the diagnostic presentation of the defendant" (p. 581).

The fact that diagnoses seem to carry so much weight is troubling to many psychologists. Forensic psychologists are usually advised not to include diagnoses in competency reports (Grisso, 1986, 2003). The same reluctance can be seen among forensic psychiatrists in the midst of increasing demands from the legal system to render formal diagnoses (American Psychiatric Association Task Force, 1992). Guidelines for practice, such as the *Specialty Guidelines for Forensic Psychology* (APA, 2013b), urge caution, reminding practitioners to focus on legally relevant factors. For example, "Forensic practitioners are encouraged to consider the problems that may arise by using a clinical diagnosis in some forensic contexts, and consider and qualify their opinions and testimony appropriately" (APA, 2013b, Guideline 10.01).

Yet representatives of the legal system routinely expect diagnoses in clinical reports, and clinicians routinely supply them, even in evaluations of competency to stand trial. In sanity evaluations, to be discussed below, diagnoses are the norm. Even though a

Table 4-2	Mental Disorders or Diagnoses Commonly Found in Evaluations Submitted to Courts*

Antisocial personality disorder:

Chronic antisocial behavior, but not due to a mental or intellectual disorder like severe intellectual disability, schizophrenia, or manic episodes.

Dementia:

A generalized, pervasive deterioration of cognitive functions due to any of various causes. Common causes are Alzheimer's disease, Parkinson's disease, cerebrovascular disease, Huntington's disease, or substance abuse. Brain tumors may also cause dementia.

Depressive disorder:

Any one of several mood disorders that typically have sadness as one of their symptoms.

Depressive personality disorder:

A personality disorder characterized by such signs as glumness, pessimism, a lack of joy, the inability to experience pleasure, and motor retardation.

Intellectual disability:

The term now preferred for mental retardation, it is characterized by intellectual functioning that is significantly below average.

Parasomnia:

Abnormal behavior or physiological events occurring during sleep; may also occur during the transitional state between sleep and waking.

Post-traumatic stress disorder (PTSD):

A disorder that results when an individual lives through or witnesses an event in which there is a threat to life or physical integrity and safety. Emotional reactions of fear, terror, or helplessness are typical at the time the event occurs.

Psychotic disorder:

Any of a number of severe mental disorders characterized by gross impairment in reality testing. Symptoms indicative of psychotic disorders are delusions; hallucinations; and markedly disorganized speech, thought, or behavior. Following are some specific forms of psychotic disorder:

Delusional disorder:

A psychotic disorder that features one or more non-bizarre delusions that persist for at least 1 month but are not due to schizophrenia. They are non-bizarre because they feature situations that could conceivably occur, but do not.

Schizophrenia:

This disorder is characterized by disturbances in thinking, emotional responsiveness, and behavior. There is marked social or occupational dysfunction. *Paranoid schizophrenia* is a subtype that includes prominent delusions or auditory hallucinations. Delusions are typically persecutory, grandiose, or both.

*Definitions adapted from the *APA Dictionary of Psychology,* 2007.

verdict of insanity is a "moral judgment" (Slobogin, 1989), its foundation is some mental disorder. Specifying the disorder, then, becomes a critical issue to many if not most courts.

Competency Restoration

Until 1972, a defendant found IST could face lifetime confinement in a mental institution. It was not uncommon for the defendant to be committed for an indefinite period of time, supposedly until rendered "competent." Early studies reported that about 50% of those found incompetent under these procedures spent the rest of their lives confined in an institution (Hess & Thomas, 1963; McGarry, 1971). It was also estimated that these IST defendants comprised at least 40% of the population in mental institutions (Steadman & Cocozza, 1974). Today, incompetent defendants represent the largest group of patients committed to mental hospitals through the legal system (Colwell & Gianesini, 2011).

In the 1972 case *Jackson v. Indiana*, the U.S. Supreme Court ruled that persons found IST may be involuntarily confined only for the reasonable period of time necessary to determine whether there is a substantial probability of their becoming competent to stand trial in the foreseeable future. If the defendant was not likely to gain competency in the foreseeable future, civil commitment proceedings must be initiated or the defendant must be released. (Civil commitment, the subject of Chapter 10, carries due process protections that make it more difficult to place a person in a mental institution against his or her will.) In the *Jackson* case, the Court left it to states to determine what are reasonable amounts of time to restore competency and how to evaluate the likelihood that competency would be achieved. Indefinite confinement is out of the question, though. States vary in the limitations they have placed on the confinement period. Some have specified time limits, while others base the length of treatment on the maximum sentence the defendant could have received if convicted.

As a result of the *Jackson* case, some persons found incompetent to stand trial who have little likelihood of being restored to competency now have their cases dismissed without prejudice, a move that gives the prosecutor the option of reinstituting charges in the event that the person regains competency. Alternatively, they may be committed to mental institutions or ordered to participate in outpatient care through civil commitment proceedings.

Drug Treatment

Most defendants deemed IST eventually are ruled competent and either plead guilty or go to trial. Melton et al. (2007) indicate that most IST defendants are indeed restorable. In a recent study, Colwell and Gianesini (2011) found that 75% of all defendants were restored to competency in an average of less than 100 days: "The studies are relatively consistent in finding that the large majority of defendants referred for treatment are recommended as 'restored' within six months, and often earlier" (p. 162). Others, such as individuals who are severely intellectually challenged or have dementia, have a well below average chance of successful restoration (Zapf & Roesch, 2011). Colwell and Gianesini recommend that unless the individual has irreversible impediments (such as progressive dementia) or moderate mental retardation, psychologists and other mental health professionals should err on the side of assuming that a defendant is restorable until it can be determined otherwise. Unfortunately, some individuals are cycled from jail, hospital, court, and the community numerous times because their mental state is in continual flux.

The government's interest in obtaining a plea or going to trial is particularly strong in a serious case, of course. It was certainly strong in the Jared Loughner case. Loughner was ruled incompetent in May 2011, four months after his crime. Examining clinicians gave the opinion that he was restorable; in August 2012 after having been ruled competent, he pled guilty and was sentenced to life imprisonment without parole.

While some IST defendants are treated in the community, those charged with serious crimes are institutionalized for the purpose of restoring them to competency. Medication is the most common type of treatment provided to incompetent defendants, whether inpatient or outpatient (Roesch et al., 1999; Zapf & Roesch, 2011). It should be noted that more than one third of states do not permit outpatient treatment restoration (Miller, 2003). In some jurisdictions, the treatment phase includes education on the legal system and the consequences of the various decisions made by criminal defendants.

When medication is the option, it is usually in the form of **psychoactive drugs,** which "exert their primary effect on the brain, thus altering mood or behavior" (Julien, 1992, p. xii). Although many of these drugs have improved in efficacy, they may still produce unwanted side effects such as nausea, headaches, and even loss of creativity in some individuals. While incompetent defendants may refuse these drugs, courts have ruled that their wishes can be overridden if the state has a strong interest in bringing the case to trial.

The battle over forced medication can be protracted, however. In the summer of 1998, Eugene Russell Weston allegedly killed two Washington, D.C., Capitol police officers and wounded two others. Found incompetent to stand trial, he languished in federal facilities for almost 3 years while his lawyers challenged the administration of psychoactive drugs. In July of 2001, a federal appeals court ruled that the government's strong interest in bringing Weston to trial overrode his right to refuse the medication. Nonetheless, the drugs have not yet made him competent. The government presumably is maintaining that progress is being made, because Weston remains hospitalized.

More recently, Jared Loughner fought the involuntary administration of psychoactive medication. His lawyers also argued that a decision to medicate him should be made in a judicial rather than administrative setting—an argument they lost. Loughner was medicated and rendered competent before pleading guilty to the murder and attempted murder charges against him, as noted above.

The U.S. Supreme Court addressed the issue of forced medication in *Sell v. United States* (2003). Sell, a former dentist, had been charged with nonviolent offenses (Medicaid and other insurance fraud, money laundering). Found incompetent to stand trial, he refused to take the psychoactive medication prescribed by attending psychiatrists to render him competent. The Supreme Court ruled that lower courts had not sufficiently examined whether Sell was a dangerous individual before approving of the forcible medication, indicating that incompetent defendants have a right to refuse the medication, but recall that this can be outweighed by the interest of the state in bringing the person to trial as happened in Weston's and Loughner's cases.

It is clear that medication is the common form of treatment afforded incompetent defendants. Some time ago, Wexler and Winick (1991) remarked that

> treatment is probably rarely tailored to the specific abilities needed to be competent to stand trial. It probably has as a goal the treatment of the patient's psychopathology, rather than the short-term goal of restoration to trial competency, or more appropriately to competency to perform the specific trial-related tasks the defendant has been found unable to do. (p. 314)

A survey of 128 forensic facilities also confirmed the suspicion that incompetent defendants did not receive treatment specifically geared to their needs to understand the legal process (Siegel & Elwork, 1990). Over half the facilities surveyed did not treat incompetent defendants any differently than the general mentally disordered population.

On the whole, studies of restoration involving medication indicate that a high percentage (75%) are restored to competency within 6 months and an even higher percentage within 1 year (e.g., Advokat, Guidry, Burnett, Manguno-Mire, & Thompson, 2012; Miller, 2003; Morris & Parker, 2008). Warren et al. (2006) found that clinicians believed defendants with organic disorders or with intellectual and learning deficits were the most likely to be unrestorable. Advokat and her colleagues discovered that a diagnosis of psychotic disorder and severe psychiatric symptomatology is closely linked to unrestorability.

Juvenile Competency

Juvenile courts and the juvenile justice process are considered civil rather than criminal and are thus distinct from criminal courts in many respects. However, when they are charged with crimes, juveniles whose cases are heard in juvenile courts are entitled to the same constitutional protections as adults (*In re Gault*, 1967), with the exception of the right to a jury (*McKeiver v. Pennsylvania*, 1971). Today, many juveniles have their cases heard in criminal courts, particularly but not necessarily when they are charged with serious crimes. In addition, juvenile courts are given authority to impose tougher sentences. As Viljoen, McLachlan, Wingrove, and Penner (2010) observed, "over the past several decades, the juvenile justice system has evolved to be much more adult-like in nature" (p. 630).

In the 1990s, at a time when juveniles faced harsher penalties at younger ages, the issue of their competence to stand trial began to capture the attention of researchers, legal commentators, and some state courts (Kruh & Grisso, 2008; Larson & Grisso, 2012). This attention has also been fueled by a growing body of research on juvenile cognitive and social development. In the case of the juvenile, competency is even more likely to involve developmental as well as mental health considerations. For example, we must ask, "Can a 12-year-old boy charged with aggravated assault appreciate the nature of the charges and the consequences he faces even if he has no evidence of a mental disorder?"

It is now well recognized that juveniles as a group differ in developmental and decision-making abilities compared with adults as a group (Grisso et al., 2003; Melton et al., 2007; Steinberg & Cauffman, 1996). As we noted when discussing APA briefs in Chapter 2, there is some debate as to the significance of these group differences in making policy decisions regarding health issues and imprisonment (Steinberg et al., 2009b, vs. Fischer et al., 2009). There is far less debate regarding the issue of adjudicative competency, although some have argued that the differences between adults and juveniles have been exaggerated (Sanborn, 2009).

In a heavily cited study, the MacArthur Foundation's Juvenile Competence Study (Grisso et al., 2003), juveniles below age 15 performed significantly worse than older juveniles or adults on measures of competency to stand trial. This led to the recognition that juvenile competency to stand trial should be assessed in a different way from adult competence.

Larson and Grisso (2012) report that the question of rendering juveniles competent—competency restoration or remediation—is gaining attention. At this point, however, not enough evidence-based practice for doing so is available. In other words, how do we make an incompetent juvenile charged with a serious crime competent to be tried, either in juvenile or adult court? In some states, the competency restoration process must—by statute—be done in the community, or in the least restrictive environment (Warren et al., 2009). Competency restoration will likely involve education, because juveniles may not understand even basic concepts, such as the role of their lawyer in the process. Juvenile defense lawyers also express concerns that their clients are unlikely to achieve adequate levels of competency in light of their developmental immaturity (Viljoen et al., 2010).

Questions relating to juveniles and their adjudicative competence abound, but the first decade of the 21st century saw considerable scholarly progress on this front. Fogel et al. (2013) refer to an explosion of research on this topic between 2000 and 2010 and have comprehensively summarized this research. In addition to a large body of developmental research on juveniles' capacities, researchers have continued to investigate the appropriateness of available instruments for use with juveniles and have made progress toward developing more.

Competency to Be Executed

One of the most controversial and ethically challenging issues relating to competency is that of assessing prisoners awaiting execution. It has long been a principle of common law that offenders must be "competent" before they are executed (Melton et al., 2007). In 1986, the U.S. Supreme Court in a Florida case—*Ford v. Wainwright*—elevated this common-law rule to a constitutional principle. In this context, a person is "incompetent" if he or she is unaware of the punishment that is about to be imposed and why he or she has to suffer it (Bohm, 1999). In ruling on this case, however, the Court did not specify procedures to be used, nor did it provide additional rights (e.g., right to a lawyer) beyond the need for a hearing on the prisoner's mental state (Melton et al., 1997). The Court has also ruled that persons with intellectual disability should not be executed (*Atkins v. Virginia*, 2002), but it did not specify how this disability was to be determined. This issue is discussed again in Chapter 12—and it is scheduled to be addressed by the Court in 2014, in *Hill v. Florida*.

In a later case, *Panetti v. Quarterman* (2007), the Court said it was not enough for a person to know he was being executed and have a factual understanding of the state's rationale for executing him; he must also appreciate that the execution was occurring because of his actions. On death row, Panetti was psychotic and delusional. He "knew" he had committed murder and was about to be executed, and a lower court had ruled that this was enough to execute him. However, the Supreme Court ruled that his delusions may have prevented him from appreciating the gravity of his crime and remanded the case to the district court to reassess this matter. As one group of clinicians noted, "Delusions cannot be ignored if they interfere with appreciating the connection between the crime and the punishment and the real reason for the execution" (Weinstock, Leong, & Silva, 2010, p. 692).

Many unanswered questions remained after the Court's decision in *Ford v. Wainwright* (1986), including what standard should be applied in deciding whether the offender was indeed competent for execution. The *Panetti* case did little to clarify the issue (Weinstock et al., 2010). Moreover, in recent years, some death penalty states have continued with their plans to execute individuals with severe mental illness. In Florida, for example, Miami killer John Ferguson—who spent 34 years on death row—was executed on August 5, 2013, despite the fact that he was diagnosed with paranoid schizophrenia and believed he was being executed because he could control the sun.

Many clinicians today refuse to participate in evaluations of competency for execution, and most will never be asked to. Those who do participate face many ethical dilemmas, aptly summarized by Mossman (1987) and Weinstock et al. (2010). For example, evaluating an offender's competency to be executed appears to conflict with the basic ethical principles to avoid harm (called the **principle of nonmaleficence**), relieve suffering, and preserve life. Also, by participating in the death penalty process, the psychologist is inappropriately improving the image of the death penalty, a social policy that remains extremely controversial.

Mossman and others (e.g., Melton et al., 1997; Weinstock et al., 2010) nevertheless believe that mental health experts *should* be involved in the assessment process, unless their repugnance toward the death penalty would make it difficult, if not impossible, to conduct an objective evaluation. They maintain that the arguments against participation can be satisfactorily addressed. If clinicians refuse to participate on the basis of moral objections to the death penalty, it is more likely that those who *do* participate will be disproportionately biased in favor of this ultimate punishment. By being involved in the process, the clinician has the opportunity to monitor the inmate's mental health needs and offer suggestions to prison officials. Conversely, the clinician who refuses to participate forgoes the opportunity to make a difference in the prisoner's life. Bonnie (1990, 1992)—who approves of participation unless the sole purpose of the examination is to pronounce the prisoner fit to die—points out that a significant proportion of death sentences are eventually set aside; assessing competency on death row can contribute to such resentencing. In fact, some death penalty states require the commutation of a death sentence to life imprisonment if a prisoner is found incompetent to be executed.

There is lack of consensus on performing competency-to-be-executed evaluations, but far more consensus on restoring an incompetent defendant to competency, if the death sentence is not set aside. Mental health practitioners are virtually unanimous in their view that they should not restore an incompetent defendant to competency at this stage, because he or she will just be put to death. Restoration would involve the administration of medication and is in direct conflict with the principle to do no harm—the medication is being administered so the prisoner will be fit to die. "Treating an incompetent to be executed prisoner to make him competent violates medical ethics" (Weinstock et al., 2010, p. 698). At present, this is a nonissue for most psychologists, because they are unable to prescribe medication in most states even if they were disposed to do so. Psychiatrists, however, may face a greater ethical dilemma in this regard.

Insanity

To paraphrase a key federal case, if a person chooses to do evil through the exercise of his or her free will, that person must bear criminal responsibility (*United States v. Brawner*, 1972). Conversely, if free will is absent, the person is not responsible. The criminal law requires that *mens rea* (intent or guilty mind) be demonstrated before an individual can be convicted of a crime. Although there are exceptions to this requirement for certain minor offenses (called **strict liability offenses**), most crimes require a showing of "evil" intent. It should be noted at the outset that lack of a guilty mind may factor into many defenses to criminal conduct, some of which will be covered later in the chapter. However, the public is acquainted with this principle in law primarily through the insanity defense.

The insanity defense may well be the most misunderstood and most disliked defense to a criminal accusation. It is an affirmative defense, one in which the individual acknowledges committing an act but declares he or she should be excused and absolved of criminal responsibility. This is what James Holmes is asserting in the *Batman* shooting case.

Despite the publicity surrounding that case, research indicates that the insanity defense is rarely used, is successful only in the most extreme cases, and even when successful is no bargain for the person acquitted. Most persons who are found **not guilty by reason of insanity** (**NGRI**) have demonstrated a serious mental disorder (A. M. Goldstein, Morse, & Packer, 2013). Yet the public often perceives the insanity defense as overused and believes the rare individual found not guilty by reason of insanity has somehow gotten away with something.

In reality, most "successful" NGRI individuals (NGRI acquittees) are led in a straight path to an institutional setting for an initial evaluation, and very few are released outright after this evaluation. The great majority are placed in a secure psychiatric hospital setting. Those released are placed on conditional release and subjected to monitoring in the community. The individual who was accused of a serious crime is especially likely to be hospitalized (Stredny, Parker, & Dibble, 2012), but long hospital stays have been documented for insanity acquittees who were charged with both serious and less serious offenses (e.g., Dirks-Lindhorst & Kondrat, 2012).

The prototype of the insanity acquittee accused of serious crime is John Hinckley, charged in 1982 with an attempt on the life of President Ronald Reagan and the shooting of Press Secretary James Brady and a police officer. More than 30 years after the crimes, Hinckley remains in a psychiatric facility, although he is allowed visits to his mother's home in nearby Virginia. Numerous less notorious individuals remain in psychiatric facilities across the country. Although there are exceptions, these individuals can remain institutionalized for a longer period of time than they would have been incarcerated if convicted of their crimes.

Public attention to the insanity defense typically peaks in the wake of a shocking, highly publicized crime, such as the Hinckley case. The federal jury's finding that Hinckley was not guilty by reason of insanity outraged and confused the public, yet the verdict was consistent with federal insanity statutes in effect at that time. The acquittal, along with a tough-on-crime stance during the 1980s, prompted Congress and many states to modify statutes, thereby making it more difficult for defendants pleading not guilty by reason of insanity. We will cover these modifications later in this chapter.

The shocking case of Andrea Yates also attracted much public attention. Yates is the Texas woman who drowned her five young children in a bathtub in 2001. She had a history of mental disorders, including diagnoses of postpartum psychosis. Even prosecutors acknowledged her illness. Nevertheless, applying the test for insanity used in Texas, jurors convicted her, apparently concluding that she knew the difference between right and wrong despite her mental illness. Yates's conviction was subsequently overturned based on a variety of procedural errors at her trial; at her second trial, before a judge rather than a jury, she was found not guilty by reason of insanity. She remains institutionalized to this day.

Had he lived, the man who killed 20 first graders and seven adults, including his mother, in Newtown, Connecticut, in December 2012 may well have pled not guilty by reason of insanity. His background was littered with evidence of psychological difficulties, and according to some (unconfirmed) reports, his mother was in the process of preparing to have him hospitalized in a psychiatric facility. Even so, he would have had to demonstrate severe mental disorder and meet the requisite test for insanity in his state. Likewise, the man who killed 32 people and wounded 25 at Virginia Tech in 2007 had a history of mental illness; had he lived, it would not have been surprising see a similar plea. The Virginia Tech case is discussed again in Chapter 10.

Abolition of the Insanity Defense

As noted above, the 1984 federal law passed after the Hinckley acquittal placed various restrictions on the insanity defense. Before discussing these modifications, we discuss the controversial issue of total abolition of this affirmative defense, which has occurred in four states—Idaho, Montana, Utah, and Kansas. A fifth state, Nevada, also abolished the defense, but its Supreme Court ruled that abolition violated both the federal and state constitutions (*Finger v. State*, 2001).

The U.S. Supreme Court has never ruled on whether abolishing the insanity defense does indeed violate the U.S. Constitution, or whether defendants have a constitutional right to raise an insanity defense. It had the opportunity to do so in 2012, but declined to hear the case (*Delling v. Idaho*, 2012). John Delling was 21 when he shot and killed two of his friends and wounded a third, all in separate incidents, one in Arizona and two in Idaho. He was diagnosed with acute paranoid schizophrenia, a disorder whose symptoms first appeared when he was in high school. Delling was initially found incompetent to stand trial, but oral and intramuscular antipsychotic medication rendered him competent.

At trial, his lawyers argued—and mental health experts confirmed—that in the grip of severe delusions, he thought his friends were taking over his brain energy, and that he had to stop them or he himself would die. Idaho had eliminated the insanity defense, but he was still entitled to show a lack of intent (mens rea). As Morse and Hoffman (2008) have stated, legal insanity and lack of mens rea are "cousins" (p. 1072), but they are not identical. In fact, they add, "Mental disorder seldom interferes with an agent's ability to act intentionally" (p. 1085). The Idaho law only required that Delling have the ability to form intent (mens rea). The court found that Delling, due to his severe mental disorder, was unable to appreciate the wrongfulness of his actions, but he still intended to kill, so he was convicted. In jurisdictions that retain the insanity defense, Delling would have had a better chance of being acquitted because the fact that he could not appreciate the wrongfulness of his actions would have been significant. Nevertheless, he would not necessarily have been acquitted.

Interestingly, at his sentencing hearing, Delling's mental disorder was viewed by the sentencing judge as an **aggravating factor** that would intensify his dangerousness, rather than as a **mitigating factor** that should lessen his responsibility for the crimes. Delling was sentenced to life without parole. He appealed his conviction, arguing that criminal defendants had a constitutional right to raise an insanity defense. Although three of nine Justices (Justices Breyer, Ginsburg, and Sotomayor) were ready to hear the case, this did not meet the "rule of four" criterion for granting certiorari. As we wrote in Chapter 2, the three Justices submitted a dissent to the denial of certiorari in this case. Amicus curiae briefs in support of Delling were filed by a number of mental health and civil liberties interest groups who hoped that the Court would take the Delling case and declare that criminal defendants had a constitutional right to offer an insanity defense, but it was not to be so. (See Table 4-3 for a representative list of U.S. Supreme Court cases relating to insanity.)

Frequency of Insanity Defense and Acquittals

As mentioned in the opening paragraph to this section, despite the publicity that accompanies major cases, it is a rare criminal defendant who invokes the insanity defense, and when raised it is usually not successful. Although there are variations across jurisdictions, it is estimated that the defense is raised in less than 1% of all felony cases (Golding, Skeem, Roesch, & Zapf, 1999; Melton et al., 2007). Interestingly, Melton et al. state, "One reason for the low plea rate is that mental health professionals are seldom willing to support a defense" (p. 203). In other words, mental health examiners who evaluate the defendants find that, even with a mental disorder, they are able to form criminal intent and can appreciate the wrongfulness of their actions.

Table 4-3	Key U.S. Supreme Court Cases Related to Insanity	
Case Name	**Year**	**Significance/Holding**
Jones v. United States	1983	Persons found NGRI may be hospitalized indefinitely for treatment of their mental illness; periodic review of their status is required.
Foucha v. Louisiana	1992	NGRI acquittees must be released if they are no longer mentally ill, even if they are considered dangerous.
Riggins v. Nevada	1992	Defendants using insanity as a defense have the right to be free from medication during their criminal trial.
Clark v. Arizona	2006	States have wide leeway in crafting tests for insanity; the Court allowed a very narrow test in this case.
Delling v. Idaho, cert. denied	2012	The Court refused to decide if the insanity defense is constitutionally required.

Again contrary to public perceptions, the cases in which the NGRI defense is raised are not necessarily the most serious. For example, in an eight-state study, only 14.3% of defendants pleading not guilty by reason of insanity had been charged with murder (Silver, Cirincione, & Steadman, 1994). Furthermore, the insanity defense is also raised in misdemeanor cases as a way to get treatment for mentally disordered individuals. Recall that we discussed this briefly with reference to the request for an evaluation of a defendant's competency to stand trial.

It is extremely difficult to obtain nationwide data on insanity defenses and acquittals because states vary widely in the availability of these statistics. Multistate surveys provide some data. In an eight-state study involving nearly 9,000 defendants who pleaded NGRI, Callahan, Steadman, McGreevy, and Robbins (1991) found an acquittal rate of 25%. Other multistate surveys have found similar acquittal rates of 20% to 25% (Cirincione, Steadman, & McGreevy, 1995; Pasewark & McGinley, 1986). In the largest nationwide data collection thus far available, Cirincione and Jacobs (1999) were able to obtain data from 36 jurisdictions (35 states and one Pennsylvania county) over the period 1974 to 1995. They identified a total of 16,379 acquittals, or a mean of 33.4 insanity acquittals per state per year. Only 15 of the 36 jurisdictions surveyed could differentiate between felony and misdemeanor acquittals. When they did, misdemeanor acquittals typically accounted for less than 10% of the total, although in one state (Oregon), 21.7% of the acquittals were for misdemeanors. Commenting on many of these findings, Melton et al. (2007) note cautiously, "As a general statement, it is not inaccurate to say that when the defense is challenged, it fails more often than it succeeds" (p. 203).

Insanity cases often do not go to trial. In an early investigation of 316 successful insanity defenses, Rogers, Cavanaugh, Seman, and Harris (1984) learned that 80% were uncontested by the prosecutor and disposed of informally without trial. Acquittals are typically followed by commitment to a psychiatric facility, usually for as long as, and sometimes longer than, imprisonment of defendants convicted on equivalent charges (Borum & Fulero, 1999). Acquittees must have periodic reviews of their status, and some states do not allow them to be held past the period of what would be a maximum penalty for their crime if convicted. In such situations, they could be recommitted under civil commitment procedures if found mentally ill and dangerous to themselves or others. This topic will be covered again in Chapter 10.

Researchers (e.g., Callahan & Silver, 1998; Manguno-Mire, Thompson, Shore, et al., 2007; Stredny et al., 2012) have studied **conditional release**, whereby acquittees are allowed back into the community with court or clinical supervision. A. M. Goldstein et al. (2013) refer to this as a form of "mental health probation" (p. 459). They observe as well that data from three states indicate that individuals who are conditionally released are less likely than convicted offenders to commit new crimes and are more likely to be rehospitalized than incarcerated.

Insanity Standards

Just as mental disorder does not equal incompetence to stand trial, neither does it equal insanity. It is possible for a person to be diagnosed with a disorder and still be criminally responsible. In order to help judges and juries decide whether someone accused of crime was indeed insane, a number of tests have been established. These tests vary widely among the states, but they usually center on one of three general models: the M'Naghten rule and the Durham rule (named after court cases), and the ALI/Brawner rule (proposed by the American Law Institute in its Model Penal Code). A modified form of this last test, called the Brawner rule, was in use in federal courts when John Hinckley was acquitted. Today, the federal courts abide by a substantially "tougher" variant of the ALI rule. A minority of states also recognize an **irresistible impulse test**.

The M'Naghten Rule: The Right and Wrong Test

The most common test for insanity today is some variant of the **M'Naghten rule**, which originated in mid-19th-century Britain. Its history has been covered in numerous sources (e.g., Finkel, 1988; A. M. Goldstein et al., 2013; Simon & Aaronson, 1988). Daniel M'Naghten believed he was being persecuted by the Tories, England's right-wing political party, and that his major persecutor was Prime Minister Robert Peel. M'Naghten fired a shot into the prime minister's carriage; fortunately for the prime minister, he was not in the carriage, but the shot killed his secretary, Edward Drummond.

There was no question that M'Naghten had committed the act, but the rule in place at that time indicated that if defendants were mentally ill, they could not resist impulses to commit deviant acts. The presiding judge directed the jury to find M'Naghten insane (Finkel, 1988). M'Naghten's acquittal led to the development of a standard that required that—at the time of the crime—defendants knew the difference between right and wrong and that what they were doing was wrong. Common-court judges began applying this test and often noted that, had M'Naghten been tried under that standard, he would *not* have been absolved of responsibility because he did know the difference between right and wrong at the time he committed the crime.

The M'Naghten rule was adopted as the standard in U.S. courts and came to be commonly referred to as the "right/wrong test." It is generally recognized today that a defendant is not responsible if he or she committed an unlawful act while

> labouring under such a defect of reason, from a disease of the mind, as not to know the nature and quality of the act he was doing; or, if he did know it, that he did not know he was doing what was wrong. (*Queen v. M'Naghten*, 1843, quoted in A. D. Brooks, 1974, p. 135)

For a time, the rule was accepted as the principal standard of criminal responsibility in virtually every American jurisdiction (Saks & Hastie, 1978). However, it was also attacked by several schools of psychiatric and psychological thought, because it was too narrow and not in keeping with current theory and practice. Psychiatrists, who were then the main examiners in matters of criminal responsibility relating to mental states, said it was impossible to convey to the judge and jury the full range of information they obtained from assessing the defendant's responsibility if it was framed solely in terms of cognitive impairment.

The Durham Rule: The Product Test

In 1954, U.S. Court of Appeals judge David Bazelon drafted what was to become the **Durham rule** (*Durham v. United States*, 1954), sometimes called the "product rule" or "product test." The Durham rule states that "an accused is not criminally responsible if his unlawful act was the product of a mental disease or mental defect" (Brooks, 1974, p. 176). The rule, therefore, focuses more on mental disorder itself than on the cognitive element of "knowing" the rightness or wrongness of a specific action. The Durham rule was later clarified in *Carter v. United States* (1957), which held that mental illness must not merely have entered into the production of the act; it must have played a necessary role.

The Durham rule was applied in federal courts and adopted by some states. Its broad scope became its major shortcoming and eventually its downfall, however. Since definitions of mental illness are often vague and subjective, the rule, according to many jurists, gave wide discretionary power to psychiatry. During the time that the Durham rule was in effect, some critics asserted that psychiatrists defined mental illness so broadly that it could be applied to most offenders. Anyone who committed an antisocial act could be viewed as mentally ill: The forbidden act was a product of the disorder. Applied in this way, the Durham rule could be and was used to exculpate large numbers of offenders who would have been held responsible under a cognitive test.

The rule also created havoc among legal scholars, clinicians, and social and behavioral scientists who tried to define "mental disease" or "defect" and to determine what acts were "products" of such conditions. Expert testimony, not surprisingly, reflected this confusion.

As Finkel (1988) quipped, "the psychiatrist was freer to jargonize" (p. 37). Eventually, the Durham rule became so unmanageable that it was discarded by most of the jurisdictions that had adopted it, including the federal courts. Some states replaced it with the ALI rule, while others returned to some variant of the M'Naghten test.

The ALI/Brawner Rule

In 1972, in *United States v. Brawner*, Judge Bazelon himself ended 18 years of unhappy experimentation with the Durham rule in federal courts. The court replaced it with a slight modification of the 1962 draft of the Model Penal Code rule formulated by the American Law Institute (the **ALI/Brawner rule**). In essence, the rule states the following:

(1) A person is not responsible for criminal conduct if at the time of such conduct as a result of mental disease or defect he lacks substantial capacity either to appreciate the criminality (wrongfulness) of his conduct or to conform his conduct to the requirements of the law.

(2) The terms "mental disease or defect" do not include an abnormality manifested only by repeated criminal or otherwise antisocial conduct.

In *Brawner*, the court also specified that the "mental disease" or "defect" must be a condition that *substantially* (a) affects mental or emotional processes or (b) impairs behavioral controls. Significantly, the ALI/Brawner rule excludes abnormality manifested only by repeated criminal or antisocial conduct. This provision was intended to disallow insanity for psychopaths and sociopaths who persistently violate social mores and often the law.

The ALI/Brawner rule was the standard in federal courts when John Hinckley was tried and found not guilty by reason of insanity. Hinckley, who was enamored of the film star Jodie Foster, lived with the strong delusions that killing the president of the United States would impress her and bind her to him forever. Hinckley was acquitted because the jury concluded that he lacked substantial capacity to conform his conduct to the requirements of the law. Put another way, his mental illness impaired his behavioral controls. Public outcry at Hinckley's acquittal then led to still more changes in insanity standards. Congress soon passed the Insanity Defense Reform Act of 1984, which, among other things, eliminated what is called the "volitional prong" of the ALI/Brawner rule—the part that indicates behavioral controls are impaired.

Today, every state that accepts the insanity defense has adopted some variant of one of the above rules. The M'Naghten rule or some version of it seems to predominate. Many states also have adopted versions of the ALI/Brawner rule, which consider an individual's capacity to appreciate the criminality of his or her conduct or to conform the conduct to the requirements of the law. Significantly, however, as of 2011, only 16 states had retained the volitional prong of the ALI/Brawner rule (A. M. Goldstein et al., 2013), which recognizes that a person is not responsible if not able to control his or her actions. The "product test" is used only in New Hampshire, while a handful of states have adopted the irresistible impulse test, which indicates that people are not criminally responsible if they are unable to control their actions. Note that this is virtually identical to the volitional prong of the ALI/Brawner rule. All states, however, require as a prerequisite the demonstration of a severe mental disorder. (See Table 4-4 for a summary of insanity standards.)

Table 4-4	Insanity Standards and Relevant Components			
	Mental Disease/ Defect	Cognitive		Volitional
		Nature and Quality	Wrongfulness	
M'Naghten	X	X	X	
Durham	X			
ALI/Brawner	X		X	X
Irresistible Impulse	X			X
Insanity Defense Reform Act	X	X	X	

Despite these elaborate attempts at establishing insanity standards, when cases involving an insanity defense get to a jury, jurors do not necessarily apply them. When a defendant pleads NGRI, the judge must give instructions to the jury as to what will qualify as insanity. Many studies have found that these instructions make little difference (e.g., Finkel, 1988, 1991; Finkel et al., 1985; Ogloff, 1991; Piel, 2012). Golding et al. (1999) suggest that the "admittedly vague and nonspecific linguistic terms of insanity standards" are at fault (p. 383). The negative public attitudes toward insanity discussed earlier may be the culprits, however, particularly in light of the fact that juries are less likely than judges to find a defendant NGRI (Callahan et al., 1991). In capital cases, jurors have been found to have antipathy to the insanity defense (Kivisto & Swan, 2011). As Finkel (2000) concludes,

> The empirical evidence leaves little doubt that jurors' constructs of sane and insane, and the law's, are significantly different. Moreover, the evidence leaves little doubt that the law's repeated attempts, via changing legal tests, to get jurors to relinquish their constructs for the law's constructs have failed. (p. 607)

Insanity Defense Reform Act of 1984 and Beyond

In addition to eliminating the volitional prong of the insanity standard, Congress in its **Insanity Defense Reform Act (IDRA) of 1984** made it more difficult for persons pleading not guilty by reason of insanity in federal courts to be acquitted. The IDRA also (a) shifts the burden of proof, (b) alters the verdict form, and (c) limits the role of the expert testifying in insanity cases. Again, many of these changes were later modeled by states in their own statutes.

Federal defendants claiming insanity have to prove that, "as a result of a severe mental disease or defect, [they are] unable to appreciate the nature and quality or the wrongfulness of [their] acts" (18 U.S.C. § 17, 1984). Prior to this change, once the defendant introduced evidence in support of insanity, the burden was on the prosecution to prove beyond a reasonable doubt that the defendant was sane. This was a critical factor in the Hinckley acquittal, because the jury had heard considerable testimony as to Hinckley's aberrant mental state; proving him sane beyond a reasonable doubt was a formidable undertaking. Now, as a result of the 1984 law, the defendant bears the burden of proving insanity by clear and convincing evidence, which is a very difficult task.

Many states followed the federal government's lead and began to require defendants to bear the burden of proving their own insanity. Today, virtually every state, similar to the federal government, places the burden of proof on defendants. That is, they must convince the judge or jury either by clear and convincing evidence or by the lesser standard of preponderance of the evidence that they were insane at the time of the crime.

The verdict form, or the way the verdict is expressed, has also changed. Rather than being judged not guilty by reason of insanity, insanity acquittees are judged not guilty *only* by reason of insanity. This is a seemingly minor but symbolically significant change that implies resistance to absolving the defendant: The defendant would be guilty if not for the mental state.

Finally, expert witnesses in federal courts and in some states are no longer allowed to give an opinion as to whether the defendant had the required mental state at the time of the criminal act. They are allowed to describe the defendant's behavior and draw a conclusion as to the alleged mental disorder, but they are not allowed to give an opinion on the ultimate legal issue. This last change is not problematic for many mental health practitioners who believe they should not be providing an ultimate opinion in any case. Nevertheless, in many *state* courts, judges still look for a recommendation from the clinician and, in fact, sometimes press for opinions.

As a whole, the above changes to both federal and state insanity statutes have made it more difficult for defendants to sustain a successful insanity defense. In addition, a minority of states have opted for still another option, the guilty but mentally ill verdict form.

Guilty but Mentally Ill (GBMI)

In response to disenchantment with the insanity defense, some states have adopted the verdict form **guilty but mentally ill (GBMI)**. This is a court verdict that allows judges and jurors a "middle ground" in the case of allegedly insane defendants—a way of reconciling their belief that a defendant "did it" with their belief that he or she "needs help." Defendants also can plead GBMI, as did Marjorie Diehl-Armstrong, but this does not guarantee them a lighter sentence. Diehl-Armstrong (see Box 4-3) was sentenced to

7 to 20 years in state prison. It should be noted that there is no GBMI verdict form or plea in the federal system.

Research on GBMI laws has found that they may not have accomplished their intended purpose of reducing the number of NGRI pleas or acquittals or providing treatment in correctional facilities. In some jurisdictions, the number of successful insanity defenses appeared to have gone down, initially, but subsequent analyses questioned whether this was due to GBMI or to other insanity defense reforms (Borum & Fulero, 1999), such as the shift in the burden of proof. A common finding in studies examining the effect of GBMI reform is the lack of special treatment provided to GBMI offenders, despite the intent of the statutes (Steadman et al., 1993).

Although GBMI statutes have remained on the books in a minority of states, they rarely receive positive reviews in the legal or psychological literature. "Virtually all commentary concerning the GBMI verdict has been scathingly negative for the reasons suggested: The verdict is unrelated to criminal responsibility, and it does not guarantee any special psychiatric treatment" (A. M. Goldstein et al., 2013, p. 458). Melton et al. (2007) assert that a possible verdict of GBMI has great potential for confusing jurors: "In short, the GBMI verdict is conceptually flawed, has significant potential for misleading the fact finder, and does not appear to achieve its goals of reducing insanity acquittals or prolonging confinement of offenders who are mentally ill and dangerous" (p. 232).

BOX 4-3

Case Study. The Pizza Deliverer Collar Bomb Case—and More

In January 2013, the U.S. Supreme Court refused to hear—without comment—the appeal of Marjorie Diehl-Armstrong, a woman diagnosed with bipolar disorder who was convicted of conspiracy and other charges in the death of a pizza delivery man. The facts of the case were bizarre. The delivery man—Brian Wells—walked into a bank in Erie, Pennsylvania, in August 2003 wearing a collar bomb and demanded money. He was apprehended by police shortly thereafter, but he told police he had been forced to wear the bomb by people he had just met. While police were awaiting the bomb squad, the bomb exploded, killing its carrier.

Witnesses in the case later indicated that Wells had been involved in the planning but had not known the bomb was real. Diehl-Armstrong was identified as the mastermind of the crime, although she denied responsibility and has maintained her innocence ever since.

Diehl-Armstrong was initially found incompetent to stand trial, but—like most other such defendants—she was later determined competent. A federal jury convicted her, and she was sentenced to life plus 30 years, a sentence that would likely guarantee she would never be released. In her 2012 appeal to the U.S. Supreme Court, she argued that the presiding

(Continued)

(Continued)

judge should not have found her competent. Her case was one of many the Supreme Court refused to hear in January 2013.

Diehl-Armstrong had an interesting history with the court system. At the time of her federal sentencing, she was serving time in a Pennsylvania prison for a separate murder that occurred around the same time as the bank robbery and may have been associated with the planning of that crime. That case dealt with the death of her boyfriend, whose body was found in a freezer in 2003. Although she argued at the time that she had been framed for his death, she eventually pled *guilty but mentally ill,* presumably believing she would receive a lighter sentence. She was sentenced to 7 to 20 years in state prison. It is not known whether she received mental health services while in prison. Interestingly, though, some research has shown that GBMI prisoners in Pennsylvania were more likely to receive treatment for their disorder than those in other states (Steadman et al., 1993).

The above-described criminal incidents were not Diehl-Armstrong's only brushes with the law. In 1984, she was charged with the killing of another man but was acquitted of that crime, possibly because she claimed she had been severely abused. In 1992, she won a malpractice suit against a hospital after her husband died. At the time of the collar-bomb bank robbery, it was alleged that she needed money to hire someone to kill her elderly father, who suffered from Alzheimer's disease. None of this was relevant to the issue before the Court in 2013, and it is unknown why the Court denied certiorari. It is likely, though, that the Court deferred to the discretion of the presiding judge at the trial court and saw no problem with the decision of the (Third Circuit) Court of Appeals, which found that the trial court was correct in ruling her competent.

Diehl-Armstrong's court-appointed lawyers said they had doubts about her ability to plan the bank robbery but also said they were finished with her case. Diehl-Armstrong, now in her early sixties, says she will continue to look for ways to appeal.

Questions for Discussion:

1. Compare the denial of certiorari in this case with the one in *Delling v. Idaho*, discussed earlier in the chapter. Of the two cases, which presented the more important issue for the Court to resolve, and why?

2. Do you think pleading guilty but mentally ill in the Pennsylvania case was a good strategy for Diehl-Armstrong to take? Why did she not follow the same strategy in the collar bomb case?

NGRI and Its Outcomes

Once committed, persons found NGRI and institutionalized are entitled to periodic review of their status. However, the state may require them to prove that they are no longer mentally ill and dangerous in order to be released. Depending upon the jurisdiction, the standard of proof may be preponderance of the evidence or clear and convincing evidence. Thus, because it is not a simple task to meet that burden, persons who are found NGRI are often held for longer periods of time than they would have been imprisoned (Golding et al., 1999). In general, they are *not* held for significantly *shorter* periods of time than persons who unsuccessfully pled not guilty by reason of insanity or persons who were convicted without using that defense (Silver, 1995). As discussed earlier, NGRI acquittees also may obtain conditional release if they meet requirements set by mental health authorities or courts, depending upon the law in a given jurisdiction. It should be mentioned that NGRI acquittees cannot be held in secure confinement if they are no longer mentally ill (*Foucha v. Louisiana,* 1992).

We cannot expect, nor would we want it to be the case, that insanity acquittees spend a lifetime in mental institutions. Mental disorders can be treated, and individuals once haunted by them can lead productive lives. However, mental illness also can go into remission, which is what happened in Foucha's case. Furthermore, many insanity acquittees have "significant lifelong psychopathological difficulties" that can be controlled only to a certain extent and that can produce variable dangerousness (Golding et al., 1999, p. 397). Nevertheless, other options exist, including community treatment and, if necessary, involuntary civil commitment—a topic to be discussed in Chapter 10. As A. M. Goldstein et al. (2013) have observed about the Foucha case, "Although there was a strong dissent [the Supreme Court ruled 5–4], the holding makes sense" (p. 459).

Clinical Assessment of Criminal Responsibility

The role of the psychiatrist or psychologist in an insanity case is essentially to *postdict.* That is, the mental health professional is asked to reconstruct a person's mental state at the time of the crime. The clinician must determine whether and what sort of disturbances existed at the behavioral, volitional, and cognitive level and clarify how those disturbances relate to the criminal act (Golding et al., 1999). Although courts and many clinicians call these "sanity evaluations," others prefer to call them evaluations of **mental state at the time of the offense (MSO)** or evaluations of **criminal responsibility (CR)**. This is because the evaluations are relevant not only to the insanity defense, but also to other defenses in which the defendant's mental state is in question. For example they relate to intoxication, duress, diminished capacity, automatism, and post-traumatic stress, to name just a few.

Interestingly, in most cases only one mental health clinician performs the evaluation, and the court tends to defer to that clinician's recommendation, if it is offered (Gowensmith et al., 2013; Melton et al., 2007). High-profile cases—those that receive national attention—are more likely to see the involvement of more than one examiner, because both the prosecutor and the defense are likely to want an examiner. In the Batman shooting case, for example, defense lawyers requested a second sanity evaluation after results of a court-ordered evaluation were submitted. Prosecutors also submitted subpoenas for the mental health records from the state hospital and from the university where Holmes was a graduate student.

Reliance on just one assessment can be problematic. MSO evaluations are widely regarded as being far more complex than the competency evaluations discussed earlier in this chapter. It is exceedingly difficult to determine what another human being was thinking or feeling at the time of a crime, an event that may have happened weeks, months, or even years previously. Indeed, in a recent study, researchers found cause to question the reliability of these evaluations (Gowensmith et al., 2013; see Box 4-4). Nevertheless, clinicians have made considerable strides in identifying methods for conducting evaluations that will be of use to the courts (Heilbrun, Grisso, & Goldstein, 2009; Melton et al., 1997, 2007). We will return to these methods in Chapter 12.

BOX 4-4 RESEARCHERS AT WORK

Are Sanity Evaluations Reliable?

Hawaii offers a natural laboratory for studying evaluations of mental state at the time of the offense, also referred to as sanity or legal sanity evaluations. In contrast to other states, where the typical defendant considering or offering an insanity defense has only one evaluation, Hawaii requires three separate, independent evaluations. This system not only provides the court with more information about a defendant but also provides researchers with the opportunity to study the reliability of these evaluations. Do different examiners reach the same conclusions about a particular case?

W. Neil Gowensmith, Daniel C. Murrie, and Marcus T. Boccaccini (2013) examined 483 evaluation reports prepared by psychologists and psychiatrists in Hawaii. The researchers found that the clinicians were unanimous in their recommendation in only 55.1% of the cases. They tended to agree the most when the defendants had a psychotic disorder or had been psychiatrically hospitalized in the recent past. They disagreed more when defendants had been under the influence of alcohol or other drugs at the time of the crime.

Among other findings, they determined the following:

- Evaluators were more likely to agree that the defendant was sane than insane.
- Evaluators agreed that the defendant was sane in 38.2% of the cases; they all agreed that the defendant was insane in 17.0% of the cases.
- The discipline of the evaluator (psychiatrist or psychologist) did not explain the difference in their opinions.
- The defendant's ethnicity did not explain the difference in their opinions.

Judges almost always went along with the majority of the panel—they did so in 91% of the cases. If judges did not go along with the majority, they tended to find the defendant legally sane rather than insane. Interestingly, judges in some instances found defendants sane when all three evaluators had recommended insanity, but they never found defendants insane when all three evaluators had recommended sanity.

Questions for Discussion:

1. The finding that all three evaluators agreed in just over half the cases raises questions about the reliability of sanity evaluations. What can be done to improve their reliability?

2. Is Hawaii's system of requiring three independent evaluations better than the typical approach of having only one court-ordered evaluation? What advantages and disadvantages do you see in this approach?

Special Conditions and Unique Defenses

In this chapter, we have focused exclusively on the insanity defense in our discussion of criminal trials and forensic evaluations. However, a number of other defenses based on mental, neurological, and physiological conditions have been raised in both criminal and civil courts, with varying degrees of success. Among these conditions are post-traumatic stress disorder, postpartum depression and postpartum psychosis, the XYY chromosomal abnormality, automatism, amnesia, battered woman syndrome, Holocaust survivor's syndrome, sexual addiction, and multiple personality disorder. Some but not all of these conditions have been classified as disorders in various editions of the DSM. Defendants also have raised defenses based on exposure to environmental contaminants, claiming that the chemicals in those contaminants precipitated their violent behavior. In criminal cases, defendants may claim to have been affected by these conditions in an effort to absolve themselves completely of criminal responsibility or to support a claim of **diminished capacity** or **diminished responsibility**. The conditions may also be raised at criminal sentencing, when the judge or jury hears evidence offered in mitigation (to lessen the gravity of the offense).

It is important to acknowledge at the outset the continuing controversy in both law and psychology with respect to these special conditions. They are neither widely accepted nor widely successful, although some have been received better than others by the courts. By the end of the 20th century, Slobogin (1999) found that testimony on battered woman syndrome, for example, was accepted in most courts. Nevertheless, Petrila (2009b) strongly questions the admission of "syndrome evidence," specifically battered woman syndrome and rape trauma syndrome, based on their very questionable scientific underpinnings.

It is more likely that the effects of abuse are regarded as a form of **post-traumatic stress disorder (PTSD)** than separate syndromes, however. Almost all courts now accept evidence of post-traumatic stress syndrome—now more appropriately referred to as post-traumatic stress *disorder*, particularly but not exclusively in veterans. In addition, many states either require or allow by statute that testimony about spousal abuse be admitted in the trials of battered women who assaulted or killed their abusers. It is noteworthy, as well, that the DSM-5 includes a section on other conditions that can be the focus of clinical attention, including spouse or partner violence (physical and sexual), neglect, and psychological abuse. Although the syndromes do not appear in the DSM as such, there is support for introducing these conditions into the legal arena.

The material in the following section outlines the scientific and clinical knowledge of the causes, effects, and legal acceptance of PTSD, which has received so much attention in both the legal and psychological literature. We also revisit briefly the two somnambulism (sleepwalking) cases introduced at the beginning of the book. They are representative of unique defenses now being introduced into criminal courts as a result of psychological research in formerly uncharted areas.

Finally, although we discuss these diagnoses in the context of criminal cases, it is important to emphasize that they are relevant to civil cases as well. For example, evidence of post-traumatic stress disorder or acute stress disorder may be introduced in employment claims or harassment claims raised in civil proceedings. This topic will reappear in Chapter 11.

Post-Traumatic Stress Disorder (PTSD)

"DSM-5 criteria for PTSD differ significantly from the DSM-IV criteria" (American Psychiatric Association, 2013, p. 812; hereinafter DSM-5). According to the DSM-5, the essential feature of post-traumatic stress disorder is "the development of characteristic symptoms following exposure to one or more traumatic events" (p. 274). Until this latest DSM revision, a person's emotional reactions to the event—such as fear, helplessness, or horror—were a necessary component. Now, emotional reactions are no longer needed. While fear-based reexperiencing, emotional, and behavioral symptoms may predominate in some individuals, others may display different mood states, negative cognitions, or dissociative symptoms (DSM-5). This and other changes in the DSM-5 led to extensive commentary when the DSM was undergoing revision (e.g., Friedman et al., 2011). Allen Francis (2013), chair of the DSM-IV Task Force, stated that the change in PTSD classification would contribute even further to an existing problem of misdiagnosis of the disorder.

Despite the above and other changes, PTSD remains an umbrella term that can be applied to many people. The directly experienced (or witnessed) traumatic events include but are not limited to "exposure to war as a combatant or civilian, threatened or actual physical assault ... threatened or actual sexual violence ... being kidnapped, being taken hostage, terrorist attack, torture, incarceration as a prisoner of war, natural or human-made disasters, and severe motor vehicle accidents" (DSM-5, p. 274). PTSD can occur in individuals as young as 1 year of age, but the criteria for diagnosis differ for children 6 and under.

The very wide range of symptoms of PTSD include but are not limited to involuntary distressing memories of the event, dissociative reactions (e.g., flashbacks), hypervigilance, self-destructive behaviors, and problems with concentration. Children may reconstruct the event in their play behavior and may have frightening dreams. Persons with PTSD may display quick flashes of temper and suicidal ideation. These are but a few of the symptoms reported in the literature as well as the DSM-5. Symptoms of PTSD usually begin within 3 months of the trauma, but there may be a delay of months or even years before full criteria for diagnosis are met. Note that what was formerly referred to as "delayed onset" is now called "delayed expression" (DSM-5, p. 276).

The traumatic event that precipitates PTSD may be experienced with no other witnesses, such as a rape or attempted rape, or it may be experienced along with other victims and bystanders, such as a flood, hurricane, mass shooting, plane crash, or war. Witnessing the event as it occurs to others (e.g., a child seeing a caretaker abused or a first responder arriving at the scene of a horrific accident) can also result in PTSD. The DSM-5 is careful to inform us, however, that witnessing media events or watching violent videos does not qualify, even in the case of children.

The traumatic event is so psychologically distressing that the person may take a very long time to recover, and sometimes never recovers completely. Even so, about one half of adults are said to recover within 3 months (DSM-5, p. 277). Studies report that between 1% and 2% of all Americans suffer from PTSD (Sutker, Uddo-Crane, & Allain, 1991). A frequently cited survey (Kessler et al., 1995) indicated that 7.8% of individuals were likely to suffer PTSD during their lifetime. The DSM-5 places lifetime prevalence slightly higher, at 8.7%, under DSM-IV criteria. It will of course be interesting to follow the research when the latest criteria are applied. When focused on specific populations such as rape victims or war veterans, research indicates much higher rates (Friel, White, & Hull, 2008).

In recent years, the research on PTSD in veterans has exploded (Gates et al., 2012). Earlier studies estimated that about 31% of Vietnam combat veterans experienced formally diagnosable symptoms of PTSD at some point during their lifetimes (Kulka et al., 1990, 1991). More recently, research has found that 16.6% of veterans of wars in Iraq (Operation Iraqi Freedom) and Afghanistan (Operation Enduring Freedom) met the criteria for PTSD 1 year after their return (C. W. Hoge, Terhakopian, Castro, Messer, & Engel, 2007). Gates et al. (2012) cite research that the prevalence in deployed U.S. military personnel may be as high as 14% to 16%. They also posit that these rates may be underestimated because of continuing stigma associated with PTSD. Addressing this stigma, the most recent (2013) recipient of the National Medal of Honor—Staff Sergeant Ty Michael Carter, who had fought in Afghanistan—acknowledged that he had experienced PTSD and urged fellow veterans suffering from similar symptoms to seek help.

The symptoms of PTSD, some of which were mentioned above, often are associated with heightened psychophysiological arousal, such as anger, irritability, and an exaggerated startle response. Hypervigilance or a degree of paranoia are not uncommon. Any of these could lead a person to respond aggressively or defensively toward others. Indeed, research indicates that persons with PTSD, including war veterans, demonstrate higher rates of aggressive behavior than persons without such a diagnosis (Collins & Bailey, 1990; National Center for PTSD, 2011). It is under these situations that a PTSD defense is most likely to be used in a criminal trial. When Sgt. Robert Bales was first charged with the murder of Afghan civilians in 2012 during his fourth military deployment, it was widely believed he would introduce evidence of PTSD. His lawyers stated publicly that he suffered from the disorder, yet they introduced no evidence of the disorder at his sentencing hearing. Bales pleaded guilty to the charges of murder and attempted murder and was sentenced in August 2013 to life without the possibility of parole.

Some 20 years ago, Appelbaum et al. (1993) posited that the problem of PTSD in the courts was "particularly acute with something as new, as 'unverifiable,' as potentially useful, and as politically charged as PTSD" (p. 230). In their study of more than 8,000 individuals who had raised insanity defenses, only 28 had PTSD as a primary diagnosis, and the defendants with PTSD were more likely to be convicted than were defendants with other mental disorders (though the difference was not significant). Since then, clinicians have made considerable progress in assessing the condition. PTSD is no longer a new concept, but many courts continue to be reluctant to accept it as a *complete* defense to criminal activity. On the other hand, evidence of PTSD can support a defense based on diminished capacity, which, if successful, could allow conviction on a lesser charge and affect sentencing. Defenses based on diminished capacity are not acceptable in all jurisdictions, however.

PTSD is also likely to be introduced at the plea-bargaining stage, although there is little research on actual plea bargaining with defendants so diagnosed. However, opinion surveys have indicated that—at least for low-level assault offenses—prosecutors are more sympathetic to veterans and find veteran defendants with PTSD less blameworthy than those without the diagnosis (Wilson, Brodsky, Neal, & Cramer, 2011). Wilson and her colleagues also found that prosecutors were more likely to offer diversion programs—that is, programs that steer people away from court processing early on—rather than jail or probation.

Automatism

In Chapter 1, we met two defendants—Kenneth Parks and Scott Falater—each of whom had killed someone close to him, supposedly while asleep. Both men admitted their violent actions, all of which by any measure were horrifying. Parks bludgeoned his mother-in-law to death and severely assaulted his father-in-law; Falater stabbed his wife

44 times with a hunting knife and later held her head underwater until she drowned. Neither defendant pleaded not guilty by reason of insanity; they did not say they had a mental disorder—the first prerequisite for a successful insanity defense. They acknowledged that they caused the deaths but said they should not be held responsible because they were not conscious of their actions at the time. As we saw in Chapter 1, the "sleepwalking defense" succeeded in Parks's case but failed in Falater's.

Although we refer loosely to the sleepwalking defense, these two defendants were actually raising the defense of *automatism* (defined in Chapter 1), which recognizes that some criminal acts may be involuntary. According to Melton et al. (2007), "The classic example of the 'automaton' is the person who commits an offense while sleeping; courts have held that such an individual does not have conscious control of his or her physical actions and therefore acts involuntarily" (p. 219). They add that other examples might include when a crime occurs if a person is involuntarily intoxicated, acting under hypnotic suggestion, or even in a state of hypoglycemia. Note that *voluntary* intoxication is not included in this list. Also, as we will discuss in Chapter 8, the notion that individuals under hypnosis act in ways that are contrary to how they would ordinarily act is not supported in the research literature.

Automatism defenses, in fact, are rarely raised in American courts; when raised, they do not typically succeed. To prevail in using such a defense, the defendant must first persuade the judge or jury that he or she was, indeed, asleep. Despite the poor record of success for automatism in American courts, it is important to remember that sleep research is developing rapidly (see Box 4-5). Many experts say it is perfectly possible for people to act without conscious awareness while they are asleep. Continuing research is likely to explore the boundaries of these actions.

BOX 4-5 RESEARCHERS AT WORK

Sleepwalking and Other Parasomnias

Mental health professionals, behavioral scientists, and sleep researchers are sometimes asked to provide expert testimony or information to the courts concerning violent and other criminal behaviors that allegedly occurred while the assailant was still asleep. In a vast majority of cases, the defendant claims he or she committed the violent act because of a sleep disorder. Interestingly, there is very little evidence of violence during *wakefulness* in individuals with sleepwalking tendencies (Cramer Bornemann et al., 2006).

Collectively, sleep disorders are classified as **parasomnias.** Parasomnias include somnambulism, confusional arousals, sleep sex (known as sexsomnia), and night terrors, and they are not

(Continued)

(Continued)

well understood (Cramer Bornemann et al., 2006). *Somnambulism* is essentially sleepwalking. *Confusional arousals* (also called sleep drunkenness) are complex (and sometimes violent) behaviors that occur after deep sleep with semiconscious awareness. They usually occur when a person is waking from a deep sleep during the first part of the night. People with this disorder seem to take more than the usual amount of time to wake up, and they display unusual behavior as they are waking. *Sexsomnia* is a condition in which a person will engage in a variety of sexual acts while still asleep. *Sleep terrors* frequently begin with a blood-curdling scream, followed by behavioral activity such as hitting the wall and running around. Although night terrors are more common in children, they also may occur in adults. People who have night terrors sometimes also sleepwalk. Of all of the parasomnias, sleepwalking—somnambulism—has been the most common defense used in the courtroom.

In most cases, parasomnias are harmless, but in rare cases, violent and injurious attacks are believed to occur while the assailant is still asleep (and therefore not conscious of what he or she is doing). Sexsomnia also has been used as a legal defense for sexual assault and rape. In a recent court case, a 42-year-old British actor claimed he was asleep when he sexually assaulted a 15-year-old girl at a house party after getting her drunk on cocktails ("'Sexsomnia' claim actor," 2012). Although the defendant used sexsomnia as his defense, the jury was not persuaded and found him guilty of rape.

According to Mahowald and Schenck (2000), "There are well-documented cases of: (1) somnambulistic homicide, filicide (murder of a son or daughter), attempted homicide and suicide, (2) murders and other crime with sleep drunkenness (confusional arousal), and (3) sleep terrors/sleepwalking with potentially violent or injurious consequences" (p. 322). Available research indicates that sleepwalking is more prevalent in children than adults (Hublin, Kaprio, Partinen, Heikkilä, & Koskenvuo, 1997). Prevalence rates range from 2.8% in girls and 2.0% in boys to 6.9% in girls and 5.7% in boys. However, in adults, sleepwalking occurs in 3.9% of men and 3.1% of women, and it occurs "weekly in 0.4% for both genders" (Hublin et al., 1997, p. 177).

Questions for Discussion:

1. Should the parasomnias be accepted as defenses to criminal conduct? Do some seem more legitimate than others? Why do you think they have not been introduced more often into criminal courts?

2. If you were a defense lawyer, would you prefer to have a client say he was suffering from PTSD at the time of the crime or was sleepwalking at the time of the crime?

Melton et al. (2007) observed that the defense of automatism had a number of advantages over the insanity defense, including the fact that demonstration of a mental illness is not required. "In light of its [automatism's] conceptual advantages and the fact that the prosecutor bears the burden of disproving involuntariness, its relative dearth in the case law is somewhat surprising" (p. 220).

SUMMARY AND CONCLUSIONS

This chapter has focused on two areas where psychology plays a key role in the processing of mentally disordered defendants: their competency to stand trial and their criminal responsibility at the time of the offense. Research and law relating to each of these important constructs were reviewed. The competency inquiry can arise in a variety of other contexts, including plea bargaining and pleading guilty, participating in a range of pretrial proceedings, and being sentenced. For that reason, many scholars now prefer to call it adjudicative competency. Competency also may be at issue in civil cases, a topic to be covered in later chapters.

Psychologists have long been involved in assessing competency to stand trial and in treating incompetent defendants. The *Dusky* standard for determining competency has remained entrenched in the law since it was first outlined by the Supreme Court in 1960, and it has been extended to other competency issues, including the competency to plead guilty or waive one's right to a lawyer.

Requiring that a defendant have "sufficient present ability" to understand the proceedings and to help her or his attorney in preparing a defense gives very little guidance to psychologists conducting competency evaluations, however, and many clinicians express frustration at the vagueness of the *Dusky* standard. A variety of forensic assessment instruments specifically geared toward the competency construct have been developed. In recent years, researchers have focused on the adjudicative competence of special populations, such as juveniles, the elderly, and the intellectually disabled. Some have also stressed the importance of considering a defendant's cultural background in all evaluations.

Most defendants found incompetent to stand trial are treated for competency restoration, sometimes in the community, and most are then found competent. Traditionally, treatment has included psychoactive drugs, sometimes to the exclusion of other forms of therapy. Contemporary treatment programs for incompetent defendants are more likely to include education about the legal process, although generally speaking, treatment for incompetent mentally disordered defendants is indistinguishable from treatment for other mentally disordered individuals.

The insanity defense—the other main topic of this chapter—is highly controversial and rife with misconceptions. It is rarely used in serious cases, and when used, it is rarely successful. Although some defendants who plead NGRI are found not guilty by judges or juries, these are the exceptions. "Successful" cases are more likely to be those that do not go to trial; in essence, both sides agree that the defendant was seriously mentally ill and not responsible at the time of the offense. Insanity acquittees typically are hospitalized, sometimes for longer periods of time than they would have served in prison if convicted.

Four states do not allow the insanity defense, and the U.S. Supreme Court has declined to say whether this violates the Constitution. All other states, along with the federal government, use specific insanity standards, such as whether the defendant knew the difference between right and wrong or could appreciate the criminality of his or her actions. Over the past 30 years, both federal and state statutes have made it more difficult for defendants to be absolved of responsibility on the basis of insanity.

The chapter ended with discussion of two special conditions that have made their way into clinical work and the courts in recent years: post-traumatic stress disorder and automatism. Although the second is not commonly raised or admitted in court, the first is frequently admitted. When post-traumatic stress disorder is parsed into specific "syndromes," however, courts are more cautious. A number of scholars have stressed that, particularly in light of criteria outlined in *Daubert*, mental health experts should be careful to assure that what they testify to is supported by evidence. In the case of syndromes, the scientific support for their validation is lacking. Automatism is infrequently used, but in light of continuing psychological research on this topic, it could appear as a psychologically based defense in future cases.

KEY CONCEPTS

Adjudicative competence

Aggravating factor

ALI/Brawner rule

Competency to
  stand trial (CST)

Conditional release

Criminal responsibility
  (CR)

Diminished capacity

Diminished responsibility

Durham rule

Guilty but mentally ill
  (GBMI)

Insanity

Insanity Defense Reform
  Act (IDRA) of 1984

Irresistible impulse test

Mens rea

Mental state at the time of
  the offense (MSO)

Mitigating factor

M'Naghten rule

Not guilty by reason of
  insanity (NGRI)

Parasomnias

Post-traumatic stress
  disorder (PTSD)

Principle of
  nonmaleficence

Psychiatric diagnoses

Psychoactive drugs

Strict liability offenses

Writ of habeas corpus

5

Eyewitness Evidence

Prosecutor:	Do you see the person who attacked you sitting in this courtroom?
Witness:	Yes.
Prosecutor:	Please point to that person.
Witness:	He's sitting right there.
Prosecutor:	Let the record show that the witness is pointing to the defendant.

The testimony of a witness, including a victim, can be the most influential piece of evidence delivered in the courtroom, particularly if the witness claims to have personally seen someone commit a crime. The impact of eyewitness testimony is even greater if other kinds of evidence (e.g., weapon or fingerprints) are sparse or unavailable. In fact, when there are no eyewitnesses, the prosecutor's case is sometimes very difficult to prove.

Jurors have often been known to accept eyewitness testimony at face value, even when it is heavily contradicted by other evidence (Loftus, 1979). People are apt to believe an account of someone who was at the scene of an incident, despite what experts may assert about the evidence.

Even judges, attorneys, and law enforcement officials tend to accept the observations of witnesses as accurate, although these professionals are probably more skeptical than laypersons. Nevertheless, research indicates that, even if they are more skeptical, they are still not aware of the specific factors that influence the accuracy of eyewitness testimony, such as the effect of stress or the length of time one has to observe an incident. In a study involving judges, law students, and undergraduates, Wise and Safer (2010) found that judges and law students were no more knowledgeable about factors that influence the accuracy of eyewitnesses than college undergraduates. In another study involving prosecutors and defense attorneys (Wise, Pawlenko, Safer, & Meyer, 2009), defense attorneys were more aware of the fallibility of eyewitnesses than prosecutors. However, both groups lacked adequate knowledge about the specific factors that influence eyewitness observation or identification. A more recent study (Wise, Safer, & Maro, 2011) found similar limited knowledge on the part of law enforcement officers. The authors concluded that judges, lawyers, and police could use better training about eyewitness fallibility. If the criminal justice system does not take advantage of the extensive research on human perception and memory, mistaken identifications of innocent persons will continue to occur.

In the mind of prosecutors, eyewitness evidence often has greater legal status than other kinds of evidence, with the exception of a confession to a crime. Experienced trial attorneys have long known that visual identification is one of the best forms of evidence that can be presented to jurors and judges. They also fully realize that the quality of eyewitness testimony often determines the outcome of a case, no matter how logically tight and persuasive the arguments presented to the jury. In fact, eyewitness testimony is sometimes the only evidence available, and it is not unusual for convictions to be based on such evidence (N. Brewer, Weber, Wooton, & Lindsay, 2012).

Eyewitness testimony is also powerful because of a common belief in the ultimate accuracy of observation and human memory. Throughout its long history, law has had to be highly dependent upon what people saw and what people said they saw. "Eyewitnesses are called upon not only to remember details of events but also to describe what people look like and to decide how confident they are in the accuracy of their memories" (Frenda, Nichols, & Loftus, 2011, p. 20). These re-creations of crime scenes, accidents, and other occurrences are almost exclusively dependent on human perception and memory, which, in legal circles, is considered to be occasionally fooled, sometimes purposely distorted, but basically accurate. Sophisticated technology that can re-create crime scenarios and provide forensic evidence down to the smallest detail is being increasingly made available to the courts, but belief in the accuracy of human perception and memory persists. "Hence, although most evidence in courts of law is circumstantial, eyewitness identification evidence is *direct* evidence of guilt" (Wells & Loftus, 2013, p. 624).

It is important to emphasize that eyewitness evidence is highly relevant in civil cases as well. The testimony of witnesses in a custody dispute, a harassment suit, or a wrongful death suit, for example, can be a crucial factor in the outcome of the case. Thus, the concepts to be discussed in this chapter are relevant to civil as well as criminal cases. Nevertheless, most of the psychological research on this topic has focused on the criminal context, and the research cited will lean heavily in that direction.

From a scientific perspective, eyewitness evidence should be approached very cautiously, yet courts do not routinely subject it to scientific scrutiny. As Wells and Loftus

(2013) observe, the criminal justice system demands a scientific model for physical evidence but is skeptical about applying it to eyewitness evidence: "Although the legal system shows considerable concern and exercises caution to avoid contaminating physical traces at a crime scene (e.g., blood, fibers), similar cautions tend not to be exercised in avoiding the contamination of human memory in eyewitnesses" (p. 627).

There has been success in getting some law enforcement agencies to make use of psychological science in their procedures for collecting eyewitness evidence, but much more needs to be done (Wells, 2006; Wells et al., 2000). Police protocols for collecting, preserving, and interpreting eyewitness evidence generally do not take into consideration the high potential for contaminating eyewitness evidence. To a very large extent, eyewitness evidence is collected in criminal investigations by nonspecialists who have little or no training on the limitations of human perception and memory. The detective or patrol officer questioning a witness may be a good cop with years on the job, but she may have little knowledge about factors that influence information provided by a witness. On the other hand, physical evidence— from either the crime scene or elsewhere— is often carefully and scientifically collected and then analyzed by highly trained individuals who are usually familiar with the research literature and skillful in the scientific method as it pertains to physical evidence.

How reliable is eyewitness evidence? Most psychologists will answer, "It depends." It may be highly reliable under some conditions and extremely unreliable in other settings. However, the psychological research on perception and memory over the past 100 years underscores the discouraging fact that in most cases the information provided by eyewitnesses is at least partially unreliable and highly susceptible to numerous influences. This is apparent not only from the psychological research, but also from recent advancements in forensic procedures that have resulted in the exoneration of many previously convicted persons. For example, of the first 40 cases in which DNA evidence was used to overturn the convictions, 36 (or 90%) involved eyewitness identification evidence in which one or more eyewitnesses falsely identified the person (Wells et al., 1998). Over a third of the wrongful convictions were the result of whites misidentifying blacks (Dwyer, Neufeld, & Scheck, 2000). More recent data underscore the continuing problem of mistaken accounts of eyewitnesses in wrongful convictions. Of the 267 DNA-based exonerations, 200 of these cases were the result of mistaken eyewitness identification, representing two thirds of the wrongful convictions (Wells & Loftus, 2013). DNA exonerations have demonstrated that eyewitnesses can be absolutely positive and yet absolutely mistaken (Wells, Memon, & Penrod, 2006).

In this chapter, we examine psychological research and theory and discover the numerous variables that influence eyewitness reports, accounts that may or may not result in courtroom testimony. Because the literature typically refers to "eyewitness testimony," we will often use "eyewitness evidence" and "eyewitness testimony" interchangeably. Ultimately, the general purpose of research in this area "is to generate scientific knowledge that will maximize the chances that a guilty defendant will be justly convicted while minimizing the chances that an innocent defendant will be mistakenly convicted" (Wells, 1978, p. 1546). At this point, though research is ongoing, there is enough evidence to urge caution in accepting too readily the accuracy of eyewitnesses.

⊠ A Brief Word on Research Methodology

Some research in eyewitness testimony examines attitudes of various participants toward witness credibility, like the research cited at the beginning of the chapter that surveyed judges, lawyers, and college students. By far the most common methodology, though, is a simulation study examining the accuracy and reliability of a witness to an event. Simulation studies place research participants in hypothetical situations under laboratory conditions. Although such studies have been criticized in relation to jury decision making, they are more accepted in eyewitness research. They are better able to approximate real-life witnessing than real-life jury decision making, which is complex and can extend for hours or days. Nevertheless, simulation studies have yielded valuable information about juries, as we will see in Chapters 6 and 7.

In addition to simulation studies, eyewitness research has the benefit of method-ologically sound data about human perception and memory, which have been developed by psychologists for nearly a century. These traditional works offer a solid foundation for the study of eyewitness observation. The contributions psychology can make in this area are substantial, and they warrant the careful attention of participants in the legal system. We look at this research first in the section below.

⊠ Human Perception and Memory

When a person recalls and identifies events, objects, and persons, two fundamental but exceedingly complicated mental processes are at work: perception and memory. In the first, sensory inputs (what one sees, hears, smells, touches, or tastes) are transformed and organized into a meaningful experience for the individual. In the second process, the transformed inputs are stored in the brain, ready to be called up when needed. Let us examine each operation in more detail.

Perception

Perceptions are reports of what a person sees or senses at any particular moment. Note that seeing is only a *part* of the process of perceiving. In fact, what one perceives is not always what one sees. You may "see" a wallet being removed from a pocket but "per-ceive" it as a gun. The eye does not relate to the brain the way a camera records on film or on a digital sensor. The eye communicates by electrochemical "blips" along neural pathways to other neuron cells and eventually to processors in various sections of the brain, specifically in the cerebral cortex. Once these blips (neural impulses) reach the cortex, they may be further coded, reorganized, and interpreted, or they may be left undeveloped. Much of this processing is beyond the conscious awareness of the person. Neurophysiological researchers have not yet discovered exactly what happens in the human brain when it receives incoming information, although there are many theories. It is clear, however, that the perception of stimuli and the person's reaction to them depend on past experiences, especially with *similar* stimuli. If you were once the beneficiary of a very painful hornet sting, you perceive those insects in a far different way from a friend who has never had such an experience. You do not merely "see" the insect. The police officer who perceives a gun rather than a wallet may have a heightened sense of danger because of past encounters. Perception, then, is an interpretive process, and it appears that our senses are not only physical organs, but social ones as well (Buckhout, 1974).

As mentioned above, there is ample evidence in the research literature that people are not consciously aware of the processes that influence their perceptions. Yet these nonconscious processes are extremely important in the representation of events or objects and therefore are crucial determinants of what witnesses report to police and recount on the witness stand. Researchers also know that the end products of these perceptual processes are often incomplete, inaccurate, and highly selective. Much external information either is not attended to, is lost in the filtering and selection of information, or is misinterpreted. Past experience or learning, expectations, and preferences all determine how this partial or incomplete information will be synthesized. Yarmey (1979) reminds us that we should also not forget that many individuals have sensory deficiencies, such as visual defects of depth perception, color blindness, difficulties in adapting to darkness, and lack of visual acuity. Even before the stimulus information is synthesized at the higher levels of perceptual interpretation, these individual defects may contaminate the information. Human sensory mechanisms are far from perfect, and this basic frailty should not be overlooked in the search for potential errors in eyewitness testimony.

Memory

Memory, the second fundamental process with which we are concerned, is usually studied in three stages: acquisition, retention, and retrieval. **Acquisition**, also called the encoding or input stage, is intimately involved with the perceptual process, and a clear demarcation between the two is difficult to make. Acquisition is the point at which perception registers in the various areas of the cortex and is initially stored. **Retention** (also called the storage stage) is when information becomes "resident in the memory" (Loftus, 1979). In the **retrieval** stage, the brain searches for the pertinent information, retrieves it, and communicates it. Any one of these three processes may not function properly, and the result is a failure to "remember," or at least remember accurately.

Eyewitness research has continually found that memory is highly malleable and easily subject to change and distortion (Loftus, 2005a; Sutton, 2011) at all three stages. The evidence is clear: Humans continually alter and reconstruct their memory of past experiences in the light of present experiences, rather than store past events permanently and unchangingly in memory. That is, people rebuild past experiences to better fit their understanding of events. Memory, especially of complex or unusual events, involves the integration of perceptual information with preexisting experiences, as well as with other subjective relevant information that may be introduced later. In this sense, memory is very much a reconstructive, integrative process, developing with the flow of new experiences and thoughts. This perspective is called the **reconstructive theory of memory**. The theory states that memory recall is subject to distortion by other intervening cognitive functions, such as individual perceptions, social influences, and knowledge, all of which often lead to errors on an ongoing basis. The theory has been well established by psychological research over the past four decades.

As is true for the perceptual processes, people are unaware of their memory processes. They are aware of the products or content of memory, but there is every reason to believe they are not aware of the transformations that have occurred during acquisition, retention, and retrieval. While eyewitnesses may remember an event or person, they are *not* conscious of the complex neurological encoding, decoding, organizing, storing, interpreting, and associating that preceded their current memory of that event or person. Moreover, there are ample opportunities for witnesses to encounter additional information after the event and then integrate it unknowingly into their original memories. The integration process represents the reconstruction aspect of memory. Therefore, even the most well-intentioned eyewitnesses may err and unconsciously distort their recall and identification. In part, this explains the radically different accounts of the same event that are provided by witnesses who are "absolutely positive" about what they saw.

Wells (1995) finds it curious that police usually exercise great caution at a crime scene, being very careful not to touch or move objects for fear of contaminating the physical evidence, but they fail to take precautions in the collection of *eyewitness* evidence. Police routinely call in special forensic teams to gather and protect the physical evidence, but they do not seem to accept the premise that eyewitness evidence, like a person's memory of the events, can be contaminated by certain interviewing strategies and misleading commentary. If police officers do not recognize the damaging effects that can occur when dealing with fragile memory, some of the procedures they use, even their way of asking a question, can yield false information. To better appreciate these damaging effects, we must explain two important concepts in eyewitness research.

Estimator and System Variables

Wells (1993) has conducted extensive research on estimator variables and system variables, particularly as they relate to the witnessing of crime. **Estimator variables** represent sources of eyewitness error that are beyond the control of the criminal justice system because they occur during or soon after the crime, and usually before investigators even arrive on the scene. Examples are the stress levels experienced by the witness at the time of the crime and the length of time the witness observed the offender. Estimator variables represent the basic nature and processes of human perception and memory. Their overall influence on witness reports can only be estimated. "Independent control over estimator variables is, for all practical purposes, impossible for actual crimes" (Wells, 1978, p. 1548). **System variables,** by contrast, can be controlled by people in the criminal justice system when gathering information from eyewitnesses. Therefore, they come into play after the witness has experienced the criminal event, and errors here are essentially preventable. Errors related to system variables are most likely to occur during two procedures: police interviews and offender identification methods. The careful and competent collection of information from eyewitnesses at these stages will minimize the potential for introducing misinformation.

Both system and estimator variables can be studied under laboratory conditions in order to discover how they can affect eyewitness reports under "real world" conditions. In 2000, Wells and his colleagues (Wells et al., 2000) reported that there had been more than 1,000 publications on eyewitness issues in psychology since 1979, and a large proportion of them have focused on system variables. This may be because system variables can be controlled and have enormous direct application on improving the gathering of evidence for the courtroom. Table 5-1 contains a representative list of estimator and system variables.

Eyewitness Estimator Variables

Court proceedings often deal with past events that were fast moving, unusual, chaotic, and threatening to the observers, such as a bank robbery in progress, an assault, or a theft. The legally relevant incident often produces a "stimulus overload" in the victim or witness, where too many things are happening too quickly and under less-than-ideal conditions for careful scrutiny. Thus far, the study of situational factors—which all qualify as estimator variables—has been a relatively neglected area, but the research to date agrees with many commonsense observations about the effects of these factors. For example, the research literature has consistently shown that describing a perpetrator is a very difficult task (Houston, Clifford, Phillips, & Memon, 2013; Meissner, Sporer, & Schooler, 2007). Meissner et al. found that descriptions of perpetrators were often non-distinct and general, resembling many people in the population.

Table 5-1	Examples of Estimator and System Variables

Estimator Variables (related to human perception and memory)

Duration of exposure to the significant event or person(s)

Frequency of exposure to the significant event or person(s)

Pace of event

Perceived significance of event

Retention interval before being asked to recall

Misinformation (e.g., obtained from others at the scene)

Disguises

Weapon focus

Emotional arousal experienced by a witness

Own-race bias

Effect of alcohol and other drugs

System Variables (controlled by information gatherers)

Misinformation provided by investigators

Malleability of witness confidence

Suggestive interviewing techniques

Coercive interrogation methods and approaches

Length of time between initial criminal event and subsequent testimony

Instructions given to witnesses prior to viewing lineup

Composition and structure of the lineup

Time Factors

Exposure Duration

Not surprisingly, the less time a witness has to observe something, the less complete the perception and recall will be. Obviously, studying a topic for a long time will mean a better exam grade, provided that the student was concentrating. It seems obvious, as well, that the longer the duration of a criminal event, the more likely a witness or victim will be to recognize a perpetrator or recall important details. In fact, there is abundant literature in the field of cognitive psychology and memory to demonstrate that the longer a subject is exposed to material, the more accurate the recall (e.g., Memon, Hope, & Bull, 2003; M. A. Palmer, Brewer, Weber, & Nagesh, 2013). For example, researchers have found that the longer subjects had to inspect slides of faces, the more accurate they later were at recognizing a given face from photographs (Laughery, Alexander, & Lane, 1971).

Frequency of Exposure

Closely related to the duration of eyewitness exposure time is frequency of exposure. The more often a witness observes an event or person, the more accurate his or her description or recognition should be. Although there is substantial support for this in the experimental literature, dating as far back as Hermann Ebbinghaus's work in 1885, frequency of exposure has not been examined in studies of eyewitness testimony. Loftus (1979) suggests that perhaps the relationship is such a commonsensical one that it has failed to draw the attention of eyewitness researchers. In addition, in "real" crime scenes, witnesses are not likely to have seen the perpetrator more than once.

Pace of Events

Another time factor that is likely to influence witness accuracy is the rate at which things happen. Fast-moving events are more difficult to process and thus to remember than slow-moving events, because of the limited processing capacity of human beings and their selective attention mechanisms. Therefore, incidents surrounded by complex activity tend to confuse, even when witnesses have a reasonably long opportunity to observe the occurrence. Consider the complex activity that occurred during the Boston Marathon bombing in April 2013. The alleged perpetrators carried bombs in backpacks and set two down along the marathon route. However, the streets were bustling with activity and there were crowds of people. Even someone following a bomber and seeing him place a backpack down on the ground may have difficulty describing the scenario accurately.

Retention Interval

Retention interval has also been shown to influence memory of events. Witnesses to crime, accidents, or civil wrongs often experience delays ranging from hours to months between seeing an event and being asked to identify an individual or tell what they observed or heard. Research has firmly established that lengthy time intervals between witnessing the event and reporting it are associated with decreased accuracy (Deffenbacher, Bornstein, McGorty, & Penrod, 2008; Sauer, Brewer, Zweck, & Weber, 2010). Witnesses, of course, generally must recall events weeks, months, or even years after they occur. If there is a discrepancy between what they reported to police and what they recount on the witness stand, this creates a problem. It is not unusual, for example, for a cross-examining attorney to ask a witness something like, "But didn't you tell police when they first interviewed you that the man you saw running out of the store was not wearing a hat? Now you say he was." Part of this inaccuracy stems from the higher probability that new information will be received and processed by the person during the longer interval, a process known as the misinformation effect, which we cover later in the chapter.

Disguises

It is common practice for offenders to disguise their appearance when committing a crime, such as by wearing a mask (such as a stocking mask), sunglasses, a hat, or a hood. These disguises qualify as estimator variables. Research indicates that even a relatively simple disguise can effectively reduce eyewitness identification accuracy (Pezdek, 2012). It appears that disguises to upper facial features, such as the eyes, forehead, or hairline, are more likely to impair eyewitness identification of the offender than those to lower facial features, such as the chin, nose, or mouth. This is because the upper facial features play a more critical role in facial recognition, with the eyes being especially important (Henderson, Williams, & Falk, 2005). Consequently, a perpetrator wearing sunglasses may be particularly difficult to identify, prompting many banks to require patrons to remove their sunglasses prior to entering. Banks now routinely extend this to hats and hoods.

Mansour et al. (2012) discovered that covering most of the face with a diaphanous stocking is as effective as completely covering the face. A diaphanous stocking is made of see-through material that distorts the face. The disguise is effective because it disrupts an eyewitness's overall image of the face and leads to misidentification of the perpetrator. According to Mansour et al., the stocking is a more effective disguise than sunglasses. It is, of course, almost guaranteed to draw attention to the individual, much more so than sunglasses that are commonly worn.

Weapon Focus

Not all details of a scene are equally remembered, because certain novel, complex, ambiguous, or arousing features draw more attention than others. Blood, masks, weapons, and aggressive actions are more likely to be noticed than clothing, hairstyle, height, facial features, or background stimuli in a crime scene. A gun pointed at a person is likely to be studied more intently than other features impinging on the person at that moment. People are quite certain about whether a gun or a knife was threatening them, but they are perhaps less certain of an assailant's clothes or facial characteristics. This phenomenon is known as weapon focus or weapon effect. Specifically, **weapon focus** refers to the concentration of a victim's or witness's attention on a threatening weapon while paying less attention to other details and events of a crime. In short, it refers to a tunneling of attention. This is relevant because the witness may be less likely to recognize the perpetrator or recall other details, such as the fact that an accomplice was waiting in a getaway vehicle.

The primary theoretical underpinning for weapon focus is James Easterbrook's (1959) observation that under high arousal, people tend to narrow their attention to the cues that are most threatening or relevant, and they correspondingly reduce their attention to other cues in the immediate environment. Therefore, highly anxious or tense individuals will not scan their environments as broadly as less anxious individuals. Easterbrook's classic theory is known as **cue utilization theory**.

The tendency to focus on some details to the exclusion of others is well illustrated by an often-cited study in which unsuspecting students sat in an anteroom waiting to participate in an experiment conducted by C. Johnson and Scott (1976). A no-weapon condition and a weapon condition were used. Participants in the no-weapon condition overheard a conversation from the experimental room concerning equipment problems, after which an individual entered the waiting room, holding a pen in greasy hands. This person, who was part of the experiment (a confederate), made a brief comment and then exited quickly. In the weapon condition, the participants overheard an angry confrontation, accompanied by sounds of bottles breaking and chairs crashing. The confederate bolted into the waiting room, holding a bloodied letter opener in blood-stained hands. As in the no-weapon condition, the confederate muttered something and then left.

When participants were interviewed about the scenario, nearly everyone in the weapon condition described a knife, while very few of the no-weapon participants could describe the pen. More important, the presence of a weapon (weapon focus compounded by emotional arousal) reduced the ability to identify the confederate from a set of 50 photographs. Apparently, the witnesses focused their attention primarily on the weapon rather than on facial features.

It should be emphasized that in both the weapon and no-weapon conditions, the confederate (the perpetrator) was only in the presence of the witnesses for about 4 seconds. More recent research findings indicate that the effects of weapon focus can be significantly reduced by longer exposure durations and shorter retention intervals (Fawcett, Russell, Peace, & Christie, 2013), distinctive facial features of the perpetrator (C. A. Carlson & Carlson, 2012), or perceived dangerousness of the perpetrator (Pickel, 2009). Kerri Pickel also found that a handgun reduced the accuracy of witnesses' descriptions of a female perpetrator more than descriptions of a male perpetrator. Apparently, the handgun is considered more unusual by eyewitnesses if it is held by a female than a male, a finding which suggests that *unusualness* is a significant factor in weapon focus in addition to perceived threat or stress level. The above research, then, suggests that weapon focus is reduced (a) as the length of the incident increases, (b) if the perpetrator has distinct facial features, and (c) if the perpetrator is perceived as especially dangerous. On the other hand, weapon focus is increased if the perpetrator is a woman.

Other researchers have also discovered the powerful role that unusualness or novelty plays in weapon focus in a variety of contexts (Hope & Wright, 2007; Saunders, 2009). As noted by Saunders, "although we know that bank robberies occur from time to time, we do not expect someone to draw a weapon when we ourselves are visiting the bank" (p. 326). Pickel (2009) contends that weapon focus occurs because the weapon is unusual to witnesses, and any unusual object could feasibly draw the attention of an eyewitness, at least temporarily. Under these conditions, Pickel points out that fewer attentional resources are available to process other visual details at the time of the crime. Therefore, a witness who is very familiar with guns may not experience weapon focus to the same degree as a witness who is unfamiliar with them.

In sum, weapon focus has received strong empirical support, particularly in scenes of short duration in which a threatening weapon is visible. Certainly, it only makes sense that when a lethal weapon is directed at anyone, arousal (fear) would be a natural (and expected) response from the victim as well as other witnesses. Moreover, recent research indicates that the weapon focus effect is probably maximized under conditions in which there is *both* an unusual or threatening object *and* high arousal. As pointed out by Hope and Wright (2007), "when a weapon is present it draws resources not only from the visual attention pool but also more general attention resources" (p. 958). In other words, a threatening weapon interferes with processing of various sources of information, and available research suggests that a weapon is more likely to do this than even an object that is novel or unusual to the eyewitness.

Emotional arousal clearly influences the degree to which accurate information will be perceived. However, recent research also suggests that the effects of high arousal on eyewitness accuracy may be even more complex than originally supposed. For example, Houston et al. (2013) discovered that, although highly emotional subjects provided a more complete *description* of a perpetrator than less emotional subjects, they were less accurate in remembering what the perpetrator actually did in a crime scene. Furthermore, they were less accurate in picking out the perpetrator in a photographic lineup. The researchers concluded, "Emotions associated with witnessing a crime are likely to impair memory for the incident and recognition of the perpetrator" (p. 127). Their findings have important implications for how statements from emotional witnesses are interpreted and how much confidence the questioning officer should have in the accuracy of statements provided by witnesses who are in a high emotional state.

Significance (or What's Happening?)

People in the midst of a crime do not always perceive that something significant is happening—they are present, but fail to realize a crime is in progress. The classic example was cited by Baron and Byrne (1981) discussing the tragic sniper incident on the University of Texas campus in 1966. Disgruntled student and veteran Charles Whitman managed to gain access to the top of the 307-foot-tall university tower with an arsenal of weapons and began firing at students below. Some heard the shots, noticed bodies falling, and immediately ran for cover. A surprising number of people simply continued along their way without perceiving the seriousness of the situation. Some individuals who survived later said they interpreted the event as a fraternity stunt and did not take it seriously. Likewise, in the 2012 theater shooting in Aurora, Colorado, some theater patrons initially interpreted the smoke bombs that were thrown by the perpetrator and even the early gunshots as special effects that were part of the entertainment for the special midnight showing of the Batman movie. As another recent example, in the Boston Marathon bombing of 2013, the sounds accompanying the first explosion were perceived by some as celebratory fireworks. When people do not understand the significance of events, relevant information can be lost. We have no way of knowing how many crimes have remained unsolved or could have been prevented because witnesses did not realize what was happening at the time of the event.

Own-Race Bias (ORB)

There is now considerable evidence that people are much better at discriminating among faces of their own race or ethnic group than they are the faces of other races or ethnic groups. This well-established phenomenon is most commonly called **own-race bias**, abbreviated ORB. Some researchers (e.g., Hugenberg, Young, Bernstein, & Sacco, 2010) refer to it as the "other-race effect" (ORE), signifying more closely that people generally are less able to identify members of another race or ethnic group than their own. This phenomenon is not restricted to the United States; it is global. Both laboratory and field research across a wide band of cultures and countries have replicated ORB, clearly confirming that the effect is a reliable and robust finding (Hugenberg et al., 2010; Messier & Brigham, 2001; Sporer, 2001). Unfortunately, the majority of eyewitness errors involve the erroneous identification of an individual who is not the perpetrator, and they appear to be increasing (Meissner & Brigham, 2001; Meissner et al., 2007).

Studies and meta-analyses have failed to find a relationship between racial attitudes or prejudice and memory for other-race faces (Meissner & Brigham, 2001), although Wells and Olson (2001) admonish that it may be premature to completely discount prejudice as a possible "moderating variable" in the effect. A **moderating variable** is one that influences—sometimes very subtly—the strength and direction of the relationship between two other variables. The moderating variable "prejudice" may be very difficult to detect in the ORB phenomenon because it is subtle in many cases, often to the point of being outside of the awareness of the person who is making the observation (Hugenberg et al., 2010; Meissner & Brigham, 2001). At this point, though, it is unwarranted to attribute misidentification of someone of another race to prejudice.

There are several theoretical explanations for ORB (Hugenberg et al., 2010). One of the more popular, called the **differential experience hypothesis**, argues that individuals will naturally have greater familiarity or experience with members of their own race and will thus be better able to detect differences among its members. Many people are raised in social environments that require them to recognize own-race faces, beginning at a very early age. Experience presumed to be a significant factor in recognition must be distinguished from mere exposure, however. Growing up in a racially and ethnically diverse neighborhood does not necessarily allow one to discern other-race facial characteristics accurately. Rather, it is the *frequency of meaningful and positive contacts* with other races that engenders perceptual skill in accurate facial discrimination (MacLin & Malpass, 2001). For example, having close friends of other races is more likely to promote facial discernment than having frequent but superficial exposure. Some support for the differential experience hypothesis is provided in studies showing that training in face familiarization dissipates the other-race effect (e.g., Hancock & Rhodes, 2008; Sangrigoli, Pallier, Argenti, Ventureyra, & de Schonen, 2005; Tanaka & Pierce, 2009).

It is also possible that people develop specific strategies, based on certain distinguishing cues of the human face, to identify same-race members (Young, Hugenberg, Bernstein, & Sacco, 2009). If the strategies used by individuals in identifying same-race members can be delineated, it is possible that the discernment of eyewitnesses may be improved prior to any identification procedure of other-race suspects. However, how crucial initial observations of suspects are and whether they might be improved by employing after-the-fact strategies remains an unanswered question.

Hugenberg et al. (2010) propose a theoretical model—called the **categorization-individual model**—that hypothesizes that the other-race effect results from some combination of experience, motivation, and personal categorization strategies. First, they point out it is well established that there are two different ways of processing faces during facial recognition: social categorization and individuation. Social **categorization** occurs quickly and spontaneously when encountering faces. It is the process of putting the encountered face into a group category, such as gender, race, and age. The next process—individuation—requires greater time and effort. A person must be motivated to do it. **Individuation** requires extracting individual identity out of the social group. If the person is not motivated to attend to the unique identity of the individual he or she has quickly put into a general category, the person may fail to be able to identify an individual from that category when expected to.

Hugenberg and his associates (2010) also include experience in their multidimensional model of face recognition. Most perceivers have substantial individual experience with their own race but do not generally have extensive experience discriminating among other-race faces. It is only when a person's identity is seen as sufficiently important that perceivers attend to it more carefully.

In sum, the literature is consistent in concluding that people have difficulty recognizing unfamiliar persons of other races. This other-race effect is obviously a critical aspect in the identification of suspects by eyewitnesses, and it may explain the misidentification of numerous suspects who were later convicted but ultimately cleared by DNA evidence. The most valid explanation for the other-race effect appears to be the differential experience hypothesis, which implies that substantial, meaningful interactions with members of a different race may promote strategies for facial discrimination. However, the lack of various effective strategies and lack of motivation for identifying different faces may also play key roles.

Effects of Alcohol and Other Drugs

Much of the research on eyewitness testimony deals with subjects who are not under the influence of alcohol or other drugs. However, police remind us that witnesses at the scene of a crime are often under the influence of some substance. J. R. Evans et al. (2009) had law enforcement officers complete a survey about their experiences with intoxicated witnesses and suspects. The officers indicated that witnesses are commonly under the influence of alcohol and that many are under the influence of multiple substances. The officers estimated that approximately 40% of the witnesses they interviewed during their investigations were under the influence of alcohol or other substances. Intriguingly, the study found that a majority of the officers believe that intoxicated witnesses provide the most detailed and accurate information right after the incident, while still intoxicated. A small minority (about 1%) thought witnesses provided the most information days or weeks later when intoxicated again.

Very few studies have examined the effects of alcohol or drugs on eyewitnesses, even though alcohol has been shown across a wide range of studies to impair memory performance both dramatically (e.g., alcohol blackout and amnesia) and subtly (J. R. Evans et al., 2009; F. T. Palmer, Flowe, Takarangi, & Humphries, 2013). On the other hand, some research suggests that alcohol seems to enhance memory under certain conditions, such as when it is consumed shortly after encoding information (Moulton et al., 2005).

Witnesses who were intoxicated at the time of an incident are less likely to be asked to testify in court compared with sober witnesses. This observation is related to the finding that jurors tend to believe that intoxicated witnesses are less credible than sober witnesses (J. R. Evans & Schreiber Compo, 2010)—and the opposing attorney would want the jury to know that the witness was intoxicated. The belief that intoxicated witnesses are less reliable than sober ones is also held by many experts (Schreiber Compo et al., 2012). However, and surprisingly, a study by Schreiber Compo et al. suggests that intoxicated witnesses may be as accurate and detailed as sober ones (see Box 5-1).

BOX 5-1 RESEARCHERS AT WORK

Do Intoxicated People Make Good Witnesses?

Common sense may suggest that persons who are intoxicated are in no shape to recall details of events they witness. Certainly, intoxicated persons must perform worse at this task than those not intoxicated. Acting on this belief, investigators may be reluctant to interview such persons when they are witnesses to crime, and the legal system, in general, may be suspicious of the accuracy of their accounts. As is sometimes the case when "common sense" gets tested under the research microscope, these assumptions do not necessarily hold.

A group of researchers (Schreiber Compo et al., 2012) placed 93 participants in one of three conditions: alcohol, placebo, or control. Careful steps were taken to ensure that participants were older than 21, had consented to the research, and were in good physical health. A medical screening procedure was used to ensure there were no contraindicators of alcohol consumption, such as pregnancy or being on prescription medication other than birth control pills. Sobriety was verified when participants first arrived, and the instruments used to produce accurate breath alcohol concentration (BrAC) were carefully calibrated.

Participants were taken to a "bar lab," where they observed a bartender preparing their drinks. Weight and gender of the participants were taken into account. Those in the alcohol group saw vodka poured into their glasses; those in the placebo group received drinks that appeared to be poured from a vodka bottle and seemed identical to the drinks of the alcohol group; those in the control group saw the bartender pour cranberry juice into their glass. The participants drank their drinks, this was repeated several times, and BrAC was measured after the last drink.

Participants were then taken to another room and asked to write down everything they recalled about the bar and the bartender. This is what they assumed was their main task. However, while they were in the room, an elaborately staged "crime" occurred. It involved an intruder, the theft of a laptop computer, and a call to University Technology Services (UTS) during which the participants heard misinformation given. UTS sent an official-looking "representative" to investigate. All participants were led to believe that this "theft" had occurred independent of their experimental task. Actually, the researchers wanted to know what they remembered about the "crime," and they were thus asked this in an interview format by the UT "representative." In debriefing, participants indicated they really thought a theft had occurred and that they were actually being interviewed about it.

The three groups did not differ significantly in the accuracy of their recollections or in their "don't know" responses. Misinformation occurred at the same level among all participants, as well. In essence, the experiment did not uncover significant differences in memory retrieval among the groups.

The researchers cautioned that this was a preliminary study, and its results should not be extended prematurely to situations outside the laboratory. The "theft" was a simple one, and participants were not placed in a stressful environment that would characterize a "real" criminal event. Nevertheless, the findings raise questions about the assumption that intoxicated individuals are deficient in memory of events compared with those who are sober.

Questions for Discussion:

1. The above study involved an elaborate research design and analysis, which are discussed only briefly here. What further information would you want to know about its methodology and results before assessing its importance?

2. Can we generalize from this study to persons who are under the influence of drugs other than alcohol?

Eyewitness System Variables

Thus far in the chapter, we have focused on estimator variables, which affect the processing of information at the time a person experiences or witnesses an event. In this section, we focus on system variables, which are relevant after the event has occurred, and which may be under the control of the legal system. As mentioned above, eyewitness research has focused more on system than estimator variables, perhaps because these can be controlled. As we note later in the chapter, the legal system has indeed taken steps to limit the negative effects of system variables, particularly in the case of pretrial identification procedures.

Some variables can qualify as both system and estimator variables. Misinformation effects are a good example of this duality, as we see below. They can occur at the scene of the event and may also be promoted during the interviewing process.

Misinformation Effect

Many studies conducted over the last 30 years show that when people see an event and are later exposed to new and misleading information about the incident, their recollections often become distorted. Perhaps more surprising is the observation that a vast majority of people are not immune to the distorting effects of misinformation (Frenda et al., 2011). The distortion may involve words, faces, or the details of witnessed events. This phenomenon is known as the **misinformation effect** (see Loftus, 2005). Such effects can qualify as system or estimator variables. To give a system variable example, a police officer investigating a crime scene may have received some mention of a tattoo from one of the witnesses. He may then ask another witness, "What color was the person's tattoo?" Even if that witness did not notice a tattoo at the time, she is apt to include that important bit of information in her subsequent statements.

Misinformation effects also can occur at the scene of the crime or accident and thus be considered estimator variables. They can spring from naturally occurring conversations before police have arrived. Co-witnesses, for example, often talk among themselves, and this has the very high potential to lead to misinformation. Witnesses may compare notes on whether a car came to a complete stop or made a rolling stop, for example. If the majority agrees that it was a rolling stop, the person who first thought it was a full stop may come to believe the others are right, and report it to police as a rolling stop. To avoid such comparing of notes, police often try to separate eyewitnesses as quickly as possible.

The misinformation effects may be particularly of concern as they relate to children. The daily conversations children have with their family members or peers often provide a common, but very powerful source of misinformation (Principe & Schindewolf, 2012). These memory-sharing conversations frequently contaminate the child's memory of what really happened. As London and Ceci (2012) note,

> It is nothing short of shocking to see children claiming to have witnessed an event that they did not, based solely on information they collected from classmates or by overhearing teachers in the hall or their mother on the phone. (p. 163)

In fact, the research conducted by Principe and Schindewolf suggests that a majority of young children (ages 3 to 6 years old) are more strongly influenced by the information provided by their peers than that provided by adults. We will discuss additional research on child witnesses shortly.

Misinformation Effects Research

Deliberately or not, police investigating a crime or the scene of an accident can introduce misinformation into the event. Deliberately or not, a lawyer may do this in the courtroom. Over the past three decades, Loftus and many other researchers have designed numerous experiments demonstrating that post-event experiences, such as exposure to additional information, can substantially affect a person's memory of the original event. In the typical experiment, research participants are shown photographs, videos, written materials, or other audio or visual displays, and then are exposed to misleading information about what they saw or read. In many studies, the simple mention of an existing object in an interview significantly increases the probability that the object will be recalled by the participant (or witness) later on. For example, asking an eyewitness to a traffic accident, "How fast was the car going when it ran the stop sign?" will enhance the recall of the stop sign, even if the witness failed to notice it in the first place. Similarly, casually mentioning an object that did not actually exist in an accident scene increases the likelihood that a witness will later report having seen that nonexistent object (Loftus, Miller, & Burns, 1978). Research participants will inadvertently integrate aspects of the misleading information into their memory from the original source material (Frenda et al., 2011).

Early in her research, Loftus (1975, 1977) discovered that witnesses *compromise* their memory when they learn of new information that conflicted with an initial observation. For example, if a witness thought he noticed a red car passing in the wrong lane and the investigating officer mentioned a green car, the witness would be likely to recall an off-colored green or blue-green car in a later report. If a witness thought a vehicle was traveling at 85 miles per hour, and the investigating officer mentioned the speed of 65, the witness would likely report later the speed to be somewhere between 65 and 85, probably closer to 65. The witness might be aware of the compromise, but it might also be an unconscious phenomenon attributable to perceptual and memory processes occurring outside awareness.

The above studies imply that law enforcement officers or attorneys can manipulate a witness's memory by introducing additional information. However, there is evidence that this is more difficult to do with important or even noticeable factors than with less important details (Loftus, 1979). Furthermore, data also suggest that misleading information provided to witnesses sometime after the event and just before a recall test will have greater impact than misleading information given immediately after the incident (Loftus et al., 1978). By the same token, interviewers wishing to maintain a consistent description of the initial incident would be wise to obtain the information immediately after the incident and then reiterate the material before and as close as possible to the time of courtroom testimony.

Although it appears that no one is immune to the distorting effects of misinformation, there is evidence that certain individuals are more vulnerable than others. For example, as will be discussed again shortly, research suggests that very young children and the elderly may be more susceptible to the effects of misinformation than adolescents or adults (Davis & Loftus, 2005; Frenda et al., 2011). In addition, recent studies have also discovered that individuals who are more intelligent, have greater perceptual and memory abilities, and have above-average facial recognition ability are better able to resist misinformation than others (Zhu et al., 2010a, 2010b). These positive features can apply to any age.

Witness Confidence and Certainty

Witness confidence is treated here as a system variable because it can be manipulated. "Eyewitness researchers tend to think of certainty as a system variable because it can be directly manipulated by legal system players through the timing and control of statements that are provided to eyewitnesses" (Smalarz & Wells, 2013, p. 161). However, it can also be considered an estimator variable as a feature of the individual. For example, some people are very firm in their convictions of what they saw—or they feel very *un*clear about it. No amount of questioning will change that confidence—or lack of it. In that sense, witness confidence can also be considered an estimator variable.

People generally assume that those who are certain about what they saw are accurate witnesses. There is some validity to this assumption. Earlier psychological studies did suggest either that certainty was unrelated to accuracy or that it was an indicator of inaccuracy. (If he's that sure, he's probably wrong.) "In fact, this idea is still endorsed by members of the legal system who have not followed closely the development of the empirical literature" (Smalarz & Wells, 2013, p. 164). Current studies have found that, in general, the more confident the eyewitness, the more accurate her decisions when identifying the culprit (N. Brewer & Wells, 2006, 2011; Smalarz & Wells, 2013). Moreover, "Highly confident decisions, rapid decisions, and decisions accompanied by relevant recollection (i.e., recall of contextual information relevant to discriminating the culprit) are more likely to be accurate than are decisions made with low confidence, slowly, or without relevant recollection" (N. Brewer & Wells, 2011, p. 24). However, it should be emphasized that many things can influence eyewitness identification certainty. For example, post-identification feedback or poorly constructed lineups—such as one in which the members were not reasonably matched in appearance—can shift the level of certainty (Douglass & Steblay, 2006). Also, some findings that appear to be relevant to adults may not extend to children. Overall, research results suggest that police investigators should pay close attention to the level of confidence of the witness when determining accuracy of offender identifications by adult witnesses.

Certainty may still be a weak indictor of accuracy, however. Psychological research has currently shifted to trying to understand the conditions under which certainty is a strong indicator and under which it is a weak indicator (Smalarz & Wells, 2013). For example, Pezdek (2012) observes that witness confidence probably decreases with the passage of time. A witness may then be less confident, but still accurate. In addition, Pezdek notes that repeatedly questioning eyewitnesses inflates their confidence without affecting the accuracy of their memory. So a witness may become even more confident but not necessarily more accurate or inaccurate.

A vast majority of the research has focused on the accuracy of identifying the offender, but little research has been directed at the witness who is positive the offender is *not* in the lineup (Smalarz & Wells, 2013). These researchers argue that witnesses' certainty in a non-identification situation is qualitatively different from witness certainty in an identification situation. People who do not identify an offender are sometimes referred to as *not-there witnesses* or **nonchoosers** (Smalarz & Wells, 2013). There are two types of nonchoosers: those who are not sure whether the perpetrator is in the lineup and those who are sure the offender is not. Those witnesses who are certain that the offender is not in the lineup obviously provide very useful information to any police investigation, because research now suggests that they are likely to be accurate. To the innocent suspect drawn into the investigation, they are invaluable. On the other hand, a non-identification from a not-sure witness might occur because the witness's memory of the incident was not that good to begin with. Much more research is needed on the relation between certainty and accuracy.

Eyewitness Confidence Malleability

Eyewitness confidence becomes a system variable when it is manipulated by agents of the law. In a survey of eyewitness experts, 95% believed that eyewitness confidence can be manipulated (Douglass & Pavletic, 2012; Kassin, Tubb, Hosch, & Memon, 2001). Douglass and Steblay (2006), for instance, found that witnesses certainty was more influenced by the feedback they received during the identification procedure (e.g., lineup or photospread) than any other system variable. Manipulation of this type is especially troublesome in the case of mistaken identification—as when a witness fingers an innocent person. In a series of well-done studies, Gary Wells and Amy Bradfield (1998, 1999) focused on the creation of false confidence by external influences, such as giving feedback to eyewitnesses after they make their identification. The researchers report, "Telling eyewitnesses who have made false identification that they identified the actual suspect or the same person that other witnesses identified leads to robust inflation in the witnesses' confidence in their identification" (p. 138). This increased confidence in eyewitnesses identification generated by external influences is referred to as the **post-identification feedback effect**.

Wells and his colleagues (Wells & Bradfield, 1999; Wells et al., 2000) find that this post-identification feedback does more than inflate the confidence level of the witnesses; it also distorts eyewitnesses' memory of how confident they were at the time of the initial identification prior to the feedback. In other words, the witnesses may believe that they were highly certain of their identification before the feedback, even though they may have wondered at the time. In addition, this confirming feedback distorts the eyewitnesses' recollection of their witnessing conditions, such as how well they were able to see the perpetrator. Most witnesses are convinced that the feedback did not influence their judgments.

Interestingly, Wells and Bradfield (1999) found it is possible to "inoculate" eyewitnesses against the post-identification feedback effect by asking them to think about the process prior to the feedback manipulation. For example, the eyewitnesses were instructed to think privately about several variables, such as how certain they were, how good their view was, and how long they took to make an identification, prior to the feedback. Wells and Bradfield found that "eyewitnesses who were instructed to think about these variables prior to the feedback manipulation were largely unaffected by the manipulation, whereas eyewitnesses who were not instructed to think about these variables were strongly affected by the manipulation" (p. 142).

Preserving the Integrity of the System

The above techniques (providing additional information, focusing on confidence) are commonly used by representatives of the legal system to procure information from witnesses. It is not illegal for police interviewing witnesses to interject information that they may not have provided spontaneously. It is also understandable that a police officer would want to promote confidence in a victim or witness and a lawyer would want her client to be confident on the witness stand. "A mistaken identification from an uncertain witness is unlikely to lead to conviction" (Smolarz & Wells, 2013, p. 173). If the legal system wishes to minimize errors and retain public confidence, it is well advised to take positive steps to seek the truth. From a very practical perspective, obtaining accurate information lessens the likelihood that innocent people will be convicted or that cases will proceed through the legal system unnecessarily. Legal psychologists have offered a number of suggestions for encouraging accuracy and protecting against misinformation.

The Cognitive Interview

One approach for improving accuracy and completeness of any eyewitness's recollection is the **cognitive interview (CI)**, a set of rules and guidelines for interviewing eyewitnesses (Wells et al., 2006). According to Memon, Meissner, and Fraser (2010), "The Cognitive Interview (or CI) is perhaps one of the most successful developments in psychology and law research in the last 25 years" (p. 340). The CI is an approach that is designed to enhance memory retrieval and communication from an eyewitness. Studies have found that police officers trained in the CI method gain a greater amount of information and more *detailed* information from eyewitnesses compared with other methods of interviewing. The method appears to be especially effective when dealing with witnesses who are older adults (Memon et al., 2010), but it can apply to all ages.

The standard police interview is often characterized by constant interruptions, excessive reliance on a predetermined list of questions, and poorly timed questioning. Although this is more likely to be the case when police are interviewing and interrogating criminal suspects—a topic we discussed in Chapter 3—a similar pattern may be used with witnesses. The questioning may not be aggressive or accusatory, but the officer is still controlling the situation. By contrast, the CI interviewer is discouraged from interrupting the witness and is instructed to allow the witness to control the flow of information by encouraging his or her own free narrative of events. The interview comprises several phases during which the interviewer engages with and establishes rapport with the witness, asks the witness to give a narrative account of the incident, and then follows with questions to encourage elaboration of some of the details the witness has reported. Research indicates that the CI improves the amount of correct information generated, compared with other interview approaches (Köhnken, Milne, Memon, & Bull, 1999).

Although we have thus far focused on just a few system variables, it should be noted that there are multiple possible sources of influence on eyewitness identification.

One predominant source involves pretrial identification procedures—specifically lineups—which have captured the attention of legal psychologists for many years. Because of the research interest in this area, we discuss these system variables in a separate section later in the chapter. For the time being, we shift our focus to two groups of eyewitnesses that have also received special attention from researchers in psychology and law.

Children as Witnesses

In the criminal justice system, children are most likely to be called upon as witnesses if they themselves have been victimized. Nearly 3 million children reportedly experienced abuse (sexual or physical) or neglect in the United States during 2010 (Klemfuss & Ceci, 2012), with at least one fifth of these reports substantiated (U.S. Department of Health and Human Services, Administration for Children & Families, 2011). Lack of substantiation does not mean that the incident did not occur, however. Although false reporting cannot be eliminated as an explanation, it could be that sufficient evidence was not obtained or that the children were not believed.

Klemfuss and Ceci (2012) note that child testimony is usually the only source of prosecuting evidence in an abuse case—particularly a sexual abuse case—because, by the nature of the crime, there are usually no other witnesses. Lawyers, judges, and sometimes police have long believed that the information acquired through the interviewing of children and their subsequent testimony is permeated with far more distortion and inaccuracy than information acquired from young and middle-aged adults (Brainerd & Reyna, 2012). However, recent research indicates that many police officers find children to be more accurate in their descriptions of crime and other incidents than many other professionals do—including eyewitness experts (G. S. Goodman & Melinder, 2007). For example, in one study of experts in forensic psychology or eyewitness testimony (Kassin et al., 2001), two thirds of the experts believed that children are generally less accurate than adults. In that same study, 94% of the experts in forensic psychology or eyewitness testimony believed that young children are also more vulnerable than adults to suggestion and other social influences. The perception of children's reporting inaccuracy extends to the general public and prospective jurors as well (Ross, Dunning, Toglia, & Ceci, 1990). To address whether these beliefs are justified, we will discuss shortly the research on child testimony.

Legal Criteria for Child Testimony

The age at which children may testify as credible and competent eyewitnesses in criminal and civil proceedings has long been controversial. In the past, many jurisdictions stipulated that 14 was the minimum age for delivering competent testimony, with exceptions being made only after a judicial inquiry into a younger child's testimonial competency. Other jurisdictions regularly allowed 10-year-olds to qualify as competent witnesses. Many states, however, required that the competency of the child witness under 12 (or even 14) be evaluated prior to allowing his or her testimony as evidence.

In recent years, however, numerous changes have been made to make it easier for a child eyewitness to testify. For example, over half the states have adopted Rule 601 of the Federal Rules of Evidence (Bulkley, 1989), which establishes a rebuttable presumption of competency for children. In other words, children, like adults, are presumed to be competent to testify. If there is doubt about their competency in light of their age, it is then evaluated. In some states, children as young as age 2 or 3 have testified (Klemfuss & Ceci, 2012; Zajac, O'Neill, & Hayne, 2012). Fortunately, most child witnesses are considerably older (Zajac et al., 2012). Under Rule 601, the normal developmental differences in memory or narration abilities between children and adults are no longer critical in determining a child's competency. Simply because a child cannot narrate an event, he or she is not precluded from testifying. However, a minimum credibility standard must still be met. Child testimony can be rejected "if a reasonable juror could believe that 'the witness is so bereft of his powers of observation, recordation, recollection, and recount as to be so untrustworthy as a witness as to make his testimony lack relevance'" (Bulkley, 1989, p. 212).

If there is doubt about the child's competency, then, she must undergo a screening process. Furthermore, in those jurisdictions that have established a statutory mandated age (e.g., a minimum age of 8 or 10), children below that age must undergo testimonial competency screening (Klemfuss & Ceci, 2012). Usually, the child is asked a brief series of questions in an effort to determine if he or she understands the oath, knows the difference between truth and lies (often referred to as truth-lie competency screening), and has the capacity to observe and recall events. "Testimonial competence refers to whether a witness has sufficient cognitive ability and moral understanding to provide useful testimony" (Klemfuss & Ceci, 2012, p. 269). If there are still questions about the child's ability to provide legal testimony, the child's competence may be assessed more thoroughly.

Competency screening and assessment are of critical importance. If a judge deems a child incompetent to testify, that child's testimony cannot be heard (Klemfuss & Ceci, 2012). If this happens and there is no other evidence to present, the case must be dismissed. On the other hand, if the court has some concerns about the child's ability but is not convinced the child is incompetent to testify, the judge may issue a warning to the jury briefly outlining her concerns about the child's ability. In most jurisdictions today, however, it is relatively rare that a child is prevented from giving testimony on the grounds of incompetency (Klemfuss & Ceci, 2012). Competency evaluation and screening are not foolproof. In addition, there is little uniformity in actual judicial practices concerning competency evaluation, and judges often make competency decisions based on few guidelines and little formal training (London & Ceci, 2012).

Psychological Research on Child Testimony

Two basic questions are posed about the testimony of children: (1) Is it truthful? and (2) Is it accurate? The first question addresses whether children are being honest, while the second addresses whether they can describe an event appropriately.

Honesty

Developmental research finds that children's understanding and moral judgments of truth and lies emerge during the preschool years (A. D. Evans & Lyon, 2012). A large collection of data emerging from forensic developmental research on child testimony indicates that the nature of the questioning and the type of memory retrieval are critical variables. For example, Lyon, Carrick, and Quas (2010) found that 4- to 6-year-old children are able to distinguish between true and false statements at a younger age than they are able to articulate an understanding of the concepts of "truth" versus "lie" or "good" versus "bad." "In practical terms, this means that many children will accept true propositions and reject false propositions even though they are incapable of articulating their understanding of the truth, lies, or falsehoods" (Lyon et al., 2010, p. 147). Thus, if some form of an oath is required of young children, they will be incapable of promising to "tell the truth" because they lack the understanding of what "tell the truth" means. However, they are usually able to *recognize* true statements and false statements by age 4 (Evans & Lyon, 2012). Again, they can do this before they are able to provide a definition or explain the difference between truth and a lie (Lyon & Saywitz, 1999).

A considerable amount of research has demonstrated that a great majority of adults—including experts—cannot reliably tell when a child is being dishonest (Block et al., 2012; G. S. Goodman et al., 2006; Nysse-Carris, Bottoms, & Salerno, 2011; Shao & Ceci, 2011). Competency screening for truth telling versus lying does not reliably predict honesty, and thus there have been some cogent arguments for excluding this part of an evaluation (Klemfuss & Ceci, 2012). Overall, studies have consistently shown that adults and experts are no better than chance at determining lying in children. Furthermore, "lying" probably does not mean the same to children and adults.

Some research suggests that children who have been maltreated may have particular difficulty telling the difference between honest and dishonest statements. Lyon et al. (2010) discovered that the manner in which maltreated or disadvantaged children are questioned about their understanding of the truth and lies plays a major role in their apparent understanding of the concepts: "Children may understand the wrongfulness of lying but not understand what lying is" (p. 148). However, it appears that most children have a better understanding of the truth than they do a lie, although the reasons for this are unclear.

Secrecy is often the norm in abusive homes, so maltreated children often have different attitudes about truth telling and lying than non-maltreated children (Lyon et al., 2010). This may also be related to low-level or marginal verbal development. According to Lyon et al., "Maltreated children might uniquely understand the wrongfulness of lying better than the meaning of lying given a home environment rich in punitiveness but lacking in linguistic stimulation" (p. 143). That is, they first learn that lies are "bad" and are punished, and they later come to understand that lies refer to false statements.

Attorneys and mental health professionals questioning children who often have trouble with the word "lie" would have better luck focusing on asking questions about "truth." Interestingly, one study (Peterson, Peterson, & Seeto, 1983) discovered that a majority of children under the age of 11 denied ever having told a lie. Ceci and Bruck (1993) have noted, though, that children sometimes do lie when the motivation for doing so is there. The researchers indicate that young children will lie if it is in their best interest or they have been induced to do so: "In this sense, they are probably no different from adults" (p. 433). For example, Bottoms et al. (2002) found that threats from loved, trusted adults can be powerful barriers to children's disclosures in forensic contexts. This finding is especially relevant in situations where sexual abusers often exert strong pressure on child victims not to tell others.

Ceci and Bruck (1993) also point out, however, that young children—even preschoolers—are capable of accurately recalling events that are forensically important and relevant: "That their reports are more vulnerable to distortion than those of older individuals, and that they can be induced to lie in response to certain motives, is not meant to imply that they are incapable of providing accurate testimony" (p. 433). Most of the research has indicated that young children are able to recall the majority of what they see or hear, even though they may not recall as much detail as older children.

According to Ceci and Bruck (1993), in order to determine the credibility of children's testimony, it is important to examine the conditions prevalent at the time the initial statement was collected from the child. They believe it is especially important to know how many times the child was questioned, who the interviewers were, the kinds of questions that were asked, and the consistency of the child's report over a period of time. In concluding an extensive review of the research, they assert,

> If the child's disclosure was made in a nonthreatening, nonsuggestible atmosphere, if the disclosure was not made after repeated interviews, if the adults who had access to the child prior to his or her testimony are not motivated to distort the child's recollections through relentless and potent suggestions and outright coaching, and if the child's original report remains highly consistent over a period of time, then the young child would be judged to be capable of providing much that is forensically relevant. (p. 433)

Accuracy as a Function of Age

It is important to emphasize, though, that children—like adults—may be telling the truth, but their information might not be accurate. The system and estimator variables that apply to adults apply to children as well. For example, a child's recognition of a perpetrator may be affected by duration of exposure or by additional information supplied by a police interviewer. As a group, however, are children less accurate than adults? The short answer is no, although they may be less detailed in their responses.

One of the earliest studies on children's testimony was a project by Marin and her colleagues (Marin, Holmes, Guth, & Kovac, 1979), which documented that, under certain circumstances, young children can indeed be as accurate in eyewitness accounts as adults. Marin's subjects were divided into four groups: kindergartners and first graders, third and fourth graders, seventh and eighth graders, and college students. When recall memory was requested by open-ended questions ("What happened?"), older subjects were able to report more material than younger ones. The younger the subject, the less detail he or she provided in describing an incident. Nevertheless, the younger subjects were *accurate* in the incomplete information they reported. When Marin's task demanded recognition memory (identifying photographs or answering yes or no to a series of questions), younger subjects were just as accurate as the older groups. Furthermore, they were no more easily misled by leading questions than the older subjects.

However, very young children (e.g., 3 years of age) seem to provide less accurate information than older children and adults across a variety of testimony tasks (free recall, answers to objective and suggestive questions, and eyewitness identifications) (G. S. Goodman & Hahn, 1987; G. S. Goodman & Reed, 1986). In this research, 6-year-olds did not differ from the adults in answering questions correctly, or in identifying an individual, but they did recall less information about the event. In addition to a list of objective (nonleading) questions, the researchers used a list of suggestive questions designed to imply incorrect information to the subjects. Both the 3-year-olds and the 6-year-olds were more influenced by these questions than the adults, indicating that young children may be more suggestible when questioned by an adult. The results do indicate, however, that if 6-year-old children are questioned in a nonsuggestive manner and provided with an unbiased lineup, they are at least as accurate as adult witnesses.

Later research confirmed these earlier findings (Bruck & Ceci, 2009, 2012). In addition, more recent studies indicate that individual differences in children's language abilities are closely related to the amount and accuracy of children's eyewitness accounts (Klemfuss & Ceci, 2012). In fact, general language skills appear to be more important than vocabulary, especially when it comes to a child's susceptibility to suggestive or misleading questioning. It should be noted that the majority of the studies on child accuracy and suggestibility have been conducted on children from economically comfortable families, rather than on children from lower-income families. However, a large percentage of abused or maltreated children who appear in court come from lower-income families (Lyon et al., 2010). In addition, maltreated children are often delayed in cognitive and language development, which may influence the information they provide compared with their non-maltreated peers (Lyon et al., 2010; Lyon & Dorado, 2008). In addition, some may be new English speakers or unable to speak English at all. As emphasized by Klemfuss and Ceci, the ability to understand an interviewer's questions requires a basic level of language skills, and the ability to respond effectively to those questions requires a basic level of productive language ability.

Reality Monitoring

In addition to studying accuracy and truth telling, research has focused on **reality monitoring**, which refers to a child's ability to distinguish actual from imagined events. Research to date suggests that children older than age 8 can usually distinguish between what is fantasy and what is "real" (Dunning, 1989). Research also shows that children as young as 4 and 6 years of age can reliably distinguish between fantasy and reality (Carrick & Quas, 2006; Ceci & Bruck, 1993). However, when children of this same age were told to imagine a pretend character was sitting in a box, they began to act as though the pretend character was real quite soon after being told. Twenty-five percent of the children were quickly convinced that the imaginary creature could become real, and many had difficulty "giving up" the creature in their mind after the experiment. This study confirms the fact that the boundaries of fantasy and reality for 4- and 6-year-olds are fragile and quickly can become blurred for them. Similar results have been reported by Bunce and Harris (2008, 2013). Bourchier and Davis (2002) found that emotions—especially fear—also encourage a blurring between fantasy and reality. This finding is especially characteristic of children who show stronger emotional reactions in general (Carrick & Quas, 2006). In summary, the extant research suggests that below the age of 8, the distinction between fantasy and the real world begins to blur for the average child (Foley & Johnson, 1985), and accuracy in testimony can be expected to decrease.

Suggestibility

Considerable research on child witnesses has focused on the extent to which they are influenced by the words of those who are questioning them. Reviewing the research in this area, Ceci and Bruck (1993) noted that there appear to be significant age differences, with preschool-aged children being more vulnerable to suggestion than either school-aged children or adults. These researchers observed that preschoolers were the most suggestible group in the great majority (15 out of 18) of the developmental studies comparing them with older children or adults. However, in a later report, Bruck and Ceci (2009) emphasize that while preschoolers tend to be more susceptible to suggestion than older children, it is largely a matter of degree. "That is, elementary school-age children show significant suggestibility effects even when preschoolers exhibit more suggestibility" (p. 160). In fact, under some conditions, there are no significant age differences at all, and in other conditions, older children are actually more suggestible than young children. For example, a repeated question may be interpreted by older children (but not younger children) as a signal that the original answer was incorrect and needed to be revised. Bruck and Ceci write, "The bottom line is that, all age groups are vulnerable to misleading suggestions, even if preschoolers are sometimes disproportionately more vulnerable" (p. 161).

Courtroom Cross-Examination of Children

In the adversarial process of justice, all criminal and civil trials involve a direct examination and a cross-examination unless the opposing attorney declines to cross examine. A direct examination is the first questioning of a witness by the party (either the plaintiff or the defendant) who called that witness to testify. It provides the opportunity for the witness to tell his or her story. Cross-examination, on the other hand, is the questioning of the witness by a party other than the direct examiner. It follows the direct examination. Generally, cross-examination is limited to matters brought out by direct examination and issues affecting the credibility of the witness.

Although cross-examinations may be detrimental to the testimonial accuracy of witnesses, children are especially vulnerable. This is particularly true of those with low levels of self-confidence, those with inadequate cognitive and language skills, and those who have a history of maltreatment. It must be emphasized that cross-examination is also a stressful experience for most anyone—professionals or adult laypersons included. Many child victims of sexual offenses who testified in court found the experience so stressful that it was highly unlikely they would report being a victim again (Zajac et al., 2013). Zajac et al. likewise reported that many parents of child witnesses indicated the cross-examination ordeal was so stressful that they would not put their children through it again.

According to Zajac et al. (2012), "Many children who undergo cross-examination are directly—and often repeatedly—accused of lying" (p. 184). Cross-examination may involve rapid delivery of questions presented with an accusatory tone, implying the child witness is not telling the truth. Defense lawyers often challenge a child witness's perceptions or understanding of the alleged event, his or her memory for details of the event, or the child's ability to communicate the details to the court. Lawyers further challenge a child's testimony by highlighting inconsistency in their statements and emphasizing the child's potential for suggestibility (Zajac et al., 2012). In addition, some lawyers try to confuse the child by using double negatives, meandering sentences, or an esoteric vocabulary (A. Cunningham & Hurley, 2007a).

In one often-cited study, Gary Wells and his associates (Wells, Turtle, & Luus, 1989) exposed 8-year-olds, 12-year-olds, and college students to a staged criminal event (a videotaped abduction of a child from a playground). One day later, the children and college students were subjected to direct questioning and cross-examination about the event. All age-groups were equally accurate about the event during direct examination, but under cross-examination, the 8-year-olds were much less accurate than the 12-year-olds or the college group. The authors attributed this finding to the 8-year-old group's greater susceptibility to misleading information. For example, during cross-examination, they were asked questions such as, "You claimed before that the playground was fairly crowded, is that correct?" (No such claim had been made.) Or they were asked, "In which hand was the man carrying his wallet?" (A wallet was never visible in the scene.) Eight-year-olds were more influenced by these misleading questions than the older witnesses. Ceci, Ross, and Toglia (1987), using 3- and 12-year-olds, found similar results. To summarize, the susceptibility of young children to suggestion and misleading information appears to be influenced by the nature of the task and the context in which it occurs. However, it should be noted that adults also can be strongly influenced by misleading questions. Very young age appears to affect the likelihood that this will occur, but—as we discuss shortly—advanced age does as well.

Communication Modality

Another important factor associated with the credibility of child witnesses is communication modality, or the medium through which the child's testimony is presented. It is clear that children's ability to answer questions in the threatening atmosphere of the courtroom is likely to differ from their ability to answer the same questions in a less formal or more familiar setting (Bala, 1999; Zajac et al., 2012). "Research findings support these concerns: children find the courtroom environment to be stressful, and their resultant anxiety appears to interfere with their ability to provide complete and accurate recall" (Zajac et al., 2012, p. 191). One of the most stressful aspects of testifying for most children is facing the accused (A. Cunningham & Hurley, 2007a). If the accused has hurt the child in the past—and may also have threatened consequences for telling—it is natural for the child to be afraid.

Courts are increasingly allowing alternate forms of testimony, particularly in noncriminal cases such as custody proceedings. In criminal cases, this is less likely to occur. The Sixth Amendment gives criminal defendants the right to confront their accusers and to cross-examine any witnesses against them. In cases involving child victims, this can be extremely traumatic to the child. The U.S. Supreme Court has allowed some accommodation, but has been reluctant to give blanket approval to alternate forms of testimony. In *Coy v. Iowa* (1988), the Court ruled that a defendant had been denied his right to confrontation because the two 13-year-old girls whom he had allegedly sexually assaulted were allowed to testify behind a screen placed between them and the defendant. In *Maryland v. Craig* (1990), however, the Court allowed closed-circuit television testimony (CCTV) in a case involving a child victim of a sexual assault who was deemed too traumatized to testify in the courtroom. Nonetheless, the Court was closely divided, and the issue remains a controversial one (Orcutt, Goodman, Tobey, Batterman-Faunce, & Thomas, 2001). State courts that have allowed the use of closed-circuit testimony, however, have generally limited it to cases of child sexual abuse (Davies, 1999). Another alternative besides CCTV is a witness or sequestration screen, which is a device positioned on or near the witness box to shield a testifying child witness from seeing the accused in the courtroom (A. Cunningham & Hurley, 2007b). Even after *Coy v. Iowa,* some judges have allowed the screens in limited circumstances. Some research suggests that CCTV actually results in bias *in favor of the defense* (Ross et al., 1990; Swim, Borgida, & McCoy, 1993) as well as bias *against the child* who testifies in this way (Orcutt et al., 2001). Other studies have found no significant difference in conviction rates between open-court testimony and CCTV (Davies & Noon, 1991; G. S. Goodman et al., 1998; Murray, 1995). The use of CCTV and videotaped testimony is more common in England, Scotland, and Australia, but these alternatives are used infrequently in the United States (McAuliff, Nicholson, Amarilio, & Ravanshenas, 2013). In the United States, there has been a discernible trend in the use of support persons. A **support person** is an adult designated by the court who provides emotional and informational support during the judicial proceedings. It is usually someone who is known to the child victim or witness. In Canada, a support person is someone who is allowed to sit or stand close to a witness younger than 18 years old while he or she testifies (A. Cunningham & Hurley, 2007b). The support person may be expected to provide three things: (1) emotional support to the child before, during, and after testimony; (2) assistance in reducing stress and anxiety; and (3) reassurance, to increase a child's sense of safety and security (A. Cunningham & Hurley, 2007b).

In the United States, both federal and state legislation permit the appointment of support persons when the courtroom proceedings involve children. In 2010, President Obama signed a 5-year reauthorization of the Child Abuse Prevention and Treatment Act, requiring all states receiving federal funds for the prevention of child abuse and neglect to provide support persons for children in child welfare cases (McAuliff et al., 2013). Title 18, Section 3509 of the U.S. Code states that "a child testifying at or attending a judicial proceeding shall have the right to be accompanied by an adult attendant to provide emotional support." Note that support persons are different from law guardians, who are appointed in some jurisdictions to protect the child's *legal* interests.

Judges usually have discretion in determining who is qualified to serve as a support person. As pointed out by McAuliff et al. (2013), support persons are very common in cases involving child sexual abuse, physical abuse, or neglect, as well as in cases of adult domestic violence. According to a national survey conducted by McAuliff and his colleagues, the consensus is that support persons decrease the child's stress and increase accuracy and credibility in general, but it was also noted that the magnitude of these effects depended on who provided the support, the age of the child, the nature of the case, and the type of emotional or informational support. It is obvious that this is an area in need of further study.

⊠ Elderly Witnesses

The preponderance of psycholegal research examining the relationship between age and testimony has focused on the eyewitness testimony of children. Research focusing on the elderly and how the public perceives them as eyewitnesses has become more prevalent in recent years, however. It appears that the testimony of older witnesses (ages 65–90) is more likely to be inaccurate compared with younger adult testimony (Aizpurua, Garcia-Bajos, & Migueles, 2009; Holliday et al., 2012; LaVoie, Mertz, & Richmond, 2007). Older adults are more susceptible than young adults to making memory errors, particularly in recollecting details of events (Saunders & Jess, 2010). More than 30 years ago, Yarmey and Kent (1980) noted that older witnesses are more cautious and less confident in their responses than younger adults.

It should be emphasized, however, that older adults vary greatly in how much they are affected by aging (Mueller-Johnson & Ceci, 2007). Some can be highly accurate in their recollection of events and maintain a strong verbal ability throughout the aging process. Interestingly, some research (e.g., Anastasi & Rhodes, 2006) has discovered that older witnesses are much more skillful at identifying faces of their own age than they are at identifying faces of other age-groups. This phenomenon, which is similar to the own-race effect discussed earlier in the chapter, is known as **own-age bias** and awaits further research. Perhaps own-age bias extends to those who are middle-aged or those who are under 30 as well.

In addition, past researchers detected that public perceptions of elderly witnesses often mirrored public perceptions of child witnesses. Yarmey (1984) found that elderly witnesses were commonly stereotyped as intellectually inferior and unable to recall events compared with younger witnesses. Ross et al. (1989) reported that college students found an 8-year-old and a 74-year-old less credible than a 21-year-old with respect to accuracy of memory (a display of own-age bias?). Somewhat more recently, Brimacombe, Quinton, Nance, and Garrioch (1997) reported a similar result, although this study found seniors were perceived by jurors as more honest than younger adults. The young and elderly witnesses were also perceived as more suggestible. The elderly witness was seen as the most honest of all the witnesses, however. Unfortunately, with the exception of the few recent studies cited above, the memory accuracy and perceptions of the elderly witness have been seriously neglected areas of psycholegal study.

✉ Pretrial Identification Methods

The identification of suspects by victims and other witnesses begins as soon after the offense as possible. Police usually obtain verbal descriptions of the perpetrators from witnesses and then show photographs or video clips to obtain a preliminary identification. Occasionally, sketch artists create images—including digital images—based on witness descriptions. In some instances, the police will have witnesses scan photos of individuals with previous records, either to identify the specific offender or to obtain an approximation of the offender's appearance. With modern technology, other identification methods have emerged—for example, witnesses now can view suspects on computers in many jurisdictions. The validity of identification techniques has been addressed by the nation's highest court in a number of early cases (e.g., *Stovall v. Denno*, 1967; *United States v. Wade*, 1967; *Simmons v. United States*, 1968).

In all of these decisions, the U.S. Supreme Court emphasized that pretrial identification methods are susceptible to bias and error. In *United States v. Wade* (1967), the Court ruled that the pretrial lineup was a critical stage in the prosecution, and therefore suspects had a Sixth Amendment right to have counsel present to assure an unbiased procedure. In a later case, however (*Kirby v. Illinois*, 1972), the Court clarified that this right to a lawyer applied to lineups *after* a person had been indicted, not to earlier lineups. In addition, the Court has ruled that convictions can be set aside if an identification procedure is impermissibly suggestive "as to give rise to a very substantial likelihood of irreparable misidentification" (*Simmons v. United States*, 1968, p. 384). Although these cases did provide some constitutional protections for criminal suspects, there remains considerable leeway for law enforcement.

Legal psychologists have long realized that pretrial identification methods are susceptible to a broad spectrum of biases and error, and some have been avidly involved in research in this area. Mistaken identification can be produced by blatant practices or more subtle innuendo. A blatant practice (e.g., placing one black man in a lineup with five white men if a victim described his assailant as a dark-skinned individual) would violate the Constitution. Subtle innuendo (e.g., a barely perceptible nod or sigh of relief when a witness has identified a suspect) may not be considered impermissibly suggestive, but it is less likely to happen if a defense lawyer is present.

In the 1970s, led by Gary Wells and others, psychologists began to examine more closely the psychology of the lineup and its ramifications for the criminal justice system, and this work has continued. Wells (1993) writes, "The function of a lineup is to learn something from the eyewitness's recognition memory that the eyewitness was not able to articulate in verbal recall" (p. 556). Notice that the words *recognition* and *recall* are important components of this description.

In the late 1990s, research in eyewitness identification relevant to pretrial identification was summarized in a document, the *Lineups White Paper* (Wells et al., 1998;

Wells, 2001). The paper included a number of recommendations suggested by the research (see Table 5-2). Shortly thereafter, then–Attorney General Janet Reno commissioned a publication entitled *Eyewitness Evidence: A Guide for Law Enforcement* (referred to as the NIJ Guide). In 2004, the American Bar Association issued its own statement of best practices for eyewitness identification procedures (Clark, 2012), which was patterned after the above.

A minority of states and many local jurisdictions have passed legislation and made changes based on these recommendations. Nevertheless, others use the "tried and supposedly true" methods of the past, perhaps because some of the above recommendations were considered impractical. Demands for reform in the system of pretrial identification procedures has not abated, however. As observed by Clark (2012), four decades of psychological research have demonstrated that the risk of false identifications could be substantially reduced if the criminal justice system were to change its procedures for identifying suspects.

Lineup Procedures and Lineup Research

There are two common types of lineups and photospreads (or computer images), and psychological research has focused on examining the advantages and disadvantages of each. In a **simultaneous lineup**, the eyewitness views everyone in the lineup (commonly six to nine persons) at one time, either live, on videotape, on computer images, or in a photospread. This simultaneous lineup procedure is the one most commonly used by police departments in the United States. A **sequential lineup** is where the eyewitness is presented with one lineup member at a time in sequence. The sequential procedure usually uses computer-assisted photographs or video clips, but in some cases it may be live. This procedure is commonly used in many countries; for instance, it is standard procedure for suspect identification in England and Wales (Horry, Memon, Wright, & Milne, 2012).

Table 5-2 **Lineups White Paper Key Recommendations**

- The person conducting the lineup or photospread should not be aware of the suspect's identity. In addition, the eyewitness should be told that the person conducting the lineup or photospread is blind to the suspect's identity.
- Eyewitnesses should be told that the perpetrator might not be in the lineup. This reduces pressure on the witness to make an identification.
- The suspect should not stand out from the nonsuspects (foils) based on the witness's previous description.
- The witness should provide a clear statement at the time of identification and prior to any feedback from police that could indicate the witness had chosen the "correct" suspect.

At the outset, it is important to note a major difference between these two approaches. The simultaneous lineup approach requires the witness to make a *relative judgment* by comparing lineup members with each other (Schuster, 2007). The sequential lineup, on the other hand, requires the witness to make an *absolute judgment* of one person. Stated another way, the witness must remember what the offender looked like and must decide whether the individual before him is or is not that person.

Wells (1993) noted that, in simultaneous lineups, eyewitnesses are susceptible to **relative judgment error**, a process "in which the eyewitness chooses the lineup member who most resembles the culprit *relative to the other members of the lineup*" (p. 560). This may occur even if the suspect is not actually in the lineup. In other words, the eyewitness selects the person who, out of all the members in the lineup, most closely "looks" like (but does not match exactly) the suspect he or she observed. Therefore, the simultaneous lineup is based on recognition rather than strictly on memory.

In the sequential lineup, the witness does not have the advantage of simultaneous comparisons before identifying a perpetrator. In fact, the sequential lineup was developed primarily to prevent witnesses from making relative judgment error, because experts and police authorities thought the chances of identifying an innocent person would be significantly reduced in a sequential format (Horry, Memon, et al., 2012; Lindsay & Wells, 1985).

Each type of lineup has disadvantages, some of which are shared. In the following sections, we cover these two predominant forms of lineups as well as the many system variables that can influence the correct identification of a suspect. We use the generic term *lineup* to apply to live lineups, photospreads, videoclips, and presentations of computer images.

Simultaneous Lineups

Physical Features of Lineup Members

Since the witness will look for a suspect who fits the description she gave to the police, the physical makeup of the members of the lineup is a crucial factor. The lineup will include the suspect along with others—called **foils**—who are not thought to be responsible for the crime. Individuals being viewed in the lineup should have as many of the relevant characteristics remembered by the witness as possible. Age, height and size, race, hairstyle, and manner of dress—especially if described by the witness—should be approximately the same for all members of the lineup. If the witness remembered the offender as a 6-foot-tall individual with blond, wavy hair and a moustache, the lineup is obviously biased if only one person in six follows that description. Depending upon how the others appear, the lineup could likely be deemed impermissively suggestive if challenged in court. For example, if the other five persons were short, dark-haired, and without facial hair, a defense lawyer would quickly call foul. On the other hand, if the suspect is slightly taller than the others, and most have blond or light-brown hair and generally match the suspect's stature, the lineup is not problematic.

Lineup Size and Composition Bias

A typical lineup comprises five individuals, but there may be more or fewer than this. If too few individuals resemble the suspect, researchers refer to this as **composition bias**.

The earliest research on composition bias occurred in the 1970s (Doob & Kirshenbaum, 1973; Wells, Leippe, & Ostrom, 1979). Building on the work of the first study, Wells et al. developed a concept they call the **functional size** of a lineup. This refers to the number of lineup members who resemble the suspect in physically relevant features, together with the suspect (similar suspects plus one). In a lineup of six, if four members resemble the suspect, the functional size is five. By contrast, **nominal size** refers to the actual number of members within the lineup, which may include some very dissimilar individuals. The nominal size of the above described lineup is six.

In the laboratory, researchers use statistical tests to determine how many members of a lineup have equal probability of being selected on the basis of crucial characteristics. Put another way, they use statistical techniques to determine a lineup's functional size. For a lineup to be considered fair, its functional size should approximate the nominal size, as in the example above. In a six-person lineup, a functional size of just three would reflect composition bias. Obtaining theoretical and statistical indices about composition bias is an interesting academic exercise for researchers, but we also must consider the reality or "ecological validity" of this approach. **Ecological validity** refers to the degree of practical or useful application of a theory or idea to the "real world." In other words, how much real-world applicability does a particular finding have? Law enforcement officials and prosecuting attorneys remind us that there are problems in including lineup members who closely resemble the suspect. First, it is often difficult to find persons (outside of members of the police department) who are willing to participate and who resemble the suspect in salient features. This is particularly a problem for medium-sized city or small-town police departments, where the subject pool is already limited. Second, law enforcement officials worry about the possibility that a high level of similarity between lineup (or photoboard) members may confuse the witnesses and distract from the accurate identification of the primary suspect.

Commitment Bias

When a witness has initially identified a face, even an incorrect one, he or she will likely choose the face again. **Commitment bias** is the tendency to stay with a decision one has previously made. It is especially operative in conditions where witnesses want to please police investigators and also presume that the police have good evidence against someone in the identification proceedings. It should be noted that, though we discuss it as it pertains to simultaneous lineups, it can occur in sequential lineups as well. Because of commitment bias, a witness who initially identifies a suspect, but with some doubts, is more likely to identify the suspect in subsequent exposures with greater conviction. Each subsequent identification promotes greater confidence because of the public and private commitment that "he is the one!" Note that this is similar to witness confidence, which was discussed earlier. In the present situation, the investigator not only encourages commitment but also tries to increase the confidence of the witness.

Thus, in an example provided by Brigham and Cairns (1988), a witness may begin the identification sequence by saying,

"I think maybe he is the one."

The police officer inquires, "Are you sure?"

The witness replies, "Yes, I'm pretty sure."

The police officer inquires further, "Pretty sure?"

The witness affirms, "Yes, I'm sure."

Between the time of this identification procedure and the trial, the witness replays the scene in his mind, thereby strengthening the commitment. This is done repeatedly as the trial date approaches. When the prosecuting attorney asks this key witness during the trial, "Are you sure this is the man?" the answer becomes, "Yes, I'm absolutely positive."

Research has revealed a number of additional aspects about lineups that are important system variables. In reference to the structure of lineups, single-suspect lineups appear to be superior to all-suspect lineups (Wells, 1993). A **single-suspect lineup** is where there is one suspect, and the other lineup members are known innocents serving as fillers, essentially foils. An **all-suspect lineup**, on the other hand, is where there are no fillers who are known to be innocent. All members in the lineup observed by the witness are potential suspects. Wells (1993) points out that a false identification is much more probable in the all-suspect lineup than in the single-suspect lineup. This is because there is no opportunity for the all-suspect approach to reveal eyewitness error, whereas the single-suspect lineup has a known-error category. In other words, the fillers represent obvious errors in the single-suspect lineup, but, because there are no known fillers in the all-suspect lineup, errors in that situation are not identifiable.

Wells (1984) also introduced the topic of the blank lineup, which received little attention until recently (M. A. Palmer, Brewer, & Weber, 2012). A **blank lineup** comprises only innocent members; it is shown to witnesses before they view a lineup that contains a suspect. The blank lineup is used primarily as a screening tool. If the eyewitness identifies someone from the blank lineup, then the police know that the eyewitness is highly susceptible to identification error during a lineup that contains the suspect. This was confirmed in the study by M. A. Palmer et al. Witnesses who made false identifications in those lineups without the suspect during a screening evaluation were also poor at identifying the "true" suspect in regular lineups. Although blank lineups would appear to be a highly effective way of avoiding misidentification, it is unlikely that they are widely used. Lineup procedures that make sense in the research laboratory may be perceived as impractical at the police station, as we mentioned above in referring to ecological validity. Table 5-3 provides a summary of the key terms and concepts associated with lineups.

Pre-lineup instructions are also important. This includes explaining to the witness that the suspect may or may not be present in the lineup. Related to this issue is the "blind" administrator procedure. A blind administrator is one who is conducting the lineup with the witness and who does not know which member of the lineup is the suspect. Sometimes this procedure is called the **double-blind lineup** because both the witness and the administrator do not know if the suspect is even in the lineup. Many believe that the inclusion of blind administrators reduces the chances of leading the witness into commitment bias and other problems of suspect identification. Recall that these methods were recommended in the NIJ Guide discussed above (see Table 5-2).

Sequential Lineups

As described earlier, in a sequential lineup, the witness views one person or image after another, not at the same time. Typically, the eyewitness must decide for each

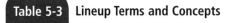

Table 5-3   **Lineup Terms and Concepts**

All-suspect lineup. One in which every person is a suspect

Blank lineup. One that does not contain the suspect

Blind administrator. Refers to the person conducting the lineup, who is unaware of the identity of the suspect or even if the suspect is in the lineup

Composition bias. Term used when too few individuals resemble the suspect in a lineup

Double-blind lineup. A lineup in which neither the administrator nor the witness is aware of whether the suspect is a member

Foil. Term for any person in the lineup who is not a suspect

Functional size. The number of individuals in the lineup who resemble the suspect, plus the suspect

Nominal size. The actual number of individuals in the lineup

Sequential lineup. Occurs when witnesses view members of a lineup, including a suspect, one at a time

Simultaneous lineup. Occurs when all members of a lineup are viewed at the same time

Single-suspect lineup. One in which only one person is the suspect; all others are foils

person whether he or she is the offender prior to being allowed to see the next person (Wells et al., 2000). A considerable amount of research conducted over the past 20 years suggests that the sequential procedure is superior in many ways compared with the simultaneous approach (Steblay, Dysart, Fulero, & Lindsay, 2001; Steblay, Dysart, & Wells, 2011).

According to Steblay, Dysart, et al. (2011), one effective way to measure lineup superiority is through a method called diagnosticity. **Diagnosticity** refers to the ratio of identifications of the suspect to identifications of innocent people. The higher the diagnosticity ratio, the stronger the evidence for superiority of the lineup method because it results in more identifications of the suspected offender and fewer errors (e.g., choosing the wrong person) (Steblay, Dysart, et al., 2011). Based on extensive review of the research literature on lineups, Steblay, Dysart, et al. (2011) conclude, "The data indicate that the sequential procedure is a more rigorous test, a higher standard, and when the witness identifies the suspects, the results can be better trusted" (p. 129). But why? It must be emphasized that there are still mistaken identifications with the sequential lineup, but the number of mistakes appears to be lower than those found for the simultaneous lineups.

The sequential lineup was first introduced in the research literature by Lindsay and Wells (1985). Over the years, the sequential lineup has gone through several modifications. For example, although witnesses originally were able to go through the lineup more than once, the recommended sequential lineup protocol today is that the witness proceeds through the sequence only once (Steblay, Dietrich, Ryan, Raczynski, & James, 2011). Unfortunately, some jurisdictions in North America that have adopted sequential lineups allow multiple laps through the sequence (Horry, Palmer, et al., 2012). This tactic potentially increases the chances for unsure or confused witnesses to identify innocent persons as offenders. For example, if they do not identify someone the first time around, they may feel pressure to do so the second or third time. Interestingly, in England, the witness is *expected* to go through the sequence twice (Horry, Memon, et al., 2012). Each lineup member is seen for about 15 seconds on a video clip. The witness must see the entire lineup—usually about nine members—twice before being asked to make a decision. However, the witness also can view the entire lineup or part of it again if he or she wishes. Horry and her colleagues discovered that witnesses who requested at least one additional viewing were 2.5 times more likely to select innocent persons as the culprit, compared with witnesses who did not request additional laps. They write, "We found clear evidence that repeated viewing of lineups increases guessing rates, which places innocent suspects at risk" (p. 264). A very similar finding was reported by Steblay, Dietrich, et al. (2011).

In some conditions, the eyewitness does not know how many photos will be shown, a procedure known as "backloading" the lineup. The witness must make a decision for each lineup member before moving on to the next and is not allowed to return to a previously rejected lineup member (Horry, Memon, et al., 2012). Horry and her colleagues (Horry, Palmer, & Brewer, 2012) found that backloading encourages witnesses to adopt a more conservative and careful approach to their decision making. They also conclude that it is essential that the witness does not know how many lineup members are to be seen. In their study, those witnesses who knew how many members were in the lineup were more willing to choose as they were nearing the end of the sequence—right or wrong.

Show-Ups

Still another, and very controversial, identification procedure is the **show-up**. "A show-up is an identification procedure in which police present a single suspect to the eyewitness(es) to see if the eyewitness(es) will identify that person as the perpetrator" (Wells, 2001, p. 795). Unlike the lineup, there are no fillers in a show-up procedure. A show-up is legal in the United States as long as it occurs soon after the offense (within hours) or under circumstances that would make a lineup impractical or impossible. Thus, police can drive a witness through a neighborhood immediately after a crime, point out a person, and ask, "Is that the guy?" Impractical circumstances are illustrated by *Stovall v. Denno* (1967), where the victim was hospitalized and in danger of dying and police brought the suspect to the victim's bedside. The U.S. Supreme Court ruled that even though some time had passed since the crime occurred, the show-up procedure was permissible because it was unlikely that the victim would have lived long enough to identify his attacker.

Psychological research clearly demonstrates that show-ups are inferior to both simultaneous and sequential lineups in terms of avoiding mistaken identification (Wells, 2001). This is not because the show-up makes witnesses more willing to identify someone. Rather, it is because, in a lineup, the error of mistakenly identifying a suspect is spread out among the foils. In the show-up situation, there is only one choice, right or wrong, and the witness knows he will be seeing only one person. Despite the limitations of the show-up, the procedure does present a practical dilemma, "pitting the suggestiveness of the procedure against the need to free innocent persons quickly and the need for public safety" (Wells, 2001, p. 796). This is little comfort to legal scholars concerned about civil liberties, however, particularly because there is little research indicating how often innocent persons are freed as the result of a show-up.

SUMMARY AND CONCLUSIONS

Eyewitness information has been, is, and will continue to be a principal source of evidence in both criminal and civil case law. However, eyewitness evidence obtained through traditional procedures of questioning and testimony is replete with potential inaccuracies and misconceptions. Even if a witness is sure of what he or she saw, that certainty may not be accurate. Human perception and memory are like unexplored labyrinths where original input becomes altered, partially lost, and transformed into an arrangement that fits our expectancies, experiences, and sometimes the disguised needs of others.

A rich store of experimental psychology addresses topics relevant to eyewitness testimony. Legal psychologists have used this foundation and have studied eyewitness research even more directly with their work in children's testimony, pretrial identification methods, and effective interviewing, among other topics. This research is often organized under the twin umbrellas of estimator and system variables. Estimator variables are specific to the individual witness and are out of the control of the legal system. They include but are not limited to age, stress levels, the significance of the event to the witness, own-race bias, and time factors such as the duration of an event. System variables come into play after an event has occurred; they can be influenced or manipulated by agents of the legal system. They include, but again are not limited to, misinformation effects, interviewing techniques, and a host of pretrial identification procedures that can influence the information provided by witnesses.

The expanding research evidence suggests that the legal system should carefully examine some of its assumptions about eyewitnesses and perhaps even entertain some small but critical changes in procedures. Despite some concerns about child testimony, a rapidly growing body of research evidence supports its accuracy, particularly on direct examination and when not influenced by leading questions. While the research indicates that children generally recall less detail about an event than adults, what they do remember is reliable. The age of the child, however, is an important variable. For example, children under 3 years of age provide less accurate information than older children, but it is not necessarily inaccurate. Likewise, the eyewitness testimony of older adults is often regarded with suspicion, but older adults vary in their accuracy, and it should not be assumed that they are unable to provide valid information. Researchers have offered numerous suggestions for improving the accuracy of eyewitnesses and diminishing the likelihood that mistaken identification will occur.

Pretrial identification procedures (e.g., lineups, photospreads, and show-ups) have been the subject of extensive research. Early findings resulted in recommendations to law enforcement, which were implemented to varying degrees in both federal and state jurisdictions. Some rejected these recommendations as impractical, however. Research strongly indicates that sequential lineups are more effective than simultaneous lineups in correctly identifying a perpetrator. When simultaneous lineups are used, however, it is recommended that the lineup administrator be blind to the identity of the suspect. Because of the potential for lineup procedures to produce false identification, this is an area of legal psychology that requires continuing attention.

KEY CONCEPTS

Acquisition

All-suspect lineup

Blank lineup

Categorization

Categorization-individual
  model

Cognitive interview (CI)

Commitment bias

Composition bias

Cue utilization theory

Diagnosticity

Differential experience
  hypothesis

Double-blind lineup

Ecological validity

Estimator variables

Foils

Functional size

Individuation

Misinformation effect

Moderating variable

Nominal size

Nonchoosers

Own-age bias

Own-race bias

Perceptions

Post-identification
  feedback effect

Reality monitoring

Reconstructive
  theory of memory

Relative judgment error

Retention

Retrieval

Sequential lineup

Show-up

Simulation studies

Simultaneous lineup

Single-suspect lineup

Support person

System variables

Weapon focus

The Trial Jury

The jury is a unique institution: It requires ordinary citizens who lack legal training to hear evidence, make sense of conflicting facts, and apply legal rules to reach a verdict about which all (or sometimes most) jurors can agree.

—Bornstein & Greene, 2011, p. 63

The trial jury is one of the most powerful components in the American system of justice, with authority to take away freedoms and autonomy from those accused of crime, bestow them, or settle disputes and impose financial liability. It is one of the few channels through which ordinary citizens can impose on society their own standards or biases concerning what is morally or socially right and wrong behavior. Although trial judges have the power to set aside a jury's guilty verdict or to reduce the monetary awards it imposes, rarely will they do so, and almost never in criminal cases. The jury's responsibility is sobering, therefore, and there is good evidence that jurors take their role in the judicial process seriously and try to make the best decision in the case before them. In fact, citizens who participate as jurors tend to come away with more favorable impressions of the legal system (M. R. Rose, Diamond, & Musick, 2012). Juries draw considerable interest from psychologists because they provide important and relevant information on how individuals perceive, interpret, understand, and remember legal evidence, and how people come to a consensus with others (Bornstein & Greene, 2011).

By the end of 2011, at least 1,500 published jury studies were available (Devine, 2012b). Two thirds of these were mock jury experiments, and the remaining one third involved research with actual trial juries. Of the studies based on actual trials, about one half involved archival data from court records, and the remainder were from surveys gathered from jurors following the trial and verdict (Devine, 2012b). Because ongoing jury deliberations are cloaked in secrecy, rarely do researchers see or hear them. Notable exceptions are the classic Chicago Jury Project (Kalven & Zeisel, 1966), which will be cited occasionally in this chapter and the next, and an occasional documentary, such as "Inside the Jury Room"—a *Frontline* report of a jury deliberating a nonviolent criminal case.

The trial jury—also called the petit jury—is the jury that considers evidence and the arguments made by attorneys and decides on a verdict in both criminal and civil cases. It is different from the *grand* jury (mentioned in Chapter 2), which is a body of citizens that determines whether there is enough evidence to prosecute an individual. Grand juries are used chiefly in the federal system, less so in the states. While all states have provisions for grand juries, only 22 states require their use (Brenner & Shaw, 2003). It should be noted that the federal grand jury is considered the most powerful investigative agency in the United States (Beal & Felman, 2011). Grand juries return an indictment (defined in Chapter 2) if they believe the evidence presented to them by the prosecutor against an accused individual is sufficient to go ahead with prosecution. Composed of as many as 23 people, grand juries almost invariably agree with the prosecutor that the evidence is sufficient. Grand jurors usually are convened for months at a time and hear a multitude of cases presented by prosecutors during their service. It must be emphasized that indictment by a grand jury is not a finding of guilt and is only the first step in what may be a long legal process.

This chapter focuses on the trial jury, including how jurors are chosen, what procedures must be followed to select them, and how the jury functions once its members are impaneled. The chapter will also cover jury size, the number of votes needed to reach a decision, and how these might affect jury deliberations. We also discuss juror comprehension, including that of instructions given to them by the presiding judge. Two special topics will be juries in death penalty trials and the controversial subject of jury nullification. The psychological processes related to how jurors and judges arrive at their decisions are covered in Chapter 7.

⬚ Overview of the Jury

In addition to the critical right to an attorney in all criminal prosecutions, the Sixth Amendment of the U.S. Constitution guarantees the right to a jury trial in criminal cases whenever the potential penalty for the offense is greater than 6 months' imprisonment or a $500 fine. The amendment, which applies to states as well as to the federal government, also guarantees that the accused shall have the right to a speedy public trial by an impartial jury from the jurisdiction where the alleged crime was committed. This right to a jury covers adults as well as juveniles tried in criminal courts. However, youths charged with crimes in juvenile or family courts have no constitutional right to a jury trial (*McKeiver v. Pennsylvania*, 1971).

The Seventh Amendment guarantees a jury in all federal *civil* cases where the damages are believed to be above a certain amount, usually $500. In civil cases, states have more leeway because the U.S. Supreme Court has not applied that amendment to the states. Some states grant no jury trials in civil cases at all, while others do in just a handful (Abraham, 1998). In both criminal and civil cases, defendants may waive the right to a trial by jury and take their chances with a judge, who serves as both a fact finder and a determiner of the issues of law. A trial by a judge rather than a jury is called a *bench trial* (noted in Chapter 2).

Despite these important and lofty constitutional guarantees, participants in the judicial process are under social, political, and economic pressure to settle a case before it gets to the trial stage. Trials, especially by jury, are time-consuming, expensive, and unpredictable, and their unpredictability often prompts even the most experienced attorneys to persuade their clients to avoid them if possible. Thus, each case must be subjected to a filtering process, replete with discretionary maneuvers that may include plea bargaining, dismissal of charges by the prosecutor or the court, or a mutually agreeable settlement by the parties in a civil suit. In jurisdictions where courts are especially overburdened, participants are encouraged to pursue alternative dispute resolution, or mediation, before approaching the court. As we noted in Chapter 2, the majority of criminal cases that are not dismissed are disposed of through plea bargaining or plea negotiation, a procedure in which the defendant pleads guilty to lesser or fewer charges, usually in exchange for a lighter sentence.

In federal courts and death penalty states, defendants may plead guilty to avoid the death sentence. In July 2013, Ariel Castro, the man accused of kidnapping three young women in Ohio, holding them captive for almost a decade, sexually and physically abusing them, and inducing at least one miscarriage by beating one victim while she was pregnant, pleaded guilty to nearly 1,000 criminal charges. By doing so, Castro avoided the possibility that prosecutors might seek the death penalty in his case. In addition, prosecutors avoided the spectacle of a lengthy trial and spared the victims of having to testify. Castro received a sentence of life without parole plus 1,000 years, guaranteeing that he would never be released from prison. However, he hanged himself with bed-sheets in his cell soon after his sentencing.

Most civil cases today also are settled or dismissed before they take the tedious journey through the entire judicial process. An estimated 75% of all civil cases are settled between the time a complaint is filed and the trial date (Abadinsky, 1995). (See Table 6-1 for some statistics on jury trials in both federal and state courts.)

Interestingly, Mize, Hannaford-Agor, and Waters (2007) report that courts across the country have increasing problems with citizens who fail to return the questionnaire mailed to prospective jurors or fail to appear for jury duty when summoned. About one fifth of all courts in their survey said that nonresponse and failure-to-appear rates are 15% or higher. Although many courts send a second qualification questionnaire or summons, there are still a significant number of citizens who fail to comply. Enforcement of jury duty is variable, with some jurisdictions preferring not to expend resources in this matter if enough jurors are eventually impaneled.

Table 6-1	Jury Trials by Numbers and Percentages
150,000	Estimated number of jury trials per year in state courts
6,000	Estimated number of jury trials per year in federal courts
50%	Percentage of *federal* criminal and civil trials in which juries are used
10%	Percentage of cases in which juries are used in *state* courts
31.8 million	Number of jury summonses issued by state courts per year
1.5 million	Number of people impaneled for jury service per year
37.6%	Percentage of Americans likely to serve as jurors in state courts over their lifetime

Sources: Litras & Golmant (2006); Mize, Hannaford-Agor, & Waters (2007); Vago (2000).

It is important to note that there has been a significant trend away from jury and bench trials in both U.S. federal and state courts over the past three decades (American College of Trial Lawyers, 2004; Higginbotham, 2010). In an extensive study, legal scholar Marc Galanter (2004) found a 60% drop in the number of trials (both federal and state) since the mid-1980s. This trend happened despite a substantial increase in complicated litigation at all levels. For example, between 1993 and 2003, the total number of felony jury trials and bench trials in state courts declined by 22% and 56%, respectively, even though the number of arrests increased or remained the same during that 10-year period in the majority of jurisdictions (C. G. Lee, 2005). In civil cases, state courts disposed of approximately 27,000 cases—tort, contract, and real property—through a jury or bench trial in 2005 (Langton & Cohen, 2008; see Table 6-2). However, there were 7.4 million civil claims *filed* in the state courts that same year.

It is no different in federal courts. There, too, far more cases are filed than go to trial. Judge Patrick E. Higginbotham (2010), senior judge of the U.S. Court of Appeals for the Fifth Circuit, finds that "federal trial courts are now more like administrative agencies than trial courts in their present efforts to discharge their duty to decide cases or controversies" (p. 747). He has witnessed a significant move toward "paper courts" in the federal court system in contrast to persons appearing in open court. Paper court is the term loosely used when a case is disposed of by means of paperwork submitted by the respective attorneys and sometimes by individuals on their own initiative. As trials have declined, private arbitrations and plea bargains have grown sharply (Higginbotham, 2010). Galanter (2004) identified a significant trend toward paper courts in state courts as well.

When cases do go to trial, defendants prefer juries to judges, at least in state courts, and most particularly for criminal cases, perhaps because there is a strong tradition in favor of being judged by a jury of one's peers when one is prosecuted for a criminal offense. However, juries seem to be preferred in civil cases as well, the exception being those that involve business interests. This could be because the litigation revolves around issues that are believed to be too complicated for the average juror to comprehend (e.g., engineering patents, complex scientific data, or trade secrets). According to Forsterlee, Horowitz, and Bourgeous (1993), "in general, jurors in civil trials are required to interconnect and recall more evidentiary elements, combine these elements in different ways, and render more decisions than their criminal jury counterparts" (p. 14). Langton and Cohen (2008) found that judges were more likely than juries to hear contract and real property cases, for example. Employment discrimination cases were more likely to be heard by juries. However, 9 out of 10 tort trials (which try civil wrongs) were resolved by juries rather than judges. Examples of tort trial topics are medical malpractice, personal injury, or damaged property. (See Table 6-2 for more information on the types of civil cases heard in state courts.)

Table 6-2 **Civil Trials in State Courts, by Case Type, 2005**

Case Type	Number	Percentage of Total Trials*
All cases	26,948	100
Tort cases	16,397	60.8
Motor vehicle	9,431	35.0
Medical malpractice	2,449	9.1
Premises liability	1,863	6.9
Intentional tort	725	2.7
Other or unknown tort	664	2.5
Conversion	378	1.4
Product liability	354	1.3
Asbestos	87	0.3
Other	268	1.0
Slander/libel	187	0.7
Professional malpractice	150	0.6
Animal attack	138	0.5
False arrest, imprisonment	58	0.2

(Continued)

Table 6-2 (Continued)		
Case Type	**Number**	**Percentage of Total Trials***
Contract cases	8,917	33.1
Seller plaintiff	2,883	10.7
Buyer plaintiff	2,591	9.6
Fraud	1,114	4.1
Rental/lease	605	2.2
Other employment dispute	558	2.1
Employment discrimination	319	1.2
Mortgage foreclosure	249	0.9
Other or unknown contract	245	0.9
Tortious interference	152	0.6
Partnership dispute	119	0.4
Subrogation	82	0.3
Real property cases	1,633	6.1
Title or boundary dispute	963	3.6
Eminent domain	542	2.0
Other or unknown real property	129	0.5

Source: Langton, L., & Cohen, T. H. (2008).

*Detail may not sum to 100% because of rounding.

More often than not, however, civil cases—like criminal cases—are settled before the trial stage. Interestingly, when cases do go to trial and juries are involved, "in a non-negligible number of cases [they] render distinctively harsh antidefendant judgments and set dramatically large awards. Virtually all of these extreme verdicts are substantially reduced or reversed by appellate courts" (Hastie, Schkade, & Payne, 1998, p. 288).

The ongoing case of the Deepwater Horizon oil rig disaster in the Gulf of Mexico on April 20, 2010, is illustrative of the complexity often found in those civil cases that receive national attention. Numerous civil claims for economic, property, and medical damages have been filed against BP, the company that owned the rig. In February 2013, a civil bench trial began in New Orleans. Although a multibillion-dollar settlement was reached soon after that, the settlement agreement itself is being challenged on appeal. Earlier, in November 2012, criminal charges against BP were resolved, with the company pleading guilty to a variety of offenses and agreeing to pay $4 billion in fines and toward research and cleanup efforts. Most recently (July 2013), Halliburton, the oil distribution corporation that worked closely with BP, admitted to criminal charges that it had covered up or destroyed evidence in the oil spill case.

Perhaps because of the enormous complexity and ambiguity inherent in some civil cases, very little psychological research attention has been directed at how jurors interpret, comprehend, and apply instructions in those cases and how they arrive at their decisions. On the other hand, those civil cases that are relatively straightforward do not attract much research attention either. Almost all the available research on jury comprehension and decision making has been directed at criminal cases.

✖ Jury Research

Social and behavioral science research on the jury has moved through a number of discernible stages, beginning in the late 1970s when jury research concentrated on the effects of jury size and on whether the jury decision must be unanimous or majority rule (Devine, Clayton, Dunford, Seying, & Pryce, 2001). In the 1980s and 1990s, jury research focused on the characteristics of jurors, jury selection, and the effects of various court procedures on jury decision making. Almost all of the foregoing research was conducted with mock jurors and is called jury simulation research. Jury simulation research refers to an experimental method used to investigate the behavior and psychological processes of individuals in small-group settings that imitate actual jury situations. Some simulation studies also recruit participants from persons who were eligible for jury duty but were not needed. (See Box 6-1 for an illustration of a recently published jury simulation study of this type.)

Scholarly reactions to early work on mock juries were not favorable. In one particularly critical article, the simulation studies were faulted on several fronts:

> It is argued that much jury simulation research, especially that involving investigation of the effects of defendant character on juror-jury decisions, can be fairly described as marked by (a) legal naivete, (b) sloppy scholarship, and (c) overgeneralization combined with inappropriate value judgments. (Vidmar, 1979, p. 96)

Too many researchers, Vidmar maintained, placed mock jurors in situations they would not realistically encounter, such as placing a short time limit on the deliberation process or having them determine the number of years an offender should serve in prison. A common methodology was to present mock jurors with brief, written case materials and have them decide an outcome, with or without some deliberation with other "jurors." Other researchers incorrectly cited earlier studies or were too confident that their findings could be generalized to the judicial system as it actually operates. The use of college students as research participants was also criticized.

BOX 6-1 RESEARCHERS AT WORK

Can Jurors Understand DNA Evidence?

Scientific research has always been relevant to many criminal and civil cases, but in the late 20th and into the 21st century, such research has exploded. Today's average juror may possess some education beyond high school—though this is not certain—but this does not mean he or she has been exposed to scientific data. DNA evidence is one example of scientific information that is increasingly relevant in both criminal and civil cases due to the expansion and sophistication of this technology.

A team of researchers (Hans, Kaye, Dann, Farley, & Albertson, 2011) was interested in learning whether jurors understood one form of DNA evidence—mitochondrial DNA (mtDNA)—and could apply it properly in deciding a criminal case. They chose mtDNA because it was a relatively novel type of evidence that had just begun to be used in criminal cases. As they noted, "a case using mtDNA as forensic evidence provided an opportunity to observe how jurors confronted a new scientific topic and what personal and other factors were associated with better understanding of the evidence" (p. 62).

Hans and her fellow researchers (2011) conducted a jury simulation study to investigate these questions. They showed a videotaped mock trial to 480 people (60 mock juries composed of 8 people each). The participants were people who had been summoned for jury duty but had not been needed and who volunteered for the experiment. The videotaped trial was an hour long and was based on an actual case in which the mtDNA evidence was offered by the prosecution. Before watching the video, the participants completed questionnaires measuring their attitudes toward expert testimony as well as toward science. After watching the video, they were given additional questionnaires and then were allowed to deliberate as a group until they reached a unanimous verdict or declared they were hung (could not agree). The average deliberation time was 39 minutes.

Results indicated that jurors as a group had good comprehension of the evidence, but there were also group differences. Not surprisingly, jurors with higher education and with more math and science courses in their background were better able to comprehend the evidence. Jurors who had suspicions or reservations about science, or who were concerned that mtDNA evidence could be contaminated, were less likely to comprehend the evidence. Group deliberations had little effect on the final verdict.

In concluding, Hans et al. (2011) noted that fears that jurors as a group could not comprehend such evidence were for the most part unwarranted. However, in cases involving complex scientific evidence, jurors might benefit from short tutorials of basic scientific concepts prior to the beginning of a trial. It was somewhat surprising to the researchers that the group deliberation process did not affect the outcome significantly. As is typical in scientific research, Hans et al. recommended further study of the impact of jury deliberation.

Questions for Discussion:

1. What are the advantages and disadvantages of simulation research relating to juries? Does the methodology used in this study allay possible concerns about disadvantages?

2. Do the findings of this study give you more or less confidence in the jury system, specifically the ability of jurors to comprehend scientific evidence?

Conducting research with actual jurors is often impractical, and other scholars have been more sympathetic to simulation research. After an extensive review of research using mock juries, Bornstein (1999) concluded that unrealistic methodology was not a major concern. The decision-making processes studied could be generalized to the decision making of real jurors. He also noted that researchers have not found differences between student and nonstudent mock juror samples. Other researchers, including some more recently, also have been favorably disposed to simulation studies using mock jurors (Diamond, 1997; Pezdek, Avilia-Mora, & Sperry, 2010; Wiener, Krauss, & Lieberman, 2011). These scholars have emphasized that studies in a second generation of research were more ecologically valid—that is, more realistic—and more method-ologically sophisticated (Diamond, 1997). Nevertheless, Diamond urged her fellow researchers to carefully analyze actual trials and not give up on efforts to conduct research with actual jurors.

In the early years of the 21st century, the next jury research phase has yet to be identified, although many studies are now being published on how jurors appraise certain evidence (e.g., expert testimony or scientific evidence), and there are many calls for more study of the deliberation process. Interestingly, Devine and his associates (2001) predicted that research with actual juries would be the new zeitgeist, but this has not yet come to pass on a widespread basis, and simulation research continues at a steady pace (Nuñez, McCrea, & Culhane, 2011; Wiener et al., 2011). One example of research with actual jurors is the Capital Jury Project, an ongoing research study of capital jury decision making (See Box 6-2 later in the chapter). Another is the Arizona Jury Reform study, which examines the impact of a jury reform measure allowing jurors to discuss the evidence among themselves while the trial is still in progress, a practice not usually permitted. Devine et al. (2001) note that the results of these projects may well change the thinking about jury procedures and process in the near future. Indeed, the results of the Capital Jury Project, which was begun in 1991, encouraged scholars across the United States to undertake similar studies (Blume, 2008).

Jury Selection

The U.S. Constitution says very little about the composition of juries other than that they must be impartial and drawn from the local geographical district where the alleged crime was committed. In interpreting the Constitution, however, the U.S. Supreme Court has issued a number of rulings relative to size and composition of juries. Jury size is a fascinating issue. In the 2013 Florida trial of George Zimmerman, only six jurors decided Zimmerman's fate. Although this small number was a surprise to many interested observers, the Supreme Court had ruled that six jurors are sufficient, even in a felony case, unless the defendant is charged with a capital crime (*Williams v. Florida*, 1970). A six-person jury must deliver a unanimous verdict, however (*Burch v. Louisiana*, 1979). (See Table 6-3 for a representative list of jury procedure cases decided by the U.S. Supreme Court.) Even though it is permissible to have six jurors, very few states allow that small a number to decide a felony case. Twelve remains the typical number for that purpose. Interestingly, the military justice system has its own

Table 6-3 Representative U.S. Supreme Court Cases on Jury Procedures

Case Name	Year	Holding/Significance
Swain v. Alabama	1965	Peremptory challenges to potential jurors are allowed.
Witherspoon v. Illinois	1968	Jurors philosophically opposed to death penalty can be removed from jury only if they make it unmistakably clear that they could not vote to convict and/or sentence defendant to death.
Williams v. Florida	1970	Allowing only six jurors in felony cases does not violate the Constitution.
McKeiver v. Pennsylvania	1971	Juveniles in juvenile court do not have a constitutional right to a jury.
Ballew v. Georgia	1978	Five-person juries in criminal cases do violate the Constitution.
Burch v. Louisiana	1979	In six-person juries, decision must be unanimous.
Wainwright v. Witt	1985	In a death penalty case, judge may remove a juror for cause, even if juror states he or she could vote to convict and/or sentence to death.
Batson v. Kentucky	1986	Prosecutors may not exercise peremptory challenges on the basis of prospective juror's race.
Georgia v. McCollum	1992	Defense lawyers may not exercise peremptory challenges on the basis of race.
J.E.B. v. Alabama	1994	Peremptory challenges may not be exercised on the basis of a potential juror's gender.
Lowenfield v. Phelps	1988	Dynamite charge is not necessarily coercive.
Penry v. Lynaugh	1989	Mitigating as well as aggravating factors must be taken into account by jurors in death sentencing.
Ring v. Arizona	2002	Jurors, not judges, must make the finding of aggravating factors.

procedural rules. In August 2013, a military jury of 13 high-ranking officials decided the fate of Army psychiatrist Nidal Malik Hasan, who was charged with murders and attempted murders of soldiers and civilians at Fort Hood, a military post near Killeen, Texas. Hasan was convicted and sentenced to death on August 28, 2013.

State and federal laws also stipulate specific procedures that must be followed and practices that must be avoided in order to assure that proper juries are constituted (Levine, 2002). These laws outline three guiding principles that govern the procedures for jury selection: (1) All citizens are expected to serve on juries if called, unless they are exempted by statute or excused; (2) the jury pool must represent a cross section of the community; and (3) biased jurors who might decide cases unfairly or with prejudice must be excluded.

The Venire and Voir Dire

Jury composition is influenced at two stages of selection, venire and voir dire. In the first stage, a pool of prospective jurors is drawn from an eligible population presumed to be representative of a local geographical area. The pool of potential jurors is called the venire. Courts have consistently ruled that jury *pools* must represent a cross section of the community or general population. However, "neither by law nor by the terms of the Constitution does a jury need to be a *microcosm* of the larger community. Systematic exclusion is forbidden, but proportional representation is not required" (Abraham, 1998, p. 122, emphasis added). Thus, the fact that one third of a community is Hispanic does not mean that one third of the jury pool nor one third of the jury itself must be.

Usually, prospective jurors are drawn from voting lists or driver's license lists representing that local geographical area. Theoretically, anyone of voting age can be expected to be called for jury duty unless he or she has served for more than a year in prison and has not been pardoned for the offense. Even when the selection process affords random representation, however, it has traditionally not been difficult to be excused from jury duty, although this cannot be said of all jurisdictions. In addition, in some states certain occupations are automatically excluded (e.g., attorneys or physicians). In most states, members of some occupational groups (e.g., teachers, police officers, firefighters) can get excused quite easily at their request. Other persons are excused from jury pools after presenting affidavits from their supervisors attesting to their indispensability or from physicians attesting to their health problems.

The names of persons in the venire appear on a list of potential jurors for a given period, and they are then eligible to be called to serve on a specific case. When this occurs, they move on to the next stage of jury selection, the voir dire. The goal of voir dire is to determine whether individuals of the venire are qualified to serve as jurors in a particular case. The voir dire is a presumptively open proceeding that allows the judge and attorneys to question the prospective jurors and possibly disqualify them from jury duty. Four states—Connecticut, North Carolina, Texas, and Wyoming—stipulate that the voir dire be entirely conducted by the attorneys (Kovera, 2013). In other states, both judges and attorneys engage in the voir dire process.

Voir dire serves three primary purposes. It helps to identify (1) who is eligible to serve based on legal requirements; (2) whether the prospective juror is able to evaluate the information provided during the trial in an impartial manner; and (3) whether the prospective juror can render a verdict based on the trial evidence, rather than on some nonlegal factors (Lieberman & Sales, 2007).

As noted by Lieberman and Sales (2007), many—perhaps most—attorneys place great importance on the voir dire process. During voir dire, attorneys can apply their own hypotheses about people in an attempt to generate the jury that will be most sympathetic to their client. These hypotheses or beliefs may come from the attorney's own experiences, lessons learned from other attorneys, or recommendations in trial tactics manuals (Lieberman, 2011). Alternatively, the attorney may hire psychological *trial consultants* (see discussion of trial consultation in Chapter 2) to help identify jurors who are most likely "to be sympathetic, hostile, or impartial to the parties involved in the case" (Lieberman, 2011, p. 49). It is at this juncture that "commonsense psychology" as espoused by attorneys, as well as findings from the research, are likely to be applied. Attorneys may also use the voir dire process to educate jurors about the central issues of the case, especially those that focus on legal questions (Lieberman & Sales, 2007). However, lawyers also use voir dire to gather information and to indoctrinate or ingratiate themselves with jurors (Blunk & Sales, 1977). This strategy to influence the jury is referred to as the "didactic purpose" of the voir dire. There is some evidence that a large proportion of the time spent in voir dire by lawyers is used to persuade the jury panel to be sympathetic to the lawyer or to the lawyer's clients (Lieberman & Sales, 2007). For example, during voir dire, "Attorneys may be excessively courteous to the panel members, use humor, express polite concern for the health of older panel members, or try to make known that they have similarities of one sort or another with jurors" (Lieberman & Sales, 2007, p. 27).

Allowable Challenges During Voir Dire

The prosecution and the defense (in civil cases, the plaintiff and the defendant) each have two options for challenging the impanelment of a prospective juror: peremptory challenges and challenges for cause. The **peremptory challenge** option lets a lawyer request the removal of a prospective juror without giving a reason. For example, the prosecuting attorney may consider a potential juror to be too analytical or too distractible. The defense attorney may simply have a hunch—based on many years' experience—that a person may not be sympathetic to her client.

> The essential nature of the peremptory challenge is that it is one exercised without a reason stated, without inquiry and without the court's control. The peremptory permits rejection for a real or imagined practicality that is less easily designated or demonstrable. (*Swain v. Alabama*, 1965, p. 220)

There are limitations on the exercise of peremptory challenges, however. The number of peremptory challenges allowed an attorney is restricted by statute or by the presiding judge, who sets the rule in a pretrial conference. In some jurisdictions, peremptories are not allowed at all, and in some the defense in a criminal trial may be allowed more peremptory challenges than the prosecution. In federal criminal trials, where the final jury size is 12, the prosecution has 6 peremptories and the defense has 10. In capital cases, each side is usually allowed 20 challenges. On the other hand, in a federal civil trial where the jury size is 6, each side has 3 peremptories. Trial judges may allow more peremptory challenges if they believe the situation warrants it. For example, when pretrial publicity is acute and extensive, judges may provide more leeway for the attorneys to play their hunches. The defense in a criminal trial is often allowed extra peremptories because it is recognized that defendants are at risk of losing their freedom in light of the awesome power of government.

The U.S. Supreme Court also has weighed in further on the issue of peremptory challenges, ruling that they may not be exercised on the basis of race (*Batson v. Kentucky,* 1986, and *Georgia v. McCollum,* 1992) or gender (*J.E.B. v. Alabama,* 1994). That is, an attorney may not remove a potential juror because she is black or because he is a man. The astute reader may ask, "If the lawyer doesn't have to give a reason, how do we know the challenge wasn't based on race or gender?" The answer is, if the presiding judge suspects that this may be the case, he or she must carefully inquire into the possibility that this is an unacceptable exercise of a peremptory challenge and must be persuaded that there is a neutral reason for challenging the juror. However, many observers have remarked that it is not difficult for a lawyer questioned by a judge to find some neutral reason that will allow the lawyer to eliminate the juror. Therefore, some proponents of jury reform—including former U.S. Supreme Court Justice Thurgood Marshall—believe peremptories themselves should not be allowed.

A **challenge for cause** can be exercised whenever it can be demonstrated that a would-be juror does not satisfy the statutory requirements for jury service (e.g., residence, occupational requirements) and has not already been eliminated from the venire. A challenge for cause also may be exercised when it can be shown that the prospective juror is so biased or prejudiced that he or she is not likely to render an impartial verdict. The presumed bias may be either for or against the defendant. If a writer is suing her publisher, for example, the publisher's attorney may want to exclude another writer from the jury. Or a juror may be eliminated because she has ties to one of the parties or attorneys through marriage or indicates prejudice against a group to which the defendant belongs. Judges may also reject a juror for cause at their own discretion without a request from either of the parties (Kovera, 2013). Finally, if a potential juror has already formed an opinion about a case, he or she can be removed for cause. An extremely controversial aspect of jury selection is found in death penalty cases where courts have ruled that jurors must be "death qualified"—meaning they must be found qualified to serve as a juror on a death penalty case. Social science research indicates that such jurors too often may not be unbiased or representative of the general population. We discuss death qualification and its accompanying research later in the chapter.

How important is voir dire to the outcome of the trial? The research literature is mixed in answering this question. "Whereas some studies provide support for the belief that voir dire is very important to the trial outcome, other studies cast doubt on this conclusion" (Lieberman & Sales, 2007, p. 28). Furthermore, research shows that, in general, attorneys are not very good at excluding unfavorable or biased jurors during the voir dire process (Kovera, 2013; Kovera, Dickinson, & Cutler, 2003; Lieberman & Sales, 2007). As we see below, even behavioral scientists do not necessarily help at this task.

Scientific Jury Selection (SJS)

The possibility that individual juror personality, group status, or demographic characteristics might affect final verdicts has led some attorneys to experiment with new techniques for voir dire. Lawyers have always used their assumptions about human nature to help them select juries, of course. For example, if one's client is a businessperson with politically conservative views who is now charged with tax fraud, one does not want left-leaning political activists on the jury. Nonetheless, the empirical evidence indicates that lawyers who rely on conventional stereotypes are poor at identifying biased jurors (Ellsworth & Reifman, 2000; Lieberman & Sales, 2007). In fact, "Jury researchers have searched in vain for individual differences—race, gender, class, attitudes, or personality—that reliably predict a person's verdict and have almost always come up empty handed" (Ellsworth & Reifman, 2000, p. 795).

Traditional hunches and guesses about potential jurors are sometimes supplemented by the time-consuming and elaborate procedures of social and behavioral scientists in the employ of attorneys. As noted in Chapter 2, this process is called *scientific jury selection* (SJS) (Saks & Hastie, 1978). Alternately, it is known as systematic jury selection (Kairys, Schulman, & Harring, 1975). This method was launched in the early 1970s. In one of the earliest examples, the defense in the Harrisburg Seven conspiracy trial hired a group of psychologists and other social scientists to help them choose jurors who would be most sympathetic to their clients.

The defense reasoning in the Harrisburg Seven case was understandable. The defendants were antiwar activists, including priests and nuns, who were accused of conspiring to blow up tunnels and kidnap presidential aide Henry Kissinger. The conservative community in which the federal trial was being held, together with the nature of the charges and the money the government was funneling into the prosecution, made acquittal unlikely. The social scientists gathered background and demographic information on each potential juror, as well as measures of attitudes, interest patterns, and possible personality characteristics. All of the information was obtained indirectly, since the researchers could not contact members of the venire or the jury itself. After the trial, in which only two of the seven defendants were convicted on minor charges, the defense publicly credited its victory in large part to the extensive help of the social scientists (Schulman, Shaver, Colman, Emrich, & Christie, 1973).

Psychologists were involved in the selection process of other juries during this time as well. In 1972, a group of five psychologists helped defense attorneys select a jury in the trial of Angela Davis, another political activist. She was charged with murder, kidnapping, and conspiracy, but was acquitted. Joan Little, a jail inmate who killed a guard who had sexually assaulted her and was threatening to do so again, was also helped by a scientific jury selection process.

Since then, a growing number of social and behavioral scientists have been refining and expanding SJS techniques, and they have participated in highly publicized trials as well as lesser-known ones. Today, attorneys use consultants knowledgeable in SJS in almost all major trials (Lieberman, 2011). Litigation or trial consulting has become a major industry, and although many consultants are psychologists, others are not, as mentioned in Chapter 2. When trial consultants advise on the selection of jurors, they may use a community survey method to measure the persuasiveness of certain arguments or evidence that might be presented during the trial. Survey questions may also include measures of community biases, pretrial publicity effects, and individual perceptions about the litigants. The gathered information presumably is to provide attorneys with an educated guess about whether a given individual will be the juror they want for their client. In some cases, the trial consultant may establish *mock juries* or shadow juries consisting of community members who follow the case and are consulted periodically in an effort to determine what specific information or strategies will be most effective in persuading jurors to see the attorney's side (Lieberman, 2011).

How helpful are these SJS methods? Opinions and findings vary (Lieberman, 2011; Suggs & Sales, 1978). "For approximately 30 years, psychologists have attempted to determine the utility of this approach by indirectly testing the effects of background characteristics on verdict decisions through experimental research and with direct examination of cases where SJS has been used" (Lieberman, 2011, p. 48). Many early SJS studies were simply inconclusive. In fact, some critics called SJS little more than "social science jury stacking" (Penrod & Cutler, 1987). Other studies indicated that it was slightly superior to random selection (Padawer-Singer, Singer, & Singer, 1974) or even to the traditional selection methods used by attorneys (Zeisel & Diamond, 1978). These early studies did not control for the quality of legal representation. In discussing their results, though, researchers acknowledged that disparity in representation was an important factor to consider. A defendant able to afford a jury or trial consultant would be likely to also afford a private defense team exclusively devoted to the case. While public defenders and private attorneys charging lower fees may be extremely capable, they cannot focus on one case alone. Moreover, few can afford to hire trial consultants to help in the case.

Unfortunately, contemporary research on SJS effectiveness remains inconclusive. This is primarily because SJS effectiveness is very difficult to measure. As pointed out by Lieberman (2011), it is especially difficult because there appears to be no meaningful definition of success. For instance, if both parties used SJS consultants in criminal trials, should the verdict be in favor of the defense or the prosecution to be considered successful? In civil trials, would a lower amount of monetary damages awarded to the plaintiff be a success—again, if both parties relied on SJS methods? Moreover, in those cases where only one side can afford a consultant, that side typically also has a highly skilled team of lawyers. If that side wins the case, was it the consultant or the lawyer who contributed most to the success of the case?

Overall, when it comes to the jury selection process, available research indicates that few juror characteristics have been found to predict with any consistency the outcome of the trial (Ellsworth & Reifman, 2000; Shaffer & Wheatman, 2000). The persuasiveness and nature of the evidence outweigh strongly any personality or specific characteristics of individual jurors. Garvey et al. (2004), for instance, in their comprehensive study of 3,000 jurors who served in criminal trials, discovered that "the strength of the evidence against a defendant is strongly and consistently related to how a juror casts his or her first vote" (p. 374). Moreover, the stronger the evidence against the defendant in a criminal case, the more likely the jurors will vote to convict. Numerous jurors have commented that they could not convict defendants because the prosecution simply did not prove its case. On the other hand, when the evidence is ambiguous or poorly presented, the characteristics of the jurors might carry greater weight in the decision-making process, although it appears that group dynamics and social pressures, rather than individual differences, play the more prominent role.

The weight that jurors give to evidence is not surprising if we remember that most people are not familiar with the judicial process and, in fact, are generally awed by it. Thus, jurors tend to be more strongly influenced by the judicial context than by their own personality and attitudes. Within the judicial context, "jurors adopt a role of 'fairness' and 'objectivity' which may be as extreme as they ever have had or will have in their lives" (Saks & Hastie, 1978, p. 70). The courtroom and the jury deliberation room may exert powerful situational pressures that mitigate the individual differences of the jurors, as we will see in the next chapter.

⬚ Jury Size and Decision Rule

Whether by historical accident or some unknown logic, the traditional jury in Great Britain, the United States, and Canada has consisted of 12 persons who must come to a unanimous decision. The U.S. Constitution is silent on the issue of jury size, and it is unclear what the framers ultimately intended (Diamond, Peery, Dolan, & Dolan, 2009). In 1966, England began to require that only 10 out of 12 jurors had to agree on a verdict (Saks, 1977), and soon after that, lawyers in the United States also began to challenge the traditional system. As a result, decision rule, which refers to the proportion of the total number of jurors required to reach a verdict, is no longer always unanimous, since some jurisdictions now allow agreement among fewer individuals (majority or quorum rule). The 12-person jury is also no longer a universal phenomenon. Three fourths of the states allow some trials with fewer than 12 members on the jury (Abraham, 1998; Diamond et al., 2009). Furthermore, approximately 80% of states today allow jury verdicts by 75% of jurors in civil cases; 20% also allow these split verdicts in noncapital criminal cases (Abraham, 1998; Diamond et al., 2009; Waters, 2004).

Jury Size

In two landmark decisions, *Williams v. Florida* (1970), which dealt with state criminal trials, and *Colgrove v. Battin* (1973), dealing with federal civil trials, the Supreme Court claimed that reduction in jury size would not alter trial results significantly. A six-person jury does not violate a person's constitutional right as laid down by the Sixth Amendment, the Court said in *Williams*, since that amendment mandates a jury "only of sufficient size to promote group deliberation, to insulate members from outside intimidation, and to provide a representative cross-section of the community" (p. 100).

In *Ballew v. Georgia* (1978), the Supreme Court once again broached the jury size issue, this time drawing a line at the minimum number of jurors to be allowed. Georgia statutes permitted a five-person jury to decide a criminal case, and the petitioner, tried on an obscenity charge, claimed that this five-person jury law deprived him of due process rights. The Supreme Court agreed, citing social and psychological research on group decision making. A year later, in *Burch v. Louisiana* (1979), the Court made it clear that a six-member jury must render a unanimous verdict. These Court decisions on jury size prompted more studies designed to discover how jury size influences the jury process and jury decision making.

Research on Jury Size

Common sense and information gleaned from the few empirical studies of jury size tell us that there are advantages and disadvantages to both small and large juries (see Table 6-4). Small groups allow more active participation from all members, because people are usually less inhibited in expressing their opinion in a small-group discussion. However, it has also been shown that small groups, to avoid upsetting the group balance, some-times inhibit expressions of disagreement among participants (Bales & Borgatta, 1955; Slater, 1958). The mere opportunity to speak is greater in a small group, however. On the other hand, research has also discovered that 6-person juries are more likely to return verdicts that are extreme as compared with 12-person juries, especially in civil trials (Horowitz & Bordens, 2002; Schkade, Sunstein, & Kahneman, 2000).

Larger groups have a number of advantages that are important to note if jury size is being considered. Large groups tend to provide the greater variety of skills and knowledge that may be necessary to arrive at a decision in a complex issue. However, larger juries, compared with smaller ones, take significantly longer to deliberate and are more likely to hang—that is, not be able to agree (Horowitz & Bordens, 2002; Saks & Marti, 1997). Large juries appear to better remember testimony given during the trial, although small juries have been shown to be better at recalling the specific arguments presented (Horowitz & Bordens, 2002; Saks, 1977).

A small number of studies have examined the effects of jury size on liability verdicts and damage awards in the context of civil trials. For example, Horowitz and Bordens (2002) found that, in mock civil trials involving 567 jury-eligible men and women, the punitive awards of 6-person juries were highly variable and unpredictable compared with those of 12-person juries. A similar result was reported by Schkade et al. (2000). Overall, it appears that 12-person juries provide more restrained and reasonable decision making than smaller groups, at least in civil trials.

As jury size increases, a more representative cross section of the community is obtained, thereby assuring minorities a better opportunity to be represented (Diamond et al., 2009). Two kinds of minorities may benefit: (1) racial, subcultural, or other demographic groups; and (2) opinion minorities. This second type of minority, which refers to those persons within a decision-making group who resist or go against the majority, has significant implications with regard to jury size.

Early but still relevant research (Asch, 1952; Roper, 1980) is illustrative. Solomon Asch, a social psychologist, found that in group situations, one minority member with even one ally greatly increases his or her resistance to persuasion by the majority. On the other hand, one minority member lacking an ally is substantially less likely to resist the majority of three or more. Thus, despite the premise of the classic film *Twelve Angry*

Table 6-4 **Advantages and Disadvantages of Small and Large Juries**

Jury Size	Advantage	Disadvantage
Small	Active participation by all. Recall arguments of attorneys.	May inhibit disagreement. Too quick to decide. Civil awards may be excessive.
Large	Variety of skills and knowledge. Recall testimony well. Better community representation. Minority (demographic and opinion) represented.	More likely to hang. Longer deliberation time. Some members are reluctant to speak out.

Men, it is unlikely that one lone individual will be able to influence others. Robert Roper tested hypotheses specifically relevant to juries. He predicted that juries with **viable minorities,** defined as at least two members not in agreement with the majority, would fail to reach a verdict more often than juries without viable minorities. He also predicted that larger juries, being more likely to contain viable minorities, would hang significantly more often than smaller ones.

Roper (1980) used a simulation design with a strong attempt at establishing ecological validity. One hundred and ten mock juries ranging from 6 to 12 members were selected from jury lists of Fayette County, Kentucky. A videotape of a criminal trial was presented in a courtroom, and the juries were then permitted to deliberate for an unlimited amount of time to reach a verdict. The decision could take one of three forms: a guilty verdict, a not guilty verdict, or a hung jury. Juries that initially reported they were deadlocked were sent back twice to try to reach a decision. If they returned a third time without a verdict, a "mistrial" as the result of a hung jury was declared.

As predicted, juries with viable minorities were more likely to end up hung than juries with nonviable minorities. In addition, the larger the jury, the more likely it was that a viable minority would emerge—hence, the more likely that the jury would be hung. The conclusions from the Roper (1980) study indicate that viable minorities are more successful at resisting conformity pressures exerted by the majority. Furthermore, larger juries over the long haul will result in significantly fewer convictions.

The Dynamite Charge

In some jurisdictions, when jurors tell the presiding judge they have reached a deadlock and it appears a retrial will be needed, the judge has the option to use the **dynamite charge.** This is also known as the shotgun instruction, the third-degree instruction, the nitroglycerin charge, the Allen charge, or the hammer instruction (Kassin, Smith, & Tulloch, 1990). Faced with the possibility of a hung jury, the judge may direct the jury to "reexamine their own views and to seriously consider each other's arguments with a disposition to be convinced" (Kassin et al., 1990, p. 538). In other words, the judge attempts to "blast" the decisional logjam into a verdict. The dynamite charge may be used in either criminal or civil trials. In *Lowenfield v. Phelps* (1988), the U.S. Supreme Court held that the dynamite charge is not necessarily coercive and reaffirmed its use on a routine basis in those jurisdictions that allow it.

The unfortunate psychological side effect of the dynamite charge, however, is that those in the minority will feel pressure from the judge to change their vote, and the majority will feel free to exert even more social pressure on the minority. Kassin et al. (1990), in an exploratory study with mock juries, found that the dynamite charge did indeed have that effect. V. L. Smith and Kassin (1993) reported a highly similar result. Their findings revealed that the dynamite charge caused jurors in the voting minority to feel coerced and to change their votes. It reduced the pressure felt by the majority, and it hastened the deliberation process in juries that favored conviction. Smith and Kassin also noted that, when the dynamite charge is used, jurors may be uncertain of their right to declare a hung jury; the charge may lead them mistakenly to believe they cannot do this. With the exception of this research, the dynamite charge issue has not been examined to any great extent by psychologists. More research needs to be done before we can assess its effect on various cases, jury compositions, and jury sizes.

Conclusions on Jury Size

Arguments about jury size are often tempered by the observation that a majority of criminal cases handled by the courts are clear-cut, where any number of individuals would probably reach the same verdict, whether it be guilty or not guilty. The sensational cases we encounter in the media, where juries sometimes deliberate for long periods (there are certainly exceptions), represent only a small percentage of all trials ushered through the courts. However, the research evidence does strongly suggest that 12-person juries, compared with smaller ones, are more likely to (1) recall more trial testimony, (2) contain members of minority groups, and (3) spend a longer (and perhaps more thoughtful) time in deliberation (Diamond et al., 2009; Saks & Marti, 1997). Perhaps the Court erred in allowing smaller trial juries. Saks and Marti emphasize that, "In holding that juries smaller than 12 are constitutional, the Supreme Court set aside 600 years of common law tradition and two centuries of constitutional history, including the reversal of its own precedents" (p. 465). Saks and Marti also note that the discernible harmful effects of shrunken juries have prompted some states to move the jury back to its original size of 12. Diamond et al. (2009) assert, "The reduction was introduced primarily in the name of efficiency, with no thought that it would impose nonmonetary costs" (p. 426). They argue that—at the very least—reducing jury size inevitably has a direct effect on the representation of minority groups on the jury, and that the most effective approach is to restore the 12-person jury.

Decision Rule

An issue closely related to that of jury size is that of decision rule—the proportion of jurors needed to agree on a verdict before it can be rendered. In other words, is it constitutionally permissible to allow a less-than-unanimous decision to convict defendants or to resolve civil matters? It surprises many people to learn that unanimity is not always required.

Currently, 48 states require unanimity in felony criminal verdicts. Oregon and Louisiana do not. In these two states, a defendant can be convicted of a felony by an 11 to 1 or 10 to 2 vote (Richey, 2013). Twenty-seven states require unanimity in misdemeanor verdicts. All states require unanimity in capital cases. Conversely, only 18 states require unanimity in civil verdicts. The size of the majority differs from jurisdiction to jurisdiction. When a jury is not required to reach a unanimous verdict, it is referred to as a **quorum jury**.

Two key U.S. Supreme Court cases, *Johnson v. Louisiana* (1972) and *Apodaca, Cooper and Madden v. Oregon* (1972), are relevant to this issue. In both cases, the Court allowed nonunanimous verdicts, especially in light of the fact that such majority or quorum verdicts would presumably result in fewer hung juries. However, as noted earlier, in *Burch v. Louisiana* (1979), the court ruled that a six-member jury must render a unanimous verdict. Many convicted offenders have challenged their convictions when verdicts were not unanimous, but with little success. In 2013, the U.S. Supreme Court denied certiorari in *Miller v. Louisiana*, which—among numerous other challenges to a conviction—challenged Louisiana's rule of allowing felony convictions by verdicts of 10–2 or 11–1. The petitioner, Miller, had been convicted by a quorum jury that had demonstrated considerable difficulty reaching a verdict. The jurors asked the presiding judge for guidance several times during the deliberation process. The judge was told, among other things, that a juror had fallen asleep and that another juror was reading and quoting from a bible. Upon hearing this, the judge ordered the bible to be removed from the jury room. Despite this and many other challenges to both jury selection and the jury's deliberation, Miller's conviction was upheld by the state appellate court. As mentioned above, the U.S. Supreme Court recently announced it would not hear the case.

It seems that nonunanimous or quorum juries are here to stay, particularly in civil cases. Moreover, despite the fact that nonunanimous juries in felony criminal cases are allowed in just two states, it does not seem that challenges to a state's rights to adopt this procedure will be successful.

Research on Decision Rule

Few empirical studies have investigated the impact of allowing juries to reach a verdict without total consensus. Of 11 such studies reviewed by Devine et al. (2001), most had been conducted during the late 1970s and early 1980s. Those studies found that juries not required to be unanimous tended to take less time to reach a verdict, took fewer polls (votes), and hung less often than those requiring unanimity. Several studies have suggested that quorum juries demonstrate better recall of the arguments and display more communication among members (Saks, 1977). However, it has also been found that quorum juries often stop deliberating the moment they reach the requisite majority (Kalven & Zeisel, 1966; Saks, 1977, 1997), thus providing less opportunity for a minority member or dissenter to argue a position or even be heard at all. Therefore, unanimous juries—like larger juries—probably have the advantage of allowing greater participation by someone with a minority view. Moreover, since the first vote of quorum juries generally predicts the final verdict (Saks, 1977), it appears that it is primarily in situations where unanimity is required that the minority can effectively alter the course set by the majority. On the other hand, unanimous juries also are more likely to block verdicts or to result in hung deliberation. In their classic work, *The American Jury*, Kalven and

Zeisel cite data indicating that, in jurisdictions requiring unanimous verdicts, 5.6% of juries were hung. This figure compared with 3.1% in jurisdictions that required only quorum verdicts.

⊠ Jury Instructions

During a trial, jurors are expected to remain passive, in the sense of having no direct involvement in the proceedings, but they are also expected to be attentive. They must listen to testimony and arguments, pay attention to demonstrations, scrutinize exhibits, and form their impressions. Traditionally, the information had to be acquired and retained through hearing and auditory memory, because jurors were prohibited from taking notes. Note taking is becoming much more common, however, particularly in complex cases. Judges increasingly are allowing—but not requiring—jurors to take notes during trials. Regardless of how it gathers its data, "The jury is expected to absorb information and spew out a decision, much like an empty sponge can be filled with liquid and squeezed to obtain what it has absorbed" (Diamond, 1993, p. 425).

After the voir dire, and once the jury has been selected, the trial follows three main phases: opening statements, the presentation of evidence, and closing arguments. In criminal trials, the prosecution usually has both the first and the last word, but this may vary by jurisdiction. Lawyers often use the opening statement phase to "connect" with the jury and summarize the position each side plans to take.

The role of the presiding judge is to enforce rules of procedure in the courtroom by controlling the manner in which evidence is presented, by ruling on objections, and by choosing between the procedural arguments of attorneys as to the proper process to be followed. It is also the judge's prerogative to control the courtroom by threatening and imposing contempt citations for disturbances or other interference with courtroom procedure.

Types of Instructions

At various points before, during, and after the trial, the presiding judge will give instructions to the jury (see Table 6-5 for definitions and illustrations). These are usually classified according to the nature of their content and when they are given. **Substantive law instructions** relate to aspects of the specific case at hand. For example, if a defendant is charged with embezzlement, the judge instructs the jury on the elements of that crime and on what must be proved by the prosecution beyond a reasonable doubt. The judge would also explain the concept of reasonable doubt. In essence, substantive law instructions include information about the law as it applies to the particular case. **Procedural instructions** are those that enlighten jurors about the various rules that apply across a wide variety of cases. For example, the judge explains the roles of judge and jury during the course of the trial or informs jurors whether their decision must be unanimous. The procedural instructions also usually include what is expected regarding the jurors' conduct during the trial, their responsibility to avoid representatives of the media, the need for their impartiality, and their duty not to discuss the case with other jurors or other persons during recess. They may also include whether the jurors can take notes during the trial. **Preliminary instructions** are given to jurors at the beginning of the trial. They are usually—but not invariably—procedural in nature. For example, the judge will routinely warn nonsequestered jurors in high-profile cases not to expose themselves to media accounts of the case and not to discuss the case with others or among themselves until it is time for deliberation.

Throughout the trial, the judge also gives a number of warnings to the jury not to consider some kinds of information in arriving at a verdict. For example, if inadmissible evidence is inadvertently or deliberately brought up in court, jurors are told simply to disregard it. In other situations, they are told the information they heard may be used in their deliberations, but only for limited purposes. Finally, when all of the evidence has been presented and both sides have made their summations, the judge gives jurors instructions pertaining to their deliberations. Both substantive and procedural instructions are given, and many repeat what has already been said. The six jurors in the Zimmerman case were given instructions that were unusually detailed and lengthy. Although Zimmerman was charged with second-degree murder (a crime that the judge defined for the jurors), prosecutors at the end of the trial requested an instruction on manslaughter as well, which the judge granted. In other words, she told jurors they could

Table 6-5 Types and Illustrations of Instructions Given to Juries by the Presiding Judge

Type of Instruction	Description	Examples
Substantive law	Inform jurors about the law relative to the case at hand.	Difference between murder and manslaughter. Explanation of preponderance of evidence.
Procedural	Inform jurors of rules and roles.	Role of judge and attorneys. Jurors must avoid media accounts.
Preliminary	Instructions given at beginning of trial.	No contact with attorneys for either side. Arrive at courthouse by given time of day.
Charging	All instructions relative to law and jurors' general duties.	Explanation of burdens of proof and which side must meet which burden.
Admonitions or curative	Intended to warn jurors or make up for ("cure") error during trial.	Disregard comment by a witness. Information may be used for one purpose, but not another.
Pattern	Standardized, uniform instructions used across different jurisdictions, typically at judge's discretion.	Defining the elements of murder. Definitions of aggravating and mitigating factors.

consider finding him guilty of the lesser charge, and she explained the elements of manslaughter compared with murder.

J. Alexander Tanford (1990) suggests placing instructions into two main categories: (1) charging instructions, and (2) admonitions: "Charging instructions explain the jury's role, describe relevant procedural and substantive law, and provide suggestions on how to organize deliberations and evaluate evidence" (p. 72). In short, they summarize the juror's duties: Listen, assess the credibility of witnesses, weigh the evidence, abide by the law, and render a decision. Note that the charging instructions may be substantive, procedural, or preliminary. They may occur at any point during the trial and sentencing.

"Admonitions are given spontaneously in an effort to prevent jurors from misusing potentially prejudicial information" (Tanford, 1990, p. 95). In the legal literature, admonitions are often called **curative instructions** because they are presumed to correct or "cure" potential errors in the trial process. There are two basic types: (1) admonitions that jurors must completely disregard information deemed by the court as being prejudicial, and (2) admonitions that jurors limit their use of certain kinds of evidence. A judge may tell the jury to disregard a witness's comment that a civil defendant has offered to settle the case, or tell a jury to disregard improper remarks made by attorneys during the trial. These are examples of curative instructions of the "disregard" type. The classic illustration occurred during the trial of Charles Manson, charged with the highly publicized Tate-LaBianca murders in California in 1969. Manson walked into the courtroom and held up a banner newspaper headline for the jurors to see. The headline was highly inflammatory, because it proclaimed that then–President Richard M. Nixon had declared that Manson was guilty. The jury was told to disregard the incident. The judge was careful, however, to poll jurors individually in an effort to determine whether they were unduly influenced by the headline.

> Limited-use evidence "refers to evidence that is introduced for certain purposes but not for others. For example, in certain cases, evidence that a defendant has prior convictions may be used to determine the credibility of statements made by the defendant . . . but may not be used to show that the defendant has committed an act. (Lieberman & Sales, 1997, p. 600)

Not surprisingly, this type of instruction—an example of **limiting instructions**—is extremely difficult for jurors to comprehend, as will be seen shortly.

In many jurisdictions, judges have adopted pattern instructions rather than instructing jurors in their own words. **Pattern instructions**, often provided by the Federal Judicial Center, are standard or uniform instructions that can be applied across different jurisdictions. Use of these instructions obviously simplifies the role of the judge. Furthermore, the content of the instructions is less likely to be challenged on appeal. On the other hand, pattern instructions typically drafted by lawyers in an effort to be legally precise are often very complex and incomprehensible to jurors (Lieberman & Sales, 1997, 2000; Tanford, 1990).

Research on Jury Instructions

Does the average juror really understand the requirements and safeguards associated with charging instructions and admonitions? Furthermore, even if the average juror does understand, will he or she do what is legally expected? Finally, what level of comprehension is acceptable? As Elwork, Alfini, and Sales (1987) have asked, what percentage of jurors must understand the instructions in order to ensure a just and fair result? These are questions social science researchers have attempted to answer. Their research is comprehensively summarized in a review by Lieberman and Sales (1997). For clarity, we will adopt Tanford's (1990) two main categories to review the research.

Charging instructions. With great regularity, research has found that jurors—even highly educated individuals—find jury instructions technical, full of ambiguity, and downright confusing (Ellsworth & Reifman, 2000; Lieberman & Sales, 1997, 2000; A. E. Smith & Haney, 2011). Smith and Haney write that in "virtually all of the reported research—regardless of the participant demographic, methodology employed, or specific legal context—jurors' comprehension of the legal instructions that are supposed to guide their decision making appears to be very low" (p. 339). This incomprehensibility has a negative effect on juror deliberation, leading jurors to discuss inappropriate topics, neglect important ones, and allow one or two jurors to control the deliberation process (Elwork, Sales, & Alfini, 1977, 1982). The lack of clarity of jury instructions also presents a serious threat to the fairness of jury trials. Although most of this comprehension research has been done with criminal juries, civil juries also demonstrate considerable difficulty in comprehension. Hastie et al. (1998), for example, found that the overall level of performance for jurors asked to define legal terms that were relevant to their decisions (and that had been defined by the judge) was very low. The median score was 5% correct, and 30% of the participants received a score of 0 correct. The researchers did find individual background factors that predicted better comprehension, however. Jurors who were younger, were better educated, and had higher income demonstrated better comprehension.

Even pattern instructions, in their effort at legal precision, have apparently become so full of jargon and qualifying clauses that they are fundamentally incomprehensible to the average citizen. Sometimes, it is even difficult to find the verb. "Legalese" by itself is not the only problem, however. A number of grammatical constructions and discourse features (e.g., poor organization within paragraphs, needless redundancy) also contribute to a misunderstanding of the text (Levi, 1990). Efforts have been made to rewrite instructions with attention to psycholinguistic principles with some success (Diamond & Levi, 1996; Elwork, Alfini, & Sales, 1987; A. E. Smith & Haney, 2011). However, even better clarity of instructions did not improve comprehension to a high level of satisfaction.

Some commentators conclude that the benefits of rewriting and simplifying may be overstated (Lieberman & Sales, 1997; Tanford, 1990). The abstract nature of the law creates its own problems. Legal concepts are often hard to understand—even for law students—because they are so abstract and so removed from any specific context or example. Accordingly, the judge should provide a context for them, refer to the actual evidence, and use numerous examples when providing instructions. As Tanford asserts, "Rewriting some instructions may be a pointless task because it is the law itself that is incomprehensible" (p. 102).

Admonitions. Recall that these are subdivided into instructions to completely disregard and instructions to limit the information to certain contexts. In either case, admonitions are problematic, as suggested by a line of research in the social and behavioral sciences.

When jurors are told to do something—like disregard what they may consider critical or enlightening evidence—they are apt to do something just the opposite, a process social psychologists call **reactance** (Brehm, 1966). Moreover, telling jurors to disregard or to segment the evidence is likely to highlight the material in their minds even more. "The empirical research clearly demonstrates that instructions to disregard are ineffective in reducing the harm caused by inadmissible evidence and improper arguments" (Tanford, 1990, p. 95). In fact, instructions to disregard may make matters worse (Wolf & Montgomery, 1977). This cognitive process is referred to in the legal literature as the **backfire effect** (Cox & Tanford, 1989). "The backfire effect occurs when jurors pay greater attention to information after it has been ruled inadmissible than if the judge had said nothing at all about the evidence and allowed jurors to consider it" (Lieberman & Arndt, 2000, p. 689). The research indicates, Lieberman and Arndt conclude, that admonitions to disregard may not only be highly ineffective in many situations, but may serve to draw jurors' attention to inadmissible evidence and essentially increase their reliance on that evidence for making their decision. Pickel (1995) found that the backfire effect occurred when jurors were instructed to ignore inadmissible evidence that indicated the defendant had a prior criminal record. However, the backfire effect did not occur when the jurors were told to disregard inadmissible "hearsay" evidence. Pickel attributed this inconsistency to the jurors' notion of what they believe is just and fair, despite what the law says. In other words, they thought it unfair to consider hearsay evidence from a third party, but perfectly justifiable to consider incriminating evidence that had slipped into the trial. Inadmissible evidence of prior conviction appears to be especially damaging to criminal defendants and most particularly when other evidence of guilt is weak (Lieberman & Sales, 1997). Lieberman and Arndt found that the backfire effect also did not occur when jurors considered the information unreliable.

Yet, despite evidence to the contrary, the courts continue to think that admonitions are effective and protect the defendant's rights (Tanford, 1990). The assumption that warnings to disregard are effective, or at least partially effective, on the thinking process and prejudice of the jury is termed, in the legal literature, the **cured-error doctrine**: A mistake was made, the jury heard something it should not have heard, and we fix this mistake by warning them not to pay attention to what they heard.

It has been suggested that, in actual cases, the group deliberation process provides checks on the jury. If the group considers information that it was told to ignore, individual jurors can put pressure on the others not to consider that information. We have little evidence that this phenomenon exists, though. Representative is a study by Rose and Ogloff (2001) in which group decision making did not improve juror application of instructions. In addition, studies that examine the after-the-fact deliberation of actual jurors, usually carried out by polling or interviewing them, support these results.

The courts also continue to believe that limiting instructions satisfy the cured-error doctrine. "[M]ost courts hold 'unquestionably' that limiting instructions should be given, and once given, 'cure' any error" (Tanford, 1990, p. 98). Empirical studies have continually shown that limiting instructions are largely ineffective concerning prior criminal convictions (Wissler & Saks, 1985), evidentiary factors (Greene & Loftus, 1986), inadmissible evidence (Sue, Smith, & Caldwell, 1973), and prior convictions of perjury (Tanford & Cox, 1987, 1988).

Nevertheless, despite the fact that social science research does not support the effectiveness of admonitions to disregard or to limit, this does not mean that judges should not issue them. In fact, failure to admonish is grounds for appeal, and a lawyer's failure to object if a request for an admonition is not forthcoming may be grounds for an appeal based on inadequate assistance of counsel. Therefore, even though a judge may be very well aware that jurors are likely not to disregard, the law requires that the judge at least make an attempt at curing the error.

Improving Juror Comprehension

Because it is clear from research that jurors often do not understand instructions, researchers have proposed methods for improving jury comprehension in this regard. For example, there is evidence that providing jurors with written copies of the instructions, particularly when this is accompanied by oral instructions from the judge, improves comprehensibility (Kramer & Koening, 1990). Heuer and Penrod (1989) did not find this improvement, although they did find that jurors receiving written instructions were more satisfied with the legal process. There is some concern that written instructions might increase deliberation time, a factor that speaks to the efficiency of the jury process. Thus far, there is no indication that providing written instructions has this effect (Lieberman & Sales, 1997).

Many experts believe that providing charging instructions about the law at the very end of the trial is a poor procedure for enhancing juror understanding of what is expected of them. Thus, the timing of the instructions is important. Elwork et al. (1977)

and Kassin and Wrightsman (1979) reported that jurors are far more likely to understand their charge and all its ramifications if instructions are communicated to them at the beginning of the trial as well as at the end. Although other researchers have not found these effects, Lieberman and Sales (1997) remark that there does not appear to be a detriment to presenting these instructions both pre- and posttrial. The possible improvement in both comprehension and juror satisfaction may lead to a reduction in juror bias, they argue.

Robbenolt, Penrod, and Heuer (1999) reviewed research on two other approaches to improving juror competence: allowing jurors to ask questions and to let them take notes. The opportunity to ask questions, if offered, has thus far been limited to misdemeanor trials and to trials in civil cases, although there are exceptions. Jurors in the 2013 murder trial of Jodi Arias were allowed to submit questions to the presiding judge, who screened them and then asked some of the defendant, who had decided to testify on her own behalf. Arias was on the stand for 18 days, some of which were spent answering about 100 jury questions. Note taking has been allowed in both misdemeanor and felony criminal cases as well as in civil trials. In most jurisdictions, the decision as to whether to allow jurors to submit questions and to take notes is left to the trial judge, but some state statutes prohibit note taking by jurors.

Robbenolt et al. (1999) reported that the research on both questioning and note taking provides little support for their advantages, but it also provides no clear evidence of harm. Field experiments conducted by Heuer and Penrod (1988, 1989, 1994) on note taking, for example, indicate that it serves as a minor memory aid but does not increase satisfaction with the trial or the verdict. However, claims that allowing jurors to take notes will distort the record, distract other jurors, or consume too much time are unwarranted. Note takers also do not have undue influence over non–note takers, nor do their notes favor one side or the other. In addition, some research studies do suggest an advantage to note taking (e.g., Horowitz & Forsterlee, 2001; Rosenhan, Eisner, & Robinson, 1994). In summary, there is no strong evidence that allowing jurors to take notes either improves or does harm to the jury process overall.

Permitting jurors to ask questions appears to promote understanding of the evidence and issues, but it does not help get at truth, increase satisfaction with the trial, or alert counsel to issues that need further development (Robbenolt et al., 1999). On the other hand, there is no evidence that jurors ask improper questions, lose their neutrality, or interfere with the trial strategies of attorneys.

Death Sentencing

At the end of 2011, a total of 36 states, the U.S. Government, and the U.S. military authorized the death penalty (Snell, 2013). Fourteen states and the District of Columbia did not. Also at the end of 2011, state prisons and the Federal Bureau of Prisons held 3,083 inmates under the sentence of death (Snell, 2013). Four states (California, Florida, Texas, and Pennsylvania) held more than half of all inmates on death row. Despite these high numbers, death comes slowly and sometimes not by execution. In 2011, a total of 24 states and the Federal Bureau of Prisons removed 137 inmates from under the sentence of death: Forty-three were executed, 24 died by other means, and 70 were removed by courts overturning sentences or convictions or were the result of commutations.

Murder trials in which the jury is asked to decide if the defendant is guilty, and if he is, whether he should be put to death, are called **capital trials**. In typical criminal trials, jurors decide only whether or not the defendant is guilty of one or more charges, and sentencing is usually left to the judge, with or without a jury recommendation. In capital trials, however, the jury makes both the guilt and sentencing decision, although in a few states the judge can override a jury's decision to spare the defendant the death penalty. If the defendant is convicted, the trial becomes a **bifurcated trial**. That is to say, the jury must first decide on guilt, then in a later proceeding decide whether the individual should be put to death. Capital trials represent one of the most difficult small-group tasks—deciding whether another person should live or die (SunWolf, 2010b). Not surprisingly, social science researchers have studied this process in great depth (see Box 6-2).

A good example of the difficult task faced by a capital jury is the Jodi Arias trial, discussed above. Arias was charged with murder in the 2008 stabbing and shooting death of her boyfriend, Travis Alexander. Although she claimed self-defense, Arias was convicted of first-degree murder in May 2013. Recall from above that she answered some 100 questions posed by the jury during her trial. The same jury, convening immediately after the conviction, could not agree on whether to sentence her to death or life in prison. As this book is going to press, a second jury is likely to be convened to make that decision. If the second jury is also unable to arrive at a decision, the death penalty will be automatically taken off the table, and a judge will sentence Arias to life.

Jury research on the death penalty has proliferated since the 1970s. During that decade, the U.S. Supreme Court first declared the death penalty, as it was then being applied, cruel and unusual punishment in violation of the Eighth Amendment (*Furman v. Georgia*, 1972). Four years later, the Court approved the death penalty if state statutes were crafted to prevent arbitrary imposition (*Gregg v. Georgia*, 1976). Most death penalty states have responded to the Court's requirements by providing for the bifurcated trial process mentioned above. The jury first must decide whether the defendant is guilty beyond a reasonable doubt. Then, in a separate proceeding, careful deliberation must be given to whether the death penalty should be imposed. This crucial role of the jury was highlighted in the Supreme Court decision (*Ring v. Arizona*, 2002) in which the Court ruled that jurors, not judges, must make a finding of the aggravating factors that will lead to a death sentence. Earlier, in *Penry v. Lynaugh* (1989), the Court ruled that **mitigating circumstances**—in that case, Penry's intellectual disability—must be taken into account.

BOX 6-2 RESEARCHERS AT WORK

The Capital Jury Project

The Capital Jury Project (CJP) is a comprehensive study of jurors who served on capital juries in 15 states. The study was designed to examine the factors that influenced their decisions, particularly related to whether to impose the death penalty (Bowers, 1995). The data were gathered through interviews with four randomly selected jurors from each capital trial after the trial was completed. The project has spurred similar research studies in many death penalty states, making this an ongoing effort to study capital sentencing.

Interviewers for the CJP were law professors, criminologists, psychologists, law students, graduate students, and political scientists. Interviews were extensive, taking 3 to 4 hours for each juror. The jurors were asked about the quality of the evidence in the case on which they sat, the demeanor of the defendant, the performance of lawyers and the judge, the legal instructions, and the process of jury deliberations, among other things. Researchers also have collected demographic data about each juror (e.g., age, gender, race, religion) and also about each juror's attitudes toward the death penalty and other criminal justice issues.

Numerous published studies have been made available since the project began in 1990. Although findings sometimes differ depending upon the state, some general conclusions are available. Here are just a few:

- The demeanor of the defendant during the trial and at the sentencing hearing has an effect on the jury's final decision; defendants who show some emotional regret are treated with some leniency, compared with those who are expressionless or arrogant in their demeanor.
- Capital jurors are strongly influenced by their own race, religion, and attitude toward the death penalty.
- Expert witnesses, particularly those called by the defense, are viewed with suspicion and seen as not credible.
- Capital jurors have considerable difficulty understanding the legal instructions provided to them by judges.
- Capital jurors have difficulty weighing aggravating and mitigating factors, and they often believe they must be in unanimous agreement on these factors.

Sources: Blume (2008); Blume, Eisenberg, & Garvey (2003).

Questions for Discussion:

1. Do the above findings from the Capital Jury Project and similar studies indicate that the death penalty should be abolished? Why or why not?

2. Discuss the pros and cons of interviewing persons who serve on juries after the case has been decided.

The process of imposing the death penalty can be a complex one and is surely taxing. Jurors must weigh aggravating and mitigating factors, but they often do not know precisely how to do this. An example of *aggravating factors* is a particularly heinous and cruel method of carrying out the crime, such as evidence that the victim was slowly tortured. *Mitigating factors* might include age, a childhood marred by extensive physical abuse, or evidence of a mental disability that had not been sufficient to acquit the defendant.

In three death penalty states (Texas, Virginia, and Oregon), predictions of future dangerousness on the part of the offender play a critical role; jurors are required by statute to consider this factor (Berry, 2010; Sites, 2007). Twenty-one death penalty states allow (but do not require) future dangerousness to be considered as an aggravating factor in capital sentencing (Sites, 2007). However, even in states that do not require or allow predictions of future dangerousness to play a role in the decision-making or capital sentencing phase, it is well known that jurors in a death penalty case spend a considerable amount of time discussing the propensity of the defendant to be violent and dangerous before they make their decision (Berry, 2010; Sites, 2007). In fact, in jurisdictions where death-qualified jurors are not encouraged or allowed to consider future dangerousness as an aggravating factor in capital cases, research finds that jurors often make future dangerousness a central component in the decision-making process (Blum, Garvey, & Johnson, 2001). As Berry asserts, these decisions are "presumably based, at least in part, on whether the juror believes that the defendant poses a personal danger to the juror himself, his friends, and his family" (pp. 902–903). Further on, we will discuss the role of clinical and actuarial predictions of dangerousness in capital cases.

The Death Qualification Process

One of the major differences between death-qualified (capital) jurors and ordinary jurors is that capital jurors must undergo a relatively rigorous selection process. For example, during the voir dire in a capital case, prosecutors poll jurors on their attitudes toward the death penalty. Prior to the late 1960s, prosecutors were allowed to automatically remove potential jurors who opposed capital punishment. In the landmark case *Witherspoon v. Illinois* (1968), however, the Supreme Court placed some limitations on this practice. It ruled that prospective jurors could be eliminated only if they made it unmistakably clear that, because of their philosophical opposition to the death penalty, they could not do one or both of the following things. First, they could not make an impartial decision as to a defendant's guilt (guilt nullifiers). Second, they could not bring themselves to sentence a convicted offender to death (penalty nullifiers). Later, the Court broadened the pool of potential "excludables" (those not allowed to serve) by allowing trial judges the discretion to exclude a juror if the judge believed the juror's views would prevent or substantially impair the performance of the juror's duties

(*Wainwright v. Witt*, 1985). In other words, even if a prospective juror says he or she is against the death penalty but could still find a defendant guilty in a capital case, a judge may believe otherwise, and the prospective juror could be excluded. It is estimated that this **death qualification** process excludes between 10% and 17% of eligible jurors (Fitzgerald & Ellsworth, 1984).

Death-Qualified Excludables

A number of studies have compared death-qualified jurors to "excludables"—those not allowed to serve on a capital jury—and suggest that capital defendants may be at a disadvantage because of the death qualification process (Bohm, 1999; Haney, 1984; SunWolf, 2010a, 2010b). "Citizens who state they could not impose the death penalty are excused by law, skewing the jury chosen toward conviction-proneness" (SunWolf, 2010a, p. 476). In addition, it is questionable whether death-qualified jurors are representative of the general population. Fitzgerald and Ellsworth (1984) found that the death qualification process significantly excludes more blacks than whites, more females than males, more low-income people than higher-income people, and more Democrats than Republicans. Death-qualified jurors also have been found to favor the prosecution and be conviction prone (Cowan, Thompson, & Ellsworth, 1984) and to be less receptive to mitigating circumstances than excludables (Luginbuhl & Middendorf, 1988). It should be noted, though, that at least one study challenges this evidence. Elliott and Robinson (1991) found that death penalty attitudes did not significantly affect verdicts.

Clinical and Statistical Prediction in Capital Cases

Recall that some states require jurors to predict the future dangerousness of an offender, while other states allow it. Research suggests, though, that whether required or allowed, future dangerousness is not far from the minds of capital jurors. During the sentencing phase of the trial, they often hear testimony on this issue. It is, however, extremely difficult to predict human behavior, even violent behavior, with acceptable accuracy—even for well-trained, experienced mental health professionals. As noted by William Berry (2010), "[T]he incontrovertible scientific evidence demonstrates that future dangerousness determinations are, at best, wildly speculative" (p. 907).

Historically, mental health professionals, when testifying at the sentencing phase of a capital case, have relied heavily on clinical prediction. *Clinical prediction* refers to the process of matching behavioral indicators with personality profiles and case histories to predict future behavior. In most cases, it is largely based on experience working with patients. To illustrate, in a well-cited Texas study of 155 capital cases in which prosecutors used experts to predict a defendant's future dangerousness, the experts were wrong in 95% of the cases (Edens et al., 2005; Texas Defender Service, 2004). A large majority of these medical and mental health experts relied almost exclusively on their clinical experience, "gut feeling," and training in making their predictions, and not on the relevant scientific research or statistical data. Consequently, predictions of dangerousness in capital cases, especially those based exclusively on clinical experience and speculation, are highly suspect. (See Box 6-3, illustrating a case in which an appellate court found clinical predictions unreliable.)

On the other hand, predictions of dangerousness based on scientific data and objective measures—actuarial predictions—are often better. They are based on statistical and experimental research on how groups of individuals with similar characteristics have acted in similar situations. However, actuarial predictions are not without their problems. Most empirically based assessment instruments and other objective measures of violence risk were not developed and validated specifically for predicting chronically dangerous individuals with high accuracy. As asserted by John Edens and his coauthors (2005), "we are unaware of any data directly addressing what most people would consider indicative of being a 'continuing threat to society'" (p. 81). Although some of the assessment measures are improving in their predictive accuracy (as will be discussed in Chapter 12), it is clear that none of them—at this stage in their development—should be used for determining life-or-death decisions in capital cases. In essence, predictions of dangerousness at capital sentencing—if they are required by the legal system—should be undertaken with extreme caution.

The U.S. Supreme Court and many state courts have assumed that jurors are perfectly capable of distinguishing between clinical and actuarial testimony and have assumed, also, that they give less weight to the clinical (Krauss & Sales, 2001). Psychological research has found the opposite, however. Jurors have a preference for expert testimony based on clinical data (Krauss & Sales, 2001; Melton et al., 2007), leading to the conclusion that clinical testimony may have an unfair advantage over actuarial-based testimony.

BOX 6-3

Case Study. Predicting Dangerousness in Capital Sentencing: Reliability of Clinical Judgment Versus Actuarial Data

Billie Wayne Coble is a Texas inmate who was twice sentenced to death, first in 1990 and again in 2008. In a triple murder, he killed his mother-in-law, father-in-law, and brother-in-law (a police officer in Waco). Coble was granted a rehearing, partly because of an unconstitutional jury charge in the first trial and partly because of the expert testimony of the state's psychiatrist at the first sentencing proceeding. At the time of the rehearing, he had spent 18 years on death row and—at age 60—was described as a model inmate who was

(Continued)

(Continued)

cooperative with corrections officers and often helped other inmates.

Coble was certainly not a model citizen prior to his imprisonment. His early childhood years were marred by negative events, and at age 15 he was diagnosed with sociopathic personality disturbance of the dissocial type. He had a history of violence, including brutalizing and molesting women and girls. He served in Vietnam but was not allowed to reenlist because he did not receive good performance reviews. The woman whose parents and brother he murdered was his third wife; during the same incident, he had kidnapped and assaulted her.

The state's expert, Dr. Richard Coons, a forensic psychiatrist who had conducted some 150 evaluations of future dangerousness and nearly 10,000 competency and sanity evaluations, had interviewed Coble prior to his first trial but had not seen him in 18 years and did not reinterview him before the 2008 hearing. His notes on the earlier interview had been lost in a flood, and he had no memory of that interview. Relying on documents provided by the prosecution, Dr. Coons testified once again that someone like Coble was at high risk of "future dangerousness," a finding that is necessary in Texas for sentencing an inmate to death. In this and other cases (e.g., *United States v. Fields*, 2007), Dr. Coons provided predictions of dangerousness based on hypothetical situations.

Dr. Coons used unstructured clinical judgment to arrive at his conclusion. He described his methodology as one that took into account the following factors: a history of violence, the person's attitude toward violence, the particulars of the offense, the person's personality and general behavior, the person's conscience,

and whether the person being assessed would be in or out of prison (*Coble v. Texas*, 2010). Questioned by Coble's attorneys, Dr. Coons admitted that he was unaware of much of the research literature on predictions of dangerousness. He said his method was subjective, and he acknowledged that other clinicians might reach different conclusions.

Dr. Mark Cunningham, a forensic psychologist who has both research and clinical experience with prisoners on death row, conducted a comprehensive violence risk assessment of Coble that included interviews, risk assessment instruments, and a review of actuarial data. Dr. Cunningham is a highly regarded scientist with an impressive publication record and professional awards and memberships. In light of a number of factors, including Coble's prison record and his age, he found Coble to be at the lowest risk for violence. Nonetheless, the jury recommended that he be sentenced to death.

The Texas Court of Criminal Appeals (*Coble v. Texas*, 2010) expressed approval of the approach taken by Dr. Cunningham and found that the testimony of Dr. Coons did not meet the standards for reliability outlined by the U.S. Supreme Court in *Daubert*, which we discussed in previous chapters. However, the court also ruled that admitting Dr. Coons's testimony amounted to harmless error: It had no substantial and injurious effect on the jury's deliberation about future dangerousness. Other arguments advanced by Coble's attorneys were also rejected.

In June of 2011, the U.S. Supreme Court denied certiorari in this case. (The APA filed an amicus brief for the case in May of 2011.) Coble attempted a third appeal to the Texas Court of Criminal Appeals, but this appeal was denied in February 2012. At this time, Coble is on death row awaiting an execution date.

Questions for Discussion:

1. Is it possible to assess future dangerousness on the basis of written records, a hypothetical situation, and no direct contact with the person whose dangerousness is being assessed?

2. In the first trial, the jury was not instructed to consider mitigating circumstances involving Coble's psychological problems, including PTSD following service in Vietnam. Why must mitigating factors be taken into account in death sentencing?

3. Should the fact that Coble was a model prisoner be taken into consideration in deciding whether to put him to death?

Psychological research continues to document both the deficiencies of clinical prediction and the juror preference for such testimony. Although we discuss this in the death penalty context here, it is problematic in numerous other contexts as well. Krauss and Sales (2001) offer several suggestions for tackling this issue. They recommend that better methods of instructing jurors should be adopted, with judges informing jurors of the natural, but misguided, preference for clinical data. They also suggest that future research explore alternative ways in which actuarial research might be presented so that it is weighed appropriately by jurors. Finally, "[f]uture empirical research will be especially important in determining how adversary procedures could eliminate or minimize the unfair advantage that accrues to clinical opinion expert testimony" (p. 305).

Capital Sentencing Instructions

The inability of jurors to comprehend instructions relating to capital sentencing is well established (e.g., Diamond & Levi, 1996; Haney & Lynch, 1994; Lynch & Haney, 2000, 2009; A. E. Smith & Haney, 2011; Wiener et al., 2004). "Poor instructional comprehension is particularly problematic in death penalty cases, where . . . Capital juries are uniquely empowered to literally decide between life and death," write A. E. Smith and Haney (p. 339). During the sentencing phase of a capital case, jurors must decide whether the person convicted should be put to death or given an alternative sentence, such as life or life without the possibility of parole. Unfortunately, in the United States, an overwhelming majority of persons who have been condemned to die were sentenced by juries that relied on flawed and poorly understood instructions (A. E. Smith & Haney, 2011). The role of the jury in capital cases has become even more crucial as the result of the Supreme Court's decision in *Ring v. Arizona* (2002). In that case, the Court ruled that a jury of one's peers—not a trial judge—must weigh the aggravating and mitigating factors to be considered in deciding whether a person should be sentenced to death (see Table 6-6 for examples). Aggravating factors, raised

Table 6-6	Examples of Aggravating and Mitigating Factors That May Be Considered at Sentencing

Aggravating Factors

Victim(s) tortured during criminal offense

Victim was a child, disabled, or elderly

Victim was vulnerable and under offender's care (e.g., violation of duty and trust)

Additional potential victims put at risk

Evidence of extensive planning of the crime

Apparent lack of remorse for the offense

Callous or egregious disposal of body

Impact of crime on victim's survivors

Mitigating Factors

Age of the offender

History of being abused as a child

History of being victim of sexual or domestic abuse

Intellectual disability

Stress experienced by offender (e.g., job loss, major health issue) at the time crime was committed

Indication that the offender is sorry for the offense

Effort to revive the victim or call for help

Serious mental disorder, such as PTSD

History of psychiatric hospitalization

Mercy recommended by victim's survivors

Note: Jurors in some jurisdictions may be *required* to take some of the above factors into account (e.g., age, intellectual disability).

by the prosecution, must be proved to the jury beyond a reasonable doubt; mitigating factors, raised by the defense, may be proved only to the juror's satisfaction. In addition, juries are free to find their own mitigating and aggravating factors. They also do not have to be unanimous in their belief that a given factor or factors are mitigating.

Wiener et al. (1995) learned that jurors having low comprehension of death penalty instructions were more likely to impose death rather than a life sentence. Interestingly, several studies find that jurors understand the term *aggravation* and the specific aggravations included in jury instructions better than they understand the term *mitigation* and specific mitigating factors (A. E. Smith & Haney, 2011). This disparity may help explain the observation that penalty phase instructions seem to be interpreted by jurors to implicitly favor death verdicts over life or life-without-parole verdicts.

In death penalty cases, it is of course especially important that jurors understand the legal questions they are to address. Luginbuhl (1992) compared juror comprehension on standard death penalty instructions—those typically given to jurors in death penalty states—and instructions that were rewritten to reflect sound linguistic principles. Comprehension was better for the rewritten instructions. These results comport with previous research suggesting that even highly conscientious jury members often miss the point in applying instructions during jury deliberations. Considering the significance of a death sentence, attempts to improve juror comprehension of these instructions would seem paramount.

✉ Jury Nullification

Jury nullification is the power of a criminal trial jury to disregard the evidence or judicial instructions because they believe the law is wrong, nonsensical, or misapplied to a particular case. It is a controversial issue. Those who support the concept maintain that it allows jurors to exercise their own conscience; those who disavow it say it can and has been abused and invites anarchy in the jury room. Norman Finkel (2000) refers to jury nullification as a dramatic exemplar of **commonsense justice**. In nullifying the law, he says, jurors are asserting, in effect, "to hell with both the law and rule of law" (p. 597). Commonsense justice is what ordinary people think is just and fair. Essentially, "it is what ordinary people think the law ought to be" (Finkel, 1995, p. 2).

Jury nullification has both a rather noble and a questionable history. In colonial times, jurors often refused to convict individuals who had been charged with violations of British laws, including John Peter Zenger, who had been charged with seditious libel. Zenger printed material that had not been authorized by the British mayor. On the other hand, jurors have also refused to convict members of the Ku Klux Klan charged in the lynching deaths of black citizens (Scheflin, 1972). In more recent times, nullification is believed to occur most often in cases that involve divisive social issues such as drug possession, euthanasia, and domestic violence (as in the rare instance when a battered woman kills her abuser—rare because abused women are more likely to be killed than to kill) (Dilworth, 1997).

After the verdict of not guilty in the infamous O.J. Simpson case, numerous commentators speculated that the jury in that case had practiced nullification. The fact that the jury deliberated for such a short period of time (less than an hour) over a highly complex case that lasted for many weeks provided fuel for those speculations. The argument was made that jurors could not possibly have attended to all they were instructed to do in that short amount of time, and that they deliberately disregarded the evidence as well as the instructions of the presiding judge. Commentators also noted that the jury may have wanted to send a message to police that racism or misconduct would not be tolerated. Other commentators reject the notion of nullification in this case. They argue that the prosecution simply did not prove every element of the crime beyond a reasonable doubt, that jurors were processing this fact as the trial unfolded, and that they had no difficulty arriving at this conclusion once they reached the jury room. Short of obtaining revelations from jurors in the case, we will never know whether nullification was indeed practiced in the Simpson case—but the trial and the resulting verdict clearly brought the issue of nullification to public consciousness.

In most instances, jurors do not realize they can in effect nullify the law and acquit the defendant regardless of the facts. In a small minority of states, the trial judge is allowed to inform the jurors that they do have that power. However, in federal courts, judges cannot inform juries of this fact (*United States v. Dougherty*, 1972). This case involved the trial of the "D.C. 9," the anti–Vietnam war protesters who broke into a government installation and poured sheep's blood over documents and carpets. The protesters appealed their conviction, arguing that jurors should have been told they could refuse to find them guilty. The appeals court did not agree, noting among other things that jurors already know about this power. Some research has questioned this assumption, however (Brody & Rivera, 1997). In addition, some studies have examined the impact of informing the jurors that they have the right to disregard the evidence and nullify the law (Devine et al., 2001). The basic finding of these studies reveals that reminding jurors of their power to nullify the law makes them more likely to use it.

In summary, jury nullification has been a hotly debated issue, but attention has been waning in recent years. Controversial not guilty verdicts can usually be explained by legal factors, such as limitations in the law, the performance of lawyers, or the strength of the evidence rather than by jury nullification. Critics of jury nullification say that jurors should not have the inherent power to throw out the laws of society in any given case, nor should they be reminded of this power, especially when evidence of the defendant's guilt is strong. However, as pointed out by Devine et al. (2001), the impact of reminding jurors that they have nullification power is complicated. What they will do with this information depends on many factors, including the nature of the evidence, the source of the reminder, the nature of the crime, the status of the defendants, and the composition of the jury. Furthermore, despite its controversial nature, jury nullification is a rare phenomenon. Most jurors try to follow the letter of the law (and obey the instructions) as closely as possible, even if they disagree with it.

SUMMARY AND CONCLUSIONS

The trial jury has been both praised as a venerable institution and vilified for delivering controversial verdicts. Social and behavioral scientists have conducted a long line of studies examining its structure as well as its deliberation processes. In addition, researchers have studied jury rules and procedures, including how jurors are selected and how judges provide them with instructions for completing their tasks. Studies that focus on jury decision making are most often simulation studies, in which participants are provided with materials or tasks that mimic the situations in which actual jurors are placed.

Although trial by jury is guaranteed by the U.S. Constitution for criminal cases and for most civil cases, the great majority of cases filed never go to trial, being settled early in the judicial process. Plaintiffs and defendants who do go to trial may choose either a jury or a judge, and juries seem to be favored over judges, at least in criminal cases. However, certain civil cases—particularly those involving complex issues—are more likely to be handled by judges alone. Trials before judges are called bench trials.

Both the case law and scholarly research have addressed the matter of jury selection. Potential jurors (the venire or jury pool) are called to service and are submitted to a selection procedure (the voir dire) for each case. Basically, the voir dire is the questioning procedure that decides whether a juror will sit on a given case. In addition to whether jurors meet the statutory requirements such as citizenship and age, lawyers and judges may reject jurors for a variety of reasons. Challenges to a juror fall into two main categories: peremptory challenges and challenges for cause. Peremptory challenges are the more controversial of the two because they do not require that the lawyer give a reason for rejecting a potential juror. Nevertheless, they cannot be exercised in a discriminatory manner, such as on the basis of race or gender. Determining that a peremptory challenge was used in a discriminatory way is not easy to do, however, a fact that has led some to call for the abolition of all peremptory challenges. In contrast, challenges for cause must be supported by a specific reason, such as the potential juror's possible bias or his or her acquaintance with one of the parties in the criminal or civil action.

Some social scientists have become involved in trial or litigation consulting, which may involve scientific jury selection (SJS). SJS presumably helps a lawyer choose jurors who are most likely to be favorably disposed toward his or her client. SJS can be an elaborate process involving community surveys and, in some cases, setting up shadow juries that follow the case and offer feedback to the lawyer. SJS is most likely to happen in major cases where the stakes are high, and it is found more in civil than in criminal cases. Despite its appeal in some quarters, however, predicting how a juror will decide a case has not been a successful enterprise.

The typical jury size in criminal cases is 12 members, but some states have juries as small as 6. It is not unusual to have juries of fewer than 12 in civil cases. Both large and small juries have advantages and disadvantages, but larger juries are at least more likely to represent a cross section of the community. Decision rule refers to the number of jurors that must agree before a final verdict is accepted. Only two states allow felony convictions by nonunanimous juries (10–2 or 11–1). Appeals by convicted offenders to this nonunanimous (or quorum) jury decision—including a recent appeal to the U.S. Supreme Court—have not been successful.

Presiding judges give juries numerous substantive and procedural instructions for fulfilling their roles and completing their tasks. Jurors are instructed on courtroom demeanor, the roles of lawyers, the elements of specific crimes, and the burdens of proof. They are warned against responding to media inquiries and discussing cases with others until the trial, including deliberation, is over. They may be told to disregard statements, and they may be given the controversial "dynamite charge" when they seem unable to reach a verdict. Research shows that jurors as a group have great difficulty comprehending some instructions—not because they are unintelligent, but because the instructions themselves may be confusing. In some jurisdictions, jurors are allowed to take notes or even pose questions for witnesses. In others, jury instructions have been rewritten in an effort to make them more comprehensible.

Capital cases pose special problems for jury selection, jury instructions, and jury deliberation. Capital jurors are called "death qualified," because they have been deemed eligible to serve on a death penalty case. "Excludables" are persons who have been prevented from serving because their opposition to the death penalty is so strong that they could not convict and/or sentence someone to death. Even if they say that they would be able to sentence someone to death despite their philosophical opposition, the presiding judge can consider them ineligible. Research has shown that death-qualified jurors are significantly different from excludables in demographics and attitudes. Some researchers indicate that this stacks the jury against the capital defendant, in part by making it less likely that a death penalty opponent will influence other jurors. An ongoing series of studies on actual capital jurors across the United States has provided important information, as well, on the decision making in these cases. Capital jurors, like many other jurors, have difficulty understanding instructions, particularly those relating to aggravating and mitigating factors. In some states, capital sentencing requires a prediction of future dangerousness on the part of the offender. Legal psychologists have long indicated that actuarial methods are better than clinical methods at assessing risk. However, prosecutors frequently offer expert testimony based on clinical predictions in death sentencing, and jurors tend to prefer clinical prediction to actuarial assessments.

Jurors generally take their tasks seriously and try to do their best. They make efforts to understand instructions, consider the evidence, and carefully weigh the testimony on both sides. Very occasionally, jurors decide to nullify the law. In other words, they deliberately make a decision that is not in keeping with what they are told to do. Jury nullification is a controversial topic—it has been used for both noble and ignoble purposes. In a few jurisdictions, jurors are told they have the right to set aside the requirements of the law and vote their conscience, but this is highly unusual and is expressly forbidden in the federal courts. Whether jurors are told or not told of this power, it is believed that true jury nullification very rarely occurs.

KEY CONCEPTS

Backfire effect

Bifurcated trial

Capital trials

Challenge for cause

Commonsense justice

Curative instructions

Cured-error doctrine

Death qualification

Decision rule

Dynamite charge

Jury nullification

Jury simulation

Limiting instructions

Mitigating circumstances

Paper court

Pattern instructions

Peremptory challenge

Preliminary instructions

Procedural instructions

Quorum jury

Reactance

Substantive law
    instructions

Trial jury

Venire

Viable minorities

Voir dire

7

Jury and Judicial Decision Making

I loved being a juror. I liked it so much I wanted to be called back again, but they said I had to wait another 7 years.

Being on a jury was the most stressful experience I've ever been through.

I f we judge from anecdotal reports from jurors, the first juror quoted above is probably atypical. Most jurors, if not as stressed as the second juror, indicate some discomfort, boredom, fatigue, or pressure associated with their service on a jury. Nevertheless, as noted in Chapter 6, they do generally come away from jury duty with a more favorable view of the legal system (Rose et al., 2012). Legal scholars and psychologists agree, though, that from start to finish, the task of a juror is a taxing and essentially cognitive one. In fact, the deliberation process toward a decision is perhaps one of the most cognitively complex tasks that most ordinary American citizens will ever be expected to perform (Gunnell & Ceci, 2010). "The ultimate task of a juror is to encode information, process it, deduce implications from it, reason as to the information's function, purpose and validity in the grand scheme of the case, and then communicate these results effectively with other jurors" (Gunnell & Ceci, 2010, p. 851).

In addition, jurors are expected not to consider extralegal factors—those not relevant to the legal issue at hand—in their decision making. Depending on the case, extralegal factors may include such things as gender, age, race, socioeconomic class, religious affiliation, or physical attractiveness of the defendant or—in civil cases—of the plaintiff and the defendant or respondent. Even pretrial publicity may be a source of extralegal bias, despite attempts by the court to restrict this information through voir dire. Basically, jurors are expected to focus exclusively on the evidence presented during the trial. Is this a reasonable expectation?

In Chapter 6, we provided an overview of the trial jury and focused on structural and procedural issues, such as jury size and instructions. In this chapter, we address what occurs when the jury retires from the courtroom into the privacy of jury chambers. Researchers have explored how jurors make their decisions and the potential influences of both legal and extralegal factors on these decisions. Later in the chapter, we will also examine whether judges are influenced by extralegal factors during their decision making.

The Jury Decision-Making Process

At the end of the evidence portion of the trial, when each side has made its closing arguments and the judge has issued instructions to the jury, the jurors are ushered to special quarters, where they are expected to deliberate in complete privacy until they reach a verdict or believe they are hopelessly deadlocked. No outside participants or information that could contaminate the deliberation are permitted in the jury room. An officer of the court—usually a sheriff's deputy or a U.S. Marshal—guards the door and, if necessary, delivers messages between the jury and the judge. In high-profile cases, juries may be sequestered for the length of the trial as well as the deliberation process. The purpose of sequestration is to protect the jury from the media and possible influences of jurors' friends and family. Judges also may fear that jurors who are not sequestered may be contacted and even threatened by associates of the defendant or the victim in a criminal case or by the other party in a civil case.

When a jury begins its deliberation, one of its first decisions is to select one person, called the foreperson or chairperson, to lead subsequent discussions and oversee the votes. This process is done among strangers, but the longer the trial, the more likely the jurors will be to know something about each other when they enter the deliberation room. Research reveals that the jury chairperson is usually male, middle-aged, of high status in the community, from a managerial or professional occupation, and experienced with regard to jury service (Devine et al., 2001; York & Cornwell, 2006). Also, the person who speaks first in the group or the first juror to mention the need to elect a chairperson is also more likely than others to be chosen to lead the group (Devine et al., 2001).

It appears that the influence of the jury chairperson on the group's decision making may be significant. He or she usually participates in the deliberation process far more than the other jurors, accounting for 25% to 35% of the speaking time (Devine et al., 2001). Research also indicates that the chairperson is viewed as significantly more influential than other jurors during deliberations (Cornwell & Hans, 2011). Juries are largely left to determine their own procedures concerning voting (called polling) on guilt or innocence or voting in favor of the plaintiff or respondent in a civil case. The chairperson often determines or influences the regularity of the voting, the timing, the format, and the sequence. The polling during jury deliberations is not to be confused with "polling the jury." **Polling the jury** is a practice whereby jurors are asked individually by the judge, after the verdict is read in the courtroom, whether they assented, and still assent, to the verdict. The procedure may be requested by either the defense or the prosecution at the time the verdict is announced. If the court finds that the verdict was not unanimous, when unanimity is required, the jury may be directed to go back into chambers for further deliberation. A jury with no apparent possibility of reaching consensus may also be discharged, ending as a hung jury, and the case may have to be retried. Recall our discussion of the dynamite charge in Chapter 6, whereby a judge may instruct the hung jury to continue its deliberation.

Once settled in the deliberation chamber, jurors may only request clarification of legal questions from the judge or ask to look at items of evidence. In some cases, they have received permission to visit or revisit the scene of a crime or accident, but they may not do so on their own without permission. If jurors have not returned a verdict by the end of their first day of deliberation, nonsequestered jurors are allowed to go home, after being admonished by the judge not to discuss the case with anyone. It is highly likely, however, that many do discuss the case with close family members. Judges also can decide to sequester the jury during the deliberation process, meaning that they are not allowed to go home until they have reached a verdict.

The empirical evidence reveals that most juries in criminal trials do not involve themselves in lengthy deliberations. In their classic research based on actual jurors, the Chicago Jury Project, Kalven and Zeisel (1966) found that, for trials lasting 1 or 2 days, 55% of the juries took 1 hour or less to reach a verdict, and 74% of the juries completed their deliberation in less than 2 hours. Most juries take a vote soon after settling into their deliberation chamber. Kalven and Zeisel also found that in 30% of the cases, jurors reached a unanimous decision after only one vote. In 90% of the cases, the majority on the first ballot won out. Nevertheless, as Bornstein and Greene (2011) put it, "we know fairly little about how individual preferences translated into a group decision, including the extent to which the majority exerts normative and/or informational influence over minority jurors" (p. 65). In addition, longer trials, more complex cases, more serious charges, and the inclusion of expert testimony usually result in longer jury deliberations (Brunnell, Chetan, & Morgan, 2009; Cornwell & Hans, 2011).

In their review of jury research, Devine et al. (2001) cite extensive data that show an interesting correlation between the initial jury vote in a criminal case and the ultimate verdict. In juries composed of 12 individuals, if 7 or fewer jurors favor conviction at the beginning of deliberation, the jury will probably acquit. In other words, the threshold for acquittal seems to be 5. Put another way, if 5 or more jurors are against conviction at the beginning of the deliberation, the chances are slim for an eventual conviction. On the other hand, if 10 or more jurors believe the defendant is guilty in the beginning of deliberation, the jury will probably convict. That is, if 2 jurors or fewer believe the defendant is not guilty, the chances are slim for eventual acquittal, and "with 8 or 9 jurors initially favoring conviction, the final verdict is basically a toss-up" (p. 692).

Twelve is the typical jury size, and thus many studies of jury decision making use that number in their methodology. As noted in the last chapter, however, some states do allow smaller juries, even for felony cases. The recent high-profile Zimmerman case, tried in Florida in the summer of 2013, was decided by six female jurors. Recall from the previous chapter that small juries are less likely to represent a cross section of the community and are also less likely to contain opinion minorities—that is, someone with different opinions from the majority. Small groups also may inhibit expressions of disagreement. On the other hand, small groups also allow for more active participation, with jury members being less inhibited. Immediately after the Zimmerman acquittal was announced, information about the jury and its decision-making process began to "leak" into the media. One juror revealed what she said was the initial vote on guilt or innocence; another juror indicated that the defendant "got away with murder" because the state did not adequately make its case. One juror allowed herself to be interviewed on national television. The case would be a fascinating study in jury decision making if studied carefully and objectively by researchers.

Jury Deliberation Styles

A growing body of research is on the approach taken by jurors as they engage in deliberation (Cornwell & Hans, 2011; Devine et al., 2001; Hastie, Penrod, & Pennington, 1983). "Deliberation style refers to the manner in which juries approach their task of reaching a verdict, particularly the initial stages" (Devine et al., 2001, p. 693). Two distinct styles have been identified: evidence-driven and verdict-driven deliberation styles.

In the **verdict-driven deliberation style**, the jury's ultimate goal is to reach a verdict as quickly as possible. The verdict-driven jury will often take a vote soon after electing a chairperson and will quickly focus their discussions on key facts that are essential to reaching a final outcome. By contrast, in the **evidence-driven deliberation style**, jurors will delay the vote until after considerable discussion focusing on evaluations of the evidence in the case. Rather than focusing on the verdict, the evidence-driven group will concentrate on developing a logical study of the evidence. Hastie et al. (1983) found that mock jurors using the evidence-driven style tended to deliberate longer, consider the evidence more carefully, and report greater satisfaction with the experience compared with mock jurors using the verdict-driven approach. However, Hastie and his colleagues could not identify how the different styles affected the final verdict.

Although deliberation style appears to be important in understanding the process of how jurors reach decisions, many questions are unanswered. For example, as noted above, how much influence does the deliberation style have on the final verdict? Are individual identifiable juror characteristics associated with deliberation style? To what extent can an individual juror who is evidence driven influence other jurors who may be more verdict driven? These are questions as yet unanswered by the research. It appears, though, that juries tend to pursue the verdict-driven approach, while the legal system prefers the evidence-driven approach, at least in principle. Devine et al. (2001) conclude from their extensive review of the jury literature, "Clearly, the evidence-driven style is closer to the normative ideal desired by the courts; in contrast, many juries adopt the verdict-driven style that seems most likely to lead to the rapid delineation of factions and steadily increasing normative pressure" (p. 701).

Cornwell and Hans (2011) suggest that an evidence-driven style should lead to high levels of participation from all members of the jury. Verdict-driven deliberations, on the other hand, are marked by early and frequent polling and pressures to conform to the majority. Recall that unanimity is not always required. However, when it is, deliberations are more likely to be evidence driven and more thorough than when majority rule is in place (Bornstein & Greene, 2011). Evidence-driven deliberations usually focus on reviewing case facts, evidence, and judicial instructions. Juries adopting this style tend not to take frequent votes, and they sometimes only rely on one final vote to formalize their evaluation of the evidence (Bornstein & Greene, 2011).

Cornwell and Hans (2011) observe that high levels of participation are generally beneficial for jury fact finding when jurors are drawn from all segments of the community: "Full participation by jurors from diverse backgrounds allows the jury to draw on personal experiences, social perspectives, and knowledge that differ across individuals and social groups" (p. 668). Furthermore, diverse juries often engage in wider-ranging deliberations that include perspectives and information that might be missed, or even avoided, by less diverse juries. For example, racially diverse jurors are more likely than those serving on single-race juries to openly discuss the racial issues involved in the case.

Juror Participation During Deliberation

It is expected that high levels of juror participation promote balance in the jury's central goal of fact finding and responsible decision making. In other words, the jury system is based on a fundamental assumption that participation by all jury members will best ensure a just verdict. Although the system cannot guarantee equal participation—some jurors clearly will be more involved than others—deliberation is negatively affected if one or more jurors withdraws from the process or says very little.

What factors might account for differences in participation levels during jury deliberation? Cornwell and Hans (2011) were interested in discovering the role demographics might play. They gathered data from jurors who served in actual felony trials in four state courts. Here again, we see an illustration of a trend toward using actual jurors, or persons who qualified for jury duty.

Cornwell and Hans (2011) used data on self-reported age, gender, race/ethnicity, income, and education, which were available from juror questionnaires. They then asked jury members for estimates of how much they had participated, after the trial was over. They found—perhaps not surprisingly—that socioeconomic level and education were correlated with participation. Jurors from higher socioeconomic levels participated more in jury deliberations than those at the lower levels, and participation increased with both education and income. Jurors who had a postgraduate education participated significantly more than those who lacked a college degree.

More surprising was the finding that middle-aged jurors participated more in deliberations than their younger and older counterparts. Gender did not play a significant role in participation.

Perhaps the most surprising finding of the Cornwell-Hans study pertains to the effects of jurors' racial and ethnic backgrounds on jury participation. Previous studies led the researchers to anticipate that minority jurors would participate less. However, they found just the opposite. Black jurors participated significantly more than white jurors, regardless of the racial breakdown of the jury. "Black jurors participated more in murder cases, drug cases, nonviolent criminal cases, and complex cases, as well as cases involving black and non-black defendants" (Cornwell & Hans, 2011, p. 691). Hispanic participation was found to be about the same as participation by non-Hispanic white jurors. In explaining these results, Cornwell and Hans noted that all the locations for the study were relatively diverse urban areas, and that the juries themselves were remarkably diverse. Previous jury studies generally used jurors who were predominately white, suggesting that a member of a racial minority in the jury room could have been more reluctant to participate.

Risky Shift or Group Polarization?

Some time ago, James Stoner (1961) discovered that when people got together in a group to arrive at a decision, they were more daring or "risky" than when they made decisions as individuals. This phenomenon, eventually called the risky-shift effect, stimulated the interest of numerous investigators who generated a collection of studies to test it, sometimes with mock jurors. As so often happens in psychological research, however, what appeared to be simple was soon discovered to be highly complex. "Risky shift" did not portray accurately the effects of groups on individual decisions (D. G. Myers & Lamm, 1976). Subsequent research illustrated that group deliberation may produce cautious decisions as well as more risky ones, depending upon the context, and thus was born the group-polarization hypothesis.

The group-polarization hypothesis states, "The average postgroup response will tend to be more extreme in the same direction as the average of the pregroup responses"

(D. G. Myers & Lamm, 1976, p. 603). This rather complicated maxim simply means that group interaction tends to draw the average individual pregroup decision more clearly in the direction in which it was already leaning. Hence, if individual members of a group were leaning toward a verdict of not guilty, the group interaction would increase their commitment toward that verdict even more. If, on the other hand, individual members tended to believe a defendant was guilty, group discussion should encourage a stronger commitment toward a guilty verdict. In civil cases, the individual jurors' beliefs that a plaintiff deserved a substantial award for damages might be reinforced in group discussion, and the ultimate group decision would award even higher damages. Thus, polarization refers to the shift toward the already-preferred pole.

D. G. Myers and Kaplan (1976) presented subjects with case materials that clearly made defendants in eight hypothetical traffic felony cases appear either guilty or not guilty. If the subjects found the defendant guilty, they were also expected to recommend punishment. The guilty–not guilty judgments were made on a scale ranging from 0 (definitely not guilty) to 20 (definitely guilty), and the punishment recommendation was given on a scale ranging from 1 (minimum punishment for the infraction) to 7 (maximum punishment).

D. G. Myers and Kaplan (1976) found that group deliberations polarized the initial-response tendencies associated with a case. Mock jurors who leaned toward guilty verdicts and punishment became harsher following deliberations. Those with lenient initial judgments became more lenient after deliberations. When jury deliberations were not allowed, however, judgments did not change from the first to the final rating.

A number of other experiments using simulated jury conditions have demonstrated the shift from pre-discussion tendency to post-discussion certainty (Bray & Kerr, 1979; Bray, Struckman-Johnson, Osborne, McFarlane, & Scott, 1978; Kaplan, 1977; Kerr, Nerenz, & Herrick, 1979). It appears that group discussion, at least under simulated conditions and with college students as mock jurors, does in fact polarize already-existing opinions or beliefs. However, a study by Kerr, Niedermeier, and Kaplan (1999) emphasizes (again) that the polarization process depends on the strength of the evidence delivered in the courtroom. They hypothesized that jury deliberation will increase (polarize) individual bias *if the evidence is ambiguous*. If, on the other hand, the evidence presented at trial is either very strong or very weak, the deliberation process will decrease individual bias and lead to a more balanced consensus in the direction of the evidence. Using several groups of four-person mock jurors, they found support for their hypotheses.

The Story Model

During the trial, a considerable amount of evidence is presented in a disjointed, question-and-answer format, sometimes over a period of several days, weeks, or—in exceptional cases—even months. In order to make a rational judgment about this extensive information, jurors try to comprehend and organize it into some meaningful whole. They do this both during the trial and during the deliberation process.

Pennington and Hastie (1986, 1992) developed a heuristic theory of how jurors organize and make sense of the vast array of evidence that is presented during the trial process and how they ultimately decide on guilt or innocence or, in civil cases, on the defendant's degree of responsibility. This popular and well-supported theory is referred to as the **story model**, and it remains the leading explanation of how jurors arrive at their decisions (Devine, 2012b). (See Table 7-1 for a summary of how the story model develops.)

Pennington and Hastie (1992) propose that jurors construct stories in the course of the trial and during the deliberation process that mediate and determine their decisions. In other words, jurors develop their own personal story of "what happened," and this conceptual structure allows them to incorporate the bits and pieces of the trial evidence into it. Overall, they try to arrive at an acceptable and plausible scenario for a crime or a civil situation. As Norman Finkel (1995) remarked, "jurors do not so much find reality as *construct* it" (p. 63). An important assumption in this model is that jurors are viewed as *active* information processors rather than *passive* recipients of information (Devine, 2012b).

The story model hypothesizes that jurors may develop several plausible but competing stories during the course of a trial, and then they try to base their decision on the story that is acceptable and best fits the evidence. Pennington and Hastie (1992) theorize that three fundamental principles determine the acceptability of the story: (1) coverage, (2) uniqueness, and (3) coherence. *Coverage* refers to the extent to which the story accounts for the evidence presented during the trial. The greater the story's coverage, the more plausible the story and the more confident the juror is about the story. *Uniqueness* refers to the extent that one story stands out from the other competing stories. If there are several stories and none is distinctive from the others, then uncertainty will result and no one story is apt to emerge. Under these conditions, the juror will be indecisive.

The third principle of story acceptability, *coherence,* is more complicated, and is determined by the interaction of three factors: (1) completeness; (2) consistency; and (3) plausibility. *Completeness* refers to the extent to which a story covers all the bases and contains the highlights of the evidence. *Consistency* refers to the internal structure of the story. More specifically, a consistent story contains few, if any, internal contradictions. In this sense, the juror wonders, "Does the story follow sequentially and make sense?" While consistency has to do with the internal aspects of the story, *plausibility* refers to the degree to which the story fits with the juror's version of the world—real or imagined. In other words, plausibility has to do with the relationship between the story and the juror's general knowledge of the world. These three factors combine to yield the coherence of a story.

Table 7-1	How the Story Model Operates

1. As a human information processor, a juror has some preconceived notion of what occurred, even though he or she is expected to judge the case based on the facts presented.

2. The juror continually constructs a story as the trial unfolds.

3. Several plausible scenarios are typically developed.

4. Evidence and testimony are woven into the juror's stories.

5. The juror is actively processing information throughout the trial; jurors are not passive recipients of information.

6. The juror decides on a final model that best dovetails with his or her cognitive belief (what must have happened).

7. The final model must cover the evidence presented, be unique (standing out from alternative models), and be coherent. Coherence is the combination of completeness, consistency, and plausibility.

8. During deliberation, the juror's model may be modified with input from other jurors.

9. The final story accepted by the juror must still be high in coverage, unique, and coherent.

Some researchers have proposed that jurors are more likely to construct one dominant story early in the trial rather than multiple stories as put forth by the story model. According to K. A. Carlson and Russo (2001), throughout the trial, jurors try to fit the various pieces of evidence into that one, dominant story. They argue that jurors try to formulate only one coherent account of the crime that is consistent with their prior beliefs, the lawyers' opening statements, and the judge's early instructions. This perspective is slightly different from the Pennington-Hastie story model because it emphasizes that only *one* story is developed early in the trial and is largely built on the strength of preexisting beliefs and biases. As the trial progresses, the typical juror will accept or reject new evidence based on how it conforms to her or his already-developed cognitive framework. Material that does not fit is rejected, and material that fits is accepted. Carlson and Russo refer to this process as **predecisional distortion**.

The hypothesis that jurors may have strong preexisting cognitive structures that could significantly slant their story making is also supported by the research of Olsen-Fulero and Fulero (1997), who have studied jury decision making in rape cases:

Overall . . . our work and recent work of others have supported the notion that jurors come to the rape judgment situation with preconceptions and attitudes that lead them to entertain particular stories about what may happen, that the stories are used to process the facts presented in the case, and that these stories are then used to arrive at a legal decision or verdict. (p. 418)

Smith (1991, 1993) has also found that prospective jurors have a preexisting conceptual prototype of certain crimes and offenders. Prospective jurors in one of her studies (1991) generally conceived of a kidnapping as characterized by ransom demands, the victim being a child, the victim being taken away, and the motive being money. Moreover, jurors tended to persist with these conceptions or stereotypes, in spite of jury instructions or points of law. In fact, her research has found that mock jurors actually have little correct information about the law. They do not enter the jury box "empty-headed," waiting for their charge. Rather, they have a preconceived notion of the crime scenario and the type of person who would commit such a crime. These personal stories of the crime and the jurors' prototypes of crime categories can influence their perceptions of the trial evidence and their verdict decisions. In addition, Finkel (1988) found that many jurors have well-established commonsense preconceptions of insanity and that these preconceptions strongly influence insanity verdicts.

V. L. Smith and Studebaker (1996) discovered that people's prior knowledge of crime categories plays a much broader role than previously known. For instance, they found that jurors' tendency to use their prior knowledge of crime categories extends not only to the verdict-determination process but also to the fact-finding phase. What jurors know—or think they know—about rape, burglary, or embezzlement, for example, affects how they will attend to the evidence presented. Furthermore, similar to jurors, *witnesses* appear to rely heavily on their offender stereotypes. That is, witnesses may fill the gaps in their memories with their preconceived notions of "criminals," and this slants their testimony significantly.

If the trial evidence matches this cognitive schema and the defendant follows the preconceived prototype, the juror is most likely to make a verdict decision along the lines of the developed story, regardless of the instructions or legal definitions. Smith (1991) found that the schemata of laypersons concerning various types of crime were contrary to the way the categories are organized under the law. Smith (1991) concludes, "These findings are consistent with research in other areas of social psychology demonstrating the potential dangers of prior knowledge or theories for accurate judgment and decision making" (p. 870).

Hindsight Bias

Another cognitive process that can potentially contaminate jury decision making is hindsight bias, which refers to biased judgments of past events after the outcome is known. It is "a projection of new knowledge into the past accompanied by a denial that the outcome information has influenced judgment" (Hawkins & Hastie, 1990, p. 311). Thus, when people learn of an outcome, they typically claim they "knew all along" what it would be. Said another way, "The hindsight bias is the tendency for people with outcome knowledge to believe falsely that they would have predicted the reported outcome of an event" (Hawkins & Hastie, 1990, p. 311). This bias potentially affects how jurors select, process, and integrate evidence for decision making.

Researchers have found evidence of hindsight bias, particularly in medical malpractice or product liability suits. In these types of cases, jurors are supposed to base their judgments on the defendant's behavior prior to the occurrence of the harm or damage. However, knowing that the defendant has curtailed his medical practice following the incident, jurors will find it extremely difficult not to blame him for the harm to the plaintiff. As another example, suppose police officers are charged with excessive force at arrest. The arrest, however, convinces an informant to come forward and help other officers solve a separate murder case. Knowledge that this occurred results in a tendency to excuse the original officers, particularly if the evidence against the officers is not strong. Again, evidentiary strength is likely to override other factors, including hindsight bias.

Influences on Jury Decision Making

Jurors are expected to decide cases on the basis of the strength of the evidence. They are not supposed to consider peripheral, irrelevant factors. As we asked at the beginning of the chapter, is this a realistic expectation? Research has uncovered many factors that seem to have some influence on a jury's final decision. In the final analysis, however, the strength of the evidence remains a key deciding factor.

Legal Trial Factors

Strength of the Evidence

"Strength of the evidence (SOE) is a global term referring to the quantity and quality of evidence presented by the plaintiff/prosecution during a trial" (Devine et al., 2001). Social and behavioral science research, both in the laboratory and in the field, have demonstrated a strong and consistent relationship between the strength of the evidence and jury verdicts (Devine et al., 2001). However, for research purposes, quantifying the strength of the evidence—also referred to as weight of the evidence—is a difficult task.

In addition, the strength or weight of the evidence is closely associated with the burden of proof. For example, precisely how much evidence is needed to reach the burden of proof required in criminal cases—beyond a reasonable doubt? Furthermore, the instructions concerning the standard of proof provided by the judge in any particular trial may be unclear to and misunderstood by jurors. Definitions of the standards of proof are not uniform across all jurisdictions, and the U.S. Supreme Court has not mandated that trial courts follow any particular definition (Horowitz & Kirkpatrick, 1996). It has, though, prohibited states from having standards that were too high, such as demanding that defendants prove their incompetency to stand trial by clear and convincing evidence (*Cooper v. Oklahoma,* 1996) rather than preponderance of the evidence.

The effect of evidentiary strength on jurors is clear-cut when the evidence is very strong or very weak. In a criminal case, when the evidence against the defendant is strong, the overwhelming tendency is to convict; when the evidence is weak, the overwhelming tendency is to acquit, regardless of the imagined scenario. However, in those cases where the evidence is ambiguous or complicated, the various aspects of the story model are most apt to come into play. Kalven and Zeisel (1966) also concluded that, when the evidence is unclear or does not favor one side, jurors would be liberated from the constraints of the evidence and become more susceptible to the influence of their own thoughts and beliefs, as well as other extralegal factors.

Effects of Expert Testimony

As we have discussed in earlier chapters, expert testimony refers to the courtroom opinion of some individual who possesses special skill or knowledge in a science, profession, or business that is not possessed by the average person. Many studies have examined the effects of expert testimony on mock juries, including the presence or absence of expert testimony, the style and content of the presentation, and the degree to which the expert's testimony is challenged (Devine, 2012b; Devine et al., 2001). The research results thus far are mixed, but much of it suggests that the overall impact of expert testimony on jury decision making is perhaps minimal (Devine, 2012b; Devine et al., 2001; Nietzel, McCarthy, & Kerr, 1999). There are situations, of course, in which expert testimony does wield some power over juror decision making, such as when it is tailored to the specific facts of the case at hand, or when it provides novel, useful information to the jury. However, in situations where the expert comes with an array of credentials and degrees, is receiving high payment to testify, or has a frequent history of testifying, he or she tends to be perceived by jurors as a "hired gun" (Cooper & Neuhaus, 2000). Experts perceived as hired guns rarely are effective in persuading jurors. If anything, they tend to engender animosity and irritation in the jurors and encourage them to rely on their preexisting opinions and beliefs.

Law professor Scott Sundby (1997) attempted to identify some empirical answers to how juries react to expert testimony (psychologists and psychiatrists) in capital cases. The study utilized data from the Capital Jury Project (see Box 6-2 in Chapter 6). One hundred and fifty-two jurors were interviewed concerning their reactions to expert testimony during the penalty phase. These jurors had served on 36 cases in which the defendant was convicted of first-degree murder, and the jury was then asked to return a sentence of death.

Sundby (1997) observed that professional expert witnesses were generally viewed negatively by jurors, especially those experts called by the defense. Many expert witnesses were seen simply as not being credible:

> The professional expert witness generally was seen as an unreliable storyteller, one likely to spin a tale for her own gain rather than for the enlightenment of

the jury. And, with only their own experience and beliefs with which to judge the story's veracity, jurors tended to discredit defense experts' testimony as being at odds with their worldview. The lay witness, in contrast, was far more likely to be perceived as a storyteller without a hidden agenda and, consequently, juries were far more receptive to the story she had to tell. (p. 1136)

To be effective, Sundby cautions, the expert's testimony must be integrated with persuasive lay testimony.

Influence of Attorneys

The iconoclastic Clarence Darrow swayed juries and stirred the imagination of budding attorneys with his courtroom antics and his rousing summations. His modern television counterparts keep viewers and television jurors alike entertained with legal cunning and acerbic wit. One need only watch local or national news coverage of actual trials to understand that these legal models are not representative of attorneys in actual courtrooms. Moreover, if the well-respected Kalven-Zeisel project (1966) accurately captures courtroom dynamics, the total impact lawyers have on the trial process is minimal.

Judges surveyed by Kalven and Zeisel (1966) concluded that prosecution and defense lawyers were equivalent in skills and in impact in slightly over three quarters of the 3,567 criminal cases they heard. Even when there was superior performance by one or the other lawyer, however, the jury's decision did not necessarily reflect it. In general, the nature of the case and the evidence presented, not the advocacy skills or the personality of the lawyers, accounted for the final verdict.

Nevertheless, it would be unwise to overlook the immense power held by attorneys in the courtroom, particularly when the evidence is ambiguous or of poor quality. Within broad limits, attorneys are able to direct and redirect testimony, making it appear credible or questionable. Furthermore, when two opposing lawyers are hopelessly ill-matched in ability or personal charm, the effect of the stronger attorney on the jury is likely to be considerable. Even though lawyers have this kind of impact within only a narrow range of cases, this small percentage still affects thousands of defendants.

During the trial process, it is the jury or the judge whom the attorneys must persuade. "Hard sells" and strong persuasive appeals are likely to prove counterproductive. Not only does this approach damage the credibility of the communicator, but it also may precipitate psychological *reactance,* discussed in Chapter 6 (Brehm, 1966). When individuals sense or perceive that their freedom of choice is being threatened or forced, they often become aroused and motivated to restore their freedom. Under these conditions, people often resort to making decisions that are opposite those desired by the communicator. Therefore, a lawyer who implies that jurors have no choice other than to absolve his or her client may soon learn that the jurors do indeed have an alternative. Although the media report anecdotal accounts of individual lawyers influencing jury decision making, research to support this happening on a widespread basis is not available.

Trials, however, are often avenues of last resort, particularly in civil cases. They occur when the respective attorneys have met an impasse in negotiations and the parties cannot agree on a settlement. Even in criminal cases, a trial may be seen as an avenue of last resort, rather than a right guaranteed by the Constitution. Because the judicial system is so dependent upon the plea-bargaining process to siphon cases from the court dockets, trial is seen as the least desirable option. In fact, even a defendant who is not guilty of the crime charged may prefer, or be persuaded, to plead guilty and avoid the expense and uncertainty of a trial.

There is little doubt, therefore, that most of what attorneys do on behalf of their clients in both criminal and civil cases is bargain and negotiate. Their ability to persuade is more likely to be tested in the pretrial arena than during the trial itself. Part of this pretrial arena includes the attorney's own client, who may be persuaded to accept a settlement or plead guilty to a lesser charge.

When they do go to trial, the best approach for attorneys in their efforts to convince the jury is to develop the evidence and arguments that support that evidence (J. Findley & Sales, 2012). On the other hand,

> In situations where jurors do not understand the evidence and arguments, or are not motivated or are unable to process the trial information, they are likely to focus on other nonlegal information such as source cues in their decision making. (J. Findley & Sales, 2012, pp. 205–206)

In those situations, the attorney's interpersonal skills and his or her ability at storytelling (recall the story model) appear key for winning the case. Likeable attorneys apparently have a significant advantage over attorneys the jurors do not like. Approaches to enhancing likeability include attorneys introducing themselves at the beginning of voir dire, appropriately addressing the court, apologizing when they are wrong, and being respectful of opposing counsel and his or her witnesses (J. Findley & Sales, 2012). Credibility may be even more persuasive. Credibility refers to such attributes as trustworthiness, honesty, and competence. However, it should be emphasized that, in the final analysis, research reveals that specific attorney characteristics are unlikely to have a consistent or powerful persuasive impact on the jury. Research has shown that the presentation of strong evidence, combined with cogent arguments that shore up that evidence, is the best approach to persuading most juries.

Defendant Characteristics

Some factors associated with a trial should not enter into the decision making of jurors or judges—they are called extralegal factors. In reality, they have nothing to do with the issue being decided. It is difficult if not impossible to "control" for the influence of these factors, only a few of which we cover here. Researchers have long focused on the extralegal factors associated with the defendants in criminal cases, but other factors include characteristics of both defendants and plaintiffs in civil trials, pretrial publicity, or even current events that may be occurring in the community at the time of the trial.

Physical Attractiveness

A long line of research in social psychology has found that most individuals believe that good-looking people, compared with physically unattractive people, possess socially desirable traits and lead more successful and fulfilling lives (Dion, Berscheid, & Walster, 1972). Moreover, transgressions or violations of the social code are tolerated more when they are committed by a physically attractive person (Dion, 1972; Efran, 1974).

Numerous early studies confirmed the significance of attractiveness to juries in both criminal and civil cases (Efran, 1974; Kulka & Kessler, 1978). Stewart (1980, 1985) found attractiveness was a factor in the decision making of trial judges: The less physically attractive the defendant, the more severe the sentence given by the judge. On the other hand, if a defendant is perceived as having used his or her attractiveness to perpetrate a crime (such as swindling a victim), this **attraction-leniency bias**, as it has come to be called, does not occur (Sigall & Ostrove, 1975).

"Attractiveness," of course, is a subjective criterion that may be associated with background variables like health, nutrition, and socioeconomic status. Moreover, as society becomes increasingly aware of the broad range of criminal activity perpetrated by the socially and economically advantaged, the connection between crime and attractiveness should become irrelevant—shouldn't it?

So far, there is little evidence in that direction, however. Research results thus far suggest that physical attractiveness could be of considerable significance in the courtroom. Gunnell and Ceci (2010) conclude from their review of the research literature that the consistency of attraction-leniency bias has withstood the test of time. Physical attractiveness, it seems, can be of considerable significance in the courtroom:

> Overall, the attraction-leniency bias has been shown to operate across decision makers (judges and jurors), types of crime, and trial type (criminal or civil), albeit it is moderated by the seriousness of the crime and the strength of evidence against the defendant. (p. 852)

Defendant's Criminal History

Juries react very strongly to knowledge about a defendant's criminal history. Prior convictions or arrests of a defendant, unrelated to the crime at hand, are inadmissible evidence during the trial. However, when jurors somehow learn that the defendant does have a history of one or more felony convictions, there is a strong tendency to find the defendant guilty (Borgida & Park, 1988; Devine, 2012b; Devine et al., 2001). This tendency happens even when the juror is told to disregard the prior criminal record through limiting instructions by the presiding judge (Lieberman & Sales, 1997). Apparently, jurors infer a criminal disposition when they learn that a defendant has committed crimes in the past (Devine, 2012b).

A fairly recent study (Givelber & Farrell, 2008) confirms the above observations as well as the complexity of the trial process. The researchers examined data from 311 noncapital felony jury trials held in four different state jurisdictions in an effort to identify factors that influenced or failed to influence judges and juries. One such factor was a defendant's criminal history. Rarely does the jury learn of a defendant's criminal background unless the defendant elects to take the stand and testify in his or her own defense.

In over half of the trials (57%) examined by Givelber and Farrell (2008), the defendant had a criminal record, but the jury did not learn of it. In about a quarter of the cases (23%), however, the defendant had a criminal record and the jury knew about it. In the Givelber and Farrell study, it was found that when the defendant had no prior criminal past—or when the defendant did, but the jury did not know this—juries convicted in 57% of the cases (Devine, 2012b). On the other hand, when the defendant had a prior criminal record and the jury learned of it, the conviction rate rose to 81% (Givelber & Farrell, 2008). Commenting on this research, Devine (2012b) affirms that criminal history seems to have a moderate but very reliable impact on jury decision making, with solid support across both simulation studies and studies that surveyed actual jurors.

Nevertheless, further analysis of the Givelber and Farrell (2008) data revealed that assuming a negative impact for criminal history may be premature, and it further underscored the complexity of factors that influence the trial process. Jurors—more than judges—are apparently favorably impressed when a defendant without a criminal record testifies on his or her own behalf or presents witnesses. It is important to emphasize that criminal defendants do not have to testify and that the defense does not have to present any witnesses. In a criminal trial, the prosecutor must make the case against the defendant. Nevertheless, when defendants did take the stand or present witnesses, jurors acquitted them 64.3% of the time; judges acquitted them only 33.3% of the time. Interestingly, when the defense presented no witnesses or the defendant did not testify, the acquittal rate was the same between judges and jurors.

Judge and jury discrepancies also disappear when the defendant and another witness testify and the defendant has a criminal past—whether or not the jury learns of it. Apparently, it is primarily the presence of credible witnesses—not the presence of a testifying defendant with an unblemished past—that triggers the judge–jury differences.

Defendant's Courtroom Behavior

How the behavior of a defendant in the courtroom affects jury verdicts has received some research attention, particularly but not exclusively in relation to capital trials. Jurors scrutinize the defendant throughout the trial, and they usually notice everything from the defendant's attire to his or her slightest facial expressions.

The most comprehensive study done to date on the influence of defendant behavior on jury decision making was conducted by Sundby (1998) using data from the California segment of the 15-state Capital Jury Project (see Box 6-2 in Chapter 6). Recall that the trial procedure in capital cases is usually bifurcated, with one part consisting of the trial phase and the second part consisting of the punishment phase. The same jurors serve as decision makers for both phases, but if the jurors cannot agree on the punishment—as happened in the Jodi Arias case—a new sentencing jury must be seated.

The Sundby (1998) project was primarily interested in how remorsefulness (or a lack of it) influences juror decisions concerning death or life-without-parole sentences. In capital cases, defendants, usually on the advice of their attorneys, often do not display remorse during their trial because remorse is an admission of guilt. Instead, they sit passively and emotionless, seemingly not caring whether they live or die. Jurors, however, look for signs of remorsefulness or responsibility for clues for their decision making. When remorse is expressed at sentencing, however, it may be considered a mitigating factor.

In the Sundby (1998) study, jurors placed a great deal of weight on sincere expressions of sorrow, especially in deciding whether to recommend death or life without parole. Nearly 70% of the jurors who voted for the death penalty during the penalty stage said that the lack of remorse by the defendant was the major reason for their death vote. Jurors scrutinized the defendant throughout the course of the trial for signs of this remorse, and they were quick to recall details about the defendant's demeanor, ranging from his attire to facial expression (Sundby, 1998). During the *early* stages of the trial process, some jurors were surprised at how "normal" the defendants appeared. Some jurors said they looked too nice to commit murder, seemed harmless, or did not look like an evil person. These early impressions, however, soon changed. The adjectives used by most capital jurors in describing the defendant during the later stages of the trial were commonly "emotionally flat," "arrogant," "cocky," and "nonchalant." Throughout the trial, jurors constantly searched for any indicators of remorse or, at least, some signs of defendants taking responsibility for their actions. This is problematic, though, because defendants during a trial are innocent until proven guilty. They should not be expected to demonstrate remorse. Such a display at sentencing—once convicted—is a different matter, but even then the individual convicted may be actually innocent. Jurors, however, did not seem to distinguish between the trial and the sentencing. The more accumulated evidence the jury could find that indicated the defendant's acceptance of responsibility for the crime, the more likely they would return a life sentence rather than death.

In his extensive review of the relevant research literature, Devine (2012b) concludes that a large and diverse set of studies have demonstrated that remorseful defendants are generally treated more leniently (although there are exceptions). In spite of the fact that many of the relevant studies used mock jurors, he notes that a well-conducted analysis by Antonio (2006) of field data, involving 1,200 capital jurors, supports remorseful leniency by "real jurors" as well.

Race of the Defendant

A sizeable amount of research has been directed at the effects of racial bias on jury decision making in both capital and noncapital trials. The research on noncapital trials across the nation has been mixed, and no clear pattern of racial bias has emerged with reference to juries. Some studies have found weak evidence that racial bias exists, usually in subtle form; other studies have not identified any significant evidence.

The research on capital trials offers a different story. Studies conducted at different times in different states and by different researchers have consistently indicated that blacks are convicted of capital crimes at a higher rate and, upon conviction, are sentenced to death at a higher rate than whites (Devine, 2012b; Eberhardt, Davies, Purdie-Vaughns, & Lynn Johnson, 2006; Snell, 2013). Although the racial disparity in capital cases is due, in part, to the nature of the evidence and the prosecutorial decision making in seeking the death penalty, a growing body of studies strongly suggests that jurors' death sentence decisions are affected by the race of the defendant and the race of the victim (Lynch & Haney, 2009, 2011). The research indicates that this racial bias depends on the composition of the jury.

As we learned in Chapter 6, the death qualification process systemically excludes certain people on the basis of their strong death penalty views. Consequently, the demographic makeup of the capital jury is "distinctive and problematic" (Lynch & Haney, 2011, p. 73). According to Lynch and Haney, survey research reveals that support for the death penalty among whites is highly associated with measures of antiblack racial prejudice and stereotyping. Among the core stereotypes is that blacks, as a group, are violently and criminally inclined. Some believe (e.g., Quillian & Pager, 2001) that this stereotype "is one of the most pervasive, well-known, and persistent stereotypes in American culture" (Lynch & Haney, 2011, p. 73) (see Box 7-1).

BOX 7-1 RESEARCHERS AT WORK

Is the White Male the Problem?

Stereotypes depicting black males as more violent and criminally inclined are especially prevalent among white males. This in itself is close to being a stereotype: Obviously, not all white males fit this pattern, and it is likely that most do not. Nevertheless, research does indicate that white males, when on capital juries, tend to push guilty verdicts and the death penalty when the case involves a black defendant. For instance, in the well-designed study by Lynch and Haney (2011), the jurors received exactly the same case and evidence:

> Yet the white men who participated as jurors in our study appear to have heard and judged a different case as a function of the race of the defendant. When they judged a black defendant—and essentially only then—they diverged significantly from their peers, both in terms of how they constructed the defendant's blameworthiness and motivation, and on whether they believed he deserved to be allowed to continue to live. (p. 91)

The data revealed that white men gave significantly less weight to the mitigating factors in the case. Overall, they appeared less able or inclined to empathize with or understand the plight of the black defendant. Other jurors—including white women—were significantly more inclined to empathize and consider mitigating factors in the case, and therefore were less predisposed toward guilty or death penalty decisions.

Perhaps more troubling was the tendency of the white males to control or dominate the discussion in the deliberation process. Other research (e.g., Bowers, Steiner, & Sandys, 2001) discovered similar results and called it the "white male dominance effect." The white male dominance effect referred to a 41% increase in the likelihood of a death sentence when there were five or more white males on the jury. What's more, during the deliberation process, white male jurors appeared to be especially influential in bringing other jurors to their punitive point of view. In fact, deliberation appears to have increased the tendency to vote for the death penalty.

In a previous study, Lynch and Haney (2009) also found that the proportion of white male jurors present on a jury elevated its tendency to vote in favor of the death penalty. They write that white male jurors "created considerable momentum in favor of death verdicts that even many initially pro-life jurors (a disproportionate number of whom were women and non-Whites) found difficult to resist" (p. 491).

Questions for Discussion:

1. The death qualification process cannot in itself account for the "white male dominance" effect in capital cases, because women become death qualified as well. What, then, can account for this effect?

2. Assuming that the white male dominance effect does exist, what are realistic solutions to this problem?

⬚ Judicial Decision Making

Despite some recent research on judicial decision making, there remains a substantial gap in our understanding of what judges do, how they think, and how they make their decisions.

> How will a judge's decision on a motion, verdict, or appeal be affected by precedents, the presence of an *amicus curiae* brief from the federal government, the plaintiff's race, a particularly eloquent brief or oral argument by the defendant's attorney, the preference and arguments of other panelists on a collegial court, the opinions of the local bar, the presentations of expert witnesses, or the demands on the judges' time? (Klein, 2010, p. xi)

Do most judges possess special reasoning skills that ordinary people lack? Do judges think the same way that ordinary citizens do? Are they biased at all when it comes to decision making?

It is important to realize that psychologists have not conducted many empirical studies of judicial behavior (Baum, 2010; Mitchell, 2010). We are very much at the early stages of our knowledge in this area. Most of the empirical studies have been conducted by legal scholars and social scientists (primarily political scientists) who have focused almost exclusively on the U.S. Supreme Court and, to a lesser extent, the appellate court judges. Trial judges, the main topic of this section, have been largely neglected, not only by psychologists but also by social scientists in general. Moreover, as noted by Mitchell, there is little reason that the research knowledge and commentary on the Supreme and appellate courts will generalize to the lower trial courts. Consequently, the topic "psychology of judicial decision making" is a very limited and incomplete one.

Functions of Trial Judges

Trial judges represent the front line in both civil and criminal trials (Vidmar, 2011). Vidmar elaborates:

> At early stages of litigation they make rulings about relevant law bearing on the dispute—for example, about whether the litigation is "ripe" for further attention by the court, about whether the claims have merit, or about whether a statute of limitations is or is not applicable. (p. 58)

They also manage a range of settlements, approve plea bargains, and preside over jury trials. They sentence defendants found guilty in criminal cases and review civil jury verdicts, sometimes adjusting damage awards up or down. As further noted by Vidmar, these various decision-making activities are potentially influenced by the judge's personality, attitudes, experiences, and cognitive biases, as well as a host of other factors. (See Box 7-2 for a discussion of the influence of diagnoses.)

Before we proceed, however, it is important to mention that the decisions made by trial judges are also influenced by considerable deference to precedent, which tends to keep personal characteristics and cognitive biases in check during judicial decision making. Vidmar (2011) comments that "judges know that if they deviate too far from prior case law or statutory guidelines, their ruling will be appealed—and likely overturned in an appellate court" (p. 58). According to Robbennolt, MacCoun, and Darley (2010), a solid understanding of judicial decision making must incorporate the knowledge that judges simultaneously attempt to balance numerous, disparate, and often conflicting objectives.

BOX 7-2 RESEARCHERS AT WORK

Are Judges Swayed by Diagnoses and Labels?

Many psychologists are leery of diagnostic labels, and they often resist using them, particularly in courts. However, as noted in earlier chapters, judges often expect to see them in the reports they receive from mental health examiners. For example, judges often want a specific diagnosis in competency evaluations, criminal responsibility evaluations, and evaluations of a defendant's "dangerousness" (Melton et al., 2007). The official diagnosis antisocial personality disorder (APD) is very closely related to the label "psychopath." In fact, the DSM-5 notes that the patterns associated with APD are also referred to as psychopathy (American Psychiatric Association, 2013, p. 659). Therefore, some mental health examiners indicate that a person has been diagnosed as a psychopath.

When judges know that an individual has been labeled a psychopath, this seems to influence their decision making. Perhaps it is not influenced in the expected direction, though.

Psychopaths are individuals who often demonstrate a distinct neurobiologically based disposition that influences their behavior. They typically exhibit lower levels of empathy, compassion, or remorse, and sometimes—but not necessarily—higher levels of violence. As a group, psychopaths engage in more antisocial behavior than the general population. Historically, some judges have considered evidence of psychopathy to be mitigating (i.e., they decreased the sentence), whereas other judges have deemed the evidence of psychopathy as aggravating (i.e., they increased the sentence).

In an effort to examine this discrepancy, Aspinwall, Brown, and Tabery (2012) enlisted 181 U.S. state trial court judges to participate in the study. All the judges read a hypothetical case where a psychiatrist explained that the defendant was a "diagnosed psychopath." However, one group of participants received the case summary, which included a statement by an expert (a neurobiologist) describing the neurobiological explanation for psychopathic antisocial behavior. In other words, the material indicated that the defendant had a biological predisposition that promoted his antisocial behavior. The other group received a case summary indicating that the defendant had a diagnosis of psychopathy but without the expert's neurobiological explanation for the cause of the disorder.

The participants were also given different information about the prosecution and defense arguments. In the prosecution condition, prosecutors argued that the evidence should be considered aggravating because the crime and the defendant's behavior all point to psychopathy. Therefore, the prosecution maintained, the defendant posed a continuing and serious threat to society. In the defense condition, the defense attorney argued that evidence should be considered mitigating because the crime and the defendant's behavior indicated that he has problems controlling his impulses due to his disorder.

Judges were then asked to indicate the extent to which the evidence concerning psychopathy mitigated, aggravated, or had no effect on the punishment they would impose. Results indicated that, while a majority of judges considered the diagnosis of psychopathy to be an aggravating factor, a surprising number (who read the neurobiologist's explanation of psychopathy) deemed it a mitigating factor. Moreover, the neurobiological reasons for psychopathy presented by the expert and the defense doubled the number of judges listing a mitigating factor. Put another way, the judges were receptive to evidence of a biological basis for the individual's disorder. Some of the judges made comments that indicated they believed it possible that "psychopaths are, in a sense, morally 'disabled' just as other people are physically disabled" (Aspinwall et al., 2012, p. 847).

The label "juvenile psychopath" has also been found to have a significant influence on judges (S. Jones & Cauffman, 2008). Once trial judges discovered a juvenile defendant was considered a psychopath by mental health experts, they were more likely to perceive the youth as less amenable to treatment and to recommend a more restrictive placement for him than a youth with no such diagnosis. The judges were also convinced that the juvenile psychopath represented more of a danger to the community than other youth.

Questions for Discussion:

1. Although psychopathy is of great interest to many legal psychologists, they also urge extreme caution in applying the label to individuals, most particularly juveniles. What might be the reasons for this caution?

2. If a person has a disorder attributed to biological causes, should this fact be considered in deciding the person's guilt in a criminal case? Should it be considered at sentencing?

Regular watchers of legal dramas on cable and network television are routinely treated to a parade of judges who are impatient, funny, kind, sarcastic, respected, corrupt, naive, efficient, brilliant, or incompetent—in other words, they are human. Schauer (2010) finds that judges share three prominent characteristics: (1) They are judges, (2) they are lawyers, and (3) they are human beings. He further posits that it is the third item on the list, and not the first and second, that offers the greatest promise for research on the psychology of judging. The assumption is that judges as humans are probably subject to many of same cognitive errors all humans make in their thinking and decision making. Schauer, however, looks at this differently. Although judges are human, their decision making may be more influenced by legal and judicial attributes than by factors that influence the decision making of laypeople. He advocates much more research in this area.

As psychologists have learned over the years, all humans rely on stereotypes and cognitive shortcuts to simplify and make sense of a complex social and legal world. Cognitive shortcuts allow for more efficient information processing, but they also create stereotypes. Judges, in spite of their education, training, and experience, are probably not immune to errors of judgment and decision making. Some empirical work clearly points in that direction. Nevertheless, as Schauer (2010) warns, precisely how much this happens remains an open question.

Research on Judge Biases

Guthrie, Rachlinski, and Wistrich (2001a, 2001b), in their oft-cited and comprehensive study of federal trial judges, used the term cognitive biases to characterize the group of decision errors sometimes made by judges. In fact, cognitive biases affect the decisions many professionals make, "including doctors, real estate appraisers, engineers, accountants, options traders, military leaders, psychologists, and even lawyers" (Guthrie et al., 2001a, p. 1). For instance, several studies have discovered that judges appear to be similar to juries in their inability to disregard legally prejudicial and impermissible facts in rendering a verdict (Landsman & Rakos, 1994; Vidmar, 2011; Wistrich, Guthrie, & Rachlinski, 2005). It is probably not as extensive as found among juries, but it still exists. Guthrie and his colleagues (2001b) focused on three cognitive biases or "cognitive illusions" to which trial judges are most likely to fall prey: (1) anchoring, (2) hindsight bias, and (3) egocentric biases.

Anchoring

Anchoring involves giving excessive weight to the initial starting value (the anchor) when decisions are to be made under conditions of uncertainty. This bias is especially prevalent in civil cases. Guthrie et al. (2001a) give the example of real estate transactions when people are trying to decide the fair market value of a house before they make an offer. In these situations, they commonly rely on the initial value available to them—the list price. The list price tends to "anchor" purchasing parties' final-price offer. Reliance on anchors is often reasonable in such a setting, because they provide important information about the "true" market value of a house. In some cases, however, the list price does not provide relevant information about the market value, but it does influence judgment and decision making. Guthrie et al. (2001a) write, "In litigation, anchors, such as damage awards requested by plaintiffs' attorneys or damage caps provided by statute, have been shown to influence the amount of damages awarded by juries" (p. 2). The researchers also discovered that judges are influenced by anchors in a similar fashion. As an example, they are aware of the awards made in similar cases and do not stray significantly from these amounts.

Hindsight Bias

As stated earlier in the chapter in discussing jurors, *hindsight bias* is the tendency to change a previous judgment or decision in the direction of newly provided information (Massoni & Vannucci, 2007). Stated another way, it is the tendency, after an event has occurred, to overestimate the extent to which the outcome could have been foreseen (VandenBos, 2007). It is one of the most pervasive errors in everyday human judgment and prediction (Bartol & Bartol, 2013), and judges are by no means immune to it. Guthrie et al. (2001a) argue that hindsight bias is a threat to accurate determinations in many areas of law. These legal scholars note that it is unusual, in ordinary life, to expect people to predict the outcome of past events; however, in law, people are asked to make this kind of judgment on a frequent basis. Because courts usually evaluate events *after* they happen, judges are continually vulnerable to hindsight bias (Guthrie et al., 2001b).

> For example, when a judge or jury sets out to determine whether a defendant was negligent, they must evaluate the reasonableness of precautions that the defendant took against causing an accident, and they make this decision knowing that there was an injury. (Guthrie et al., 2001a, p. 2)

Research has shown that precautions that seem reasonable to people *before* an accident may seem negligent afterward. Another example is found when a prosecutor's approach, which appeared skillful during the trial, seems less competent after the jury decides not to convict. The opposite also occurs—that is, something initially believed to be unreasonable is later thought to be acceptable. The prosecutor's brazen attack on the witness is outrageous, until the prosecutor wins the case. She is then praised for her stellar performance.

In their study, Guthrie et al. (2001b) found that judges are indeed susceptible to hindsight bias. The researchers determined that judges could not help but rely on information that was not available before a relevant event occurred, but that later became available. This susceptibility to hindsight bias, the researchers write, is troubling because judges are frequently expected to suppress their knowledge of some set of facts before making decisions.

> When deciding whether to suppress evidence found during a police search, for example, judges are expected to ignore their knowledge of the outcome of the search for purposes of determining whether the police had probable cause to conduct the search. (Guthrie et al., 2001b, pp. 804–805)

Egocentric Biases

In Garrison Keillor's hometown, "all of the children are above average," as many public radio listeners know. This illustrates the long-standing psychological knowledge that people are often self-serving about their own abilities and competence (as well as those of their children). "People routinely estimate that they are above average on a variety of desirable characteristics, including health, driving, productivity, and the likelihood that their marriage will succeed" (Guthrie et al., 2001a, p. 3). Because of these **egocentric biases**, litigants and their attorneys probably overestimate their own abilities and the merits of their cases. These biases are also likely to undermine settlement efforts because each side remains optimistic about its chances of winning at trial.

Guthrie et al. (2001b) reasoned that judges, like most humans, are also likely to be inclined to interpret information in self-serving or egocentric ways. Moreover, these judicial biases might make it difficult for judges to realize they can make mistakes, "issue unfair rulings, make choices that reflect personal biases, or even be subject to cognitive illusions of judgment" (Guthrie et al., 2001a, p. 3). Guthrie et al. (2001b) found that judges, on rating their prior decisions (the number of cases that have been overturned in their careers), exhibited a significant self-serving bias. In sum, they believed they were better in their decisions than their record revealed. The authors concluded that judges, like all other human beings, will rely on cognitive shortcuts and biases that may induce decision errors.

To illustrate the potential for judge errors further, Wallace and Kassin (2012) recruited 132 judges from three states to participate in an experiment involving errors in judgment around confession evidence. The judges were presented with one of six versions of a two-page criminal case summary taken from actual cases containing confession evidence. The case involved burglary and the murder of a young woman. The researchers manipulated three levels of confession by the defendant and two levels of evidence (see Table 7-2). After reading the case summary, the judges were asked to complete a questionnaire on how they would rule.

Results revealed that judges found that the high-pressure confession was coerced and therefore improperly admitted into evidence. However—and as found in previous

Table 7-2   Confession and Evidence Conditions in Wallace and Kassin's (2012) Experiment

Confession Condition	Description
No confession	Suspect did not confess to the crime.
High coercion	Suspect questioned for 15 hours; suspect claimed threats. High-pressure tactics, including police waving gun.
Low coercion	Suspect questioned for 30 minutes; suspect claimed coercion, but no behavioral indicators; videotape did not indicate high coercion.
Evidence Condition	
Strong evidence	Lab analysis found hair on victim consistent with defendant's hair. Jewelry found in defendant's home.
Weak evidence	Hair analysis results inconclusive. No items belonging to victim in defendant's home.

studies on juries—the improper confession, even if not admitted, significantly increased the judges' conviction of the defendant, even in the weak evidence condition.

> The fact that judges exhibited the same bias that mock jurors have in past studies is interesting and adds to a growing body of research suggesting that some of the biases observed in lay decision makers are rooted in such basic social cognition processes that they tend to afflict professional judges as well. (Wallace & Kassin, 2012, p. 156)

The researchers contend that the bias is so "fundamental" that no one is immune, including trial judges.

Racial and Other Group Biases

In addition to the cognitive biases discussed above, judges may have racial biases as well as gender, ethnic, religious, and other biases against persons belonging to specific groups. Both anecdotal and research evidence of such biases—particularly gender bias— was not uncommon in the past, but there has been less evidence in recent years, likely because of gender diversity in the judicial profession. Anecdotes continue to be told, including the one about the judge who sentenced a male teacher to a mild probationary sentence for the rape of a 14-year-old girl, stating that the girl herself was physically advanced for her age. Recent research, however, has not documented the *systematic* gender discrimination of the past.

Racial bias has been somewhat documented, however. For example, judges have been found to be as prone as other persons to stereotyping of blacks (Rachlinski, Johnson, Wistrich, & Guthrie, 2009; Vidmar, 2011). That is, judges in some studies imposed harsher penalties on black defendants than on white defendants. In a study by Blair, Judd, and Chapleau (2004), blacks who were rated as having the most "Afrocentric" features received significantly longer sentences than blacks having fewer of these features, even after other factors were controlled in the study.

However, Vidmar (2011) admonishes that the above studies did not involve "real-world contexts" but were laboratory experiments that may have distorted the results. The typical methodology in such studies is to ask participants to read case materials or view portions of a simulated trial. Vidmar asserts that "in actual trials, judges weigh inadmissible evidence along with many other pieces of evidence, including arguments by opposing legal counsel, so any effects of implicit biases may be negligible" (p. 59). In actual cases, compared with simulation studies, judges have more detailed information or deal with settled legal doctrines, and they have more time to consider and deliberate. However, Vidmar also believes that the potential effects of race on sentencing may be "subtle and invidious" (p. 59) and difficult to clearly identify.

SUMMARY AND CONCLUSIONS

The decision-making processes of juries and judges, particularly juries, has been researched extensively by social scientists, resulting in an impressive store of studies from various academic disciplines. Reviews of the literature indicate that well over 1,500 jury studies have been published (Devine, 2011b). Most—about two thirds—are mock jury experiments. Some have participants who either served on juries or were called for jury duty, but most use typical research participants recruited from the community or college classrooms. Studies of judicial decision making are fewer in number, but they are more likely to use "real" judges. The judges are surveyed about their attitudes or actual decisions, or they are asked to read case materials and make decisions based on the facts of the case presented. The chapter focused primarily on the decision making of jurors, but increasingly more information about judicial decision making is becoming available.

Juries adopt deliberation styles, with the two most common being verdict driven and evidence driven. It appears that most juries use the former, which indicates a desire to reach consensus or unanimity as soon as possible. The law prefers juries to use the evidence-driven approach, which implies a very careful review of the evidence presented as well as conscientious deliberation among a group of individuals who are unlikely to have known one another before the trial began. Verdict-driven juries spend less time deliberating and are more likely to pressure jurors with a minority opinion to bend to the majority. Nevertheless, researchers do not suggest that justice is not served by the verdict-driven jury. There is concern, however, when some jurors may not feel free to participate or may not be listened to. Research has found that diversified juries (in socioeconomic status, race, gender, and age) are the most likely to ensure the integrity of the jury system.

Jury deliberation is likely to result in group polarization—or a move toward the decision favored by the majority of the jurors. Deliberation is also likely to adopt a story model, in which jurors create their versions of what must have occurred. This is particularly likely to occur if the evidence for neither side is strong. Jurors are free to create their cognitive picture of the scene that unfolded, be it a crime or a civil wrong. Although the strength of the evidence is a dominant factor in the outcome of the case, when evidence is not strong, the story model predominates. This is logical, if one considers the likelihood that clear-cut cases will result in a plea bargain or a settlement rather than a trial, despite the constitutional guarantee of a trial.

If jurors are influenced by the strength of the evidence (if it is there), they do not seem to be heavily influenced by expert testimony or by the proficiency of the attorneys. They are, however, influenced by extralegal factors such as characteristics of the defendant. Surprisingly, physical attractiveness remains a strong factor in jury decision making, with numerous studies confirming it as an important component. Perhaps no characteristic of the defendant is as powerful as his or her criminal history, however. When jurors are made aware of a criminal history, even if told to disregard this fact, they find it difficult to do so. The courtroom behavior of the defendant has been studied particularly in the context of capital cases, where jurors expect to see some evidence of regret or compassion from the defendant.

Factors influencing judges have been studied in different ways, but a major approach has been to consider cognitive biases they may hold, often similar to the biases of other human beings. Anchoring bias relates primarily to damage awards in civil cases, but it may be relevant to sentencing as well. It refers to a tendency to rely on information from past awards (or sentences) to establish an award or sentence in the case at hand. Hindsight bias is a human cognitive feature that is difficult to avoid. A judge often must make a decision already knowing the outcome of a situation. The most frequently cited illustration is a judge's need to decide on the legality of a search after the search has uncovered incriminating evidence—this is, of course, a routine decision judges must make, because the search would not be challenged if evidence had not been uncovered. However, the nature of the evidence (e.g., highly incriminatory) may influence the judge's decision, even though it should not. Finally, judges—like other humans—are subject to egocentric biases, in which they believe in the correctness of their own decisions, and racial bias, which is often subtle and very difficult to detect. Research on judicial decision making is beginning to attract a considerable amount of attention in the literature on psychology and law, but it remains largely uncharted territory.

KEY CONCEPTS

Anchoring

Attraction-leniency bias

Cognitive biases

Egocentric biases

Evidence-driven
  deliberation style

Extralegal factors

Group-polarization
  hypothesis

Hindsight bias

Polling the jury

Predecisional distortion

Risky-shift effect

Story model

Verdict-driven deliberation
  style

Controversial Evidence in the Courtroom

Profiling, Psychological Autopsies, and Hypnosis

The relationship between psychology and law is no stranger to controversy. We have seen evidence of this in previous chapters, beginning with Chapter 1, where the relation between the two disciplines was described as challenging. Legal psychologists often wish judges, lawyers, and legislators would pay closer attention to research findings or recognize the limits of their expertise. Psychologists cannot absolutely predict dangerousness, for example, although some lawyers and judges expect them to do so. For their part, legal practitioners wish the mental health professionals would be more attuned to the statutes; the rules that govern the law; and the need to operate efficiently, often with limited resources.

Increasingly, since the *Daubert* decision, courts in particular are challenging the evidence and the scientific findings offered by mental health professionals as well as experts in all other sciences. Mental health professionals testifying in court, for example, are expected to document that they use valid techniques and measures as well as evidence-based practices, despite the fact that judges seem to rely most heavily on the credentials of the expert testifying and the general acceptance of techniques used among the scientific community (Skeem et al., 2009). Judicial scrutiny is nowhere more apparent,

249

though, than in the case of controversial methods, such as profiling, hypnosis, and equivalent death analyses (also known as psychological autopsies). This chapter reviews psychological research on these topics along with statutes and court decisions relevant to their use.

⬙ Overview of Profiling

Profiling is broadly defined as "a technique that identifies behavioral, cognitive, emotional, and demographic characteristics of known and unknown individuals, based on clues gleaned from a wide range of information" (Bartol & Bartol, 2013, p. xiii). The term "behavioral analysis" is often preferred by those who have trained in the technique, but "profiling" continues to be widely used as well. The information derived for profiling purposes includes, but is not limited to, crime scene investigations, interviews, documents, databases, behavioral observation, and even suicide notes. A majority of readers are probably familiar with profiling in criminal cases—generally called criminal profiling—but few are familiar with the use of profiling in civil cases.

Profiling can be divided into five major categories: (1) crime scene profiling; (2) geographic profiling; (3) psychological profiling; (4) suspect-based profiling; and (5) equivocal death analysis—also called the psychological autopsy (see Table 8-1 for definitions). The five profiling categories are not mutually exclusive, because they somewhat overlap in definition and purpose. However, the classification helps in understanding the many topics carrying the label "profiling." Of the five, crime scene profiling and the psychological autopsy are the most likely to be associated with court proceedings and thus will take up our attention in this chapter.

The remaining three types of profiling procedures are usually restricted to the investigative and public safety realms of law enforcement and rarely are used as a source of evidence in courtroom proceedings, although they may be. Nevertheless, psychologists—including those engaged in psychology/law activities—are interested in exploring their effects.

This is especially the case with **suspect-based profiling**, which has the potential of singling out individuals of certain racial, ethnic, religious, or cultural groups. In suspect-based profiling, law enforcement makes use of characteristics that are believed to be associated with certain crimes, such as terrorist activities or drug trafficking. Consequently, suspect-based profiling is commonly associated with "racial profiling," defined as police-initiated action that is based "on the race, ethnicity, or national origin rather than the behavior of an individual or information that led police to a particular individual" suspected of criminal activity (Ramirez, McDevitt, & Farrell, 2000, p. 53). The racial profiling controversy began within the context of traffic stops, but now has expanded to airport security, shoplifting, immigration, and

Table 8-1	Definitions of the Five Types of Profiling
Profiling Type	**Description**
Crime scene	The process of identifying behavioral patterns, motivations, and demographic variables of an *unknown* offender based on the evidence gathered at the crime scene.
Geographic	A method of identifying the area of probable residency and the probable area of the next crime of an *unknown* offender. The process is based on the analysis of the location and spatial relationships among various crime sites.
Psychological	The process of identifying and predicting the level of dangerousness of *known* or *unknown* individuals. The process usually involves two slightly different assessment procedures: threat assessment and risk assessment. Threat assessment is a process to determine the credibility and seriousness of an expressed threat being carried out. The person may be *known* or *unknown*. Risk assessment, on the other hand, is a process to determine the probability of a *known* individual harming others or self.
Suspect-based (also known as prospective profiling)	Refers to identifying the psychological and behavioral features of *unknown* persons who may be planning to commit a particular crime, such as drug trafficking, school shooting, shoplifting, bombing, or terrorist activities. The process is based on systematic collection of behavioral, personality, cognitive, and demographic data gathered on previous offenders who have committed similar crimes.
Psychological autopsy (also called equivocal death analysis or reconstructive death analysis)	The postmortem reconstruction of the emotional life, behavior, and thought patterns of a *known* but *deceased* person. It is most often used in civil trials when an equivocal death has occurred, but it may also come into play in criminal cases.

the quality of law enforcement practices (Withrow & Dailey, 2012). Most recently, in 2013, a federal judge declared unconstitutional the "stop and frisk" policies of the New York Police Department (NYPD), citing persuasive evidence that they constitute racial profiling because they single out persons on the basis of their race.

It is important to point out that police are allowed to stop and briefly question someone if they have reasonable, articulable suspicion that a crime has occurred, is in progress, or is about to happen (*Terry v. Ohio*, 1968). They are also allowed to conduct a pat-down search during these "Terry stops" for their own protection. However, in the case of the NYPD, the judge noted that African Americans and Latinos were disproportionately stopped, and often for behavior that would not raise police suspicion if displayed by whites. In general, the courts have consistently ruled that the police may not stop persons on the basis of race, national origin, or ethnicity alone—these factors do not constitute articulable suspicion. However, the courts have frequently allowed law enforcement to consider race if used in combination with other factors to establish reason for a brief stop (Withrow & Dailey, 2012).

With the exception of racial profiling—which is illegal—profiling has been designated by some scholars as an acceptable technique that is primarily an art without scientific foundation. Other scholars consider it a young, developing science destined to improve. Some forms of profiling have garnered supportive but cautious research evidence (such as **geographic and psychological profiling**), while crime scene profiling that is clinically based and psychological autopsies are viewed less enthusiastically by research psychologists. Suspect-based profiling, of course, must be very carefully done to avoid a focus on illegal characteristics like race or ethnicity. What's more, some "profilers" are highly respected researchers or practitioners, careful not to make outlandish claims or predictions; unfortunately, many others who claim to be profilers are not so cautious.

Crime Scene Profiling

Crime scene profiling is the process of identifying behavioral patterns, motivations, and demographic variables associated with an *unknown* offender based on evidence gathered at the crime scene. In other words, the crime scene is examined for clues that might lead to the person responsible. In some cases, police have a suspect in mind and may communicate this to the profiler. This can be problematic if it takes attention away from the search for other suspects.

Many police departments use crime scene profiling to some extent, particularly for a series of crimes or especially heinous, hard-to-solve crimes. They either consult a professional "lay" profiler or enroll officers in official training programs, such as that offered by the FBI and other professional law enforcement agencies. Although not all departments consult profilers, many do. Those agencies who do so believe it works or at least helps move along an investigation, particularly when difficult cases are involved. There are also many police agencies and officers who are not convinced profiling is helpful (Snook, Cullen, Bennell, Taylor, & Gendreau, 2008). Questions raised in this chapter relate to whether profiling should be restricted to this investigative phase of a case or should be admitted into court proceedings as evidence beyond the ken of the average person, thus requiring the help of an expert witness. For example, should a profiler be allowed to testify that a given individual does, or does not, fit the profile of a child molester? Should a profiler need special credentials, such as being certified as a behavioral analyst for the FBI, before testimony is accepted? The answer to these questions depends on a number of factors, and—not surprisingly—there is considerable variation in court decisions.

Three Basic Approaches to Profiling

There are three basic approaches to crime scene profiling: (1) clinical, (2) statistical, and (3) a combination of the two. Clinically inclined profilers construct their profile on the basis of their training, experience, knowledge, and intuition or "gut feelings." However, research has discovered that there are very few instances where the report by the profiler, compiled before the case is solved, reveals a high degree of accuracy that led to the arrest and conviction of the offender (Bartol & Bartol, 2013). **Clinically produced profiles** miss the mark in many ways, and they may actually steer police away from the real perpetrator. Many professional, experienced profilers agree that clinical profiling is far from a science in its current form (Copson et al., 1997). According to Copson et al., much contemporary profiling involves "a leap of logic, and observing or predicting something which goes beyond what is known at that point" (p. 14). Snook and his colleagues (2008) observe that clinically oriented profiling "is not a generally accepted scientific technique, is not reliable, cannot prove the guilt of the defendant, and does not provide explanations that are outside the normal understanding of the jury" (p. 1266). It is also highly vulnerable to the numerous cognitive biases of the profiler. As Snook et al. also point out, some courts have referred to clinically based profiling as "junk science."

Statistical, researched-based profiling, on the other hand, is largely based on an empirical and systematic analysis of offenders who have previously committed crimes that are considered similar to those being investigated. Although it is early in its development, this approach holds great promise. Research-based profiling controls for cognitive biases and is scientific in focus, but it does have its limitations. For example, it fails to put "flesh" on the offender by not incorporating the unique, human, and intriguing features of the behavioral pattern of the offender. After all, every offender is different and somewhat unique. The scientific, statistical approach to profiling is sometimes considered boring and dry. Hence, the clinical profile, permeated with speculations about the motivations and uniqueness of the offender's pattern of crimes, is often considered the more exciting and captivating approach. This is especially the case among the public who read forensic novels; watch the entertainment media on profiling; and listen to profilers on the news media who explain the offender's motivations, mind, and methods. The clinical approach is the preferred method of most individuals who call themselves profilers, especially those in the United States. The statistical approach has been preferred by profilers in Europe, New Zealand, and Canada, and is *slowly* becoming accepted in the United States.

The third approach is the **combination method of profiling,** which includes features of both clinical and scientific methods. A blend of both approaches has considerable potential so long as it includes a healthy helping of scientific research on human behavior and a solid foundation in statistical analyses of offender patterns. It holds great promise for improved profiling accuracy in the future, especially if it continually tests and examines the reliability and validity of the approach.

We will examine in the next few sections how crime scene profiling has fared in the legal system. We begin with one aspect that has been troubling for more than a decade, the so-called *CSI* effect.

The *CSI* Effect: Fact or Fiction?

In criminal courts, it is not uncommon for prosecutors—and sometimes defense attorneys—to want to introduce profiling evidence, often in the form of expert testimony. They also want to introduce scientific evidence such as results obtained from DNA or ballistics analyses. However, some prosecutors complain that popular television shows about forensic-science evidence (e.g., *Crime Scene Investigation* or *CSI*, *Criminal Minds*, and *Bones*) make jurors expect too much of the prosecution and, more generally, the government (Cole & Dioso-Villa, 2009; Shelton, 2010). Prosecutors argue that juries are wrongfully acquitting defendants when the prosecution does not present the kind of irrefutable evidence that they see on these forensically related shows. Basically, "It was claimed [by prosecutors] that jurors confused the idealized portrayal of the capabilities of forensic science on television with the actual capabilities of forensic science in the contemporary criminal justice system" (Cole & Dioso-Villa, 2009, p. 1335). This confusion, as it pertains to juries, is called the *CSI* effect, and it is assumed to render jurors less likely to convict. The mass media quickly began to characterize the *CSI* effect as a well-established phenomenon among juries, despite no empirical evidence to support this (Cole & Dioso-Villa, 2009). Thus, the *CSI* effect encompasses not only crime scene profiling, but also other techniques and procedures presumably found in the well-equipped forensic laboratories portrayed in the media.

The belief that a *CSI* effect exists has apparently become prevalent in some legal circles (Mancini, 2011). Mancini illustrates with the anecdote that the Ohio Bar Association Jury Instructions Committee changed the jury instructions to warn impaneled jury members "to disregard any impressions they may have developed from viewing programs such as *CSI* when forming their verdicts (p. 157). The chief justice of the Massachusetts Supreme Judicial Court asserted that talk about *"CSI"* should be banned in courtrooms across the state (Tamber, 2009). Moreover, in at least one criminal case (*Charles and Drake v. State*, 2010), convictions were overturned because of the nature of questioning during voir dire. The trial judge in that case told jurors that he assumed that many of them watched so-called realistic forensic crime shows. He then told jurors that if they believed they could not convict a defendant without *CSI*-type scientific evidence, they should stand and be removed from further consideration for jury duty. When the defendants were convicted, defense lawyers appealed the convictions, arguing that the trial judge biased the case in favor of the prosecution by suggesting that such hard-and-fast evidence was not needed. The appellate court agreed.

> Thus, we conclude that the judge abused his discretion by suggesting to the panel that "convicting" Drake and Charles was the only option in the present case; this suggestive question poisoned the venire, thereby depriving Drake and Charles of a fair and impartial jury. (*Charles and Drake v. State*, 2010, p. 735)

In a nonscientific but nonetheless interesting survey, Judge Donald E. Shelton (2010), a state trial judge in Ann Arbor, Michigan, polled more than 1,000 summoned jurors in two jurisdictions in an effort to gauge their expectations of scientific forensic evidence in the courtroom. The survey revealed that they did indeed expect the introduction of modern scientific evidence in criminal trials. However, those individuals who frequently watched *CSI* had significantly higher expectations for all types of scientific evidence than people who did not watch that program. Nevertheless, although the show increased juror expectations for scientific evidence to be presented during the trial, they still believed they could render a proper verdict even in the absence of sound scientific evidence. In other words, according to Shelton, the jurors said they would not base their decisions on whether or not the scientific evidence played a prominent role in the trial. The jurors simply thought that in today's electronic age there should be more high-quality scientific evidence presented during the trial. These high expectations are what Judge Shelton referred to as the "tech effect," which he claims springs from the public's awareness of the role modern technology can play in the criminal adjudication process. From his perspective, the tech effect was not from *CSI* alone but from various sources of mass media in general. Shelton concluded, "The strong prosecutor depiction of the *CSI* Effect, which asserts that jurors who watch *CSI* will wrongfully acquit defendants, does not have an empirical basis" (p. 23). However, does a survey of prospective jurors in just two jurisdictions close the debate on the influence of the *CSI* effect on the jury?

Psychological research has yet to uncover whether the *CSI* effect has a significant impact on jury decision making. Baskin and Sommers (2010) reviewed the available research and concluded, "The answer to the question of whether juror decisions regarding verdicts in criminal cases arise out of or in spite of the CSI Effect, or whether they bear any relationship to crime show viewing, remains elusive" (p. 98).

Moreover, the specific impact of *profiling* portrayed in the media has not been directly tested. Most media offerings with investigative themes encompass a range of crime solving, including the collection and examination of physical evidence at the crime scene such as DNA evidence, fingerprint analysis, toxic and fabric material analyses, blood spatter, and skeletal remains. Criminal profiling or behavioral analysis is not the central focus in the *CSI* series, but it is on shows like *Criminal Minds*. Consequently, further studies are needed to determine the extent to which profiling movies and TV shows influenced jurors who actually served on a trial, especially if a profiler served as an expert witness. It is likely that profiling-focused TV programs have significant influence on creating misconceptions among the public on what profiling can do (see Table 8-2), but the extent to which this carries into the jury room remains in question.

Regardless of whether the *CSI* effect occurs and influences a jury, a profiler with extensive experience and credentials is likely to do so. The profiler or behavioral analyst

Table 8-2	Misconceptions and Reality Concerning Profiling
Misconception	**Reality**
Profilers predict personality and the criminal mind.	Personality prediction and criminal mind assessments have highly questionable validity and reliability. Statements about personality and "the criminal mind" are often not helpful to investigators. Profilers should focus on behavioral patterns.
Profilers solve crimes.	Profilers provide information that may or may not be helpful to police investigators. Very rarely do they solve crimes. Profilers who are not law enforcement officers should not consider themselves an arm of law enforcement.
Profiling is an established scientific enterprise.	Although the scientific approach to profiling is recommended in the legal psychology literature, profiling is in its early stages and is far from being established as a science.

Source: Adapted from Rainbow & Gregory (2011) and Bartol & Bartol (2013).

who testifies that the evidence gathered at a murder crime scene clearly represents the "signature" of the defendant can be extremely persuasive to many jurors. A signature is a unique behavioral pattern that a serial offender leaves at the crime scene for investigators to find. (See Table 8-3 for this and other terminology associated with crime scene profiling.) The signature may involve certain items that are left at or removed from the scene, or symbolic patterns such as writings on the wall. Usually, it is the offender's "calling card" to inform police that the crime scene is his work.

Is crime scene profiling testimony admitted into courts, should it be, and what types of testimony should be allowed? As we shall see, courts are more accepting of profiling when it is used as an investigative tool to help police in solving a crime, and usually less accepting when a behavioral consultant wants to testify in the courtroom that a defendant "fits the profile" of those who commit a particular crime. This is generally considered inadmissible character evidence.

Courts across the globe have grappled with whether to allow criminal profiling evidence, as well as what type to allow. The answer sometimes depends on how the evidence is described. In some courts, for example, "behavioral analysis" is looked on more favorably than "profiling," even though they are basically different terms for the very same procedure. As Risinger and Loop (2002) have observed, "Though courts have generally rejected testimony concerning profiling frankly so offered, they have often bent over backwards to admit profiling-based testimony, or testimony of profilers, when it could be labeled differently" (sec. IC, para. 254).

Paths to Admission of Evidence

Alison, West, and Goodwill (2004) observed that attempts to introduce profiling in court have taken two different paths. In one path, attorneys for either side try to introduce the original report prepared by the profiler to illustrate or suggest to a jury that the defendant matches or does not match it. The prosecution, of course, claims that the profile matches the defendant. When the defense attorney introduces a profile, it is to argue that the profile does *not* match his or her client. Canter, Alison, Alison, and Wentink (2004) refer to this path as **profile–defendant correspondence (P-DC)**.

Although many trial courts are skeptical of profiling evidence, others routinely accept profiling evidence and testimony, particularly if the expert does not directly compare the defendant to a particular profile (Bosco, Zappala, & Santtila, 2010; George, 2008). For example, testimony that a defendant fits or does not fit the profile of a sexual sadist or a child molester is more likely to be rejected by the courts than testimony about typical characteristics of such offenders as a group. In the latter case, the expert testifies that child molesters tend to have certain characteristics but does not say that the defendant has them. The jury is left to draw its own conclusions.

In the second path identified by Canter et al. (2004), **profile–crime correspondence (P-CC)**, profilers report the similarity between two or more *crimes*, which would suggest that the same individual has committed them. This also has been referred to as **case linkage** or **similarity analysis**. Alison et al. (2004) report that P-DC is more controversial than P-CC because of its prejudicial effect, in that "[it] necessitates direct commentary about

Table 8-3 **Terms Commonly Used in Clinical Crime Scene Profiling**

Term	Definition
Modus operandi (MO)	Refers to the actions and methods an offender uses to commit a crime.
Personation	Refers to any behavior that goes beyond what is necessary to successfully commit a crime.
Signature	The unique markers left at a crime scene that indicate the work of a specific serial offender.
Staging	The intentional alteration of a crime scene prior to the arrival of the police in order to hide some aspect of the crime.
Trophy	An item taken from the crime scene or from the victim that symbolizes the offender's triumph over the victim. A **souvenir** is a meaningful item taken by the offender to remember the incident.
Undoing	A behavioral pattern evident at the crime scene in which the offender tried to psychologically "undo" the crime.
Organized crime scene	Crime scene that indicates planning and premeditation on the part of the offender. The scene shows that the offender maintained control of his emotions as well as the victim.
Disorganized crime scene	Crime scene that demonstrates that the offender committed the crime without premeditation or planning. In other words, the scene suggests the offender acted on impulse or in a rage.

the defendant, whereas [P-CC] considers the similarity between offenses" (p. 79). Despite this, however, research and scholarly criticism about linkage analysis appears regularly in the legal and social science literature. Critics observe that even elaborate databases designed to facilitate linking crimes (e.g., ViClas; ViCAP) have not reached the stage of development whereby their reliability and validity can be firmly established (Bennell, Snook, MacDonald, House, & Taylor, 2012; Risinger & Loop, 2002; Snook, Luther, House, Bennell, & Taylor, 2012). We discuss case linkage again later in the chapter.

Profiling as Expert Evidence

Most legal experts and researchers do not object strongly to allowing profiling—regardless of the path—to be part of the *investigation process*. They are far more skeptical about profiling testimony in the courtroom.

According to Kocsis (2009), "it is prudent to avoid the use of profiling *in the courtroom* and to instead confine its application to its more traditional investigative context" (p. 258, emphasis added). In addition, Kocsis and others (e.g., Risinger & Loop, 2002) recommend that, if they do allow profiling testimony, courts exercise extreme caution in admitting the evidence, considering the fact that profiling is in its very early stages as a science.

As discussed throughout this book, trial judges and juries are the triers of fact. They hear and weigh evidence and decide whether there is sufficient evidence to (depending on the context) proceed with a case, convict someone of a crime, or find a defendant negligent in a civil court. Because neither judges nor jurors are omniscient or all knowing, they sometimes benefit from the knowledge that may be imparted by an expert witness. Today, as indicated above, many trial courts—especially in the United States—do admit profiling evidence of various types, and this seems to occur particularly when such evidence is offered by the prosecution (George, 2008). Nevertheless, appellate courts sometimes reverse these decisions. It is by no means certain that this will happen, however. In fact, after a comprehensive review of legal cases involving profiling testimony in the United States, George found that profiling evidence was alive and well in U.S. courtrooms, even after review by appellate courts. Courts in other countries are more cautious (Bourque et al., 2008; Youngs, 2009).

Recall from Chapter 1 that expert witnesses provide knowledge that is "beyond the ken" of the average layperson. Scientific knowledge clearly fits into this category. Most people are not knowledgeable of the intricacies of blood analysis, the effects of environmental contaminants, chemical reactions, medical procedures, or myriad other topics that are the province of the natural and physical sciences. Do the social and behavioral sciences come under the same umbrella? The quick answer to that is "yes," but social and behavioral scientists often have more hurdles to overcome than the "hard" scientists if they wish to testify in court. With reference to profiling evidence, a key question becomes, "Is it scientific?" As we shall see shortly, though, some courts have placed more weight on the credentials and experience of the experts than on the scientific validity of their methods and techniques. That is, the evidence is accepted not so much because it is scientific but because it is offered by individuals with long-standing experience in criminal investigative procedures.

Despite the fact that profiling evidence is admitted in many courts, there is considerable debate in the legal and psychological literature as to whether it should be. Some argue that profiles may be helpful as investigatory tools but should not be allowed in the courts (e.g., George, 2008; Kocsis, 2009; Risinger & Loop, 2002), while others are in favor of admitting profiling evidence (e.g., Ingram, 1998; Woskett, Coyle, & Lincoln, 2007). Arguments against profiling typically include the undue influence of the expert, particularly if testifying for the prosecution; lack of scientific validity of the techniques used; and the prejudicial nature of the information provided. Some critics note that, even if the expert does not indicate directly that a person "fits a profile," the jury may be led to that conclusion quite naturally.

Perhaps due to the influence of the FBI and its training programs, profiling remains far more accepted in U.S. courts than in other countries. This is largely because of the societal recognition of FBI credentials and the psychological impact they carry with U.S. courts. As George (2008) points out, many profilers either work for the FBI or are past agents; consequently, they are more likely to testify for the prosecution. In Australia, profiling evidence is generally not accepted. "(M)ore caution has been exercised over its admissibility especially regarding the expertise of its practitioners" (Woskett et al., 2007, p. 306). In Canada, several recent cases suggest that the scientific reliability of the behavioral aspects of profiling has not been sufficiently established to be accepted in the courtroom. This led the Canadian Human Rights Commission (2011) to issue several recommendations for developing performance criteria and undertaking research on the effectiveness of behavioral profiling (Bourque et al., 2008).

In England, a prominent case—*R. v. Stagg* (1994)—is said to have dealt a blow to criminal or offender profiling in court. The presiding judge in that case said offender profiling was not generally accepted by the psychological profession, and he did not allow the profiler to take the stand to bolster the prosecution's case. While acknowledging that a profile could be used in developing lines of inquiry and helping police in investigations, the judge stated that it should not be used to identify a suspect. Interestingly, though, he expressed doubt about the usefulness of offender profiles *even during the investigation process* (Ormerod & Sturman, 2005). Nevertheless, police can exercise broad discretion over their investigative methods, and consulting a profiler is but one path to take in solving a crime. In the *Stagg* case, however, investigators appear to have given undue weight to the opinions of the profiler, and the profiler in turn seems to have perceived himself as part of the prosecution team (Ormerod & Sturman, 2005).

Profiling Credentials

A number of court cases have revolved around the credentials of the expert being called to testify. It should be understood that there is as yet no accrediting group for profilers, and many behavioral experts resist that moniker, now preferring titles like "behavioral analyst" or "criminal investigative analyst." There is also no standard way to prepare a profile report, although some researchers and practitioners have provided a variety of helpful protocols. Although in the United States, anyone can call him- or herself a profiler, not anyone can claim the credentials of a trained analyst. Nevertheless, the lack of standardization and the paucity of empirical research on the techniques used—even by those with specific training—are major reasons why caution is urged with respect to legal proceedings.

With few exceptions, in the United States, FBI-trained crime scene analysts, or those now trained under the International Criminal Investigative Analysis Fellowship (ICIAF), are accepted as "experts" in that field. According to its website, the ICIAF remains one of the few organizations in the world that trains and certifies profilers. Participants in the training must be police officers with at least 10 years of experience doing basic police work and at least 2 or more years in violent crime investigation. However, their testimony may be limited to certain aspects, as will be noted again below. Many courts are not amenable to allowing *law enforcement agents* to testify about someone's personality or motivation for committing a crime, referred to as **motivational analysis**.

Even here there are exceptions, however, as we mention later in the chapter. However, U.S. courts are more accepting of testimony directly related to crime scene analysis, or features of the crime scene such as staging or organized and disorganized crime scenes (see Table 8-3). This is probably because it is seen as directly within their area of expertise. In fact, in a military case, *United States v. Meeks* (1992), **crime scene analysis** itself was recognized as a body of specialized knowledge beyond the ken of the average person, thus allowing the expert to help the fact finder in arriving at a decision. The expert, FBI profiler Judson Ray, was allowed to testify on psychological aspects as well, such as that the offender went to the crime scene with sex and killing on his mind (George, 2008). In addition, in *Delaware v. Pennell* (1989, 1991), an FBI agent's testimony did not even have to meet the test of scientific acceptability because his own experience in criminal investigation was sufficient to make him an expert.

There have been cases, however, in which even highly credentialed agents have had their testimony rejected by trial courts. At least part of this is due to the *Daubert* decision. For example, soon after *Daubert*, a trial court in an Ohio case (*State v. Lowe*, 1991) did not allow the testimony of well-known profiler John Douglas. The appellate court upheld this exclusion. Although it recognized that Douglas had considerable experience in the field of homicide investigation, the court said his method was intuitive rather than scientific, and this method did not amount to sufficient evidence of reliability. As required by *Daubert*, the trial judge seems to have taken a closer look at the reliability of expert testimony, and the appellate court agreed with the judge.

Some profilers have attained a certain celebrity status, have written books based on their experiences, and have made themselves available for media and cable news interviews relative to high-profile cases. Other self-described profilers, some with few academic credentials, become involved in high-interest cases, like those of the Beltway Snipers, JonBenét Ramsey, Kaylee Anthony, and Madeleine McCann. Each of these nationally followed cases saw profilers emerge to make appearances on cable networks, and some were willing to testify in courts. It is important to emphasize that consulting with law enforcement during the *investigative phase* of a case does not require sterling credentials or extensive experience. Standards for testifying in court as an *expert,* however, are far more demanding than providing opinions or speculations to the public through the media. Even practitioners, researchers, and scholars with solid credentials can run into problems during presentation of the evidence when cross-examined in the courtroom.

As mentioned above, courts outside of the United States have been more guarded about accepting credentials of profilers or finding their testimony persuasive (Youngs, 2009). In one Australian case (*R. v. Hillier*, 2003), the court was skeptical about the methodology of a behavioral consultant who had studied profiling in the United States:

> [T]he fact that profiling may sometimes prove to be a valid investigative tool does not justify a conclusion that its exponents may leap majestically over the limitations of modern psychology and psychiatry and give expert evidence as to the personality and conduct of a particular person. (p. 105)

The court also said, cogently, "Amongst the many factors which may lead an expert witness into error is a malady which, if encountered in a new car salesperson, might be described as gross product enthusiasm" (p. 105).

In England and Wales, commentators have been concerned about the misuse of profiling by police or in courts, particularly after the facts of the highly publicized *R. v. Stagg* (1994) case mentioned above. Stagg was accused of brutally stabbing to death a young mother who was walking with her 2-year-old child in a park in 1992. Stagg, who fit the profile that had been given to police by the profiler, denied the crime, but he was detained for 14 months before he was freed by a judge the first day of his trial. As mentioned above, the judge was extremely critical of the profiler's involvement in the investigation of the case. Over a decade later, after someone else had confessed to the crime, Metropolitan Police apologized to Stagg for falsely accusing him of the murder.

Courts in the UK in general have been extremely skeptical of profiling, both as to whether it is widely accepted and as to whether it is scientific. Gudjonsson and Copson (1997) studied 90 trials and found that only two individual profilers were admitted as experts. In Canada, where the standards for admissibility of expert testimony are similar though not identical to those outlined in *Daubert,* many courts also have expressed skepticism about various profiling evidence. In one case (*R. v. Klymchuk*, 2005), a Canadian appellate court seemed particularly concerned that the testimony of a behavioral analyst trained by the FBI would have undue influence over the jury, which was likely to regard profiling as scientific and infallible as a result of its extensive coverage in the popular media.

It is well established that investigators and other experts can discuss the facts of the crime scene, including what they observed, the **modus operandi**—the actions and methods the offender uses to commit the crime—presence of a signature, and possible staging of the crime. When investigators conclude that a homicide has been staged to look like a burglary, for example, this testimony is usually allowed. However, when they cross a line and provide evidence on motives or lead a jury to draw inferences about guilt, they are on shakier ground.

Linkage Analysis in the Courtroom

Another troubling issue is the use of linkage analysis to draw connections between various crimes. Like much crime scene profiling, this is acceptable during the investigatory phase. Law enforcement officials have always looked for similarities in methods of perpetrating crimes in the event that several were committed by the same individual. Did the burglar gain access through a basement window in several different cases? What kinds of items were left behind? Were various victims' bodies posed in a crude fashion? In recent years, with the help of sophisticated investigative technology and computerized databases, linkage analysis has become even more firmly entrenched in police procedures. However, the questions remain, how reliable is it, and does it meet the test of scientific acceptance in court?

One of the first noteworthy court cases dealing with linkage analysis was *State v. Pennell* (1989, 1991). It involved the torture and killings of three women. Two of the crimes were clearly linked to the defendant by physical evidence alone. The third crime occurred sometime after details of the first two cases were reported in the media, and thus could have been a "copycat" killing. Prosecutors wanted to convict Pennell of all three crimes. FBI agent John Douglas made the link at the trial stage by noting what he believed were common signatures found at the scene. Pennell was convicted. He appealed his conviction, arguing among other things that linkage analysis was not generally acceptable in the scientific community. (Note that this was before *Daubert,* at a time when the *Frye* general acceptance standard dominated.)

The Delaware Supreme Court, however, allowed the testimony about the common signature (which essentially supported linkage analysis) on the basis of Douglas's many years of experience as an FBI analyst. As noted above, his years of experience were sufficient to qualify him as an expert, so the Court seemed to assume that his knowledge was reliable. However, the Court indicated that it was strongly opposed to *profile evidence*, which it said was extremely prejudicial. Interestingly, George (2008) suggests that Douglas and his colleagues in the FBI "created a new application of profiling called 'linkage analysis' with the explicit goal of gaining admission as expert witnesses" (p. 231). As mentioned earlier in the chapter, the terminology used in presenting the evidence is what makes the difference to some courts; to the Delaware court, "signature" and "linkage" testimony was acceptable, whereas "profiling" testimony would not have been.

Motivations, Mind, and Personality Statements Not Allowable

Investigators and other experts can discuss the facts of the crime scene, and they are on somewhat shakier ground with linkage analysis. However, when they tread on peripheral territory such as the possible motivation of the perpetrator, the criminal mind, or the psychological characteristics of defendants, they are even more likely to be seriously challenged.

This is particularly true in Canada, where "the unanimous position of Canadian courts on the behavioural aspects of profiling is that its scientificity is not so established as to meet requirements of admissibility" (Bourque et al., 2009, p. 4). Thus, in a key Canadian case (*R. v. Ranger*, 2003), an appeals court ruled that some testimony from a detective in the behavioral sciences unit of the police was admissible, but some was not. Specifically, testimony that a crime scene was staged to look like a break-in was allowed, but testimony on the motivation of the offender was not. The Court of Appeal stressed that expert evidence of crime scene analysis should be limited to the "what" of a case and not include the "why" or the "who" (Kari, 2005). These issues, the court said, were beyond the scope of properly admissible evidence. The court also expressed concern that this testimony would be perceived by the jury as having more weight than it deserved because of the detective's status as an expert witness. Recall that standards for admissibility of expert testimony include a weighing of the probative versus prejudicial value. In this case, the appeals court believed her testimony had undue influence over the jury.

In the United States, however, expert testimony on the psychological characteristics of criminal defendants has been admitted with less difficulty, depending on how it is cloaked. Individuals with impressive credentials, particularly those trained in FBI-sponsored programs, get considerable leeway, and particularly at the trial stage, though there are exceptions. In one notable case (*State v. Haynes*, 1988), a profiler testified at length about the traits and characteristics of "anger-retaliatory" murderers, leading the jury to conclude that the defendant matched those characteristics. The Court of Appeals ruled that this offender-profiling testimony was not scientific, could not be considered reliable, and should not have been admitted. It also indicated that the expert testimony was more prejudicial than probative, and that it amounted to inadmissible character evidence as well.

In summary, trial courts after *Daubert* have been more aware of their gatekeeping role and have made efforts to scrutinize more carefully the scientific status of the profiler's testimony. They have been more likely to reject evidence that is not scientifically based. However, there is little consistency across jurisdictions, and the decisions of appellate courts are unpredictable as well.

✖ The Psychological Autopsy

The psychological autopsy is a technique that is used in both civil and criminal courts, most particularly the former. It can be valuable in insurance benefits claims, worker's compensation cases, testamentary capacity cases, product liability determinations, or malpractice claims. Psychological autopsies often come into play when the death appears to be equivocal—that is, when the manner of death is unknown or undetermined. Consequently, it is sometimes referred to as reconstructive death analysis or **equivocal death analysis**. This postmortem analysis was developed during the 1970s by psychologists Edwin S. Shneidman and Norman L. Farberow and medical examiner Theodore J. Murphy at the Los Angeles Suicide Prevention Center.

The psychological autopsy is a form of profiling because it involves the discovery and reconstruction of a deceased person's life based on the evidence left behind by that person. Typically, it entails having a mental health professional revisit the person's lifestyle, cognitive processes, and recent emotional and behavioral patterns prior to his or her death. The psychological autopsy is not as concerned with the cause of death as with the **mode of death**. The *cause* of death refers to the body system failures that directly triggered the death, such as a gunshot wound to the brain, lack of oxygen, heart attack, or stroke. The *mode* of death falls into one of five categories: (1) suicide, (2) homicide, (3) accidental, (4) natural causes, or (5) undetermined.

Psychological autopsies have been conducted on people ranging from Adolf Hitler to Mohamed Atta, the alleged ringleader of the 9/11 hijackers (Lankford, 2012). Some of these autopsies are very detailed and written after careful review of numerous documents and interview data, but they may also be exercises in speculation. Despite evidence that Atta may have experienced depression, shame, and social isolation, as noted by Lankford, for example, we will never know whether his actions were motivated more by these factors than by the religious and political ideology that others have attributed to him (Gambetta, 2005; Townsend, 2007).

To what extent do courts accept expert testimony on psychological autopsies? Historically, the courts have been willing to allow such evidence as long as it falls within the rules of procedure for admitting expert testimony. In civil cases, the psychological autopsy has been commonly used to determine whether benefits are owed to the decedent's beneficiaries. These cases most frequently involve life insurance payments because many policies state that a suicide precludes benefits. However, some policies will allow payments if it can be established that the death was an "insane suicide" (J. L. Knoll, 2008). An insane suicide is a legal term defined by the U.S. Supreme Court in *Mutual Life Insurance Company v. Terry* (1872), which implies the decedent was so emotionally distraught that he or she did not have a rational appreciation of his or her actions (Jacobs & Klein-Benheim, 1995; J. L. Knoll, 2008). In these cases, a psychological autopsy could be an invaluable tool in establishing the state of the person just before the suicide.

Examples of Psychological Autopsy Applications in Civil Cases

Worker's compensation insurance provides a good illustration of the relevance of the psychological autopsy. Although the cases do not start in the civil courtroom—they are typically handled by employment review boards—denials of benefits can result in a more formalized civil case. (We discuss employment compensation claims in Chapter 11.) The courts have generally interpreted worker's compensation laws to include mental and emotional as well as the physical consequences of work-related injury (Jacobs & Klein-Benheim, 1995). Emotional trauma related to the job, even in the absence of physical trauma, has been sufficient for receiving compensation under such laws (Jacobs & Klein-Benheim, 1995). In the cases of suicide, the worker's dependents are entitled to compensation if three conditions are met. First, the emotional distress must have arisen out of and occurred in the course of employment. Second, there must be a causal connection established between the nature of the employment and the suicide. Third, it must be shown that the employee was of such unsoundness of mind as to make him or her irresponsible for the act of suicide. The courts generally have not interpreted suicide by itself to be an irrational act. It must be established that the person was not in control at the time of the act. Obviously, this is where a psychological autopsy would be most helpful.

In other civil litigations, psychological autopsies are presented as evidence when a decedent's testamentary capacity is questioned. In these instances, a will is contested on the grounds that the deceased lacked the capacity to execute or change a will at some point before his or her death, or was unduly influenced by another person. In such cases, a psychologist or mental health professional may be asked to perform a psychological autopsy and offer an opinion concerning the mental status and capacity of the deceased at the time the will was signed. (Testamentary capacity also will be covered again in Chapter 11.)

In other legal contexts, the psychological autopsy is frequently conducted to reconstruct the possible reasons for a suicide and ultimately to establish legal culpability on the part of other persons and organizations. For example, it may be necessary to ascertain whether certain kinds of harassment by fellow workers or supervisors led to the suicide of the affected person. Failure of the company or organization to have adequate policies and procedures in place for handling problems of this nature may be sufficient reason to find the company liable. Far too often, bullying or cyberbullying has led to a tragic suicidal death of the victim, usually a teen or young adult. In these cases, it is sometimes necessary to determine—if possible—the thoughts and emotional state of the deceased prior to the suicide.

In product liability cases, numerous lawsuits, claiming that the drugs they produce caused suicides, have been brought against pharmaceutical companies. In fact, pharmaceutical-company lawsuits represent the most common product liability cases. For example, in November 2012, the Supreme Court of New York awarded a $1.5 million malpractice verdict to the family of a man who committed suicide while taking antidepressant drugs. In 2010, Forest Laboratories settled 54 lawsuits (totaling over $313 million) over their antidepressants (Celexa, Levothroid, and Lexapro) that were tied to suicides in children and adolescents. In February of 2013, Pfizer settled lawsuits for $273 million that claimed their smoking-cessation drug (Chantix) significantly increased the risk of suicide. To reduce the number of suits, some drugs, such as antidepressants, come with black box warnings stating that they can cause suicidal thoughts and behaviors. Clearly, it is important to determine what prompted the suicide: the drug or something else.

The U.S. Food and Drug Administration (FDA) has warned that suicidal thoughts or actions may be produced by at least 130 prescription drugs (Lavigne, McCarthy, Chapman, Petrilla, & Knox, 2012). In addition to the often-cited causes like antidepressants and smoking-cessation drugs, other drugs tied to suicide include those used for asthma, neuropathic pain, and anxiety. However, pharmaceutical-company lawsuits may begin to wane in the near future. On July 7, 2013, in a 5–4 vote, the U.S. Supreme Court in *Mutual Pharmaceutical Company v. Bartlett* (2013) struck down a lower court's ruling and the award for the victim's adverse reaction to a prescribed drug. The Court further ruled—in line with its earlier ruling in 2011 (*PLIVA, Inc. v. Mensing*, 2011)—that generic drug companies are exempt from lawsuits as long as they scrupulously follow federal law concerning drug composition, warning labels, manner of administration, dosage form, and strength. The Court's ruling holds, regardless of whether the drug caused serious injury or death or prompted the victim to commit suicide. Justice Sotomayor—in her written dissent against the ruling—believed the Court majority's decision was based on "an implicit and undefended assumption that federal law gives the pharmaceutical companies the right to sell a federally approved drug free from common-law liability" (*Mutual Pharmaceutical*, 2013, p. 1 of dissenting opinion). It is unclear at this writing to what extent product-liability lawsuits involving prescribed drugs will be affected by the Supreme Court's ruling in future cases.

Psychological Autopsies in Legal Proceedings

Unfortunately, psychological autopsies are unstandardized, with little agreement on precisely how they should be conducted. There is no "gold standard" on how to perform one. Not surprisingly, courts have been very cautious about allowing them into evidence. However, many lawyers have argued that—particularly in insurance cases where suspected suicides are in question—a psychological autopsy is important. A case out of England, *R. v. Guilfoyle* (2001), illustrates very well the tenuous scientific state of the psychological autopsy. Guilfoyle was charged with the murder of his pregnant wife, who was found hanging in their garage. A suicide note was found on the scene, but upon investigation police found evidence to charge the husband, who was subsequently convicted. In appealing his conviction, Guilfoyle tried to introduce new evidence in the form of a psychological autopsy completed by psychologist David Canter, who concluded that Paula Guilfoyle had indeed committed suicide.

The Court of Appeal ruled that the psychologist's opinion was *inadmissible,* partly because there was no way of testing the reliability of the testimony—for example, there was no substantial body of academic writing approving Canter's methodology. In addition, they noted that Canter had not up to that point conducted psychological autopsies, although this in itself would not be a bar to presenting evidence if it were otherwise reliable. As the court noted, "the present academic status of psychological autopsies is not, in our judgment, such as to permit them to be admitted as a basis for expert opinion before a jury" (*R. v. Guilfoyle*, n. 25).

Although the psychological autopsy is suspect in many court cases, it is occasionally allowed, as it was in *Jackson v. State* (1989). A Florida woman was charged with mental child abuse after her 17-year-old daughter, a nude dancer, shot herself. The mother had forged the girl's birth certificate to make it appear to the club that she was old enough to dance, and had apparently forced her daughter to take on this job. A psychiatrist had conducted a psychological autopsy on the girl, with results that were very incriminating against the mother. To establish the scientific nature of the autopsy, the psychiatrist told the court that psychological autopsies have been accepted in the field of psychiatry and that hospitals often require them in the case of suicides.

The mother was convicted of mental child abuse but appealed her conviction. Her attorney argued that the psychiatrist's testimony should not have been allowed because the autopsy was not reliable—being based on testimony about the state of mind of someone the psychiatrist had never met. The appellate court affirmed the conviction, and indicated that the autopsy testimony by the psychiatrist was no different from expert testimony in testamentary capacity cases, where clinicians had also not interviewed the subjects of their reports.

In *Sysyn v. State* (2000), another Florida case, the trial court had *not* allowed psychological autopsy evidence. The defendant in the case was charged with killing an individual whom she believed to be purposefully goading her into killing her (the victim and the defendant were both female). The defendant believed that the victim was a prostitute and a drug addict and may have had AIDS. The defendant said that, while driving a car in which the victim was a passenger, she felt a sharp object in her arm, which she assumed to be a needle. At that point, the defendant said she took a handgun from the victim and shot her in the head. A psychologist was ready to testify that, based on a psychological autopsy, the victim was indeed suicidal, but the trial court did not allow this testimony. On appeal, the appeals court ruled that the lower court had not abused its discretion and therefore did not second-guess the decision to disallow the evidence.

In still another case, a defense attorney challenged the admission of a psychological autopsy that was damaging to the attorney's client. However, the court (*United States v. St. Jean*, 1995) ruled that an expert providing information derived from a psychological autopsy had testimony that was helpful to the trier of fact. The judge also ruled that the procedure was accepted in the mental health community.

As the above cases indicate, and as we have seen in other profiling instances, prosecutors have more success than defense attorneys when it comes to getting profile evidence admitted. Similarly, it is likely that psychological autopsies are admitted in civil courts more than they are in criminal cases.

The psychological autopsy is controversial among many psychologists because it does not yet have an established methodology or empirical research to support it. There are typical procedures used, such as interviews with significant persons, review of available records, diaries or social media postings, and even downloaded material or websites that had been visited by the victim. Some clinicians highlight the importance of making a trip to the person's home and place of work. If a suicide note has been left, this is a valuable source of information as well (Haines, Williams, & Lester, 2011). Others have noted that determining the authenticity of a suicide note can be highly challenging (Bennell, Jones, & Taylor, 2011). Despite the relative infancy of the psychological autopsy, some researchers emphasize that substantial progress has been made toward developing a standardized procedure that will give this type of autopsy greater scientific status (J. L. Knoll, 2009; Snider, Hane, & Berman, 2006).

Forensic Hypnosis

It has long been believed that there is something intriguingly magical about hypnosis. It is a procedure whereby a trained clinician or hypnotist suggests that a participant experience various changes in sensation, perception, cognition, emotion, or control over behavioral patterns (VandeBos, 2007). Hypnosis has been used as entertainment, as a method of psychotherapy, as a procedure in several branches of medicine, and as a means of enhancing the memory of eyewitnesses and victims in the criminal justice system.

Beginning in the late 1970s, *forensic* hypnosis was especially popular as a memory-enhancement procedure for use by law enforcement (Wagstaff, Brunas-Wagstaff, Cole, & Wheatcroft, 2004). Wagstaff (2008) writes that the popular image of a hypnotized person is someone in a "trance state," possibly with unusual powers, and under the control of the hypnotist. The person has little awareness of what is going on around him or her. If this belief is true, then fully controlled, unaware hypnotized persons "can be made to offend against their wills or become unwitting victims of crime and abuse" (p. 1277). Moreover, if hypnotized people are not in control of their cognitions and willpower, they can presumably be induced to tell the truth, perhaps against their own best interest.

For well over a century, another widely held belief has been that hypnosis can exhume long-forgotten or buried memories. This belief has frequently been bolstered by anecdotal or clinical claims describing cases where previously inaccessible memories have been brought to light by the mysterious hypnotic trance. The ability to recover long-forgotten memories through hypnosis is the most deeply held hypnosis-related belief in the eyes of the public, the media, and even many mental health professionals (Wagstaff, 2008).

There are different ways of enhancing or reviving memory. Certain techniques, such as free association, fantasy, or other recall strategies, are common and acceptable; this is referred to as **nonhypnotic hypermnesia**. Enhancement or revival of memory through hypnosis is more controversial. It produces a state known as **hypnotic hypermnesia**. The increased appearance of this technique in the courtroom during the 1960s engendered considerable controversy and precipitated a wealth of research addressing the validity and application of hypnotic hypermnesia in forensic settings (Pettinati, 1988).

Not everyone can be hypnotized. The ability to be hypnotized is often assumed to be an enduring and stable attribute, which peaks during the life cycle in late childhood and declines gradually thereafter (Scheflin, Spiegel, & Spiegel, 1999). Psychological experts who embrace hypnosis as a valuable forensic tool believe that the ability to be hypnotized follows a normal distribution curve similar to intelligence, with most people falling somewhere in the middle. About 10% of the general population cannot be hypnotized, and 5% to 10% are highly suggestible (Hilgard, 1965). Almost everyone (90%) can experience at least some effects of hypnosis. Among the factors that are important in inducing hypnosis are (1) the level of trust the subject places on the hypnotist, (2) the subject's motivation and desire to cooperate, (3) the kind of preconceived notions the subject has about hypnosis, and (4) the context and reasons for the hypnosis (e.g., entertainment or critical information gathering). Trust, motivation, a strong belief in the powers of hypnotism, and a serious context (such as a criminal investigation) enable most people to become hypnotized. Apparently, what distinguishes truly being hypnotized from simple behavioral compliance is the person's ability to experience suggested alterations in perception, memory, and mood (Orne, Whitehouse, Dinges, & Orne, 1988).

Relaxation and better concentration are the initial goals of hypnosis. Subjects are sitting or lying down, and the hypnotist continually emphasizes quietness, calmness, and drowsiness while keeping the person concentrated on a target (a candle, a button, a swinging object, or virtually any object that promotes sustained attention). The subject, asked to concentrate only on the target and the hypnotist's voice, is encouraged to drift to sleep, all the while hearing what the hypnotist is saying. The hypnotist generally will suggest different behaviors, moods, or thoughts, and with each behavior or alteration, the subject falls into a deeper trance, or at least becomes increasingly convinced that hypnotism is in effect. Subjects are encouraged to involve themselves in various imaginative scenes, a process that adds to the positive aspects of hypnosis. In fact, "the subject's willingness to accept fantasy as reality during the hypnotic experience, together with the often dramatic vividness of recollections in hypnosis, may inspire great confidence that the recalled material is true to fact" (Orne et al., 1988, p. 25). This characteristic of hypnosis can be very troubling in forensic investigations that are dependent upon accurate recollections of witnesses or victims, as we shall see.

Major Theoretical Perspectives on Hypnosis

Despite its long history, hypnosis is still at a relatively early state of scientific development, and its application far exceeds our scientific knowledge about the phenomenon. We still do not know precisely what hypnosis is. We have little knowledge of why one person is readily susceptible and why another is not. We know that hypnosis is not the same as sleep or the same state as that found during sleepwalking.

While hypnosis lacks scientific elucidation, there are at least two major theoretical perspectives directed at explaining the mechanisms behind its effects. One perspective is generally referred to as the **hypnotic trance theory**, which assumes that hypnosis represents a special state of consciousness that promotes a high level of responsiveness to suggestions and changes in bodily feelings. Under this special state of consciousness (some argue that it taps the unconscious), the subject may be able to regress to childhood and vividly remember or act out events that have been repressed or at least put on the very back burner of memory. While in the trance, subjects may be instructed to feel little or no pain, or to perform acts that they are unable to do when not hypnotized. Individuals can be instructed to sense, feel, smell, see, or hear things not normally possible outside of hypnosis; even memory can be enhanced and drastically improved in some situations. Generally speaking, the deeper the "hypnotic trance," the more intense, detailed, and vivid a scene becomes to the subject. Historically, the chief spokesperson for this position has been Ernest Hilgard.

The second position advanced to explain hypnosis is the **cognitive behavioral viewpoint**, which maintains that subjects are not in a special state of consciousness when they appear hypnotized. Rather, hypnosis is a product of certain attitudes, motivations, and expectancies toward the "hypnotic state." Specifically, people who have a positive attitude toward hypnosis are motivated to be hypnotized and expect to be hypnotized.

They play the role suggested to them by the hypnotist; when the hypnotist suggests to them that they feel relaxed, they will try and probably will feel relaxed.

Theodore X. Barber, the chief advocate of the cognitive behavioral perspective (Barber, Spanos, & Chaves, 1974) has postulated that the good hypnotic subject is one who not only has the proper mixture of attitude, motivation, and expectancy, but also has the ability to think and imagine with the hypnotist. The good hypnotic subject is like the person who watches a motion picture and feels the emotions and experiences of the persons on the screen. Barber argues that hypnosis is, in most respects, a highly similar experience. The hypnotic subject feels the intense and vivid experiences that are suggested by the hypnotist.

Martin Orne (1970; Orne, Dinges, & Orne, 1984) hypothesized a similar viewpoint to the cognitive behavioral theory, suggesting that role playing accounts for much of the so-called hypnotic phenomenon. That is, subjects act the way they *think* a truly hypnotized individual would act. Orne and his colleagues (1988) believe that "a prerequisite for hypnosis is the willingness to adopt the role of the 'hypnotic subject,' with its implicit social contract for uncritical acceptance of appropriate suggestions administered by the hypnotist" (p. 23). The "hypnotic subject" is willing to relinquish his or her sense of reality temporarily, hold any critical thinking in abeyance, and concentrate on what the hypnotist says. Orne has found in his research (e.g., Orne, M. T., Dinges, & Orne 1984; Orne et al., 1988) that the material described under so-called hypnotic trances is often inaccurate and embellished with many intervening events that occur between the initial incident and the hypnotic session. It appears that hypnotic subjects may be very susceptible to distortions, suggestions, imagination, and leading questions. This is problematic in part because, particularly if the interviewer is a police officer convinced of the powers of hypnosis, he or she is apt to inadvertently suggest events or details that were not present at the crime scene. The hypnotized witness or victim, eager to please the interviewer, can easily imagine a scene decorated with subjective fantasies and thoughts in line with the suggestions of the questioner. Under these conditions, the hypnotized subject may begin to be convinced of the accuracy and power of hypnosis to the same degree as the hypnotist. Furthermore, the subject may become convinced of the accuracy of his or her account of the imagined scene.

When hypnosis is used as a tool to aid the recall of events that may be either several hours or several years old, the fundamental assumption is that human perception and memory function like a videotape. All the events and details are stored accurately and simply must be recalled or brought to consciousness. We have seen, however, that this assumption is faulty. Human perception and memory are flawed and permeated with inaccuracies and distortions. The frailties of perception and memory, combined with the highly suggestive medium under which hypnosis is conducted, provide a situation where critical inaccuracies have a high probability of occurring.

Research on Forensic Hypnosis

The accuracy of one's recall under the influence of hypnosis is of major concern to the courts, which are ideally focused on seeking the truth. Psychological research has explored the extent to which this recall is valid. In addition, people wonder whether hypnotic subjects can be forced to do something they would otherwise not do. In other words, as Wagstaff (2008) observes, people ask, can hypnotized persons be induced to commit immoral, criminal, or self-injurious acts of which they would normally be incapable? Although some hypnosis literature maintains that people have unwittingly been hypnotized into committing criminal acts—if they in fact occurred—such incidents are extremely rare and undocumented. There are many other explanations besides hypnosis to explain such events. Moreover, there is growing consensus among researchers in the field of hypnosis that hypnotized people do not lose consciousness, control of their behavior, or their normal sense of conscience (Scheflin, 2014; Wagstaff, 2008). In other words, a hypnotized person would not do something he or she would not otherwise do if not hypnotized.

What does the research tell us about the reliability and validity of information gained under hypnosis in forensic settings? So far, the studies on forensic hypnosis have focused on three areas: (1) accuracy of recall, (2) posthypnotic confidence of the victim or witness, and (3) suggestibility of the victim or witness during hypnosis.

Accuracy of Recall

One way hypnosis is used by forensic investigators is to help individuals remember the details of events that happened in the past—a week, a month, or even years previously. In some instances, the investigation may require digging deep into the past for details of events that happened to the individual at an early age. In short, the hypnotized individual is asked to relive an experience from childhood. When hypnosis is used in this way, the procedure is known as **hypnotic age regression**. For example, in some instances, the victim or witness of a crime may become so emotionally or physically traumatized by the event that he or she has great difficulty remembering it or even identifying who was involved. This is especially the case if the crime happened a long time ago, such as we might find in cases involving sexual abuse during childhood. The hope is that, with the aid of hypnosis, a victim or witness can "regress" back to those early events and reconstruct them with more accuracy than would be found in nonhypnotic memories. However, the research does not seem to support the view that hypnosis enhances memory for events that happened during our childhood. "On the basis of available data from properly controlled experiments and studies in which the researchers had access to biographical records, there is no support for the view that hypnotic age regression improves accurate recollection of childhood memories" (Orne et al., 1988, p. 36). In fact, there is reason to believe that memories acquired through hypnotic age regression are often far less accurate than nonhypnotic memories.

What about enhancing memory of recent events? Here, too, the research is not supportive. Although some studies have indicated that hypnosis may improve short-term memory, the effect is generally unreliable and subject to considerable error (Kebbell & Wagstaff, 1998; Scoboria, Mazzoni, Kirsch, & Milling, 2002). More recent research (e.g., Scheflin, 2014) suggests that some current hypnotic techniques are more evidence-based, however.

Confidence

Hypnosis has the uncanny ability to instill a high degree of confidence in our recall of the things we remember under its spell. A highly hypnotizable subject might conclude, "I never realized that's the way it happened. I must have repressed it. It was so vivid when I was hypnotized. After experiencing it under hypnosis, I am convinced now that that's the way it happened." However, the research is quite consistent in showing that a high degree of confidence in the veracity of hypnotic material is often a poor fit with the actual facts when independent evidence is available (Scoboria et al., 2002; Wagstaff et al., 2004). Unfortunately, this increased false confidence may permanently distort eyewitness testimony (Pettinati, 1988), or "cement" the subject's memory of the event to the extent that he or she believes it to be more credible than ordinary memory (Scheflin, 2014; Scheflin et al., 1999). Moreover, the inclination to confabulate and to make up missing information seems to be greater under hypnosis (Orne et al., 1988). In effect, hypnosis does increase the amount of information and peripheral details recalled, but much of it is incorrect or made up. Consequently, the information gathered from hypnosis is often a subtle mixture of both fact and fantasy (Perry, Laurence, D'Eon, & Tallant, 1988).

Suggestibility

Memory under hypnosis is highly malleable, often producing "pseudo-memories," especially in highly hypnotizable subjects (Haber & Haber, 2000). Consequently, leading or suggestive questions or subtle cues communicated, often inadvertently, by the hypnotist or others involved in the investigation can have a dramatic effect on posthypnotic recall. In effect, hypnosis seems to sensitize many subjects and make them more susceptible to leading questions than nonhypnotized persons (Kebbell & Wagstaff, 1998). Although much more research needs to be done, the current research suggests that there is a very high risk that counterfactual or inaccurate information will be incorporated into memory during the hypnotic process, especially among highly hypnotizable persons.

Hypnosis also fails to increase recognition accuracy beyond motivated nonhypnotic performance (Wagstaff, 2008). Therefore, attempts to improve the recognition of suspects by witnesses and victims through hypnosis are unlikely to improve identifications beyond what could be accomplished by standard investigative procedures.

Some studies have challenged the research that presents hypnosis in a negative light, however (Brown, Scheflin, & Hammon, 1998). Scheflin et al. (1999), responding to a study by Laurence and Perry (1983) finding inaccurate memories after hypnosis, emphasized that only a minority of the highly hypnotizable subjects continued to report these pseudo-memories after 7 days. The implication is that interviewing or reinterviewing hypnotized individuals after that time period might make it less likely that inaccurate memories would be retained. McCann and Sheehan (1988) conducted an experiment whose results suggested that implanting false memories with hypnosis was far less facile than had been presumed. Proponents of the use of hypnosis to refresh memory also maintain that the artificial, laboratory settings of experiments on hypnosis cannot replicate the emotions and motivations of real victims and witnesses. However, hypnosis, with safeguards, may be a critically important aid to refreshing memory in persons who have been traumatized and suffer from amnesia (Scheflin et al., 1999).

Despite the problems encountered in the research literature, there continues to be support for the practice. It is significant that some psychologists continue to argue that hypnosis can improve memory (Wagstaff, 2008). Indeed, some research does reveal that hypnosis and similar procedures can sometimes enhance memory recall, especially for personally meaningful and emotion-laden material (W. C. Webster & Hammon, 2011). Scheflin (2014) reports that law enforment in recent years has documented cases in which hypnosis was crucial to the solving of criminal cases. However, the research also notes that although memory recall may be enhanced, there tends to be an increase in false recollections and misinformation.

Many police in a number of countries continue to use hypnosis for memory enhancement of witnesses and victims, convinced it is useful in the discovery of evidence. Wagstaff (2008) points out that the use of hypnosis and similar techniques appears to produce better results than routine police interviewing in many cases. Hypnosis-like procedures encourage less interruption and provide the witness or victim an opportunity to elaborate freely when giving his or her account of the incident. The procedure also encourages relaxation and better concentration of the witness. Because of the success of a number of interview procedures that retain some *features* of hypnosis, such as relaxation, focused attention, and concentration, some police agencies are inclined to use these approaches in evidence interviews rather than full-blown hypnosis. As noted above, this may be a better alternative for obtaining accurate information.

One popular approach is the *cognitive interview* (discussed in Chapter 5), which utilizes techniques such as rapport building, focused attention, and encouragement to report everything without interruption. As noted by Wagstaff (2008), "because of the practical problems associated with the use of hypnosis, the cognitive interview has generally displaced hypnosis as the preferred mode of memory facilitation in police investigations in the United Kingdom and United States" (p. 1287). Wagstaff believes that encouraging the witness or victim to relax, concentrate on aspects of the incident, and say what comes into his or her mind without interruption holds great promise for forensic interviewing in the future.

Legal Status of Hypnosis

Should evidence that has been obtained with the aid of hypnosis be admitted into courts? Obviously, those who question the reliability and validity of this evidence respond vehemently in the negative. Another consideration, one not often mentioned, is its influence on the jury. Some research has found that jurors are more likely to believe testimony if they are specifically told it was elicited under hypnosis (Wagstaff, Vella, & Perfect, 1992). "In other words, it seems that because of the common belief that hypnosis is a special, even 'unfakable,' memory aid, jurors may give greater credence to hypnotically elicited testimony" (Wagstaff, 2009). Wagstaff notes that the power of the word *hypnosis* should not be underestimated.

Courts in different jurisdictions have adopted one of several approaches to hypnotic testimony (Scheflin, 2014; Topham, 1997). They are per se exclusion, per se admissibility, the procedural safeguards approach, and the totality of circumstances approach. The latter two approaches are similar and in some literature are treated simultaneously.

According to Webert (2003), many courts do exclude all hypnotically induced testimony based on the belief that it is unreliable as a technique for eliciting accurate testimony: "A minority of courts have found the dangers of hypnotically enhanced testimony so compelling that all testimony from a previously hypnotized witness is excluded, even those memories recalled prior to hypnosis" (p. 1301). Courts in about 25 states have adopted this **per se exclusion** standard—choosing to disallow evidence obtained during or after a hypnotic session.

Other courts are more receptive. The first court case that opened the door to hypnotically refreshed recollection was *Harding v. State*, a 1968 Maryland case. The "open admissibility" or **per se admissibility** standard set in that case has been adopted in only three states, however (Scheflin, 2014). This rule was modified in one important way by the U.S. Supreme Court in *Rock v. Arkansas* (1986). In that case, the Court ruled that a per se exclusion of a criminal defendant's statement, taken under hypnosis, violated the defendant's Sixth Amendment right to a fair trial. In other words, a court cannot *automatically* exclude a defendant's statement that was obtained while under hypnosis, if the defendant himself wished to introduce it. Nevertheless, jurisdictions are still free to apply the per se exclusion rule to hypnotically obtained evidence from *victims* or *witnesses*. This prohibition on evidence obtained under hypnosis typically applies to the posthypnotic identification of criminal suspects. In other words, if a victim were to identify her or his aggressor after being hypnotized, the identification would be suppressed in a jurisdiction that uses the per se exclusion standard (McConkey & Sheehan, 1995).

The **procedural safeguards approach** was first articulated by the New Jersey Supreme Court in a 1981 case, *State v. Hurd.* That court gave a list of factors to be considered by a trial court before allowing hypnotically refreshed testimony:

- The hypnotic session had to be conducted by an experienced psychologist or psychiatrist;
- The hypnotist should have been independent, not affiliated with either party in the litigation;
- Information given to the hypnotist by the parties or by law enforcement should be recorded;
- A detailed record of the subject's prehypnotic memories must be kept;
- All contact between the subject and the hypnotist during the session must be recorded; and
- During all phases of the hypnosis, only the hypnotist and the subject may be present.

The New Jersey court ruled, as well, that the trial judge had to consider the reliability of the testimony and the general acceptability of the technique among the scientific community. Note that this decision was issued before the *Daubert* ruling.

The procedural safeguards approach was surpassed somewhat by both *Daubert* and the **totality of circumstances approach**, which is in effect in 14 states and 11 federal circuits (Scheflin, 2014). This approach essentially allows judges to rule on the merits of the hypnotic sessions by focusing on a variety of factors, such as reliability, the qualifications of the hypnotist, the purpose of the hypnosis, and the presence of a permanent record, among others. It actually encourages judges to take into account all of the safeguards outlined by the New Jersey court, and more. "The totality-of-the-circumstances approach is preferable to the strict procedural safeguards theory because the presence or absence of procedural safeguards may not always mitigate the problems associated with hypnotically-induced testimony" (Topham, 1997, p. 439).

The totality of circumstances rule was articulated in *Borawick v. Shay* (1996), a federal case involving the alleged recollection of repressed memories of child sexual abuse. The plaintiff, Joan Borawick, was an adult when she sought medical treatment for chronic physical illness. She had a history of suffering panic attacks and had received treatment over many years. In 1987, her physician referred her to a hypnotist, with whom she underwent 12 to 14 sessions. The hypnotist was not licensed as a clinical psychologist, did not hold a medical degree, and had no education beyond high school.

One year after her last hypnosis session, Borawick recalled being sexually abused by her aunt and uncle during summer visits when she was 4 and 7 years old. She also recalled sexual abuse by many other individuals, including her father and friends of her father. She recalled such abuse from as early as age 3 and also remembered being forced to drink blood during a ritual involving a dead pig. Borawick filed suit against her aunt and uncle, the Shays, in 1992, more than 3 years after her final session with the hypnotist. Though she sought to introduce evidence from her therapeutic sessions, the courts refused to admit the evidence. The lower court applied criteria similar to those used by the New Jersey court in the *Hurd* case—note that even the first requirement (a qualified hypnotist) was not met. Borawick appealed the lower court's decision with no success.

The Second Circuit Court of Appeals applied a totality of circumstances approach. Interestingly, it found that some of the criteria in the safeguard approach might be too rigid, and more flexibility should be considered. On the other hand, the court said, if hypnotically obtained information were to be admitted only because it met procedural safeguards, the jury might give it more weight than was warranted. Therefore, a careful pretrial assessment of the testimony, on a case-by-case basis, was needed. Although it agreed that in Borawick's case the evidence should not be admitted, it recommended a case-by-case totality analysis in future cases involving hypnosis. Proponents of hypnosis like this decision, because it is far more receptive to hypnosis than other approaches, with the exception of the rarely taken "per se admissibility" approach.

The debate over the admissibility of evidence obtained during hypnosis intensified throughout the 1990s and well beyond (Scheflin, 2014). Opponents (e.g., Orne et al., 1996) emphasized that lack of validity haunts such evidence and that nonprofessional uses and documented abuses are too egregious to open the door to this testimony. They fear, also, that "disguised hypnosis" in the form of relaxation techniques or guided imagery is becoming all too common during police interviews. Supporters of hypnosis that is performed by competent and experienced professionals following strict guidelines tell a different story. They argue that the per se exclusion rule is an unfair restriction on a common forensic practice and on the rights of victims and witnesses to testify. Thus, they much prefer that courts consider hypnosis evidence on a case-by-case basis.

The research evidence is quite conclusive on the unreliability of hypnosis as an accurate, memory-restoring technique in forensic settings, however. It may be a helpful therapeutic tool, but, as stated by Orne and his colleagues (1988), empirical studies "compel the conclusion that hypnotically induced memories should never be permitted to form the basis for testimony by witnesses or victims in a court of law" (p. 51). That said, employing hypnosis to provide leads, especially those that can be corroborated by independent sources, is reasonable. In addition, hypnosis can serve as an information facilitator for individuals who are fearful or embarrassed to report, or who are motivated by guilt to repress (Orne et al., 1988). But overall, information gathered through standard forensic investigative techniques that utilize aspects of the cognitive interview are substantially more fruitful than material acquired through the risky business of "pure" hypnosis.

SUMMARY AND CONCLUSIONS

Many psychological techniques, approaches, and measures are developed for research purposes or for use in psychological practice. They are not necessarily evidence based or so broadly accepted that they are ready for widespread dissemination, even within the scientific community. In addition, many techniques serve good purposes in clinical practice or the research laboratory, but do not meet the rigid standards set by the courts for the admission of expert evidence. This chapter reviewed three such techniques: crime scene profiling, psychological autopsies, and hypnosis. Although each has its merits and its strong supporters, each also illustrates controversial evidence that is sometimes accepted, but more often rejected, by both criminal and civil courts.

Crime scene profiling is one form of profiling, a broad category that includes geographical, suspect-based, and psychological profiling as well as equivalent death analysis, also called the psychological autopsy. The chapter discusses crime scene profiling and the psychological autopsy, because they are the most likely forms of profiling to be offered as evidence presented by expert witnesses.

Crime scene profiling gathers data from the crime scene in order to obtain information about an unknown offender. The information most valuable to profilers is anything that reflects unique characteristics or behaviors of a crime perpetrator. Many law enforcement agencies consult profilers for help with difficult cases, and many other agencies obtain the assistance of professional profilers specifically trained by agencies such as the FBI. Crime scene profiling, when it is competently done, is a valuable tool in the investigative process, although it also has the potential of leading investigative officers astray and away from the true perpetrator.

A key question in psychology and law is whether profiling evidence should be admitted into courts. As a general rule, courts in the United States have been more accepting of this type of evidence than courts in other countries. The credentials of the profilers—many of whom prefer to call themselves behavioral analysts—often determine whether profiling evidence will be admitted. Two main forms of crime scene profiling were discussed: clinically based and actuarial profiling. Clinically based profiling largely centers on the profiler's past experience, training (clinically based), and hunches. It is often replete with comments about an offender's motives or psychological characteristics, and is on far less solid research ground than actuarial profiling. Actuarial profiling views cases through a large database of similar offenses, but some have observed that even the large databases are not without sources of error. The ideal crime scene profiling approach should include both clinical and actuarial data, but the latter is clearly the more objective method.

Regardless of whether the profiling is clinical or actuarial, courts are reluctant to allow expert testimony on a defendant's motives, and they generally do not allow testimony that a defendant fits the profile of a particular type of offender. There is also some resistance to linkage analysis, which is a way of looking at common features in different crimes and linking them to one defendant. Like crime scene profiling in general, linkage analysis is more acceptable during the investigatory stages of criminal cases than as evidence during a criminal trial.

The psychological autopsy—also referred to as equivalent death analysis or reconstructive death analysis—is appearing increasingly in courts, most particularly in civil courts. Psychological autopsies are so called because they attempt to shed light on psychological factors that led to a person's death. Rather than seeking the cause of death, they seek the mode or manner. Most are conducted to determine whether the death was a suicide. They often appear in civil cases when survivors wish to obtain insurance benefits or attribute the death of their loved ones to the negligence of some person or entity. There is no standard way to conduct a psychological autopsy, which is one reason why some courts are reluctant to admit them as evidence. Those who believe psychological autopsies should be welcomed in courts have sought to improve their respectability by establishing guidelines for their preparation.

Hypnosis has had a rocky history regarding efforts to have it introduced into courts. Although competent hypnotists may make use of the technique in their clinical practice, hypnotically induced memories do not fare well in the legal system. Many jurisdictions do not allow evidence of hypnotically refreshed testimony, based on research findings that such memories are not accurate. This is referred to as the per se exclusion rule. However, if the defendant wishes to introduce statements that he or she made under hypnosis, the courts must consider allowing this on a case-by-case basis. In other words, a per se exclusion of all hypnotic testimony is not acceptable in that circumstance. Very few jurisdictions have a per se admissibility rule, meaning that information gained under hypnosis is acceptable. About one third of states and the federal courts consider hypnotically refreshed testimony on a case-by-case basis.

KEY CONCEPTS

Case linkage	Combination method of profiling	Equivocal death analysis
Clinically produced profiles	Crime scene analysis	Geographic profiling
Cognitive behavioral viewpoint	Crime scene profiling	Hypnotic age regression
	CSI effect	Hypnotic hypermnesia

Hypnotic trance theory

Mode of death

Modus operandi

Motivational analysis

Nonhypnotic hypermnesia

Per se admissibility

Per se exclusion

Procedural safeguards approach

Profile–crime correspondence (P-CC)

Profile–defendant correspondence (P-DC)

Profiling

Psychological profiling

Signature

Souvenir

Statistical, research-based profiling

Suspect-based profiling

Totality of circumstances approach

Psychology and the Family Court

A popular television sitcom of the 1950s, *Father Knows Best,* depicted a typical family as living in the ethnically homogeneous suburbs and led by a loving, wise father who worked in an office and was greeted on arriving home by an equally loving and wise mother, usually wearing an apron. Their three wholesome and sometimes mischievous children provided them with frequent but minor dilemmas to solve. In the 1960s and 1970s, families depicted in the entertainment media changed slightly, reflecting more ethnic and racial diversity while also poking fun at the imperfections of the parents and tackling more challenging problems facing the young. Fast-forward to a 2013 sitcom—*Modern Family.* Focused on three families—a couple who are both in a second marriage and the families of the man's adult children—the show reflects divorce, blended families, interracial adoption, gay relationships, and parental efforts to be wise but "cool." Although critics have argued that the real modern family is still not accurately depicted, the show reflects society better than sitcoms of the 1950s, when viewers wondered why their own imperfect families were not like those they saw on television.

Conceptions and definitions of family and of marriage have changed dramatically, and the laws that deal with them have changed accordingly. (See Table 9-1 for key U.S. Supreme Court decisions in family law.) Family courts in most states today are very different from what they were even 30 years ago. An expanded definition of family has meant not only increasing caseloads but also shifts in responsibilities to other specialized courts. For example, whereas early family courts almost invariably heard juvenile

Table 9-1	Representative U.S. Supreme Court Cases in Family Law	
Case Name	**Date**	**Holding/Significance**
Griswold v. Connecticut	1965	Right to privacy for married couples includes right to birth control.
Loving v. Virginia	1967	Interracial couples have a right to marry.
Eisenstadt v. Baird	1972	Unmarried individuals have right to birth control.
Stanley v. Illinois	1972	Unmarried father cannot be deprived of custody upon death of children's mother unless proven unfit.
Troxel v. Granville	2000	Parents have right to limit visitations with grandparents.
Hollingsworth v. Perry	2013	The ruling let stand a California Supreme Court decision declaring unconstitutional a provision banning same-sex marriage in that state.
United States v. Windsor	2013	Legally married same-sex couples cannot be deprived of federal benefits.

delinquency cases, many states now have a separate system of juvenile and family courts. In the words of a family court judge, "the modern family law courtroom is a busy, somewhat frantic, and under-resourced place" (Juhas, 2011, p. 126). He notes that today's family court, in most jurisdictions, is not specifically designed to handle only one type of case, such as divorce or parental separation. Rather, "there may be custody requests, property disputes, discovery motions, free-standing domestic violence restraining orders and requests for child and spousal support, and so forth, all to be handled in the space of a few hours" (p. 125).

In essence, any issue relating to family law can be addressed by family courts. This may include legal issues involving marriage; civil unions; and the termination of relationships, including divorce, annulment, property settlements, alimony, child custody, termination of parental rights, and visitation rights. Family law also may include aspects of elder law, estate planning, surrogacy, and situations involving the end of life, among many others. Family law is sometimes, but not always, separated from child welfare law or social services law, which relates to neglected, abused, or dependent children (S. L. Brooks, 1999; National Association of Counsel for Children, 2006). Furthermore, it is sometimes—but again, not always—separated from juvenile law, which focuses on children and adolescents who are neglected or have violated the law, or are at serious risk of violating it.

Legal psychologists consult and conduct research in virtually every area of family law. In this chapter, we examine an area in which psychology has played an extremely significant contributing role: the dissolution of a marriage or civil union and its consequences. This includes research and participation in conciliation court and alternate dispute resolution, child custody matters, relocation issues, parental rights, parenting coordination programs, and the psychological impact of divorce and custody arrangements. Topics related to elder law, the care of the disabled, and issues revolving around the end of life will be covered in Chapter 11.

⬚ The Modern Family Court

The family court system can be regarded as a spin-off of the juvenile court system, which began at the turn of the 20th century, in 1899. Illinois was the first state to establish a separate system designed to meet the needs of children who were deemed either in need of care and protection or in danger of engaging in crime and delinquency. The history of the juvenile justice system has been amply covered elsewhere (e.g., Bernard, 1992). Family courts came on the scene much later, following a period of extensive growth and development in family-related legal issues. A few family courts were established in some states quite early. For example, in 1937, the National Council of Juvenile and Family Court Judges (NCJFC) was founded, suggesting that at least some states had family courts back then.

Although there was some early experimentation with family courts or family court dockets, it was not until the 1970s that the movement for a separate court to handle family law cases began to take hold across the United States (Adam & Brady, 2013). Family courts developed quickly through the 1980s and 1990s, often separating from the juvenile courts of the past. Today, family courts do not typically deal with juvenile delinquency—though many still do—but they routinely deal with child neglect, divorce and custody, the emancipation of minors, juvenile health issues, and many other matters relating to the family in a complex society. Thus,

> The huge increase in cases and the development of a significant body of case law about the family has led most states to develop dedicated family law benches, designed to deal effectively and appropriately with the complex issues facing families dealing with divorce and parental separation. (Adam & Brady, 2013, p. 28)

Perhaps not surprisingly, family courts can be dangerous places because of the anger and dissatisfaction of the litigants. Some commentators have asserted that judges and lawyers are more likely to be killed or injured by family law litigants than by criminal court defendants (Kreeger, 2003), although this has not been documented in recent years. Many courtrooms today—including family courts—have increased security measures, including metal detectors and scanners at entry points. Nevertheless, emotions run high in family court, and verbal clashes and minor physical altercations are not uncommon. Mental health professionals—some of whom have offices within or adjacent to courthouses—have become invaluable in offering assistance to family court judges, lawyers, litigants, and—ultimately—the children themselves. Below, we describe some of the prominent changes in the family courts that directly affect the roles and increase the responsibilities of psychologists and other mental health professionals.

⬔ Changes in Family Court in Recent Years

The family court has experienced many changes and been confronted with wide-ranging demands, particularly over the past few decades. These include increases in caseloads and responsibilities, more reliance on mental health professionals, and a significant shift in a basic doctrine associated with custody in divorce cases.

Nature of Caseloads and Responsibilities

New definitions of marriage and family as well as changes in family structure have had major effects on the work of family courts. Approximately 50% of today's first marriages and 60% of second marriages end in divorce (Amato, 2010; Mirecki, Chou, Elliott, & Schneider, 2013). When children are involved, the divorce becomes increasingly more complicated, especially when there are two, three, or more divorces and sometimes children of each partner in various relationships to the divorcing parties (Bridge, 2006). Referring to changes in family structure, Bridge comments, "a whole new category of 'never-marrieds' (either because they would not or could not) were developing, maturing, raising kids, separating, dying, and coming to courts to resolve conflict, just like other families" (p. 191). In addition, more families from diverse cultural heritages have brought different attitudes toward marriage, gender roles, and family-upbringing practices.

In recent years, the family courts also have seen a significant increase in families formed through nontraditional means, including families with same-sex parents, families with children born through reproductive technology, and families with grandparents or other extended family members being the sole caregivers and raising minor children. In addition, factors like high levels of unemployment, housing shortages, economic issues, and the separation from extended family may prompt one or both parents to relocate to a distant place (Grossman & Okun, 2003), raising a host of issues involving custody and visitation. Relocation is an important topic for mental health professionals and will be discussed in more detail later in the chapter.

Increases in the number of parents who are not married also contribute to the complexity of issues faced by family courts. In the 1960s, it was estimated that only 5% of newborns were born to unmarried mothers. Those mothers were often in their teens, and many were persuaded or coerced to place their babies for adoption—a relatively simple process that did not tax the resources of the court (generally a probate court). In 2012, by contrast, one half of all births were to unmarried mothers; they were generally older than the mothers of past decades and not as likely to place their children for adoption (Adam & Brady, 2013). We must stress that families headed by single parents do not routinely come before family courts; however, when they do (e.g., mother seeks financial support from father or relatives petition for custody), the courts may be unprepared to deal with the uncharted territory. As one judge has stated, the law does not provide a structure and forum for deciding the issues of nontraditional families (Keeger, 2003).

Finally, the fatherhood movement—wherein biological fathers began to assert more rights with respect to custody, visitation, and decisions involving their children—has had a similar effect of increasing the caseloads of family courts. (See Box 9-1 for discussion of a recent U.S. Supreme Court case relevant to adoption, unmarried parents, and fatherhood.)

BOX 9-1

Case Study. Adoptive Parents Versus Baby Girl: The Baby Veronica Case

As recently as the 1960s and 1970s, Native American children in the United States who came into the care of the child welfare system were placed either temporarily or permanently in non-Indian foster homes and adoptive homes. It is believed that most of these children were not taught or kept in touch with their cultural heritage. In an effort to place limits on this process, Congress in 1979 passed the Indian Child Welfare Act (ICWA). The law did not stop the practice of placing Native American children in non-Indian homes; rather, it required that such placements be approved by tribal councils. This federal law was a crucial aspect of the heart-wrenching case discussed here.

Baby Veronica was born in Oklahoma 30 years after the ICWA was passed, on September 15, 2009, to an unmarried woman. The baby's biological father was a Cherokee Indian, but the mother was not. Present at the birth were a husband and wife from South Carolina who had prearranged to adopt the baby. The adoptive couple had connected with the biological mother through a private adoption agency. The biological mother had two other children, and she believed the couple would provide a stable and warm home for this new baby.

The biological parents were initially engaged to be married, and the biological father had been informed of the pregnancy. Accounts of the facts of the case diverge at this point. The biological father said he was ready to marry the mother and did not want the adoption to happen. The mother said the father had not been willing to provide any child support and had agreed to the adoption. The biological father also had a child from a previous relationship—a 6-year-old daughter for whom he was providing child support.

The court records suggest that those involved in the adoption process were not forthcoming about the child's Native American background. This was an important point to subsequent courts, because it appeared to violate the ICWA.

(Continued)

(Continued)

When the father in this case learned that the adoption had proceeded, he sought custody of his infant daughter, who had lived with her adoptive parents since her birth. A hearing was held in family court in Oklahoma, and that court voided the adoption and ordered that the baby be handed over to the biological father. A clinical psychologist had testified that this transfer would be damaging to the child and recommended that the baby be allowed to remain with her adoptive parents. However, a child welfare worker familiar with the father and his family testified that he would provide the baby with a good home.

Baby Veronica was removed from her adoptive parents' home on New Year's Eve, 2011, when she was about 15 months old. The adoptive couple went public with their attempt to regain custody of the baby girl, granting media interviews and going through legal channels. In July 2012, the South Carolina Supreme Court affirmed the decision of the family court in Oklahoma that had voided the adoption. The determining factor was the fact that the Cherokee Nation had no knowledge of the adoption, contrary to requirements of the ICWA.

In early 2013, the U.S. Supreme Court ruled that the ICWA did not apply to this case and sent the issue back to the South Carolina Supreme Court, which then ruled in favor of the adoptive parents and ordered the father to surrender the child, suggesting that he and the adoptive parents might work together to make visitation arrangements. At that time, the child was almost 4 years old and had been living with her biological father and grandparents for 2 years. Although the father initially stated he would not surrender his daughter, he did comply, and as of this writing, the child is back with her adoptive parents. It is not known whether visitation arrangements with the father and his family have been made.

Questions for Discussion:

1. Do you believe the final decision made by the South Carolina Supreme Court was in the best interests of baby Veronica?

2. Should an unmarried biological father have equal rights to an unmarried biological mother in making decisions relative to their child?

In addition to the diversity in caseloads discussed above, family courts have witnessed dramatic increases in self-representation of litigants. In the 1970s and 1980s, family law litigants usually had an attorney who represented them in court. Now, across the United States it is estimated that both litigants proceed on their own in over 50% of family court cases (Adam & Brady, 2013). In some states, approximately 70% of the litigants in family court are self-represented (Juhas, 2011). This self-representation can be seen even in those cases involving domestic violence in which prosecutors have not filed criminal charges. "In domestic violence cases, the self-represented can climb to a staggering 90% or more" (Juhas, 2011, p. 125). The shift to self-represented litigants has posed an enormous challenge for family court judges, because they must assure that the rights of the parties on both sides are protected. In some states, various professionals—such as law guardians or child advocates—are assigned to represent the interests of minor children who may be affected by the dispute.

Expanding Roles of Mental Health Professionals

Mental health professionals were traditionally consulted by courts in divorce cases primarily to help in making custody and custody-related decisions. This continues to be a major area of their involvement in family court, and we will discuss custody evaluations in detail shortly. For the present, it is important to note that the roles of mental health professionals have expanded to include other areas. It is noteworthy, though, that psychologists are the experts most preferred by both judges and attorneys in cases involving child custody evaluations and a wide spectrum of other family court issues (Bow et al., 2011). This preference is largely due to the strong developmental focus or research background of many of the psychologists consulted in child custody and family matters.

Today, because of increasing litigation and the toll it takes on the family, courts often require the parties to make good-faith attempts to resolve matters on their own, without having final solutions imposed upon them. Increasingly, the court looks to mental health professionals for help in this process. "In many courts mental health experts (as well as other professionals) have proven invaluable in early intervention case resolution conferences shortly after a case was filed, but before litigation starts in earnest" (Juhas, 2011, p. 127).

Family court judges also seek more guidance on issues relating to child and adolescent development. This may have something to do with the increases in self-representation that were mentioned above. If there is no lawyer to represent the parties, and no advocate to represent the children, judges may feel a particular obligation to develop their knowledge of factors to be weighed in making decisions. As expressed by L. D. Elrod and Dale (2008), "Untrained in the dynamics of interpersonal relationships and the developmental needs of children, judges increasingly look to mental health professionals and the social sciences for help in determining the child's best interest" (p. 383). Family court judge Judith Kreeger (2003) expressed a similar view: "Most family court judges are well educated and experienced in family law, but we have little formal education in the family systems, mental health, and child development issues that underlie and often drive family disputes" (p. 260).

Psychologists and other mental health professionals provide invaluable information about how children, adolescents, and adults interrelate and how family members influence each other in their adjustment and aspirations (Grossman & Okun, 2003). These professionals offer an understanding of how family dynamics and family systems operate in today's rapidly changing multicultural society. For example, mental health professionals are now concentrating on studying family dynamics within multilevel **systems theory**. "A fundamental assumption of systems theory is that one cannot fully understand a complex system by isolating one part" (Magnavita, 2012, p. 3). The complex system of a family cannot be fully understood without looking at all the interrelationships operating on the system at any given time. **Attachment theory**, based on John Bowlby's (1982) original formulations, has also made contributions in recent years. This theory emphasizes the dynamics of human relationships, especially those between child and parents or caregivers. Basically, Bowlby's theory argues that an infant needs to develop a relationship with at least one primary caregiver for social and emotional development to occur normally. According to Lee, Borelli, and West (2011), "child custody evaluators have expressed growing interest in utilizing attachment theory and its accompanying research to inform their evaluations" (p. 232).

The Association of Family and Conciliation Courts (AFCC) has played a major role in expanding the development of innovations in family services to litigants and their families (Press, 2013). These family services include conciliation services, custody and visitation mediation, and parenting coordination. We discuss these topics in greater detail in the section on divorce and custody decision making in this chapter.

Demise of the Tender Years Doctrine

At the outset, it must be emphasized that family courts do not decide the custody of minor children in most divorces. As a general rule, custody is uncontested; in the ideal situation, the parents have agreed as to which of them will have custody, and the court formally approves of the arrangement. Large-scale studies have revealed that courts make the ultimate decision in only 6% to 20% of custody cases, the remaining being resolved by joint agreement between the divorcing parents, with or without the help of out-of-court dispute resolution or mediation (Melton et al., 1997, 2007).

When custody is contested, however, or when previous custodial arrangements are challenged by one of the parties, the court must make the final decision. Traditionally, two standards or doctrines guided them in this task. One was the best interests of the child standard, and the other was the tender years doctrine. As we will see, both have often been criticized, they sometimes conflict with one another, and the latter has virtually disappeared.

The **best interests of the child (BIC) standard** has its origins in *In re Bort*, an 1881 Kansas Supreme Court case. The Kansas court held, "We understand the law to be, when the custody of children is the question, that the best interest of the children is the paramount fact. Rights of father and mother sink into insignificance before that" (cited in Gould & Martindale, 2013, p. 102). The **tender years doctrine** was articulated by an Illinois appellate court in 1899, in *People v. Hickey*:

> In awarding care and custody of children of divorced persons, an infant of tender years will generally be left with the mother, where no objection is shown to exist as to her, even if the father be without blame, *because of the father's inability to bestow on it that tender care which nature requires, and which it is the*

peculiar province of the mother to supply; and this rule will apply with much force in cases of female children of a more advanced age. (Einhorn, 1986, p. 128)

Prior to the 1970s, courts generally applied the tender years doctrine, which presumes the mother will get custody. These courts often melded it with the BIC standard by indicating that remaining with the mother was in the child's best interest. They assumed that fostering the mother–child relationship, particularly before age 7, was critical to the child's development; thus, the mother was deserving of custody unless it was demonstrated that she was unfit. Courts and legislatures reasoned that small children needed mothering more than fathering, especially during their formative years (Adam & Brady, 2013). Consequently, in almost all contested custody cases, the mother was awarded custody of the children, and the father was often awarded visitation (L. D. Elrod & Dale, 2008). Unmarried fathers did not have legal rights to their children and seldom sought parenting time or custody (Gould & Martindale, 2013). Custody issues involving same-sex parents were of course unheard of, because same-sex civil unions or marriages had not been legally recognized.

Gradually, however, courts began to question the wisdom of the tender years doctrine as a general principle. Although many judges continued to embrace their personal beliefs that mothers presumptively deserved custody unless found unfit, when custody was contested, courts began to consider more carefully what would be in the best interest of the child or children in each specific case (Gould & Martindale, 2013). Today, although mothers continue to be awarded custody in the great majority of contested cases (Gould & Martindale, 2013), the decision is not based on the tender years doctrine—it has virtually disappeared in all states except Mississippi. Santilli and Roberts (1990) noted that the doctrine was abolished or abandoned largely on the basis of three challenges. First, it was seen as a violation of the equal protection provided under the Fourteenth Amendment, giving automatic preference to the mother rather than the father without a rational basis for doing so. Second, the doctrine violated equal rights amendments found in many state constitutions. Third, it made a number of psychological assumptions about parenting that may or may not be valid. The BIC standard is now the predominant approach taken in family courts in deciding a range of issues involving the welfare of dependent children. The BIC standard, too, is controversial, however. As observed by Gould and Martindale (2013), the vagueness of the standard "often leaves judges to make decisions on personal experiences and beliefs rather than on scientific knowledge about what is best for the child" (p. 104).

⋈ Divorce and Child Custody

The divorce rate in the United States began to increase in 1963 and did not stop climbing until 1981 (Adam & Brady, 2013). During those 18 years, the divorce rate tripled. Even though divorce rates have stabilized somewhat since 1981, they remain relatively high. What happened between 1963 and 1981 that contributed to the dramatic increase in divorce rates? Simply put, divorce became easier to obtain.

In 1963, married couples—even if both partners agreed—could not easily get a divorce. In most states, divorces were handled by probate courts, and these courts granted a divorce only if the party seeking it could prove convincingly that the other spouse was guilty of serious marital misconduct or inability to perform marital duties (e.g., spouse was imprisoned). More specifically, "the typical grounds for divorce were adultery, impotence, physical or mental cruelty, habitual drunkenness, desertion, or gross neglect of duty" (L. H. Elrod, 2002, p. 221). The couple's problems would be described in open court and documented in court records. Moreover, it was not unusual for one of the twosome to agree to be "the bad guy," providing the other with the needed grounds for obtaining the divorce that both parties wanted. Consequently, divorces may have been even more emotionally draining and psychologically costly to the family than they are today.

In 1969, California became the first state to allow a divorce for irreconcilable differences (which essentially created a **no-fault divorce** option), as long as the breakup was mutually agreeable. In 1970, the National Conference of Commissioners on Uniform State Laws adopted the Uniform Marriage and Divorce Act, which outlined a no-fault divorce law requiring only a judicial finding that the marriage was irretrievably broken. Although only eight states adopted the act in its entirety, many state legislatures adopted some of its provisions and added other factors they considered important (L. D. Elrod & Dale, 2008). Soon, no-fault divorce statutes appeared across the nation, and by 1985 all 50 states allowed no-fault divorce (L. H. Elrod, 2002).

In the United States today, approximately half of all first marriages end in divorce within 15 years (U.S. Bureau of the Census, 2011), representing one of the highest rates in the industrialized world (Kourlis, 2012). Another 20% of marriages end in divorce for couples married over 15 years, indicating that the effects of parental divorce are not limited to young children (Uphold-Carrier & Utz, 2012). It is estimated that over 40% of all children will experience the divorce of their parents during their childhood or adolescence (Krauss & Sales, 2000), and about half of U.S. children spend at least part of their childhood living with a single parent (M. E. Lamb & Malloy, 2013). Additional data from the National Survey of Family Growth reveal that divorce rates are higher for some groups than for others (Amato, 2010). For example, 42% of non-Hispanic whites and Hispanics divorce within the first 15 years of marriage, compared with 55% of African Americans (Amato, 2010). In addition, Hispanics and African Americans are more likely than non-Hispanic whites to end their marriages in permanent separations rather than go through the process of divorce.

Under the no-fault divorce system, judges are no longer required to determine whether couples are innocent or guilty of marital misconduct. In addition, when minor children are involved, no-fault divorce proceedings permit the judge to make decisions about custody and parenting based on what is in the child's best interest (Adam & Brady, 2013). This would happen only if the partners themselves could not amicably agree on custody.

The Best Interests of the Child Standard Revisited

The decision as to who will have custody over a minor child may arise in several contexts, not just divorce (K. D. Hess & Brinson, 1999). First, parents or other relatives of the child may be involved in a custody dispute following not only a divorce but also the death of one or both parents. Second, a state agency may be seeking to assume temporary or permanent custody over the children of parents who are allegedly neglectful or abusive. Third, and more rarely, in a variety of situations surrogate parents, unwed fathers, domestic partners, or friends may seek to gain custody, as we saw in Box 9-1. The great majority of the psychological research in this area has focused on the determination of custody in divorce situations. As noted earlier, in making these custody decisions, courts are often aided by mental health professionals.

The best interests of the child standard, as noted above, is the predominant guide used by family courts when rendering custody decisions. The BIC standard is also applied in subsequent matters related to custody, such as parental relocation wishes or visitation rights. Although there is no uniform definition subscribed to by all jurisdictions (or even by mental health professionals), the term generally refers to the view that parents' legal rights should be secondary to what is best for the child. However, arriving at BIC determinations can be problematic, and the standard has been applied unpredictably. Critics say its vagueness also encourages parents to dispute rather than come to an agreement about custody (Maccoby, 2005). More specifically, because it is vague there is no way to predict which parent is likely to win the custody battle; so each parent believes that her or his arguments for gaining custody are justified and chances of winning are good. Critics also say it exacerbates parental conflict and creates problems in parenting and co-parenting, "which psychological science clearly shows to be key factors predicting children's psychological difficulties in response to the parents' separation and divorce" (Emery, Otto, & O'Donohue, 2005, p. 1).

In an effort to address the vagueness and unpredictability of the BIC standard, approximately 16 states and the District of Columbia list in their statutes some factors to guide courts in determining custody (Child Welfare Information Gateway, 2010). The factors are related to the circumstances of the child and both the circumstances and capacity of the child's potential caregivers. The five most often listed in state statutes are the following:

(1) The emotional ties and relationships between the child and his or her parents, siblings, family and household members, or other caregivers;

(2) The capacity of the parents to provide a safe home and adequate food, clothing, and medical care;

(3)   The mental and physical health needs of the child;

(4)   The mental and physical health of the parents; and

(5)   The presence of domestic violence in the home.

Listing factors to consider may be helpful, but it does not do away completely with the vagueness of the BIC standard. Furthermore, the subjectivity of the judge making the ultimate decision—or the mental health professional recommending it—cannot be overlooked. Consider, for example, the varying interpretations that could be made of "safe home," "emotional ties," and "mental health needs of the child."

Factor 5—which is of course a negative factor—is considered in all states, whether or not they list other specific factors, and it may be the easiest factor to weigh, as long as it is documented. During the 1970s and 1980s, domestic violence came into the forefront of public attention, and research in the area proliferated. Once public awareness became widespread and the growing research demonstrated the dramatic and long-term detrimental effects of domestic violence on children, it became common to consider it in custody decision making. Some studies suggest that 60% of litigating parents report domestic violence of some kind (L. D. Elrod & Dale, 2008). In each specific case, however, the judge must assess the validity of the claims.

Judges also must decide the relative value of each factor, which is not addressed in the law. In other words, are custody evaluators expected to give equal weight to each factor, or should one or two trump the others in the list? Some states have expanded the list to a dozen or more factors without much clarification. For example, a popular additional factor is what is known as the "friendly parent," or the **"friendly parent doctrine"** (L. D. Elrod & Dale, 2008). The friendly parent is the one more likely to promote and encourage the child's contact with the other parent, with the assumption that both parents should remain in the child's life. Judges consider this in nearly all states and are expected to give preference to the parent who exhibits it (Stahl, 2014).

The friendly parent doctrine may stem partly from the alleged post-divorce phenomenon identified as **parental alienation syndrome (PAS)**. According to L. D. Elrod and Dale (2008), "The original theory depicted a vindictive, hostile parent systematically programming the child to view the other parent as evil, dangerous, or unnecessary to the child" (p. 384). PAS is attributed to the parent who is trying to turn the child against the other parent. Like many other psychological syndromes, PAS is highly controversial and, so far, unsubstantiated. Many experts believe it is based on "junk science" and argue that it should be totally excluded from court (Bruch, 2001; Emery, 2005). Others are more receptive to its consideration (R. Bond, 2008). In the more receptive view, having PAS would weigh against a parent seeking custody of his or her child. PAS was at one point considered for inclusion in the DSM-5—probably not as a syndrome but as a disorder—but was apparently considered too undocumented. The

DSM-5 includes a section pertaining to problems related to the primary support group, including disruption of family by separation or divorce, but no diagnostic category is attached (American Psychiatric Association, 2013).

It is a common observation that divorcing parents, or parents battling for custody, sometimes encourage their children to choose sides against their spouse (Meier, 2009), but perhaps not to the extent that a "syndrome" can be identified. "Custody-contesting parents have probably always run the gamut from those who have taken the high road and sought to protect their children from their own conflict, to those who have actively enlisted the children in their battles against the other parent" (Meier, 2009, p. 233). Some children are undeniably caught in the middle of the parental conflict. Mental health professionals who conduct custody evaluations must be constantly alert to this possibility.

Attempts at Improving the BIC Standard: The Approximation Rule

In an effort to remedy problems with the BIC standard, the American Law Institute proposed that in contested custody cases, the courts allocate custodial time to each parent that approximates the proportion of time each spent performing caretaking functions in the past (Warshak, 2007). Consequently, the proposal, known as the **approximation rule**, primarily relies on one factor: amount of past caretaking. Since the approximation rule typically avoids an investigation of other factors that may contribute to the child's well-being, proponents of the rule argue that it makes the outcome of custody disputes more predictable and reduces the incidence of custody trials. At first blush, this seems to be a clear, objective standard. However, some experts believe the BIC standard is not as "broken" as critics say, and the approximation rule is itself problematic. "The limited evidence does not support the premise that the best-interests standard encourages high rates of litigation, and there is no evidence that the approximation rule will make a significant dent in the already low rate of custody trials" (Warshak, 2007, p. 124). Furthermore, the approximation rule looks backward and does not consider changes in a child's developmental status or future living arrangements. It is conceivable, for example, that the mother *was* the primary caretaker in the past, but the father has a new job that would facilitate his spending more time with his 8-year-old son. Applying the approximation rule would favor the mother in the custody decision making.

Thus, no unitary standard or doctrine—be it tender years, best interest, friendly parent, or approximation rule—makes the custody decision an easy one. Considering the best interests of the child is vital, but the BIC standard is not without subjectivity and must be applied carefully on a case-by-case basis. Before we proceed, it is important to briefly describe the various custodial arrangements that are possible as a result of child custody evaluations.

Custodial Arrangements

In most states, there are four basic custodial arrangements: sole custody, divided custody, joint custody, and split custody. These are based on two fundamental categories of parental decision making authority: legal and physical. **Legal parental authority** refers to decisions about the child's long-term welfare, education, medical care, religious upbringing, and other issues significantly affecting his or her life. **Physical authority** involves decisions affecting only the child's daily activities, such as deciding whether the child can stay overnight at a friend's house, attend a party, or have access to the parent's car. In some situations, however, the dividing line between legal and physical authority is blurred, as when a 15-year-old wants to work 20 hours a week to earn extra spending money. It could be argued that, although this seems to relate to the child's day-to-day life, the decision may have long-term implications if schoolwork suffers as a result. The type of authority—legal or physical—exercised over the child will vary according to the custodial arrangement.

The most common arrangement is **sole custody**, where one parent has both legal and physical authority and the other parent does not, although the noncustodial parent usually retains visitation rights. Children in the United States are overwhelmingly in sole custody of their mothers, whether or not courts have made the custody decision. In 2009, for example, 82% of custodial parents were mothers with sole custody (U.S. Census Bureau, 2011).

Another arrangement is **divided custody**, where each parent is afforded legal and physical decision-making powers, but on an alternating basis. That is, the parental decision-making authority shifts (usually on a 6-month basis), depending on which parent the child is living with as well as the location of the child's school district. If the parents live close to each other within the child's district, the "shift" may be as often as every 5 days or weekly. While the child is with one parent, that parent makes both the legal and physical decisions for the child. **Joint custody** is where both parents share legal authority but the children live predominantly with one parent, who will have the physical authority to make the day-to-day decisions. Making decisions relating to physical authority is often troublesome in joint custody arrangements, however, and it can result in conflict and disagreement between the parents. One resolution of this problem is an arrangement called **limited joint custody**, where both parents share legal authority but one parent is given exclusive physical authority and the other is awarded liberal visitation rights. **Split custody** is a custodial arrangement where the legal and physical authority over one or more children is awarded to one parent, and the legal and physical authority over the remaining children is awarded to the other. Normally, each parent is given reciprocal visitation rights. Although there may be variants of any of the above arrangements, one of the four is generally observed. Nevertheless, courts today look for arrangements that will involve both parents, if possible. Most states "recognize some form of joint or shared parenting that apportions parental time and responsibility in a way designed to provide frequent and continuing contact with both parents" (Connell, 2010, p. 494).

In addition, researchers, clinicians, and legal professionals have begun to see a greater role for children and their wishes. This shift has been attributed to the UN Convention on the Rights of the Child (CRC), which encourages children's participation in decision making about matters that affect their own lives (Saywitz, Camparo, & Romanoff, 2010). As Saywitz et al. remark, "there are a number of studies that suggest children want to participate in the decision-making process and can provide both accurate and meaningful information, although they do not want to be responsible for the outcome of the case" (p. 543).

✉ Psychological Effects of Divorce and Custodial Arrangements

Legal psychologists and researchers as well as practitioners from many mental health disciplines have studied the effects of both divorce and custodial arrangements on children. As will be seen below, early studies indicated the effects of divorce were largely negative and that some custodial arrangements were clearly "better" than others; later research has indicated that the issues are far more complex. (See Table 9-2 for a summary of research findings relevant to child custody arrangements.)

Table 9-2 **Key Research Findings on Effects of Divorce and Custody Arrangements**
• As a general principle, children are better off in two-parent, stable homes.   • Most children at all ages are negatively affected by divorce, at least in the short term.   • The degree of trauma experienced by the child is affected by his or her developmental age; young children may experience separation anxiety, while school-age children may express preference for one parent over the other.   • Adolescents given input into the custody decision adjust better to divorce than those on whom custody is imposed.   • The conflict that *precedes* the divorce may be just as traumatic as, or more traumatic than, the conflict associated with the divorce itself.   • As a group, children are resilient and are able to adjust to parental divorce; a majority (approximately 75%) adjust to parental divorce over the long term.   • Children are better off in a stable, single-parent home than in a conflict-ridden two-parent home.   • Children with same-sex parents are as likely to be well adjusted as children of opposite-sex parents.   • A key factor predicting children's long-term positive adjustment to divorce is a respectful and cooperative relationship between divorced parents.   • Joint custody is the optimal custody arrangement for both parents and children.   • Joint custody is problematic when there is hostility between parents, when one parent relocates, or when one parent withdraws from involvement with the child.   • Multiple transitions (moves, remarriages) have negative effects on children's adjustment to divorce.   • Financial standard of living declines precipitously for many women following divorce.   • A warm relationship with at least one parent predicts a child's positive adjustment to divorce.

Effects of Divorce

There is considerable agreement that, on average, children from divorced and remarried families have more adjustment problems than do those in nondivorced, two-parent families, but there is less agreement on the size of these effects (Bauserman, 2012; Hetherington, Bridges, & Insabella, 1998). It is widely believed, and supported by empirical research, that divorce itself is likely to have negative effects on most children (Krauss & Sales, 2000; M. E. Lamb & Malloy, 2013), at least in the short term. In their summary of the research literature, Gould and Martindale (2013) assert, "Research findings have generally indicated that children are best served when they have strong and healthy relationships with both parents" (p. 123). The breakup of a marriage threatens and can damage such positive relationships. In another comprehensive summary of the research literature, M. E. Lamb and Malloy conclude, "Researchers have clearly demonstrated that, on average, children benefit from being raised in two biological or adoptive parent families rather than separated, divorced, or never-married single-parent households" (p. 572).

Some studies suggest that children who experienced divorce are more likely to exhibit poorer academic performance, delayed psychological development, difficulties with cognitive skills, and poor physical and mental health compared with children from intact two-parent homes (Amato, 2001, 2010; Kim, 2011; Uphold-Carrier & Utz, 2012). In addition, these problems tend to continue into adulthood for many of these children and adolescents. Paul Amato (2010) writes,

> adults with divorced parents tend to obtain less education, have lower levels of psychological well-being, report more problems in their own marriages, feel less close to their parents (especially fathers), and are at greater risk of seeing their own marriages end in divorce. (p. 653)

Over the past three decades, the most heavily cited empirical studies on the effects of divorce are the Virginia Longitudinal Study of Divorce conducted by Hetherington, Cox, and Cox (1979) and the Wallerstein (1980, 1989) ongoing studies of divorced families in Northern California. Psychologist Judith Wallerstein followed 131 children from 60 divorced families for 25 years, conducting interviews every 5 years (Wallerstein & Lewis, 2004). She found that many of the children were extremely distressed after the divorce, and the distress and psychological problems accompanying the divorce were still evident 15 years later. Many problems centered on the inability to form meaningful, intimate relationships. About 60% of the children never married.

The Virginia project was a study of 72 white, middle-class 4- and 5-year-old children and their divorced parents. The researchers learned that marital discord and divorce often result in an increase in behavioral problems, and that the nature of these problems is largely dependent on the age of the child (Hetherington, 1979). Hetherington and her colleagues continued this research, following some 400 families over a 30-year period (Hetherington & Kelly, 2002). After studying almost 1,400 families and more than 2,500 children for as long as three decades, Hetherington and Kelly concluded that the negative impact of divorce on both children and parents has been exaggerated. They assert that only one fifth of children experience any long-term psychological damage after the divorce, a conclusion that appears to contrast with the one arrived at by Wallerstein. Hetherington and Kelly found that the vast majority of children adjusted reasonably well within 2 years after the divorce. Other later research also began to suggest that young children experienced greater short-term harmful effects from both divorce and custody arrangements, while older children experienced more long-term effects (Rohman, Sales, & Lou, 1990; Sales, Manber, & Rohman, 1992).

The results of earlier studies of the effects of divorce on children are not as unequivocal as they may appear, however. More recent research indicates there are many complex factors that influence the degree of trauma and whether there are long-lasting effects of parental divorce on children. For example, "Approximately 25% of children in post-separation and divorced families give evidence of adjustment problems, compared to 12–15% in married families" (M. E. Lamb & Malloy, 2013, p. 572). These data clearly suggest that a majority of children from divorced families exhibit no psychopathology or behavioral problems over the long term, although they probably experience some immediate distress at the time of the divorce. Children seem to be more competent, resilient, and adaptive than adults generally assume. In fact, many parents have more difficulty adjusting to divorce than the children do. But for those children who *do* experience stress over a longer period of time, what factors play a prominent role?

It is now well documented that the marital distress that *precedes* divorce often has considerable negative effects on the entire family. As Strohschein (2012) reminds us, "our understanding of the effect of divorce on child outcomes remains incomplete unless we attend to what is happening in children's lives in the period leading up to divorce" (p. 501). Divorce should be viewed as a process rather than a single event. This is especially apparent in cases of domestic violence, where conflict and abuse often occur over extended periods of time. High conflict is associated with poorer child outcomes following divorce, especially when the conflict has its roots in pre-separation relationships and continues at high levels months or longer after the divorce. Amato (2000, 2010) argues that marital dissolution is an ongoing process that unfolds over time, beginning when couples are still married and ending years after the legal divorce proceedings. He notes that the divorce itself probably has few direct effects on children. "Instead, the short-term stresses and long-term strains that precede and follow marital disruption increase the risk of a variety of behavior, emotional, interpersonal, and academic problems among children" (Amato, 2010, p. 656). Amato also emphasizes that the amount of conflict between the parents plays a major role in the overall adjustment and sense of well-being in the children. For example, some research evidence suggests that children of divorced families appear to have a higher level of well-being than do children of high-conflict *intact* families (Booth & Amato, 2001; Bryan, 1999; Strohschein, 2005). Therefore, it is clear that high hostility or conflict between parents is detrimental to children, both in intact families and during and after divorce. This is attenuated somewhat if the child does not perceive him- or herself as being at the root of the conflict. Second, warm parent–child relationships and parenting skills in at least one parent—and preferably both—are predictive of positive adjustment to divorce.

Amato (2010) further points out that it is the number of transitions experienced by children that influences their sense of well-being and adjustment patterns. This is referred to as the **multiple-transition perspective**. These multiple transitions are illustrated by the fact that about 75% of divorced mothers and 80% of divorced fathers remarry. Moreover, as mentioned earlier, the divorce rate for remarriages is even higher than for first marriages (Amato, 2010; Hetherington et al., 1998; Mirecki et al., 2013). Therefore, children not only likely suffer the emotional upheaval of family discord and custody battles associated with the initial divorce; many also experience a series of marital transitions and household breakups in subsequent divorces. The multiple-transition perspective holds considerable promise for researchers trying to understand the long-term effects of divorce and subsequent custodial arrangements.

Financial Burdens After Divorce

Divorce is associated with other adverse circumstances besides the process of pre-separation conflict, separation, and custody battles. Often, the family financial situation is affected by the loss of a major source of income. "Even in the best of circumstances . . . it is more expensive to maintain two households than one, and the standards of living thus tend to decline" (M. E. Lamb & Malloy, 2013, p. 574). A significant amount of research reveals that a woman's standard of living declines precipitously after divorce (Warrener, Koivunen, & Postmus, 2013). Related to the immediate financial decline are factors like the lack of quality, affordable child care; housing affordability; and pediatric medical care. Of additional concern are the daily demands associated with being the sole caregiver, which often interfere with opportunities for better-paying, full-time employment. The after-divorce decline in the standard of living obviously affects the "success" of a sole custody arrangement and the adjustments necessary in other custodial arrangements.

The Developmental Age Factor

James Bray (1990, 1991), in his work on the effects of divorce, emphasizes that children's reactions to parental separation, divorce, and remarriage differ significantly as a function of age. Bray posits that these events are not necessarily worse for children of certain ages, only that children of various ages have different reactions and, in some case, different behavior disorders as a result. He notes that there is as yet no direct evidence on the effects of custodial or visitation arrangements for infants (birth to 6 months), although research on the effects of daycare on infants may provide helpful information for making custody decisions. The daycare research suggests that very young children can adapt to short and regular separations from custodial parents. However, M. E. Lamb and Kelly (2009) and M. E. Lamb and Malloy (2013) emphasize that the separation should be relatively short, as infants need to interact with both parents in a variety of contexts—such as feeding, playing, diapering, soothing, putting to bed—to ensure that the parent–infant relationship is strengthened.

During the preschool ages (3 to 5 years), children may experience separation anxiety (fear of a parent leaving) if their parents also become particularly tense and upset about the parent–child separation. As Bray (1991) argues, children are generally highly susceptible to the feelings of parents at this age and react, sometimes strongly, to any conflict between them. During the school-age and preadolescent period, children develop clear preferences for one or the other parent and are very sensitive to subtle pressures and loyalty conflicts between parents (Bray, 1991). Further, Bray finds that children at this age are usually not able to fully understand divorce or to separate themselves psychologically from parental influence. However, during adolescence, children are usually able to understand the divorce process and tend not to be overly influenced by parental wishes or reactions.

Effects of Custodial Arrangements

Children's adjustment to various custodial arrangements depends on many factors, including the age and gender of the child, the length of time the divorce process takes place, family economic resources, parental conflict before and after the divorce, and the resilience and personality differences of the children.

Although sole custody is the predominant arrangement, joint custody has increasingly become the more recommended in the literature. This is because recent studies in developmental and family psychology find that—in most cases—joint custody is in the best interest of the child (Adam & Brady, 2013; L. D. Elrod & Spector, 2011). Due to the research findings concerning the benefits of two cooperating parents, many states have adopted joint custody presumptions for their courts in the determining of custody arrangements (Gould & Martindale, 2013). In addition, research suggests that children and adolescents with divorced parents appear to be better adjusted when they are in joint custody arrangements compared with sole custody (Bauserman, 2002, 2012).

Parental satisfaction also appears to be higher in joint custody arrangements. According to research conducted by Bauserman (2012), joint custody fathers are more involved with their children and most satisfied with their relationship with the children. In addition, they are also more satisfied with the child custody arrangement overall. Joint custody mothers reported experiencing less parenting burden and stress, and both joint custody mothers and fathers reported less conflict with their ex-spouse. Moreover, Bauserman discovered that joint custody did not have to involve joint *physical* custody to be associated with overall satisfaction—legal custody was sufficient. For example, legal custody was awarded to both parents, but the children live predominantly with one, while the other has liberal visitation periods and assumes physical custody during specified periods, such as summer vacation. Bauserman also found that re-litigation was lower in joint custody compared with other custody arrangements. One of the primary benefits of joint custody is that it provides "a way of giving children access to both parents while allowing parents freedom of divorce" (Adam & Brady, 2013, p. 31).

Although some evidence indicates that, in most instances, joint custody arrangements appear to be psychologically healthier for the children involved than sole custody, at least three warnings are in order. First, joint custody may be contraindicated when certain family process variables, such as hostility between the parents, are present and continue to be present for some time after the divorce. In fact, parental hostility was usually considered the variable that contributed significantly to the "failure" of joint custody; if parents were not hostile toward one another, joint custody would work (Buchanan, Maccoby, & Dornbusch, 1991; Johnston, 1996; Maccoby, Buchanan, Mnookin, & Dornsbusch, 1993). Likewise, Gould and Martindale (2013) posit that "attempting to promote cooperation via joint custody in every case may be beyond the cooperation capacities of the parents and result in conflict that is harmful to children" (p. 105).

Second, joint custody may not be possible if a parent moves away. Relocation often leads to children having less and less contact with their nonresident parents as time goes by. If the relocation distance is substantial, many fathers in particular drift away from their children after divorce, perhaps because they are deprived of the opportunity to be parents rather than simply visitors. Third, if joint custody is to be successful, both parents must be involved. Both parents not only need to spend adequate amounts of time with their children; they also need to be involved in a diverse array of activities with them (M. E. Lamb & Malloy, 2013).

It is also important to ensure that **parenting plans** encourage similar meaningful child–parent relationships to develop and flourish after divorce. (Parenting plans are an important component of custody decision making; they include not only custody arrangements but also visitation rights for the noncustodial parent and for close relatives to the child.) However, it must be emphasized that children often do not benefit when they begin to spend considerable time with parents who were previously neither highly involved nor supportive in the child's psychological development (M. E. Lamb & Malloy, 2013). This "forced contact" with a parent who did not previously spend much time with the child is perhaps what supporters of the approximation rule, mentioned above, hoped to avoid.

✉ Roles of Mental Health Professionals in Child Custody

Psychologists and other mental health professionals who are involved in child custody cases may be differentiated on the basis of whether their primary role is as a consultant or an evaluator (see Table 9-3). As consultants, they usually serve as either (1) case-blind "teachers" who are asked to provide relevant information on the research literature on specific topics before the court; or (2) trial consultants, who are either retained in a non-testifying capacity to advise the attorney on strategies or information concerning the case, or as an expert willing to testify on behalf of the attorney's client. As an evaluator, they may be court-appointed, neutral evaluators or work-product evaluators. We begin with the court-appointed child custody evaluator.

Court-Appointed Neutral Evaluators

Fortunately, most divorcing parents settle their parenting issues informally, with or without the aid of a mediator, without direct court intervention or before a trial. Melton et al. (2007) estimate that about 90% of the litigants engaging in child custody disputes settle without a court hearing. Of the cases that do not settle, only a small percentage of them lead to a child custody evaluation. As **court-appointed neutral evaluators**, mental health professionals help the court make decisions on custodial arrangements.

The overwhelming majority of child custody evaluations are court ordered (Bow, 2006). The child custody evaluator is appointed by the court after the parties agree on the person chosen. If the parties cannot agree on the evaluator, the court may appoint a different evaluator who it believes will be sufficiently impartial and objective. Although the family court often encourages the parties to make a good-faith attempt to resolve the

Table 9-3	Consulting and Evaluating Roles in Child Custody Matters
Consultants	Provide relevant information about research to courts.
	Assist lawyers in non-testifying or testifying capacity.
Evaluators	Serve as neutral, court-appointed examiner.
	Evaluate work product of other mental health professionals.

matter on their own, the neutral evaluator is typically brought into the case when an early settlement does not appear likely. If the parties do not have attorneys, the neutral evaluator may be the only professional working with them. The primary goal of the neutral evaluator is to evaluate the family functioning, parenting styles, and relationships as objectively as possible. The secondary goal is to talk to the parties and describe for them what he or she is seeing in the family. According to Judge Mark Juhas (2011), the neutral evaluator's information may have the effect of allowing the parents to

> pull together for their children, as opposed to becoming further polarized. . . . The neutral evaluator is in a unique position to either help guide the family through the process of a mutually satisfactory resolution, or guide the family directly into the courthouse depending on how they approach their task. (p. 128)

He notes that "courts are asking and expecting experts to do their work with an eye toward resolution of the case as well as educating both the bench and the litigants on many different facets of the family" (p. 127).

It should be noted that the term **parenting plan evaluations** is sometimes preferred rather than *child custody evaluations*. This may be because mental health professionals are asked to assess parenting skills for a variety of reasons not limited to making custody decisions. For example, parenting can be assessed in cases involving a possible termination of a parent's rights, a custodial parent's wish to relocate across the country, or an adolescent's request to be judged an emancipated minor. Because both the general literature and psychological guidelines continue to use the term "child custody evaluations," we retain that usage as well.

Child custody evaluations are extremely difficult and challenging to conduct. Numerous commentators have remarked that they are emotionally charged and pose many ethical dilemmas (Connell, 2010; Kaser-Boyd, 2009; Stahl, 2014)—it is not unusual to see them referred to as "minefields." They are among the most dangerous and risky endeavors for psychologists, because of the high levels of stress, threat of litigation, risk of licensing board complaints, and risk of personal harm (Kirkland & Kirkland, 2001). "Family law cases involve complex and emotionally charged disputes over highly personal matters, and the parties are often deeply invested in a specific outcome" (American Psychological Association, 2010, p. 864). Kirkland and Kirkland report that approximately 10% of all new cases of ethics violations compiled by the American Psychological Association involve custody evaluation complaints. Moreover, Austin, Dale, et al. (2011) note that there is a high percentage of difficult personalities (and even personality disorders) among the population of child custody litigants who require court-ordered custody evaluations.

In a survey of psychologists who conduct child custody evaluations, 35% had received at least one board or ethics complaint, 10% had at least two complaints, and

10% had experienced a malpractice suit pertaining to child custody work (Bow, 2006; Bow & Quinnell, 2001). Although these complaints and suits may have been dismissed, as respondents indicated in their commentary, they are still a source of stress and financial strain to the practitioner as well as to the parties involved in the custody proceeding. Interestingly, approximately 10% of the survey participants indicated they no longer perform child custody evaluations. Bow and Quinnell's study also revealed that almost all of the psychologists in their sample included a recommendation in their evaluation concerning the **"ultimate issue."** That is, the psychologists offered their opinion to the court on which parent should obtain custody.

In a more recent survey of 213 experienced child custody evaluators, Ackerman and Brey Pritzl (2011) found that almost half of the evaluators had at least one licensure board complaint filed against them, and 20% had three or more complaints filed against them. It is noteworthy, though, that none of the respondents in the survey indicated they had more serious complaints against them, such as those from the state ethics board, or had malpractice suits filed against them.

Conducting Child Custody/Parenting Evaluations

Conducting a competent child custody evaluation requires the skillful integration of both science and clinical acumen (Gould & Martindale, 2013). The evaluator must be able to integrate current research with clinical experience. According to the APA (2010) *Guidelines for Child Custody Evaluations in Family Law Proceedings*, "The most useful and influential evaluations focus upon skills, deficits, values, and tendencies relevant to parenting attributes and a child's psychological needs" (p. 864). The APA *Guidelines* strongly emphasize that psychologists who conduct child custody evaluations maintain an up-to-date understanding of child development and family dynamics, child and family psychopathology, the impact of divorce on children, and the specialized child custody research literature. As observed by R. F. Kelly and Ramsey (2009), "a judge faced with a difficult case may highly value a custody evaluation, especially if the judge believes that the custody evaluation is scientifically grounded" (p. 287). The *Guidelines* also stress that psychologists strive to remain familiar with specific laws and court rulings governing the practice and nature of child custody adjudication within the locality where they conduct the evaluation. For example, if courts in that jurisdiction look favorably on the "friendly parent" rule discussed above, the examiner should be aware of that.

In some child custody cases, psychologists are asked by the family court to evaluate situations of special concern, such as allegations of sexual abuse and domestic violence or possible mental disorder in one of the parents. In sexual abuse cases, psychologists surveyed have rated the interview with the alleged victim as the most important procedure used, followed by an interview with the alleged perpetrator and a review of the records (Bow, 2006; Bow, Quinnell, Zaroff, & Assemany, 2002). In domestic violence cases, psychologists and social workers used several methods of data collection, including interviews, a review of police and medical records, and some psychological testing (Bow & Boxer, 2003).

Families in which domestic violence occurs present many logistic and ethical problems for examiners. Kaser-Boyd (2009) finds that some parents try to hide evidence of violence out of fear that they will lose custody of their children, even before divorce proceedings. This is because examiners are required to report child abuse to authorities; if abuse is reported, Child Protective Services may step in and remove the children from both parents. Kaser-Boyd also notes that battered women have many reasons to fear the custody evaluation process. Due to the trauma they have experienced, they may not perform well on psychological tests. Moreover, when the violence happens in the children's presence, the mother may be accused of failing to protect them. Custody evaluators must keep these factors in mind in interpreting test results, and they must be familiar with the general research on family violence.

The issue of mental illness also may arise in the most extreme of custody-related proceedings, the **termination of parental rights**. This is when a court decides that a parent is unfit to care for the child or children in his or her custody and places the child in the custody of the state or other party. Depending upon the law in a given state, termination of parental rights also may release the child for adoption. It should be emphasized that the threshold for terminating parental rights is high, and a parent's nonfitness must be demonstrated, usually by at least clear and convincing evidence. The imprisonment of a parent is not cause for a termination of parental rights. Some states have a lower threshold for mental illness, mental deficiency, habitual use of alcohol or drugs, or debauchery (Melton et al., 1997, 2007). With respect to mental illness, case law indicates that courts must evaluate parental competency and the risk to the children, not just the presence of mental illness. Nevertheless, in some situations parental unfitness has been assumed from a mental illness diagnosis without close examination of how the disorder specifically impacts the person's parenting (Benjet, Azar, & Kuersten-Hogan, 2003).

Criticisms of Child Custody Evaluations

In its *Guidelines for Child Custody Evaluations in Family Law Proceedings* (APA, 2010b), the APA recommends that psychologists employ multiple methods of data gathering. "Direct methods of data gathering typically include such components as psychological testing, clinical interview, and behavior observation" (Guideline 10). Tests and inventories are apparently being used even more than before. Ackerman and Brey Pritzl (2011) found that, compared with 10 years previously, there was a substantial increase in the number of psychological tests administered to both adults and children during the custody evaluation process. Interestingly, however, there has been increasing criticism of their use.

Criticism has focused on the lack of validity and reliability studies on many of the testing instruments specifically used for custody evaluations. For example, projective tests, sentence completion, the Bricklin Perceptual Series, and the Perception of Relationships Test (PORT) are gaining in popularity yet lack adequate research on their validity. (**Projective tests**—such as the Children's Apperception Test [CAT]—are personality assessment procedures that consist of a series of ambiguous stimuli designed to elicit unique responses from the child.) In their cogent and incisive assessment of child custody evaluations, Emery et al. (2005) argue that tests and inventories "specifically developed to assess questions relevant to child custody are completely inadequate on scientific grounds" (p. 1). Also criticizing the use of standard measures, O'Donohue et al. (2009) make a plea for better measures of such relevant constructs as attachment, parenting skills, parental conflict, environmental stability, and the emotional stability of the parents.

Some mental health professionals and attorneys have questioned the usefulness of child custody evaluations, even when psychological tests are not used by the evaluator. "These professionals have seriously questioned the adequacy of research supporting child custody determinations, the role of the evaluator, and the appropriateness of addressing the ultimate issue" (Bow, 2006, p. 25). Recall that the *ultimate issue* refers to the final decision that must be made by the court. Examples of the ultimate issue in the present context include who should have custody, whether a parent's rights should be terminated, and whether visitation should be allowed. Courts often ask for such recommendations from the evaluating professionals, and many professionals are willing to provide them (Melton et al., 2007). When child custody recommendations are made by the psychologist, they should be based on sound psychological data and address the psychological best interests of the child (American Psychological Association, 2010). The psychologist should seek to avoid relying on personal biases or unsupported beliefs.

The literature on how custody or parenting evaluations are performed—descriptive literature with data obtained from surveys or examinations of case records—is quite extensive. However, R. F. Kelly and Ramsey (2009) recommend additional and more far-reaching research endeavors examining the *outcome* for children from divorce. This would help determine whether evaluators and courts are accurate in their predictions of the best custodial arrangements. In other words, did they get it right? R. F. Kelley and Ramsey also point out that little reliable information is available on the number of custody evaluations conducted or how they are used. We know how they are done, but we do not know how many are performed, how extensively they are used by the courts, or how the children fared after the court's decision.

The Work-Product Evaluator

Child custody evaluators should approach their task with the expectation that their work product and opinions may be reviewed by another expert, known as the

work-product evaluator. There are no available data on how often this happens, and it is believed to occur infrequently, but evaluators must always be prepared for the possibility that another professional will review their work. The work-product evaluator most often is appointed by the court after one of the lawyers perceives that there may be potential problems with "the evaluator's methodology, bias, or that the opinions do not seem to correspond with the facts and circumstances of the case" (Austin, Dale, et al., 2011, p. 48).

The work-product evaluator is expected to conduct an objective appraisal of the custody report and formulate opinions about the strengths and weakness of the report (Austin, Dale, et al., 2011). This review "may be the only check and balance for a substandard evaluation" before it goes to court (Gould-Saltman, 2011, p. 139). The work-product evaluator or reviewer typically reviews interview notes, parent–child observation notes, psychological testing data, and pertinent records and reports (Austin, Kirkpatrick, & Flens, 2011). This information will help him or her discover things that the previous evaluator may have overlooked, was unaware of, or for some reason did not pursue. The reviewer also assesses whether the evaluator followed the relevant professional guidelines and standards of practice in conducting an assessment of the family. It is expected, as well, that the child custody evaluator followed, in principle, one of several professional guidelines for custody evaluations, such as those listed in Table 9-4.

Psychologists also should observe the code of conduct outlined in the *Ethical Principles of Psychologists and Code of Conduct* (American Psychological Association, 2002, 2010). Interestingly, there have been no professional guidelines or model standards established for work-product evaluators by any professional organizations to date (Austin, Kirkpatrick, et al., 2011).

Table 9-4   **Examples of Professional Guidelines for Conducting Custody Evaluations**

Title of Guidelines	Professional Group or Organization
Guidelines for Child Custody Evaluations in Family Law Proceedings	American Psychological Association, 2010
Model Standards of Practice for Child Custody Evaluation	Association of Family and Conciliation Courts, 2006
Guidelines for Psychological Evaluations in Child Protection Matters	American Psychological Association, 2013a
Specialty Guidelines for Forensic Psychology	American Psychological Association, 2013b
Practice Parameters for the Forensic Evaluation of Children and Adolescents Who May Have Been Physically or Sexually Abused	American Academy of Child and Adolescent Psychiatry, 1997

Ultimately, the primary goal of the work-product reviewer is to determine whether the parenting plan recommended by the child custody evaluator is likely to be beneficial to the child. That is, if the evaluator makes a custody recommendation, he or she also may make recommendations regarding visitation rights of the noncustodial parent, visits with grandparents or other relatives, counseling for children or parents, or even enrollment in a particular school. Like the original evaluator, the work-product evaluator is expected to follow the best interests of the child standard. In addition to assisting the court, the work-product evaluator may be asked to explain to the attorney or parent-litigants the strengths and weaknesses of the original report, and to provide better recommendations for resolving the case.

Case-Blind Consultants

Case-blind consultants are appointed by the court to provide their knowledge about up-to-date research and professional literature pertaining to the family or child development. Because the research on family and child development is expanding rapidly, the case-blind consultant has the important task of educating the court on some specific, relevant issue or topic, such as dealing with children with special needs. In most cases, the consultant offers expert testimony "that is explicitly designed to inform and educate the court about specialized, technical, or research-based knowledge as opposed to case-specific testimony" (Austin, Dale, et al., 2011, p. 57). The case-blind consultant is distinctly different from the consultant who is expected to provide "fact-specific" testimony based on knowledge of the case (Mnookin & Gross, 2003). By definition, the case-blind consultant has little or no knowledge of the court documents or details about the case.

The Trial Consultant (Non-Testifying and Testifying)

The final role in child custody cases is the **trial consultant** (see Chapter 6) who provides services for an attorney or a legal team as either a non-testifying or testifying expert. The range of services the *non-testifying* trial consultant provides includes educating the attorney and his or her client about the research literature on topics involved in the case, helping with trial strategy, and drafting questions for direct and cross-examination of witnesses (Austin, Dale, et al., 2011). The non-testifying trial consultant may also interview the attorney's client for information pertinent to trial preparation, engage in expert witness preparation, identify (for the legal team) appropriate expert witnesses, review the forensic work products for trial preparation, and formulate responses to foreseeable strategies of opposing counsel (Gould, Martindale, Tippins, & Wittmann, 2011). Sometimes the consultant will sit at the attorney's table during the trial to give advice as needed but will not testify. In addition, "the work product produced by the non-testifying consultant would be covered by attorney–client work product privilege and could not be discovered by another attorney" (Austin, Dale, et al., 2011, p. 59).

The *testifying* consultant may not be perceived as objective in the same way as a court-appointed, neutral expert; although still credible, he or she is generally expected to be supportive of the legal position of the retaining attorney (Austin, Dale, et al., 2011). Moreover, the testifying consultant has an obligation "to limit opinions to those that can be expressed with a reasonable degree of professional certainty" (Gould et al., 2011, p. 44). In some cases, the cross-examining attorney may attempt to depict the retained consultant as a subjective "hired gun," but in most litigated custody cases, the testifying consultant is not seen in this way (Gould et al., 2011). Rather, he or she is more often than not seen as credible. Nevertheless, when a consultant is called to testify by one of the litigating parents, it is only logical that one would assume he or she would offer evidence supportive of that parent's custody request.

All the roles listed above should be consistent with the ethical principles and standards of the profession. For example, some ethical problems may emerge if the testifying consultant also functions as a behind-the-scenes trial consultant to a legal team. In the eyes of some experts and legal scholars, this is a **dual relationship** that raises questions about ethical propriety. In general, the recommendation is to serve as one or the other, but not both.

> While the roles of trial consultant and testifying expert witness share many functions, the field of forensic psychology has evolved to a point where there is an emerging consensus that keeping these roles distinct is beneficial for the forensic practitioner, for attorneys advocating for clients, for the courts, and for litigants themselves. (Gould et al., 2011, p. 45)

Another example of a strongly frowned upon dual relationship is the psychologist who functions as a child custody evaluator for a current or former psychotherapy client, or a psychologist who engages in psychotherapy with a current or former child custody examinee. Psychologists are specifically cautioned to avoid these dual or multiple roles in the field's standards and guidelines (APA, 2002, Standard 3.05; APA, 2010, Guideline 7).

Alternative Dispute Resolution (ADR)

For centuries, the adversarial method has served as the fundamental approach for resolving disputes in most Western societies (Bridge, 2006). It is assumed that truth will emerge if the two opposing sides present their cases, are allowed to challenge each other, and have a neutral decision maker (judge or jury) determine the final outcome. However, nonadversarial alternative practices began to develop in civil disputes and even in minor criminal matters in the 1960s, including in family law. California, for example, created a **conciliation court** designed to assist couples in reconciling and preserving their marriage. Other states soon followed the practice. Couples who decided to reconcile after counseling signed a Reconciliation Agreement, which the court adopted as an order (Adam & Brady, 2013). However, as the number of divorces increased, the original purpose of the conciliation court soon expanded to a wide spectrum of other services focused on achieving a mutually acceptable disposition.

In many cases, litigants struggled with financial, social, emotional, psychological, and relational conflicts that were not appropriate for judges to resolve (Adam & Brady, 2013). It soon became apparent that those cases were better managed through a variety of nonadversarial or alternative dispute resolution procedures. This included mediation of custody, pretrial custody recommendations, settlement conferences, parent education, and counseling. In these nonjudicial settings, litigants were able to discuss personal matters and related struggles that usually are not permitted in court proceedings. As pointed out by Adam and Brady, "the ability of litigants to vent their feelings often helps with the healing process and, simultaneously, fosters nonjudicial resolution of the underlying legal issue" (p. 32). Collectively, these nonadversarial attempts to resolve relational conflicts in divorce proceedings are known as court-connected **alternative dispute resolution** programs or ADR programs. While a number of such out-of-court alternatives exist nationwide, we will only discuss three of the most common: divorce mediation, collaborative divorce, and parenting coordination.

Divorce Mediation

Divorce mediation began as a pilot program in the Los Angeles Conciliation Court in 1973, and by 1980, California *mandated* mediation in all child custody disputes (Boyarin, 2012). By 1990, divorce mediation programs had spread to 38 states and Washington, D.C. Mediation is a process of trying to resolve divorce disputes with the help of a professional mediator. A primary objective of the process is to reduce the adversarial relations between the divorcing parties. Proponents of mediation maintain that adversarial maneuvering by the parties often prolongs court involvement and affects minor children in a negative way. Adversary proceedings, particularly relative to custody determinations, often further strain already-fragile relationships between the divorcing parents.

"Mediation was originally intended as a voluntary and informal process designed to empower parties to explore the resolution of their disputes on their own terms rather than within the existing adversarial and legally rigid formal process" (Boyarin, 2012, p. 380). The goal is not *reconciliation* but *negotiation of a fair agreement* between the parties. As mentioned previously, divorce settlements have been traditionally reached either through the often-bruising litigation or through out-of-court negotiations between the parties' lawyers. Divorce mediation differs from these traditional strategies in three fundamental ways: (1) The communication takes place with a single professional mediator, (2) the mediation is based on an assumption of cooperation, and

(3) the parties make their own decisions (Emery & Wyer, 1987). The third feature also distinguishes mediation from arbitration (Emery & Wyer, 1987), because mediators have no authority to impose decisions on the parties. They act as neutral agents who provide opinions and guidance in the search for a settlement. Divorce mediation concentrates heavily on self-determination of both parties.

Professional mediators, who are members of the Family Mediation Association, must have a minimum of 40 hours' training. They are frequently trained psychologists or social workers, and sometimes attorneys. Regardless of the background and training of the mediator, the "process has to lead to a fair (as perceived by the parties), efficient, stable, wise, and well-informed resolution" (Boyarin, 2012, p. 382).

Early research in this area uncovered a variety of positive effects of divorce mediation. The process kept a significant number of families out of court, and custody agreements reached through mediation took half the time of in-court litigation (Emery, Mathews, & Kitzmann, 1994; Emery & Wyer, 1987). Between one half and three quarters of couples who went through mediation were believed to reach mutually satisfactory agreements. Mediation seemed to lead to greater compliance with child support and to greater cooperation between parents (Pearson & Thoennes, 1989). Available data also suggest that court mediators worked primarily with divorcing partners who had attempted but failed to reach a settlement out of court. Joint custody was the most common mediation agreement. Mediation also appeared to reduce substantially the amount of re-litigation (going back to court) on custody arrangements later on (Emery & Wyer, 1987).

At this point, and despite the popularity of mediation, not enough is known about who succeeds in the process, and researchers find there are many unanswered questions about what specific factors best predict successful mediation (Ballard, Holtzworth-Munroe, Applegate, & D'Onofrio, 2011). It is known, however, that up to 60% of couples coming to mediation report some physical aggression between spouses prior to participating in mediation (Ballard et al., 2011; Mathis & Tanner, 1998). It comes as no surprise, therefore, that Ballard et al. found that cases involving domestic violence and high levels of parental conflict were less likely to reach full agreement than cases with no evidence of domestic violence or extensive parental conflict.

Although divorce mediation is not a universal remedy, there is a good amount of evidence that parents participating in the process and who come to full agreement are more satisfied, are more flexible in adapting to their children's changing needs, and appear to be more involved with their children after divorce (Ballard et al., 2011; Beck, Sales, & Emery, 2004).

Collaborative Divorce

Despite some concerns, there appears to be continued support among legal and mental health professionals for the mediation approach, particularly when children are involved

(Ballard et al., 2011; C. M. Lee, Beauregard, & Hunsley, 1998). Mediation presents a way to avoid the acerbic courtroom battle that devastates the family, and rather than do away with it altogether, many believe mediation should be "fixed." Some scholars suggest alternative paradigms. Tesler (1999), for example, champions "collaborative divorce," which she argues is superior to the traditional mediation approach. Although mediation can work for some couples, she cites several weaknesses, including many of those discussed above. Collaborative practice is a respectful, cooperative, voluntary process designed to resolve divorce issues without the need to go to court.

In **collaborative divorce**, both lawyers and mental health professionals are committed to finding a solution that will be satisfactory to both sides. Both parties agree to continue to work toward this outcome; should one party threaten litigation, both attorneys are obliged to withdraw from the case. Consultants and experts are retained jointly, so that there is no pitting of one expert against another. "In contrast to litigation, collaborative practitioners use a problem-solving approach to resolve disputes by maintaining transparency, building on shared interests, minimizing coercive influences, trading relative advantages, and staying on the clients' legal and personal goals" (Otis, 2011, p. 229). Mental health professionals play very prominent roles in the practice (Otis, 2011). Mosten (2011) predicts that, in the near future, "collaborative practice will become part of the professional education and license qualifications for mental health and financial professionals" (p. 283). In the long run, collaborative practice will provide significant opportunities for many new professionals in mental health.

Parenting Coordination

Parenting coordination (PC) is a form of dispute resolution for parents engaged in *high levels of conflict* following a divorce. PC comes into play in parental disputes "where the parents are not able to resolve their child-related disputes on their own and constantly revert to relying on the courts to intervene" (Boyarin, 2012, p. 384). A family court may recommend this process when it is determined that ongoing parental conflicts could be detrimental to a child's post-divorce adjustment and sense of well-being. PC is a process that tends to be more directive and coercive than divorce mediation. As observed by Matthew Sullivan (2013), "Parenting coordination has developed as an alternative to the more adversarial processes in the family courts for the most chronically conflicted co-parents" (p. 58). The conflicts usually center on child custody and visitation issues. In most cases, the court will assign a coordinator to manage and resolve the quarrel or disagreement, and to implement the existing parental or court-mandated plan. Typically, this person is a psychologist or other mental health professional, but sometimes a family law attorney or a retired judge is assigned the role by the court. The coordinator is expected to have training in mediation, family law, family systems, psychopathology, and child development (J. B. Kelly, 2008). The role is post-adjudication (after a divorce or other court ruling) but often includes some judicial authority to decide specific day-to-day co-parenting issues.

It should be emphasized that parenting coordination does *not* include clinical services, such as psychotherapy, counseling, or formal psychological assessment. Rather, the coordinator's tasks are to understand the details and perspectives of the dispute and work toward a satisfactory settlement in the best interests of the child. The coordinator is expected to sustain a posture of objectivity and to preserve the distinctions between coordinator and other professional roles (J. B. Kelly, 2008).

Currently, parenting coordination is practiced in more than 30 states and several Canadian provinces (Fidler, 2012; Sullivan, 2013), but specific legislation regulating it has been passed in only 8 states (Parks, Tindall, & Yingling, 2011). In addition, its effectiveness in resolving the disputes of feuding parents has yet to be demonstrated or satisfactorily researched (Sullivan, 2013).

✖ Contemporary Special Issues in Custody Decision Making

This chapter began with a discussion of changes in family court caseloads over the past 30 years. As family court judges themselves have observed, they are faced today with a multitude of situations that rarely needed to be addressed in the past. Some of these are discussed below.

Parental Relocation

Frequently, one parent wishes to move with his or her children to a new location following separation or divorce. In a vast majority of cases, the other parent is still involved in some capacity with the child, even if it only entails occasional visitation. Generally, noncustodial parents may relocate to pursue other interests without permission of the court or the custodial parent. On the other hand, if the *custodial parent* wishes to move, he or she usually may do so only with the consent of the former spouse or the approval of the court. If the noncustodial parent opposes the relocation of the custodial parent, it creates a conflict between the custodial parent's need for self-determination and the noncustodial parent's interest in maintaining meaningful contact with the child. The situation becomes more complicated when one joint-custody parent opposes the move of the other joint-custody parent who desires to relocate with the children (or some of the children). There is rarely an easy answer. If the noncustodial parent or the joint-custody parent opposes the move, the parent wishing to move must request permission from the family court. In technical terms, the family court generally calls this a **relocation request**.

During the 1970s and late 1980s, the courts in most states made it difficult for parents with primary custody to move with their children. However, beginning in 1990 (*Gruber v. Gruber*, 1990), "the next dozen years brought a furious level of activity in state appellate courts and legislative responses to the relocation problem" (Austin, 2008a, p. 139). In the *Gruber* case, in Pennsylvania, the custodial parent was denied the right to move to another state by the trial court. When Gruber appealed this decision, the appellate court set out a three-part test for courts to apply in deciding this difficult issue. First, would the move advance the quality of life for the custodial parent and the child or children? Second, what are the motives of the custodial parent in moving as well as those of the noncustodial parent in opposing the move? Third, what is the availability of realistic visiting arrangements for the noncustodial parent? Shortly after the decision, the Pennsylvania legislature added 10 more factors to be considered by courts in this matter. This is obviously a difficult task for family courts to address.

The more recent trend has been to permit custodial parents to relocate, although the conditions imposed as well as the tests used by courts to make the decision vary from state to state (J. B. Kelly & Lamb, 2003). While U.S. jurisdictions have adopted statutes in the past two decades promoting joint custody, shared parental responsibility, and continuing contact with both parents following separation and divorce, meeting these expectations is not always possible. Divorced and never-married parents move far more frequently than two-parent, never-divorced parent families (Austin, 2008a). One study indicated that custodial mothers moved, on average, four times during the first 6 years after divorce, and another revealed that nearly half of young adults recalled moving as children within the first year after separation of their parents (Booth & Amato, 2001; J. B. Kelly & Lamb, 2003). Some studies discovered that 3% of the custodial parents moved out of the area within 12 weeks after the divorce was finalized, 10% moved away within a year, and 17% moved within 2 years (Braver, Ellman, & Fabricius, 2003). In an extensive review of the research literature on relocation, William Austin (2008a) concluded that frequency of residential moves is related to school achievement and behavioral problems, "so that a threshold of mobility of three or more moves doubles the likelihood of behavioral and emotional problems" (pp. 140–141). Clearly, the issue of relocation of a child with one of the parents following divorce or the end of a never-married relationship between parents is becoming increasingly important to mental health professionals as well as the family courts.

Relocation is particularly problematic when the court has previously granted a joint custody arrangement during the divorce process, because the court must now decide whether to maintain this arrangement. Regardless of the custody arrangement, though, the family court must focus on the potential harm to the relationship between the child and the nonresidential or nonrelocating parent (Austin, 2008a; J. B. Kelly & Lamb, 2003). Relocation requests "may pit a custodial parent's reasonable wish to better her circumstances by moving against a noncustodial parent's reasonable desire to maintain the frequent contact with his minor child that is a normal and perhaps essential element of any parental relationship" (Braver et al., 2003, p. 206). Relocations usually result in a significant reduction in contact between children and nonmoving parents, resulting in anger, anguish, and sometimes further litigation (J. B. Kelly & Lamb, 2003).

Increasingly, mental health professionals are asked by family courts to conduct a relocation evaluation. In these cases, the evaluator must be familiar with jurisdiction-specific statutory requirements and case law decisions pertaining to relocation (Gould & Martindale, 2013; Stahl, 2010). Most states have statutes and case law that stipulate what factors are to be considered before their courts decide whether a child may relocate with his or her parent. However, family court judge Kreeger (2003) laments that the "dichotomy between legal standards and psychological knowledge is particularly harmful in relocation cases" (p. 261). Many of the statutes and legal standards show an enormous lack of understanding about the harmful effects on children that can occur if separated by distance from the other parent. Researchers are beginning to recognize that a relocation move is only one factor in a long line of events, experiences, and changes that are likely to have a considerable impact on a child's life (Gould & Martindale, 2013; Shear, 1996). "A request to move away must not be examined in isolation but as part of the larger story of a child's emerging life" (Gould & Martindale, 2013, p. 124). The developmental age of the child, the geographical distance of the proposed move, the extent of the noncustodial parent's involvement in the child's daily activities, and the history of parental conflict are some of the key factors that warrant careful consideration in the relocation evaluation (Austin, 2008a, 2008b).

Many developmental psychologists believe it would be ideal if divorced parents wishing to relocate could wait until their children are at least 2 or 3 years old, because the children would then be better equipped with the cognitive and language skills necessary to maintain long-distance relationships. On the other hand, child development research suggests that there are two groups of children who are most likely harmed by relocation: children age 6 and under and children 12 and older (Austin, 2008a; Gould & Martindale, 2013). The primary reasons for these age-groups being especially vulnerable stem from disruptive attachments, either from the loss of a significant parent or from the loss of important friends and peer groups.

As indicated in the *Gruber* case, however, the child's best interests are often inextricably tied to the health and well-being of the custodial parent. If the custodial parent has better career opportunities in another state, for example, these bode well for a better economic opportunity for the family as well as the psychological health of the custodial parent. With increasing job mobility in society, these factors should be taken into account in deciding whether or not to allow the relocation.

Incarcerated Parents

In the late 20th century, rising incarceration rates were accompanied by the troubling reality that many children were left in free society while their parents—including sometimes their sole custodial parent—were in jail or prison. Although relatives often cared for these children, mother–child and father–child bonds were at risk of being broken. A parent's imprisonment is reason to remove that child from the sole physical and legal custody of the parent. However, it is not enough reason to terminate parental rights unless the parent has been convicted of a serious crime against his child or children. Imprisoned parents also have not lost their right to contact with their children. In a recent New York case, for example, an imprisoned biological father won his case for regular visits with his 3-year-old son. Although the biological parents were not married, the father had established a relationship with the child and wished to maintain that relationship during his prison term (*Granger v. Misercola*, 2013). The New York Court of Appeals ruled that there was a presumption that imprisoned parents could receive visits from their children. That presumption could be overcome by a showing that these visits or the travel involved would be damaging to the child. In the *Granger* case, there was no such showing.

The issue involving imprisoned parents is particularly troubling with respect to women offenders, because they are more likely than men to have dependent children who were in their care before their imprisonment. In addition, because there are fewer prisons for women, they are more likely to be incarcerated farther from their homes. Some prisons today offer programs for children of incarcerated parents, as well as parenting courses for the inmates, both female and male. A few jails and prisons allow incarcerated women with short sentences to have their young children (usually under 1 year) remain with them in special family units. Such nursery programs have been evaluated positively in the literature, with results showing lower recidivism rates as well as better social and psychological adjustment for both parent and child.

Never-Married Parents

A large number of children are born out of wedlock (Emery et al., 2005; Gould & Martindale, 2013). In recent years, custody disputes between never-married parents have often led to family court litigation and child custody evaluations, which can sometimes require unique factors to be considered. For example, unmarried mothers are frequently helped with childcare by grandparents and other extended family members. In fact, some unmarried parents have their child reared by relatives almost exclusively. In these cases, the introduction of the biological father into the custody equation may result in feelings of displacement by those family members and relatives who have been contributing to the care of the children on an ongoing basis.

Same-Sex Parents

The number of lesbian, gay, bisexual, and transgender (LGBT) individuals in the United States is very difficult to approximate. Statistics tend to underestimate the numbers, because many people who are LGBT choose not to disclose their sexual orientation (Burkholder & Burbank, 2012). Recent surveys estimate that about 1% of all households in the United States are headed by same-sex couples, with 19% reported having children. A large percentage (84%) of the couples with children live with their biological children, either from previous heterosexual relationships or from sperm donation. A small percentage of the children are stepchildren or adopted (Burkholder & Burbank, 2012).

Currently, there exists a patchwork of recognition and nonrecognition of same-sex marriages, civil unions, and domestic partnerships in the United States (Stein, 2012). Although the U.S. Supreme Court has not declared same-sex marriage to be a constitutional right, its two landmark rulings in 2013 (*United States v. Windsor* and *Hollingsworth v. Perry*) were significant victories for same-sex couples. At this writing, 16 states and the District of Columbia recognize the right of same-sex couples to marry.

Research literature over the past two decades indicates that there is no detrimental impact on children reared by same-sex parents (Raley, 2010). Children raised in homes with gay and lesbian parents are not disadvantaged with respect to gender development, personal development, or social relationships. Although there is some anecdotal evidence that these children may feel the effects of teasing or peer harassment, on the whole, "In study after study, the offspring of lesbian and gay parents have been found to be at least as well adjusted overall as those of other parents" (Patterson, 2009, p. 732). In fact, children raised by same-sex couples do not differ significantly from those raised by opposite-sex couples in victimization, social skills, peer relations, or psychological functioning (Rivers, Poteat, & Noret, 2008; Wainwright & Patterson, 2008).

Overall, the research finds that parent–child relationship quality is significantly more important than parental sexual orientation (Wainwright & Patterson, 2008). As Patterson notes, the social science research on children living with gay and lesbian parents is very clear-cut. In a policy statement, the American Psychological Association (2004) affirmed that children's psychological well-being was unrelated to parental sexual orientation, and that children of gay and lesbian parents were as likely to flourish as children of heterosexual parents. Although early research focused primarily on children living with female same-sex couples (e.g., Wainwright & Patterson, 2006, 2008) more recent research suggests families led by two fathers are equally solid.

Same-sex couples may—like heterosexual couples—decide to dissolve their relationship. When this occurs and they cannot agree on a satisfactory custodial arrangement, the family court is often expected to determine the best arrangement for the litigating parties. Although the research finds that same-sex couples are more likely to agree on custodial arrangements than heterosexual couples (Dodge, 2006), same-sex couples who do not agree present unique challenges for the family court. As observed by Raley (2010), child custody disputes involving same-sex parents are sometimes further complicated by biological, psychological, social, and legal factors.

In some of these cases, a gay or lesbian parent coming from a dissolved heterosexual marriage seeks custody of the minor children. In others, where a heterosexual marriage is not at issue, a same-sex partner has adopted his or her partner's child, or the partners together have adopted one or more children (see Box 9-2 for a case illustration). Upon dissolution of the relationship, one person seeks to remain in the child's life as sole or joint parent or seeks visitation rights. In addition, some divorces between same-sex couples have already occurred in those states that recognize marriage equality; in some of these cases, minor children have been involved.

BOX 9-2

Case Study. Custody and Child Abduction

Lisa Miller and Janet Jenkins met in 1997 when both women were living in Virginia. In December 2000, they traveled to Vermont, the first state to pass a law allowing civil unions, legal arrangements that sanctioned marriage-like relationships between same-sex couples. (Vermont has since recognized the right of same-sex couples to marry.) Miller and Jenkins had a civil union ceremony and returned to their home in Virginia to live. In 2001, Miller became pregnant through artificial insemination with sperm from an anonymous donor (Lindevaldsen, 2009). Lisa Miller gave birth to a daughter, Isabella, on April 16, 2002, and Janet Jenkins cut the umbilical cord. Several months later, the family moved to Vermont, presumably because the state was more receptive to lesbian relationships. In nearly the first year and a half of Isabella's life, she lived with two mothers and frequently saw her grandparents as well.

When Isabella was 17 months old, the two women ended their relationship. Miller returned to Virginia with the child, and filed court forms in Vermont to dissolve the civil union—an action that was the near-equivalent of obtaining a divorce decree. Jenkins, still living in Vermont, did not object to the dissolution of the civil union, but sought physical and legal custody of Isabella through the Vermont family court (Lindevaldsen, 2009). That court awarded custody to Miller and granted Jenkins parent–child contact. Miller was directed to allow Jenkins weeklong visitations with Isabella frequently throughout the year. Two weeks after the decision, Miller asked a circuit court in Frederick County, Virginia, to declare her the sole parent, and it did that, ruling also that Jenkins had no right to custody or visitation. Consequently, Miller—after Jenkins's first weekend of visitation—did not adhere to the Vermont family court's order,

(Continued)

(Continued)

nor did she allow Jenkins any physical or telephone contact with the child. Jenkins was paying child support and frequently drove the 10 hours to Virginia only to be rebuffed in her attempt to see Isabella. At that point, the Vermont court found Miller in contempt for refusing to comply with the court order for visitation rights.

Meanwhile, the Virginia Court of Appeals held that the lower Virginia court should not have ruled on the child's parentage. The court also ruled that the Vermont court had appropriate and sole jurisdiction, and that Virginia must give full force to the Vermont court's orders. Miller then appealed to the Virginia Supreme Court, but the appeal was dismissed on procedural grounds. Thus, the Vermont court's visitation order remained in force.

At an early point in these legal wranglings, Lisa Miller questioned her lesbianism, joined an evangelical Christian Church, and denounced homosexuality. In Virginia, Isabella was enrolled in a Christian school, and Miller obtained a teaching job at Liberty Christian Academy in Lynchburg, a Baptist School founded by the Reverend Jerry Falwell. Encouraged and supported by like-minded pastors and friends, Lisa Miller continued to defy the visitation orders of both the Vermont and Virginia courts. In November 2007, the Vermont court ordered that physical and legal custody of Isabella be transferred to non-biological mother Jenkins, effective January 1, 2010. The reversal of custody was a groundbreaking decision because of the civil union aspect of the case as well as the removal of custody from the biological mother. However, the judge said he was

making the decision in the best interests of the child, and that this was the only way she would have contact with both women; Janet Jenkins had agreed to allow regular visitations. (Recall the "friendly parent" doctrine referred to earlier in the chapter.) Lisa Miller appealed the decision to the Vermont Supreme Court, which upheld the lower court's ruling that physical and legal custody be awarded to Jenkins.

The Miller-Jenkins saga did not end with this court decision. With the help of members of her church and apparent support from representatives of Liberty University (Eckholm, 2012), Lisa Miller left the state with Isabella, traveled to Buffalo, New York, crossed into Canada, and from there flew to Mexico and ultimately to Nicaragua, where she adopted aliases for the two of them: Sarah for herself, and Lydia for the child. The case is now one of child abduction and remains an FBI open case.

Isabella appears on posters of the National Center for Missing and Exploited Children. People familiar with the situation have described her as living a lonely life, "long on prayer but isolated" (Eckholm, 2012, para. 3). She has been told that the woman she once called "Mama" will never go to heaven because she is living in sin with women (Eckholm, 2012). In August 2012, the Mennonite pastor Kenneth Miller (no relation to Lisa Miller) was found guilty in federal district court of aiding and abetting in the abduction of Isabella by helping Lisa Miller violate court orders. He was sentenced in March 2013 to 27 months in prison, but that sentence will likely be appealed. Lisa and Isabella remain in hiding.

Questions for Discussion:

1. Do you believe the lower court in Virginia was correct in declaring Lisa Miller the sole parent of this child?

2. The family court in Vermont seems to have applied the friendly parent doctrine in awarding custody to Janet Jenkins. Do you agree that this was a correct decision?

3. Which factors would you consider in deciding whether the best interests of the child were served in this case?

4. Using Internet resources, obtain more information about this case and discuss on the basis of what you have learned.

Debates have occurred in the legal literature as to whether a parent's sexual orientation should be a factor to consider in making decisions that affect minor children, such as awarding custody or making foster care and adoption placements. Patterson (2009) reviewed the developing law in jurisdictions across the United States and noted that laws relating to custody, visitation, and adoption with respect to gay and lesbian individuals vary widely:

At one end of the scale is a state such as Massachusetts, in which . . . parental sexual orientation is deemed irrelevant for purposes of foster care, child custody, and visitation proceedings. At the other end, in a state such as Missouri, the law does not recognize same-sex marriages and also disadvantages lesbian and gay parents in custody and visitation proceedings. (p. 731)

With the Supreme Court's 2013 decisions, and rapidly changing laws across the United States, it is likely that discrepancies in outcomes between cases involving heterosexual and same-sex couples will be seen less and less.

SUMMARY AND CONCLUSIONS

Definitions and conceptions of "family" have changed dramatically over the last half century. Whereas the typical family in the mid-20th century was thought to comprise a mother, father, and two or more biological or adopted children, today's family may not meet that description.

Families today, living under one roof, may be "blended," including children of one or both adults from a previous marriage; led by two mothers or two fathers; led by a sole parent, female or male; or composed of extended relatives, such as grandparents, uncles, aunts, and cousins. The parents in today's family may or may not be married, and the head of the family may even be an older brother or sister.

Family courts are specialized courts that must deal with a wide range of matters involving the modern family. Their caseloads have increased, and the disputes they process have changed dramatically in recent years. Although some family courts process delinquency cases, the trend today is to separate the family court from the juvenile court. Family courts primarily settle disputes involving divorce, separation, child custody, child neglect, and termination of parental rights. Cases of serious child neglect or abuse are more likely to be heard in misdemeanor or felony courts.

Mental health professionals have an increasing role in today's family court. They are primarily either consultants or evaluators. As consultants, they inform judges and lawyers about recent research, such as studies on child development or the effects of divorce on children. They may also serve as trial consultants or as expert witnesses in the courtroom itself. Their most common role is that of an evaluator in child custody situations. Although child custody is agreed upon by the parties in the vast majority of divorce situations, when custody is contested, judges typically appoint a mental health professional to evaluate the situation. Mental health professionals may be asked to make custody and other recommendations based on a best interest of the child (BIC) standard. Mental health professionals also may be used as work-product evaluators, reviewing an earlier assessment from a fellow professional.

Psychological research on the effects on children of divorce, family makeup, and various custodial arrangements has proliferated over the past 30 years. Early research found largely negative effects of divorce, but later research indicated long-term effects were not invariably negative, especially if divorcing parents refrained from hostility toward one another. A child's developmental age is also a factor; young children may exhibit separation anxiety, and school-age children often prefer one parent to another or play the parents against each other. However, custody arrangements must be factored in as well. Research indicates that joint custody, where both parents share equal responsibility for the children, is the "model" solution. Nevertheless, joint custody is not workable in situations where parents demonstrate hostility toward one another, one parent wishes to relocate, or one parent tends to be uninvolved in the children's lives. Research has also shown that children of same-sex couples are as well-adjusted as children of heterosexual couples. There is no support in the research literature for the contention that children are harmed by being in a stable home with two mothers or two fathers. These and other findings from the psychological research must be taken into account by mental health professionals conducting custody evaluations.

Child custody evaluations arguably represent the most controversial role of the mental health professional in family court. There is a wealth of descriptive information about how these are conducted, and professional organizations offer guidelines for practitioners. Most evaluations include interviews with children, parents, and collateral sources like relatives and teachers. Psychological measures or tests are often administered. Increasingly, mental health professionals are urged to pay attention to the wishes of the children themselves. Despite professional efforts to improve the quality of child custody evaluations, critics still maintain that they are intrusive and lend themselves to too much subjectivity. Nevertheless, family court judges request the assistance of mental health practitioners, because the judges themselves are often at a loss for how to make these difficult decisions without clinical input.

Because custody disputes take their toll on everyone in the family, family law often recommends—and some statutes require—some effort at mediation. Divorce mediation, wherein mediators are mental health professionals like psychologists and social workers, but also may be lawyers, exists in all states. Collaborative divorce, where many professionals try to help the two parties achieve a satisfactory agreement, is also gaining attention. When satisfactory arrangements cannot be achieved through mediation or collaboration, parenting coordinators may be appointed to keep disputes between the opposing parties at a minimum.

Psychological research in recent years has examined special topics relating to divorce. In addition to studying the effects of divorce and custody arrangements, researchers have examined the effects of relocation, which occurs more frequently in today's mobile society. Relocation that occurs when one parent moves a significant distance can be detrimental, particularly to children below age 6 and over age 12, and most particularly if the noncustodial parent ceases to be a meaningful part of the children's lives. In recent years, perhaps in recognition of the increased mobility in our society, judges have been more receptive to granting relocation requests. However, both statutes and case law in many states require that judges consider a range of factors before making a final decision. Mental health practitioners consulting with the courts often focus on the psychological effects of a potential move on the children but should not ignore the psychological effect on the custodial and noncustodial parent as well. In the final analysis, the best interest of the child is the wisest unitary standard to use, but as emphasized in the chapter, it is often subjectively applied.

As noted above, research on same-sex parenting is universal in its finding that children raised by same-sex parents are not significantly different in adjustment, personality features, social skills, or peer relations than children of heterosexual couples. Therefore, it is unlikely that there would be significant differences in their adjustments to divorce and to relocation. Cases in which one or both former partners protest the custody or visitation arrangements ordered by the courts, as illustrated in the case study in this chapter, can be particularly wrenching for the child or children involved. This would be true whether parents are of the same sex or different sexes.

KEY CONCEPTS

Alternative dispute resolution

Approximation rule

Attachment theory

Best interests of the child (BIC) standard

Case-blind consultants

Collaborative divorce

Conciliation court

Court-appointed neutral evaluators

Divided custody

Divorce mediation

Dual relationship

Friendly parent doctrine

Joint custody

Legal parental authority

Limited joint custody

Multiple-transition perspective

No-fault divorce

Parental alienation syndrome (PAS)

Parenting coordination (PC)

Parenting plan evaluations

Parenting plans

Physical authority

Projective tests

Relocation request

Sole custody

Split custody

Systems theory

Tender years doctrine

Termination of parental rights

Trial consultant

Ultimate issue

Work-product evaluator

10

Involuntary Civil Commitment

Questions of civil liberties and individual rights need to remain an essential focus of psychology and law scholars and practitioners.

—Petrila, 2009b, p. 402

Civil liberty concerns, as evidenced by the extensive due process protections afforded to those facing involuntary commitment, and the state's interest in protecting all of its citizens, are fundamentally at odds.

—Manahan, 2004, p. 30

Mentally disordered individuals who are presumed to be unable to care for themselves are often seen in our communities. Many are homeless, and a high percentage have co-occurring substance abuse disorders. The media often give attention to their plight, particularly when they are on the streets or in inadequate or temporary shelters. In recent years, the ranks of the homeless mentally ill have expanded to include both male and female veterans, often suffering with symptoms of PTSD, clinical depression, or suicidal ideation.

It is important to point out that mentally disordered individuals as a group are not harmful to others, but there are exceptions. Although most do not engage in violence, some—especially those with paranoid disorders—are significantly at risk of doing harm (Silver, Piquero, Jennings, Piquero, & Leiber, 2011). Mentally ill individuals are not necessarily dangerous to themselves either, though they may be in need of supervision such as oversight of medications or compliance with treatment. To what extent should the law permit the involuntary hospitalization of those with mental disorders for their own protection and the protection of others? To what extent should they be forced to obtain treatment in the community? When should restrictions be placed on their freedom? These questions have stymied legal scholars since the mid-20th century and remain crucial topics in psychology and law today, with little sign of universal agreement. The two quotes at the beginning of the chapter, reflecting disparate views on this topic, are illustrative.

In Chapter 4, we covered the commitment of individuals who are incompetent to stand trial for the purpose of restoring them to competency, as well as the commitment of persons found not guilty by reason of insanity. In this chapter, we focus on a different category of individuals, those who have not been charged with criminal offenses, although they may be. In general, their offending, if it occurs, is minor, but some are at risk of committing serious violent offenses.

Petrila (2009b) suggests that the topic of involuntary civil commitment has fallen under the radar in recent years. Many psychologists are unaware of legal changes that have occurred in this arena, particularly in the standards required for committing people to inpatient care against their will. This may be because civil commitment is more likely to involve the medical profession, specifically psychiatrists. The medical profession is more likely to be complicit in the restriction of rights, believing this to be in the best interest of those they have diagnosed as mentally ill (Kress, 2006; Pfeffer, 2008). However, many scholars remind mental health professions of the continual need to protect the constitutional rights of those who are subject to institutionalization and coerced treatment (e.g., La Fond, 2011; Morse, 2006; Petrila, 2009b).

We also cover in the chapter a seemingly intractable problem—the so-called **sexually violent predator (SVP)**. SVPs are individuals who are *not necessarily mentally disordered* in the clinical sense of the term. The SVP is, by legal definition, someone who (1) has been convicted of committing a sexually violent crime, (2) is determined under the law to have some mental abnormality, and (3) is considered a danger to the public because of the likelihood that he will commit more sexual offenses. SVPs are discussed in this chapter because 20 states have laws enabling the civil commitment of these individuals, against their will, after the expiration of their prison sentences (McLawsen, Scalora, & Darrow, 2012). Furthermore, in a recent case (*United States v. Comstock*, 2010), the U.S. Supreme Court ruled that it was the prerogative of Congress to allow the involuntary civil commitment of SVPs in the federal system. Thus, SVPs can be committed involuntarily at the expiration of their sentences under both federal law and the laws of many states. As we will see in this chapter, SVP laws have been criticized for their overreach, and they raise ethical issues for many clinicians (La Fond, 2011).

⬜ A Brief History

In the United States, commitment of persons to mental institutions against their will and for long periods can be traced to the historical periods representing the so-called **cult of the asylum** (Rothman, 1971) and **cult of curability** (Deutsch, 1949) during the 19th century. Prior to this time, persons who displayed "strange" behavior were kept in their own homes or turned out onto the streets, where many joined the ranks of vagrants and eventually were held in workhouses or jails. In some cases, bizarre "treatments" were attempted. Julien (1992) notes that persons displaying what would now be called schizophrenic behavior were treated by such methods as "twirling them on a stool until they lost consciousness or dropping them through a trap door into an icy lake" (p. 217).

In the 19th century, institutional confinement began to emerge as a first resort (Dershowitz, 1974, p. 803). The legal doctrine of *parens patriae*—in which the state acts as parent or protector of the individual—allowed government to restrict the freedom of supposedly mentally ill individuals in their own best interest. It was assumed that the presumably safe, protective, and nonstressful environment of the asylum offered the best treatment (and thus a cure) that society could give to "lunatics" (a pejorative term that has since been expunged from all federal statutes). In reality, of course, institutional confinement was anything but nonstressful, and it did not cure anything. Critics such as Rothman (1980) also argued that institutionalization was more a matter of convenience than genuine concern for the well-being of the mentally disordered. Family members could conveniently place their relatives in an institutionalized setting without formally showing a mental disorder, inability to care for one's self, or dangerousness to self or others, although the certification of one or two medical doctors was generally required.

In the first two thirds of the 20th century, until approximately the late 1960s, mentally disordered individuals who could not be cared for by their families or friends continued to be committed to mental institutions or psychiatric hospitals where it was not unusual for them to remain throughout their lives. The appalling conditions under which they were sometimes kept have been amply documented elsewhere, both in court cases and in scholarly literature to the present day (Lareau, 2013; Rothman, 1971, 1980). Books and movies like *One Flew Over the Cuckoo's Nest* and documentaries like *Titicut Follies* received widespread public attention and critical acclaim.

Due Process Changes

In the 1960s, courts began to pay more attention to individual rights, and gradually involuntary commitment became known as a deprivation of the liberty guaranteed by the Constitution. People could be committed to mental institutions against their will *only* with careful attention to procedural safeguards. In addition, even if they were appropriately committed, there would be limits placed on their continuing confinement.

The U.S. Supreme Court case that firmly established due process as a crucial consideration in involuntary civil commitment was *O'Connor v. Donaldson* (1975). Donaldson, who supposedly had paranoid schizophrenia, was committed to a mental institution in Florida at the request of his father for care, maintenance, and treatment. He was hospitalized for nearly 15 years despite his repeated requests to be released. Although considered mentally ill, at no time was he a danger to himself or others. There was no violence or evidence of suicidal ideation in his background. Furthermore, throughout those years, Donaldson apparently had received custodial care, but no treatment to improve his condition. The superintendent of the institution said Donaldson had received "milieu therapy," but "witnesses from the hospital staff conceded that, in the context of this case, 'milieu therapy' was a euphemism for confinement in the 'milieu' of a mental hospital" (*O'Connor v. Donaldson*, 1975, p. 563).

The Supreme Court opinion emphasized that a finding of "mental illness" alone cannot justify involuntary custodial confinement of nondangerous individuals, nor can "mere public intolerance or animosity" constitutionally justify the deprivation of physical liberty. The Court ruled that, in light of the fact that no treatment was available to Donaldson and that he was not dangerous to himself or others, he should be released.

The Supreme Court's decision, along with lower court decisions in many states, led to changes in statutes across the country. By 1978, all but two states had afforded greater protections for those faced with civil commitment (Turkheimer & Parry, 1992). Laws now required adversarial hearings before a judicial officer, legal representation for those subject to being committed, and a showing of mental illness and need for treatment along with dangerousness to self or others or **grave disability** (which presumes one cannot take care of oneself). Although courts generally required that the state demonstrate a need for treatment if institutionalization was warranted, they did not necessarily require that treatment be provided if it was not available (Lareau, 2013). The revised statutes of the late 20th century also began to require periodic administrative review of the need for continued institutionalization.

The strictest of the standards—those that were the most difficult for the government to meet—required a showing of *imminent* danger as well as a consideration of a less restrictive alternative to hospitalization. This was primarily fueled by a civil liberties–oriented movement toward deinstitutionalization, but partly also by new health care approaches, such as managed care, which sought to limit hospitalization as a general principle (Hiday, 2003). Outpatient treatment in the community, either ordered by the court or on strong recommendation from hospital clinicians, became more frequent. We discuss outpatient treatment in more detail later in the chapter.

Social science research in the 20th century—both before and after the statutory changes—revealed that candidates for involuntary civil commitment were disproportionately poor or indigent, uneducated, and unemployed or employed in low-status occupations. They did not seem to be disproportionately male or female, although some research suggested that the interaction between age and gender was significant. That is, older women and younger men were more likely to be institutionalized than older men and younger women (Hiday, 1988). Ethnic and racial minorities did not seem to be disproportionately at risk for civil commitment, once economic status, age, and gender were controlled.

Outcomes of Statutory Changes

After the statutory changes, the typical stay in a public mental institution following involuntary civil commitment was less than a month, but a substantial number of short-timers were continually at risk of recommitment—they were referred to as "frequent flyers" (Parry, Turkheimer, Hundley, & Creskoff, 1991). Turkheimer and Parry (1992) observed that persons recommitted were rarely considered dangerous; rather, they were highly likely to be recommitted as gravely disabled, and there were very likely no less drastic alternatives available for them in the community. Hiday (1988), reviewing the empirical research on civil commitment, observed that by the 1960s, the more flagrant and widespread abuses of the past no longer occurred. Nonetheless, many questions were raised about conditions of confinement and the quality of treatment received in mental institutions, including the rights of patients to refuse medications and the efficacy of various treatment approaches.

Despite the civil liberties approach that characterized the rights-oriented statutory changes, many legal scholars concluded that they did not accomplish what had been intended. Turkheimer and Parry (1992), for example, identified two major problems. First, the strict standards and procedural protections (e.g., lawyers, prior notice of hearings) that were adopted were not honored in practice. Civil commitment hearings, Turkheimer and Parry discovered, were not being carried out as they were meant to be: The empirical research "has been virtually unanimous in demonstrating that attorneys, judges, and clinical examiners do not perform in a manner consistent with revised commitment standards and procedures" (p. 646). Civil commitment hearings were often perfunctory, dominated by paternalistic practitioners and lacking in any demonstration of zealous advocacy on the part of attorneys representing those at risk of being committed or recommitted. This was particularly acute in the case of recommitment hearings, which received less attention in the research literature. A second problem identified by Turkheimer and Parry was more society-wide: The promise of community treatment had not been fulfilled. "[A]n important reason for the gap [between the letter of the law and the practice of it] in civil commitment hearings is the unwillingness of hearing participants to release patients into a community that is unable to care for them" (p. 647).

Other legal scholars reported that in some states, stricter commitment standards contributed to a **criminalization of the mentally ill**, a thesis that reverberated in later scholarly writings as well (H. R. Lamb & Weinberger, 2005). That is, individuals not eligible for civil commitment were charged with minor crimes such as disorderly conduct or unlawful trespassing in order to justify detaining them in jail, arguably for their own protection (Bonowitz & Bonowitz, 1981; Teplin, 2000; Teplin & Pruett, 1992). Other researchers found little support for such a phenomenon, however, and believed that the documented increases in the mentally disordered population in jail could be attributed to numerous social factors that could not be linked directly to restrictive commitment statutes (Arvanites, 1988; Hiday, 1988). Although differences of opinion continue as to the cause, many scholars today would agree with Lareau (2013) that jails and prisons "have become the de facto psychiatric hospitals of today" (p. 309).

Loosening the Standards

Gradually, around the turn of the 21st century, commentators began to notice a trend toward more flexible standards for involuntary civil commitment, with states changing their standards or courts interpreting them broadly, providing states with more power over the lives of the mentally disordered (Litwack & Schlesinger, 1999; Morse, 1998). For example, some courts ruled that commitment need not be based on *recent overt* acts, on threats of violence, or on *imminent* dangerousness (Litwack & Schlesinger, 1999), opening the way for states to modify their standard. This did not mean that psychiatric hospitals became overfilled—in fact, many were closed due to lack of funds or deteriorating physical conditions—but it did suggest that it was easier for states to commit individuals for shorter periods of time.

State power over the mentally disordered was particularly evident in the case of sex offenders (Janus & Meehl, 1997), and this power remains controversial to this day (McLawsen et al., 2012; Melton et al., 2007; Petrila, 2009b). The U.S. Supreme Court's pronouncements on this issue, in *Kansas v. Hendricks* (1997) and *Kansas v. Crane* (2002), will be discussed later in the chapter. We now move ahead some 20 years for an indication of what has and has not changed.

⊠ Modern Commitment Statutes

It is frequently noted that the number of individuals held in psychiatric facilities on any one day is fewer than ever before, but the total number of yearly admissions is far greater. It has been estimated, for example, that there are 660,000 admissions to psychiatric hospitals in any given year (Lareau, 2013; Winick, 2005). However, the number of beds available per 100,000 population decreased from 339 in 1955 to 22 in 2000 (Lareau, 2013). These statistics can be explained by numerous and sometimes overlapping factors, including the closure of inpatient psychiatric facilities, effective treatment with medication, shorter durations of stays, the availability of outpatient treatment, and—in some cases—more stringent standards for continuing hospitalization. Although most statutes specify an outside limit before additional review is needed (e.g., 3 months or 6 months), no state places a limit on the number of recommitments of one individual (Melton et al., 2007). That is, the frequent flyers can be recommitted in an unlimited number of subsequent hearings, as long as the commitment criteria are met.

Involuntary civil commitment laws exist today in all states and the District of Columbia. These laws identify the standards and procedures to be followed prior to and during commitment, but they differ in many respects. For example, although all jurisdictions require a showing of mental disorder or mental illness, these terms are defined variably and sometimes not defined at all (Lareau, 2013). During the due process movement of the 1960s and 1970s, most states required that there be "imminent danger" of harm to oneself or to others, often also requiring evidence of a recent overt act. Today, the imminent danger standard has survived in just a handful of states (Pfeffer, 2008). As noted in Box 10-1, the Commonwealth of Virginia was one of the last states to require imminent danger before it changed its law following the Virginia Tech shooting of 2007. All statutes, however, require at least clear and convincing evidence of the need for hospitalization, as mandated by the Supreme Court in *Addington v. Texas* (1970). (See Table 10-1 for a list of this and other cases relevant to civil commitment.)

Table 10-1	Key U.S. Supreme Court Cases Relating to Civil Commitment	
Case Name	**Year**	**Holding/Significance**
O'Connor v. Donaldson	1975	Case disallowed the indefinite commitment, without treatment, of mentally ill individuals who are not dangerous to themselves or others.
Addington v. Texas	1979	Need for commitment must be proved by clear and convincing evidence; preponderance of the evidence is not enough.
Zinermon v. Burch	1990	Persons committing themselves must be competent to do so.
Kansas v. Hendricks	1997	Allows civil commitment of sexually violent predators (SVPs) following expiration of their prison sentence.
Kansas v. Crane	2002	State must demonstrate that SVPs have some mental abnormality and some inability to control their actions.
United States v. Comstock	2010	Congress was within its prerogative to adopt SVP legislation; therefore, civil commitment of SVPs is acceptable in the federal system.

Danger to Self or Others

Involuntary civil commitment of the inpatient type requires a showing of danger, sometimes worded as harm to self or others. In other words, there is a prediction that, if not hospitalized, the individual will hurt herself or someone else. A recent suicide attempt or self-mutilation is behavior indicative of self-harm. In some jurisdictions, courts have looked at substance abuse and other self-destructive behaviors, such as those associated with eating disorders (Rustad, Junquera, Chaves, & Eth, 2012; Testa & West, 2010). States differ on whether the danger must be imminent and whether it must be documented by a recent overt act, but as observed above, the imminent danger standard has largely disappeared. In the typical statute today, dangerousness refers to a substantial likelihood of harm or a significant risk of harm. Interestingly, some states include emotional harm or danger to property as criteria for institutionalization (Lareau, 2013).

BOX 10-1

Case Study. Civil Commitment and the Law: Lessons From the Virginia Tech Shooting

Egregious, high-profile criminal cases often lead to major changes in both state and federal laws. Illustrations abound. Cases of child sexual abuse led to laws requiring the registration of sex offenders as well as the SVP laws discussed in this chapter; stalking cases led to anti-stalking legislation, including cyberstalking and cyberbullying; the Newtown, Connecticut, killings in December 2012 led to some changes in gun laws in some states. The mass shooting at Virginia Tech in April 2007 led to changes in laws regarding civil commitment in the Commonwealth of Virginia.

Seung-Hui Cho, a graduate student, killed 32 individuals and wounded about 35 others in the April massacre, after which he also killed himself. As illustrated in a report by a review panel shortly after the tragedy (Virginia Tech Review Panel, 2007), there were numerous indicators of mental disturbance in his background, the beginnings of which apparently coincided with serious physical health problems at age 3.

Cho, one of two children of Korean parents who emigrated to the United States, was a special needs child with hardworking, loving parents. However, he was very quiet and found it difficult to interact socially with peers and even to communicate with his parents. In middle school, he was diagnosed with a social anxiety disorder and with selective mutism. (He rarely spoke, and when he did, his voice was very low.) He was withdrawn, showed signs of depression, and was eventually prescribed an antidepressant. Cho was an eighth grader at the time of the infamous school shootings at Columbine High School in Colorado, and he wrote a disturbing paper in which he indicated he wanted to repeat Columbine, committing homicide and suicide (Virginia Tech Review Panel, 2007).

Chu received counseling while living at home with his parents, and he had individualized education programs (IEPs) throughout his middle and high school years. His verbal communication was minimal, but he graduated from high school with very good grades. He scored 540 on his verbal and 620 on his math SATs. These grades and scores got him into Virginia Tech. The school was unaware of his counseling, medication history, or special needs (Virginia Tech Review Panel, 2007). There was apparently no indication of violence in his background.

When he left for college in the fall of 2003, Cho was not on medication and had refused continued counseling—as a young adult, he was free to do so. At Virginia Tech, he was known as an isolated, noncommunicative student who had a series of roommates, most of whom interacted very little with him. In his junior year, he became more withdrawn and began displaying behavior that caused concern among both students and faculty. For example, he went to a party and repeatedly stabbed a carpet with a knife; he wrote stories with hostile, violent themes; at least one of his professors believed he was bullying her; and students apparently dropped a class he was in because they were uncomfortable with his bizarre behavior. Professors recommended that he obtain counseling.

In December 2005, about 16 months before the Virginia Tech shooting, campus police received a complaint from a student that he had been sending her strange, self-deprecating, but not threatening messages. He also texted someone that he might as well kill himself. Campus police contacted Cho, and a pre-screener with the department (a social worker) recommended that he be hospitalized under a temporary detention order because he was an imminent danger to himself. Cho was hospitalized overnight. Prior to the issuance of an extended commitment order, an independent evaluator (a psychiatrist) believed Cho was *not* an imminent danger. This evaluator had no access to Cho's prior mental health records and sought no

collateral information, saying later that there were not enough resources to do so. At Cho's commitment hearing, he himself was the only witness; the court reviewed the records, agreed with the prescreener that Cho was likely an imminent danger, but also noted that Virginia law required that a less restrictive alternative to hospitalization be offered. Therefore, the judge issued an order for outpatient treatment. Apparently, Cho never followed up to receive that treatment. Fourteen months later, he committed his atrocities (Virginia Tech Review Panel, 2007).

The Virginia Tech mass shooting prompted a review of Virginia's civil commitment statutes and a change from the "imminent danger" standard to one of "substantial likelihood or significant risk of harm." Had that standard been in effect when Cho's commitment hearing occurred, the independent examiner *might* have been more willing to support institutional confinement. Nonetheless, as the Virginia Tech Panel (2007) report revealed, lack of communication about Cho's mental status, confidentiality of records, and lack of sufficient resources also were significant factors leading up to the tragedy.

Questions for Discussion:

1. Compare and contrast the two standards, "imminent danger" and "substantial likelihood of harm." Does the latter standard sufficiently protect the rights of the person facing involuntary commitment?

2. Discuss the difficulties in enforcing an order of outpatient treatment.

3. If Virginia Tech had been aware of Cho's counseling, medication history, and special needs, would that have been reason to deny him admission?

Grave Disability

Every state allows the involuntary civil commitment of nonsuicidal individuals under a standard that indicates they are so mentally disturbed or disabled that they are not able to care for their own needs in a community setting (Melton et al., 2007). In some states, the concept of *grave disability* is subsumed under a dangerousness standard, under the assumption that a person unable to meet her own needs is, by definition, dangerous to herself (Lareau, 2013). Grave disability standards sometimes outline the specific needs the individual is unable to meet, such as food, clothing, shelter, medical care, and the ability to secure personal safety (Melton et al., 2007).

Some research suggests that grave disability is being used more and more as a standard for commitment, and most particularly recommitment. Pokorny, Shull, and Nicholson (1999), studying commitments and extended commitments of 490 patients, found that dangerousness followed by disability were the critical variables accounting for *initial admission*. For the recommitment or *extended commitment* process, however, the patient's degree of disability played a more important role than dangerousness. Nevertheless, the dangerousness standard is the more controversial of the two because it requires a prediction of the future behavior of the person facing commitment proceedings. The possibility of dangerousness also raises questions about the responsibility of mental health professionals to take steps to avert the danger. We will discuss these topics below, following a section on civil commitment proceedings.

✕ Civil Commitment Proceedings

In a review of the literature on civil commitment proceedings at the end of the 20th century, Turkheimer and Parry (1992) identified a litany of problems. Among them were the following:

- Attorneys were poorly prepared and often did not perform adversarial roles.
- Judges deferred to mental health recommendations or discouraged attorneys from challenging these professionals and questioning other persons who may have observed the behavior of the person facing commitment.
- Least restrictive alternatives to hospitalization were not considered.
- Examinations by mental health practitioners were perfunctory or nonexistent.
- Respondents were not advised of their rights, including rights to be represented by counsel.

There are strong indications that these problems continue to exist. Consider the following comment: "If there has been any constant in modern mental disability law in its thirty-five-year history, it is the near-universal reality that counsel assigned to represent individuals at involuntary civil commitment cases is likely to be ineffective" (Perlin, 2008, p. 241). The author goes on to say that the quality of counsel in most jurisdictions has been "mediocre or worse" (p. 243) and that legal challenges to the status quo have been rare. Only a handful of states have created specialized legal services for persons being subjected to commitment against their will, and the quality of these services is largely unexamined.

Although the law requires an adversarial hearing for civil commitment, hearings are often informal and hinge on opinions of physicians or psychiatrists who are not always cross-examined. It must be emphasized again that psychologists are far less likely than other mental health professionals to participate in these proceedings. Family members, social workers, employers, or friends may also testify, but it is not uncommon for a judge to make a decision based solely on clinical testimony or written reports. In its report on the Virginia Tech shootings (Virginia Tech Panel, 2007), the panel of experts noted that they had done a survey of civil commitment hearings conducted in that state in May of that year. Although this is not an empirically sound research project, it is illustrative that 60% of these hearings lasted no more than 15 minutes, and only 4% required more than 30 minutes.

Interestingly, Melton et al. (2007) state that "the mental health attorney has no clear ethical mandate. . . . Does the lawyer zealously advocate the wishes of a client who seems to behave irrationally?" (p. 352). Melton and his colleagues do favor the adversarial model in civil commitment proceedings, noting that it is crucial that clinicians be cross-examined and that the courts abide by civil commitment criteria, such as establishing dangerousness or grave disability by clear and convincing evidence. Nevertheless, they suggest that it is permissible for lawyers to stop short of zealously advocating their client's freedom in his or her best interest unless the client is competent.

Recall the two quotes at the beginning of this chapter, coming from seemingly disparate perspectives. There is clear evidence in the literature of tension between, on the one hand, scholars and practitioners concerned about protecting individual rights and, on the other, scholars and practitioners who believe that restricting those rights may be in the best interest of the individuals as well as society. Attorneys representing civil commitment candidates may be afraid their clients will not get the help they need if they are not civilly committed. Furthermore, they may not want to appear socially irresponsible in arguing for the release of persons they believe unable to function on their own (Turkheimer & Parry, 1992). Finally, they may be worried that the individuals they are representing can pose a threat to society or specific people if released. This leads us to a related topic, the obligation of mental health practitioners to issue warnings if they believe someone in their care is likely to do harm.

◤ Duty to Warn or Protect

The year 2012 was an especially tragic one on the national landscape. Although gun violence is an everyday occurrence in some towns and cities, mass shootings such as those in Colorado, Wisconsin, and Connecticut prompted an ongoing national discourse on how to prevent and respond to gun violence. Unfortunately, much of the attention focused on keeping weapons out of the hands of the mentally ill, implying that this group of individuals might be especially dangerous. As we have learned, the mentally ill *as a group* are no more likely to be violent than anyone else, but some categories of mental illness put an individual at greater risk of committing violent acts. Extreme violence is still the exception, but when it becomes known that the perpetrator had contact with the mental health system and perhaps even expressed a desire to perform violent acts, there is public outrage: Why weren't steps taken to institutionalize this individual and provide treatment before his behavior became so erratic that others died at his hands?

Clinicians in many states are under statutory obligations to warn or to protect specific individuals who might be at risk of being harmed by a clinician's patients. These laws are collectively known as *Tarasoff* laws after a well-known case (*Tarasoff v. Regents of the University of California*, 1974, 1976). They can be very different from state to state, however. For example, some require clinicians to warn potential victims, while others allow this but do not require it. Some laws involve no direct warning to the potential victim(s) but require or allow practitioners to notify police or other officials The decade of the 1980s was one in which the *Tarasoff* doctrine was widely applied, while the 1990s saw an interesting trend of rejecting or severely limiting the doctrine in many states (Felthous, 2001). Where the statutes exist, they trigger a duty to protect only if there is a clearly identifiable potential victim or if there is a very serious threat to public safety as a result of the patient's potential violence. The statutes also protect therapists from liability if they have taken reasonable steps to protect. However, in some jurisdictions, mental health practitioners can be held liable for not warning potential victims of violence at the hands of their patients (Gutheil & Appelbaum, 2000). Court decisions and statutes also vary widely in whether they require that clinicians warn identifiable third parties or control the potentially violent behavior of their patients in other ways, such as by hospitalization (Felthous & Kachigian, 2001). Table 10-2 provides a breakdown of states with and without *Tarasoff*-like laws.

In spite of these different legal standards within jurisdictions, many mental health professionals have interpreted the "spirit" of *Tarasoff* as a national standard of practice. That is, it is the professional responsibility of clinicians to take reasonable steps to protect a "reasonably identifiable victim" from serious threats from their clients. Thus, even without the requirement, mental health practitioners are likely to contact their

Table 10-2	Tarasoff-Like Laws in Various Jurisdictions	
States *requiring* clinicians to warn or protect* potential victims under certain conditions		
Arizona	Massachusetts	Oklahoma
California	Mississippi	Pennsylvania
Colorado	Minnesota	South Carolina
Delaware	Michigan	Tennessee
Idaho	Missouri	Vermont
Indiana	Montana	Washington
Kentucky	Nebraska	Wisconsin
Louisiana	New Hampshire	Utah
Maryland	New Jersey	
New York	Ohio	
Jurisdictions *allowing or encouraging* clinicians to warn or protect, but not requiring it		
Alaska	Florida	Rhode Island
Connecticut	Illinois	Texas
District of Columbia	Oregon	West Virginia
States with no specific *Tarasoff*-like law		
Alabama	Kansas	North Dakota
Arkansas	Maine	South Dakota
Georgia	Nevada	Virginia
Hawaii	New Mexico	Wyoming
Iowa	North Carolina	

*Warn or protect refers to either warning victims directly or protecting victims, such as by reporting concerns to law enforcement or initiating emergency hospitalization of the client/patient. In light of rapid changes in related legislation (e.g., gun safety laws) some modifications may apply.

supervisors, a threat assessment center, or even local law enforcement officers if they fear that the public safety or a specific individual is at risk. This does pose some ethical problems for clinicians, though. Particularly at risk is the patient–therapist relationship, in which the therapist has assured the patient that confidentiality will be maintained.

The respective arguments for and against the duty to warn have taken on new meaning in recent years, with evidence that mental health practitioners had contact with mass shooters in so many cases. In Colorado, a psychiatrist was alarmed at the behavior of the alleged shooter in the Batman case and had apparently called in a threat assessment team at the university he was attending. Even so, at least one individual whose loved one was a shooting victim has sued the psychiatrist for failing to protect the public. At this writing, the suit has not been settled, and there is of course no guarantee that it will be successful. Duty-to-protect lawsuits have been filed against numerous mental health professionals in less dramatic cases.

Research on Dangerousness

Researchers have expended considerable energy in their attempts to study violence among the mentally disordered, with some researchers in recent years suggesting there is more violence than previously thought (e.g., Douglas, Guy, & Hart, 2009; Silver, Felson, & VanEseltine, 2008; Silver, Piquero, Jennings, Piquero, & Leiber, 2011). As we noted in Chapter 4, some persons with certain serious mental illnesses—such as psychosis—have been found particularly at risk of serious aggressive behavior (Douglas et al., 2009). Nevertheless, it is important to keep in mind the cautionary statement of Heilbrun, Douglas, and Yasuhara (2009) that "the association between mental illness and violence remains unsettled" (p. 334).

For our purpose in this chapter, we focus on civilly committed individuals, whose violence potential has not been studied extensively. Exceptions are early studies from North Carolina (Hiday, 1990) and multistate studies from the MacArthur Foundation (Monahan et al., 2001; Steadman et al., 1998). Hiday followed over a 6-month period 727 individuals brought into civil commitment proceedings in North Carolina for mental illness and dangerousness. Psychiatrists had evaluated two thirds of them as dangerous. In her follow-up study, Hiday found no reports of violent acts or threats for three quarters of the individuals. In addition, a separate group of studies has examined outcomes of people ordered to receive outpatient treatment, a topic to be discussed shortly.

MacArthur Violence Risk Assessment Study

The MacArthur Violence Risk Assessment Study (Monahan et al., 2001; Steadman et al., 1998)—perhaps the most comprehensive study of this nature—focused on more than 1,000 acute, civil psychiatric patients at three different sites. Participants were white, African American, and Hispanic persons 18 to 40 years old. Extensive data on demographic and historical factors were collected, and diagnoses were recorded. (See Box 10-2 for more information on this study.)

BOX 10-2 RESEARCHERS AT WORK

MacArthur Violence Risk Assessment Study: Can We Predict Violence in Those Civilly Committed?

Henry Steadman, John Monahan, and their associates conducted what has become the most heavily cited research study on predicting violence in persons civilly committed (Steadman et al., 1998). The study used as participants more than 1,000 civil psychiatric patients who had been admitted or committed due to an acute psychiatric disorder.

During their hospitalization, the participants were measured on 134 wide-ranging risk factors. These included factors such as frequency of abuse as a child, frequency of parents fighting with each other, persecutory delusions, violent fantasies, suicide attempts, drug use, total number of people in social network, number of negative and positive persons in social network, and homelessness. The MacArthur researchers hypothesized that the risk factors measured while the patients were in the institution would help predict their level of violence once discharged. Thus, the study had two core goals: "to do the best 'science' on violence risk assessment possible and to produce a violence risk assessment 'tool' that clinicians in today's world of managed mental health services could actually use" (Monahan et al., 2001, p. 9). Without such assistance, Monahan and his colleagues stated, the ability of clinicians to predict violence was "modest at best" (p. 13).

For the next phase, the researchers interviewed the former patients and those who knew them in the community once they were discharged. Interviews were conducted every 10 weeks for a 1-year period. Steadman et al. (1998) reported that 50% of the patients completed all five follow-up interviews, and 84% completed at least one. During the interviews, patients and informants were asked whether and how often the patient had engaged in any of eight categories of aggressive behavior over the past 10 weeks. The categories were based on the Conflict Tactics Scale (Straus, 1995; Straus & Gelles, 1990) and its expansion (Lidz, Mulvey, & Gardner, 1993).

Of primary importance was the finding that no single risk factor, standing alone, was a significant predictor of violence. Furthermore, no single risk factor had to be present for the individual to demonstrate violent behavior.

> Our data are most consistent with the view that the propensity for violence is the result of the accumulation of risk factors, no one of which is either necessary or sufficient for a person to behave aggressively toward others. People will be violent by virtue of the presence of different sets of risk factors. There is no single path in a person's life that leads to an act of violence. (Monahan et al., 2001, p. 142)

The tool that was ultimately produced by the MacArthur researchers was the Multiple ICT (Iterative Classification Tree), which soon developed into the actuarial instrument COVR

(Continued)

(Continued)

(Classification of Violence Risk; Monahan et al., 2005). It places people in 12 different risk groups (6 low risk, 4 high risk, and 2 average risk). Monahan et al. (2001) found that almost half of their participants were in the low-risk group; the remaining participants were about evenly divided between high- and average-risk groups.

Questions for Discussion:

1. The above is only a brief description of a complex study. What other aspects of the methodology would you want to know before judging the importance of the study?

2. Why do most forensic psychologists prefer to say they are assessing risk rather than predicting violence?

3. Psychologists are more likely to be involved in research concerning civilly committed persons than to participate in commitment proceedings. What are some explanations for this?

Steadman and Monahan's seminal research was followed by additional studies on civilly committed populations. Skeem and Mulvey (2001) examined the strength of the PCL-SV (Hart, Cox, & Hare, 1995) in predicting risk and found that the instrument predicted violent behavior, but only modestly when other factors were controlled for (e.g., recent violence, criminal history, substance abuse, and personality disorders). Furthermore, despite the fact that we now have more sophisticated instruments available for assessing the likelihood of violent behavior, none is perfect. As Petrila (2009b) has observed, the new approaches "still have wide margins of error *when applied to the individual*" (p. 389). That is, mental health clinicians may be able to provide probabilities, but they cannot definitively say that a given individual is dangerous.

In sum, there is no sure way of predicting which civilly committed individuals will harm themselves or others when released, or which will harm others if not committed. It seems that approximately half are low risk—and even among those who are not, the "right" risk factors must be aligned. Put another way, the situation will influence, perhaps even dictate, whether someone is dangerous to self or others. Thus, many researchers, legal psychologists, and clinicians prefer to advocate outpatient commitment and monitoring of individuals at risk of violent behavior, as we discuss in the following section. This may occur either as an initial commitment or after a person has spent some time in an institutional setting.

✉ Involuntary Outpatient Commitments

In some, but not all states, mentally ill individuals are ordered to seek treatment in the community. Also called "assisted commitment" or "nonhospitalization orders," this mechanism is intended to keep individuals out of institutional settings while providing mental health treatment on a regular basis. Lareau (2013) summarizes three contexts in which outpatient commitment is delivered as (1) the least restrictive alternative to institutionalization, (2) conditional release, and (3) preventive commitment. In those states that require a **least restrictive alternative**, an outpatient order may be placed on an individual who may not need the restrictiveness of a hospital setting but does require continuing treatment. The **conditional release**, as Lareau notes, is a form of "step-down treatment" (p. 316) for the individual who has spent some time in a hospital setting—as we mentioned in Chapter 4, this may be considered a form of "mental health probation." Individuals on conditional release—such as insanity acquittees—are expected to meet specific criteria, such as meeting with therapists, as a condition of remaining in the community. Of the three forms of outpatient commitment, conditional release is the one that likely received the most intensive court monitoring (Lareau, 2013).

The third context is the rarest and the most controversial: **preventive commitment**. It "typically employs commitment standards that are less stringent and less protective of civil rights than customary civil commitment standards" (Lareau, 2013, p. 317), and it is available in about 10 states (Melton et al., 2007). The point of this approach is to intervene before the individual deteriorates to the point of requiring hospitalization (Parry, cited in Lareau, 2013). Preventive commitment is controversial because the individual does not meet the criteria for other forms of involuntary civil commitment, such as grave disability or dangerousness to self. However, those who support it believe it is a good option for individuals who would not otherwise voluntarily seek assistance but whose mental states are such that deterioration is inevitable without treatment (Hiday, 2003).

Kendra's Law and Its Spin-Offs

The modern trend in the direction of outpatient commitment can be traced to New York's passage of "Kendra's Law," which specifies a version of **assisted outpatient treatment** (AOT). This is a way of requiring that some mentally disordered individuals receive treatment in the community. In 1999, Kendra Webdale, a 32-year-old journalist, was pushed to her death, into the path of a subway train, by a man who had been diagnosed with schizophrenia and had a history of violence, but was not taking medication. The law named after her allows judges to order individuals to receive psychiatric treatment in the community for up to 6 months or be subject to institutionalization. All but a handful of states now have similar laws, with varying lengths of commitment. They mandate community treatment, but they do not mandate medication—the decision whether or not to medicate is left to the treatment provider.

Critics of these laws maintain they infringe on civil liberties by coercing individuals to receive treatment under the assumption that they are dangerous to society. Critics also say the laws are applied disproportionately on the basis of race or socioeconomic status. An independent study of New York's law (Swartz, Swanson, Steadman, Robbins, & Monahan, 2009) indicated the law was effective in reducing violence and affording treatment to the mentally disordered, and it found no evidence of racial bias. The study itself has been criticized because, though it compared AOT populations to non-AOT populations, it was not a randomized trial. The New York law and others patterned after it in other states are likely to remain, but they are also likely to be challenged on civil liberties grounds and watched closely for continuing evidence of effectiveness.

Whether or not a state has an AOT law in effect, mental health professionals may strongly *recommend* outpatient treatment once patients have been released from psychiatric hospitals. Patients may be given the names of community treatment providers, and an initial follow-up appointment may be made. Russell Eugene Weston, Jr.—the man who shot three Capitol Police officers in 1998, killing two—had been scheduled to receive such treatment. Weston had a history of mental health problems, first noticed by his family in his late adolescence (Manahan, 2004), and he periodically received psychiatric treatment. Approximately 2 years before the Capitol shootings, discussed in Chapter 4, Weston had been civilly committed to a state psychiatric hospital in Montana because he presented a danger to himself and others. He was released after 2 months when, with the help of medication, signs of violent behavior had dissipated (Manahan, 2004). The hospital arranged for Weston to obtain outpatient treatment in Illinois, where he was moving, but Weston, denying he had mental health problems and aware that the outpatient treatment was voluntary, did not pursue the treatment.

Outpatient commitment in all its contexts has received considerable attention in recent years, with some research emphasizing its ineffectiveness (Pfeffer, 2008). For the most part, studies have reported positive results and cost-effectiveness (Hiday & Scheid-Cook, 1987, 1989; Swanson et al., 1999, 2001; Swanson et al., 2013; Swartz et al., 2009). Extended commitment periods and frequent monitoring in the community both are believed to be especially important, however. Monitoring of outpatient treatment is most likely to happen if the treatment is conditional to remaining free after release from an institutional setting. Otherwise, the supervision of individuals under outpatient treatment orders is likely to be sporadic for many reasons, including lack of monitoring resources and lack of treatment opportunities. Furthermore, to achieve maximum effectiveness, outpatient programs should be longer in duration, spanning years rather than months (Durham & La Fond, 1990). The typical outpatient treatment order is in effect for 30 to 90 days. As mentioned above, New York's Kendra's Law allowed judges to order a 6-month treatment period. In 2013, Kendra's Law was modified to extend the period of supervision to 1 year.

In summary, then, the research on outpatient treatment is more positive if treatment is extended to periods of at least 6 months or even a year or more. Studies demonstrate that persons treated in the community recover faster, have fewer relapses, deteriorate less from dependency fostered by hospitalization, maintain employment better, and cost the state about half as much money as similar patients treated in hospitals (Swartz et al., 2009). Hiday and Scheid-Cook (1987, 1989) contend that outpatient treatment orders are particularly appropriate for the chronically mentally ill who would otherwise be caught in the "revolving door" of hospitalization, release, and rehospitalization. Their extensive 6-month follow-up study of 1,266 adults who had gone through civil commitment hearings in North Carolina found that persons committed to outpatient treatment, compared with those who had been institutionalized and then released, were more likely to be employed, to have maintained contact with community mental health centers, and to have more social contacts at the end of the 6-month period. However, both substance abuse and lack of compliance with medication have been identified as factors that limit the effectiveness of involuntary outpatient treatment and are associated with offending by persons with serious mental disorders (Bonta, Law, & Hanson, 1998; Borum, Swanson, Swartz, & Hiday, 1997).

Research in the early 2000s has continued to support both the frequency and the efficacy of outpatient treatment. It is also emphasized, however, that careful monitoring and frequent contacts with the outpatients are necessary.

Voluntary Commitments

In the 20th century, the literature on civil commitment often made a sharp demarcation between voluntary and involuntary commitment. An estimated 25% to 30% of all patients in public mental institutions were believed to have been committed involuntarily (Monahan & Shah, 1989; Wexler, 1990). Was the majority, then, composed of people who committed themselves on their own volition? Not necessarily, because an unknown number had probably occurred under the threat of formal commitment proceedings (Carroll, 1990). Moreover, some presumably *involuntary* commitments were actually voluntary. That is, the person wanted to be hospitalized, but the involuntary commitment process was used in order to assure that treatment would be expedited (Farabee, Shen, & Sanchez, 2002).

Interestingly, questions also were raised as to whether the mentally disordered were even competent to make the decision to commit themselves. This question was prompted by a 1990 U.S. Supreme Court decision (*Zinermon v. Burch*). Burch had been found wandering along a Florida highway, bloodied, bruised, and disoriented. He was taken to a private mental health care facility designated by the state to receive patients suffering from mental illness. There, he signed forms consenting to admission and treatment on a short-term basis. Staff at the facility diagnosed his condition as paranoid schizophrenia and gave him psychotropic medication. After 3 days, it was determined that Burch needed long-term treatment, so he was referred to a state mental hospital. Once again, he signed forms requesting admission and authorizing treatment. Still another form authorizing treatment was signed 2 weeks later. There was ample evidence in the record that he was disoriented, confused, and bizarre in both action and appearance during each form-signing episode. Burch remained in the institution for 5 months, during which time no hearing was held regarding either his hospitalization or his treatment. Following his release, he complained that he had been admitted inappropriately and did not recall signing voluntary forms.

The U.S. Supreme Court ruled, in a 5–4 decision, that in this case Burch had a substantive right to be competent before consenting to voluntary hospitalization and a consequent procedural right to a hearing to determine whether this competency existed. In other words, before being allowed to commit himself to a mental institution, he should have been given a hearing to determine whether he was able to make that decision. The Court stopped short of making this a constitutional requirement for all voluntary admissions.

Nevertheless, mental health practitioners feared that the *Burch* case would be interpreted as requiring hearings in all voluntary commitments and that the voluntary process would become nearly indistinguishable from the involuntary (Winick, 1991). This has not come to pass. As Melton et al. (2007) indicate, even after the *Burch* case, psychiatric facilities likely do not make much effort to determine whether an individual seeking admission to a psychiatric hospital has the capacity to make that decision. Melton et al. add that commentators "suggest that many 'voluntary' patients are in fact patients who either are subtly coerced into accepting the label [voluntary admission] or in fact are unable to understand its implications" (p. 809).

◼ Informed Consent and the Right to Refuse Treatment

Informed consent is a crucial concept in the law. Most people are aware of it in the context of medical procedures. For example, surgical patients agree to have surgery after being given basic information about the procedures to be performed and told of possible risks. Informed consent is also relevant to mental health practitioners in many different ways. It is at issue when mental health professionals seek to prescribe medication or initiate psychological treatment. It also comes into play when psychological evaluations are conducted. These include but are not limited to evaluations of competency, mental state at the time of the offense, disability, or parenting (child custody evaluations).

The minimal legal requirements for giving informed consent are

1   That the person be a competent adult;

2   That there be no duress or coercion;

3   That the person be told of any risks involved; and

4   That the person be told of the likely consequences of not accepting the care that is offered or of refusing to cooperate in the evaluation process.

All professional guidelines make reference to the importance of obtaining informed consent. For example, the *Guidelines for Child Custody Evaluations in Family Law Proceedings* (APA, 2010b) state,

> Obtaining appropriately informed consent honors the legal rights and personal dignity of examinees and other individuals. This process allows persons to determine not only whether they will participate in a child custody evaluation but also whether they will make various disclosures during the course of an examination or other request for information. (Standard 9)

Likewise, the *Specialty Guidelines for Forensic Psychology* (APA, 2013b) emphasize the importance of informing the recipients of forensic services about the nature and parameters of these services (Guideline 6). Obtaining informed consent of research participants is crucial as well (see APA, 2002, Ethics Code, Standards 8.02–8.05).

Note that adulthood has traditionally been considered a legal requirement; by definition, a child cannot provide informed consent. Courts have sometimes allowed exceptions to this rule, particularly in cases involving adolescents seeking certain medical procedures. Like children and adolescents, persons who are severely developmentally disabled or mentally disordered may be incapable of giving informed consent to medical procedures, tests, or treatment. The concept, then, becomes particularly relevant in the case of the mentally disordered individual who refuses treatment, as will be seen in the next section. Some scholars also believe that informed consent is meaningless in the case of persons who are institutionalized against their will—such as in mental hospitals, jails, and prisons. In these cases, "consent" if given may be the result of coercion.

Receiving and Refusing Treatment

Involuntary confinement of the mentally disordered has raised important questions about their legal rights to receive and to refuse treatment. "Treatment generally refers to a process of a diagnosis, intervention, and prognosis designed to relieve pain or suffering or to effect a cure" (Cohen, 2008, section 6.2(1)). Thus, the right to receive treatment represents an affirmative obligation on the part of the state to "do something" designed to improve the individual's mental condition. Recall the *O'Connor v. Donaldson* (1975) case discussed earlier in the chapter. Donaldson had received nothing but custodial care throughout his 15 years in a mental institution. He was not considered a danger to himself or others. The U.S. Supreme Court ruled that—absent treatment to address his condition—he should be released.

The state is not obliged to "cure" an individual, because the treatment provided may not be effective. Additionally, the legal right to receive treatment does not require the state-of-the-art treatment available for that particular mental disorder (Cohen, 2008). All that is needed is a good faith effort to provide patients with an individualized treatment program that includes periodic evaluation.

The legal right to *refuse* treatment recognizes that involuntary medication violates the patient's autonomy and bodily integrity. Under the doctrine of informed consent, a competent person has the right to refuse medication and life-sustaining artificial nutrition and hydration (*Cruzan v. Director, Missouri Department of Health,* 1990). The Supreme Court has recognized, though, that there may be a governmental interest that supersedes the right to refuse medication. For example, in *Washington v. Harper* (1990), the Court allowed the forced medication of an inmate on the premise that it was needed to control his dangerous behavior. Furthermore, as mentioned in Chapter 4 and illustrated by the Loughner case, courts have allowed the forced medication of criminal defendants to make them competent to stand trial, at least in serious cases and when the presiding judge has carefully considered the arguments for and against the forced medication.

However, just as a person must be competent to consent to treatment, he or she also must be competent to refuse. Are mentally disordered individuals competent to make decisions about treatment regimens deemed to be in their best interest? This question has been addressed by many psychological researchers (e.g., Appelbaum & Grisso, 1995; Petrila, 2006). Not surprisingly, the answer is often "it depends." Research has found that persons with some disorders (e.g., schizophrenia and Alzheimer's disease) have more deficits in decisional capacity than those with other mental disorders. However, even persons without any mental disorder may have such deficits. "A notion that normal subjects without psychiatric disorders have normal decision-making capacity is not necessarily valid" (Jeste & Saks, 2006, p. 608).

MacArthur Competence Study

An often-cited series of studies sponsored by the MacArthur Foundation (e.g., Appelbaum & Grisso, 1995; Grisso & Appelbaum, 1995; Grisso, Appelbaum, Mulvey, & Fletcher, 1995) has demonstrated that even persons with mental disorders can perform adequately on measures of decision-making ability. The researchers assessed and compared decision-making competence in three groups: patients hospitalized with mental disorders (schizophrenia and depression), patients hospitalized with medical illness, and nonpatients recruited from the community. Of the three groups, only schizophrenic patients with severe psychological symptoms performed poorly; the majority of schizophrenic patients performed adequately. Patients with depression demonstrated intermediate levels of decision making. The researchers also discovered that, for the schizophrenic patients, decision making improved after a 2-week period of treatment, with decreased symptoms. This led to a recommendation that patients be reassessed periodically for decision-making ability.

The MacArthur Competency to Consent research described above indicates that decision-making capability is not evenly distributed among individuals with mental disorders. Clearly, questions can be raised about the competency of schizophrenic patients with severe symptoms to make rational decisions about their own treatment. However, simply because a mentally disordered person cannot make a rational decision about medication, we should not assume that decisions to medicate should be made without oversight. Although psychoactive drug treatment today has made life more tolerable for many people, there are special concerns associated with administering it to individuals who are in an institution or whose freedom in the community is contingent upon taking medication. Public psychiatric facilities, primarily because their residents tend to come from disadvantaged and powerless groups in society, are especially susceptible to taking the path of least resistance in treating patients (A. D. Brooks, 1986). Psychoactive medication, which makes patients easier to control, is just such a path. In community settings, the mentally disordered who experience adverse side effects find themselves in a no-win situation, because by refusing to take the drugs, they risk reinstitutionalization. Cycles of taking and refusing to take drugs are not uncommon.

The MacArthur studies discussed above led to the development of the MacArthur Competence Assessment Tool–Treatment (MacCAT-T), which is the most comprehensive tool available for measuring one's ability to consent to treatment. It has an interview format that allows clinicians to test decision-making competence in four legally relevant areas: abilities to state a choice, to understand relevant information, to appreciate the nature of one's own situation, and to reason with information.

Psychologists have developed other instruments to measure decision-making capacity in various contexts. The predominant instruments measure the competence to consent to participating in research or treatment. Some 20 such instruments have been published, and they "exist on a spectrum from brief, highly structured, and more easily administered and scored, to lengthier, less structured, and requiring more guidance in administration and interpretation" (Jeste & Saks, 2006, p. 613). The instruments are described and assessed in a number of different sources (e.g., Jeste & Saks, 2006; Melton et al., 2007).

⬚ Civil Commitment of Sex Offenders

In the last quarter of the 20th century, sex-offending rates began to climb, and research in that area proliferated. It must be recognized, though, that sex offending is a broad category. It encompasses behavior as varied as sexual assault, sexual trafficking, exhibitionism, accessing child pornography, and prostitution, among other offenses. While all of these are crimes, not all share the same degree of seriousness. High-profile cases in recent years have kept sex offending at the forefront of public attention. In 2013, Ariel Castro pleaded guilty to multiple counts of felonies—including rape, kidnapping, and attempted murder—after a woman he had allegedly abducted and held hostage for nearly a decade managed to escape. Two other women and the 6-year-old child of one of the three were found in the same house. Other shocking cases involving abductions and rapes of children and adolescents (e.g., Elizabeth Smart and Jaycee Duggard) have received extensive publicity.

Sex offenders, particularly those who assault children, are reviled by the public, in the media, and—if they are imprisoned—by other prisoners. In the last 30 years, many state and federal laws have increased penalties on these offenders, and concerns that they could reoffend once released prompted laws requiring them to notify police of their whereabouts. Almost all jurisdictions require some form of registration to track the residency of convicted offenders; the most serious must register for life. However—and of particular relevance to this chapter—20 states along with the federal government have laws that allow sex offenders to be civilly committed to psychiatric facilities beyond their prison sentence, presumably for rehabilitative purposes. In several key cases, the U.S. Supreme Court has put its stamp of approval on these laws (*Kansas v. Crane*, 2002; *Kansas v. Hendricks*, 1997; *United States v. Comstock*, 2010).

The typical statute of this nature allows the civil commitment of convicted sex offenders after they have served their criminal sentence, if they are deemed to be a threat to public safety because of their predicted sexual offending. Like the other civil commitment statutes discussed earlier in the chapter, these laws require proof of present mental illness (which may be broadly defined) as well as dangerousness, and they provide for adversarial court proceedings. However, while such involuntary commitments are not automatic, "the operative rule in sex offender commitments seems to be that if at least one expert says that the respondent is dangerous, then a finding to that effect will be made by the court" (Janus & Meehl, 1997). Today, it is estimated that some 4,500 individuals are being held past their sentences under SVP laws (Aviv, 2013).

Leroy Hendricks serves as a good illustration of the type of offender sexual predator statutes were meant to incapacitate. Hendricks was a pedophile and rapist whose history of sexual offenses against children dated back to 1955. He had served both jail and prison sentences and had been treated in a state mental hospital. In 1984, he was convicted of taking "indecent liberties" with two 10-year-old boys. In the mid-1990s, when he was scheduled for release after serving almost 10 years of his sentence, the state of Kansas committed him to a state mental institution. Hendricks himself said during his commitment proceeding that he was not cured, that he could not control his sexual urges, and that only his death would guarantee that he would stop victimizing children. (See Box 10-3 for additional discussion of this case.)

BOX 10-3

Case Study. Sexually Violent Predators— Two Cases From Kansas: *Kansas v. Hendricks* (1997) and *Kansas v. Crane* (2002)

Leroy Hendricks and Michael Crane approached the U.S. Supreme Court 5 years apart with very different stories. Although they were both committed to psychiatric facilities under the state's SVP law, their crimes were not the same. As mentioned in the text, Hendricks was a convicted pedophile and rapist. At his commitment hearing, he stated that only his own death would stop him from offending against children. Crane was convicted of lewd and lascivious behavior and aggravated sexual battery, acts that were committed on the same day. He first exposed himself to an attendant in a tanning salon. Later that day, he exposed himself to a video store clerk, grabbed her, and demanded that she perform oral sex. When she refused, he ran off. Crane had apparently committed similar acts with increasing frequency, and psychologists testified that he suffered from exhibitionism and antisocial personality disorder.

Both men were subjected to civil commitment proceedings and were sent to psychiatric facilities at the completion of their prison sentences. In both cases, the state supreme court ruled that the civil commitments did not satisfy legal criteria. In Hendricks's case, he did not have a diagnosed mental illness; in Crane's case, although he had received a diagnosis, it was not demonstrated that he could not control his behavior—something the Kansas court believed necessary.

The U.S. Supreme Court allowed the commitment of Hendricks, stating that demonstrating "some type of abnormality" was sufficient to civilly commit a sex offender beyond his sentence. In other words, a diagnosed mental illness was not required. In the case of Crane, the Court sent the case back for further proceedings. Civil commitment of this type did not require that the person have absolutely no control over his behavior; rather, it would have to be demonstrated that there was serious difficulty in doing so.

In the Hendricks case, the Court also emphasized that the Kansas statute provided for a yearly review of the commitment, which served as some protection for the person committed. The statute did not require sex offender treatment. However, the Court also stressed that even if treatment were not offered for the offender's condition, the commitment was justified in the interest of public safety.

As a result of these two Kansas cases, it is not too difficult to confine sex offenders past

(Continued)

(Continued)

the serving of their prison sentence. As stated in the chapter, it is estimated that more than 4,000 individuals are being held in this way. The statutes typically do not require a serious mental disorder or evidence of dangerousness to others. If mental health practitioners support the confinement based on some degree of abnormality and difficulty controlling one's behavior, the offender may be confined on the basis of what he might do, using less stringent criteria than are used for others who are civilly committed. In addition, the SVP statutes recommend but do not necessarily require sex offender treatment, and the duration period between reviews is often longer than is the case for "ordinary" civil commitment. As noted in the chapter, many mental health practitioners believe these differences are unacceptable and have resulted in ensnaring sex offenders who are not all dangerous predators for extended periods of time.

Questions for Discussion:

1. If the state had no SVP legislation, could either of these two men be committed under typical civil commitment statutes?

2. Does the civil commitment of sex offenders past their sentence consist of punishment if they are not provided with treatment?

3. Discuss the pros and cons of civilly committing (a) Leroy Hendricks and (b) Michael Crane to psychiatric facilities.

There is no doubt that some persons committed under SVP laws may terrify the public. Leroy Hendricks is a case in point. Not all sex offenders are alike, however, and it appears that some are undeservedly given the dangerous sexual predator label. In an incisive article, Rachel Aviv (2013) tells the story of "John," a 31-year-old man convicted of downloading child pornography from the Internet and using the Internet to persuade a minor to have sex. John logged on to a chat room and unknowingly engaged in conversations with a federal agent; he then arranged to meet two "teenage" girls who were in reality federal agents. He pled guilty and was sentenced to 53 months in federal prison. Conditionally released, John later violated the terms of this release by downloading more child pornography. He was returned to prison for 2 years. At the end of his sentence, he was civilly committed as a sexually violent predator and sent to a treatment center operated by the Federal Bureau of Prisons. A determinative factor in his commitment was his score on the STATIC-99—a measure developed for rapists and child molesters—and testimony by a forensic psychologist that he was an accident waiting to happen.

Given the facts described above, most observers would probably agree that John did something wrong by downloading the child pornography and trying to link up with underage girls, although some would question the length of the sentence for a noncontact crime. Is John a sexually violent predator? Ten years ago, it was estimated that between 1,300 and 2,209 persons were being held under sexually violent predator statutes nationwide (La Fond, 2003). In 2013, Aviv reported that the number had increased to more than 4,500.

Despite the fact that SVP laws are not uncommon, few studies have examined systematically both the process of civil commitment and which sex offenders are sent to psychiatric facilities. McLawsen et al. (2012) summarized the available studies and reported their own results from Nebraska. They found that sex offenders in studies from Minnesota, Washington State, Arizona, Wisconsin, Florida, and California had been assessed as posing a moderate to high risk of sexual recidivism, while sex offenders from Nebraska had a medium to moderate risk. The most common diagnosis in Nebraska was paraphilia, a general category that includes sexual attraction to children. In other states, while paraphilia was a common diagnosis, other common diagnoses were psychopathy and personality disorders. All studies indicated that persons who are civilly committed under SVP laws have lower proportions of serious mental illnesses than other civilly committed groups (McLawsen et al., 2012).

Many mental health practitioners have ethical concerns about recommending the civil commitment of sex offenders past the expiration of their prison sentences (e.g., Petrila, 2009b). Some are concerned about the risk assessment instruments used by mental health boards in deciding whether to hospitalize an individual at the end of his sentence (e.g., McLawsen et al., 2012). Others are concerned about the lack of provision for treatment found in many SVP statutes. Although the laws indicate the offenders are being hospitalized for rehabilitative purposes, treatment is not guaranteed. If individuals are civilly committed, they should at the very least be provided with treatment. Although the literature is mixed with respect to the effectiveness of sex offender treatment, "overall, treated sex offenders fare better than untreated offenders" (Burdon & Gallagher, 2002, p. 98).

There remain many questions about the civil commitment of sex offenders under these laws. As McLawsen et al. (2012) conclude, much more research is needed from more jurisdictions examining commitment proceedings, the risks and diagnostic profiles of the offenders who are committed, and the quality of the treatment received within the psychiatric facilities.

SUMMARY AND CONCLUSIONS

A historical overview of involuntary civil commitment in the United States suggests that the most outrageous abuses of the past have disappeared. No longer is it common for patients to be placed in public mental institutions without regard for their constitutional rights or to be kept there indefinitely under unsanitary, physically deteriorating conditions. Moreover, today's statutes require that candidates for civil commitment, in addition to having a mental illness, must be proven gravely disabled or dangerous to others or to themselves.

Reviews of the civil commitment literature indicate, however, that restrictive criteria have lessened in recent years—very few states, for example, now require proof of *imminent* danger. In addition, the spirit of the more restrictive commitment statutes may be violated. Civil commitment proceedings in many jurisdictions are perfunctory and non-adversarial and continue to give deference to mental health practitioners. Lawyers for persons subject to civil commitment proceedings often do not approach their task with the zealous advocacy expected in an adversarial proceeding. They may believe commitment is in the best interest of their client and may be concerned about lack of treatment opportunities within the community.

On the other hand, civil commitments are shorter in length, although recommitments are not unusual. The total number of individual commitments per year far exceeds the total number of beds. Although some commitments are voluntary in nature—that is, an individual presents himself for commitment or agrees to be institutionalized—most research attention has focused on civil liberties of those who are committed against their will.

Outpatient commitment, also known as assisted outpatient treatment (AOT) or order of nonhospitalization, is a viable alternative to institutionalization if it operates effectively. AOT can be used either in place of psychiatric hospitalization or after a period of such hospitalization. Research indicates that treatment that includes regular monitoring of the individual and that extends over a period of at least six months—and preferably a year—is in the best interest of many mentally disordered individuals.

A key controversial issue facing psychologists and other clinicians since the 1970s has been the duty to warn or protect persons who might be at risk of violence from a patient. Some version of this duty is now found in the statutes or case law of most jurisdictions. Although the duty has become a fact of life, and is even embraced by some clinicians for its therapeutic implications, other clinicians are concerned about its ethical implications.

Much of the attention regarding civil commitment has now focused on sexually violent predators (SVPs) at the end of their prison sentence. Laws allowing this require showing that the person has some type of abnormality—not necessarily a diagnosed mental disorder—and a significant inability to control his behavior. Although SVP statutes generally provide for periodic review of the hospitalization, they do not all provide for sex offender treatment. Furthermore, despite the name, SVP laws do not apply only to those who have committed sexually *violent* crimes. The rising numbers of civil commitments of those who are considered sexually dangerous is of concern to many mental health practitioners as well as others concerned about the protection of civil liberties and the overreach of the state in these matters.

KEY CONCEPTS

Assisted outpatient
treatment (AOT)

Conditional release

Criminalization of the
mentally ill

Cult of curability

Cult of the asylum

Grave disability

Informed consent

Least restrictive alternative

Parens patriae

Preventive commitment

Sexually violent predator
(SVP)

CHAPTER

11

Psychology in Civil Litigation

W e are a litigious society, seeking redress through the courts for a wide range of alleged wrongs done to us by others. In civil law, these wrongs are referred to as **torts**. We sue our neighbors, our employers, our schools, our contractors, police who arrest us, our physicians, and sometimes even our parents. We sue hospitals, educational institutions, and pharmaceutical companies. We sue for libel, for invasion of privacy, for false arrest, for sexual harassment, and for toxic harm, to name but a few examples. Although some civil suits are frivolous, political science research indicates that most have some merit and that safeguards exist, enabling the dismissal of unsubstantiated claims early in the process (see generally, Bonsignore et al., 2006; Doherty, Reville, & Zakaras, 2012). Moreover, although courts may be overwhelmed by the volume of litigation, the law provides access to the courts at least until a judge or magistrate reviews the initial documents.

The great majority of civil cases are settled out of court, with and without the dispute resolution or mediation processes discussed in other chapters. Psychologists can participate in these early stages of a case by evaluating plaintiffs and respondents, guiding the mediation process, or consulting with lawyers. Later, if a case goes to trial, the psychologist or other mental health professional may testify as an expert witness. The jury or judge makes two final decisions: (1) They determine the liability—that is, whether the defendant (sometimes called the respondent) is responsible for the harm; and (2) they determine the damages if the defendant is found responsible.

The **plaintiff**—the person filing a suit in civil court—typically wants more than an apology from the **respondent** or **defendant**, who is the person or entity that allegedly harmed the plaintiff. In some cases, plaintiffs want the ongoing behavior to stop, in which case they seek an **injunction**. In most cases, plaintiffs want some form of financial compensation, or **damages**. Damages fall into two major categories: **compensatory damages** are intended to make up for the harm suffered by the plaintiff, sometimes also referred to as a way of making the person whole; **punitive damages** are assessed when the harm done is so grave that the judge or jury believes the defendant needs extra punishment. Punitive damages are also intended to deter the defendant and others from committing similar harmful acts in the future (Lenton, 2007). To be awarded damages, regardless of the type, the plaintiff must first be able to demonstrate some physical harm or mental injury as a result of the actions of the defendant. The plaintiff also must show that the defendant either intended the harm or was at least negligent. For example, the jogger who was mauled by the much-maligned pit bull and sues the owner does not have to prove that the owner intended the harm; however, it must be shown that the owner was negligent, such as by not adequately training or containing the animal.

Civil cases are sometimes perceived as easy to win because, in all but a few situations, they require only a finding of *preponderance of evidence*. Some exceptions will be mentioned later in the chapter. None requires a finding of proof beyond a reasonable doubt, such as what is expected in criminal trials. However, civil cases may be time-consuming and emotionally exhausting, and plaintiffs who win them often have difficulty collecting the money to which they are entitled. In addition, though trial judges typically do not modify the damages awarded to the plaintiff when the plaintiff wins, appeals court judges are more likely to do so, particularly when the awards are considered excessive. For these reasons, plaintiffs are encouraged to pursue early dispute resolution or out-of-court settlements.

The ability to obtain damages for emotional suffering *alone* is a relatively new concept in the law. It was not until the latter half of the 20th century that courts allowed plaintiffs to seek damages for mental injury without some evidence of physical injury (Foote & Lareau, 2013). Mental injury may also be referred to as emotional distress, emotional harm, or psychic or psychological trauma. Foote and Lareau observe, though, that if there is no physical injury, the plaintiff claiming emotional distress usually must show some physical manifestation of this emotional distress, such as headaches or nausea.

Not all the civil issues discussed in this chapter involve civil wrongs, or torts, however. Litigants approach courts—often specialized courts—with claims for employment benefits, health benefits, insurance, or veterans benefits that they believe have been unjustly denied. In some cases, these claims require evidence of psychological harm, such as post-traumatic stress. Others believe they have been discriminated against in hiring or denied promotions based on their disabilities, in violation of federal and state laws, and the disabilities may be psychologically related.

Another area in which legal psychologists—both practitioners and researchers—may be involved is the assessment of various competencies or capacities. We discussed competencies that were relevant to criminal law (e.g., competency to stand trial, competency to understand *Miranda* warnings, competency to be executed) in earlier chapters. In the present chapter, we address competency in the civil arena, where the term *capacity* is usually preferred (Moye, Marson, & Edelstein, 2013). As Moye et al. observed,

> Capacity issues arise most frequently when an individual makes a decision that puts his or her health, assets, property, or self at risk and lacks the insight or the willingness to accept help. In these situations, clinicians or family members may raise the question of whether this person has capacity and are often seeking authority for surrogate decision making on behalf of the identified person. (p. 159)

Thus, there may be questions about whether a person had testamentary capacity (ability to make out a will) or had capacity to manage her financial affairs or to refuse medical treatment. Recall our discussion of informed consent in Chapter 10. Providing informed consent presumes that one has the ability (or capacity) to do so.

In summary, the civil law in general provides multiple opportunities for psychologists to interact with the legal system. We have already addressed some of these, particularly in the last few chapters. In this chapter, we focus on topics that relate directly to civil capacities and to the employment and educational spheres.

⊠ Civil Capacities

As indicated above, there is sometimes confusion about the terms *competency* and *capacity*. Some experts recommend that "competency" be used only to refer to a *legal* finding and that "capacity" be used to refer to *clinical* findings (American Bar Commission on Law and Aging and the American Psychological Association, 2008; hereafter cited as ABA-APA, 2008). Most clinicians interchange the terms, and they most often use the term competency. In earlier chapters, we discussed various competencies in relation to legal findings (such as competency to stand trial or competency to waive constitutional rights). In this chapter, we will use the clinical term "capacity," as recommended by the American Bar Association in consultation with the American Psychological Association.

Civil capacity refers to the ability to make decisions about money, property, and health care, and to communicate them. By far the most frequently litigated form is **testamentary capacity**, which refers primarily to the cognitive ability to make a will (ABA-APA, 2008).

Testamentary Capacity

The next generation will likely witness a substantial increase in the need for civil capacity evaluations on the basis of dramatic demographic changes, such as the shift toward a society of elderly individuals in whose hands there is a disproportionate amount of societal wealth (Foot, 2002; Shulman, Cohen, & Hull, 2005). It is estimated that $41 trillion in wealth will be transferred before 2050 via inheritance (Peisah & Shulman, 2012). The fastest-growing group of older adults is the 85-plus age range, which is expected to grow from 4.2 million in 2000 to 12.9 million by 2020, an over 200% increase (Administration on Aging, 2006). "All these trends conspire to produce a significant, if not dramatic, increase in will challenges and concomitant requests for capacity assessments both contemporaneous and retrospective" (Peisah & Shulman, 2012, p. 95). In addition, a high prevalence of dementia in older adults "combined with the growing complexity of modern families will . . . contribute to the increase in challenges to wills" (Shulman et al., 2005, p. 63).

Currently, the courts and legal professionals are increasingly turning to psychologists for opinions regarding the decision-making capacity of older adults (ABA-APA, 2008). "Often these complex cases require fine-grained cognitive and functional evaluation that balances promoting autonomy while protecting a vulnerable adult from harm" (ABA-APA, 2008, p. 9).

Assessing testamentary capacity requires the evaluation of four basic attributes: (1) the knowledge that one is making a will, (2) knowing the nature and extent of one's property, (3) awareness of the nature and relationship of those who may be beneficiaries, and (4) knowledge of the manner in which the property is distributed. Although people of every age and cognitive ability execute their wills and other vital documents, challenges to the validity of these documents are most likely to occur in the cases of those who are elderly and vulnerable, mentally disordered, or experiencing cognitive decline.

Forming and Executing a Will

Interestingly, there is some debate as to just how cognitively complex the task of making a will is. According to Melton et al. (2007), testamentary capacity does not demand high cognitive skills. It does not refer to a general ability to conduct one's affairs. They maintain that "only a low threshold of functioning is required" (p. 396). On the other hand, Shulman et al. (2005) say that testamentary capacity represents an advanced activity of daily living and is mediated by higher cognitive functions: "This is different from household activities of daily living such as shopping, housework, meal preparation or basic ADL's [activities of daily living] such as bathing and dressing" (p. 64).

Psychologists and other mental health professionals who assess the elderly and those with cognitive or mental impairments often classify functioning into two broad categories: (1) *Activities of daily living* (ADLs), such as grooming, toileting, eating, and dressing; and (2) *instrumental activities of daily living* (IADLs), such as abilities to manage finances, health, and functioning in the home and community. According to Shulman et al. (2005), testamentary capacity falls in the second category. The psychologist assessing it must have sufficient clinical experience and knowledge of complex cognitive functioning to be able to render a skillful and meaningful forensic report. The cognitive and general brain functions to be assessed by the clinician include judgment, impulsivity, planning, and appreciation of the nature of complex interpersonal relationships (Shulman et al., 2005). In addition, "testators must know a reasonable approximation of the overall worth of their estate and which individuals are the 'natural objects' of the bounty, usually blood relatives (Raub & Ciccone, 2012, p. 287). (**Testator** is the term for the person who has written and executed a last will and testament that is in effect at the time of death.)

Wills are not invalidated just because a person has a mental disorder, is intellectually disabled, or is addicted to alcohol or other drugs (Melton et al., 2007). However, these factors can be relevant if there is concern that they contributed to a person's incapacity at the time the will was signed. When wills are challenged, dementia is the most common condition cited, followed by alcohol abuse and neurological and psychiatric conditions (Shulman et al., 2005). **Dementia** refers to a pervasive loss of cognitive function beyond what might be expected from normal aging. However, even persons with mild or moderate dementia have intervals of lucidity, and the clinician must determine if this was the case at the time the will was constructed and signed.

When most people write their wills, mental health practitioners are not consulted. However, if a testamentary capacity evaluation is requested at the time an individual is executing a will, some experts recommend that a video recording be made of the evaluation: "A video recording can present compelling information that may be relevant to a court's effort in the future to determine if the person possessed testamentary capacity at the time of writing the will" (Raub & Ciccone, 2012, p. 289). In fact, even without the presence of a mental health professional, it is still a good idea for the execution of the document to be videotaped if there is suspicion that the will may be challenged in the future.

Most often, however, psychologists, neuropsychologists, or other mental health professionals are asked to give *retrospective* opinions after a person has died, and the will is "being challenged on the basis of lack of testamentary capacity or undue influence" (Shulman et al., 2005, p. 64). (See Box 11-1 for a case relevant to this issue.)

BOX 11-1

Case Study. The Marshall/Astor Story

In a recent high-profile case, the will of the very wealthy socialite and philanthropist Brooke Astor—who died in 2007 at age 105—was settled in 2012 after a public airing of circumstances surrounding the last years of her life. Astor had drafted a will in 2002 in which she left significant portions of her estate (estimated at $100 million) to various educational, cultural, and social institutions. In 2003 and twice in 2004, she amended that will, decreasing the charitable contributions and leaving more to her son, Anthony Marshall. One of the amendments also gave Marshall outright control of the estate. Although Astor was diagnosed with Alzheimer's disease some years before her death, the record indicated that she was mentally competent when she signed the original will in 2002. However, she apparently had diminished capacity at the time the changes were made. In addition, the charities and individuals who challenged the amendments to her will maintained she was under undue influence of her son, who was at the time her legal guardian.

In an unfortunate family saga, Anthony Marshall's son Philip sued his father for guardianship of Philip's grandmother, maintaining that she was the victim of elder abuse and was held in squalid conditions in her Upper East Side apartment in New York. Although claims of elder abuse were not substantiated, Astor was eventually removed from her son's care and lived the last years of her life among friends who were prominent in political and social circles.

A settlement of the civil suit involving the will was reached in 2012 without necessitating a protracted trial. The settlement preserved the 2002 will and nullified the later amendments. Various charities and public and private institutions received the bulk of Astor's fortune, but relatives and others also benefited.

In a separate *criminal* matter, Astor's son, Anthony Marshall, along with a family lawyer, Francis X. Morrissey, Jr., were convicted on several charges associated with looting her assets. They were found guilty of fraud-related crimes, including tricking her into altering her will, and were given prison terms of 1 to 3 years. Both began serving their terms in late June 2013. Marshall, wheelchair bound and suffering from Parkinson's disease and congestive heart failure, was sent to a medical unit similar to a skilled nursing facility on prison grounds. After serving 8 weeks of his sentence, the 89-year-old was released from prison on medical parole.

Questions for Discussion:

1. What roles might a mental health practitioner play in a case like the one described above?

2. Discuss the societal costs and benefits of sending Anthony Marshall to prison.

3. What factors should be taken into account in deciding whether to release a person from prison under a program of medical parole, which is sometimes referred to as compassionate release?

Psychologists have been largely left to their own devices and methods for assessing testamentary capacity, but the procedure most often relied on is highly similar to a psychological autopsy (Drogin & Barrett, 2013; Parry & Drogin, 2007; see also Chapter 8). If a will is challenged, the burden of proof in most jurisdictions is clear and convincing evidence of incapacity, and it rests with the party alleging the deficiency (Raub & Ciccone, 2012). In other words, the party or parties challenging the will must provide clear and convincing evidence that the testator did not have testamentary capacity at the time the will was written.

Testamentary Capacity Concerning Other Legal Documents

While testamentary capacity is a term typically reserved for the execution of wills, it may also be applied to other contexts involving legal documents. Examples are the capacity to make health care decisions or to manage finances (see also Table 11-1). With regard to health care decision making, it has become more common for people to write **advance directives**, which are their directions and wishes in the event that they become physically or mentally incapacitated. In these cases, a court or a party in a legal proceeding challenging the advance directive may request that a psychologist evaluate a person's capacities before he or she became incapacitated. In other cases, the question of capacity may arise at the time the person is making the initial directive. Some requests for the capacity to make decisions on health care may come from a physician. In other cases, the request may come from the court or a lawyer.

Likewise, with respect to both health care and finances, many people today have executed a **durable power of attorney (POA)**. In this document, the individual appoints an agent or agents to manage financial affairs, make health care decisions, and conduct other business. It may be in effect immediately or in the event the person becomes incapacitated.

Although a durable power of attorney is a written document that remains valid even if the person should later become unable to make his or her own decisions, the family may believe the agent should not have been assigned and is not acting in the best interest of the incapacitated person. The family may argue, for instance, that the agent in question had "undue influence" on the person at the time the power of attorney document was executed. **Undue influence** refers to "the intentional use of social influence, deception, and manipulation to gain control of the decision making of another" (ABA-APA, 2008, p. 15). Cognitive impairment often leads to an increase in susceptibility to and dependence on others. Therefore, a psychologist may be asked to assess the person's capacity at the time he or she executed the durable power of attorney document.

Guardianship is a relationship created by state law in which a court provides one person (the guardian) the duty and power to make personal or property decisions for the incapacitated person. In the absence of a signed power of attorney document, or in combination with it, a family member may ask for legal guardianship. As pointed out by the ABA-APA (2008), when a petition for guardianship is filed, psychologists may be asked to evaluate whether this person can be independently responsible for his or her life. In answer to this inquiry, psychologists will provide considerable help to the court by assessing *specific* domains that will enable the judge to fashion a "limited order." A limited order limits the authority of the guardian to only those areas where the person needs assistance, such as managing the checkbook and paying bills (ABA-APA, 2008). For example, the court may be interested in the person's **donative capacity**, which refers to the capacity to give appropriate gifts to charity, organizations, friends, or relatives.

Capacity to make a gift has been defined by courts to require an understanding of the nature and purpose of the gift, an understanding of the nature and extent of the property to be given, a knowledge of the natural objects of the donor's bounty, and an understanding of the nature and effect of the gift. (ABA-APA, 2008, p. 17)

Most states have moved toward a preference for limited guardianship, judging a person to lack capacity only in specific areas. (See Table 11-1 for illustrations of other capacities that may be specified in a limited order.)

In assessing the many testamentary capacities, mental health professionals must consider whether certain impairments are temporary, declining, permanent, or reversible. The critical point is the time at which the person is executing (or, if looked at retroactively, has executed) a document. However, a court would also want to know the likelihood that a person's incapacity was temporary, such as might be the case of a demented person who retains lucid periods. In that case, the person might not have been incapacitated when the document was signed. Drogin and Barrett (2013) write,

Numerous disorders can result in impairments that interfere with testamentary capacity, including delusional disorder, schizophrenia, substance abuse, and a

---

Table 11-1   **Some Types of Capacity Recognized by the Courts**

Contractual capacity: Capacity to enter into contracts, such as purchasing products or services on extended plans. The person must be able to understand the nature and effect of the act or business being transacted.

Capacity to convey real property: Capacity to sell one's property, such as a house, land, or valuable coin collection. The person must be able to understand the nature and effect of the transaction at the time it is executed.

Capacity to execute a durable power of attorney: Capacity to assign someone to make financial or health decisions on one's behalf. Some states have held that the standard is similar to that for making a will.

Capacity to consent to medical care: Capacity to agree to medical procedures and approaches, including experimental drugs and clinical trials. Informed consent is a critical component of this capacity.

Capacity to refuse medical treatment: Capacity to decline additional medical treatment, refuse surgery, or decline drug treatment. Informed consent is a critical component of this capacity.

Capacity to execute health care advance directive: Capacity to make health-related decisions ahead of the fact in the event that one becomes incapacitated in the future.

Capacity to consent to sexual relations: Capacity to engage willfully in sexual intercourse or other sexual relations. It is most likely to be assessed in persons who are mentally disordered, intellectually disabled, or evidencing some form of dementia.

Capacity to drive: Capacity to operate a motor vehicle, which is often set out by state law. It involves the physical or mental ability to operate a motor vehicle with safety on the highways.

Capacity to mediate: As noted by the ABA-APA (2008), "Mediation is increasingly being used as a means of dispute resolution in a broad range of issue that might otherwise go to court" (p. 20). This capacity refers to whether the person understands the mediation process, who the parties mediating are, the role of the mediator, and the issues at hand.

host of physiologically based conditions that might permanently or even temporarily affect the examinee's ability to distinguish between fantasy and reality.
(pp. 297–298)

They point out that the issue of temporary incapacity is critical in such evaluations
because the person may have executed the advance directive or other document during
a "lucid interval" in which symptoms were not prominent.

End-of-Life Issues

The average life span of people in the Western world has increased steadily over the past
century. In the United States, the average age of death is 78, whereas in 1900 it was 47
(Groopman, 2013). It is not unusual today to have relatives or close acquaintances in
their nineties, and many people know of at least one centenarian. Unfortunately, many
individuals who reach their eighties and nineties also experience deficits in their cognitive abilities, the most serious of which are represented by dementias, including
Alzheimer's disease, vascular dementia, and dementias associated with chronic diseases
like Parkinson's and Huntington's.

As we discussed above, when elderly people sign documents that have a significant
effect on their lives or the lives of others, the law may question the validity of these decisions. This is not limited to the elderly, of course; decision making by persons with
mental disorders, for example, was a topic addressed in Chapters 4 and 10. Other mental
impairments—temporary neurological conditions or situational depression associated
with a debilitating physical disease—may also cloud one's judgment and affect the capacity for making informed decisions, regardless of one's age. With the advent of the 21st
century, however, some individuals with debilitating, terminal diseases—even if they
were relatively young—began to argue for a right to decide to bring their life to an end.
This has led to some need for mental health professionals to evaluate whether they have
the capacity to make that decision.

Hastened Death

In May 2013, Vermont became the third state in the United States to pass legislation
enabling individuals suffering from a terminal illness to obtain prescription medication
to end their lives. Oregon had passed a similar law in 1997, and another went into effect
in the state of Washington in 2009. In all three cases, the patients must be residents of
the state and have an estimated survival period of less than 6 months. Critics of these
laws refer to them as "assisted suicide" or "physician-assisted suicide" laws, but supporters prefer to call them "death with dignity" laws. In fact, the legislation specifically states

that the actions allowed by the laws shall not be construed as suicide, assisted suicide, mercy killing, or homicide. Courts in Montana and New Mexico have also supported the right of a competent terminally ill person to obtain help in dying.

An individual's right to self-determination in medical matters has long been recognized under the law. In a court opinion issued a century ago, Justice Benjamin Cardozo, who later became a Justice of the U.S. Supreme Court, wrote that "every human being of adult years and sound mind has a right to determine what shall be done with his own body" (*Schloendorff v. Society of New York Hospital*, 1914, cited in Moye et al., 2013, p. 161). In the late 20th century, many courts acknowledged the rights of competent individuals to refuse medical treatment. Nevertheless, these same courts also invariably made reference to the government's interest in preserving life (Cantor, 1989). The U.S. Supreme Court allowed families to withdraw life support with evidence that this would be within the person's wishes (*Cruzan v. Director, Missouri Department of Health*, 1990). Court decisions such as these encouraged state legislatures to enact legislation authorizing the use of living wills and health care advance directive instruments (Winick, 1998). Thus, when individuals have made clear, preferably in writing, the type of care they would and would not accept were they to become physically noncommunicative or mentally incompetent, treatment providers are presumably bound to respect their wishes. In most jurisdictions, clear indication of a desire to avoid being kept alive on life-support systems—in the form of a living will or advance directives—will lead a court to abide by the individual's wishes, even when challenged by the family. The most common method of doing this is to withdraw life-sustaining treatment, such as hydration or nutrition. DNR (do not resuscitate) orders are also common.

Another, less commonly known method is aggressive palliative care, which refers to hastening death by giving drugs that are known to pose a high risk that a patient will not tolerate them (Benjamin, Werth, & Gostin, 2000). For individuals who are not comatose or on life support, death also can be hastened directly through terminal sedation or ingesting drugs prescribed by a physician. This is the action sanctioned by the "death with dignity" laws. Courts and legislatures are much less willing to let patients take that approach, however. Although Oregon, Washington, and Vermont have done so, legislatures in other states (e.g., Massachusetts) have rejected bills allowing that option. In Montana, an effort to have physician-assisted death recognized as a constitutional right under the state constitution failed (*Baxter v. Montana*, 2009). However, the supreme court of Montana ruled that it did not contradict public policy if a physician prescribed lethal drugs to a patient. As a result, a physician in that state can prescribe life-ending medication at the request of a competent patient without fear of criminal prosecution.

In two separate cases, the U.S. Supreme Court refused to establish a constitutional right to "physician-assisted suicide," by ruling that a state's *prohibition* against assisting, causing, or aiding a suicide did not violate the Constitution (*Vacco v. Quill*, 1997; *Washington v. Glucksberg*, 1997). Note that the 1997 Supreme Court decision in the Washington case spurred that state to change its law in the opposite direction—Washington now has a law similar to Oregon's. The Supreme Court also has upheld Oregon's law (*Gonzales v. Oregon*, 2006). Interestingly, in 2012, a physician who was instrumental in having Oregon's 1997 law passed was able to benefit by that law. He died at age 83 after ingesting a lethal chemical potion that he had requested from his own physician.

In the few states that have passed laws allowing physicians to help a patient hasten his or her death, a number of safeguards protect both the patient and the physicians or mental health practitioners involved in the case. For example, the laws require the attending physician to consult with a second physician, and they provide for mental health consultation if any of the physicians has doubt about the patient's mental competence or judgment. The laws do not, however, require the input of a psychiatrist or psychologist if the physicians do not have such doubts. (See Table 11-2 for features of the Vermont law.)

At about the time Oregon adopted its legislation, the American Psychological Association (2003) convened a working group on assisted suicide and end-of-life issues. Like similar working groups, its members were tasked with reviewing research and making policy recommendations for psychologists on these topics. The group was unable to make recommendations, noting the diversity of opinion on the matter. They did, however, comment on research indicating there are "fluctuations in the will to live," suggesting that even if someone decides he or she wishes to die, the person could change his or her mind. Given the diverse views on the issue, the group demurred from making recommendations other than to encourage psychologists to follow closely the developments in end-of-life issues.

The involvement of psychologists in hastened death decisions is relatively recent and one that many prefer not to address. It is unknown how many psychologists are indeed consulted on these matters in the states that have passed death with dignity laws. As noted above, these laws do not require consultation with mental health professionals unless the physician has reason to believe the individual may not be capable of making the decision. Even in that situation, the mental health professional is perhaps more likely to be a psychiatrist than a psychologist.

It is widely believed that some people at the last stages of their lives have simply been able to get help in dying from a trusted physician, but how often this occurs is not documented. It is likely that physicians in every state have done this. Supporters of death with dignity laws say that making this a legal practice gives peace of mind to both patients and the medical profession, because there is no fear of being subjected to criminal penalties.

Table 11-2 Key Points in Vermont "Death with Dignity" Act

The patient wanting a physician's help ending his or her own death must

- Make two oral requests at least 15 days apart.
- Submit a written request for medication witnessed by two persons, one of whom is not related or an heir. A form, "Request for medication to hasten my death," is provided if the patient wishes to use it.

Provisions relating to the physician:

- Inform the patient of diagnosis, prognosis, results and risk of medication, and alternatives.
- Obtain a second medical opinion from another physician.
- Verify that the patient's judgment is not impaired; alternatively, the physician may refer the patient for evaluation by a psychiatrist, psychologist, or clinical social worker.
- Refer patient for psychological counseling, if indicated.
- Recommend that the patient notify his or her family.
- See proof of Vermont residency.
- Document all steps and verify patient's wish prior to writing a prescription.
- The physician may dispense the lethal drug directly or provide a written prescription; however, the physician may not inject the patient or otherwise help the patient take the drug.

Time periods:

- The patient must be determined to have less than 6 months to live.
- The physician must wait 48 hours after the second oral request before providing the lethal drug or prescription.

Other provisions:

- The attending physician may sign the death certificate.
- The attending physician and health care institution are immune from subsequent legal actions; health care institutions may have policies prohibiting this practice.
- There is no mandate for physicians to provide this service to a patient.
- This action (on the part of the physician and patient) does not for any purpose qualify as suicide, assisted suicide, mercy killing, or homicide.
- The State Department of Health is mandated to collect data and generate and release an annual statistical report.

Source: 18 VSA Chapter 113, "Rights of Mentally Competent Patients Suffering a Terminal Condition."

The issue, however, is whether the law should outrightly support a competent person's wish to end his or her own life. Furthermore, those who oppose death with dignity legislation express concern that some individuals will feel obliged to request life-ending medication in order not to become burdens to those who care for them. On the other hand, those who support this legislation believe that persons with terminal illnesses should be allowed to choose the method by which they will die, with no recriminations or punishments given to their physicians or survivors.

There are numerous arguments for and against these laws, and the philosophical and ethical issues this raises are debated in the psychological and legal literature (e.g.,

Benjamin et al., 2000; Winick, 1998). In an excellent summary article, Rosenfeld (2000) identifies a broad range of methodological concerns and areas in which more research is needed. These include physician attitudes and practices; adequate measures of depression and psychological distress in patients; better measures of demographic variables, including race, religion, and acculturation or ethnic identity; and distinctions among medical conditions, to name but a few untapped research possibilities.

⊠ Psychology in the Employment Sphere

Psychologists provide a wide variety of services in employment. Prominent among them are industrial/organizational (I/O) psychologists, who have specialized knowledge and training regarding behavior in the workplace. They can be found in private and public organizations, including corporations, government agencies, and health and educational entities. Other psychologists—who do not necessarily self-identify as I/O psychologists—may consult in activities as varied as job analyses, research on consumer behavior and attitudes, recruitment and selection of employees, training, and offering counseling services or workshops for supervisors and employees. They may also perform threat assessments to reduce the likelihood of violence in the workplace. An extensive research and theoretical literature is available in each of these areas. For illustrative purposes, we focus on three areas closely associated with legal psychology and the workplace: (1) assessments in employment compensation and personal injury claims, (2) the Americans with Disabilities Act and its amended version, and (3) psychological research on sexual harassment.

Employment Compensation and Personal Injury Claims

In late February 2003, a fire broke out in The Station, a nightclub in West Warwick, Rhode Island. One hundred people were killed and more than 200 were injured. The fire was subsequently attributed to pyrotechnics set off by the performing band, causing insulation in the building's walls to ignite. Some victims died or were injured as a result of being trampled in the panic that ensued as nightclub patrons rushed for the exit. The tragedy was followed by criminal investigations as well as civil suits. It was clear that no one intended the deaths to occur, but there were questions about the culpability of various individuals. One of the nightclub owners was charged with and pled guilty to involuntary manslaughter and served time in prison until 2008, when he was released on parole.

In civil suits filed after the fire, a number of entities—including the band, various equipment manufacturers, and a media outlet whose photographers allegedly interfered with attempts by patrons to exit the club—offered financial settlements to victims and their families. The story of the Rhode Island fire has been documented in media accounts as well as the legal literature. Relevant to our discussion here is the fact that—in addition to a prison sentence for one owner—the nightclub owners were given a steep civil fine for failing to carry worker's compensation insurance for their employees, some of whom were on the list of victims.

Employment compensation laws were passed to avoid extensive tort actions on the part of employees who were injured in the course of their work. In passing these laws, Congress and state legislatures also recognized the formidable task faced by the injured worker pitted against his or her powerful employer. Under tort law, as noted in the beginning of the chapter, the employee would have to prove some fault on the part of the employer. This was a long, involved process that rarely resulted in a successful claim and often left the worker and his or her family in poverty (Melton et al., 1997, 2007). By contrast, under the employment compensation system, employers agree to insure their workers, and workers agree not to seek the greater compensation that they might possibly achieve if they filed a civil suit and succeeded in proving some negligence on the part of the employer. The laws do not completely foreclose the possibility of a civil suit against the employer, but they do give strong incentive to the employee to take advantage of the system in place.

The legal process in employment compensation cases is less formalized than it would be in a civil courtroom. Typically, a hearing officer or a hearing board reviews the record and assesses the validity of the employee's claim. If the employee was indeed hurt on the job, he is entitled to receive lost wages and some compensation for the injury. The hearing board's decision is subject to review by a higher court if the employee wishes to appeal. Although this system does not give the individual all wages he or she has lost— typically two thirds (Melton et al., 2007)—it does provide certainty and also covers medical expenses. "Today, all states and the federal government have workers' compensation laws, and the vast majority of all civilian employees are covered" (Melton et al., 2007, p. 403). A business's failure to purchase worker's compensation insurance can result in fines, as happened in the Rhode Island nightclub case.

Employment compensation claims primarily involve physical injuries that occurred on the job, but psychological injury or emotional distress may be asserted as well. This, of course, is where the mental health practitioner comes in. The worker may claim, for example, that as a result of the physical injury (e.g., being stabbed by a fellow worker who had been identified as a threat to others), he is terrified of being revictimized and has other symptoms that may rise to the level of PTSD or an acute stress disorder. Some workers also have been successful in claiming that the mental injury came first and was followed by physical injury. For example, a worker may say that the stress and strain created by an extremely difficult working situation and unreasonably long hours led to a heart attack. When employees claim mental injury based on a mental stimulus, they are less likely to be successful, however (Melton et al., 2007). For example, it is more difficult to claim successfully that stress and strain resulted in clinical depression or anxiety than to claim that stress and strain resulted in a heart attack (physical injury). On the whole, however, compensation for emotional damages is much more difficult to obtain than compensation for physical injuries. Being stabbed on the job by a fellow worker or falling off a scaffold that was improperly attached to a building both produce physical injuries that are unlikely to be denied compensation.

It should be noted that evaluations of mental injury also occur in a variety of **personal injury** litigation that is not necessarily employment related. For example, mental health is included in "pain and suffering" and "emotional distress" claims by individuals who were injured in car accidents, bitten by a neighbor's dog, or traumatized by a school shooting. In each of these situations, as in the employment compensation cases, the mental health practitioner must evaluate the validity of the person's claim.

Melton et al. (2007) state that evaluations of mental injury have many similarities to the insanity evaluations that were discussed in Chapter 4. Like these evaluations of mental state at the time of the offense (MSO), they are retrospective and complex. However, unlike MSO evaluations, mental injury evaluations also require a current-state assessment and a prospective assessment. The psychologist must make some judgment about the plaintiff's past, present, and future functioning: Will the plaintiff be able to function as he or she did prior to and at the time of the claim? In some jurisdictions, courts are willing to consider a plaintiff's lost enjoyment of life (LEL), a topic we will discuss again shortly. In addition, because of the interplay between physical and emotional factors in the typical mental injury case, evaluations by both psychologists and persons with medical degrees, such as psychiatrists, are warranted.

The Americans with Disabilities Act

In 1990, Congress passed the **Americans with Disabilities Act** (**ADA**), a far-reaching public law affecting all levels of state and local governments, about 5 million private businesses, and some 43 million Americans defined by the law as physically or mentally disabled. The act was intended to correct long-standing discrimination in the areas of employment, housing, public accommodations, and education. In the same year, Congress changed the name of a law that was specifically applied to education (the Education for All Handicapped Children Act) and called it the Individuals with Disabilities Education Act (IDEA), revised in 2004 to be the Individuals with Disabilities Education Improvement Act (IDEIA). The two laws—the ADA and the IDEIA—have much in common in that they both try to protect vulnerable individuals from discrimination. We cover the IDEIA in more detail later in the chapter.

The ADA prohibits employers from discriminating against persons with physical or mental disabilities who can perform the essential functions of the job they hold or desire to hold. More specifically, the act outlaws disability discrimination in hiring, training, compensation, and benefits (Foote, 2013). The law does not spell out clearly who qualifies as disabled, but it does specifically *exclude* some from that category (e.g., persons with sexual disorders, compulsive gamblers, and people with psychoactive substance abuse disorder resulting from current illegal use of drugs). Reasonable accommodations must be made in the case of a worker who qualifies as disabled under the law. If a worker claims that she has been discriminated against on the basis of her disability, the claim is first evaluated according to guidelines issued by the Equal Employment Opportunity Commission (EEOC), the government agency charged with interpreting the law in this area. Depending upon the outcome of the case, it may then reach the courts, including the U.S. Supreme Court. It should be noted that most claims by employees against their employers are won by the employer. It is estimated that employees win in one fourth of the instances (Foote, 2013; Goodman-Delahunty & Foote, 2011).

In the years since the initial passage of the ADA, the courts addressed many unanswered questions dealing with the law. A general consensus among legal scholars is that the ADA has been severely limited (Foote, 2013; Melton et al., 2007; Petrila, 2009b). The Supreme Court itself, in three cases known as the *Sutton* trilogy (*Albertson's Inc. v. Kirkingburg*, 1999; *Murphy v. United Parcel Service*, 1999; *Sutton v. United Air Lines*, 1999), required courts to evaluate a worker's disability (e.g., myopia, high blood pressure) in its corrected state, even if it had not been corrected. In other words, if a person says he has excessively high blood pressure because of stressful job conditions, the court must consider the extent to which effective medication would reduce that problem. The Court also ruled, in *Toyota v. Williams* (2002), that the disability covered by the law had to be one that restricted "major life activities," or activities that are of central importance to most people's lives (e.g., walking or feeding oneself). In that case, the Court ruled that carpal tunnel syndrome was not considered such a disability. In another case (*Chevron v. Echazabal*, 2002), the Court said a company can refuse to hire a person with a disability for a job that could exacerbate the problem. Echazabal had applied for a job with Chevron. During his physical exam, he was found to have a liver condition that Chevron's doctors said would be worsened by exposure to toxins at the oil refinery. As a result of these and other court decisions, it was estimated that the ADA went from protecting 43 million American when it was first passed to protecting a mere 13.5 million (Rozalski, Katsiyannis, Ryan, Collins, & Stewart, 2010).

Partly in response to this narrow interpretation of the original ADA, Congress passed the Americans with Disabilities Act Amendments Act of 2008 (ADAAA), which provided a broader view of disabilities that was more in line with the original law (Petrila, 2009b). "The additional language in the ADA amendments of 2008 is a significant attempt to redefine disability" (Rozalski et al., 2010, p. 24). Congress had concerns about the *Sutton* trilogy's rule that disabilities must be viewed in their corrected state as well as concerns about the application only to major life activities suggested by the *Toyota* case. At this point, it is too early to tell whether the Amended Act has had a significant effect on the number of individuals who once again qualify as disabled, or the likelihood of their success at challenging the actions of employers. We address below the provisions of the ADA that are most relevant to psychological issues.

Medical Questions and Screening Preemployment

The laws prohibit questions pertaining to past medical history or questions that elicit information about disabilities, unless an applicant has been given a conditional job offer. In other words, an employer must offer a job before inquiring whether the job applicant has a disability that may affect job performance. Recall that Echazabal's eligibility for employment by Chevron was questioned only after he took his physical, a normal procedure required of potential employees, but not until they have advanced in the application process. In his case, his liver disease precluded him from obtaining a job because of concern about his exposure to toxic materials.

The preemployment questioning is pertinent to mental health professionals who provide candidate screening for local, state, and federal agencies, such as law enforcement. Many psychological tests and inventories used for candidate screening have items that inquire about medical history or center on medical or health problems. Although some psychologists are reluctant to use any test or inventory in this manner because of concerns about litigation (Camara & Merenda, 2000), others continue to use the tests but delete those items that delve into medical history or administer them only after a conditional offer has been made. Still others have adopted newer tests and inventories that do not include health questions.

Reasonable Accommodations

Both the original ADA and the ADAAA mandate that employers and organizations provide reasonable accommodations or assistance to qualified individuals to enable them to perform essential functions of their jobs or use their services (Carpenter & Paetzold, 2013). The implications here are enormous as they relate to possible mental disorders. Many employees have brought claims against employers who fired them, alleging that they were let go because of a mental impairment. Examples of mental impairment according to the ADA include major depression, bipolar disorder, anxiety disorders (including post-traumatic stress disorder), and schizophrenia or psychosis.

Under the ADA and ADAAA, employers are expected to make reasonable accommodations, which may include such things as allowing breaks for the employee to take needed medication or some release time for psychotherapy sessions. In general, courts have supported the right of employers to require that an individual seek and participate in treatment as a condition of continued employment. Foote (2013) notes that various mood disorders, such as depression, can have a significant impact on one's job performance but can also respond well to effective treatment.

A major question remains, though, as to which mental disorders qualify as disabilities under the ADA and its amendment. As noted above, the ADA already *excludes* certain disorders (e.g., sexual disorders, psychoactive substance abuse), but it is not altogether clear which are *included*. Psychologists and other mental health practitioners must guard against assuming that every diagnosis in the DSM-5 qualifies as a disability. Doing so would lead to increasing challenges to the validity of these labels and the instruments and methods used to produce them (Foote, 2013). Rather than relying on diagnostic categories, the assessment of an individual should address the extent to which he or she is hindered in the ability to do the job and whether reasonable accommodation would solve this problem. A psychological evaluation of an individual who claims an ADA-defined mental or psychological disability begins with the mental health professional investigating how the person functions at home, at work, and in a variety of other settings (Foote, 2013). The length of time the psychological impairment lasts is important because impairments of several weeks or months do not constitute disability. The psychological impairment does constitute a disability if it is chronic or is consistently episodic.

Another vexing problem for psychological assessment pertains to the issue of workers who engage in misconduct or who threaten others in the workplace. The ADA and EEOC regulations do recognize that making direct threats to others is cause for dismissal from the job. A direct threat is defined as "a significant risk of substantial harm to the health and safety of the individual or others that cannot be eliminated or reduced by reasonable accommodation" (EEOC regulations, quoted in Foote, 2013, p. 275). As emphasized by Foote, the risk of violence must be high to qualify as a direct threat. In some cases, employers may be worried about veiled threats, comments made by an employee, or behavior patterns that change such as temper eruptions. In that case, a mental health examiner may be asked to assess the likelihood that the employee presents a danger to the workplace. Violence in the workplace—though not to be ignored—is less common than behaviors that create a hostile work environment.

Harassment and Hostile Work Environments

Title VII of the Civil Rights Act of 1964, amended in 1971, prohibits discrimination in the workplace on the basis of race, color, religion, sex, or national origin. The EEOC, charged with setting guidelines for the enforcement of employment laws, includes age, disability, and protected activity in the list of categories that are subject to discrimination. This far-reaching law has enabled employees to bring federal suits against employers in both public and private organizations on grounds that they were harassed and subjected to a hostile work environment, because harassment is a form of discrimination. A hostile work environment is created when the behavior of others in the workplace (e.g., supervisors, coworkers) interferes with a person's job performance. Under the law, employers are vicariously responsible for the discriminatory actions of supervisors.

Until very recently, the precise meaning of "supervisor" had not been determined, and courts issued different opinions on the matter. Some ruled that a supervisor could be anyone who directly oversaw a person's daily work. Others ruled that "supervisor" was limited to those with the power to hire, fire, promote, demote, transfer, or discipline an individual. In June 2013, the U.S. Supreme Court in *Vance v. Ball State University* took the narrow approach in a case that involved racial harassment. The Court ruled that a supervisor was one empowered to take tangible employment actions, such as hiring and firing, demoting, or making changes that would bring about a significant change in responsibilities or benefits. In the *Vance* case, because the individual who delivered discriminatory comments and created a hostile work environment was not a supervisor according to that definition, the university did not bear vicarious responsibility for her actions.

The employer may still be held liable if the harasser is a fellow employee—not a supervisor. In that case, however, the plaintiff must demonstrate that the employer was negligent. In other words, if the employer knew or should have known about the conduct but failed to address it, the employer can be held responsible. Again in the *Vance* case, negligence on the part of the university would be difficult to prove because many steps were apparently taken to address and solve the problem.

Suits alleging harassment in the workplace can and do arise in numerous contexts. Although each type is important, we will address sexual and gender harassment in this section, primarily because psychologists are most likely to be consulted in such cases.

Sexual harassment may be broadly defined as unwelcome sexual advances, requests for sexual favors, and other unwanted verbal or physical conduct of a sexual nature (Hellkamp & Lewis, 1995). Civil claims of sexual harassment arise most frequently in employment and educational contexts, where harassment qualifies as discrimination in violation of Title VII of the Civil Rights Acts of 1964, amended in 1971. Specifically, as noted above, harassment creates a hostile work environment. Schools also can be held responsible for student-on-student sexual and other harassment under Title IX of the Education Amendments of 1972 if the school board displays deliberate indifference to harassment, has knowledge of it, and the harassment is so serious that it deprives victims of access to educational opportunities (*Davis v. Monroe County Board of Education,* 1999). School districts today often approach this issue by addressing it with anti-bullying programs integrated into the curriculum. Unfortunately, there is also anecdotal evidence that some schools attempt to "solve" their bullying and harassment problems by encouraging the victims to transfer to other schools rather than taking appropriate action against the perpetrators.

It cannot be emphasized enough that workplace harassment, including sexual harassment, violates the law. Despite efforts to educate society about its consequences and ramifications, this behavior continues to be highly problematic in many work environments. In August 2013, the mayor of San Diego resigned from office after 16 women testified about his harassing behavior, which included unwanted touches and suggestions with sexual overtones. In the spring of 2013, evidence of widespread sexual harassment and assault in the military came to public attention with the release of a report issued by the Department of Defense. It was estimated that over a 1-year period, more than 26,000 cases of sexual assault or harassment against both women and men had occurred. Fewer than one fifth were reported, and in only 238 cases were the perpetrators punished. Investigative reporters also have learned that military personnel who do report assault or harassment often see their careers ruined; they may be reassigned, labeled with mental illnesses, discharged from the military, and denied lifetime health care benefits.

To qualify as illegal, the harassing behavior displayed must be more than irritating or mildly offensive. It must be severe and pervasive, so much so that it alters conditions of the victim's employment, creating a hostile work environment. As noted above, employers are vicariously liable for the conduct of supervisors, and they are liable for worker-on-worker harassment if they—the employers—were negligent and failed to take steps to address the behavior. The harassing conduct also must be objectively offensive—or offensive to a reasonable person—as well as subjectively offensive to the plaintiff (*Harris v. Forklift Systems, Inc.*, 1993; see Box 11-2). In sexual harassment suits, plaintiffs often seek compensation for mental anguish and pain and suffering (e.g., anger, anxiety, loss of self-esteem, fear, or feelings of humiliation), but extensive psychological harm need not be demonstrated for a plaintiff to prevail (*Harris v. Forklift Systems, Inc.*, 1993). In other words, the Supreme Court has recognized that some victims of sexual harassment may experience its negative effects without also experiencing debilitating psychological deterioration.

BOX 11-2

Case Study. Sex-Based Harassment in the Workplace: *Harris v. Forklift Systems, Inc.*

Teresa Harris worked as a manager in an equipment rental company during the mid-1980s. According to the facts of the case, the president of the company—Charles Hardy—displayed behavior toward her and other women that included unwanted sexual advances and gender harassment. In front of other employees, he called her "a dumb-ass woman" and said he needed a man as rental manager. He once suggested that he and Harris go to a local hotel to negotiate a raise. He threw objects on the ground and asked her and other women to pick them up, and he was known to ask them to get coins from his front pants pockets.

Harris complained, Hardy apologized and claimed he did not realize he was being offensive, and he promised he would stop. His behavior soon reappeared, however. Harris quit the job and then sued her former employer under Title VII of the Civil Rights Act on the basis that Hardy had created a hostile and abusive work environment.

(Continued)

(Continued)

The lower court found this was a "close case," but ruled that the comments and behavior were not so severe that they affected Teresa Harris's psychological well-being. She had not presented evidence of serious emotional damage. The U.S. Supreme Court, however, ruled that she did not have to do so. The Court reiterated that the conduct in question has to be more than merely offensive; it must be severe and pervasive enough that it alters the conditions of the victim's employment. Furthermore, the victim must subjectively perceive the environment to be abusive. Both of these conditions were met in the above case.

However, the plaintiff does not have to demonstrate that she or he suffered extreme psychological damage. The conduct of the harasser is what is at issue in sexual harassment cases.

In a pithy comment, Justice Sandra Day O'Connor wrote, "Title VII comes into play before the harassing conduct leads to a nervous breakdown." She added that, although evidence of concrete psychological harm is relevant, it is not required.

Questions for Discussion:

1. Teresa Harris complained to Hardy that she found his behavior offensive. Did she have an obligation to do that before filing suit?

2. Considering the behaviors described in the first paragraph, would you as a judge weigh any as more serious than others? Should you?

3. Should evidence of psychological harm be relevant in sexual harassment cases?

Although serious psychological harm need not be demonstrated to support a sexual harassment claim, in accordance with *Harris v. Forklift Systems, Inc.* (1993), many victims do experience significant distress, and this is relevant when assessing damages to the plaintiff. For example, the victim may claim that the actions of the defendant not only were irritating or embarrassing but also led to a mental disorder, such as a major depressive disorder (Kovera & Cass, 2002) or PTSD. In such a situation, a mental health practitioner will be asked to conduct a psychological evaluation and to testify about the results.

Gender Harassment

In more recent years, scholars have brought attention to the reality of **gender harassment**, arguing that it, too, is a serious form of discrimination (Franke, 1995; Leskinen, Cortina, & Kabat, 2011). They say as well that it should be covered under sexual harassment law, which thus far is very narrowly defined by many courts. Gender harassment is behavior directed at individuals who appear to violate gender ideals, such as women working in a previously all-male environment. Unlike "traditional," narrowly defined sexual harassment, gender harassment does not involve unwanted sexual attention and an implication that the victim be cooperative; rather, it is behavior that conveys a degrading attitude toward the individual or group at whom it is directed. It creates a hostile work environment, and some courts are willing to consider it sexual harassment. Nevertheless, opinion surveys indicate that people perceive it as less serious than the unwanted sexual attention form and are also less likely to report it (Leskinen et al., 2011). An example of sexual harassment narrowly defined is the supervisor who touches employees inappropriately or demands sexual favors; an example of gender harassment is the fellow worker who continually tells jokes degrading to women or displays a pattern of making sexist comments, such as telling women they lack mathematical ability or should be home cooking dinner for their husbands. The U.S. Supreme Court has indicated that hostility in the workplace, even without sexual advances, qualifies as discrimination (*Oncale v. Sundowner Offshore Services*, 1998). Despite the Court's brief comment that sexual advances are not needed in order for behavior to qualify as sexual harassment, the term *sexual harassment* "conjures up narrow notions of unwanted sexual advances; it fails to include gender harassment in the minds of many" (Leskinen et al., 2011, p. 38).

Many legal scholars point out that much sexual harassment in the workplace is not sexually motivated; rather, it is designed to preserve the sex segregation of jobs, particularly male jobs that pay the most and are most likely to bring promotion (Schultz, 2006). Leskinen et al. (2011), in a study of women in the military and the legal profession (lawyers from a federal judicial circuit), found that most women from both groups reported no or minimal experiences of harassment. For those who did experience harassment, the vast majority did not involve unwanted sexual advances. Rather, the women were exposed to crude or sexist comments and behavior. When compared with women who had not experienced harassment, they were less satisfied in their work and experienced less psychological well-being (military), and more stress and less satisfaction with professional relationships (lawyers). Based on these findings, Leskinen et al. recommend that research and practicing psychologists pay careful attention to gender harassment and its effect in the workplace.

Wrongful Death and Personal Injury Suits

Those whose relatives and loved ones have experienced sudden deaths often go to court to claim benefits that they believe are rightfully theirs. Alternatively, those who have experienced a disaster—or in some cases their survivors—may want to attribute direct blame to a person or entity they hold responsible for their pain and suffering. Most recently, in the aftermath of the Batman shooting case in Aurora, Colorado, at least 10 suits have been filed in federal courts against the company that owned the theater, alleging that the company did not adequately protect theatergoers from harm. Representatives of the company responded that they could not possibly have anticipated the massacre that occurred. Although some of these suits were dismissed immediately by the courts, others were allowed to go forward. Likewise, some 150 families or victims of the Fort Hood shooting in 2009, when army psychiatrist Nidal Hasan opened fire in a medical building, are suing the government for negligence, claiming government officials should have known that he was a danger to others and should have taken necessary steps to prevent his actions. Hasan was charged with 13 counts of premeditated murder and 32 counts of premeditated attempted murder. He represented himself at his trial in the summer of 2013, was found guilty, and was subsequently sentenced to death.

Some of the most controversial wrongful death suits have been filed against manufacturers of products, including tobacco and guns. Class action suits against the tobacco industry in the 1970s resulted in massive settlements, some marketing changes by the cigarette industry, and education efforts directed at preventing or eliminating tobacco use. Suits against gun manufacturers have been less successful. After the D.C. Beltway shootings in 2002, survivors of victims received a settlement from manufacturers of the rifle used in the deaths. However, in 2005, Congress passed a law severely limiting the ability of victims to sue gun manufacturers. As noted in Chapter 8, suits against pharmaceutical companies also often involve wrongful death claims. However, as noted, the Supreme Court recently placed severe limits on those claims (*Mutual Pharmaceutical Company v. Bartlett*, 2013).

Historically, there have been wide variations in the size of awards across otherwise similar wrongful death cases (Lenton, 2007). Part of the problem lies in the ambiguous instructions given to jurors in these cases. "Jurors in wrongful death cases are provided very little instruction regarding how these damage awards should be determined, so there is a great deal of room for individual and group psychology to influence the judgment" (Lenton, 2007, p. 1194). Research examining the psychology of wrongful death awards has concentrated on the characteristics of the plaintiff, decedent, and defendant with an eye toward learning about the possible role of prejudice and stereotypes in these decisions (Covati, Foley, & Coffman, 2001; J. Goodman, Loftus, Miller, & Greene, 1991; Lenton, 2007). For example, Lenton discovered in his research that "the lives of older persons, those without children, and individuals of low SES [socioeconomic status] were deemed to be worth less money than the lives of young persons, parents, and individuals of high SES" (p. 1210).

Psychologists may be involved in wrongful death suits when plaintiffs claim extreme emotional distress, such as post-traumatic stress disorder or depression, following the death of a loved one. This is similar to the emotional distress associated with employment compensation and harassment claims discussed above. Like the person who has directly experienced and survived a wrongful act, the survivor of the person who has died may need to provide documentation of the pain and suffering experienced as a result of the death. Psychologists also may be asked to assess the state of mind of the deceased individual. In that case, the psychological autopsy described in Chapter 8 may be required. As noted in that chapter, many courts are reluctant to admit the psychological autopsy into evidence in light of its relatively new status and lack of scientific methodology. It does appear to be admitted more in civil than criminal cases, however.

Loss of Enjoyment of Life

Another issue in personal injury cases is the awarding of damages for lost enjoyment of life (LEL), also referred to as "hedonic damages." LEL damages are intended to compensate "for the limitations on the person's life created by the injury" (*Thompson v. National Railroad Passenger Corp.*, 1980, p. 824). According to Berlá, Andrews, and Berlá (1999),

> The loss of enjoyment of life is a forensic concept rooted in wrongful death claims that developed along two lines. One track, the wrongful death cases, defined the concept as the loss of pleasure of being alive—a loss commencing at death. The other track, which developed later from personal injury suits, defined the concept as the loss of particular pleasure one could no longer experience in life. (p. 311)

Although LEL is somewhat vague, it can be measured. For example, Andrews, Meyer, and Berlá (1996) developed the Lost Pleasure of Life Scale. These researchers asked psychologists experienced in disability evaluations to judge the severity of impact that a large number of behavioral descriptors of impairment (e.g., loss of bladder control, inability to play with children) would have on a person's enjoyment of life (Poser, Bornstein, & McGorty, 2003). The impairments are clustered into four broad categories of activity (see Table 11-3). It is unknown to what extent psychologists evaluating wrongful death and personal injury claims are using the scale in their practice, but it does offer some guidance for assessing the psychological injuries experienced by plaintiffs in these civil suits.

Table 11-3	Categories and Descriptions of Impairments Experienced by Plaintiffs in Suits Claiming Lost Enjoyment of Life (LEL)	
Category	**Examples**	
Practical	Limitations on eating, sleeping, traveling, dressing, shopping	
Emotional/psychological	Loss of satisfaction derived from any activity that enhances a person's physical well-being, sense of self-worth, dignity, integrity, and sense of mastery	
Social	Decreased participation in previously rewarding social activities	
Occupational	Loss of vocational or career identity	

Source: Adapted from Berlá et al. (1999).

✖ Psychology in the Educational Sphere

Mental health professionals, including, of course, educational, developmental, and school psychologists, have much to offer both schools and the law. The services they provide fall mostly under the umbrella of assessment—such as assessing language abilities, disabilities, or whether a student is a threat to himself or others. Although psychologists also consult with teachers and administrators on dealing with classroom behavior problems, including harassment and bullying, assessment seems to be their major function. "The primary use of psychological assessment in U.S. schools is for the diagnosis and classification of educational disabilities" (Braden, 2013, p. 295). Braden adds that school psychologists report that the largest single activity they perform is the assessment of intelligence, achievement, and social-emotional disorders.

Braden (2013) also lists six distinct but related purposes that drive psychological assessment in the educational system. They are screening, diagnosis, intervention, evaluation, selection, and certification. Students considered at risk (e.g., of psychological disorders, academic failure, depression) may need *screening* to see if they qualify for certain prevention programs available through the school system. Screening also may be needed in an effort to determine whether a student poses a credible threat to himself or others in the school, possibly requiring temporary suspension and referral to an outside agency. *Diagnosis* involves assessing students specifically for psychoeducational problems, such as learning disabilities. Assessment also serves *intervention* purposes, in that results of the assessment may help educational professionals choose among several possible treatment strategies to employ with a child. Students are assessed for *evaluation* purposes when the school system wishes to determine the outcome of a particular educational approach, such as changes made to a curriculum. Assessment serves a *selection* purpose when students are chosen for particular programs, such as programs for gifted students or students with special needs. Finally, assessment for *certification* is least likely to be needed, but may be relevant if someone other than teachers is needed to certify student learning, as for graduation or promotion to higher grades (Braden, 2013).

The emphasis on assessment in its various iterations may well be attributed to the passage of laws with many similarities to the ADA discussed earlier in the chapter. Although assessment has always been an important activity for school psychologists, both federal and state laws in recent years have sought greater accountability and more oversight of public education across the United States. Consequently, the role of the school psychologist has expanded quite dramatically.

Individuals with Disabilities Education Act (IDEA)

As noted earlier in the chapter, at about the same time it passed the Americans with Disabilities Act, Congress reaffirmed the right of all disabled children to the same free public education as their nondisabled peers. In the process, it changed the name of the Education for All Handicapped Children Act to the Individuals with Disabilities Education Act (IDEA) of 1990. This was amended in 2004 and is now sometimes referred to as the Individuals with Disabilities Education Improvement Act (IDEIA). The law applies to children with both physical and mental disabilities and includes— among others—intellectual disability (formerly mental retardation), hearing and visual impairments, autism, serious emotional disturbance, and traumatic brain injuries. Children with these special needs are entitled to be educated in the least restrictive environment and to be provided with rehabilitation services, such as speech therapy and special classroom aides. An **individualized education program** (IEP) is prepared for each child, as mentioned in the previous chapter. The IDEA is a complex law that we do not address in detail here. For our purposes, we emphasize the legal context and the role of the educational or school psychologist.

The IEP is typically prepared by an interdisciplinary team that may include psychologists of various specialties in addition to educators and medical personnel. The program or plan must address whether the child has a qualifying disability and, if so, what methods and resources are necessary to ensure that he or she will be educated. The least restrictive setting must be considered. Parents or guardians should be apprised of the procedure and have a right to challenge the program as well as subsequent decisions about its implementation.

Under education law, school districts are responsible for the public education of each child enrolled there. This includes children with special needs, as affirmed in the IDEA. Courts have generally ruled that educational needs can be separated from medical needs, however. Thus, if a child requires treatment in a medical or therapeutic setting, the school district is responsible only for that portion of the costs that covers the child's education. Precisely how to allocate those costs is not always clear, though, and the IDEA itself does not offer sufficient guidelines. In a recent illustrative case (*Jefferson County School District v. Elizabeth E.*, 2013), a school district in Colorado was sued for failing to pay for a residential placement that was deemed necessary to treat a child's mental illness. The local public school had not been effective for the child, who had exhibited a variety of serious emotional problems during her elementary school years. The district then reached a negotiated settlement with the child's parents and agreed to pay half the cost of a specialized residential treatment and education program in another state, where she remained for 2 years. After those 2 years, the parents removed her from the program, saying it was no longer effective. The parents then chose and enrolled their daughter in a different residential program in a different state. When they asked the school district for reimbursement, it refused to contribute to the costs, saying the child was no longer a resident of Colorado. Moreover, the parents had not consulted with the district before moving the child. Two lower courts—a district court and an appellate court—ruled that the school district bore some responsibility for payment under the

IDEA but did not agree on how to determine the specific costs. The school district appealed, but the U.S. Supreme Court denied certiorari without comment in 2013. Although this is a complex case that we do not discuss in detail here, it is important to stress that the law mandates that school districts meet the educational needs of the children in their district.

Children with special needs are not the only ones who are assessed by the school psychologist, as the beginning of this section indicates. Furthermore, school psychologists as well as community psychologists and other mental health professionals may consult with school officials on a case-by-case basis, as needs arise. For example, in incidents involving a traumatic event, such as the sudden death of a school principal or a school violence incident such as a shooting, mental health professionals provide support and clinical services to students, teachers, and staff, and often to community members as well. The services provided by mental health professionals in these emergency situations are not likely to raise legal questions.

SUMMARY AND CONCLUSIONS

The law affords many opportunities for people to go to court and seek redress. A fundamental principle in law is access to the courts. There is, of course, no guarantee that this access will result in a satisfactory outcome. In the civil context—which covers topics discussed in this chapter as well as earlier chapters—plaintiffs appearing before judges, juries, or hearing officers or hearing bodies often do not win their cases. Research suggests, however, that they are satisfied if some settlement has been reached and if they perceive they have been treated fairly.

Many civil suits fall under the category of torts, or civil wrongs. This is when one party, the plaintiff, alleges that the other party, the respondent or defendant, has harmed him or her in some way. The harm may be intended, or it may be the result of negligence on the part of the respondent. Therefore, the person suing must persuade the judge or jury that there was harm as well as fault on the part of the person being sued. The standard of proof in most civil suits is preponderance of the evidence, not proof beyond a reasonable doubt as required in criminal cases. In some contexts, clear and convincing evidence must be demonstrated by the plaintiff. For example, most jurisdictions require clear and convincing evidence of someone's incapacity to execute legal documents.

Psychologists often assess the cognitive capacities of individuals to make decisions, including but not limited to decisions relating to wills, financial agreements, donating one's possessions or property, entering contracts, and consenting to medical treatment. Testamentary capacity, referring primarily to the capacity to execute a will, does not involve complex cognitive skills. Most wills are straightforward and are not challenged.

However, some researchers maintain that higher cognitive abilities are required than have traditionally been presumed. In addition, executing wills or other legal documents may be challenged in particular if the testator (person making the will) is cognitively deficient, elderly, or mentally disordered. It is recommended that the execution of legal documents be videotaped in these circumstances. Legal documents also may be challenged if there is suspicion that the individual was under undue influence of another party or parties.

In recent years, the capacity of individuals to make the decision to seek help in ending their lives has been addressed by some psychologists who may be consulted in these decisions. Although only a few states have laws sanctioning this decision, it may become more common in the future and is likely to continue to be a controversial issue.

Psychologists participate in torts most particularly when the plaintiffs allege some mental suffering or emotional distress as the result of the actions of the defendant. Mental suffering may also be an element of employment compensation claims, where employees collect benefits from injuries suffered in the workplace. In accordance with the employment compensation system, the employer is not held to be at fault, but agrees to compensate the worker for lost wages and to cover medical costs. It should be noted that violations of the law by the employer (e.g., failure to install needed safety equipment) fall under a different category than employment compensation claims. In other words, an employee can sue an employer under tort law for failing to protect. In addition, criminal charges may be brought against the employer.

Harassment torts comprise a substantial portion of suits against employers. Under federal law barring discrimination in employment on the basis of race, sex, religion, and ethnicity, employers are held liable for the actions of supervisors as well as for those of nonsupervisory employees. In the latter case, however, employers are responsible only if they become aware of the problem and fail to address it. Sexual harassment may be viewed both narrowly and broadly. Narrowly, it involves a pattern of behavior that implies an invitation to sexual activity, such as inappropriate touching or ogling. Broadly defined, sexual harassment includes sexist and derogatory comments that are not typically interpreted as an invitation to sexual activity. The broader view is referred to as gender harassment, and many scholars believe it occurs more frequently than the narrower form. Both types of harassment must be perceived as offensive, must be pervasive, and must create a hostile work environment. Evidence of the behavior itself is sufficient to win a suit, but many victims also claim extreme emotional distress as a result of the harassment. Although psychologists are most likely to be consulted if there is a claim of extreme emotional distress, any degree of emotional suffering may require psychological documentation.

Another employment-related civil action is the claim of discrimination based on the ADA and its amendments. When employers refuse to hire or promote individuals because of their disabilities, or when they fire or demote them, they may be in violation of the law, which requires that reasonable accommodations be made for persons with disabilities. After the passage of the original ADA in 1990, courts severely limited its application, resulting in drastic decreases in the number of persons who were protected by the law. In 2008, amendments were passed that restored the earlier protections, but it is still too early to determine whether these have had the desired effects.

The chapter ended with a brief discussion of psychology in the educational sphere, focusing on assessment issues. The primary work of psychologists in the educational system has long been assessment, but this is even more the case since the passage of federal and state laws seeking to make schools more accountable for meeting the educational needs of all students. Students with disabilities are covered under a separate law, the Individuals with Disabilities Education Improvement Act (IDEIA) of 2004. Although assessment is not the only task performed by mental health professionals within the educational system, it is the task most closely related to legal issues.

KEY CONCEPTS

Advance directives

Americans with
    Disabilities Act (ADA)

Civil capacity

Compensatory damages

Contractual capacity

Damages

Defendant (civil cases)

Dementia

Donative capacity

Durable power of
    attorney (POA)

Employment
    compensation claims

Gender harassment

Guardianship

Individualized education
    program (IEP)

Injunction

Lost enjoyment of
    life (LEL)

Personal injury

Plaintiff

Punitive damages

Respondent

Sexual harassment

Testamentary capacity

Testator

Torts

Undue influence

12

Psychological
Assessment and the Law

*Dr. Coons . . . did not perform any psychiatric assessment of appellant after his
18 years of nonviolent behavior on death row, nor did he refer to any psychological testing that might have occurred in that time frame.*

—Coble v. Texas, 2010

*The record is "devoid of evidence demonstrating either the scientific validity or
reliability of the GSS as a measure of susceptibility to suggestion or appropriate
applications of the test results."*

—Commonwealth v. Soares, 2001

P sychological assessment and psychological testing have become indispensable to
the legal system, but courts can give them careful scrutiny, as the above quotes
demonstrate. The number of commercially available assessment measures and
tests for forensic applications has increased dramatically in recent years (Ogloff &
Douglas, 2013). In fact, during the past two decades, forensic psychology has become
largely an assessment-focused enterprise (Skeem & Monahan, 2011). This is not to say
that legal psychologists have expended all their energy in that direction, as we have
demonstrated throughout the text. However, assessment and testing play an important
role in many civil and criminal matters, and a broadening spectrum of psychological
tests and assessment instruments designed to help mental health professionals evaluate
legally relevant questions is available.

The terms *assessment* and *testing* are not synonymous. **Psychological assessment**, which also may be called **psychological evaluation**, refers to *all* the techniques used to measure and evaluate an individual's past, present, or future psychological status. Its primary goal is to reduce the complexity of human behavior to a manageable set of variables so that present behavior can be appraised, some parameters of future behavior can be predicted, and appropriate intervention strategies can be undertaken. It is a procedure or approach that involves the gathering and integration of information from various sources in order to make a decision or recommendation. It usually includes interviews, observations, reviews of case files and records, and various measuring procedures that typically include psychological tests.

Psychological testing, then, is only one component of the assessment process. Psychological tests are standardized measuring instruments developed to measure specific abilities or skills. They come in different formats and have specified goals. Several tests at a time, usually called "test batteries," are sometimes administered to an individual or group. Depending on the specific goal of the instrument, the test may be intended to measure intelligence or specific cognitive abilities, such as reasoning, comprehension, or abstract thinking (VandenBos, 2007). A psychological test may also be designed to measure specific aptitude, such as mechanical ability, manual coordination, or dexterity; or achievement, such as reading, spelling, mathematics, or knowledge of a specific topic (such as the role of a judge or defense attorney in a criminal case). A psychological test may also be used to measure personality traits or disorders. Such tests are usually self-administered and are referred to as "inventories." The Minnesota Multiphasic Personality Inventory (MMPI-2), for example, is a **personality inventory**.

Thus, to use an illustration that encompasses both psychological assessment and psychological testing, a child custody assessment or evaluation may include (1) mental status and bio-historical interviews of the adults and minor child(ren); (2) psychological testing of the child(ren) and possibly the adults as well; (3) observations of the interaction among the adults and the minor child(ren); (4) a review of the available reports and previous assessments; and (5) interviews with significant others, such as grandparents or teachers. Likewise, the capacity assessments discussed in the previous chapter may also include interviews and observations, record reviews, and cognitive tests.

In civil cases, psychological assessment and testing have long been used to determine whether individuals are able to care for themselves or are in need of psychological treatment. Courts today must make judgments about the need for confinement in a mental institution or for treatment services within the community. To make appropriate decisions, they turn to mental health professionals for guidance. Heilbrun (1992) notes that psychologists are increasingly asked to assess competencies to consent to medical treatment or research and to enter into a contractual relationship. They are also participating in the disability determination process, civil capacities evaluations, and the process of determining compensation for mental injuries, as we discussed in the last chapter. In family law, in addition to psychological assessment in child custody decisions, psychologists are consulted in abuse and neglect determinations, juvenile delinquency dispositions, and end-of-life issues.

Increasingly, as we have noted, assessment and testing procedures are used to determine parental suitability for child custody, to appraise a person's ability and capacity to make wills, or to determine eligibility for federal and state benefits on the basis of mental or emotional incapacity. Work-related personal injury litigation, where plaintiffs seek compensation for an injury allegedly suffered on the job due to negligence on the part of an employer, is a rapidly growing area where assessment plays an integral part. Forensic assessment is also crucial in determining the extent of emotional injury. Claims of emotional injury in the form of pain and suffering, mental anguish, or emotional harm are often raised in personal injury, harassment, discrimination, disability, and malpractice cases (Heilbrun, Grisso, Goldstein, & Laduke, 2013; Kane, Nelson, Dvoskin, & Pitt, 2013).

Psychological assessment and testing are frequently used throughout the educational system, not only to measure intelligence and aptitude, but also to diagnose learning disabilities and to aid in the creation of IEPs (Braden, 2013). They also appear in the screening and selection of personnel in business and industry and in the military (Klimoski & Wilkinson, 2013; Wasserman, 2013).

Within medical settings, psychologists can encounter many unique opportunities for collaboration with physicians (Sweet, Tovian, Guidotti Breting, & Suchy, 2013). Psychologists may provide a wide range of assessments and interventions, often in place of more costly or unnecessary medical assessment and treatment. For example, they are involved in assessment in such areas as "cardiac disorders, epilepsy, neurodegenerative disorders (e.g., Parkinson's disease, Alzheimer's disease), stroke, traumatic brain injury, chronic pain treatment, dental problems, and organ transplant programs" (Sweet et al., 2013, p. 319). Each of these opportunities is accompanied by some possibility that an assessment may be relevant in a future legal proceeding.

Psychological assessment is also extremely important in adult inpatient and outpatient mental health settings. Sellbom, Marion, and Bagby (2013) write, "The primary purpose of psychological assessments in adult inpatient and outpatient mental health settings is to evaluate patients' cognitions, affect, behavior, personality traits, strengths, and weaknesses in order to make judgments, diagnoses, predictions, and treatment recommendations" (p. 241). Child mental health settings also rely heavily on psychological assessments. "Routine psychological assessment in child mental health settings focuses on the identification and quantification of symptom dimensions and problem behaviors and the collection of information relevant to the development of treatment strategies" (Wrobel & Lachar, 2013, p. 261). As in the medical area, assessments in mental health settings may be offered (and challenged) as evidence in future litigation.

In criminal law, specifically relating to criminal courts, forensic assessments are important in at least five areas. First, they play a major role in the arrest and pretrial process for both adults and juveniles, when a psychologist may evaluate a defendant's competency to waive legal rights, plead guilty, or stand trial. In the case of a juvenile, he or she may be evaluated before a decision is made to transfer the individual out of the juvenile system and into criminal court. Second, assessment is used to help courts determine a defendant's dangerousness to self or others for the purposes of making bail decisions. Third, when a defendant raises an insanity defense or a diminished capacity defense, evidence obtained from evaluations of his or her mental state at the time of the crime is crucial. Fourth, the victim of the crime may undergo assessment as evidence that a crime did indeed occur, such as in the case of children. Fifth, assessment may provide invaluable information in the sentencing phase of a criminal trial, particularly when the judge is interested in knowing about an offender's future dangerousness or amenability to rehabilitation. This is especially the case for juvenile offenders. In sex offense cases, for example, where limited sex offender programs are available, a judge might order the offender to be examined to see whether he would be a good candidate for such a program. In those jurisdictions that allow the civil commitment of sexually violent predators at the end of their prison sentences—a topic covered in Chapter 10—the dangerousness of the offender is assessed. Such an assessment also is made when capital punishment is an option, as we discussed in Chapter 6.

Assessment also has a place outside of the court process. Both police and correctional psychologists make extensive use of these techniques. Some criminal justice agencies rely on the psychologist to help make screening, selection, and promotional decisions. Law enforcement candidates and already-employed personnel are often assessed and given psychological tests or inventories designed to help determine their suitability for promotion or their fitness for duty after a traumatic event, such as experiencing a mass shooting incident. Correctional psychologists assess inmates when they first enter the prison system and at various points during their sentence. The psychological assessment of correctional officers is less common, although there is little doubt that it should be considered if corrections is to employ competent, adjusted, and adaptable personnel (Megargee, 2013).

Over the years, psychological assessment and testing techniques have generated a spectrum of social concerns and considerable legal scrutiny in both civil and criminal cases. In the civil arena, questions of unfair employment practices, discrimination, and invasion of privacy have been at the forefront. As we saw in the previous chapter, for example, some tests have run afoul of the ADA because they inappropriately inquired about a person's medical history. In criminal cases, the issue of self-incrimination has been extremely troubling. As a result of court challenges (e.g., *Estelle v. Smith*, 1981), mental health examiners must not only obtain informed consent from a criminal defendant, but must also warn him that information obtained may be used against him. However, when a court orders the psychological assessment or evaluation of a criminal defendant, the defendant has little option but to comply.

One purpose of this chapter is to acquaint readers with the many legal areas in which psychological assessment plays an important role. Another purpose is to familiarize readers with the dominant instruments used. It should be noted before we proceed that many of the psychological assessment and testing instruments have been carefully developed, are backed by considerable research, and have reasonable validity. In large part, they follow the criteria set forth in the *Standards for Educational and Psychological Testing* (American Educational Research Association, American Psychological Association, and National Council on Measurement in Education, 1999). Many others, however—even those that are commercially sold—lack the reliability, validity, and research support that they should have. We also wish to emphasize that many of the well-researched psychological assessment instruments have not been validated *for a forensic context*. A test may be a good measure of cognitive skills but not necessarily a good measure of one's ability to assist one's attorney.

Forensic Classifications of Assessment and Testing

Heilbrun, Rogers, and Otto (2000; Otto & Heilbrun, 2002) proposed three general categories of psychological assessment and testing instruments and techniques: (1) clinical measures and assessment techniques, (2) forensically relevant instruments (FRIs), and (3) forensic assessment instruments (FAIs). The three categories reflect the degree of direct relevance the various tests and techniques have to specific legal issues, with the third being the most directly relevant.

Tests in the first category, **clinical measures and assessment techniques**, were developed for the assessment, diagnosis, or treatment planning of clinical, school, or other populations. While important, they were not developed *specifically* in response to legal questions or forensic concerns. They have been developed to assess such things as learning disabilities, emotional or mental disorders, personality traits, aptitude, academic achievement, occupational success, and psychopathology. Consequently, when instruments in this category are used in courts and other legal settings, it is important that the examiner be particularly skillful and trained in applying the results of the instrument *to the legal questions at hand*. Far too often, however, psychologists seem to administer tests indiscriminately, without a clear idea of how the information gathered will address the substantive issues related to the law (Melton et al., 2007).

In the second category, **forensically relevant instruments (FRIs)**, Otto and Heilbrun (2002) place those measures that assess clinical constructs that are often pertinent to evaluating persons in the legal system. While these instruments and techniques were designed for research and the identification of certain behavioral, emotional, or mental characteristics, they have considerable direct applicability and relevance to the legal system as well. Examples include instruments and techniques to assess psychopathy, malingering or lying, neuropsychological issues, and violence risk potential.

The third category, **forensic assessment instruments (FAIs)**, "are measures that are directly relevant to a specific legal standard and reflect and focus on specific capacities, abilities, or knowledge that are embodied by the law" (Otto & Heilbrun, 2002, p. 9). Examples include those measures designed to evaluate a criminal defendant's competence to stand trial; one's capacity to understand *Miranda* warnings; or an older person's ability to manage legal, financial, and health care matters. The most common forensic assessments in criminal law are assessments of competence to stand trial (CST) (Stafford & Sellbom, 2013). However, many mental health practitioners do not make use of the FAIs specifically designed for this purpose.

Although this third category—forensic assessment instruments—is most directly relevant to legal issues, these measures are not easy to develop. Changes in the law over time, variations in the law across jurisdictions, and the need to dovetail the testing instrument to correspond to legal changes as they relate to psychological function make it a challenge to create and validate FAIs. (See Table 12-1 for examples of specific instruments in each of the three categories.)

Clinical Measures and Assessment Techniques

Clinical measures fall into two dominant categories: those that measure cognitive skills and those that measure personality attributes. Within each category, we will find specialized tests designed to measure specific attributes such as artistic ability, or mental health disorders such as depression or psychosis.

Table 12-1 Categories, Descriptions, and Examples of Psychological Assessment Measures

Category	Description	Examples
Clinical	Psychological measures designed for general cognitive or personality assessment	WAIS-III; CAS, MMPI-2; MMPI-2-RF; TAT; Rorschach (RIM); Beck Depression Inventory
Forensically relevant	Identify psychological characteristics pertinent to legal issues	SIR-2; Halstead-Reitan Neuropsychological Battery; Luria-Nebraska Neuropsychological Battery; HCR-20; PCL-R; COVR
Forensic assessment instruments	Designed specifically to measure abilities directly relevant to the legal system	CMR; CMR-R; MVS; MacCAT-CA

Cognitive Tests and Techniques

When mental processes such as thinking, learning, perceiving, problem solving, and remembering are measured and evaluated, cognitive assessment is occurring. Ideally, this is accomplished by some combination of interviewing, behavioral observation, and testing. Many cognitive "assessments," however, are more accurately called cognitive "testing," since they only consist of the use of an intelligence or IQ test. The Wechsler Abbreviated Scale of Intelligence (WASI; Wechsler, 2003) is a good example of these. The Das-Hagliere Cognitive Assessment System (CAS) is another. The CAS "is a cognitive processing battery intended for use with children and adolescents 5 through 17 years of age" (Wasserman, 2013, p. 452). The CAS is considered unique among cognitive ability measures because it is comprehensive and has undergone high levels of research in its development. Other cognitive instruments include the Differential Ability Scales–Second Edition, the Kaufman Assessment Battery for Children–Second Edition, and the Reynolds Intellectual Assessment Scales.

According to Wasserman (2013), "there are numerous substantive reasons to give intelligence tests" (p. 482). The most common reasons for psychologists working in education and health care are to "facilitate diagnosis, determine the nature of difficulty, and establish capacity/potential" (pp. 482–483). These goals may shift in the future as school districts and health facilities undergo changes in curriculum, federal requirements, and legal classification guidelines.

Most states have discontinued the use of cognitive ability testing of *all* students in their school systems. For some students, though, some testing of this sort is desirable. For example, results of cognitive ability tests *may* be required before placing children in advanced or gifted programs, and they are a critical component in the assessment of disabilities and the establishment of IEPs, as we discussed in Chapter 11. Wasserman (2013) points out that school psychologists today spend about two thirds of their time testing for eligibility for special education programs. Furthermore, cognitive tests often appear in family law and criminal law contexts. A juvenile, for example, may be given a cognitive ability test, the results of which are used to argue against his being transferred to an adult criminal court.

Cognitive ability scores also appear in reports of pretrial competency and sanity evaluations, presentence investigation reports submitted to sentencing judges, and prison records. Finally, cognitive ability tests are destined to take on a critical role in the death penalty context, because the Supreme Court has ruled that offenders who are "mentally retarded" (the term previously used for those who are intellectually disabled) may not be put to death (*Atkins v. Virginia*, 2002). As observed in Chapter 4, the Court did not specify how disability should be determined; this is left to states. In July 2013, the state of Georgia once again came close to executing Warren Hill, a man with an IQ of 70, despite the fact that seven experts who examined him agreed that he was intellectually disabled. Georgia requires in this context that intellectual disability be proved beyond a reasonable doubt, a near-impossible standard to meet. Hill's execution has been stayed by courts at least four times in 2012 and 2013. In the fall of 2013, the U.S. Supreme Court agreed to hear a very similar case, *Hall v. Florida*. Hall, who has an IQ of 71, has been on death row for 35 years. The case is scheduled for oral arguments before the Court in early 2014.

Personality and Psychopathology Assessment

The term *personality* means different things to different psychologists, but common themes run through their definitions. The definitions of most psychologists focus on relatively enduring psychological attributes of a person that can generally differentiate that particular person from others. For example, some individuals are more anxious and tense than others across a variety of situations. In police work, it is commonly known that some officers respond to stress and life-threatening situations with greater levels of anxiety and agitation. We might observe this in any context—sports, the corporate environment, or the college classroom. Some people consistently are more anxious under stress, and they may also take longer to return to their usual day-to-day anxiety levels after a particularly stressful experience. The personality variable in this instance is anxiety, more commonly called "nervousness." Like other personality variables—for example, defensiveness or extraversion—it can be measured by various personality inventories. For our purposes, **personality** will be defined as "the combination of all of the relatively enduring dimensions of individual differences on which [the person] can be measured" (Byrne, 1974, p. 26).

Traditionally, personality testing has been divided into two very broad categories: projective and objective. They are distinguished principally by the clarity of the stimuli used to obtain responses from the person taking the test. It should be mentioned, though, that the dichotomy between projective and objective measures is considered by some scholars to be an oversimplification and to reflect a biased understanding of personality measures (Viglione & Rivera, 2013). In fact, some psychologists have recommended that we retire the terms "objective" and "projective" altogether (Meyer & Kurtz, 2006). However, the terms continue to be widely used in both the research literature and clinical practice. Consequently, we describe the two categories but caution that they should not be perceived as strictly polar opposites. Rather, they are beginning to merge into a continuum, with many assessment instruments falling somewhere in the middle. For example, projective testing has become somewhat more objective in its scoring in recent years, and performance-based personality assessment—to be discussed again below—tries to incorporate some of the best aspects of projective and objective testing into its procedures (Viglione & Rivera, 2013).

Projective assessment measures are designed with the assumption that personality attributes are best revealed when a person responds to ambiguous stimuli. The principle is that individuals will "project" their personality onto an image or stimulus that could be interpreted as anything. Depending on the procedure, some of the projective stimuli are abstract, such as inkblots, while others are more concrete, such as photographs or sketches that the person is asked to interpret or tell a story about. The most commonly used instrument representing the first category is the Rorschach (also called the Rorschach Inkblot Method, or RIM), while the second category is best represented by the Thematic Apperception Test (TAT), or the Children's Apperception Test (CAT). Although historically the scoring of responses by the examiner was highly subjective, in recent years there has been a growing body of research supporting the validity of reliability-scored Rorschach indices (Sellbom et al., 2013). Essentially, the modern scoring of RIM has become more objective.

Objective assessment measures of personality and psychopathology are commonly used in clinical practice. Basically, an assessment tool is objective to the extent that examiners can apply a scoring key and objectively score the performance or response pattern. When the examiner follows the required steps for administration, any bias and subjectivity on the part of the examiner is eliminated or greatly reduced. The vast majority of objective personality tests (or **inventories**) have a "self-report" format, meaning that the subjects are expected to answer "yes" or "no," or "true" or "false" to brief statements or descriptions referring to their behavior, beliefs, or attitudes. As we described previously, the most frequently used self-report test associated with the law is the Minnesota Multiphasic Personality Inventory–2 (MMPI-2), a 566-item personality inventory used across a wide variety of clinical and employment settings. The MMPI was originally developed for the diagnosis of patients in psychiatric settings. The revised version (MMPI-2) has been constructed to be more useful for personnel selection, medical settings, correctional settings, and a multitude of other settings (Naglieri & Graham, 2013). In fact, the MMPI-2 and the Rorschach Inkblot Method are the two most widely researched and frequently used personality assessment instruments in clinical settings or evaluations of the mental disorders of offenders (Hogan, 2005; Weiner, 2013).

Performance-based assessment measures of personality combine some of the better features of both projective and objective measures, as mentioned above. They are a relatively new development in psychological assessment. "Performance-based personality measures require an individual to perform a task that is designed to elicit information about the personality in action" (Viglione & Rivera, 2013, p. 600). Psychologists Donald Viglione and Bridget Rivera further describe these tests as bringing out the individual characteristics of relevant behavior, association, perceptions, emotions, and interpersonal aspects of personality that can be observed, measured, and documented by the examining psychologist. According to Viglione and Rivera, one meaningful aspect of performance assessments is that they make an individual unique compared with other personality measures. Performance measures are highly diverse in their assessment designs and administrations, and many are in the early stages of development.

Several research studies have examined the types of measures used by psychologists in various forensic settings. Boccaccini and Brodsky (1999) surveyed experienced forensic psychologists who assessed emotional injuries in civil suits. They found that the personality inventories most commonly used were the MMPI (used by 94% of the respondents), the Millon Clinical Multiaxial Inventory (39%), the Rorschach (28%), the Beck Depression Inventory (18%), the Trauma Symptom Inventory (15%), and the Personality Assessment Inventory (14%). All but the Rorschach are objective measures. It should be noted that in the Boccaccini-Brodsky survey, psychologists were especially drawn to the Trauma Symptom Survey Inventory because of its convincing normative data, validity scales, and research support.

Budd, Felix, Poindexter, Naik-Polan, and Sloss (2002), in their survey of mental health practitioners who evaluated abused or neglected children, discovered that "projective personality measures" were used in over 90% of these child protection cases. Objective personality inventories were used in only 19% of the cases. This finding probably can be explained by the fact that children tend to respond better to projective measures, and there is a limited number of valid objective personality measures designed specifically for children.

In 2008, the MMPI-2-RF (Restructured Form) was published (Ben-Porath & Tellegen, 2008). According to Sweet et al. (2013), "The MMPI-2-RF . . . represents an important development in multidimensional measures for both psychiatric symptoms and reactions to medical problems" (p. 335). The instrument is a 338-item, restructured version of the MMPI-2, and it contains 51 scales.

Sellbom et al. (2013) find that "clinicians seem to be polarized as to whether they should use performance-based tests or rely solely on objectively scored instruments" (p. 248). However, most clinicians realize that either objective measures or performance-based testing *by themselves* are usually insufficient to answer referrals or court-ordered evaluations concerning differential diagnoses or treatment recommendations. They know they must use multiple assessment tools, including tests, inventories, interviews, and other sources of data. The clinical interview is (and always has been) a particularly popular source of information in the assessment of personality and psychopathology (Craig, 2013).

Evidence-Based Assessment and Psychopathology

Clinical measures of psychopathology—such as the diagnosis of a mental disorder—must be heavily evidence based (Sellbom et al., 2013). In 2006, the American Psychological

Association (APA) strongly advocated for **evidence-based psychological practice**, extending from intervention and psychotherapy to assessment and testing (APA Presidential Task Force on Evidence-Based Practice, 2006). The APA defined evidence-based practice in psychology as "the integration of the best available research with clinical expertise in the context of patient characteristics, culture, and preferences" (p. 284). The definition closely resembles the definition of evidence-based practice by the Institute of Medicine, outlined several years earlier. Best research evidence refers to valid scientific results relevant to intervention strategies and assessment instruments.

Sellbom et al.'s (2013) emphasis on evidence-based measures certainly holds for court referrals to the psychologist for opinions and recommendations on the mental disorder of a defendant or other litigants. Moreover, the assessment of mental disorders should be systematically linked to the psychiatric symptoms described in the DSM-IV-TR or the newly revised DSM-5, both of which are usually recognized by the legal system as containing acceptable definitions of mental disorders. The DSM criteria are then evaluated using empirically validated instruments designed for the mental disorder(s) in question. This approach encourages psychologists to do an evaluation that is tailored to each individual's presenting problem and specific symptoms. In addition, "an evidence-based approach to psychological assessment requires empirical support for any conclusions or recommendations, as opposed to relying solely on clinical impression and judgment" (Sellbom et al., 2013, p. 242). The MMPI-2-RF, for example, has a set of scales that measure psychopathology that are believed to dovetail well with many of the DSM-5 disorders.

◼ Forensically Relevant Instruments

Instruments in this category, as explained previously, are not designed to assess cognitive ability, personality features, or mental disorders, nor do they assess performance on specific legal standards. Rather, they focus on clinical constructs that are often pertinent to evaluating persons in the legal system (Otto & Heilbrun, 2002). Although it could be argued that identification of mental disorders falls into this category, it is primarily an undertaking that fits better under the clinical assessments discussed above. In this section, we will briefly review forensically relevant instruments that measure feigning, neuropsychological impairments, risk to self or others, and psychopathy.

Assessment of Feigning (or Gross Exaggeration of Symptoms)

At the outset, we must make a distinction between *feigning* and *malingering*. Although each of these terms is used colloquially for faking, there is a subtle difference. The term **feigning** is often used in forensic psychology to refer to "the deliberate fabrication or gross exaggeration of psychological and physical symptoms *without any assumption* *about its goals*" (Rogers & Bender, 2013, p. 518, emphasis added). **Malingering**, on the other hand, is "the deliberate fabrication or gross exaggeration of psychological or physical symptoms *for the fulfillment of an external goal*" (Rogers & Bender, 2013, p. 518, emphasis added).

The motivation or goal behind malingering is often to obtain financial compensation or benefits, to avoid work, or to evade criminal prosecution or conviction. Malingering is not rare; it is estimated to occur in about 15% to 17% of all forensic cases (Rogers & Bender, 2013; Rogers, Salekin, Sewell, Goldstein, & Leonard, 1998), but it is extremely difficult to detect. The courts often ask mental health professionals to provide their expert opinion regarding the possibility of malingering, because failing to detect it can lead to incorrect legal determinations. Forensic assessments are highly dependent on the openness and honesty of examinees' responses (Rogers & Bender, 2013). In fact, Rogers and Bender assert that determinations of malingering frequently supersede all other forensic, clinical issues of importance: "When a forensic psychologist concludes an individual is malingering, this opinion is likely to invalidate all claims by that person while simultaneously undercutting his or her credibility" (p. 520).

As noted above, though, malingering is not easy to detect; feigning is less complex. It is relatively easy to uncover that someone is fabricating or exaggerating an illness (or hiding a disorder or disability), but the reasons and motivations for doing so are difficult. The evaluation of malingering—which requires that the motivation for doing this be determined—requires a comprehensive and skillful assessment. The evaluation should never rely on only one psychological test or measure (Rogers & Shuman, 2005). These evaluations are most common in two major areas: (1) feigned mental disorders, and (2) feigned cognitive impairment. Note that the word "feigned" is used, but the evaluation must go beyond identifying the exaggeration itself if it is to be useful to the courts.

According to Rogers and Bender (2013), the forensic instruments available today are not designed to identify the reasons, motivations, or intentions for the exaggeration or fabrication of psychological or physical symptoms. In other words, they cannot tell us *why* the person is fabricating symptoms, only *that* she or he is. As Rogers and Bender emphasize: "*Importantly, tests are feigning measures and not malingering measures*" (p. 518). They go on to assert, "As currently developed and validated, they can evaluate grossly exaggerated presentations but not examinees' multifaceted motivations" (p. 518). Similarly, Gaines, Giles, and Morgan (2012) write that psychological "instruments alone can never be used to make a classification of malingering" (p. 437). However, they also posit that feigning evidence from psychological instruments "can then be used as collateral confirmation when there is additional evidence of actual malingering" (p. 437). Therefore, classifying someone as malingering will require additional information from clinical interviews, behavioral observations, medical records, interviews with other professionals (including health care workers and physicians) and others who know the person well, and—when necessary—additional psychological measures (such as the

Personality Assessment Inventory, or PAI, and the MMPI-2-RF). It will also require solid knowledge of the research literature on the subject.

The two major areas—the assessment of feigned mental disorders and feigned cognitive impairment—also require different approaches for identification. The most common instrument for detecting **feigned mental disorders** is the Structured Interview of Reported Symptoms–2 (SIRS-2) (Rogers, 2008a). The SIRS-2 is often called the "gold standard" or "premier measure for detecting feigned mental disorders" (Boccaccini, Murrie, & Duncan, 2006; Green & Rosenfeld, 2011; Green, Rosenfeld, & Belfi, 2012), but it cannot by itself determine malingering, only feigning. The scales include questions that mental health professionals would generally ask in cases where *suspicions* of malingering are present, but considerably more information is necessary to suggest malingering. Moreover, the scales are geared to minimize the risk that a respondent will be inappropriately identified as feigning symptoms (Melton et al., 2007). Overall, empirical research focusing on the ability of the scales to distinguish malingering about mental disorders has demonstrated that the SIRS-2 is better than other instruments at detecting feigning.

In **feigned cognitive impairment**, "malingerers must convince the examiner that their efforts are sincere and their ostensible impairments are genuine" (Rogers & Bender, 2013, p. 527). According to Rogers, detection strategies for feigned cognitive impairment can be placed into two general categories: unlikely presentations and excessive impairment. **Unlikely presentations** are response patterns that are unusual and rare for patients with genuine cognitive impairment. An example would be a person performing equally on both easy and difficult items, or giving unexpected answers on questions that require forced-choice answers (e.g., a list of three or four choices the person must select from). **Excessive impairment** refers to the tendency of individuals who are faking cognitive impairment to perform much lower on various tests than expected for cognitively impaired populations. This is the more commonly used of the two strategies. Rogers (2008a) argues that the overriding goal of feigned cognitive assessment is the measurement of *correct* responses. Malingerers are unlikely to consider gradations of difficulty, but concentrate instead on making as many errors as they consider reflective of the disorder on the task. In other words, they fail simple cognitive tasks that are generally successfully completed by most cognitively impaired individuals.

In most civil cases involving cognitive impairment (or physical neurological impairment), a comprehensive evaluation by a neuropsychologist is needed (Boone, 2013; Mossman, Wygant, & Gervais, 2012). As will be seen below, such evaluations are increasingly sought in criminal matters as well.

Assessment of Neuropsychological Impairment

Neuropsychology deals with studying and assessing the functioning and dysfunctioning of the human nervous system, particularly the brain. In general, forensic neuropsychology is concerned with the diagnosis and consequence of brain damage within a legal context.

At present, clinical neuropsychologists are called upon routinely to assist the "trier of fact" (e.g., judges, juries) in understanding the behavioral, emotional, motivational, and cognitive sequelae following insults to the brain as well as to delineate the importance of biopsychosocial variables in modulating brain function and dysfunction. (Heilbronner, 2004, p. 312)

According to many experts, forensic neuropsychology is the most rapidly developing subspecialty within clinical neuropsychology, and some believe it is outpacing other specializations in forensic psychology and forensic psychiatry in terms of professional growth (Heilbronner, 2004; Kaufmann, 2008, 2012; LaDuke, DeMatteo, Heilbrun, & Swirsky-Sacchetti, 2012). The psychological assessment of brain injury and nervous system functioning has become almost indispensable to the law (Heilbrun et al., 2003; LaDuke et al., 2012). For many years, forensic neuropsychology has offered assessment services almost exclusively within the realm of civil law, to the neglect of the criminal law area (LaDuke et al., 2012). However, there has been a discernible trend in recent years for many more forensic neuropsychologists to offer assessments in criminal matters (Sweet & Meyer, 2012). For example, in a 2011 survey conducted by LaDuke and his associates, two thirds of the forensic neuropsychologists reported providing evaluation services to the criminal justice system, a pattern that has historically been unusual for neuropsychological professionals. The researchers concluded, "Overall, the majority of neuropsychologists appear to conduct forensic assessments in both civil and criminal legal cases, while a sizeable minority restricts their forensic experience to civil cases" (p. 507).

In civil matters, neuropsychologists are most often consulted in cases involving workers' compensation, disability determination, educational due process within public school systems, personal injury, child custody, impaired professional ability and fitness for duty, and mental competency such as the capacity to make a health care decision. Best estimates indicate there are thousands of neuropsychological evaluations conducted each year within this legal context (Heilbronner, 2004).

In criminal litigation, neuropsychologists are most often used to assist in determining competency to stand trial, criminal responsibility, and factors that might contribute to the mitigation of a sentence (LaDuke et al., 2012; Otero, Podell, DeFina, & Goldberg, 2013). The language "mental disease or defect," which appears in the law related to insanity, is broadly interpreted to include not only psychological disorders but neurological or physiological ones as well. Neuropsychologists, therefore, can help in determining what effect known brain damage may have on the capacities and behavior of a defendant. In addition to brain damage, other neurological disorders also can have an impact on one's behavior. Recall the example of defendants with sleep disorders in Chapter 1. Although a neurological problem may not completely absolve the individual of responsibility for an offense, it may diminish that responsibility and reduce the sentence if he is convicted of the crime.

Despite neuropsychology's entry into criminal courts, a vast majority of the forensic neuropsychological evaluations are still done in civil law cases, where they often focus on **traumatic brain injury (TBI)**. A TBI is caused by a bump, blow, or jolt to the head or a penetrating head injury that disrupts normal functioning of the brain. Cognitive impairment represents a significant proportion of these civil cases. Each year, an estimated 1.7 million people in the United States sustain a TBI, resulting in about 53,000 deaths (Coronado et al., 2011; Faul, Xu, Wald, & Coronado, 2010). According to recent statistics, the most common causes of TBIs are transportation accidents (48.9%), followed by falls (25.8%), firearms (9.7%), assaults (7.5%), and other causes (8%) (Bigler & Brooks, 2009).

In civil matters, the forensic neuropsychologist tries to answer three basic questions for the court and attorneys: (1) Is there brain damage? (2) What was the cause of this brain damage? And (3) what effects will this brain damage or dysfunction have on the behavioral, affective (emotional), and cognitive life of this individual? Lorena was returning the tourist van to company headquarters when its brakes failed on a curved incline, causing the van to veer off the road and onto its side. Lorena suffered a serious head injury. In addition to deciding whether the company was negligent in maintaining upkeep of the van, the court also must find the answers to the above questions. In the criminal context (not relevant in Lorena's case), an additional question is, what effect did the brain damage have on the individual's behavior? Specifically, did it preclude or diminish the defendant's ability to form the necessary mental intent needed to commit the crime?

Neuropsychological assessment techniques vary widely. The nature of the examinations ranges from a relatively brief clinical interview to a comprehensive examination that includes extensive neuropsychological test administration (Otero et al., 2013). The examination may include an evaluation of general intelligence, language, memory, attention, thought processes, perceptual-motor functioning, and emotional status. Most neuropsychologists apparently prefer to use various combinations of tests, depending on the individual being tested and the legal questions asked. Overall, no single test is adequate for the detection or diagnosis of all suspected brain damage, primarily because of the enormous complexity of the brain (Martell, 1992). Modern technology, such as magnetic resonance imaging (MRI), fMRI, positron emission tomography (PET), computed tomography (CT), magnetoencephalography (MEG), and diffusion tensor imaging, has enabled neuropsychologists to study the brain's functioning more directly, and also has somewhat reduced the need for some of the standardized neuropsychological testing (Naglieri & Graham, 2013; Otero et al., 2013). However, some of the standard and more traditional neuropsychological tests are indispensable for identifying inabilities or the abilities necessary for thinking, learning, and behaving (Naglieri & Otero, 2011; Otero et al., 2013). "It is through standardized neuropsychological instruments and other methods that the forensic psychologist presents evidence to support or refute the presence of central nervous system dysfunction" (Otero et al., 2013, pp. 507–508).

One of the major tasks for neuropsychologists making forensic assessments is to separate preexisting brain dysfunctions from dysfunctions resulting from a current injury. Conditions that existed prior to the trauma in question are sometimes subtle, complicated, and difficult to identify—even by those who know the individual well—and are more common than supposed. In the illustration above, Lorena may have had a preexisting brain injury as the result of a fall in the past that was not detected. Evidence of that injury could reduce the degree of responsibility attributed to the van company. It is important to note, though, that in criminal cases, preexisting trauma in a victim is not as relevant: For example, an aggressor is responsible for the harm, even though he was unaware that the victim had experienced prior blows to the head and was susceptible to dying from still another trauma.

Another important objective is to make certain that indicators of neurological impairment gathered from neuropsychological assessment are not the result of other factors in an otherwise healthy individual. For example, the apparent impairment may simply be the natural result of advancing age rather than something attributable to an injury on the job.

Risk Assessment

Forensic risk assessment is a procedure or technique for estimating the probability that an individual will engage in antisocial, dangerous, or criminal behavior. In the criminal justice and juvenile justice systems, risk assessment may be ordered by the court to determine the likelihood of recidivism or parole violations, especially in cases involving sex offenders. A person's dangerousness also may be assessed in domestic violence cases, where judges consider preventive detention to keep the accused incapacitated before trial. These are but two illustrations. In the mental health system, risk assessment is often requested for decisions involving civil commitment, commitment as a sexually violent predator, or tort liability of mental health professionals for their patient's violence. Risk assessments are also becoming more common for workplace violence and violent terrorism (Skeem & Monahan, 2011).

Risk assessment measures focus on predictions of violence or, more broadly, dangerousness. Dangerousness is generally defined as the potential for individuals to do harm either to themselves or to others. Psychologists resist saying that they can "predict" such behavior, however. They prefer to discuss probabilities. Therefore, risk assessment measures are usually designed to evaluate the level of threat an individual poses to him- or herself or to other people's safety. However, it can be complicated to satisfy the legal criterion of dangerousness, as many jurisdictions have extremely diverse criteria (Melton et al., 2007; Ogloff & Douglas, 2013). This was alluded to in Chapter 10, when we discussed various criteria for involuntary civil commitment. As but one example, harm to property or causing emotional harm may satisfy criteria in some jurisdictions, whereas only serious physical violence or risks of sexual offending satisfy the criteria in other jurisdictions (Ogloff & Douglas, 2013). Some state statutes now explicitly require that specific assessment instruments be used in determining dangerousness or risk (Skeem & Monahan, 2011). For instance, Virginia's Sexually Violent Predator statute not only "mandates the use of a specific instrument but also specifies the cutoff score on that instrument that must be achieved to proceed further in the commitment process" (Skeem & Monahan, 2011, p. 38). Virginia was the only state that designates both a specific actuarial risk assessment instrument (the STATIC-99) and a cutoff score (5) in a statute. However, the Virginia Joint Legislative Audit and Review Commission (2011), in a report to the governor and general assembly of that state, later concluded that specifying the test and a cutoff score was a flawed approach and recommended that this be eliminated from the statute.

Risk assessment instruments now exist on a continuum, "with completely unstructured (clinical) assessment occupying one pole of the continuum, completely structured (actuarial) assessment occupying the other pole, and several forms of partially structured assessment lying between the two" (Skeem & Monahan, 2011, p. 39). Recall the *Coble* case, covered in Box 6-3, where one expert used clinical assessment and the other used actuarial measures. Completely structured or **actuarial assessment** is based on how *groups* of individuals with similar characteristics have acted in the past. The fundamental statistic employed in actuarial prediction is the *base rate*, which is defined as the statistical prevalence of a particular behavior in a given group over a set period of time, usually 1 year. Insurance companies have compiled extensive statistics on who gets into traffic accidents. These statistics may show, for example, that 20-year-old males who have mediocre academic records and drive a Trans-Am have a very high probability of being involved in a traffic accident within a 2-year period. In fact, the base rate for this group may be 40%. If Devon falls into this group, he will pay much higher insurance rates than Justine, a 20-year-old woman with an outstanding academic record and a 9-year-old minivan. The thing to remember is that actuarial prediction is based on *statistics* compiled on *certain groups* of people.

Unstructured clinical judgment, on the other hand, is based on experience and knowledge with dealing with a certain clientele. A mental health professional may assert, "Based on my experience in dealing with Charles and others like him, I predict that he will assault someone again within a year." Recall also from Box 6-3 that Dr. Coons outlined a methodology that included impressions of an individual—including not only his past behavior, but also his "conscience." Unstructured clinical judgment has been extensively criticized in the professional literature as unscientific, too often based on "gut feelings," and reflective of a "tea leaves" approach to the prediction of dangerousness (*Coble v. Texas*, 2010).

Of the three types of prediction, clinical prediction is without doubt the most intuitive and subjective. While clinical experience may be an invaluable source of ideas and useful in acquiring certain skills, it is also fraught with an extensive range of biases and inaccuracies (Grove & Meehl, 1996).

Structured clinical (professional) judgment is a combination of the two. It takes relevant knowledge and statistical and scientific data that actuarial assessment can provide and combines it with the knowledge and experience of the trained clinician during the risk assessment process. It represents the middle of the risk assessment continuum.

Of the three approaches, the unstructured or clinical one has the least amount of scientific support for accuracy in prediction (Skeem & Monahan, 2011). Actuarial predictions are almost always more accurate than clinical ones, based on the scientific literature (Grove & Meehl, 1996). Robyn Dawes, David Faust, and Paul Meehl (1989) reviewed nearly 100 comparative studies in the social sciences. They concluded, "In virtually every one of these studies, the actuarial method has equaled or surpassed the clinical method, sometimes slightly and sometimes substantially" (p. 1669). Some studies suggested that psychologists who relied on unstructured clinical judgment were incorrect 2 out of every 3 times when trying to predict an individual's future violent behavior (Vitacco, Erickson, Kurus, & Apple, 2012).

Structured clinical judgment presumably combines the best of the knowledge obtained from professional practice and empirical knowledge; it offers decision-making *guidelines* to clinicians for use in assessing risks in a variety of contexts. Guidelines have been developed to assess risk of spousal violence (Kropp, Hart, Webster, & Eaves, 1995), violence in mentally disordered populations (Webster, Douglas, Eaves, & Hart, 1997), and sexual violence (Boer, Hart, Kropp, & Webster, 1997). Borum (1996) has published an extremely helpful article on guidelines, and Litwack and Schlesinger (1999) cite numerous sources for these guidelines.

The structured professional judgment approach is illustrated by the Historical/Clinical/Risk Management Scale (HCR-20), developed by Christopher Webster and his colleagues (1997; Webster, Harris, Rice, Cormier, & Quinsey, 1994). The HCR-20 scale purports to identify the presence or absence of violence risk factors in adults. As is apparent from the title of the scale, the HCR-20 bases its predictive power on three major areas: (1) past or historical (H) factors, (2) clinical or current (C) factors, and (3) risk management (R) factors. Historical items include "previous violence," "age at first violent incident," and "early adjustment at home." Other "H" items are relationship instability, employment problems, substance use problems, and major mental illness. Clinical or "C" items include lack of insight, negative attitudes (antisocial, hostile, angry), and "active symptoms of major mental illness" (Webster et al., 1997, p. 263). Risk or "R" factors are related to the future circumstances of the individuals being evaluated, such as whether the person is likely to have adequate housing, meals, daily activities, and finances. Research indicates that individuals without these basics are at higher risk for violence than those who have these needs managed and taken care of. Researchers of the HCR-20 found that the historical (H) items are the strongest for predicting future violent actions (Webster et al., 1997), and C items are second strongest (Borum, 1996). The HCR-20 has been increasingly introduced in court and administrative proceedings, mostly revolving around sexually violent persons' commitment or potential release from a secure setting to parole (Vitacco et al., 2012).

An instrument receiving continuing research attention is the Classification of Violence Risk (COVR; Monahan et al., 2005), which was discussed briefly in Chapter 10. That instrument was developed to measure risk in civilly committed populations. As we noted, results from research on the COVR indicate that an accumulation of risk factors, rather than any one risk factor, is present in people with a propensity for violence. As Monahan and his colleagues (2001) observe, "no one [risk factor] is necessary or sufficient for a person to behave aggressively toward others" (p. 142).

Another important risk assessment tool is the Violence Risk Appraisal Guide (VRAG), developed by Harris, Rice, and Quinsey (1993; Quinsey, Harris, Rice, & Cormier, 2006). The VRAG is based on data from 618 men with prior histories of significant violence who were initially confined at the Oak Ridge Division of the Penetanguishene Mental Health Centre (now called the Waypoint Centre for Mental Health Care) in Ontario, Canada. Oak Ridge is a maximum-security facility providing assessment and treatment for persons referred from the courts, correctional services, and other provincial psychiatric hospitals. Twelve variables believed to predict future violence make up the VRAG. The variables include separation from parents by age 16 or younger, schizophrenia, elementary school maladjustment, alcohol abuse history, and symptoms of psychopathy. Researchers discovered that the VRAG's best predictor of violent recidivism was the score on the PCL-R, and that the scale overall is a useful instrument for predicting criminal violence among men who had already been apprehended for violent crime (Rice, 1997). Sexual Violence Risk–20 (SVR-20; Boer, Hart, Kropp, & Webster, 2007; Hart & Boer, 2010) uses structured guidance to predict sexual violence.

Assessment of Psychopathy

Considerable research has revealed a strong association between psychopathy and serious criminal behavior, including violence. Consequently, psychopathy plays a central role in risk assessments conducted as part of psycholegal evaluations in criminal and civil contexts (Hart & Storey, 2013). The term **psychopath** is used to describe a person who exhibits a collection of psychological, interpersonal, and neuropsychological characteristics that distinguish him or her from the general population. The core behavioral features of psychopaths include the following:

(1) Poor judgment and failure to learn from experience

(2) Trouble evaluating the potential consequences of their actions

(3) Lack of guilt or remorsefulness for cruel or antisocial actions

(4) Callousness and lack of empathy

(5) Low anxiety or nervousness in high-pressure situations

(6) Cycles of unreliability and impulsiveness

(7) Superficial charm

(8) Frequent deceitfulness or lying

(9) Failure to follow a well-defined life plan

(10) Inability to love or give genuine affection to others

Not all psychopaths exhibit all these features, but most show many of them. The above characteristics they do have tend to be stable across their lifetimes. However, Hart and Storey (2013) admonish forensic psychologists who conduct risk assessments, "The presence of psychopathy is neither necessary nor sufficient to conclude that someone is at high risk for future violence, because not all people with psychopathy are violent and not all people who commit violence have psychopathy" (p. 562).

Hart and Storey (2013) divide procedures for assessing psychopathy into three categories: (1) structured diagnostic interviews, (2) self-report questionnaires and inventories, and (3) expert rating scales. Structured diagnostic interviews obtain information from the person being evaluated via an interview consisting of a predetermined set of questions or topics. The collected interview material is then scored, resulting in standardized and reliable diagnoses.

Currently, one of the most popular measuring instruments for adult *criminal* psychopathy is the Psychopathy Checklist–Revised (PCL-R; Hare, 2003). It is basically an expert rating scale, meaning that only persons trained in its use should administer it. The PCL-R assesses the emotional, interpersonal, behavior, and social deviance aspects of criminal psychopathy from various sources, including parents, other family members, friends, and arrest and court records.

The PCL-R has been heavily researched and has been used extensively. It is estimated that the PCL-R is used in about 60,000 to 80,000 evaluations each year (Otto & Heilbrun, 2002). So far, the research has strongly supported the reliability and validity of the PCL-R for distinguishing *criminal* psychopaths from the general population or non-psychopaths

(Hare, 1996, 1998; Hare, Forth, & Strachan, 1992). The PCL-R is a 20-item clinical rating scale based on information obtained through a semi-structured interview and personal files (usually prison files) on the individual. It usually takes several hours to administer, again by a highly trained mental health professional. Scores are assessed on a 3-point scale, depending on the degree to which the individual matches the description of a high score for each of the psychopathic traits. Total scores can range from 0 to 40. Cutoff scores of 30 on the PCL-R have been found to be useful diagnostic indicators of psychopathy, although some clinicians have used scores ranging from 25 to 33 (Simourd & Hoge, 2000). It is important to note that the PCL-R is considered primarily a *dimensional* measure of criminal psychopathy rather than a categorical measure in which a person is classified as either a psychopath or a non-psychopath. In other words, the more psychopathic features a person displays, the more likely a person falls into the psychopathy end of the continuum.

The PCL:SV is a 12-item scale, derived from the PCL-R, that has two primary purposes: (1) to screen for psychopathy in forensic settings, and (2) to assess and diagnose psychopathy outside of forensic settings (Hart et al., 1995). Scores of 18 or higher on the PCL:SV are suggestive of psychopathy, and scores of 13 to 17 indicate "potential" psychopathy (Hart et al., 1995). The PCL:SV has been shown to predict post-release violence among forensic psychiatric patients (Hill, Rogers, & Bickford, 1996; Monahan et al., 2001; Strand, Belfrage, Fransson, & Levander, 1999). The instrument takes about an hour to an hour and a half to administer. Unlike the PCL-R, the PCL:SV can be completed without access to criminal record information. Therefore, the assessment tool is suitable for use in civil psychiatric evaluations and personnel selection, such as of law enforcement, correctional, or military recruits (Hart et al., 1995).

Forensic Assessment Instruments

Forensic assessment instruments are designed to measure a specific legal standard and target specific capacities, abilities, or knowledge that the court considers important in making decisions about some issues of the law. We will cover two examples of forensic assessment instruments in this section: (1) ability to understand the *Miranda* warning, and (2) assessments of competency to stand trial. Although both of these topics were covered in earlier chapters, we did not at that time focus on the nature of these assessment processes.

Forensic Assessment of the Capacity to Comprehend *Miranda* Warnings

It is estimated that at least 318,000 custodial suspects are involved annually in police interrogations without fully making a knowing and intelligent waiver of their *Miranda* warnings (Frumkin, Lally, & Sexton, 2012; Rogers, 2008b). Often, courts have looked to forensic mental health professionals to assist them in determining whether a *Miranda* waiver was knowingly, intelligently, and voluntarily made (Frumkin et al., 2012). Consequently, many articles (e.g., Frumkin, 2008, 2010; A. Goldstein & Goldstein, 2010; Grisso, 2003) have been written on how to assess defendants' ability to waive their rights and advance a valid waiver. One of the more common series of tests designed for evaluation of defendants' ability or competence to waive their *Miranda* rights are the four instruments labeled the Instruments for Assessing and Appreciation of Miranda Rights developed by Grisso (1998a). The four are the Comprehension of Miranda Rights (CMR), Comprehension of Miranda Rights–Recognition (CMR-R), Comprehension of Miranda Vocabulary (CMV), and Function of Rights in Interrogation (FRI). Similar instruments later developed by Rogers and his colleagues include the Miranda Statements Scale (MSS; Rogers, 2005), the Miranda Vocabulary Scale (MVS; Rogers, 2006b), and the Miranda Rights Scale (MRS; Rogers, 2006a). As yet, these instruments are unpublished but are referred to in literature discussing them (e.g., Rogers, Harrison, Rogstad, LaFortune, & Hazelwood, 2010).

We do not discuss each of these individually, but on the whole they are designed to assess to what extent defendants comprehend or understand what they are told. For example, the defendant must be able to distinguish statements that mean the same as or something different from each element of the warning. For example, "You have the right to an attorney" does not mean only during a trial. Some of the scales also ask the defendant to define words in the *Miranda* warning to assess his or her understanding of the legal vocabulary often used in the warning. Words like "attorney," "provided," "waive," and "indigent" may not be familiar to some defendants.

The FRI and the MRS are intended to assess the defendant's capacity to appreciate the significance of the rights within the context of police questioning, the attorney–client relationship, and court proceedings. Many defendants believe that anything they tell their lawyers can be reported to the presiding judge. The FRI uses hypothetical police vignettes to assess whether the defendant understands the adversarial nature of interrogation and the function of rights to silence and counsel in the context of interrogation and arrest. The MRS asks defendants to address advantages and disadvantages on such issues as relinquishing their right to silence and their right to an attorney (Rogers et al., 2010).

The Miranda Rights Comprehension Instruments (MCRI; N. E. S. Goldstein et al., 2012) was recently revised from the earlier instruments developed by Grisso and his colleagues to reflect the vocabulary currently used in *Miranda* warnings and a fifth element of the warning, which has been added in many jurisdictions. This fifth element explicitly informs defendants that they can stop the questioning at any time to consult with an attorney. The MCRI also provides updated norms for comparing the defendant's level to the relevant population in general.

A different type of instrument, the Gudjonsson Suggestibility Scales (GSS; Gudjonsson, 1997), has been put forth by some clinicians as a helpful measure of a person's susceptibility to psychological coercion during the interrogation process. Leading questions by police or an investigator's reactions to a suspect's answers may prompt highly suggestible suspects to change their answers or even to give a false confession. The GSS has attracted an impressive body of research, but some courts have been critical of its reliability and validity, as the quote at the beginning of this chapter illustrates. However, in a recent study of pretrial defendants—including some who were mentally disordered—Rogers et al. (2010) found that suggestibility as measured by the GSS was unrelated to comprehension of *Miranda* rights.

Forensic Assessments of Competency to Stand Trial

Evaluation of competence to stand trial requires two levels of assessment (Stafford & Sellbom, 2013). The first level requires the psychologist to evaluate the defendant's understanding of the legal situation and the options available. The second level requires an assessment directed at whether the defendant has a mental disorder or cognitive impairment, or is malingering.

The current legal standard for competence to stand trial has not changed since the U.S. Supreme Court in *Dusky v. United States* (1960) outlined the necessary criteria for the standard more than 50 years ago. As noted in Chapter 4, the Court in that case stated, "The test will be whether [the defendant] has sufficient present ability to consult with his lawyer with a reasonable degree of rational understanding, and whether he has a rational as well as factual understanding of the proceedings against him" (p. 179).

The MacArthur Competence Assessment Tool–Criminal Adjudication (MacCAT-CA; Hoge, Bonnie, Poythress, & Monahan, 1999) is an objective, standardized instrument developed to evaluate the defendant's competence to assist counsel, and decision competence. The instrument is specifically designed to address the criteria recommended by *Dusky*. The MacCAT-CA consists of 22 structured interview items that are divided into three subscales of psycholegal abilities: understanding, reasoning, and appreciation. *Understanding* refers to the capacity for factual understanding of the legal system and the adjudication process. *Reasoning* refers to the ability to distinguish more relevant from less relevant factual information and the ability to reason about two legal options: pleading guilty or not guilty. *Appreciation* in this context is the defendant's capacity to understand his or her own legal circumstances.

The examiner begins the test by reading a hypothetical vignette (about an aggravated assault at a pool hall) to the defendant. The defendant is then asked 16 questions about the vignette as it pertains to the legal process (understanding and reasoning). The last 6 questions are specifically geared to test a defendant's understanding of his or her own circumstances (appreciation). The MacCAT–CA is considered appropriate for use with both felony and misdemeanor defendants, ages 18 or older. The instrument represents a solid approach for evaluating adjudicative competency, but it is not equipped to assess psychopathology or mental disorders in the defendant (Skeem, Golding, & Emke-Francis, 2004).

Forensic Evaluations in Delinquency Cases

Juvenile issues have been mentioned in various chapters in the book, but—with the exception of material on comprehension of *Miranda* rights—we have not focused on assessment measures. We do so here because assessment of juveniles is a major enterprise for psychologists, and a strong research literature exists to support it. In their comprehensive review of forensic evaluation in delinquency cases, Thomas Grisso and Christina Riggs Romaine (2013) conclude, "A solid body of empirical knowledge and literature has begun to develop, and a consensus is clearly emerging regarding best practices in juvenile forensic assessments" (p. 363). Such consensus has not yet emerged with regard to the assessment of other populations.

Juvenile delinquency is an imprecise social and legal label for a wide range of law- and norm-violating behavior. Legally, the term refers to behavior against the criminal code committed by an individual who has not reached adulthood. Immediately, a problem arises as to what is meant by "adulthood." Although the legal definition has traditionally been restricted to persons under age 18, the age varies by state. In some states, when persons reach the age of 17, they are no longer considered "juveniles," though they may be handled as "youthful offenders" by the criminal courts.

The cases of most juveniles charged with violating the law are heard in juvenile or family court, which is guided by a rehabilitative rather than a punitive policy. However, the juvenile or family court may decide that it believes the juvenile should be tried in adult criminal court. All states allow juveniles to be tried in criminal court under certain circumstances (Office of Juvenile Justice and Delinquency Prevention, 2011). In these cases, psychologists are often asked to perform evaluations addressing criteria for waiver of juvenile court jurisdiction, thus allowing youths to be tried in the criminal court. Although juveniles may be transferred for a wide variety of offenses, transfer is typically reserved for the most serious cases and the most serious juvenile offenders. In a comprehensive, four-state study of juvenile transfers, Snyder, Sickmund, and Poe-Yamagata (2000) found that weapon use, victim injury, age of the offender, and nature of the court history were important variables in transfer decision making. Thus, if a juvenile charged with a public order offense is transferred to criminal court, the juvenile probably is close to the age where he would no longer be under the jurisdiction of the juvenile court. Alternatively, he may have a history of more serious offending.

"Psychologists have been providing specialized evaluations for the courts in delinquency cases for about 100 years" (Grisso & Riggs Romaine, 2013, p. 359). This has been over a half century longer than they have been conducting adult competence to stand trial and criminal responsibility evaluations. The most frequent evaluations by psychologists in delinquency cases are those that involve assessing the youth's psychological needs and rehabilitation potential (Grisso & Riggs Romaine, 2013). There are two forensic contexts in which these evaluations are normally requested by the court. One is during the pretrial stage, when the court may request a psychological assessment of the youth's possible need for emergency mental health intervention. The second is during the posttrial stage of the delinquency proceedings, when the court may request help in deciding on an appropriate disposition of the case, usually involving some form of intervention or treatment plan. However, the same as for adults, psychologists also may be asked to assess a juvenile's competency to understand and waive constitutional rights and competency to participate in the proceedings—otherwise known as adjudicative competency.

Concerning evaluations for the court disposition decision, Grisso (1998b) has outlined four fundamental questions that the psychological evaluation is expected to answer:

(1) What are the important characteristics of the delinquent? This involves some reporting on personality features, family background, peer relationships, mental or intellectual problems, performance in school, substance abuse, and offending history.

(2) What needs to change? That is, what factors may have contributed to the delinquent behavior, and how can they be changed to prevent future offending?

(3) What types of intervention or psychological treatment could be applied that might result in rehabilitation?

(4) What is the likelihood of change once these interventions or treatments are put into place?

It is very important that a well-rounded developmental perspective be a major consideration in any forensic evaluation of youth.

Age and Developmental Considerations

Thomas Grisso (1997, 1998b, 2005) has provided excellent reviews of the research in this area. Grisso (2005) notes that many studies address *adolescent* cognitive development and decision-making skills, but far more research focusing on *delinquents* and the particular situations facing them is needed. He contends that the research literature on the developmental abilities of adolescents as a group should not be generalized to the developmental abilities of delinquents, whose life experiences often have placed them at a cognitive disadvantage. Delinquent offenders also are more likely than adolescents as a group to have learning disabilities, low intellectual functioning, and emotional disturbances, all of which place them at risk of not being competent to stand trial in criminal courts.

With respect to age, it seems clear that children age 13 and below are at a significantly greater risk than adults for not being able to play the role of defendant. Youths aged 14 to 16, on the other hand, vary considerably. Some seem to have developed legally relevant cognitive abilities, while others are significantly developmentally delayed. As Grisso and others (e.g., Grisso & Schwartz, 2000) have emphasized, for this age-group, age per se is a poor indicator of their competence to stand trial. Approximately 50% of all juveniles referred to juvenile court are age 15 or younger (Knoll & Sickmund (2012).

Adolescent Judgment and Decision Making

In addition to the importance of studying delinquents separately from general adolescents, as Grisso recommends, it is also important to recognize results from the general literature on adolescence. A large number of developmental and neuropsychological studies conducted over the past 15 years are relevant. Developmental psychology and neuropsychology have played an increasingly crucial role in juvenile crime policy because decisions about whether and when juvenile offenders should be punished as adults have been hotly debated and often contested (Bonnie & Scott, 2013). The limits of adolescent capacity to interpret and regulate emotional states, to resist peer pressure, and to engage in mature decisions have a direct relevance to decision making in the forensic context (R. D. Hoge, 2012). Therefore, one important role of forensic assessments of adolescents is the documentation of the cognitive and emotional limitations of the youth in question (Hoge, 2012). Grisso and Riggs Romaine (2013) write, "Forensic examiners . . . will increasingly be asked to address youths' competence to stand trial or degree of culpability, as well as questions of rehabilitation needs, with reference to these developmentally related questions about youths' decisional capacities" (p. 374).

In three recent decisions mentioned earlier in the book (*Graham v. Florida*, 2010; *Miller v. Alabama*, 2012; *Roper v. Simmons*, 2005), the U.S. Supreme Court referred to psychological and brain research in rulings on the sentencing of juveniles. Specifically, both the death penalty and mandatory life without parole were found unconstitutional for individuals who committed their crimes as juveniles, under the Eighth Amendment prohibiting cruel and unusual punishment (Bonnie & Scott, 2013). Justice Kagan, in writing the majority opinion in *Miller v. Alabama*—the case that put an end to the mandatory life-without-parole sentencing of juveniles convicted of murder—noted that developments in psychology and brain science continue to show fundamental differences between juvenile and adult brain development.

The research to date underscores the fact the adolescent judgment and decision making are significantly different from that of adults. It is universally known that adolescence—for many if not most adolescents—is a time of heightened risk taking and unchecked recklessness. "It is well established that adolescents are more likely than children or adults to take risks, as evinced by elevated rates of experimentation with alcohol, tobacco, and drugs, unprotected sexual activity, violent and nonviolenct crime, and reckless driving" (Albert, Chein, & Steinberg, 2013, p. 114). This high level of teenage vulnerability to risk taking is believed to be based on two major factors: developmental changes in the brain during adolescent development and strong peer influence at this time. In reference to the first factor, the frontal lobes—those areas of the brain that play important roles in executive function, advanced cognitive processes, planning, control of impulses, and weighing the consequences of decisions before acting—exhibit key changes as humans move from adolescence to adulthood (Bonnie & Scott, 2013; Lamb & Malloy, 2013). "Indeed, it appears that the brain changes characteristic of adolescence are among the most dramatic and important to occur during the lifespan" (Steinberg, 2010, p. 160). Due to these rapid changes in brain development, the adolescent brain is at its peak for sensation seeking and concurrent poor impulse control. In general, adolescents tend to live for the moment. They tend to be impatient, seeking immediate rewards rather than long-term ones. Moreover, they also tend to be more emotionally volatile than adults (Lamb & Malloy, 2013). As summarized by Michael Lamb and Lindsay Malloy, "adolescents experience a surge in emotion and reward seeking without a concomitant increase in the ability to self-regulate" (p. 582).

In addition, a growing body of research concludes that brain changes during adolescence result in a high neurobehavioral propensity to need the company of other adolescents (Albert et al., 2013; Burnett, Sebastian, Cohen Kadosh, & Blakemore, 2011; Somerville, 2013). It is a well-known observation that teenagers spend an enormous amount of time with other teenagers; it is less well known that they may be biologically programmed for this contact. The neurobehavioral desire for peer companionship clearly reaches its peak period during midadolescence for the average teenager (Steinberg, 2010). As emphasized by Albert et al. (2013),

> Peer relations are never more salient than in adolescence. In addition to a puberty-related spike in interest in opposite-sex [or same-sex] relationships, adolescents spend more time than children or adults interacting with peers, report the highest degree of happiness in peer contexts, and assign the greatest priority to peer norms for behavior. (p. 116)

Albert and Steinberg cogently argue that peer influence is one of the primary factors contributing to adolescents' heightened tendency to make risky decisions and demonstrate poor judgment. Basically, the presence of peers increases the adolescent tendency toward short-term benefits of risky choices over the long-term value of safe alternatives (Albert et al., 2013; Albert & Steinberg, 2011b). This tendency occurs at a time when they lack the judgment to exercise self-control and to evaluate the future consequences of their behavior. Studies indicate that about 90% of teenage boys admit to committing criminal offenses for which they could be incarcerated (Scott & Steinberg, 2008). Most often, they commit these crimes in the company of their peers.

Moreover, educational programs designed to reduce adolescent risk taking and criminal activity are often ineffective (Bartol & Bartol, 2013). "The problem is not what they know, but what they do" (Sunstein, 2008, p. 147). Although many adolescents understand cognitively the risk associated with their behaviors by about age 14, the impulse controls required to reduce these risky behaviors are simply not equivalent to those of adults until at least the age 21 (Pharo, Sim, Grapham, Gross, & Hayne, 2011). Essentially, teenagers are cognitively very able to learn and understand much of what they are exposed to but have difficulty—due to brain maturation factors—controlling their behavior at times, especially in the presence of peers. In fact, adolescents do not differ much from adults in their capacity to rationally evaluate risk information, especially in the absence of peers (Albert & Steinberg, 2011a). As teenagers get older, risk-taking behavior and peer influences slowly decrease, but they continue to some extent until around age 24.

The mental health professional involved in assessment of the juvenile offender must recognize normal developmental factors and be very familiar with the expanding research literature. It is clear that adolescents who are involved in the criminal justice system often have impaired intellectual abilities, mental health problems, and substance abuse issues (Lamb & Malloy, 2013). When arrested, they may become confused about their involvement and the seriousness of the crime, they may wish to protect peer co-offenders, and they may fully embrace the short-term consequences of avoiding uncomfortable interrogations over the long-term consequences of a confession (Lamb & Malloy, 2013). As discussed in Chapter 3, research indicates that many do not understand their constitutional rights, including those protected by the *Miranda* warning (N. E. S. Goldstein et al., 2013; Grisso, 1998a; Rogers, 2008b, 2011). Studies of interrogations of juveniles also reveal high percentages (6% to 14%) of adolescents who falsely confessed during interrogation (Gudjonsson, Sigurdsson, Asgeirsdottir, & Sigfusdottir, 2009). Lamb and Malloy assert that "juvenile interrogation falls at the intersection of developmental psychology and the law, and it is an area in desperate need of reform" (p. 584).

SUMMARY AND CONCLUSIONS

The goal of psychological testing and assessment is to reduce the complexity of human mental processes and behavior to a manageable set of variables, so that the current status of individuals can be appraised, interventions and treatment approaches can be recommended, and—to some extent—the individuals' future behavior can be predicted. Many mental health experts accept some futility in the predictions of behavior, particularly dangerous behavior. Therefore, and especially with respect to violence, they prefer to describe their work as assessing risk. Whether assessing risk or assessing psychological status, tests and inventories can be invaluable tools to the psychologist consulting with courts, law enforcement, the educational system, both physical and mental health agencies, the correctional system, and business and industry.

The first part of the chapter was organized around three general classifications of assessment and testing instruments and techniques: (1) clinical measures and assessment techniques, (2) forensically relevant instruments (FRIs), and (3) forensic assessment instruments (FAIs). The three categories reflect the degree of direct relevance the various instruments have to specific legal issues and topics. The number of commercially available psychological instruments that have clear forensic applications has increased dramatically, and the heavily used measures within these three categories were listed and briefly described in the chapter.

Clinical measures include cognitive and personality assessment. In the former category are standardized "intelligence tests" that have a long history of use as well as very recently designed but validated measures of intellectual achievement. Cognitive measures continue to be used extensively in the educational context, particularly with respect to determining eligibility for special education programs. They are often requested by courts dealing with juveniles and with defendants or offenders who are suspected of being intellectually disabled. Personality measures have traditionally been categorized as objective or projective, but this distinction is less firm than in the past, and some recent measures can be better placed on a continuum, displaying features of both. These are called performance-based assessment measures. Clinical assessment of mental disorders is often requested of mental health professionals. Psychologists engaged in this enterprise must be familiar with diagnoses in the DSM-5 or other classification systems.

Forensically relevant measures identify psychological characteristics that are pertinent to legal issues. Instruments to assess malingering are prominent, but as the chapter indicated, these assessments are extremely complex. Most existing measures assess feigning, not malingering, though courts are interested in knowing the motivations behind the "faking" behavior. Other examples of forensically relevant measures include measures of psychopathy and neurological assessments, such as assessments of traumatic brain injury (TBI).

Forensic assessment instruments were designed specifically to measure abilities directly relevant to the law, such as the comprehension of one's legal rights or one's competency to understand the legal process and assist one's attorney.

The chapter ended with a discussion of the forensic assessment of juveniles, which represents a topic of rapidly developing research endeavors. Experts in this area have emphasized that a consensus is emerging on the best practices to take in assessing juvenile abilities. It is now widely acknowledged that juveniles differ from adults in brain development; although they may be cognitively mature, they are more likely as a group to be emotionally immature. Decision making by juveniles, especially spontaneous decisions and those made under peer influences, cannot be regarded in the same way as decision making by adults. For these reasons, courts have given more leeway to juveniles, recommending that they should be spared the most severe punishments, such as the death penalty and mandatory life without parole, allowing them the possibility to demonstrate rehabilitation.

KEY CONCEPTS

Actuarial assessment

Clinical measures and assessment techniques

Evidence-based psychological practice

Excessive impairment

Feigned cognitive impairment

Feigned mental disorders

Feigning

Forensic assessment instruments (FAIs)

Forensically relevant instruments (FRIs)

Inventories

Malingering

Neuropsychology

Objective assessment measures

Performance-based assessment measures

Personality

Personality inventory

Projective assessment measures

Psychological assessment

Psychological evaluation

Psychological testing

Psychopath

Structured clinical judgment

Traumatic brain injury (TBI)

Unlikely presentations

Unstructured clinical judgment

Cases Cited

Addington v. Texas, 99 S.Ct. 1804 (1979).

Alabama v. Shelton, 535 U.S. 654 (2002).

Albertson's Inc. v. Kirkingburg, 527 U.S. 555 (1999).

Apodaca, Cooper, and Madden v. Oregon, 406 U.S. 404 (1972).

Argersinger v. Hamlin, 407 U.S. 25 (1972).

Arizona v. Falater, No. CR1997-000928-A (Ariz. Super.Ct. Maricopa County 1997).

Arizona v. Fulminante, 499 U.S. 279 (1991).

Ashcraft v. Tennessee, 322 U.S. 143 (1944).

Atkins v. Virginia, 536 U.S. 304 (2002).

Ballew v. Georgia, 435 U.S. 223 (1978).

Batson v. Kentucky, 476 U.S. 79 (1986).

Baxter v. Montana, P.3d WL 5155363 (Mont. 2009).

Berghuis v. Thompkins, 130 S.Ct. 2250 (2010).

Berkemer v. McCarty, 468 U.S. 420 (1984).

Borawick v. Shay, 68 F.3d 597 (2d Cir. 1995); cert. denied, 116 S.Ct. 1869 (1996).

Bowers v. Hardwick, 478 U.S. 186 (1986).

Boyer v. Louisiana 569 U.S. _____ (2013).

Brewer v. Williams, 430 U.S. 386 (1977).

Brown v. Mississippi, 297 U.S. 278 (1936).

Burch v. Louisiana, 441 U.S. 130 (1979).

California v. Prysock, 453 U.S. 355 (1981).

Carter v. United States, 252 F.2d 608 (D.C. Cir. 1957).

Charles and Drake v. State, 414 Md. 726 (2010).

Chevron v. Echazabal, 536 U.S. 73 (2002).

Clark v. Arizona, 126 S. Ct. 2709 (2006).

Coble v. Texas, 313 S.W.3d 274 (Tex.Crim.App. 2010); certiorari denied 131 S.Ct. 3030 (2011).

Colgrove v. Battin, 413 U.S. 149 (1973).

Commonwealth v. Soares, 51 Mass. App. Ct. 273 (2001).

Cooper v. Oklahoma, 116 S.Ct. 1373 (1996).

Coy v. Iowa, 108 S.Ct. 2798 (1988).

Crane v. Kentucky, 476 U.S. 683 (1986).

Cruzan v. Director, Missouri Department of Health, 497 U.S. 261 (1990).

Daubert v. Merrell Dow Pharmaceuticals, Inc., 509 U.S. 579 (1993).

Davis v. Monroe County Board of Education, 526 U.S. 629 (1999).

Davis v. United States, 512 U.S. 452 (1994).

Delaware v. Pennell, 584 A.2d 513, Del. Super.Ct. (1989).

Delaware v. Pennell, 602 A.2d 48 (Del. 1991).

Delling v. Idaho, cert. denied 133 S.Ct. 504 (2012).

Dickerson v. United States, 530 U.S. 428 (2000).

District of Columbia v. Heller, 554 U.S. 570 (2008).

Donaldson v. Montana, 2012 MT 288 (2012).

Drope v. Missouri, 420 U.S. 162 (1975).

Duckworth v. Eagan, 109 S.Ct. 2875 (1989).

Durham v. United States, 214 F.2d 862 (D.C. Cir. 1954).

Dusky v. United States, 362 U.S. 402 (1960).

Eisenstadt v. Baird, 405 U.S. 438, 454 (1972).

Escobedo v. Illinois, 378 U.S. 478 (1964).

Estelle v. Smith, 451 U.S. 454 (1981).

Fare v. Michael C., 442 U.S. 707 (1979).

Finger v. State, 27 P.3d 66 (Nev. 2001).

Fisher v. University of Texas, 570 U.S. _____ (2013).

Florida v. Powell, 130 S.Ct. 1195 (2010).

Ford v. Wainwright, 477 U.S. 399 (1986).

Foucha v. Louisiana, 504 U.S. 71 (1992).

Frye v. United States, 54 App. D.C. 46, 47 293 F. 1013, 1014 (1923).

Furman v. Georgia, 408 U.S. 238 (1972).

General Elec. Co. v. Joiner, 522 U.S. 136 (1997).

Georgia v. McCollum, 505 U.S. 42 (1992).

Gideon v. Wainwright, 372 U.S. 335 (1963).

Godinez v. Moran, 113 S.Ct. 2680 (1993).

Gonzales v. Oregon, 546 U.S. 243 (2006).

Graham v. Florida, 130 S.Ct. 2011 (2010).

Granger v. Misercola, 990 N.E. 2d 110 (2013).

Gregg v. Georgia, 428 U.S. 153 (1976).

Griswold v. Connecticut, 381 U.S. 479, 486 (1965).

Gruber v. Gruber, 583 A.2d 434 (Pa. Super. 1990).

Harding v. State, 5 Md. App. 230, 246 (1968).

Harris v. Forklift System, Inc. 510 U.S. 17 (1993).

Hodgson v. Minnesota, 497 U.S. 417 (1990).

Hollingsworth v. Perry, 570 U.S. _____ (2013).

In re Bort, 25 Kan. 215 (1881).

In re Gault, 387 U.S. 1 (1967).

Indiana v. Edwards, 554 U.S. 164 (2008).

J.D.B. v. North Carolina, 564 U.S. _____ (2011).

J.E.B. v. Alabama ex rel. T.B., 511 U.S. 127 (1994).

Jackson v. Indiana, 406 U.S. 715 (1972).

Jackson v. State, 553 So.2d 719 (1989).

Jefferson County School District v. Elizabeth E., 702 F.3d 1227 (10th Cir. 2012); cert. denied (2013).

Jenkins v. United States, 307 F.2d 637 (D.C. Cir. 1962 en banc).

Jones v. United States, 383 U.S. 541 (1966).

Kansas v. Crane, 535 U.S. 407 (2002).

Kansas v. Hendricks, 521 U.S. 117, S.Ct. 2072 (1997).

Kirby v. Illinois, 406 U.S. 682 (1972).

Kumho Tire Co., Ltd. v. Carmichael, 119 S.Ct. 1167 (1999).

Loving v. Virginia, 388 U.S. 1, 12 (1967).

Lowenfield v. Phelps, 108 S.Ct. 546 (1988).

M'Naghten, 10 Clark & Fin. 200, 210, 8 Eng. Rep. 718 (1843).

Maryland v. Craig, 497 U.S. 836 (1990).

McDonald v. City of Chicago, 561 U.S. (2010).

McKeiver v. Pennsylvania, 403 U.S. 538 (1971).

Medina v. California, 505 U.S. 437 (1992).

Michigan v. Kowalski, case number 141932 (MI S.Ct., July 30, 2012).

Miller v. Alabama and Jackson v. Hobbs, 132 S.Ct. 2455 (2012).

Miller v. Louisiana, 83 So.3d 178 (La. App. 5th Cir. 2011); cert. denied (2013).

Miller-Jenkins v. Miller-Jenkins, 12 A.3d 768, 771–772 (Vt. 2010).

Miller-Jenkins v. Miller-Jenkins, 661 S.E.2d 822 (Va. 2008).

Miranda v. Arizona, 384 U.S. 436 (1966).

Murphy v. United Parcel Service, 527 U.S. 516 (1999).

Mutual Life Insurance Company v. Terry, 82 U.S. 580 (1872).

Mutual Pharmaceutical Company v. Bartlett, 570 U.S. _____ (2013).

New York v. Quarles, 467 U.S. 649 (1984).

O'Connor v. Donaldson, 422 U.S. 563 (1975).

Oncale v. Sundowner Offshore Services, 523 U.S. 75 (1998).

Panetti v. Quarterman, 551 U.S. 930 (2007).

Pate v. Robinson, 383 U.S. 375 (1966).

Penry v. Lynaugh, 492 U.S. 302 (1989).

People v. Hickey, 86 Ill. App. 20 (1899).

Perry v. New Hampshire, 132 S.Ct. 716 (2012).

PLIVA, Inc. v. Mensing, 131 S.Ct. 2567, 564 U.S. _____ (2011).

R. v. Guilfoyle, 2 Cr. App. Rep. 57 (2001).

R. v. Hillier, ACTSC 50 (2003, Australia).

R. v. Klymchuck, 203 C.C.C.3d 341 (2005, Ont. C.A.).

R. v. Ranger, 178 C.C.C.3d 375 (2003).

R. v. Stagg, C.C.C. 14 (1994).

Regina v. Parks, 2 S.C.R. 871 (1992).

Rhode Island v. Innis, 446 U.S. 291 (1980).

Riggins v. Nevada, 504 U.S. 127 (1992).

Ring v. Arizona, 536 U.S. 584 (2002).

Rock v. Arkansas, 483 U.S. 44 (1986).

Roper v. Simmons, 125 S.Ct. 1183 (2005).

Salinas v. Texas, 133 S.Ct. 928 (2013).

Sell v. United States, 539 U.S. 166 (2003).

Shelby County v. Holder, 570 U.S. _____ (2013).

Simmons v. United States, 390 U.S. 377 (1968).

Spano v. New York, 360 U.S. 315 (1959).

Stanley v. Illinois, 405 U.S. 645 (1972).

State v. Fortin, 162 N.J. 517 (2000).

State v. Free, 798 A.2d 83 (N.J Super. Ct. App. Div. (2002).

State v. Haynes, WL 99189, Ohio Ct. App. (1988).

State v. Hurd, 86 N.J. 525, 432 A.2d 86 (1981).

State v. Lowe, 75 Ohio App. 3d 404, 599 N.E.2d 783, Ohio Ct. App. (1991).

State v. Pennell, 584 A.2d 513, Del. Super.Ct. (1989).

State v. Pennell, 602 A.2d 48, Del. (1991).

Stovall v. Denno, 388 U.S. 293 (1967).

Sutton v. United Airlines 527 U.S. 471 (1999).

Swain v. Alabama, 380 U.S. 202 (1965).

Sysyn v. State, 756 So.2d 1058; Fla. App. Lexis 4238 (2000).

Tarasoff v. Regents of the Univ. of Cal., 529 P.2d 553 (Cal. 1974), vac., reheard en banc, & aff'd 131 Cal. Rptr. 14, 551 P.2d 334 (1976).

Terry v. Ohio, 392 U.S. 1 (1968).

Thompson v. National Railroad Passenger Corp., 621 F.2d 814 (1980).

Thompson v. Oklahoma, 487 U.S. 815 (1988).

Tibbals v. Carter and Ryan v. Gonzales, 568 U.S. _____ (2013).

Toyota v. Williams, 534 U.S. 184 (2002).

Troxel v. Granville, 530 U.S. 57, 58 (2000).

United States v. Brawner, 471 F.2d 969 (D.C. Cir. 1972).

United States v. Comstock, 560 U.S., 130 S.Ct. 1949 (2010).

United States v. Dougherty, 473 F.2d 1113 (D.C. Cir. 1972).

United States v. Fields, 483 F.3d 313 (2007).

United States v. Meeks, 35 M. J. 64, 65 (C.M.A. 1992).

United States v. St. Jean, 1995 WL 106960 (1995).

United States v. Wade, 388 U.S. 218 (1967).

United States v. Windsor, 570 U.S.____ (2013).

Vacco v. Quill, 521 U.S. 793 (1997).

Vance v. Ball State University, 570 U.S. ____ (2013).

Wainwright v. Witt, 105 S.Ct. 844 (1985).

Washington v. Glucksberg, 117 S.Ct. 2258 (1997).

Washington v. Harper, 494 U.S. 210 (1990).

Williams v. Florida, 399 U.S. 78 (1970).

Witherspoon v. Illinois, 391 U.S. 510 (1968).

Yarborough v. Alvarado, 541 U.S. 652 (2004).

Zinermon v. Burch, 110 S.Ct. 975 (1990).

References

Abadinsky, H. (1995). *Law and justice* (2nd ed.). Nelson-Hall Publishers.

Abadinsky, H. (2007). *Law and justice* (6th ed.). Englewood Cliffs, NJ: Prentice Hall.

Abraham, H. J. (1998). *The judicial process* (7th ed.). New York: Oxford University Press.

Ackerman, M. J., & Brey Pritzl, T. (2011). Child custody evaluation practices: A 20-year follow-up. *Family Court Review, 49,* 618–628.

Adam, K. S., & Brady, S. N. (2013). Fifty years of judging in family law: The Cleavers have left the building. *Family Court Review, 51,* 28–33.

Administration on Aging. (2006). *A profile of older Americans: 2006.* Washington, DC: Department of Health and Human Services.

Advokat, C. D., Guidry, D., Burnett, D. M. R., Manguno-Mire, G., & Thompson, J. W. (2012). Competency restoration treatment: Differences between defendants declared competent or incompetent to stand trial. *Journal of the American Academy of Psychiatry and Law, 40,* 89–97.

Aizpurua, A., Garcia-Bajos, E., & Migueles, M. (2009). False memories for a robbery in young and older adults. *Applied Cognitive Psychology, 23,* 174–187.

Albert, D., Chein, J., & Steinberg, L. (2013). The teenage brain: Peer influences on adolescent decision making. *Current Directions in Psychological Science, 22,* 114–120.

Albert, D., & Steinberg, L. (2011a). Judgment and decision making in adolescence. *Journal of Research on Adolescence, 21,* 211–224.

Albert, D., & Steinberg, L. (2011b). Peer influences on adolescent risk behavior. In M. T. Bardo, D. H. Fishbein, & R. Milch (Eds.), *Inhibitory control and drug abuse prevention: From research to translation* (pp. 211–228). New York: Springer.

Alison, L. J., West, A., & Goodwill, A. (2004). The academic and the practitioner: Pragmatists' views of offender profiling. *Psychology, Public Policy, and Law, 10,* 71–101.

Amato, P. R. (2000). The consequences of divorce for adults and children. *Journal of Marriage and the Family, 62,* 1269–1287.

Amato, P. R. (2001). Children of divorce in the 1990s: An update of the Amato and Keith (1991) meta-analysis. *Journal of Family Psychology, 15,* 355–370.

Amato, P. R. (2010). Research on divorce: Continuing trends and new developments. *Journal of Marriage and Family, 72,* 650–666.

American Academy of Child and Adolescent Psychiatry. (1997). Practice parameters for the forensic evaluation of children and adolescents who may have been physically or sexually abused. *Journal of the American Academy of Child & Adolescent Psychiatry, 36,* 423–442.

American Bar Association Commission on Law and Aging and the American Psychological Association. (2008). *Assessment of older adults with diminished capacity: A handbook for psychologists.* Washington, DC: American Bar Association.

American College of Trial Lawyers. (2004). *The "vanishing trial": The college, the profession, the civil justice system.* Irvine, CA: Author.

American Educational Research Association, American Psychological Association, and

National Council on Measurement in Education. (1999). *Standards for educational and psychological testing.* Washington, DC: American Educational Research Association.

American Psychiatric Association. (2013). *Diagnostic and statistical manual of mental disorders* (5th ed.). Arlington, VA: Author.

American Psychiatric Association Task Force. (1992). *The use of psychiatric diagnosis in the legal process.* Washington, DC: American Psychiatric Association.

American Psychological Association. (2002). Ethical principles of psychologists and code of conduct. *American Psychologist, 57,* 1060–1073.

American Psychological Association. (2003, October 25). *Report: End-of-life issues and assisted suicide. Public Interest APA Online.* Washington, DC: Author.

American Psychological Association. (2010a). Amendments to the 2002 "Ethical Principles of Psychologists and Code of Conduct." *American Psychologist, 65,* 493.

American Psychological Association. (2010b). Guidelines for child custody evaluations in family law proceedings. *American Psychologist, 65,* 863–867.

American Psychological Association. (2011). Guidelines for assessment of and intervention with persons with disabilities. *American Psychologist, 67,* 43–62.

American Psychological Association. (2013a). Guidelines for psychological evaluations in child protection matters. *American Psychologist, 68,* 20–31.

American Psychological Association. (2013b). Specialty guidelines for forensic psychology. *American Psychologist, 68,* 7–19.

Anastasi, J. S., & Rhodes, M. G. (2006). Evidence for an own-age bias in face recognition. *North American Journal of Psychology, 8,* 237–252.

Andrews, P., Meyer, R. G., & Berlà, E. P. (1996). Development of the Lost Pleasure of Life Scale. *Law and Human Behavior, 20,* 99–111.

Antonio, M. E. (2006). Arbitrariness and the death penalty: How the defendant's appearance during trial influences capital jurors' punishment decision. *Behavioral Sciences & the Law, 24,* 215–234.

APA Presidential Task Force on Evidence-Based Practice. (2006). Evidence-based practice in psychology. *American Psychologist, 61,* 271–285.

Appelbaum, P. S., & Grisso, T. (1995). The MacArthur Treatment Competence Study: I. Mental illness and competence to consent to treatment. *Law and Human Behavior, 19,* 105–126.

Appelbaum, P. S., Jick, R. Z., Grisso, T., Givelbar, D., Silver, E., & Steadman, H. J. (1993). Use of posttraumatic stress to support an insanity defense. *American Journal of Psychiatry, 150,* 229–234.

Appleby, S. C., Hasel, L. E., & Kassin, S. M. (2013). Police-induced confessions: An empirical analysis of their content and impact. *Psychology, Crime & Law, 19,* 111–128.

Arvanites, T. M. (1988). The impact of state mental hospital deinstitutionalization on commitments for incompetency to stand trial. *Criminology, 26,* 307–320.

Asch, S. E. (1952). *Social psychology.* Englewood Cliffs, NJ: Prentice Hall.

Aspinwall, L. G., Brown, T. R., & Tabery, J. (2012). The double-edged sword: Does biomechanism increase or decrease judges' sentencing of psychopaths? *Science, 337,* 846–849.

Association of Family and Conciliation Courts. (2006). *Model standards of practice for child custody evaluation.* Madison, WI: Author.

Atkinson, J. (2010). The law of relocation of children. *Behavioral Sciences & the Law, 28,* 563–579.

Austin, W. G. (2008a). Relocation, research, and forensic evaluation: Part I. Effects of residential mobility on children of divorce. *Family Court Review, 46,* 136–149.

Austin, W. G. (2008b). Relocation, research, and forensic evaluation: Part II. Research support for the relocation risk assessment model. *Family Court Review, 46,* 347–365.

Austin, W. G., Dale, M. D., Kirkpatrick, H. D., & Flens, J. R. (2011). Forensic expert roles and services in child custody litigation: Work product review and case consultation. *Journal of Child Custody, 8,* 47–83.

Austin, W. G., Kirkpatrick, H. D., & Flens, J. R. (2011). The emerging forensic role for work product review and case analysis in child access and parenting plan disputes. *Family Court Review, 49,* 737–749.

Aviv, R. (2013, January 14). The science of sex abuse: Is it right to imprison people for heinous crimes they have not yet committed? *The New Yorker,* pp. 36–45.

Bala, N. (1999). Child witnesses in the Canadian criminal courts: Recognizing their capacities and needs. *Psychology, Public Policy, and Law, 5,* 323–354.

Bales, R. F., & Borgatta, E. F. (1955). Size of group as a factor in the interaction profile. In A. P. Hare, E. F. Borgatta, & R. F. Bales (Eds.), *Small groups: Studies in social interaction* (pp. 495–512). New York: Knopf.

Ballard, R. H., Holtzworth-Munroe, A., Applegate, A. G., & D'Onofrio, B. (2011). Factors affecting the outcome of divorce and paternity mediations. *Family Court Review, 49,* 16–33.

Barber, T. X., Spanos, N. R., & Chaves, J. F. (1974). *Hypnosis, imagination, and human potentialities.* New York: Pergamon Press.

Barland, G. H. (1988). The polygraph test in the USA and elsewhere. In A. Gale (Ed.), *The polygraph test: Lies, truth, and science* (pp. 73–95). London: Sage.

Barland, G. H., & Raskin, D. C. (1973). Detection of deception. In W. F. Prokasy & D. C. Raskin (Eds.), *Electrodermal activity in psychological research* (pp. 417–477). New York: Academic Press.

Baron, R. A., & Byrne, D. (1981). *Social psychology: Understanding human interaction* (3rd ed.). Boston: Allyn & Bacon.

Baron, R. A., & Byrne, D. (2000). *Social psychology* (9th ed.). Boston: Allyn & Bacon.

Bartol, C. R., & Bartol, A. M. (2013). *Criminal and behavioral profiling.* Los Angeles: SAGE.

Baskin, D. R., & Sommers, I. B. (2010). Crime-show-viewing habits and public attitudes toward forensic evidence: The "CSI effect" revisited. *The Justice System Journal, 31,* 97–113.

Baum, L. (2010). Motivation and judicial behavior: Expanding the scope of inquiry. In D. E. Klein & G. Mitchell (Eds.), *The psychology of judicial decision making* (pp. 3–25). New York: Oxford University Press.

Bauserman, R. (2002). Child adjustment in joint custody versus sole custody arrangements: A meta-analytical review. *Journal of Family Psychology, 16,* 91–102.

Bauserman, R. (2012). A meta-analysis of parental satisfaction, adjustment, and conflict in joint custody and sole custody following divorce. *Journal of Divorce & Remarriage, 53,* 464–488.

Beal, S. S., & Felman, J. E. (2011). Enlisting and deploying federal grand juries in the war on terrorism. In R. A. Fairfax, Jr. (Ed.), *Grand jury 2.0: Modern perspectives on the grand jury* (pp. 3–24). Durham, NC: Carolina Academic Press.

Beck, C. J. A., Sales, B. D., & Emery, R. E. (2004). Research on the impact of family mediation. In J. Folberg, A. L. Milne, & P. Salem (Eds.), *Divorce and family mediation* (pp. 447–482). New York: Guilford Press.

Belenko, S. (1998). *Research on drug courts: A critical review.* New York: National Center on Addiction and Substance Abuse.

Benjamin, G. A. H., Werth, J. L., & Gostin, L. O. (Eds.). (2000). Special theme: Hastened death. *Psychology, Public Policy, and Law, 6,* 262–267.

Benjet, C., Azar, S. T., & Kuersten-Hogan, R. (2003). Evaluating the parental fitness of psychiatrically diagnosed individuals: Advocating a functional-contextual analysis of parenting. *Journal of Family Psychology, 17,* 238–251.

Bennell, C., Jones, N. J., & Taylor, A. (2011). Determining the authenticity of suicide notes: Can training improve human judgment? *Criminal Justice and Behavior, 38,* 669–689.

Bennell, C., Snook, B., MacDonald, S., House, J. C., & Taylor, P. J. (2012). Computerized crime linkage systems: A critical review and research agenda. *Criminal Justice and Behavior, 39,* 620–634.

Ben-Porath, Y. S., & Tellegen, A. (2008). *Minnesota Multiphasic Personality Inventory-2-Restructured Form: Manual for administration, scoring, and interpretation.* Minneapolis: University of Minnesota Press.

Ben-Shakhar, G. (2002). A critical review of the control questions test (CQT). In M. Kleiner (Ed.), *Handbook of polygraph testing* (pp. 103–126). San Diego, CA: Academic Press.

Ben-Shakhar, G., Bar-Hillel, M., & Lieblich, I. (1986). Trial by polygraph: Scientific and juridical issues in lie detection. *Behavioral Sciences & the Law, 4,* 459–479.

Ben-Shakhar, G., & Elaad, E. (2002). The guilty knowledge test (GKT) as an application of psychophysiology: Future prospects and obstacles. The comparison questions test. In M. Kleiner (Ed.), *Handbook of polygraph testing* (pp. 87–102). San Diego, CA: Academic Press.

Ben-Shakhar, G., & Furedy, J. J. (1990). *Theories and applications in the detection of deception: A psychophysiological and international perspective.* New York: Springer-Verlag.

Berlà, E. P., Andrews, P., & Berlà, K. A. (1999). Loss of pleasure of life: Conceptual, vocational, and forensic perspectives. *Journal of Career Assessment, 7,* 200–321.

Bernard, T. (1992). *The cycle of juvenile justice.* New York: Oxford University Press.

Berry, W. W. (2010). Ending death by dangerousness: A path to the de facto abolition of the death penalty. *Arizona Law Review, 52,* 889–924.

Bersoff, D. N., & Ogden, D. W. (1991). APA amicus curiae briefs: Furthering lesbian and gay male civil rights. *American Psychologist, 46,* 950–956.

Bigler, E. D., & Brooks, M. (2009). Traumatic brain injury and forensic neuropsychology. *Journal of Head Trauma Rehabilitation, 24,* 76–87.

Black, H. C. (1990). *Black's law dictionary* (6th ed.). St. Paul, MN: West Publishing.

Blair, I. V., Judd, C. M., & Chapleau, K. M. (2004). The influence of Afrocentric facial features in criminal sentencing. *Psychological Science, 15,* 674–679.

Blake, D. D., Weathers, F. W., & Nagy, L. M. (1995). The development of a clinician-administered PTSD scale. *Journal of Traumatic Stress, 8,* 75–90.

Blanck, P. D., & Berven, H. M. (1999). Evidence of disability after *Daubert. Psychology, Public Policy, and Law, 5,* 16–40.

Block, S. D., Shestowsky, D., Segovia, D. A., Goodman, G. S., Schaaf, J. M., & Weed Alexander, K. (2012). "That never happened": Adults' discernment of children's true and false memory reports. *Law and Human Behavior, 36,* 365–374.

Blum, J. H., Garvey, S. P., & Johnson, S. L. (2001). Future dangerousness in capital cases: Always at issue. *Cornell Law Review, 86,* 397–438.

Blume, J. H. (2008). *An overview of significant findings from the Capital Jury Project and other empirical studies of the death penalty relevant to jury selection, presentation of evidence and jury instructions in capital cases.* Retrieved October 25, 2013, from http://web.knoxnews .com/pdf/112208carjack2.pdf

Blume, J. H., Eisenberg, T., & Garvey, S. P. (2003). Lessons from the Capital Jury Project. In S. Garvey (Ed.), *Beyond repair? America's death penalty* (pp. 144–177). Durham, NC: Duke University Press.

Blunk, R., & Sales, B. D. (1977). Persuasion during the voir dire. In B. D. Sales (Ed.), *Psychology in the legal process* (pp. 39–58). New York: Spectrum.

Boccaccini, M. T., & Brodsky, S. L. (1999). Diagnostic test usage by forensic psychologists in emotional injury cases. *Professional Psychology: Research and Practice, 30,* 253–259.

Boccaccini, M. T., Murrie, D. C., & Duncan, S. A. (2006). Screening for malingering in a criminal-forensic sample with the Personality Assessment Inventory. *Psychological Assessment, 18,* 415–423.

Boer, D. P., Hart, S. D., Kropp, P. R., & Webster, C. D. (1997). *Manual for the Sexual Violence Risk-20.* Vancouver, B.C., Canada: The British Columbia Institute Against Family Violence.

Bohm, R. M. (1999). *Deathquest: An introduction to the theory and practice of capital punishment in the United States.* Cincinnati, OH: Anderson.

Bolocofsky, D. N. (1989). Use and abuse of mental health experts in child custody determinations. *Behavioral Sciences & the Law, 7,* 197–213.

Boltz, M. G., Dyer, R. L., & Miller, A. R. (2010). Are you lying to me? Temporal cues for deception. *Journal of Language and Social Psychology, 29*, 458–466.

Bond, C. F., Jr., & DePaulo, B. M. (2006). Accuracy of deception judgments. *Personality and Social Psychology Review, 10*, 214–234.

Bond, R. (2008). The lingering debate over the parental alienation syndrome phenomenon. *Journal of Child Custody, 4*, 37–54.

Bonnie, R. J. (1990). Dilemmas in administering the death penalty: Conscientious abstentions, professional ethics, and the needs of the legal system. *Law and Human Behavior, 14*, 67–90.

Bonnie, R. J. (1992). The competence of criminal defendants: A theoretical reformulation. *Behavioral Sciences & the Law, 10*, 291–316.

Bonnie, R. J., & Grisso, T. (2000). Adjudicative competence and youth offenders. In T. Grisso & R. G. Schwartz (Eds.), *Youth on trial: A developmental perspective on juvenile justice* (pp. 73–103). Chicago: University of Chicago Press.

Bonnie, R. J., & Scott, E. S. (2013). The teenage brain: Adolescent brain research and the law. *Current Directions in Psychological Science, 22*, 158–161.

Bonowitz, J. C., & Bonowitz, J. S. (1981). Diversion of the mentally ill into the criminal justice system: The police intervention perspective. *American Journal of Psychiatry, 138*, 973–976.

Bonsignore, J. J., Arons, S., Katsh, E., Pipkin, R. M., d'Errico, P., et al. (2006). *Before the law: An introduction to the legal process*. Belmont, CA: Wadsworth/Cengage.

Bonta, J., Law, M., & Hanson, K. (1998). The prediction of criminal and violent recidivism among mentally disordered offenders: A meta-analysis. *Psychological Bulletin, 3*, 123–142.

Boone, K. B. (2013). *Clinical practice of forensic neuropsychology: An evidence-based approach*. New York: Guilford Press.

Booth, A., & Amato, P. R. (2001). Parental predivorce relations and offspring postdivorce well-being. *Journal of Marriage and Family, 63*, 197–212.

Borgida, E., & Park, R. (1988). The entrapment defenses: Juror comprehension and decision making. *Law and Human Behavior, 12*, 19–31.

Bornstein, B. H. (1999). The ecological validity of jury simulations: Is the jury still out? *Law and Human Behavior, 23*, 75–91.

Bornstein, B. H., & Greene, E. (2011). Jury decision making: Implications for and from psychology. *Current Directions in Psychological Science, 20*, 63–67.

Borum, R. (1996). Improving the clinical practice of violence risk assessment: Technology, guidelines, and training. *American Psychologist, 51*, 945–956.

Borum, R., & Fulero, S. M. (1999). Empirical research on the insanity defense and attempted reforms: Evidence toward informed policy. *Law and Human Behavior, 23*, 375–394.

Bosco, D., Zappala, A., & Santtila, P. (2010). The admissibility of offender profiling in the courtroom: A review of legal issues and court opinions. *International Journal of Law and Psychiatry, 33*, 184–191.

Bottoms, B. L., Goodman, G. S., Schwartz-Kenney, B. M., & Thomas, S. N. (2002). Understanding children's use of secrecy in the context of eyewitness reports. *Law and Human Behavior, 26*, 285–313.

Bourchier, A., & Davis, A. (2002). Children's understanding of the pretence–reality distinction: A review of current theory and evidence. *Developmental Science, 5*, 397–426.

Bourque, J., LeBlanc, S., Utzschneider, A., & Wright, C. (2009, March). *The effectiveness of profiling from a national security perspective*. Ottawa, ON: Canadian Human Rights Commission.

Bow, J. N. (2006). Review of empirical research on child custody practice. *Journal of Child Custody, 3*, 23–50.

Bow, J. N. (2010). Use of third party information in child custody evaluations. *Behavioral Sciences & the Law, 28*, 511–521.

Bow, J. N., & Boxer, P. (2003). Assessing allegations of domestic violence in child custody evaluations. *Journal of Interpersonal Violence, 18*, 1394–1410.

Bow, J. N., Gottlieb, M. C., & Gould-Saltman, D. (2011). Attorneys' beliefs and opinions about child custody evaluations. *Family Court Review, 49*, 301–312.

Bow, J. N., & Quinnell, F. A. (2001). Psychologists' current practices and procedures in child custody evaluations: Five years post American Psychological Association guidelines. *Professional Psychology: Research and Practice, 32*, 261–268.

Bow, J. N., Quinnell, F. A., Zaroff, M., & Assemany, A. (2002). Assessment of sexual abuse allegation in child custody cases. *Professional Psychology: Research and Practice, 33*, 566–575.

Bowers, W. J. (1995). The Capital Jury Project: Rationale, design, and preview of early findings. *Indiana Law Review, 70*, 1043–1068.

Bowers, W. J., Steiner, B. D., & Sandys, M. (2001). Death sentencing in black and white: An empirical analysis of the role of jurors' race and jury racial composition. *University of Pennsylvania Constitutional Law, 3*, 171–274.

Bowlby, J. (1982). *Attachment and loss: Vol. 1. Attachment.* New York: Basic Books.

Boyarin, Y. (2012). Court-connected ADR—A time of crisis, a time of change. *Family Court Review, 50*, 377–404.

Braden, J. P. (2013). Psychological assessment in school settings. In I. B. Weiner (Ed.), *Handbook of psychology: Vol. 10. Assessment* (2nd ed., pp. 291–314). Hoboken, NJ: Wiley.

Brainerd, C. J., & Reyna, V. F. (2012). Reliability of children's testimony in the era of developmental reversals. *Developmental Review, 32*, 224–267.

Braver, S. L., Ellman, I. M., & Fabricius, W. V. (2003). Relocation of children after divorce and children's best interests: New evidence and legal considerations. *Journal of Family Psychology, 17*, 206–219.

Bray, J. H. (1990). Impact of divorce on the family. In R. E. Rakel (Ed.), *Textbook of family practice* (4th ed.). Philadelphia: W. B. Saunders.

Bray, J. H. (1991). Psychosocial factors affecting custodial and visitation arrangements. *Behavioral Sciences & the Law, 9*, 419–437.

Bray, R. M., & Kerr, N. L. (1979). Use of simulation method in the study of jury behavior: Some methodological considerations. *Law and Human Behavior, 3*, 107–120.

Bray, R. M., Struckman-Johnson, C., Osborne, M. D., McFarlane, J. B., & Scott, J. (1978). The effects of defendant status on the decisions of students and community juries. *Social Psychology, 41*, 256–260.

Brehm, J. W. (1966). *A theory of psychological reactance.* New York: Academic Press.

Brenner, S. W., & Shaw, L. (2003). *State grand juries.* Dayton, OH: University of Dayton School of Law.

Brewer, N., Weber, N., Wooton, D., & Lindsay, D. S. (2012). Identifying the bad guy in a lineup using confidence judgments under deadline pressure. *Psychological Science, 23*, 1208–1214.

Brewer, N., & Wells, G. L. (2006). The confidence–accuracy relationship in eyewitness identification: Effects of lineup instructions, foil similarity, and target-absent base rates. *Journal of Experimental Psychology: Applied, 12*, 11–30.

Brewer, N., & Wells, G. L. (2011). Eyewitness identification. *Current Directions in Psychological Science, 20*, 24–27.

Bridge, B. J. (2006). Solving the family court puzzle: Integrating research, policy, and practice. *Family Court Review, 44*, 190–199.

Brigham, J. C., & Cairns, D. L. (1988). The effect of mugshot inspections on eyewitness identification accuracy. *Journal of Applied Social Psychology, 18*, 1394–1410.

Brodsky, S. L. (2004). *Coping with cross-examination and other pathways to effective testimony.* Washington, DC: American Psychological Association.

Brody, D. C., & Rivera, C. (1997). Examining the Dougherty "all-knowing" assumption: Do jurors know about their nullification power? *Criminal Law Bulletin, 33*, 151–167.

Brooks, A. D. (1974). *Law, psychiatry and the mental health system.* Boston: Little, Brown.

Brooks, A. D. (1986). Law and antipsychotic medications. *Behavioral Sciences & the Law, 4*, 247–263.

Brooks, S. L. (1999). Therapeutic jurisprudence and preventive law in child welfare proceedings: A family systems approach. *Psychology, Public Policy, and Law, 5,* 951–965.

Brown, D., Scheflin, A. W., & Hammond, D. C. (1998). *Memory, trauma treatment, and the law.* New York: Norton.

Bruch, C. S. (2001). Parental alienation syndrome and parental alienation: Getting it wrong in child custody cases. *Family Law Quarterly, 35,* 527–552.

Bruck, M., & Ceci, S. J. (2009). Reliability of child witnesses' reports. In J. L. Skeem, K. S. Douglas, & S. O. Lilienfeld (Eds.), *Psychological science in the courtroom: Consensus and controversy* (pp. 149–174). New York: Guilford Press.

Bruck, M., & Ceci, S. J. (2012). Forensic developmental psychology in the courtroom. In D. Faust (Ed.), *Coping with psychiatric and psychological testimony* (pp. 723–737). New York: Oxford University Press.

Brunnell, T., Chetan, D., & Morgan, N. C. (2009). Factors affecting the length of time a jury deliberates: Case characteristics and jury composition. *Review of Law & Economics, 5,* 555–578.

Bryan, P. E. (1999). "Collaborative divorce": Meaningful reform or another quick fix? *Psychology, Public Policy, and Law, 5,* 1001–1017.

Buchanan, C., Maccoby, E., & Dornbusch, S. (1991). Caught between parents: Adolescents' experience in divorced homes. *Child Development, 62,* 1008–1029.

Buck, J., Louden, J. E., Hall, T., Huss, M., Meissner, C., & Pivovarova, E. (2012, Summer). Gender differences in professional development among AP-LS members: Results of the Professional Development of Women survey. *Division 41, American Psychological Association Newsletter,* 1–12. Retrieved October 29, 2013, from http://www.ap-ls.org/publications/newsletters/Summer2012.pdf

Buckhout, R. (1974). Eyewitness testimony. *Scientific American, 321,* 23–31.

Budd, K. S., Felix, E. D., Poindexter, L. M., Naik-Polan, A. T., & Sloss, C. F. (2002). Clinical assessment of children in child protection cases: An empirical analysis. *Professional Psychology: Research and Practice, 33,* 3–12.

Bulkley, J. S. (1989). The impact of new child witness research on sexual abuse prosecutions. In S. J. Ceci, D. F. Ross, & M. P. Toglia (Eds.), *Perspectives on children's testimony* (pp. 208–229). New York: Springer-Verlag.

Bull, R. H. (1988). What is the lie-detection test? In A. Gale (Ed.), *The polygraph test: Lies, truth and science* (pp. 10–18). Newbury Park, CA: Sage.

Bunce, L., & Harris, M. (2008). "I saw the real Father Christmas!" Children's everyday uses of real, really, and pretend. *British Journal of Developmental Psychology, 26,* 445–455.

Bunce, L., & Harris, M. (2013). "He hasn't got the real toolkit!" Young children's reasoning about real/not real status. *Developmental Psychology, 49,* 1494–1504.

Burdon, W. M., & Gallagher, C. A. (2002). Coercion and sex offenders: Controlling sex-offending behavior through incapacitation and treatment. *Criminal Justice and Behavior, 29,* 87–109.

Burgoon, J. K., Blair, J. P., & Strom, R. E. (2008). Cognitive biases and nonverbal cue availability in detecting deception. *Human Communication Research, 34,* 572–599.

Burkholder, G. J., & Burbank, P. (2012, October). Caring for lesbian, gay, bisexual, and transsexual parents and their children. *International Journal of Childbirth Education, 27*(4), 12–18.

Burnett, S., Sebastian, C., Cohen Kadosh, K., & Blakemore, S. J. (2011). The social brain in adolescence: Evidence from functional magnetic resonance imaging and behavioural studies. *Neuroscience & Biobehavioral Reviews, 35,* 1654–1664.

Byrne, D. (1974). *An introduction to personality* (2nd ed.). Englewood Cliffs, NJ: Prentice Hall.

Callahan, L. A., & Silver, E. (1998). Factors associated with the conditional release of persons acquitted by reason of insanity: A decision tree approach. *Law and Human Behavior, 22,* 147–163.

Callahan, L. A., Steadman, H. J., McGreevy, M. A., & Robbins, P. C. (1991). The volume and characteristics of insanity defense pleas: An eight-state study. *Bulletin of Psychiatry and the Law, 19,* 331–338.

Camara, W. J., & Merenda, P. F. (2000). Using personality tests in pre-employment screening. *Psychology, Public Policy, and Law, 6,* 1164–1186.

Canter, D. V., Alison, L. J., Alison, E., & Wentink, N. (2004). The organized/disorganized typology of serial murder: Myth or model? *Psychology, Public Policy, and Law, 10,* 293–320.

Cantor, N. L. (1989). The permanently unconscious patient, non-feeding and euthanasia. *American Journal of Law and Medicine, 15,* 381–437.

Carlson, C. A., & Carlson, M. A. (2012). A distinctiveness-driven reversal of the weapon-focused effect. *Applied Psychology in Criminal Justice, 8,* 36–53.

Carlson, K. A., & Russo, J. E. (2001). Biased interpretation of evidence by mock jurors. *Journal of Experimental Psychology: Applied, 7,* 91–103.

Carpenter, N. C., & Paetzold, R. L. (2013). An examination of factors influencing responses to requests for disability accommodations. *Rehabilitation Psychology, 58,* 18–27.

Carrick, N., & Quas, J. (2006). Effects of discrete emotions on young children's ability to discern fantasy and reality. *Developmental Psychology, 42,* 1278–1288.

Carrión, R. E., Keenan, J. P., & Sebanz, N. (2010). A truth that's told with bad intent: An ERP study of deception. *Cognition, 114,* 105–110.

Carroll, J. F. (1990). Treating drug addicts with mental health problems in a therapeutic community. *Journal of Chemical Dependency Treatment, 3,* 237–259.

Ceci, S. J., & Bruck, M. (1993). Suggestibility of the child witness: A historical review and synthesis. *Psychological Bulletin, 113,* 403–439.

Ceci, S. J., Ross, D. F., & Toglia, M. P. (1987). Age differences in suggestibility: Narrowing the uncertainties. In S. J. Ceci, M. P. Toglia, & D. F. Ross (Eds.), *Children's eyewitness memory* (pp. 79–91). New York: Springer-Verlag.

Child Welfare Information Gateway. (2010, March). *Determining the best interests of the child: Summary of state laws.* Retrieved October 29, 2013, from https://www .childwelfare.gov/systemwide/laws_policies/ statutes/best_interest.cfm

Christy, A., Clark, C., Frei, A., & Rynearson-Moody, S. (2012). Challenges of diverting veterans to trauma informed care: The heterogeneity of Intercept 2. *Criminal Justice and Behavior, 39,* 461–474.

Cirincione, C., & Jacobs, C. (1999). Identifying insanity acquittals: Is it any easier? *Law and Human Behavior, 23,* 487–497.

Cirincione, C., Steadman, H., & McGreevy, M. (1995). Rates of insanity acquittals and the factors associated with successful insanity pleas. *Bulletin of the American Academy of Psychiatry and Law, 23,* 399–409.

Clark, S. E. (2012). Costs and benefits of eyewitness identification reform: Psychological science and public policy. *Perspectives on Psychological Science, 7,* 238–259.

Clear, T. R., & Cole, G. F. (2000). *American corrections* (5th ed.). Belmont, CA: West/Wadsworth.

Cochrane, R. E., Grisso, T., & Frederick, R. I. (2001). The relationship between criminal charges, diagnoses, and psycholegal opinions among federal defendants. *Behavioral Sciences & the Law, 19,* 565–582.

Cohen, F. (2008). *The mentally disordered inmate and the law* (2nd ed.). Kingston, NJ: Civic Research Institute.

Cohen, T. H., & Reaves, B. A. (2006). *Felony defendants in large urban counties, 2002.* Washington, DC: U.S. Department of Justice, Office of Justice Programs, Bureau of Justice Statistics.

Cole, S. A., & Dioso-Villa, R. (2009). Investigating the "CSI effect" effect: Media and litigation crisis in criminal law. *Stanford Law Review, 61,* 1335–1373.

Collins, J. J., & Bailey, S. L. (1990). Traumatic stress disorder and violent behavior. *Journal of Traumatic Stress, 3,* 203–220.

Colwell, L. H., & Gianesini, J. (2011). Demographic, criminogenic, and psychiatry factors that predict competency restoration. *Journal of the*

American Academy of Psychiatry and Law, 39, 297–306.

Committee on Ethical Guidelines for Forensic Psychologists. (1991). Specialty guidelines for forensic psychologists. *Law and Human Behavior, 15*, 655–665.

Conley, J. M. (2000). Epilogue: A legal and cultural commentary on the psychology of jury instructions. *Psychology, Public Policy, and Law, 6*, 822–831.

Connell, M. (2010). Parenting plan evaluation standards and guidelines for psychologists: Setting the frame. *Behavioral Sciences & the Law, 28*, 492–510.

Consigli, J. E. (2002). Post-conviction sex offender testing and the American Polygraph Association. In M. Kleiner (Ed.), *Handbook of polygraph testing* (pp. 237–250). San Diego, CA: Academic Press.

Cooper, J., & Neuhaus, I. M. (2000). The "hired gun" effect: Assessing the effect of pay, frequency of testifying, and credentials on the perception of expert testimony. *Law and Human Behavior, 24*, 149–171.

Copson, G., Badcock, R., Boon, J., & Britton, P. (1997). Articulating a systematic approach to clinical crime profiling. *Criminal Behaviour and Mental Health, 7*, 13–17.

Cornwell, E. Y., & Hans, V. P. (2011). Representation through participation: A multilevel analysis of jury deliberations. *Law & Society Review, 45*, 667–698.

Coronado, V. G., Xu, L., Basavaraju, S. V., McGuire, L. C., Wald, M. M., Faul, M. E., et al. (2011, May). *Surveillance for traumatic brain injury–related deaths—United States, 1997–2007.* Atlanta, GA: Centers for Disease Control and Prevention, Division of Injury Response.

Covati, C. J., Foley, L. A., & Coffman, K. A. (2001). Surviving spouse's demeanor and role theory in a wrongful death civil trial. *American Journal of Forensic Psychology, 19*, 41–56.

Cowan, C. L., Thompson, W. C., & Ellsworth, P. C. (1984). The effects of death qualification on jurors' predisposition to convict and on the quality of the deliberation. *Law and Human Behavior, 8*, 53–79.

Cox, M., & Tanford, S. (1989). An alternative method of capital jury selection. *Law and Human Behavior, 13*, 167–183.

Craig, R. J. (2013). Assessing personality and psychopathology with interviews. In J. R. Graham, J. A. Naglieri, & I. B. Weiner (Eds.), *Handbook of psychology: Vol. 10. Assessment psychology* (2nd ed., pp. 558–582). Hoboken, NJ: Wiley.

Cramer Bornemann, M. A., Mahowald, M. W., & Schenck, C. H. (2006). Parasomnias: Clinical features and forensic implications. *Chest, 130*, 605–610.

Cruise, K. R., & Rogers, R. (1998). An analysis of competency to stand trial: An integration of case law and clinical knowledge. *Behavioral Sciences & the Law, 16*, 35–50.

Cunningham, A., & Hurley, P. (2007a). *A full and candid account: Overview of issues related to child testimony.* London, Ont., Canada: Centre for Children and Families in the Justice System.

Cunningham, A., & Hurley, P. (2007b). *A full and candid account: Using special accommodations and testimonial aid to facilitate the testimony of children.* London, Ont., Canada: Centre for Children and Families in the Justice System.

Davies, G. (1999). The impact of television on the presentation and reception of children's testimony. *International Journal of Law and Psychiatry, 22*, 241–256.

Davies, G., & Noon, E. (1991). *An evaluation of the live link for child witnesses.* London: Home Office.

Davis, D., & Loftus, E. F. (2005). Age and functioning in the legal system: Perception, memory, and judgment in victims, witnesses and jurors. In I. Noy & W. Karwowski (Eds.), *Handbook of forensic human factors and ergonomics.* London: Taylor & Francis.

Dawes, R. M., Faust, D., & Meehl, P. E. (1989). Clinical vs. actuarial judgment. *Science, 243*, 1668–1674.

Deffenbacher, K. A., Bornstein, B. H., McGorty, E. K., & Penrod, S. D. (2008). Forgetting the once-seen face: Estimating the strength of an eyewitness's memory representation. *Journal of Experimental Psychology: Applied, 14,* 139–150.

DeMatteo, D., & Heilbrun, K. (2012, April). (Eds.). Diversion from standard prosecution. Special issue, *Criminal Justice and Behavior.*

DeMatteo, D., Marczk, G., Krauss, D. A., & Burl, J. (2009). Educational and training models in forensic psychology. *Training and Education in Professional Psychology, 3,* 184–191.

DeMatteo, D., Marlowe, D. B., Festinger, D. S., & Arabia, P. L. (2009). Outcome trajectories in drug courts: Do all participants have serious drug problems? *Criminal Justice and Behavior, 36,* 354–368.

DePaulo, B. M., Lindsay, J. J., Malone, B. E., Muhlenbruck, L., Charlton, K., & Cooper, H. (2003). Cues to deception. *Psychological Bulletin, 129,* 74–118.

Dershowitz, A. M. (1974). The origins of preventive confinement in Anglo-American law: Part 2. The American experience. *University of Cincinnati Law Review, 43,* 781–846.

Deutsch, A. (1949). *The mentally ill in America.* New York: Columbia University Press.

Devine, D. J. (2012a, Summer). Jurors and the Internet: Where are the data? *Newsletter of the American Psychology-Law Society,* 16–17.

Devine, D. (2012b). *Jury decision making: The state of the science.* New York: NYU Press.

Devine, D. J., Clayton, L. D., Dunford, B. B., Seying, R., & Pryce, J. (2001). Jury decision making: 45 years of empirical research on deliberating groups. *Psychology, Public Policy, and Law, 7,* 622–727.

Diamond, S. S. (1993). Instructing on death: Psychologists, juries, and judges. *American Psychologist, 48,* 423–434.

Diamond, S. S. (1997). Illuminations and shadows from jury simulations. *Law and Human Behavior, 21,* 561–571.

Diamond, S. S., & Levi, J. N. (1996). Improving decisions on death by revising and testing jury instructions. *Judicature, 79,* 224–232.

Diamond, S. S., Peery, D., Dolan, F. J., & Dolan, E. (2009). Achieving diversity on the jury: Jury size and the peremptory challenge. *Journal of Empirical Legal Studies, 6,* 425–449.

Dilworth, D. C. (1997, August). Federal judges can remove jurors who refused to convict. *Trial, 33,* 17–20.

Dion, K. K. (1972). Physical attractiveness and evaluations of children's transgressions. *Journal of Personality and Social Psychology, 24,* 207–213.

Dion, K. K., Berscheid, E., & Walster, E. (1972). What is beautiful is good. *Journal of Personality and Social Psychology, 24,* 285–290.

Dirks-Lindhorst, P. A., & Kondrat, D. (2012). Tough on crime or beating the system: An evaluation of Missouri Department of Mental Health's not guilty by reason of insanity murder acquittees. *Homicide Studies, 16,* 129–150.

Dodge, J. A. (2006). Same-sex marriage and divorce: A proposal for child custody mediation. *Family Court Review, 44,* 87–103.

Doherty, J. W., Reville, R. T., & Zakaras, L. (2012). *Would increased transparency improve the civil justice system?* Santa Monica, CA: Rand/UCLA.

Doob, A. N., & Kirshenbaum, H. M. (1973). Bias in police lineups: Partial remembering. *Journal of Police Science and Administration, 1,* 287–293.

Douglas, K. S., Guy, L. S., & Hart, S. D. (2009). Psychosis as a risk factor for violence to others: A meta-analysis. *Psychological Bulletin, 135,* 679–706.

Douglass, A. B., & Pavletic, A. (2012). Eyewitness confidence malleability. In B. Cutler (Ed.), *Conviction of the innocent: Lessons from psychological research* (pp. 149–163). Washington, DC: American Psychological Association.

Douglass, A. B., & Steblay, N. (2006). Memory distortion in eyewitnesses: A meta-analysis of the post-identification feedback effect. *Applied Cognitive Psychology, 20,* 859–869.

Drizin, S., & Leo, R. A. (2004). The problem of false confessions in the post-DNA world. *North Carolina Law Review, 82,* 891–1007.

Drogin, E. Y., & Barrett, C. L. (2013). Trial consultation. In R. K. Otto & I. B. Weiner (Eds.),

Handbook of psychology: Vol. 11. Forensic psychology (2nd ed., pp. 648–663). Hoboken, NJ: Wiley.

Drogin, E. Y., Dattilio, F. M., Sadoff, R. L., & Gutheil, T. G. (2011). *Handbook of forensic assessment: Psychological and psychiatric perspectives*. Hoboken, NJ: Wiley.

Dror, I. E., & Bucht, R. (2012). Psychological perspectives on problems with forensic science evidence. In B. Cutler (Ed.), *Conviction of the innocent: Lessons from psychological research* (pp. 257–276). Washington, DC: American Psychological Association.

Dunning, D. (1989). Research on children's eyewitness testimony: Perspectives on its past and future. In S. J. Ceci, D. F. Ross, & M. P. Toglia (Eds.), *Perspectives on children's testimony* (pp. 230–248). New York: Springer-Verlag.

Durham, M. L., & La Fond, J. Q. (1990). A search for the missing premise of involuntary therapeutic commitment: Effective treatment of the mentally ill. In D. B. Wexler (Ed.), *Therapeutic jurisprudence* (pp. 133–163). Durham, NC: Carolina Academic Press.

Dwyer, J., Neufeld, P., & Scheck, B. (2000). *Actual innocence: Five days to execution and other dispatches from the wrongly convicted*. New York: Doubleday.

Easterbrook, J. A. (1959). The effect of emotion on cue utilization and the organization of behavior. *Psychological Review, 66*, 181–201.

Eberhardt, J. L., Davies, P. G., Purdie-Vaughns, V. J., & Lynn Johnson, S. (2006). Looking deathworthy: Perceived stereotypicality of black defendants predicts capital-sentencing outcomes. *Psychological Science, 17*, 383–460.

Eckholm, E. (2012). *Which mother for Isabella? Civil union ends in an abduction and questions.* Retrieved October 29, 2013, from http://www .nytimes.com/2012/07/29/us/a-civil-union-ends-in-an-abduction-and-questions .html?_r=0

Edens, J. F., Buffington-Vollum, J. K., Keilen, A., Roskamp, P., & Anthony, C. (2005). Predictions of future dangerousness in capital murder trials: Is it time to "disinvent the wheel"? *Law and Human Behavior, 29*, 55–86.

Edens, J. F., Skeem, J. L., & Kennealy, P. J. (2009). The Psychopathy Checklist in the courtroom: Consensus and controversies. In J. L. Skeem, K. S. Douglas, & S. O. Lilienfeld (Eds.), *Psychological science in the courtroom: Consensus and controversy* (pp. 175–201). New York: Guilford Press.

Edens, J. F., Smith, S. T., Magyar, M. S., Mullen, K., Pitta, A., & Petrila, J. (2012). "Hired guns," "Charlatans," and their "voodoo psychobabble": Case law references to various forms of perceived bias among mental health expert witnesses. *Psychological Services, 9*, 259–271.

Efran, M. C. (1974). The effect of physical appearance on the judgment of guilt, interpersonal attraction, and severity of recommended punishment in a simulated jury task. *Journal of Research in Personality, 8*, 5 54.

Einhorn, J. (1986). Child custody in historical perspective: A study of changing social perceptions of divorce and child custody in Anglo-American law. *Behavioral Sciences & the Law, 4*, 119–135.

Elliott, R., & Robinson, R. J. (1991). Death penalty attitudes and the tendency to convict or acquit: Some data. *Law and Human Behavior, 15*, 389–404.

Ellsworth, P. C., & Reifman, A. (2000). Juror comprehension and public policy: Perceived problems and proposed solutions. *Psychology, Public Policy, and Law, 6*, 788–821.

Elrod, L. D., & Dale, M. D. (2008). Paradigm shifts and pendulum swings in child custody: The interests of children in the balance. *Family Law Quarterly, 42*, 381–418.

Elrod, L. D., & Spector, R. G. (2011). A review of the year in family law: Working toward more uniformity in laws relating to families. *Family Law Quarterly, 44*, 443–511.

Elrod, L. H. (2002). Divorce and annulment. In K. L. Hall (Ed.), *The Oxford companion to law* (pp. 221–222). New York: Oxford University Press.

Elwork, A., Alfini, J. J., & Sales, B. D. (1987). Toward understandable jury instructions. In L. S. Wrightsman, S. M. Kassin, & C. E. Willis (Eds.), *In the jury box: Controversies in the courtroom* (pp. 161–179). Newbury Park, CA: Sage.

Elwork, A., Sales, B. D., & Alfini, J. J. (1977). Juridic decisions: In ignorance of the law or in light of it? *Law and Human Behavior, 1,* 163–189.

Elwork, A., Sales, B. D., & Alfini, J. J. (1982). *Making jury instructions understandable.* Indianapolis, IN: Miche/Bobbs-Merrill.

Emery, R. E. (2005). Parental alienation syndrome: Proponents bear the burden of proof. *Family Court Review, 43,* 8–13.

Emery, R. E., Mathews, S., & Kitzmann, R. (1994). Child custody mediation and litigation: Parents' satisfaction 1 year after settlement. *Journal of Consulting and Clinical Psychology, 62,* 124–129.

Emery, R. E., Otto, R. K., & O'Donohue, W. T. (2005). A critical assessment of child custody evaluations: Limited science and a flawed system. *Psychological Science in the Public Interest, 6,* 1–29.

Emery, R. E., & Wyer, M. M. (1987). Divorce mediation. *American Psychologist, 42,* 472–480.

Esses, V. M., & Webster, C. D. (1988). Physical attractiveness, dangerousness, and the Canadian Criminal Code. *Journal of Applied Social Psychology, 18,* 1017–1031.

Evans, A. D., & Lyon, T. D. (2012). Assessing children's competency to take the oath in court: The influence of question type on children's accuracy. *Law and Human Behavior, 36,* 195–205.

Evans, J. R., Meissner, C. A., Brandon, S. E., Russano, M. B., & Kleinman, S. M. (2010). Criminal vs. HUMINT interrogations: The importance of psychological science to improving interrogative practice. *Journal of Psychiatry & Law, 38*(1–2), 215–249.

Evans, J. R., Meissner, C. A., Ross, A. B., Houston, K. A., Russano, M. B., & Hogan, A. J. (2013). Obtaining guilty knowledge in human intelligence interrogations: Comparing accusatorial and informational-gathering approaches with a novel experimental paradigm. *Journal of Applied Research in Memory and Cognition, 2,* 83–88.

Evans, J. R., & Schreiber Compo, N. (2010). Mock jurors' perceptions of identification made by intoxicated witnesses. *Psychology, Crime & Law, 16,* 191–210.

Evans, J. R., Schreiber Compo, N., & Russano, M. B. (2009). Intoxicated witnesses and suspects: Procedures and prevalence according to law enforcement. *Psychology, Public Policy, and Law, 15,* 194–221.

Faigman, D. L., & Monahan, J. (2009). Standards of legal admissibility and their implications for psychological science. In J. L. Skeem, K. S. Douglas, & S. O. Lilienfeld (Eds.), *Psychological science in the courtroom: Consensus and controversy* (pp. 3–25). New York: Guilford Press.

Fanniff, A. M., Otto, R. K., & Petrila, J. (2010). Competence to proceed in SVP commitment hearings: Irrelevant or a fundamental due process right? *Behavioral Sciences & the Law, 28,* 647–670.

Farabee, D., Shen, H., & Sanchez, S. (2002). Perceived coercion and treatment need among mentally ill parolees. *Criminal Justice and Behavior, 29,* 76–86.

Faul, M., Xu, L., Wald, M. M., & Coronado, V. G. (2010, March). *Traumatic brain injury in the United States: Emergency department visits, hospitalizations, and deaths.* Atlanta, GA: Centers for Disease Control and Prevention, National Center for Injury Prevention.

Fawcett, J. M., Russell, E. J., Peace, K. A., & Christie, J. (2013). Of guns and geese: A meta-analytic review of the "weapon focus" literature. *Psychology, Crime & Law, 19,* 35–66.

Felthous, A. R. (2001). Introduction to this issue: The clinician's duty to warn or protect. *Behavioral Sciences & the Law, 19,* 321–324.

Felthous, A. R., & Kachigian, C. (2001). To warn and to control: Two distinct legal obligations or variations of a single duty to protect? *Behavioral Sciences & the Law, 19,* 355–373.

Fidler, B. J. (2012). Parenting coordination: Lessons learned and key practice issues. *Canadian Family Law Quarterly, 3*, 237–273.

Findley, J., & Sales, B. D. (2012). *In the science of attorney advocacy: How courtroom behavior affects jury decision making.* Washington, DC: American Psychological Association.

Findley, K. A., & Scott, M. S. (2006). The multiple dimensions of tunnel vision in criminal cases. *Wisconsin Law Review, 2*, 291–397.

Finkel, N. J. (1988). *Insanity on trial.* New York: Plenum.

Finkel, N. J. (1991). The insanity defense: A comparison of verdict schemas. *Law and Human Behavior, 15*, 533–555.

Finkel, N. J. (1995). *Commonsense justice: Jurors' notions of the law.* Cambridge, MA: Harvard University Press.

Finkel, N. J. (2000). Commonsense justice and jury instructions: Instructive and reciprocating connections. *Psychology, Public Policy, and Law, 6*, 591–628.

Finkel, N., Shaw, R., Bercaw, S., & Kock, J. (1985). Insanity defenses: From the jurors' perspective. *Law and Psychology Review, 9*, 77–92.

Finkelman, J. M. (2010). Litigation consulting: Expanding beyond jury selection to trial strategy and tactics. *Consulting Psychology Journal: Practice and Research, 62*, 12–20.

Fischer, K. W., Stein, Z., & Heikkinen, K. (2009). Narrow assessments misrepresent development and misguide policy: Comment on Steinberg, Cauffman, Woolard, Graham, and Banich (2009). *American Psychologist, 64*, 595–600.

Fitzgerald, R. E., & Ellsworth, P. C. (1984). Due process vs. crime control: Death qualification and jury attitudes. *Law and Human Behavior, 8*, 31–51.

Fogel, M. H., Schiffman, W., Mumley, D., Tillbrook, C., & Grisso, T. (2013). Ten year research update (2001–2010): Evaluations for competence to stand trial (Adjudicative competence). *Behavioral Sciences & the Law, 31,* 165–191.

Foley, M. A., & Johnson, M. K. (1985). Confusion between memories for performed and imagined actions. *Child Development, 56*, 1145–1155.

Follingstad, D. (2010). Increasing complexity: Resisting simplification in forensic psychology. *Forensic Psychology Unbound, 2*, 10–22.

Foot, D. (2002). *Boom, bust, and echo.* Toronto, Ont., Canada: Stoddart.

Foote, W. E. (2013). Forensic evaluations in Americans with Disabilities Act cases. In R. K. Otto & I. B. Weiner (Eds.), *Handbook of psychology: Vol. 11. Forensic psychology* (2nd ed., pp. 271–294). Hoboken, NJ: Wiley.

Foote, W. E., & Lareau, C. R. (2013). Psychological evaluation of emotional damages in tort cases. In R. K. Otto & I. B. Weiner (Eds.), *Handbook of psychology: Vol. 11. Forensic psychology* (2nd ed., pp. 172–200). Hoboken, NJ: Wiley.

Forsterlee, L., Horowitz, I. A., & Bourgeous, M. J. (1993). Juror competence in civil trials: Effects of preinstruction and evidence technicality. *Journal of Applied Psychology, 78*, 14–21.

Francis, A. (2013). *DSM–5 is guide not bible—ignore its ten worst changes.* Retrieved November 15, 2013, from http://www.psychologytoday.com/blog/dsm5-in-distress/201212

Frank, J. (1949). *Courts on trial: Myth and reality in American justice.* Princeton, NJ: Princeton University Press.

Franke, K. M. (1995). The central mistake of sex discrimination law: The disaggregation of sex from gender. *University of Pennsylvania Law Review, 144*, 1–99.

Frenda, S. J., Nichols, R. M., & Loftus, E. F. (2011). Current issues and advances in misinformation research. *Current Directions in Psychological Science, 20*, 20–23.

Friedman, M. J., Resick, P. A., Bryant, R. A., Strain, J., Horowitz, M., & Spiegel, D. (2011). Classification of trauma and stress-related disorders in DSM-5. *Depression and Anxiety, 28*, 737–749.

Friel, A., White, T., & Hull, A. (2008). Posttraumatic stress disorder and criminal responsibility. *Journal of Forensic Psychiatry and Psychology, 19*, 64–85.

Frumkin, I. B. (2008). Psychological evaluation in *Miranda* waiver and confession cases. In R. L. Denney & J. P. Sullivan (Eds.), *Clinical neuropsychology in the criminal forensic setting* (pp. 135–175). New York: Guilford Press.

Frumkin, I. B. (2010). Evaluations of competency to waive *Miranda* rights and coerced or false confessions: Common pitfalls in expert testimony. In G. D. Lassiter & C. Meissner (Eds.), *Police interrogations and false confessions: Current research, practice, and policy recommendations* (pp. 191–209). Washington, DC: American Psychological Association.

Frumkin, I. B., Lally, S. J., & Sexton, J. E. (2012). The Grisso tests for assessing understanding and appreciation of *Miranda* warnings with a forensic sample. *Behavioral Sciences & the Law, 30*, 673–692.

Gaines, M. V., Giles, C. L., & Morgan, R. (2012). The detection of feigning using multiple PAI scale elevations: A new index. *Assessment, 20*, 437–447.

Galanter, M. (2004). The vanishing trial: An examination of trials and related matters in federal and state courts. *Journal of Empirical Legal Studies, 1*, 459–570.

Gambetta, D. (2005). *Making sense of suicide missions.* Oxford, UK: Oxford University Press.

Garvey, S. P., Hannaford-Agor, P., Hans, V. P., Mott, N. L., Munsterman, G. T., & Wells, M. T. (2004). Juror first votes in criminal trials. *Journal of Empirical Legal Studies, 2*, 371–398.

Gates, M. A., Holowka, D. W., Vasterling, J J., Keane, T. M., Marx, B. P., & Rosen, R. C. (2012). Posttraumatic stress disorder in veterans and military personnel: Epidemiology, screening, and case recognition. *Psychological Services, 9*, 361–382.

George, J. A. (2008). Offender profiling and expert testimony: Scientifically valid or glorified results? *Vanderbilt Law Review, 61*(1), 221–260.

Givelber, D. J., & Farrell, A. S. (2008). Judge and juries: The defense case and differences in acquittal rates. *Law & Social Inquiry, 33*, 31–52.

Golding, S. L., & Roesch, R. (1987). The assessment of criminal responsibility: A historical approach to a current controversy. In I. B. Weiner & A. K. Hess (Eds.), *Handbook of forensic psychology* (pp. 395–436). New York: Wiley.

Golding, S. L., Skeem, J. L., Roesch, R., & Zapf, P. A. (1999). The assessment of criminal responsibility: Current controversies. In I. B. Weiner & A. K. Hess (Eds.), *The Handbook of forensic psychology* (2nd ed., pp. 379–408). New York: Wiley.

Goldkamp, J. S., & Irons-Guynn, C. (2000). *Emerging judicial strategies for the mentally ill in the criminal caseload: Mental health courts in Fort Lauderdale, Seattle, San Bernardino, and Anchorage.* Washington, DC: U.S. Department of Justice, Office of Justice Programs, Bureau of Justice Statistics.

Goldkamp, J. S., & Weiland, D. (1993). *Assessing the impact of Dade County's felony drug court.* Washington, DC: National Institute of Justice.

Goldstein, A., & Goldstein, N. (2010). Evaluating capacity to waive *Miranda* rights. New York: Oxford University Press.

Goldstein, A. M., Morse, S. J., & Packer, I. K. (2013). Evaluation of criminal responsibility. In I. B. Weiner (Ed.), *Handbook of Psychology* (2nd ed., pp. 440–472). Hoboken, NJ: Wiley.

Goldstein, N. E. S., Goldstein, A. M., Zelle, H., & Conde, L. O. (2013). Capacity to waive Miranda rights and the assessment of susceptibility to police coercion. In R. K. Otto & I. B. Weiner (Eds.), *Handbook of psychology: Vol. 11. Forensic psychology* (2nd ed., pp. 381–411). Hoboken, NJ: Wiley.

Goldstein, N. E. S., Zelle, H., & Grisso, T. (2012). *The Miranda rights comprehension instruments: Manual.* Sarasota, FL: Professional Resources Press.

Goodman, G. S., & Hahn, A. (1987). Evaluating eyewitness testimony. In I. B. Weiner & A. K. Hess (Eds.), *Handbook of forensic psychology* (pp. 258–292). New York: Wiley.

Goodman, G. S., & Melinder, A. (2007). Child witness research and forensic interviews of young children: A review. *Legal and Criminological Psychology, 12*, 1–19.

Goodman, G. S., Myers, J. E. B., Qin, J., Quas, J. A., Castelli, P., Redlich, A. D., et al. (2006). Hearsay versus children's testimony: Effects of truthful and deceptive statements on jurors decisions. *Law and Human Behavior, 30*, 363–401.

Goodman, G. S., & Reed, R. S. (1986). Age differences in eyewitness testimony. *Law and Human Behavior, 10*, 317–332.

Goodman, G. S., Tobey, A. E., Batterman-Faunce, J. M., Orcutt, H., Thomas, S., Shapiro, C., et al. (1998). Face-to-face confrontation: Effects of closed-circuit technology on children's eyewitness testimony and jurors' decisions. *Law and Human Behavior, 22*, 165–203.

Goodman, J., Loftus, E. F., Miller, M., & Greene, E. (1991). Money, sex, and death: Gender bias in wrongful death damage awards. *Law and Society Review, 25*, 252–285.

Goodman-Delahunty, J. (1997). Forensic psychological expertise in the wake of *Daubert. Law and Human Behavior, 21*, 121–140.

Goodman-Delahunty, J., & Foote, W. E. (2011). *Workplace discrimination and harassment.* London: Oxford University Press.

Gould, J. W., & Martindale, D. A. (2013). Child custody evaluations: Current literature and practical applications. In R. K. Otto & I. B. Weiner (Eds.), *Handbook of psychology: Vol. 11. Forensic psychology* (2nd ed., pp. 101–138). Hoboken, NJ: Wiley.

Gould, J. W., Martindale, D. A., Tippins, T., & Wittmann, J. (2011). Testifying experts and nontestifying trial consultants: Appreciating the differences. *Journal of Child Custody, 8*, 32–46.

Gould-Saltman, D. (2011). A view from the crossroad: Considerations for mental health professionals consulting with attorneys (by a judge, and former lawyer . . . with a degree in psychology). *Journal of Child Custody, 8*, 135–141.

Gowensmith, W. N., Murrie, D. C., & Boccaccini, M. T. (2012). Field reliability of competence to stand trial opinions: How often do evaluators agree, and what do judges decide when evaluators disagree? *Law and Human Behavior, 36*, 130–139.

Gowensmith, W. N., Murrie, D. C., & Boccaccini, M. T. (2013). How reliable are forensic evaluations of legal sanity? *Law and Human Behavior, 37*, 98–106.

Grady, D., & Carey, B. (2013, November 5). Medical ethics have been violated at detention sites, a new report says. *New York Times*, p. A16.

Granhag, P. A., & Strömwall, L. A. (2002). Repeated interrogations: Verbal and nonverbal cues to deception. *Applied Cognitive Psychology, 16*, 243–257.

Green, D., & Rosenfeld, B. (2011). Evaluating the gold standard: A review and meta-analysis of the Structured Interview of Reported Symptoms. *Psychological Assessment, 23*, 95–107.

Green, D., Rosenfeld, B., & Belfi, B. (2012). New and improved? A comparison of the original and revised versions of the Structured Interview of Reported Symptoms. *Assessment, 20*, 210–218.

Greene, E., & Loftus, E. F. (1985). When crimes are joined at trial. *Law and Human Behavior, 9*, 193–207.

Greenfield, D. P., Dougherty, E. J., Jackson, R. M., Podboy, J. W., & Zimmermann, M. L. (2001). Retrospective evaluation of *Miranda* reading levels and waiver competency. *American Journal of Forensic Psychology, 19*, 75–86.

Griffin, P. (2011, Winter). Presidential column. *AP-LS News, 31*(1), 2.

Griffin, P., Addie, S., Adams, B., & Firestine, K. (2011). *Trying juveniles as adults: An analysis of state transfer laws and reporting.* Washington, DC: Office of Juvenile Justice and Delinquency Prevention.

Grisso, T. (1981). *Juveniles' waiver of rights: Legal and psychological competence.* New York: Plenum.

Grisso, T. (1986). *Evaluating competencies: Forensic assessments and instruments.* New York: Plenum.

Grisso, T. (1988). *Competency to stand trial evaluations: A manual for practice.* Sarasota, FL: Professional Resource Exchange.

Grisso, T. (1997). The competence of adolescents as trial defendants. *Psychology, Public Policy, and Law, 3*, 32–48.

Grisso, T. (1998a). *Assessing understanding and appreciation of Miranda rights: Manual and materials.* Sarasota, FL: Professional Resources Press.

Grisso, T. (1998b). *Forensic evaluation of juveniles.* Sarasota, FL: Professional Resources Press.

Grisso, T. (2003). *Evaluating competencies: Forensic assessments and instruments* (2nd ed.). New York: Kluwer.

Grisso, T. (2005). *Evaluating juveniles' adjudicative competence.* Sarasota, FL: Professional Resources Press.

Grisso, T., & Appelbaum, P. S. (1995). The MacArthur Treatment Competence Study: III. Abilities of patients to consent to psychiatric and medical treatment. *Law and Human Behavior, 19,* 149–174.

Grisso, T., Appelbaum, P., Mulvey, E., & Fletcher, K. (1995). The MacArthur Treatment Competence Study II: Measures of abilities related to competence to consent to treatment. *Law and Human Behavior, 19,* 127–148.

Grisso, T., & Riggs Romaine, C. L. (2013). Forensic evaluation in delinquency cases. In R. K. Otto & I. B. Weiner (Eds.), *Handbook of psychology: Vol. 11. Forensic psychology* (2nd ed., pp. 359–380). Hoboken, NJ: Wiley.

Grisso, T., & Saks, M. J. (1991). Psychology's influence on constitutional interpretation. *Law and Human Behavior, 15,* 205–211.

Grisso, T., & Schwartz, R. G. (Eds.). (2000). *Youth on trial.* Chicago: University of Chicago Press.

Grisso, T., Steinberg, L., Woolard, J., Cauffman, E. S., Graham, S., Lexcen, F., . . . Schwartz, R. (2003). Juveniles' competence to stand trial: A comparison of adolescents' and adults' capacities as trial defendants. *Law and Human Behavior, 27,* 333–363.

Groopman, J. (2013, June 24). Before night falls. *The New Yorker,* pp. 18–23.

Grossman, N. S., & Okun, B. F. (2003). Family psychology and family law: Introduction to the special issue. *Journal of Family Psychology, 17,* 163–168.

Grove, W. M., & Meehl, P. E. (1996). Comparative efficiency of informal (subjective, impressionistic) and formal (mechanical, algorithmic) prediction procedures: The clinical-statistical controversy. *Psychology, Public Policy, and Law, 2,* 293–323.

Gudjonsson, G. H. (1984). A new scale of interrogative suggestibility. *Personality and Individual Differences, 5,* 303–314.

Gudjonsson, G. H. (1992). *The psychology of interrogations, confessions and testimony.* London: Wiley.

Gudjonsson, G. H. (1997). *The Gudjonsson Suggestibility Scale manual.* London: Psychology Press.

Gudjonsson, G. H., & Copson, G. (1997). The role of the expert in criminal investigation. In J. L. Jackson & D. A. Bekerian (Eds.), *Offender profiling: Theory, research and practice* (pp. 61–76). Chichester, UK: Wiley.

Gudjonsson, G. H., & Sigurdsson, J. F. (1999). The Gudjonsson Confession Questionnaire–Revised (GCQ-R): Factor structure and its relationship with personality. *Personality and Individual Differences, 27,* 953–968.

Gudjonsson, G. H., Sigurdsson, J. F., Asgeirsdottir, B. B., & Sigfusdottir, I. D. (2006). Custodial interrogation, false confession and individual differences: A national study among Icelandic youth. *Personality and Individual Differences, 41,* 49–59.

Gudjonsson, G. H., Sigurdsson, J. F., & Einarsson, E. (2004). The role of personality in relation to confessions and denials. *Psychology, Crime, & Law, 10,* 125–135.

Gunnell, J. J., & Ceci, S. J. (2010). When emotionality trumps reason: A study of individual processing style and juror bias. *Behavioral Sciences & the Law, 28,* 850–877.

Gutheil, T., & Appelbaum, P. (2000). *Clinical handbook of psychiatry and the law* (3rd ed.). Baltimore: Williams & Wilkins.

Guthrie, C., Rachlinski, J. J., & Wistrich, A. J. (2001a, April). Inside the judicial mind. *Dispute Resolution Alert, 1*(7), 1–4.

Guthrie, C., Rachlinski, J. J., & Wistrich, A. J. (2001b, May). Inside the judicial mind. *Cornell Law Review, 86,* 777–823.

Haber, R. N., & Haber, L. (2000). Experiencing, remembering, and reporting events. *Psychology, Public Policy, and Law, 6,* 1057–1097.

Haines, J., Williams, C. L., & Lester, D. (2011). The characteristics of those who do and do not leave suicide notes: Is the method valid? *Omega: Journal of Death & Dying, 63,* 79–94.

Halleck, S. (1980). *Law in the practice of psychiatry.* Washington, DC: National Institute of Mental Health.

Hancock, K. J., & Rhodes, G. (2008). Contact, configural coding, and the other-race effect in face recognition. *British Journal of Psychology, 99,* 45–56.

Haney, C. (1980). Psychology and legal change: On the limits of a factual jurisprudence. *Law and Human Behavior, 4,* 147–199.

Haney, C. (1984). Examining death qualification: Further analysis of the process effect. *Law and Human Behavior, 8,* 133–151.

Haney, C., & Lynch, M. (1994). Comprehending life and death matters. *Law and Human Behavior, 18,* 411–436.

Hans, V., Kaye, D. H., Dann, B. M., Farley, E. J., & Albertson, S. (2011). Science in the jury box: Jurors' comprehension of mitochondrial DNA evidence. *Law and Human Behavior, 35,* 60–71.

Hare, R. D. (1996). Psychopathy: A clinical construct whose time has come. *Criminal Justice and Behavior, 23,* 25–54.

Hare, R. D. (1998). The Hare PCL-R: Some issues concerning its use and misuse. *Legal and Criminal Psychology, 3,* 99–119.

Hare, R. D. (2003). *Manual for the Hare Psychopathy Checklist–Revised* (2nd ed.). Toronto, Ont., Canada: Multi-Health Systems.

Hare, R. D., Forth, A. E., & Strachan, K. E. (1992). Psychopathy and crime across the life span. In R. D. Peters, R. J. McMahon, & V. L. Quinsey (Eds.), *Aggression and violence throughout the life span* (pp. 285–300). Newbury Park, CA: Sage.

Harris, G. T., Rice, M., & Quinsey, V. (1993). Violent recidivism of mentally disordered offenders: The development of a statistical prediction instrument. *Criminal Justice and Behavior, 20,* 315–335.

Hart, S. D., & Boer, D. P. (2010). Structured professional guidelines for sexual violence risk assessment: The Sexual Violence Risk–20 (SVR-20) and Risk for Sexual Violence Protocol (RSVP). In R. K. Otto & K. S. Douglas (Eds.), *Handbook of violence risk assessment* (pp. 269–294). New York: Routledge/Taylor & Francis.

Hart, S. D., Cox, D., & Hare, R. D. (1995). *The Hare Psychopathy Checklist: Screening version.* Toronto, Ont., Canada: Multi-Health Systems.

Hart, S. D., & Storey, J. E. (2013). Clinical and forensic issues in the assessment of psychopathy. In R. K. Otto & I. B. Weiner (Eds.) *Handbook of psychology: Vol. 11. Forensic psychology* (2nd ed., pp. 556–578). Hoboken, NJ: Wiley.

Hasselbrack, A. M. (2001). Opting in to mental health courts. *Corrections Compendium,* Sample Issue, 4–5.

Hastie, R., Penrod, S. D., & Pennington, N. (1983). *Inside the jury.* Cambridge, MA: Harvard University Press.

Hastie, R., Schkade, D., & Payne, J. (1998). A study of juror and jury judgments in civil cases: Deciding liability for punitive damages. *Law and Human Behavior, 22,* 287–314.

Hawkins, S. A., & Hastie, R. (1990). Hindsight: Biased judgments of past events after the outcomes are known. *Psychological Bulletin, 107,* 311–327.

Heilbronner, R. L. (2004). A status report on the practice of forensic neuropsychology. *Clinical Neuropsychologist, 18,* 312–326.

Heilbrun, K. (1992). The role of psychological testing in forensic assessment. *Law and Human Behavior, 16,* 257–272.

Heilbrun, K., & Brooks, S. (2010). Forensic psychology and forensic science: A proposed agenda for the next decade. *Psychology, Public Policy, and Law, 16,* 219–253.

Heilbrun, K., Dematteo, D., Yashuhara, K., Brooks-Holliday, S., Shah, S., King, C., et al. (2012). Community-based alternatives for justice-involved individuals with severe mental illness: Review of the relevant research. *Criminal Justice and Behavior, 39,* 351–419.

Heilbrun, K., Douglas, K. S., & Yasuhara, K. (2009). Violence risk assessment: Core controversies. In J. L. Skeem, K. S. Douglas, & S. O. Lilienfeld

(Eds.), *Psychological science in the courtroom: Consensus and controversy* (pp. 333–357). New York: Guilford Press.

Heilbrun, K., Grisso, T., & Goldstein, A. (2009). *The foundations of forensic mental health assessment.* New York: Oxford University Press.

Heilbrun, K., Grisso, T., Goldstein, A. M., & Laduke, C. (2013). Foundations of forensic mental health assessment. In R. Roesch & P. A. Zapf (Eds.), *Forensic assessments in criminal and civil law: A handbook for lawyers* (pp. 1–26). New York: Oxford University Press.

Heilbrun, K., Marczyk, G. R., DeMatteo, D., Zillmer, E. A., Harris, J., & Jennings, T. (2003). Principles of forensic mental health assessment: Implications for neuropsychological assessment in forensic contexts. *Assessment, 10,* 329–342.

Heilbrun, K. S., Rogers, R., & Otto, R. K. (2000). Forensic assessment: Current status and future directions. In J. R. P. Ogloff (Ed.), *Psychology and law: Reviewing the discipline* (pp. 119–146). New York: Kluwer/Plenum.

Hellkamp, D. T., & Lewis, J. E. (1995). The consulting psychologist as an expert witness in sexual harassment and retaliation. *Consulting Psychologist Journal: Practice and Research, 47,* 150–159.

Henderson, J. M., Williams, C. C., & Falk, R. J. (2005). Eye movements are functional during face learning. *Memory & Cognition, 33,* 98–106.

Hess, A. K. (1999). Serving as an expert witness. In A. K. Hess & I. B. Weiner (Eds.), *The handbook of forensic psychology* (2nd ed., pp. 521–555). New York: Wiley.

Hess, A. K. (2006). Defining forensic psychology. In I. B. Weiner & A. K. Hess (Eds.), *The handbook of forensic psychology* (3rd ed., pp. 28–58). Hoboken, NJ: Wiley.

Hess, J. H., & Thomas, H. E. (1963). Incompetency to stand trial: Procedures, results and problems. *American Journal of Psychiatry, 119,* 713–720.

Hess, K. D., & Brinson, P. (1999). Mediating domestic law issues. In A. K. Hess & I. B. Weiner

(Eds.), *The handbook of forensic psychology* (2nd ed., pp. 63–103). New York: Wiley.

Hetherington, E. M. (1979). Divorce: A child's perspective. *American Psychologist, 34,* 851–858.

Hetherington, E. M., Bridges, M., & Insabella, G. M. (1998). What matters? What does not? Five perspectives on the association between marital transitions and children's adjustment. *American Psychologist, 53,* 167–184.

Hetherington, E. M., Cox, M., & Cox, R. (1979). Family interaction and the social, emotional, and cognitive development of children following divorce. In V. Vaughn & T. Brazelton (Eds.), *The family: Setting priorities* (pp. 148–176). New York: Science & Medicine.

Hetherington, E. M., & Kelly, J. (2002). *For better or worse: Divorce reconsidered.* New York: Norton.

Heuer, L., & Penrod, S. D. (1988). Increasing jurors' participation in trials: A field experiment with jury note taking and question asking. *Law and Human Behavior, 12,* 409–430.

Heuer, L., & Penrod, S. D. (1989). Instructing jurors: A field experiment with written and preliminary instructions. *Law and Human Behavior, 13,* 231–261.

Heuer, L., & Penrod, S. D. (1994). Juror note taking and question asking during trial: A national field experiment. *Law and Human Behavior, 18,* 121–150.

Hiday, V. A. (1988). Civil commitment: A review of empirical research. *Behavioral Sciences & the Law, 6,* 15–44.

Hiday, V. A. (1990). Dangerousness of civil commitment candidates. *Law and Human Behavior, 14,* 551–567.

Hiday, V. A. (2003). Outpatient commitment: The state of empirical research on its outcomes. *Psychology, Public Policy, and Law, 9,* 8–32.

Hiday, V. A., & Scheid-Cook, T. L. (1987). The North Carolina experience with outpatient commitment: A critical appraisal. *International Journal of Law and Psychiatry, 10,* 215–232.

Hiday, V. A., & Scheid-Cook, T. L. (1989). A follow-up of chronic patients committed to outpatient treatment. *Hospital and Community Psychiatry, 40,* 52–58.

Higginbotham, P. E. (2010). The present plight of the United States district courts. *Duke Law Journal, 60,* 745–764.

Hilgard, E. R. (1965). *Hypnotic susceptibility.* New York: Harcourt Brace Jovanovich.

Hill, C., Rogers, R., & Bickford, M. (1996). Predicting aggressive and socially disruptive behavior in a maximum security forensic psychiatric hospital. *Journal of Forensic Sciences, 51,* 56–59.

Hogan, T. P. (2005). 50 widely used psychological tests. In G. P. Koocher, J. C. Norcross, & S. S. Hill III (Eds.), *Psychologists' desk reference* (2nd ed., pp. 101–104). New York: Oxford University Press.

Hoge, C. W., Terhakopian, A., Castro, C. A., Messer, S. C., & Engel, C. C. (2007). Association of post-traumatic stress disorder with somatic symptoms, health care visits, and absenteeism among Iraq War veterans. *American Journal of Psychiatry, 164,* 150 153.

Hoge, R. D. (2012). Forensic assessments of juveniles: Practice and legal considerations. *Criminal Justice and Behavior, 39,* 1255–1270.

Hoge, S. K., Bonnie, R. J., Poythress, N., & Monahan, J. (1992). Attorney–client decision-making in criminal cases: Client competence and participation as perceived by their attorneys. *Behavioral Sciences & the Law, 10,* 385–394.

Hoge, S. K., Bonnie, R. J., Poythress, N., & Monahan, J. (1999). *The MacArthur Competence Assessment Tool—Criminal adjudication.* Odessa, FL: Psychological Assessment Resources.

Hoge, S. K., Bonnie, R. G., Poythress, N., Monahan, J., Eisenberg, M., & Feucht-Haviar, T. (1997). The MacArthur Adjudicative Competence Study: Development and validation of a research instrument. *Law and Human Behavior, 21,* 141–179.

Holliday, R. E., Humphries, J. E., Milne, R., Memon, A., Houlder, L., Lyons, A., et al. (2012). Reducing misinformation effects in older adults with cognitive interview mnemonics. *Psychology and Aging, 27,* 1191–1203.

Hope, L., & Wright, D. (2007). Beyond unusual? Examining the role of attention in the weapon focus effect. *Applied Cognitive Psychology, 21,* 951–961.

Horowitz, I. A., & Bordens, K. S. (2002). The effects of jury size, evidence complexity, and note taking on jury process and performance in civil trial. *Journal of Applied Psychology, 87,* 121–130.

Horowitz, I. A., & Forsterlee, L. (2001). The effects of note-taking and trial transcript access on mock jury decisions in a complex civil trial. *Law and Human Behavior, 25,* 373–391.

Horowitz, I. A., & Kirkpatrick, L. C. (1996). A concept in search of a definition: The effects of reasonable doubt instructions on certainty of guilt standards and jury verdicts. *Law and Human Behavior, 20,* 655–670.

Horry, R., Memon, A., Wright, D. B., & Milne, R. (2012). Predictors of eyewitness identification decisions from video lineups in England: A field study. *Law and Human Behavior, 36,* 257–265.

Horry, R., Palmer, M. A., & Brewer, N. (2012). Backloading in the sequential lineup prevents within-lineup criterion shifts that undermine eyewitness identification performance. *Journal of Experimental Psychology: Applied, 18,* 346–360.

Houston, K. A., Clifford, B. R., Phillips, L. H., & Memon, A. (2013). The emotional eyewitness: The effects of emotion on specific aspects of eyewitness recall and recognition performance. *Emotion, 13,* 118–128.

Hublin, C., Kaprio, J., Partinen, M., Heikkilä, K., & Koskenvuo, M. (1997). Prevalence and genetics of sleepwalking: A population-based twin study. *Neurology, 48,* 177–181.

Hugenberg, K., Young, S. G., Bernstein, M. J., & Sacco, D. F. (2010). The categorization-individuation model: An integrative account of the other-race recognition deficit. *Psychological Review, 117,* 1168–1187.

Hunt, J. W. (2010). *Admissibility of expert testimony in state courts.* Minneapolis, MN: Aircraft Builders Council.

Iacono, W. G. (2009). Psychophysiological detection of deception and guilty knowledge. In J. L. Skeem, K. S. Douglas, & S. O. Lilienfeld (Eds.), *Psychological science in the courtroom:*

Consensus and controversy (pp. 224–241). New York: Guilford Press.

Iacono, W. G., & Lykken, D. T. (1997). The validity of the lie detector: Two surveys of scientific opinion. *Journal of Applied Psychology, 82,* 426–433.

Iacono, W. G., & Patrick, C. J. (2014). Employing polygraph assessment. In I. B. Weiner & R. K. Otto (Eds.), The handbook of forensic psychology (4th ed., pp. 613-658. New York: Wiley.

Inbau, F. E., & Reid, J. E. (1967). *Criminal interrogation and confessions.* Baltimore: Williams & Wilkins.

Inbau, F. E., Reid, J. E., Buckley, J. P., & Jayne, B. C. (2004). *Criminal interrogation and confessions* (4th ed.). Gaithersburg, MD: Aspen.

Inbau, F. E., Reid, J. E., Buckley, J. P., & Jayne, B. C. (2013). *Criminal interrogation and confessions* (5th ed.). Burlington, MA: Jones & Bartlett Learning.

Ingram, S. (1998). If the profile fits: Admitting criminal psychological profiles into evidence in criminal trials. *Journal of Urban and Contemporary Law, 54,* 239–267.

Jacobs, D., & Klein-Benheim, M. (1995). The psychological autopsy: A useful tool for determining proximate causation in suicide cases. *Bulletin of the American Academy of Psychiatry and Law, 23,* 165–182.

James, F., Jr. (1965). *Civil procedure.* Boston: Little, Brown.

Janus, E. S., & Meehl, P. E. (1997). Assessing the legal standard for predictions of dangerousness in sex offender commitment proceedings. *Psychology, Public Policy, and Law, 3,* 33–64.

Jeste, D. V., & Saks, E. R. (2006). Decisional capacity in mental illness and substance use disorders: Empirical database and policy implications. *Behavioral Sciences & the Law, 24,* 607–628.

Johnson, C., & Scott, B. (1976). *Eyewitness testimony and suspect identification as a function of arousal, sex of witness, and scheduling of interrogation.* Paper presented at a meeting of the American Psychological Association, Washington, DC.

Johnston, J. (1996). Children's adjustment in sole custody compared to joint custody families and principles for custody decision making. *Family and Conciliation Courts Review, 33,* 415–425.

Jones, S., & Cauffman, E. (2008). Juvenile psychopathy and judicial decision making: An empirical analysis of an ethical dilemma. *Behavioral Sciences & the Law, 26,* 151–165.

Juhas, M. (2011). Commentary on forensic mental health consulting: Is more better? *Journal of Child Custody, 8,* 124–134.

Julien, R. M. (1992). A primer of drug action (6th ed.). New York: W. H. Freeman.

Kairys, D., Schulman J., & Harring, S. (1975). *The jury system: New methods for reducing prejudice.* Philadelphia: National Jury Project and National Lawyers Guild.

Kalven, H., Jr., & Zeisel, H. (1966). *The American jury.* Boston: Little, Brown.

Kane, A. W., Nelson, E. M., Dvoskin, J. A., & Pitt, S. E. (2013). Evaluations for personal injury claims. In R. Roesch & P. A. Zapf (Eds.), *Forensic assessments in criminal and civil law: A handbook for lawyers* (pp. 148–160). New York: Oxford University Press.

Kaplan, M. F. (1977). Discussion polarization effects in a modified jury decision paradigm: Informational influences. *Sociometry, 40,* 262–271.

Kari, S. (2005, December). Judge cautions against TV-type evidence. *Law Times.* Ottawa, Ont.: Thomson Reuters Canada.

Kaser-Boyd, N. (2009). Child abuse and domestic violence in divorce and child custody: Ethical issues. *Professional Psychology: Research and Practice, 40,* 548–549.

Kassin, S. M. (1997). The psychology of confession evidence. *American Psychologist, 52,* 221–233.

Kassin, S. M. (2008). Expert testimony on the psychology of confessions: A pyramidal framework of the relevant science. In E. Borgida &

T. S. Fiske (Eds.), *Beyond common sense: Psychological science in the courtroom* (pp. 195–218). Oxford, UK: Blackwell.

Kassin, S. M. (2012a). Paradigm shift in the study of human lie-detection: Bridging the gap between science and practice. *Journal of Applied Research in Memory and Cognition, 1,* 118–119.

Kassin, S. M. (2012b). Why confessions trump innocence. *American Psychologist, 67,* 431–445.

Kassin, S. M., Drizin, S., Grisso, T., Gudjonsson, G. H., Leo, R. A., & Redlich, A. D. (2010). Police-induced confessions: Risk factors and recommendations. *Law and Human Behavior, 34,* 3–38.

Kassin, S. M., Dror, I. E., & Kukucka, J. (2013). The forensic confirmation bias: Problems, perspectives, and proposed solutions. *Journal of Applied Research in Memory and Cognition, 2,* 42–52.

Kassin, S. M., Goldstein, C. G., & Savitsky, K. (2003). Behavior confirmation in the interrogation room: On the dangers of presuming guilt. *Law and Human Behavior, 27,* 187–203.

Kassin, S. M., & Gudjonsson, G. H. (2004). The psychology of confession evidence: A review of the literature and issues. *Psychological Science in the Public Interest, 5,* 35–69.

Kassin, S. M., & Kiechel, K. L. (1996). The social psychology of false confessions: Compliance, internalization, and confabulation. *Psychological Science, 7,* 125–128.

Kassin, S. M., Leo, R. A., Meissner, C. A., Richman, K. D., Colwell, L. H., Leach, A. M., et al. (2007). Police interviewing and interrogation: A self-report survey of police practices and beliefs. *Law and Human Behavior, 31,* 381–400.

Kassin, S. M., Smith, V. L., & Tulloch, W. F. (1990). The dynamic charge: Effects on the perceptions and deliberation behavior of mock jurors. *Law and Human Behavior, 14,* 537–550.

Kassin, S. M., Tubb, V. A., Hosch, H. M., & Memon, A. (2001). On the "general acceptance" of eyewitness testimony research: A new survey of the experts. *American Psychologist, 56,* 405–416.

Kassin, S. M., & Wrightsman, L. S. (1979). On the requirements of proof: The timing of judicial instruction and mock juror verdicts. *Journal of Personality and Social Psychology, 37,* 1877–1887.

Kassin, S. M., & Wrightsman, L. S. (1985). Confession evidence. In S. M. Kassin & L. S. Wrightsman (Eds.), *The psychology of evidence and trial procedure.* Beverly Hills, CA: Sage.

Kaufmann, P. M. (2008). Admissibility of neuropsychological evidence in criminal cases: Competency, insanity, culpability, and mitigation. In R. L. Denny & J. P. Sullivan (Eds.), *Clinical neuropsychology in the criminal forensic setting* (pp. 55–90). New York: Guilford Press.

Kaufmann, P. M. (2012). Admissibility of expert opinions based on neuropsychological evidence. In G. J. Larrabee (Ed.), *Forensic neuropsychology: A scientific approach* (2nd ed., pp. 70–100). New York: Oxford University Press.

Kebbell, M. R., & Wagstaff, G. F. (1998). Hypnotic interviewing: The best way to interview eyewitnesses? *Behavioral Sciences & the Law, 16,* 115–129.

Keeler, E. (1984). *Lie detector man.* Boston: Telshare.

Kelly, J. B. (2008). Preparing for the parenting coordination role: Training needs for mental health and legal professionals. *Journal of Child Custody, 5,* 140–159.

Kelly, J. B., & Lamb, M. E. (2003). Developmental issues in relocation cases involving young children: When, whether, and how? *Journal of Family Psychology, 17,* 193–205.

Kelly, R. F., & Ramsey, S. H. (2009). Child custody evaluations: The need for systems-level outcome assessments. *Family Court Review, 47,* 286–363.

Kelman, H. C., & Hamilton, V. L. (1989). *Crimes of obedience.* New Haven, CT: Yale University Press.

Kerlinger, F. N. (1973). *Foundations of behavioral research* (2nd ed.). New York: Holt, Rinehart & Winston.

Kerr, N. L., Nerenz, D., & Herrick, D. (1979). Role playing and the study of jury behavior. *Sociological Methods and Research, 7,* 337–355.

Kerr, N. L., Niedermeier, K. E., & Kaplan, M. F. (1999). Bias in jurors vs. bias in juries: New evidence from the SDS perspective. *Organizational Behavior and Human Decisions Processes, 80,* 70–86.

Kessler, R. C., Sonnega, A., Bromet, E., Hughes, M., & Nelson, C. B. (1995). Post-traumatic stress disorder in the National Comorbidity Survey. *Archives of General Psychiatry, 52,* 1048–1060.

Kim, H. S. (2011). Consequences of parental divorce for child development. *American Sociological Review, 76,* 487–511.

King, L., & Snook, B. (2009). Peering inside a Canadian interrogation room: An examination of the Reid model of interrogation, influence tactics, and coercive strategies. *Criminal Justice and Behavior, 36,* 674–694.

Kirkland, K., & Kirkland, K. (2001). Frequency of child custody evaluations complaints and related disciplinary action: A survey of the association of state and provincial psychology boards. *Professional Psychology: Research and Practice, 32,* 171–174.

Kivisto, A. J., & Swan, S. A. (2011). Attitudes toward the insanity defense in capital cases: (Im)partiality from Witherspoon to Witt. *Journal of Forensic Psychology Practice, 11,* 311–329.

Klein, D. E. (2010). Introduction. In D. Klein & G. Mitchell (Eds.), *The psychology of judicial decision making* (pp. xi–xv). New York: Oxford University Press.

Klein, D. E., & Mitchell, G. (Eds.). (2010). *The psychology of judicial decision making.* New York: Oxford University Press.

Kleiner, M. (2002). Physiological detection of deception in psychological perspectives: A theoretical proposal. In M. Kleiner (Ed.), *Handbook of polygraph testing* (pp. 127–182). San Diego, CA: Academic Press.

Klemfuss, J. Z., & Ceci, S. J. (2012). Legal and psychological perspectives on children's competence to testify in court. *Developmental Review, 32,* 268–286.

Klimoski, R. J., & Wilkinson, T. R. (2013). Psychological assessment in industrial/organizational settings. In J. R. Graham, J. A. Naglier, & I. B. Weiner (Eds.), *Handbook of psychology: Vol. 10. Assessment psychology* (2nd ed., pp. 347–372). Hoboken, NJ: Wiley.

Knoll, C., & Sickmund, M. (2012, October). *Delinquency cases in juvenile court, 2009.* Washington, DC: Office of Juvenile Justice and Delinquency Prevention.

Knoll, J. L. (2008). The psychological autopsy, Part I: Applications and methods. *Journal of Psychiatric Practice, 14,* 393–397.

Knoll, J. L. (2009). The psychological autopsy, Part II: Toward a standardized protocol. *Journal of Psychiatric Practice, 15,* 52–59.

Koch, W. J., Nader, R., & Haring, M. (2009). The science and pseudoscience of assessing psychological injuries. In J. L. Skeem, K. S. Douglas, & S. O. Lilienfeld (Eds.), *Psychological science in the courtroom: Consensus and controversy* (pp. 263–283). New York: Guilford Press.

Kocsis, R. N. (2009). Criminal profiling: Facts, fictions, and courtroom admissibility. In J. L. Skeem, K. S. Douglas, & S. O. Lilienfeld (Eds.), *Psychological science in the courtroom: Consensus and controversy* (pp. 245–262). New York: Guilford Press.

Köhnken, G., Milne, R., Memon, A., & Bull, R. (1999). A meta-analysis on the effects of the cognitive interview. *Psychology, Crime & Law, 5,* 3–27.

Kourlis, R. L. (2012). It is just good business: The case for supporting reform in the divorce court. *Family Court Review, 50,* 549–557.

Kovera, M. B. (2013). Voir dire and jury selection. In R. K. Otto & I. B. Weiner (Eds.), *Handbook of Psychology: Vol. 11. Forensic psychology* (2nd ed., pp. 630–647). Hoboken, NJ: Wiley.

Kovera, M. B., & Cass, S. A. (2002). Compelled mental health examination, liability decisions, and damage awards in sexual harassment cases. *Psychology, Public Policy, and Law, 8,* 96–114.

Kovera, M. B., Dickinson, J. J., & Cutler, B. L. (2003). Voir dire and jury selection. In A. M. Goldstein (Ed.), *Handbook of psychology: Forensic psychology* (pp. 161–175). New York: Wiley.

Kramer, G., & Koening, D. (1990). Do jurors understand criminal jury instructions? Analyzing the results of the Michigan Juror Comprehension Project. *University of Michigan Journal of Law Reform, 23,* 401–437.

Krauss, D. A., & Sales, B. D. (2000). Legal standards, expertise, and experts in the resolution of contested child custody cases. *Psychology, Public Policy, and Law, 6,* 843–879.

Krauss, D. A., & Sales, B. D. (2001). The effects of clinical and scientific expert testimony on juror decision making in capital sentencing. *Psychology, Public Policy, and Law, 7,* 267–310.

Kreeger, J. L. (2003). Family psychology and family law—a family court judge's perspective: Comment on the special issue. *Journal of Family Psychology, 17,* 260–262.

Kress, K. (2006). Rotting with their rights on. *Behavioral Sciences & the Law, 24,* 573–598.

Kropp, P. R., Hart, S. D., Webster, C. W., & Eaves, D. (1995). *Manual for the Spousal Assault Risk Assessment guide* (2nd ed.). Vancouver, B.C., Canada: British Columbia Institute on Family Violence.

Kruh, I., & Grisso, T. (2008). *Evaluation of juveniles' competence to stand trial.* New York: Oxford University Press.

Kuhn, T. S. (1970). *The structure of scientific revolutions* (2nd ed.). Chicago: University of Chicago Press.

Kulik, C. J., Perry, E. L., & Pepper, M. B. (2003). Here comes the judge: The influence of judge personal characteristics on federal sexual harassment case outcome. *Law and Human Behavior, 27,* 69–97.

Kulka, R. A., & Kessler, J. B. (1978). Is justice really blind? The influence of litigant physical attractiveness on juridical judgment. *Journal of Applied Psychology, 8,* 366–381.

Kulka, R. A., Schlenger, W. E., Fairbank, J. A., Hough, R. L., Jordan, B. K., Marmar, C. R., et al. (1990). *Trauma and the Vietnam War generation: Report of findings from the National Vietnam Veterans Readjustment Study.* New York: Brunner/Mazel.

Kulka, R. A., Schlenger, W. E., Fairbank, J. A., Jordan, B. K., Hough, R. L., Marmar, C. R., et al. (1991). Assessment of post-traumatic stress disorder in the community: Prospects and pitfalls from recent studies of Vietnam veterans. *Psychological Assessment: A Journal of Consulting and Clinical Psychology, 4,* 547–560.

LaDuke, C., DeMatteo, D., Heilbrun, K., & Swirsky-Sacchetti, T. (2012). Clinical neuropsychology in forensic contexts: Practitioners' experience, training, and practice. *Professional Psychology, 43,* 503–509.

La Fond, J. Q. (2003). Outpatient commitment's next frontier: Sexual predators. *Psychology, Public Policy, and Law, 9,* 159–182.

La Fond, J. Q. (2011). Sexual offender commitment laws in the USA: The inevitable failure of misusing civil commitment to prevent future crimes. In B. McSherry & P. Keyer (Eds.), *Dangerous people: Policy, prediction, and practice: International perspectives on forensic mental health* (pp. 51–61). New York: Routledge/Taylor & Francis Group.

Lamb, M. E., & Kelly, J. B. (2009). Improving the quality of parent–child contact in separating families with infants and young children: Empirical research foundations. In R. M. Galatzer-Levy, L. Kraus, & J. Galatzer-Levy (Eds.), *The scientific basis of child custody decisions* (2nd ed., pp. 187–214). Hoboken, NJ: Wiley.

Lamb, M. E., & Malloy, L. C. (2013). Child development and the law. In R. M. Lerner, M. A. Easterbrook, J. Mistry, & I. B. Weiner (Eds.), *Handbook of psychology: Vol. 6. Developmental psychology* (2nd ed., pp. 571–593). Hoboken, NJ: Wiley.

Lamb, H. R., & Weinberger, L. E. (2005). The shift of psychiatric inpatient care from hospitals to jails and prisons. *Journal of the*

American Academy of Psychiatry and the Law, 33, 529–534.

Lancaster, G. L. J., Vrij, A., Hope, L., & Waller, B. (2013). Sorting the liars from the truth tellers: The benefits of asking unanticipated questions on lie detection. *Applied Cognitive Psychology, 27,* 107–114.

Landsman, S., & Rakos, R. F. (1994). A preliminary inquiry into the effect of potentially biasing information on judges and jurors in civil litigation. *Behavioral Sciences & the Law, 12,* 113–126.

Langleben, D. D., & Moriarty, J. C. (2013). Using brain imaging for lie detection: Where science, law, and policy collide. *Psychology, Public Policy, and Law, 19,* 222–234.

Langton, L., & Cohen, T. H. (2008, October). *Civil bench and jury trials in state courts, 2005.* Washington, DC: U.S. Department of Justice, Bureau of Statistics.

Lankford, A. (2012). A psychological autopsy of 9/11 ringleader Mohamed Atta. *Journal of Police and Criminal Psychology, 27,* 150–159.

Lareau, C. R. (2013). Civil commitment and involuntary hospitalization of the mentally ill. In R. K. Otto & I. B. Weiner (Eds.), *Handbook of psychology: Vol. 11. Forensic psychology* (2nd ed., pp. 308–331). Hoboken, NJ: Wiley.

Larson, K., & Grisso, T. (2012, Summer). Juvenile competence to stand trial: Issues in research, policy, and practice. *American Psychology-Law Society Newsletter,* pp. 18–20.

Laughery, K. R., Alexander, J. E., & Lane, A. B. (1971). Recognition of human faces: Effects of target exposure time, target position, pose position, and type of photograph. *Journal of Applied Psychology, 55,* 477–483.

Laurence, J. R., & Perry, C. (1983). Hypnotically created memory among highly hypnotizable subjects. *Science, 222,* 523–524.

Lavigne, J. E., McCarthy, M., Chapman, R., Petrilla, A., & Knox, K. L. (2012). Exposure to prescription drugs labeled for risk of adverse effects of suicidal behavior or ideation among 100 Air Force personnel who died by suicide, 2006–2009. *Suicide and Life-Threatening Behavior, 42,* 561–566.

LaVoie, D. J., Mertz, H. K., & Richmond, T. L. (2007). False memory susceptibility in older adults: Implications for the elderly eyewitness. In M. Toglia, J. D. Read, D. F. Ross, & R. C. L. Lindsay (Eds.), *The handbook of eyewitness psychology: Vol. 1. Memory for events* (pp. 605–625). Mahwah, NJ: Lawrence Erlbaum.

Lee, C. G., with LaFountain, R. C. (2005, October). Felony caseloads in the NACM network. *Caseload highlights: Vol. 12.* Willamsburg, VA: National Center for State Courts.

Lee, C. M., Beauregard, C. P. M., & Hunsley, J. (1998). Lawyers' opinions regarding child custody mediation and assessment services: Implications for psychological practice. *Professional Psychology: Research and Practice, 29,* 115–120.

Lee, S. M., Borelli, J. L., & West, J. L. (2011). Children's attachment relationships: Can attachment data be used in child custody evaluations? *Journal of Child Custody, 8,* 212–242.

Lenton, A. P. (2007). Matters of life and death: Justice in judgments of wrongful death. *Journal of Applied Social Psychology, 37,* 1191–1218.

Leo, R. A. (2008). *Police interrogation and American justice.* Cambridge, MA: Harvard University Press.

Leo, R. A., & Drizin, S. A. (2010). The three errors: Pathways to false confession and wrongful conviction. In G. D. Lassiter & P. A. Meissner (Eds.), *Police interrogation and false confessions: Current research, practice, and policy recommendations* (pp. 9–30). Washington, DC: American Psychological Association.

Leskinen, E. A., Cortina, L. M., & Kabat, D. B. (2011). Gender harassment: Broadening our understanding of sex-based harassment at work. *Law and Human Behavior, 35,* 25–39.

Levi, J. (1990). The study of language in the judicial process. In J. Levi & A. G. Walker (Eds.), *Language in the judicial process* (pp. 3–38). New York: Plenum.

Levine, J. P. (2002). Jury: Right to jury trial. In K. L. Hall (Ed.), *The Oxford companion to American law* (pp. 454–458). New York: Oxford University Press.

Levitt, G. A., Vora, I., Tyler, K., Arenzon, L., Drachman, D., & Ramos, G. (2010). Civil commitment outcomes of incompetent defendants. *Journal of the American Academy of Psychiatry and the Law, 38,* 349–358.

Lidz, C. W., Mulvey, E. P., & Gardner, W. (1993). The accuracy of predictions of violence to others. *Journal of the American Medical Association, 269,* 1007–1011.

Lieberman, J. D. (2011). The utility of scientific jury selection: Still murky after 30 years. *Current Directions in Psychological Science, 20,* 48–52.

Lieberman, J. D., & Arndt, J. (2000). Understanding the limits of limiting instructions: Social psychological explanations for the failures of instructions to disregard pretrial publicity and other inadmissible evidence. *Psychology, Public Policy, and Law, 6,* 677–711.

Lieberman, J. D., & Sales, B. D. (1997). What social science teaches us about the jury instruction process. *Psychology, Public Policy, and Law, 3,* 589–644.

Lieberman, J. D., & Sales, B. D. (2000). Jury instructions: Past, present, and future. *Psychology, Public Policy, and Law, 6,* 587–590.

Lieberman, J. D., & Sales, B. D. (2007). The purpose and effectiveness of voir dire. In J. D. Lieberman & B. D. Sales (Eds.), *Scientific jury selection* (pp. 17–37). Washington, DC: American Psychological Association.

Lindevaldsen, R. M. (2009). Same-sex relationships and the full faith and credit clause: Reducing America to the lowest common denominator. *William & Mary Journal of Women and the Law, 16,* 29–82.

Lindsay, R. C. L., & Wells, G. L. (1985). Improving eyewitness identifications from lineups: Simultaneous versus sequential lineup presentation. *Journal of Applied Psychology, 70,* 556–564.

Litras, M., & Golmant, J. R. (2006). A comparative study of juror utilization in U.S. District Courts. *Journal of Empirical Legal Studies, 3,* 99–120.

Litwack, T. R., & Schlesinger, L. B. (1999). Dangerousness risk assessments: Research, legal, and clinical considerations. In A. K. Hess & I. B. Weiner (Eds.), *The Handbook of forensic psychology* (2nd ed., pp. 171–217). New York: Wiley.

Loftus, E. F. (1975). Leading questions and the eyewitness report. *Cognitive Psychology, 7,* 560–572.

Loftus, E. F. (1977). Shifting human color memory. *Memory and Cognition, 5,* 696–699.

Loftus, E. F. (1979). *Eyewitness testimony.* Cambridge, MA: Harvard University Press.

Loftus, E. F., Miller, D. G., & Burns, H. J. (1978). Semantic integration of verbal information into a visual memory. *Journal of Experimental Psychology: Human Learning and Memory, 4,* 19–31.

London, K., & Ceci, S. J. (2012). Competence, credibility, and reliability of children's forensic reports: Introduction to special issue on child witness research. *Developmental Review, 32,* 161–164.

Luginbuhl, J. (1992). Comprehension of judges' instructions in the penalty phase of a capital trial. *Law and Human Behavior, 16,* 203–218.

Luginbuhl, J., & Middendorf, K. (1988). Death penalty beliefs and jurors' responses to aggravating and mitigating circumstances in capital trials. *Law and Human Behavior, 12,* 263–281.

Luskin, M. L. (2013). More of the same? Treatment in mental health courts. *Law and Human Behavior, 37,* 255–266.

Lykken, D. T. (1959). The GSR in the detection of guilt. *American Journal of Psychology, 43,* 385–388.

Lykken, D. T. (1988). The case against polygraph testing. In A. Gale (Ed.), *The polygraph test: Lies, truth and science* (pp. 111–125). London: Sage.

Lykken, D. T. (1998). *A tremor in the blood: Uses and abuses of the lie detector* (2nd ed.). New York: Plenum.

Lynch, M., & Haney, C. (2000). Discrimination and instructional comprehension: Guided discretion, racial bias, and the death penalty. *Law and Human Behavior, 24,* 337–358.

Lynch, M., & Haney, C. (2009). Capital jury deliberation: Effects on death sentencing, comprehension, and discrimination. *Law and Human Behavior, 33*, 481–496.

Lynch, M., & Haney, C. (2011). Mapping the racial bias of the white male capital juror: Jury composition and the "empathetic divide." *Law & Society Review, 45*, 69–101.

Lyon, T. D., Carrick, N., & Quas, J. A. (2010). Young children's competency to take the oath: Effects of task, maltreatment, and age. *Law and Human Behavior, 34*, 141–149.

Lyon, T. D., & Dorado, J. (2008). Truth induction in young maltreated children: The effects of oath-taking and reassurance on true and false disclosures. *Child Abuse & Neglect, 32*, 738–748.

Lyon, T. D., & Saywitz, K. J. (1999). Young maltreated children's competence to take the oath. *Applied Developmental Science, 3*, 16–27.

Maccoby, E. E. (2005). A cogent case for a new child custody standard. *Psychological Science in the Public Interest, 6*, i–ii.

Maccoby, E., Buchanan, C., Mnookin, R., & Dornsbusch, S. (1993). Postdivorce roles of mother and father in the lives of their children. *Journal of Family Psychology, 1*, 24–38.

MacLaren, V. V. (2001). A quantitative review of the guilty knowledge test. *Journal of Applied Psychology, 86*, 674–683.

MacLin, O. H., & Malpass, R. S. (2001). Racial categorization of faces: The ambiguous race face effect. *Psychology, Public Policy, and Law, 7*, 98–118.

Magnavita, J. J. (2012). Advancing clinical science by using system theory as the framework for expanding family psychology with unified psychotherapy. *Couple and Family Psychology: Research and Practice, 1*, 3–13.

Mahowald, M. W., & Schenck, C. H. (2000). Parasomnias: Sleepwalking in the law. *Sleep Medicine Reviews, 4*, 321–339.

Manahan, V. J. (2004). When our system of involuntary civil commitment fails individuals with mental illness: Russell Weston and the case for effective monitoring and medication delivery mechanisms. *Law & Psychology Review, 28*, 1–33.

Mancini, D. E. (2011). The CSI effect reconsidered: Is it moderated by need for cognition? *North American Journal of Psychology, 13*, 155–174.

Manguno-Mire, G. M., Thompson, J. W., Bertman-Pate, L. J., Burnett, D. R., & Thompson, H. W. (2007). Are release recommendations for NGRI acquittees informed by relevant data? *Behavioral Sciences & the Law, 25*, 43–55.

Manguno-Mire, G. M., Thompson, J. W., Shore, J. H., Croy, C. D., Artecona, J. F., & Pickering, J. W. (2007). The use of telemedicine to evaluate competence to stand trial: A preliminary randomized controlled study. *Journal of the American Academy of Psychiatry and the Law, 35*, 481–489.

Mansour, J. K., Beaudry, J. L., Bertrand, M. I., Kalmet, N., Melsom, E. I., & Lindsay, R. C. L. (2012). Impact of disguise on identification decisions and confidence with simultaneous and sequential lineups. *Law and Human Behavior, 36*, 513–526.

Marin, B. V., Holmes, D. L., Guth, M., & Kovac, P. (1979). The potential of children as eyewitnesses: A comparison of children and adults on eyewitness tasks. *Law and Human Behavior, 3*, 295–306.

Marlowe, D. B., Festinger, D. S., Dugosh, K. L., Benasutti, K. M., Fox, G., & Fox, J. R. (2012). Adaptive programming improves outcomes in drug court: An experimental trial. *Criminal Justice and Behavior, 39*, 514–532.

Marshall, J. (1972). Trial, testimony and truth. In S. S. Nagel (Ed.), *The rights of the accused: In law and action* (Vol. 1). Beverly Hills, CA: Sage.

Martell, D. A. (1992). Forensic neuropsychology and the criminal law. *Law and Human Behavior, 16*, 313–336.

Massoni, G., & Vannucci, M. (2007). Hindsight bias, the misinformation effect, and false autobiographical memories. *Social Cognition, 25*, 203–220.

Mathis, R. D., & Tanner, Z. (1998). Effects of unscreened spouse violence on mediated agreements. *American Journal of Family Therapy, 26*, 251–260.

Mazzoni, G., & Vannucci, M. (2007). Hindsight bias, the misinformation effect, and false autobiographical memories. *Social Cognition, 25*, 203–220.

McAuliff, B. D., & Groscup, J. L. (2009). Daubert and psychological science in court: Judging validity from the bench, bar, and jury box. In J. L. Skeem, K. S. Douglas, & S. O. Lilienfeld (Eds.), *Psychological science in the courtroom: Consensus and controversy* (pp. 26–52). New York: Guilford Press.

McAuliff, B. D., Nicholson, E., Amarilio, D., & Ravanshenas, D. (2013). Supporting children in U.S. legal proceedings: Descriptive and attitudinal data from a national survey of victim/witness assistants. *Psychology, Public Policy, and Law, 19*, 98–113.

McCann, J. T. (1998a). Broadening the typology of false confessions. *American Psychologist, 53*, 319–320.

McCann, J. T. (1998b). A conceptual framework for identifying various types of confessions. *Behavioral Sciences & the Law, 16*, 441–453.

McCann, T., & Sheehan, P. W. (1988). Hypnotically induced pseudomemories—Sampling their conditions among hypnotizable subjects. *Journal of Personality and Social Psychology, 54*, 339–346.

McConkey, K. M., & Sheehan, P. W. (1995). *Hypnosis, memory, and behavior in criminal investigation.* New York: Guilford Press.

McDermott, B. E., Scott, C. L., Busse, D., Andrade, F., Zozaya, M., & Quanbeck, C. D. (2008). The conditional release of insanity acquittees: Three decades of decision-making. *Journal of the American Academy of Psychiatry and the Law, 36*, 329–336.

McGarry, A. L. (1971). The fate of psychiatric offenders returned for trial. *American Journal of Psychiatry, 127*, 1181–1184.

McLawsen, J. E., Scalora, M. J., & Darrow, C. (2012). Civilly committed sex offenders: A description and interstate comparison of populations. *Psychology, Public Policy, and Law, 18*, 453–476.

Megargee, E. I. (2013). Psychological assessment in correctional settings. In J. R. Graham, J. A. Naglieri, & I. B. Weiner (Eds.), *Handbook of psychology: Vol. 10. Assessment psychology* (2nd ed., pp. 394–424). Hoboken, NJ: Wiley.

Meier, J. S. (2009). A historical perspective on parental alienation syndrome and parental alienation. *Journal of Child Custody, 6*, 232–257.

Meissner, C. A., & Brigham, J. C. (2001). Thirty years of investigating the own-race bias in memory for faces: A meta-analytic review. *Psychology, Public Policy, and Law, 7*, 3–35.

Meissner, C. A., & Brigham, J. C. (2005). Memory for own- and other-race faces: A dual process approach. *Applied Cognitive Psychology, 19*, 545–567.

Meissner, C. A., Hartwig, M., & Russano, M. B. (2010). The need for a positive psychological approach and collaborative effort for improving practice in the interrogation room. *Law and Human Behavior, 34*, 43–45.

Meissner, C. A., Redlich, A. D., Bhatt, S., & Brandon, S. E. (2012). Interview and interrogation methods and their effects on true and false confessions. *Campbell Systematic Reviews, 13*, 1–53.

Meissner, C. A., Sporer, S. L., & Schooler, J. W. (2007). Person descriptions as eyewitness evidence. In R. Lindsay, D. Ross, J. Read, & M. Toglia (Eds.), *Handbook of eyewitness psychology: Vol. 2. Memory for people* (pp. 3–34). Mahwah, NJ: Lawrence Erlbaum.

Melton, G. B., Petrila, J., Poythress, N. G., & Slobogin, C. (1997). *Psychological evaluations for the courts: A handbook for mental health professionals and lawyers* (2nd ed.). New York: Guilford Press.

Melton, G. B., Petrila, J., Poythress, N., & Slobogin, C. (2007). *Psychological evaluations for the courts: A handbook for attorneys and mental health professionals* (3rd. ed). New York: Guilford Press.

Melton, G. B., Weithorn, L., & Slobogin, C. (1985). *Community mental health centers and the courts: An evaluation of community based forensic services.* Lincoln: University of Nebraska Press.

Memon, A., Hope, L., & Bull, R. (2003). Exposure duration: Effects on eyewitness accuracy and confidence. *British Journal of Psychology, 94,* 339–354.

Memon, A., Meissner, C. A., & Fraser, J. (2010). The cognitive interview: A meta-analytic review and study space analysis of the past 25 years. *Psychology, Public Policy, and Law, 4,* 340–372.

Meyer, G. J., & Kurtz, J. E. (2006). Advancing personality assessment terminology: Time to retire "objective" and "projective" as personality test descriptors. *Journal of Personality Assessment, 87,* 223–225.

Miethe, T. D., Lu, H., & Reese, E. (2000). Reintegrative shaming and recidivism risks in drug court: Explanations for some unexpected findings. *Crime & Delinquency, 46,* 522–541.

Miller, R. D. (2003). Hospitalization of criminal defendants for evaluation of competence to stand trial or for restoration of competence: Clinical and legal issues. *Behavioral Sciences & the Law, 21,* 369–391.

Mirecki, R. M., Chou, J. L., Elliott, M., & Schneider, C. M. (2013). What factors influence marital satisfaction? Differences between first and second marriages. *Journal of Divorce & Remarriage, 54,* 78–93.

Mitchell, G. (2010). Evaluating judges. In D. Klein & G. Mitchell (Eds.), *The psychology of judicial decision making* (pp. 221–248). New York: Oxford University Press.

Mize, G. E., Hannaford-Agor, P. L., & Waters, N. L. (2007, April). *The state-of-the-states survey of jury improvement efforts: Executive summary.* Williamsburg, VA: National Center for State Courts, Center for Jury Studies.

Mnookin, J. L., & Gross, S. R. (2003). Expert information and expert testimony: A preliminary taxonomy. *Seton Hall Law Review, 34,* 139–185.

Monahan, J., & Shah, S. A. (1989). Dangerousness and commitment of the mentally disordered in the United States. *Schizophrenia Bulletin, 15,* 541–553.

Monahan, J., Steadman, H. J., Robbins, P. C., Appelbaum, P., Banks, S., Grisso, T., et al.

(2005). An actuarial method of violence risk assessment for persons with mental disorders. *Psychiatric Services, 56,* 810–815.

Monahan, J., Steadman, H. J., Silver, E., Appelbaum, P. S., Robbins, P. C., Mulvey, E. P., . . . Banks, S. (2001). *Rethinking risk assessment: The MacArthur Study of Mental Disorder and Violence.* New York: Oxford University Press.

Moore, T. E., & Gagnier, K. (2008). "You can talk if you want to": Is the police caution on the "right to silence" understandable? *Criminal Reports, 51,* 233–249.

Morris, D. R., & Parker, G. F. (2008). Jackson's Indiana: State hospital competence restoration in Indiana. *Journal of the American Academy of Psychiatry and the Law, 36,* 522–534.

Morse, S. J. (1998). Fear of danger, flight from culpability. *Psychology, Public Policy, and Law, 4,* 250–267.

Morse, S. J. (2006). Steel traps and unattainable aspirations: A comment on Kress. *Behavioral Sciences & the Law, 24,* 599–606.

Morse, S. J., & Hoffman, M. B. (2008). The uneasy entente between legal insanity and mens rea: Beyond *Clark v. Arizona. Journal of Criminal Law & Criminology, 97,* 1071–1149.

Mossman, D. (1987). Assessing and restoring competency to be executed: Should psychologists participate? *Behavioral Sciences & the Law, 5,* 397–409.

Mossman, D. (2013). When forensic examiners disagree: Bias, or just inaccuracy? *Psychology, Public Policy, and Law, 19,* 40–55.

Mossman, D., Wygant, D. B., & Gervais, R. O. (2012). Estimating the accuracy of neurocognitive effort measures in the absence of a "gold standard." *Psychological Assessment, 24,* 815–822.

Mosten, F. S. (2011). The future of collaborative practice: A vision for 2030. *Family Court Review, 49,* 282–292.

Moulton, P. L., Petros, T. V., Apostal, K. J., Park, R. V., Ronning, E. A., King, B. M., et al. (2005). Alcohol-induced impairment and enhancement of memory: A test of the interference theory. *Physiology & Behavior, 85,* 240–245.

Moye, J., Marson, D. C., & Edelstein, B. (2013). Assessment of capacity in an aging society. *American Psychologist, 68*, 158–171.

Mueller-Johnson, K., & Ceci, S. J. (2007). The elderly eyewitness: A review and prospectus. In M. Toglia, J. D. Read, D. F. Ross, & R. C. L. Lindsay (Eds.), *The handbook of eyewitness psychology: Vol. 1. Memory for events* (pp. 577–603). Mahwah, NJ: Lawrence Erlbaum.

Mulvey, E. P., & Schubert, C. A. (2012, December). *Transfer of juveniles to adult court: Effects of a broad policy in one court.* Washington, DC: Office of Juvenile Justice and Delinquency Prevention.

Murray, K. (1995). *Live television link: An evaluation of its use by child witnesses in Scottish criminal trials.* Edinburgh, Scotland: Central Research Unit, The Scottish Office.

Myers, B., & Arena, M. P. (2001). Trial consultation: A new direction in applied psychology. *Professional Psychology: Research and Practice, 32*, 386–391.

Myers, D. G., & Kaplan, M. F. (1976). Group-induced polarization in simulated juries. *Personality and Social Psychology Bulletin, 2*, 63–66.

Myers, D. G., & Lamm, H. (1976). The group polarization phenomenon. *Psychological Bulletin, 83*, 602–627.

Naglieri, J. A., & Graham, J. R. (2013). Current status and future directions of assessment psychology. In J. R. Graham, J. A. Naglier, & I. B. Weiner (Eds.), *Handbook of Psychology: Vol. 10. Assessment psychology* (2nd ed., pp. 645–658). Hoboken, NJ: Wiley.

Naglieri, J. A., & Otero, T. (2011). Cognitive Assessment System: Redefining intelligence from a neuropsychological perspective. In A. Davis (Ed.), *Handbook of pediatric neuropsychology* (pp. 320–333). New York: Springer.

Narchet, F. M., Meissner, C. A., & Russano, M. B. (2011). Modeling the influence of investigator bias on the elicitation of true and false confessions. *Law and Human Behavior, 35*, 452–465.

National Association of Counsel for Children. (2006). *Child welfare law office guidebook.* Denver, CO: Author.

National Center for PTSD. (2011, May 25). *PTSD overview.* Retrieved November 15, 2013, from http://www.ptsd.va.gov/professional/pages/fslist_ptsd_overview.asp

National Institute of Justice. (2012, May). *Drug Courts.* Washington, DC: Author.

Neubauer, D. W. (2002). *America's courts and the criminal justice system* (7th ed.). Belmont, CA: Wadsworth.

Nicholson, R. A., & Kugler, K. E. (1991). Competent and incompetent criminal defendants: A quantitative review of comparative research. *Psychological Bulletin, 109*, 355–370.

Nietzel, M. T., McCarthy, D. M., & Kerr, M. J. (1999). Juries: The current state of the empirical literature. In R. Roesch, S. D. Hart, & J. R. P. Ogloff (Eds.), *Psychology and law: The state of the discipline* (pp. 23–52). New York: Kluwer Academic/Plenum.

Nuñez, N., McCrea, S. M., & Culhane, S. E. (2011). Jury decision making research: Are researchers focusing on the mouse and not the elephant in the room. *Behavioral Sciences & the Law, 29*, 439–451.

Nysse-Carris, K. L., Bottoms, B. L., & Salerno, J. M. (2011). Experts' and novices' abilities to detect children's high-stakes lies of omission. *Psychology, Public Policy, and Law, 17*, 76–98.

O'Connell, M. J., Garmoe, W., & Goldstein, N. E. (2005). Miranda comprehension in adults with mental retardation and the effects of feedback style on suggestibility. *Law and Human Behavior, 29*, 359–369.

O'Donohue, W. T., Bietz, K., & Tolle, L. (2009). Controversies in child custody evaluations. In J. L. Skeem, K. S. Douglas, & S. O. Lilienfeld (Eds.), *Psychological science in the courtroom: Consensus and controversy* (pp. 284–308). New York: Guilford Press.

Office of Juvenile Justice and Delinquency Prevention. (2011). *Statistical briefing book.* Washington, DC: Department of Justice, Author.

Ogloff, J. R. P. (1991). A comparison of insanity defense standards on juror decision making. *Law and Human Behavior, 15*, 509–531.

Ogloff, J. R. P. (1999). Ethical and legal contours of forensic psychology. In R. Roesch, S. D. Hart, & J. R. P. Ogloff (Eds.), *Psychology and law: The state of the discipline* (pp. 405–422). New York: Kluwer Academic.

Ogloff, J. R. P., & Douglas, K. S. (2013). Forensic psychological assessments. In J. R. Graham, J. A. Naglieri, & I. B. Weiner (Eds.), *Handbook of psychology: Vol. 10. Assessment psychology* (2nd ed., pp. 373–393). Hoboken, NJ: Wiley.

Okorodudu, C., Strickland, W. J., Van Hoorn, J. L., & Wiggins, E. C. (2007). A call to action: APA's 2007 resolution against torture. *Monitor, 38*, 22.

Olsen-Fulero, L., & Fulero, S. M. (1997). Commonsense rape judgments: An empathy-complexity theory of rape juror story making. *Psychology, Public Policy, and Law, 3*, 402–427.

Olson, E. A., & Charman, S. D. (2011). "But can you prove it?" Examining the quality of innocent suspects' alibis. *Psychology, Crime & Law, 18*, 453–471.

Orcutt, H. K., Goodman, G. S., Tobey, A. E., Batterman-Faunce, J. M., & Thomas, S. (2001). Detecting deception in children's testimony: Factfinders abilities to reach the truth in open court and close-circuit trials. *Law and Human Behavior, 25*, 339–372.

Ormerod, D., & Sturman, J. (2005). Working with the courts: Advice for expert witnesses. In L. Alison (Ed.), *The forensic psychologist's casebook: Psychological profiling and criminal investigation* (pp. 170–193). Portland, OR: Willan.

Orne, M. T. (1970). Hypnosis, motivation and the ecological validity of the psychological experiment. *Nebraska Symposium on Motivation, 18*, 187–265.

Orne, M. T., Dinges, D. F., & Orne, E. C. (1984). On the differential diagnosis of multiple personality in the forensic context. *International Journal of Clinical and Experimental Hypnosis, 32*, 118–169.

Orne, M. T., Whitehouse, W. G., Dinges, D. F., & Orne, E. C. (1988). Reconstructing memory through hypnosis: Forensic and clinical implications. In H. M. Pettinati (Ed.), *Hypnosis and memory* (pp. 21–63). New York: Guilford Press.

Otero, T. M., Podell, K., DeFina, P., & Goldberg, E. (2013). Assessment of neuropsychological functioning. In J. R. Graham, J. A. Naglier, & I. B. Weiner (Eds.), *Handbook of Psychology: Vol. 10. Assessment psychology* (2nd ed., pp. 503–533). Hoboken, NJ: Wiley.

Otis, M. R. (2011). Expanding collaborative divorce through the social sciences. *Family Court Review, 49*, 229–238.

Otto, R. K., & Heilbrun, K. (2002). The practice of forensic psychology: A look toward the future in light of the past. *American Psychologist, 57*, 5–18.

Packer, I. K., & Borum, R. (2013). Forensic training and practice. In R. K. Otto & I. B. Weiner (Eds.), *Handbook of psychology: Vol. 11. Forensic psychology* (2nd ed., pp. 16–36). Hoboken, NJ: Wiley.

Padawer-Singer, A. M., Singer, A. N., & Singer, R. L. J. (1974). Voir dire by two lawyers: An essential safeguard. *Judicature, 57*, 386–391.

Palmer, F. T., Flowe, H. D., Takarangi, M. K. T., & Humphries, J. E. (2013). Intoxicated witnesses and suspects: An archival analysis of their involvement in criminal case processing. *Law and Human Behavior, 37*, 54–59.

Palmer, M. A., Brewer, N., & Weber, N. (2012). The information gained from witnesses' responses to an initial "blank" lineup. *Law and Human Behavior, 36*, 439–447.

Palmer, M. A., Brewer, N., Weber, N., & Nagesh, A. (2013). The confidence–accuracy relationship for eyewitness identification decisions: Effects of exposure duration, retention interval, and divided attention. *Journal of Experimental Psychology: Applied, 19*, 55–71.

Parks, L. S., Tindall, H. L., & Yingling, L. C. (2011). Defining parenting coordination with state laws. *Family Court Review, 49*, 629–641.

Parry, J., & Drogin, E. Y. (2007). *Mental disability law, evidence and testimony: A comprehensive reference manual for lawyers, judges, and mental disability professionals*. Washington, DC: American Bar Association.

Pasework, R., & McGinley, H. (1986). Insanity plea: National survey of frequency and success. *Journal of Psychiatry and Law, 13*, 101–108.

Patterson, C. J. (2009). Children of lesbian and gay parents: Psychology, law, and policy. *American Psychologist, 64*, 727–736.

Pearson, J., & Thoennes, N. (1989). Custody after divorce: Demographic and attitudinal patterns. *American Journal of Orthopsychiatry, 60*, 233–249.

Peisah, C., & Shulman, K. I. (2012). Testamentary capacity. In G. J. Demakis (Ed.), *Civil capacities in clinical neuropsychology: Research findings and practice application* (pp. 95–120). New York: Oxford University Press.

Pember, D., & Calvert, C. (2012). *Mass media law* (18th ed.). New York: McGraw-Hill.

Pennington, N., & Hastie, R. (1986). Evidence evaluation in complex decision making. *Journal of Personality and Social Psychology, 51*, 242–258.

Pennington, N., & Hastie, R. (1992). Explaining the evidence: Tests of the story model for juror decision making. *Journal of Personality and Social Psychology, 62*, 189–206.

Penrod, S., & Cutler, B. L. (1987). Assessing the competence of juries. In I. B. Weiner & A. K. Hess (Eds.), *Handbook of forensic psychology* (pp. 293–318). New York: Wiley.

Perillo, J. T., & Kassin, S. M. (2011). Inside interrogation: The lie, the bluff, and false confessions. *Law and Human Behavior, 35*, 327–337.

Perlin, M. L. (2008). "I might need a good lawyer, could be your funeral, my trial": Global clinical legal education and the right to counsel in civil commitment cases. *Washington University Journal of Law and Policy, 28*, 241–264.

Perry, C. W., Laurence, J. R., D'Eon, J., & Tallant, B. (1988). Hypnotic age regression techniques in the elicitation of memories: Applied uses and abuses. In H. M. Pettinati (Ed.), *Hypnosis and memory* (pp. 128–154). New York: Guilford Press.

Peterson, C. C., Peterson, J. L., & Seeto, D. (1983). Developmental changes in the ideas about lying. *Child Development, 54*, 1529–1535.

Petrila, J. P. (Ed.). (2006). Capacity to consent: A snapshot of contemporary legal and clinical issues. Special Issue, *Behavioral Sciences & the Law, 24*, 719.

Petrila, J. P. (2009a). Congress restores the Americans with Disabilities Act to its original intent. *Psychiatric Services, 60*, 878–879.

Petrila, J. P. (2009b). Finding common ground between scientific psychology and the law. In J. L. Skeem, K. S. Douglas, & S. O. Lilienfeld (Eds.), *Psychological science in the courtroom: Consensus and controversy* (pp. 387–407). New York: Guilford Press.

Pettinati, H. M. (Ed.). (1988). *Hypnosis and memory*. New York: Guilford Press.

Pezdek, K. (2012). Fallible eyewitness memory and identification. In B. Cutler (Ed.), *Conviction of the innocent: Lessons from psychological research* (pp. 105–124). Washington, DC: American Psychological Association.

Pezdeck, K., Avilia-Mora, E., & Sperry, K. (2010). Does trial presentation medium matter in jury simulation research? Evaluating the effectiveness of eyewitness expert testimony. *Applied Cognitive Psychology, 24*, 673–690.

Pfeffer, A. (2008). Note: "Imminent danger" and inconsistency: The need for national reform of the "imminent danger" standard for involuntary civil commitment in the wake of the Virginia Tech tragedy. *Cardozo Law Review, 30*, 277–318.

Pharo, H., Sim, C., Grapham, M., Gross, J., & Hayne, H. (2011). Risky business: Executive function, personality, and reckless behavior during adolescence and emerging adulthood. *Behavioral Neuroscience, 125*, 970–978.

Pickel, K. L. (1995). Inducing jurors to disregard inadmissible evidence: A legal explanation does not help. *Law and Human Behavior, 19*, 407–424.

Pickel, K. L. (2009). The weapon focus effect on memory for female versus male perpetrators. *Memory, 17*, 664–678.

Piel, J. (2012). In the aftermath of *State v. Becker*: A review of state and federal jury instructions on insanity acquittal disposition. *Journal of the*

American Academy of Psychiatry and Law, 40, 537–546.

Pirelli, G., Gottdiener, W. H., & Zapf, P. A. (2011). A meta-analytic review of competency to stand trial research. *Psychology, Public Policy, and Law, 17,* 1–53.

Pokorny, L., Shull, R. D., & Nicholson, R. A. (1999). Dangerousness and disability as predictors of psychiatric patients' legal status. *Behavioral Sciences & the Law, 17,* 253–267.

Popper, K. (1962). *Conjectures and refutations: The growth of scientific knowledge.* New York: Basic Books.

Popper, K. (1968). *The logic of scientific discovery.* New York: Harper & Row.

Poser, S., Bornstein, B. H., & McGorty, E. K. (2003). Measuring damages for lost enjoyment of life: The view from the bench and the jury box. *Law and Human Behavior, 27,* 53–68.

Poythress, N. G. (1979). A proposal for training in forensic psychology. *American Psychologist, 34,* 612–621.

Poythress, N. G., Bonnie, R. J., Hoge, S. K., Monahan, J., & Oberlander, L. B. (1994). Client abilities to assist counsel and make decisions in criminal cases: Findings from three studies. *Law and Human Behavior, 18,* 437–452.

Poythress, N. G., & Zapf, P. A. (2009). Controversies in evaluating competence to stand trial. In J. L. Skeem, K. S. Douglas, & S. O. Lilienfeld (Eds.), *Psychological science in the courtroom: Consensus and controversy* (pp. 309–329). New York: Guilford Press.

Press, S. (2013). Family court services: A reflection of 50 years of contributions. *Family Court Review, 51,* 48–55.

Principe, G. F., & Schindewolf, E. (2012). Natural conversations as a source of false memories in children: Implications for the testimony of young witnesses. *Developmental Review, 32,* 205–223.

Quillian, L., & Pager, D. (2001). Black neighbors, higher crime? The role of racial stereotypes in evaluations of neighborhood crime. *American Journal of Sociology, 107,* 717–769.

Quinsey, V., Harris, G., Rice, M., & Cormier, C. (2006). *Violent offenders: Appraising and managing risk* (2nd ed.). Washington, DC: American Psychological Association.

Rachlinski, J., Johnson, S., Wistrich, A., & Guthrie, C. (2009). Does unconscious racial bias affect trial judges? *Notre Dame Law Review, 84,* 1195–1246.

Rainbow, L., & Gregory, A. (2011). What behavioural investigative advisers actually do. In L. Alison & I. Rainbow (Eds.), *Professionalizing offender profiling* (pp. 18–34). London: Routledge.

Raley, J. A. (2010). Factors to explore in doing child custody evaluations involving gay and lesbian parents. *Journal of Child Custody, 7,* 176–191.

Ramirez, D. A., McDevitt, J., & Farrell, A. (2000, November). *A resource guide on racial profiling data collection systems: Promising practices and lessons learned.* Boston: Northeastern University Press.

Raskin, D. C. (1988). Does science support polygraph testing? In A. Gale (Ed.), *The polygraph test: Lies, truth and science* (pp. 96–110). London: Sage.

Raub, J., & Ciccone, J. R. (2012). Testamentary capacity. *Journal of the American Academy of Psychiatry and the Law, 40,* 287–289.

Redding, R. E., Floyd, M. Y., & Hawk, G. L. (2001). What judges and lawyers think about the testimony of mental health experts: A survey of the courts and bar. *Behavioral Sciences & the Law, 19,* 583–594.

Redlich, A. D. (2010). False confessions, false guilty pleas: Similarities and differences. In G. D. Lassiter & P. A. Meissner (Eds.), *Police interrogation and false confessions: Current research, practice, and policy recommendations* (pp. 49–66). Washington, DC: American Psychological Association.

Redlich, A. D., Kulish, R., & Steadman, H. J. (2011). Comparing true and false confessions among persons with serious mental illness. *Psychology, Public Policy, and Law, 17,* 394–418.

Redlich, A. D., & Meissner, C. A. (2009). Techniques and controversies in the interrogation of suspects.

In J. L. Skeem, K. S. Douglas, & S. O. Lilienfeld (Eds.), *Psychological science in the courtroom: Consensus and controversy* (pp. 124–148). New York: Guilford Press.

Reinhard, M., Scharmach, M., & Müller, P. (2013). It's not what you are, it's what you know: Experience, beliefs, and the detection of deception in employment interviews. *Journal of Applied Social Psychology, 43,* 467–479.

Reisner, A. D., Piel, J., & Makey, M., Jr. (2013). Competency to stand trial and defendants who lack insight into their mental illness. *Journal of the American Academy of Psychiatry and Law, 41,* 85–91.

Reppucci, N. D., Meyer, J., & Kostelnik, J. (2010). Custodial interrogation of juveniles: Results of a national survey of police. In G. D. Lassiter & C. A. Meissner (Eds.), *Police interrogations and false confessions: Current research, practice, and policy recommendations* (pp. 67–80). Washington, DC: American Psychological Association.

Rice, M. E. (1997). Violent offender research and implications for the criminal justice system. *American Psychologist, 52,* 414–423.

Richey, W. (2013, February 19). Unanimous juries for criminal convictions? Supreme Court declines case. *Christian Science Monitor,* p. 2.

Risinger, D. M., & Loop, J. L. (2002). Three card monte, Monty Hall, modus operandi and "offender profiling": Some lessons of modern cognitive science for the law of evidence. *Cardozo Law Review, 24,* 193–211.

Rivers, I., Poteat, V. P., & Noret, N. (2008). Victimization, social support, and psychological function among children of same-sex and opposite-sex couples in the United Kingdom. *Developmental Psychology, 44,* 127–134.

Robbennolt, J. K., MacCoun, R. J., & Darley, J. M. (2010). Multiple constraint satisfaction in judging. In D. Klein & G. Mitchell (Eds.), *The psychology of judicial decision making* (pp. 27–40). New York: Oxford University Press.

Robbennolt, J. K., Penrod, S., & Heuer, L. (1999). Assessing and aiding civil juror competence. In A. K. Hess & I. B. Weiner (Eds.), *The handbook of forensic psychology* (2nd ed., pp. 273–302). New York: Wiley.

Robinson, R., & Acklin, M. W. (2010). Fitness in paradise: Quality of forensic reports submitted to the Hawaii judiciary. *International Journal of Law and Psychiatry, 33,* 131–137.

Roesch, R., & Golding, S. (1980). *Competency to stand trial.* Urbana–Champaign: University of Illinois Press.

Roesch, R., Zapf, P. A., Golding, S. L., & Skeem, J. L. (1999). Defining and assessing competency to stand trial. In A. K. Hess & I. B. Weiner (Eds.), *The handbook of forensic psychology* (2nd ed., pp. 327–349). New York: Wiley.

Rogers, R. (2005). *Miranda Statements Scale* (Unpublished measure). Denton: University of North Texas.

Rogers, R. (2006a). *Miranda Rights Scale* (Unpublished measure). Denton: University of North Texas.

Rogers, R. (2006b). *Miranda Vocabulary Scale* (Unpublished measure). Denton: University of North Texas.

Rogers, R. (2008a). Detection strategies for malingering and defensiveness. In R. Rogers (Ed.), *Clinical assessment of malingering and deception* (3rd ed., pp. 14–38). New York: Guilford Press.

Rogers, R. (2008b). A little knowledge is a dangerous thing . . . emerging Miranda research and professional roles for psychologists. *American Psychologist, 63,* 776–787.

Rogers, R. (2011). Getting it wrong about Miranda rights: False beliefs, impaired reasoning, and professional neglect. *American Psychologist, 66,* 728–736.

Rogers, R., & Bender, S. D. (2013). Evaluation of malingering and related response styles. In R. K. Otto & I. B. Weiner (Eds.). *Handbook of psychology: Vol. 11. Forensic psychology* (2nd ed., pp. 517–540). Hoboken, NJ: Wiley.

Rogers, R., Cavanaugh, J. L., Seman, W., & Harris, M. (1984). Legal outcome and clinical findings: A study of insanity evaluations. *Bulletin of the American Academy of Psychiatry and Law, 12,* 75–83.

Rogers, R., & Ewing, C. P. (2003). The prohibition of ultimate opinions: A misguided enterprise. *Journal of Forensic Psychology Practice, 3*, 65–75.

Rogers, R., Harrison, K. S., Rogstad, J. E., LaFortune, K. A., & Hazelwood, L. L. (2010). The role of suggestibility in determinations of Miranda abilities: A study of the Gudjonsson Suggestibility Scales. *Law and Human Behavior, 34*, 66–78.

Rogers, R., Rogstad, J., Gillard, N., Drogin, E., Blackwood, H., & Shuman, D. (2010). "Everyone knows their Miranda rights": Implicit assumptions and countervailing evidence. *Psychology, Public Policy, and Law, 16*, 300–318.

Rogers, R., Rogstad, J. E., Steadman, J. A., & Drogin, E. Y. (2011). In plain English: Avoiding recognized problems with Miranda miscomprehension. *Psychology, Public Policy, and Law, 17*, 264–285.

Rogers, R., Salekin, R. T., Sewell, K. W., Goldstein, A. M., & Leonard, K. (1998). A comparison of forensic and nonforensic malingerers: A prototypical analysis of explanatory models. *Law and Human Behavior, 22*, 353–367.

Rogers, R., & Shuman, D. W. (2005). *Fundamentals of forensic practice: Mental health and criminal law*. New York: Springer.

Roper, R. (1980). Jury size and verdict consistency: "The line has to be drawn somewhere"? *Law and Society Review, 14*, 977–995.

Rose, M. R., Diamond, S. S., & Musick, M. A. (2012). Selected to serve: An analysis of lifetime jury participation. *Journal of Empirical Legal Issues, 9*, 33–55.

Rose, V. G., & Ogloff, J. R. (2001). Evaluating the comprehensibility of jury instructions: A method and an example. *Law and Human Behavior, 25*, 409–431.

Rosenfeld, B. (2000). Methodological issues in assisted suicide and euthanasia research. *Psychology, Public Policy, and Law, 6*, 559–574.

Rosenfeld, B., & Ritchie, K. (1998). Competence to stand trial: Clinician reliability and the role of offense severity. *Journal of Forensic Science, 43*, 151–157.

Rosenhan, D. L., Eisner, S. L., & Robinson, R. J. (1994). Notetaking can aid juror recall. *Law and Human Behavior, 18*, 53–61.

Ross, D. F., Dunning, D., Toglia, M. P., & Ceci, S. J. (1989). Age stereotypes, communication modality, and mock jurors' perceptions of the child witness. In S. J. Ceci, D. F. Ross, & M. P. Toglia (Eds.), *Perspectives on children's testimony* (pp. 37–56). New York: Springer-Verlag.

Ross, D. F., Dunning, D., Toglia, M. P., & Ceci, S. J. (1990). The child in the eyes of the jury: Assessing mock jurors' perceptions of the child witness. *Law and Human Behavior, 14*, 5–23.

Rotgers, F., & Barrett, D. (1996). *Daubert v. Merrell Dow* and expert testimony by clinical psychologists: Implications and recommendations for practice. *Professional Psychology: Research and Practice, 27*, 467–474.

Rothman, D. J. (1971). *The discovery of the asylum: Social order and disorder in the new republic*. Boston: Little, Brown.

Rothman, D. J. (1980). *Conscience and convenience*. Boston: Little, Brown.

Rozalski, M., Katsiyannis, A., Ryan, J., Collins, T., & Stewart, A. (2010). Americans with Disabilities Act Amendments of 2008. *Journal of Disability Policy Studies, 21*, 22–28.

Rustad, J. K., Junquera, P., Chaves, L., & Eth, S. (2012). Civil commitment among patients with alcohol and drug abuse: Practical, conceptual, and ethical issues. *Addictive Disorders and Their Treatment, 11*, 136–145.

Ryba, N. L., Brodsky, S. L., & Shlosberg, A. (2007). Evaluations of the capacity to waive Miranda rights: A survey of practitioners' use of the Grisso instruments. *Assessment, 14*, 300–309.

Saks, M. J. (1977). *Jury verdicts*. Lexington, MA: Lexington Books.

Saks, M. J. (1990). Expert witnesses, nonexpert witnesses and nonwitness experts. *Law and Human Behavior, 14*, 291–313.

Saks, M. J. (1993). Improving APA science translation amicus briefs. *Law and Human Behavior, 17*, 235–247.

Saks, M. J. (1997). What do jury experiments tell us about how juries (should) make decisions?

Southern California Interdisciplinary Law Journal, 6, 1–53.

Saks, M. J., & Hastie, R. (1978). *Social psychology in court.* New York: Van Nostrand Reinhold.

Saks, M. J., & Marti, M. W. (1997). A meta-analysis of the effects of jury size. *Law and Human Behavior, 21,* 451–466.

Sales, B., Manber, R., & Rohman, L. (1992). Social science research and child custody decision-making. *Applied and Preventive Psychology, 1,* 23–40.

Sanborn, J. B., Jr. (2009). Juveniles' competency to stand trial: Wading through the rhetoric and the evidence. *Journal of Criminal Law and Criminology, 99,* 135–214.

Sangrigoli, S., Pallier, C., Argenti, A.-M., Ventureyra, V. A. G., & de Schonen, S. (2005). Reversibility of the other-race effect in face recognition during childhood. *Psychological Science, 16,* 440–444.

Santilli, L. E., & Roberts, M. C. (1990). Custody decisions in Alabama before and after the abolition of the tender years doctrine. *Law and Human Behavior, 14,* 123–136.

Sauer, J. D., Brewer, N., Zweck, T., & Weber, N. (2010). The effect of retention interval on the confidence-accuracy relationship for eyewitness identification. *Law and Human Behavior, 34,* 337–347.

Saunders, J. (2009). Memory impairment in the weapon focus effect. *Memory & Cognition, 37,* 326–335.

Saunders, J., & Jess, A. (2010). The effects of age on remembering and knowing misinformation. *Memory, 18,* 1–11.

Saywitz, K., Camparo, L. B., & Romanoff, A. (2010). Interviewing children in custody cases: Implications of research and policy for practice. *Behavioral Sciences & the Law, 28,* 542–562.

Schauer, F. (2010). Is there a psychology of judging? In D. Klein & G. Mitchell (Eds.), *The psychology of judicial decision making* (pp. 103–120). New York: Oxford University Press.

Scheflin, A. (1972). Jury nullification—The right to say no. *Southern California Law Review, 45.*

Scheflin, A. (2001). Hypnosis and the courts: A study of judicial error. *Journal of Forensic Psychology Practice, 1,* 101–111.

Scheflin, A. W. (2006). Forensic uses of hypnosis. In I. B. Weiner & A. K. Hess (Eds.), *The handbook of forensic psychology* (3rd ed., pp. 589–628). Hoboken, NJ: Wiley.

Scheflin, A. W. (2014). Applying hypnosis in forensic contexts. In I. B. Weiner & R. K. Otto (Eds.), The handbook of forensic psychology (4th ed., pp. 659-708). New York: Wiley.

Scheflin, A. W., Spiegel, H., & Spiegel, D. (1999). Forensic uses of hypnosis. In A. K. Hess & I. B. Weiner (Eds.), *The handbook of forensic psychology* (2nd ed., pp. 474–498). New York: Wiley.

Schkade, D., Sunstein, C., & Kahneman, D. (2000). Empirical study: Deliberating about dollars: The severity shift. *Columbia Law Review, 100,* 1139–1212.

Schreiber Compo, N., Evans, J. R., Carol, R. N., Villalaba, D., Ham, L. S., Garcia, T., et al. (2012). Intoxicated eyewitnesses: Better than their reputation? *Law and Human Behavior, 36,* 77–86.

Schulman, J., Shaver, P., Colman, R., Emrich, B., & Christie, R. (1973). Jury selection for the Harrisburg conspiracy trial. *Psychology Today, 6,* 37–44, 77–84.

Schultz, V. (2006). Understanding sexual harassment law in action: What has gone wrong and what we can do about it. *Thomas Jefferson Law Review, 29,* 1–53.

Schuster, B. (2007, October). Police lineups: Making eyewitness identification more reliable. *National Institute of Justice Journal, 258,* 2–9.

Schwitzgebel, R. L., & Schwitzgebel, R. K. (1980). *Law and psychological practice.* New York: Wiley.

Scoboria, A., Mazzoni, G., Kirsch, I., & Milling, L. S. (2002). Immediate and persisting effects of misleading questions and hypnosis on memory reports. *Journal of Experimental Psychology: Applied, 8,* 26–32.

Scott, E., & Steinberg, L. (2008). *Rethinking juvenile justice.* Cambridge, MA: Harvard University Press.

Sellbom, M., Marion, B. E., & Bagby, M. (2013). Psychological assessment in adult mental health settings. In J. R. Graham, J. A. Naglieri, & I. B. Weiner (Eds.), *Handbook of psychology: Vol. 10. Assessment psychology* (2nd ed., pp. 241–259). Hoboken, NJ: Wiley.

"Sexsomnia" claim actor Simon Morris guilty of raping girl. (2012, December 17). *BBC News.* Retrieved October 24, 2013, from http://www.bbc.co.uk/news/uk-wales-south-east-wales-20758315

Shaffer, D. R., & Wheatman, S. R. (2000). Does personality influence reactions to judicial instructions? Some preliminary findings and possible implications. *Psychology, Public Policy, and Law, 6,* 655–676.

Shao, Y., & Ceci, S. J. (2011). Adult credibility assessments of misinformed, deceptive, and truthful children. *Applied Cognitive Psychology, 25,* 135–145.

Shear, L. E. (1996). Life stories, doctrines, and decision making: Three high courts confront the move-away dilemma. *Family & Conciliation Court Review, 34,* 439–458.

Shelton, D. E. (2010). Juror expectations for scientific evidence in criminal cases: Perceptions and reality about the "CSI effect" myth. *Thomas M. Cooley Law Review, 27,* 1–35.

Shulman, K. I., Cohen, C. A., & Hull. I. (2005). Psychiatric issues in retrospective challenges of testamentary capacity. *International Journal of Geriatric Psychiatry, 20,* 63–69.

Shuman, D. W., & Sales, B. D. (1999). The impact of Daubert and its progeny on the admissibility of behavioral and social science evidence. *Psychology, Public Policy, and Law, 5,* 3–15.

Siegel, A. M., & Elwork, A. (1990). Treating incompetence to stand trial. *Law and Human Behavior, 14,* 57–65.

Sigall, H., & Ostrove, N. (1975). Beautiful but dangerous: Effects of offender attractiveness and nature of the crime on juridic judgment. *Journal of Personality and Social Psychology, 31,* 410–414.

Silver, E. (1995). Punishment or treatment? Comparing the lengths of confinement of successful and unsuccessful insanity defendants. *Law and Human Behavior, 19,* 375–388.

Silver, E., Cirincione, C., & Steadman, H. (1994). Demythologizing inaccurate perceptions of the insanity defense. *Law and Human Behavior, 18,* 63–70.

Simon, R., & Aaronson, D. E. (1988). *The insanity defense.* New York: Praeger.

Simourd, D. J., & Hoge, R. D. (2000). Criminal psychopathy: A risk-and-need perspective. *Criminal Justice and Behavior, 27,* 256–272.

Singer, M. T., & Nievod, A. (1987). Consulting and testifying in court. In I. B. Weiner and A. K. Hess (Eds.), *Handbook of forensic psychology* (pp. 529–554). New York: Wiley.

Sites, B. (2007). The danger of future dangerousness in death penalty use. *Florida State University Law Review, 34,* 959–996.

Skeem, J. L., Douglas, K. S., & Lilienfeld, S. O. (Eds.). (2009). *Psychological science in the courtroom: Consensus and controversy.* New York: Guilford Press.

Skeem, J. L., Golding, S. L., Cohn, N. B., & Berge, G. (1998). Logic and reliability of evaluations of competency to stand trial. *Law and Human Behavior, 22,* 519–547.

Skeem, J. L., Golding, S. L., & Emke-Francis, P. (2004). Assessing adjudicative competency: Using legal and empirical principles to inform practice. In W. T. Donohue & E. R. Levensky (Eds.), *Forensic psychology: A handbook for mental health and legal professionals* (pp. 175–211). New York: Academic Press.

Skeem, J. L., & Monahan, J. (2011). Current directions in violence risk assessment. *Current Directions in Psychological Science, 20,* 38–42.

Skeem, J. L., & Mulvey, E. P. (2001). Psychopathy and community violence among civil psychiatric patients: Results from the MacArthur Violence Risk Assessment Study. *Journal of Consulting and Clinical Psychology, 69,* 358–374.

Slater, P. E. (1958). Contrasting correlates of group size. *Sociometry, 21,* 129–139.

Slobogin, C. (1989). The "ultimate issue" issue. *Behavioral Sciences & the Law, 7,* 259–266.

Slobogin, C. (1999). The admissibility of behavioral science information in criminal trials: From primitivism to Daubert to voice. *Psychology, Public Policy, and Law, 5*, 100–119.

Smalarz, L., & Wells, G. L. (2013). Eyewitness certainty as a system variable. In B. L. Cutler (Ed.), *Reform of eyewitness identification procedures* (pp. 161–178). Washington, DC: American Psychological Association.

Smith, A. E., & Haney, C. (2011). Getting to the point: attempting to improve juror comprehension of capital penalty phase instructions. *Law and Human Behavior, 35*, 339–350.

Smith, B. M. (1967). The polygraph. *Scientific American, 216*, 25–31.

Smith, S. R. (1989). Mental health expert witnesses: Of science and crystal balls. *Behavioral Sciences & the Law, 7*, 145–180.

Smith, V. L. (1991). Prototypes in the courtroom: Lay representations of legal concepts. *Journal of Personality and Social Psychology, 61*, 857–872.

Smith, V. L. (1993). When prior knowledge and law collide: Helping jurors use the law. *Law and Human Behavior, 17*, 507–536.

Smith, V. L., & Kassin, S. M. (1993). Effects of the dynamite charge on the deliberations of deadlocked mock juries. *Law and Human Behavior, 17*, 625–643.

Smith, V. L., & Studebaker, C. A. (1996). What do you expect? The influence of people's prior knowledge of crime categories on fact finding. *Law and Human Behavior, 20*, 517–532.

Snell, T. L. (2013, July). *Capital punishment, 2011—Statistical tables*. Washington, DC: U.S. Department of Justice, Bureau of Justice Statistics.

Snider, J. F., Hane, S., & Berman, A. L. (2006). Standardizing the psychological autopsy: Addressing the Daubert standard. *Suicide and Life-Threatening Behavior, 36*, 511–518.

Snook, B., Cullen, R. M., Bennell, C., Taylor, P. J., & Gendreau, P. (2008). The criminal profiling illusion: What's behind the smoke and mirrors? *Criminal Justice and Behavior, 35*, 1257–1276.

Snook, B., Luther, K., House, J. C., Bennell, C., & Taylor, P. J. (2012). The Violent Crime Linkage Analysis System: A test of inter-rater reliability. *Criminal Justice and Behavior, 34*, 437–453.

Snyder, H. N., Sickmund, M., & Poe-Yamagata, E. (2000). *Juvenile transfers to criminal court in the 1990s: Lessons learned from four studies.* Washington, DC: U.S. Department of Justice, Office of Juvenile Justice and Delinquency Prevention.

Somerville, L. H. (2013). The teenage brain: Sensitivity to social evaluation. *Current Directions in Psychological Science, 22*, 121–127.

Sporer, S. L. (2001). The cross-race effect: Beyond recognition of faces in the laboratory. *Psychology, Public Policy, and Law, 7*, 170–200.

Stafford, K. P., & Sellbom, M. G. (2013). Assessment of competence to stand trial. In R. K. Otto & I. B. Weiner (Eds.), *Handbook of psychology: Vol. 11. Forensic psychology* (2nd ed., pp. 412–439). Hoboken, NJ: Wiley.

Stahl, P. M. (2010). *Conducting child custody evaluations: From basic to complex issues.* Thousand Oaks, CA: Sage.

Stahl, P. M. (2014). Conducting child custody and parenting evaluations. In I. B. Weiner & R. K. Otto (Eds.), The handbook of forensic psychology (4th ed., pp. 137-169). Hoboken, NJ: Wiley).

Stark-Wroblewski, K., Wiggins, T. L., & Ryan, J. J. (2006). Assessing student interest and familiarity with professional psychology specialty areas. *Journal of Institutional Psychology, 33*, 273–277.

Steadman, H. J. (1979). *Beating a rap?* Chicago: University of Chicago Press.

Steadman, H. J., & Cocozza, J. J. (1974). *Careers of the criminally insane.* Lexington, MA: Lexington Books.

Steadman, H. J., McCarty, D. W., & Morrissey, J. P. (1989). *The mentally ill in jail: Planning for essential services.* New York: Guilford Press.

Steadman, H., McGreevy, M., Morrissey, J., Callahan, L., Robbins, P., & Cirincione, C. (1993). *Before and after Hinckley: Evaluating insanity defense reform.* New York: Guilford Press.

Steadman, H. J., Mulvey, E. P., Monahan, J., Robbins, P. C., Appelbaum, P. S., Grisso, T., . . . Silver, E. (1998). Violence by people discharged from acute psychiatric inpatient facilities and by others in the same neighborhoods. *Archives of General Psychiatry, 55*, 393–401.

Steblay, N. K., Dietrich, H. L., Ryan, S. L., Raczynski, J. L., & James, K. A. (2011). Sequential lineup laps and eyewitness accuracy. *Law and Human Behavior, 35*, 262–274.

Steblay, N. K., Dysart, J. E., Fulero, S., & Lindsay, R. C. L. (2001). Eyewitness accuracy in rates in sequential and simultaneous lineup presentations: A meta-analysis comparison. *Law and Human Behavior, 25*, 459–473.

Steblay, N. K., Dysart, J. E., & Wells, G. L. (2011). Seventy-two test of the sequential lineup superiority effect: A meta-analysis and policy discussion. *Psychology, Public Policy, and Law, 17*, 99–139.

Stein, E. (2012). The topography of legal recognition of same-sex relationships. *Family Court Review, 50*, 181–204.

Steinberg, L. (2010). A behavioral scientist looks at the science of adolescent brain development. *Brain and Cognition, 72*, 160–164.

Steinberg, L., & Cauffman, E. (1996). Maturity of judgment in adolescence: Psychosocial factors in adolescent decision making. *Law and Human Behavior, 20*, 249–272.

Steinberg, L., Cauffman, E., Woolard, J., Graham, S., & Banich, M. (2009a). Are adolescents less mature than adults? Minors' access to abortion, the juvenile death penalty, and the alleged APA "flip-flop." *American Psychologist, 64*, 583–594.

Steinberg, L., Cauffman, E., Woolard, J., Graham, S., & Banich, M. (2009b). Reconciling the complexity of human development with the reality of legal policy: Reply to Fischer, Stein, and Heikkinen (2009). *American Psychologist, 64*, 601–604.

Stewart, J. E. (1980). Defendant's attractiveness as a factor in the outcome of criminal trials: An observational study. *Journal of Applied Social Psychology, 10*, 348–361.

Stewart, J. E. (1985). Appearance and punishment: The attraction-leniency effect in the courtroom. *Journal of Social Psychology, 125*, 373–378.

Stone, A. (1975). *Mental health and law: A system in transition.* Washington, DC: U.S. Government Printing Office.

Stoner, J. A. F. (1961). *A comparison of individual and group decisions involving risk.* Unpublished master's thesis, School of Industrial Management, MIT.

Strand, S., Belfrage, H., Fransson, G., & Levander, S. (1999). Clinical and risk management factors in risk prediction of mentally disordered offenders—more important than historical data? *Legal and Criminological Psychology, 4*, 67–76.

Straus, M. A. (1995). *Manual for the Conflict Tactics Scales.* Durham: Family Resource Laboratory, University of New Hampshire.

Straus, M. A., & Gelles, R. (1990). *Physical violence in American families.* New Brunswick, NJ: Transaction Press.

Stredny, R. V., Parker, A. L. S., & Dibble, A. E. (2012). Evaluator agreement in placement recommendations for insanity acquittees. *Behavioral Sciences & the Law, 30*, 297–307.

Strier, F. (1999). Whither trial consulting? Issues and projections. *Law and Human Behavior, 23*, 93–115.

Strohschein, L. (2005). Parental divorce and child mental health trajectories. *Journal of Marriage and Family, 67*, 1286–1300.

Strohschein, L. (2012). Parental divorce and child mental health: Accounting for predisruption differences. *Journal of Divorce & Remarriage, 53*, 489–502.

Strömwall, L. A., Harwig, M., & Granhag, P. A. (2006). To act truthfully: Nonverbal behaviour and strategies during a police interrogation. *Psychology, Crime & Law, 12*, 207–219.

Sue, S., Smith, R. E., & Caldwell, C. (1973). Effects of inadmissible evidence on the decisions of simulated jurors: A moral dilemma. *Journal of Applied Social Psychology, 3*, 345–353.

Suggs, D., & Sales, B. D. (1978). The art and science of conducting the voir dire. *Professional Psychology, 9*, 367–388.

Sullivan, M. J. (2013). Parenting coordination: Coming of age? *Family Court Review, 51*, 56–62.

Sundby, S. E. (1997). The jury as critic: An empirical look at how capital juries perceive expert and lay testimony. *Virginia Law Review, 83,* 1109–1188.

Sundby, S. E. (1998). The capital jury and absolution: The intersection of trial strategy, remorse, and the death penalty. *Cornell Law Review, 83,* 1557–1598.

Sunstein, C. R. (2008). Adolescent risk-taking and social meaning: A commentary. *Developmental Review, 28,* 145–152.

SunWolf. (2010a). Counterfactual thinking in the jury room. *Small Group Research, 41,* 474–494.

SunWolf. (2010b). Investigating jury deliberation in a capital murder case. *Small Group Research, 41,* 380–385.

Sutker, P. B., Uddo-Crane, M., & Allain, A. N. (1991). Clinical and research assessment of posttraumatic stress disorder: A conceptual overview. *Psychological Assessment: A Journal of Consulting and Clinical Psychology, 3,* 520–530.

Sutton, J. (2011). Influences on memory. *Memory Studies, 4,* 355–359.

Swanson, J. W., Van Dorn, R. A., Swartz, M. S., Robbins, P. C., Steadman, H. J., McGuire, T. G., et al. (2013, July). The cost of assisted outpatient treatment: Can it save states money? *American Journal of Psychiatry.* Doi: 10.1176/appi.ajp.2013.12091152

Swartz, M. S., Swanson, J. W., Steadman, H. J., Robbins, P. C., & Monahan, J. (2009). *New York State Assisted Outpatient Treatment Program evaluation.* Durham, NC: Duke University School of Medicine.

Sweet, J. J., & Meyer, D. G. (2012). Trends in forensic practice and research. In G. J. Larrabee (Ed.), *Forensic neuropsychology: A scientific approach* (2nd ed., pp. 501–516). New York: Oxford University Press.

Sweet, J. J., Tovian, S. M., Guidotti Breting, L. M., & Suchy, Y. (2013). Psychological assessment in medical settings. In J. R. Graham, J. A. Naglieri, & I. B. Weiner (Eds.), *Handbook of psychology: Vol. 10. Assessment psychology* (2nd ed., pp. 315–346). Hoboken, NJ: Wiley.

Swim, J. K., Borgida, E., & McCoy, K. (1993). Videotaped versus in-court witness testimony: Does protecting the child witness jeopardize due process? *Journal of Applied Social Psychology, 23,* 603–631.

Tanaka, J. W., Pierce, L. J. (2009). The neural plasticity of other-race face recognition. *Cognitive, Affective, and Behavioral Neuroscience, 9,* 122–131.

Tanford, J. A. (1990). The law and psychology of jury instructions. *Nebraska Law Review, 69,* 71–111.

Tanford, S., & Cox, M. (1987). Decision processes in civil cases: The impact of impeachment evidence on liability and credibility judgments. *Social Behavior, 2,* 165–182.

Tanford, S., & Cox, M. (1988). The effects of impeachment evidence and limiting instructions on individual and group decision making. *Law and Human Behavior, 12,* 477–497.

Teplin, L. A. (2000, July). Keeping the peace: Police discretion and mentally ill persons. *National Institute of Justice Journal,* 8–15.

Teplin, L. A., & Pruett, N. S. (1992). Police as streetcorner psychiatrists: Managing the mentally ill. *International Journal of Law and Psychiatry, 15,* 139–156.

Tesler, P. H. (1999). Collaborative law: A new paradigm for divorce lawyers. *Psychology, Public Policy, and Law, 5,* 967–1000.

Testa, M., & West, S. G. (2010). Civil commitment in the United States. *Psychiatry, 7,* 30–40.

Texas Defender Service. (2004). *Deadly speculation: Misleading Texas capital juries with false predictions of future dangerousness.* Houston and Austin, TX: Author.

Thomas, J. (2013, January/February). Veterans treatment courts quickly expanded. *National Psychologist, 22*(1), 1.

Topham, K. L. (1997). Borawick v. Shay: The admissibility of hypnotically-induced memories. *Golden Gate University Law Review, 27,* 423–458.

Townsend, E. (2007). Suicide terrorists: Are they suicidal? *Suicide and Life-Threatening Behavior, 37,* 35–49.

Trovillo, P. V. (1939). A history in lie detection. *Journal of Criminal Law and Criminology, 29,* 848–881.

Turkheimer, E., & Parry, C. D. H. (1992). Why the gap? Practice and policy in civil commitment hearings. *American Psychologist, 47*, 646–655.

Tyler, T. R. (1990). *Why people obey the law.* New Haven, CT: Yale University Press.

Uphold-Carrier, H., & Utz, R. (2012). Parental divorce among young and adult children: A long-term quantitative analysis of mental health and family solidarity. *Journal of Divorce & Remarriage, 53*, 247–266.

U.S. Census Bureau. (2011, December). *Custodial mothers and fathers and their child support: 2009.* Washington, DC: U.S. Department of Commerce, U.S. Census Bureau.

U.S. Department of Health and Human Services, Administration for Children & Families. (2011). *Child maltreatment 2010.* Retrieved November 9, 2013, from http://www.acf.hhs.gov/programs/cb/stats_research/index.htm#ca

U.S. House of Representatives. (2010, December). *Federal Rules of Evidence.* Washington, DC: U.S. Government Printing Office.

Vago, S. (2000). *Law and society* (6th ed.). Upper Saddle River, NJ: Prentice Hall.

VandenBos, G. R. (Ed.). (2007). *APA dictionary of psychology.* Washington, DC: American Psychological Association.

Van Koppen, P. J. (2012). Deception detection in police interrogations: Closing in on the context of criminal investigations. *Journal of Applied Research in Memory and Cognition, 1*, 124–125.

Varela, J. G., Boccaccini, M. T., Gonzalez, E., Gharagozloo, L., & Johnson, S. M. (2011). Do defense attorney referrals for competence to stand trial evaluations depend on whether the client speaks English or Spanish? *Law and Human Behavior, 35*, 501–511.

Vidmar, N. (1979). The other issues in jury simulation research: A commentary with particular reference to defendant character studies. *Law and Human Behavior, 3*, 1–6.

Vidmar, N. (2011). The psychology of trial judging. *Current Directions in Psychological Science, 20*, 58–62.

Viglione, D. J., & Rivera, B. (2013). Performance assessment of personality and psychopathology. In J. R. Graham, J. A. Nagleri, & I. B. Weiner (Eds.), *Handbook of psychology: Vol. 10. Assessment psychology* (2nd ed., pp. 600–621). Hoboken, NJ: Wiley.

Viljoen, J. L., McLachlan, K., Wingrove, T., & Penner, E. (2010). Defense attorneys' concerns about the competence of adolescent defendants. *Behavioral Sciences & the Law, 28*, 630–646.

Viljoen, J. L., & Zapf, P. A. (2002). Fitness to stand trial: A comparison of referred and non-referred defendants. *International Journal of Forensic Mental Health, 1*, 127–138.

Viljoen, J. L., Zapf, P., & Roesch, R. (2007). Adjudicative competence and comprehension of Miranda rights in adolescent defendants: A comparison of legal standards. *Behavioral Sciences & the Law, 25*, 1–19.

Virginia Joint Legislative Audit and Review Commission. (2011, November). *Report to the governor and the General Assembly of Virginia: Review of the civil commitment of sexually violent predators.* Richmond, VA: Author.

Virginia Tech Review Panel. (2007). *Mass shootings at Virginia Tech.* Retrieved November 15, 2013, from http://www.governor.virginia.gov/TempContent/techPanelReport-docs/FullReport.pdf

Vitacco, M. J., Erickson, S. K., Kurus, S., & Apple, B. N. (2012). The role of the Violence Risk Appraisal Guide and Historical, Clinical, Risk-20 in U.S. courts: A case law survey. *Psychology, Public Policy, and Law, 18*, 361–391.

Vrij, A. (2008). *Detecting lies and deceit: Pitfalls and opportunities* (2nd ed.). Chichester, UK: Wiley.

Vrij, A., Akehurst, L., & Knight, S. (2006). Police officers', social workers', teachers' and the general public's beliefs about deception in children, adolescents and adults. *Legal and Criminological Psychology, 11*, 297–312.

Vrij, A., & Granhag, P. A. (2007). Interviewing to detect deception. In S. A. Christianson (Ed.), *Offenders' memories of violent crimes* (pp. 279–304). Chichester, UK: Wiley.

Vrij, A., & Granhag, P. A. (2012). Eliciting cues to deception and truth: What matters are the questions asked. *Journal of Applied Research in Memory and Cognition, 1*, 110–117.

Vrij, A., Granhag, P. A., & Mann, S. (2010). Good liars. *Journal of Psychiatry & Law, 38*, 77–98.

Vrij, A., Leal, S., Granhag, P. A., Mann, S., Fisher, R. P., Hillman, J., et al. (2009). Outsmarting the liars: The benefit of asking unanticipated questions. *Law and Human Behavior, 33*, 159–166.

Vrij, A., Mann, S. A., & Fisher, R. P. (2006). An empirical test of the Behavior Analysis Interview. *Law and Human Behavior, 30*, 329–345.

Vrij, A., Mann, S. A., Fisher, R. P., Leal, S., Milne, R., & Bull, R. (2008). Increasing cognitive load to facilitate lie detection: The benefit of recalling an event in reverse order. *Law and Human Behavior, 32*, 253–265.

Wagstaff, G. F. (2008). Hypnosis and the law: Examining the stereotypes. *Criminal Justice and Behavior, 35*, 1277–1294.

Wagstaff, G. F. (2009). Is there a future for investigative hypnosis? *Journal of Investigative Psychology and Offender Profiling, 6*, 43–57.

Wagstaff, G. F., Brunas-Wagstaff, J., Cole, J., & Wheatcroft, J. (2004). New direction in forensic hypnosis: Facilitating memory with a focused meditation technique. *Contemporary Hypnosis, 21*, 14–28.

Wagstaff, G. F., Vella, M., & Perfect, T. (1992). The effect of hypnotically elicited testimony on jurors' judgments of guilt and innocence. *Journal of Social Psychology, 132*, 591–595.

Wainwright, J. L., & Patterson, C. J. (2006). Delinquency, victimization, and substance use among adolescents with female same-sex parents. *Journal of Family Psychology, 20*, 526–530.

Wainwright, J. L., & Patterson, C. J. (2008). Peer relations among adolescents with female same-sex parents. *Developmental Psychology, 44*, 117–126.

Wallace, D. B., & Kassin, S. M. (2012). Harmless error analysis: How do judges respond to confession errors? *Law and Human Behavior, 36*, 151–157.

Wallerstein, J. S. (1989, January 23). Children after divorce: Wounds that don't heal. *The New York Times Magazine*, pp. 19–21, 41–44.

Wallerstein, J. S., & Kelly, J. (1980). *Surviving the break-up: How children and parents cope with divorce*. New York: Basic Books.

Wallerstein, J. S., & Lewis, J. M. (2004). The unexpected legacy of divorce: Report of a 25-year study. *Psychoanalytic Psychology, 21*, 353–370.

Warren, J. I., DuVal, J., Komarovskaya, I., Chauhan, P., Buffinton-Vollum, J., & Ryan, E. (2009). Developing a forensic delivery system for juveniles adjudicated incompetent to stand trial. *International Journal of Forensic Mental Health, 8*, 245–262.

Warren, J. I., Murrie, D. C., Stejskal, W., Colwell, L. H., Morris, J., Chauhan, P., et al. (2006). Opinion formation in evaluating the adjudicative competence and restorability of criminal defendants: A review of 8,000 evaluations. *Behavioral Sciences & the Law, 24*, 113–132.

Warren, J. L., Fitch, W. L., Dietz, P. E., & Rosenfeld, B. D. (1991). Criminal offense, psychiatric diagnosis, and psycholegal opinion: An analysis of 894 pretrial referrals. *Bulletin of the American Academy of Psychiatry and Law, 19*, 63–69.

Warren, J. L., Rosenfeld, B., Fitch, W. L., & Hawk, G. (1997). Forensic mental health clinical evaluation: An analysis of interstate and intersystemic differences. *Law and Human Behavior, 21*, 377–390.

Warrener, C., Koivunen, J. M., & Postmus, J. L. (2013). Economic self-sufficiency among divorced women: Impact of depression, abuse, and efficacy. *Journal of Divorce & Remarriage, 54*, 163–175.

Warshak, R. A. (2007). The approximation rule, child development research, and children's best interests after divorce. *Child Development Perspectives, 1*, 119–125.

Wasserman, J. D. (2013). Assessment of intellectual functioning. In J. R. Graham, J. A. Naglieri, & I. B. Weiner (Eds.), *Handbook of psychology: Vol. 10. Assessment psychology* (2nd ed., pp. 451–501). Hoboken, NJ: Wiley.

Waters, N. L. (2004, August). *Does jury size matter? A review of the literature.* Williamsburg, VA: The National Center for State Courts.

Watson, C., Weiss, K. J., & Pouncey, C. (2010). False confessions, expert testimony, and admissibility. *Journal of the American Academy of Psychiatry and the Law, 38,* 174–186.

Webert, D. R. (2003). Are the courts in a trance? Approaches to the admissibility of hypnotically enhanced witness testimony in the light of empirical evidence. *American Criminal Law Review, 40,* 1301–1327.

Webster, C. D., Douglas, K. S., Eaves, D., & Hart, S. D. (1997). *HCR-20: Assessing risk for violence, version 2.* Burnaby, BC, Canada: Simon Fraser University.

Webster, C. D., Harris, G. T., Rice, M. E., Cormier, C., & Quinsey, V. L. (1994). *The violence prediction scheme: Assessing dangerousness in high-risk men.* Toronto: University of Toronto Press.

Webster, W. C., & Hammon, D. C. (2011). Solving crimes with hypnosis. *American Journal of Clinical Hypnosis, 53,* 249–263.

Weiner, I. B. (2013). The assessment process. In J. R. Graham, J. A. Naglieri, & I. B. Weiner (Eds.), *Handbook of psychology: Vol. 10. Assessment psychology* (2nd ed., pp. 3–25). Hoboken, NJ: Wiley.

Weiner, I. B., & Otto, R. (2014). *Handbook of forensic psychology* (4th ed.). Hoboken: Wiley.

Weinstock, R., Leong, G. B., & Silva, J. A. (2010). Competence to be executed: An ethical analysis post Panetti. *Behavioral Sciences & the Law, 28,* 690–706.

Weiss, K. J., Watson, C., Markov, D., Del Busto, E., Foubister, N., & Doghrami, K. (2011, Summer). Parasomnias, violence and the law. *Journal of Psychiatry & Law, 39,* 249–286.

Wells, G. L. (1978). Applied eyewitness testimony research: System variables and estimator variables. *Journal of Personality and Social Psychology, 36,* 1546–1557.

Wells, G. L. (1984). The psychology of lineup identification. *Journal of Applied Social Psychology, 14,* 89–103.

Wells, G. L. (1993). What do we know about eyewitness identification? *American Psychologist, 48,* 553–571.

Wells, G. L. (1995). Scientific study of witness memory: Implications for public and legal policy. *Psychology, Public Policy, and Law, 1,* 726–736.

Wells, G. L. (2001). Police lineups: Data, theory, and practice. *Psychology, Public Policy, and Law, 7,* 791–801.

Wells, G. L. (2006). Eyewitness identification: Systematic reforms. *Wisconsin Law Review, 2006,* 615–643.

Wells, G. L., & Bradfield, A. L. (1998). "Good, you identified the suspect": Feedback to eyewitnesses distorts their reports of the witnessing experience. *Journal of Applied Psychology, 83,* 360–376.

Wells, G. L., & Bradfield, A. L. (1999). Distortions in eyewitnesses' recollections: Can the post-identification-feedback effect be moderated? *Psychological Science, 10,* 138–144.

Wells, G. L., Leippe, M. R., & Ostrom, T. M. (1979). Guidelines for empirically assessing the fairness of a lineup. *Law and Human Behavior, 3,* 285–294.

Wells, G. L., & Loftus, E. F. (2013). Eyewitness memory for people and events. In R. K. Otto & I. B. Weiner (Ed.), *Handbook of psychology: Vol. 11. Forensic psychology* (2nd ed., pp. 617–629). Hoboken, NJ: Wiley.

Wells, G. L., Malpass, R. S., Lindsay, R. C. L., Fisher, R. P., Turtle, J. W., & Fulero, S. (2000). From the lab to the police station: A successful application of eyewitness research. *American Psychologist, 55,* 581–598.

Wells, G. L., Memon, A., & Penrod, S. D. (2006). Eyewitness evidence: Improving its probative value. *Psychological Science in the Public Interest, 7,* 45–75.

Wells, G. L., & Olson, E. A. (2001). The other-race effect in eyewitness identification: What do we do about it? *Psychology, Public Policy, and Law, 7,* 230–246.

Wells, G. L., Small, M., Penrod, S., Malpass, R. S., Fulero, S. M., & Brimacombe, C. A. E.

(1998). Eyewitness identification procedures: Recommendations for lineups and photospreads. *Law and Human Behavior, 22,* 603–647.

Wells, G. L., Turtle, J. W., & Luus, C. A. E. (1989). The perceived credibility of child eyewitnesses: What happens when they use their own words? In S. J. Ceci, D. F. Ross, & M. P. Toglia (Eds.), *Perspectives on children's testimony* (pp. 23–36). New York: Springer-Verlag.

Wechsler, D. (2003). *Manual for the Wechsler Intelligence Scale for Children—Fourth edition.* San Antonio, TX: The Psychological Corporation.

Wexler, D. B. (Ed.). (1990). *Therapeutic jurisprudence.* Durham, NC: Carolina Academic Press.

Wexler, D. B., & Winick, B. J. (1991). *Essays in therapeutic jurisprudence.* Durham, NC: Carolina Academic Press.

Wiener, R. L., Krauss, D. A., & Lieberman, J. D. (2011). Mock jury research: Where do we go from here? *Behavioral Sciences & the Law, 29,* 467–479.

Wiener, R. L., Pritchard, C. C., & Weston, M. (1995). Comprehensibility of approved jury instructions in capital murder cases. *Journal of Applied Psychology, 80,* 455–467.

Wilson, J. K., Brodsky, S. L., Neal, T. M. S., & Cramer, R. J. (2011). Prosecutor pretrial attitudes and plea-bargaining behavior toward veterans with posttraumatic stress disorder. *Psychological Services, 8,* 319–331.

Winick, B. J. (1991). Competency to consent to voluntary hospitalization: A therapeutic jurisprudence analysis of Zinermon v. Burch. In D. B. Wexler (Ed.), *Essays in therapeutic jurisprudence* (pp. 83–132). Durham, NC: Carolina Academic Press.

Winick, B. J. (1998). Foreword: Planning for the future through advance directive instruments. *Psychology, Public Policy, and Law, 4,* 579–609.

Winick, B. J. (2005). *Civil commitment: A therapeutic jurisprudence model.* Durham, NC: Carolina Academic Press.

Wise, R. A., Pawlenko, N. B., Safer, M. A., & Meyer, D. (2009). What U.S. prosecutors and defense attorneys know and believe about eyewitness testimony. *Applied Cognitive Psychology, 23,* 1266–1281.

Wise, R. A., & Safer, M. A. (2010). A comparison of what U.S. judges and students know and believe about eyewitness testimony. *Journal of Applied Social Psychology, 40,* 1400–1422.

Wise, R. A., Safer, M. A., & Maro, C. M. (2011). What U.S. law enforcement officers know and believe about eyewitness factors, eyewitness interview and identification procedures. *Applied Cognitive Psychology, 25,* 488–500.

Wissler, R. L., & Saks, M. J. (1985). On the inefficacy of limiting instructions: When jurors use prior conviction evidence to decide on guilt. *Law and Human Behavior, 9,* 37–48.

Wistrich, A. J., Guthrie, C., & Rachlinski, J. J. (2005). Can judges ignore inadmissible information? The difficulty of deliberately disregarding. *University of Pennsylvania Law Review, 153,* 1251–1345.

Withrow, B. L., & Dailey, S. D. (2012). Racial profiling litigation: Current status and emerging controversies. *Journal of Contemporary Criminal Justice, 28,* 122–145.

Wolf, S., & Montgomery, D. A. (1977). Effects of inadmissible evidence and level of judicial admonishment to disregard on the judgments of mock jurors. *Journal of Applied Social Psychology, 7,* 205–219.

Woskett, J., Coyle, I. R., & Lincoln, R. (2007). The probity of profiling: Opinions of Australian lawyers on the utility of criminal profiling in court. *Psychiatry, Psychology and Law, 14,* 306–314.

Wrobel, N. H., & Lachar, D. (2013). Psychological assessment in child mental health settings. In J. R. Graham, J. A. Naglier, & I. B. Weiner (Eds.), *Handbook of psychology: Vol. 10. Assessment psychology* (2nd ed., pp. 261–290). Hoboken, NJ: Wiley.

Yarmey, A. D. (1979). *The psychology of eyewitness testimony.* New York: The Free Press.

Yarmey, A. D. (1984). Age as a factor in eyewitness memory. In G. L. Wells & E. F. Loftus (Eds.), *Eyewitness testimony* (pp. 256–272). New York: Cambridge University Press.

Yarmey, A. D., & Kent, J. (1980). Eyewitness identification by elderly and young adults. *Law and Human Behavior, 4*, 359–371.

York, E., & Cornwell, B. (2006). Status on trial: Social characteristics and influence in the jury room. *Social Forces, 85*, 455–477.

Young, S. G., Hugenberg, K., Bernstein, M. J., & Sacco, D. F. (2009). Interracial contexts debilitate same-race face recognition. *Journal of Experimental Social Psychology, 45*, 1123–1126.

Youngs, D. (2009). Investigative psychology in the courtroom: Beyond the offender profile. *Journal of Investigative Psychology and Offender Profiling, 6*, 1–9.

Zaitchik, M. C., Berman, G. L., Whitworth, D., & Platania, J. (2007). The time is now: The emerging need for master's-level training in forensic psychology. *Journal of Forensic Psychology Practice, 7*, 65–71.

Zajac, R., Garry, M., London, K., Goodyear-Smith, F., & Hayne, H. (2013). Misconceptions about childhood sexual abuse and child witnesses: Implications for psychological experts in the courtroom. *Memory, 21*, 608–617.

Zajac, R., O'Neill, S., & Hayne, H. (2012). Disorder in the courtroom? Child witness under cross-examination. *Developmental Review, 32*, 181–204.

Zapf, P. A., & Roesch, R. (2006). Competency to stand trial: A guide for evaluators. In I. B. Weiner & A. K. Hess (Eds.), *The handbook of forensic psychology* (3rd ed., pp. 305–331). Hoboken, NJ: Wiley.

Zapf, P. A., & Roesch, R. (2011). Future directions in the restoration of competency to stand trial. *Current Directions in Psychological Science, 20*, 43–47.

Zeisel, H., & Diamond, S. (1978). The effect of peremptory challenges on the jury and verdict. *Stanford Law Review, 30*, 491–531.

Zhang, K., Frumkin, L. A., Stedman, A., & Lawson, G. (2013). Deception in context: Coding nonverbal cues, situational variables and risk of detection. *Journal of Police and Criminal Psychology, 28*, 150–161.

Zhu, B., Chen, C., Loftus, E. F., Lin, C., He, Q., Chen, C., et al. (2010a). Individual differences in false memory from misinformation: Cognitive factors. *Memory, 18*, 543–555.

Zhu, B., Chen, C., Loftus, E. F., Lin, C., He, Q., Chen, C., et al. (2010b). Individual differences in false memory from misinformation: Personality characteristics and their interactions with cognitive abilities. *Personality and Individual Differences, 48*, 889–894.

Glossary

Accusatorial approach. Refers to the primary way of questioning suspects in criminal investigations. This interrogation process assumes the suspect is guilty, and a primary goal is to obtain a confession. See also Information-gathering approach.

Acquisition. Also called the encoding or input stage. The point at which perception registers in the various areas of the cortex and subcortical regions of the brain.

Actuarial assessment. Completely structured assessment based on how groups of individuals with similar characteristics have acted in the past.

Adjudicative competence. Refers to the ability to understand and participate in a wide variety of court proceedings.

Administrative law. Law created and enforced by representatives of the numerous administrative agencies of national, state, or local governments.

Advance directives. Document specifying one's wishes and directions in the event of physical or mental incapacitation.

Adversarial model. A process adopted by the American judicial system as the most effective way to arrive at the truth in legal disputes or controversies. Two sides each make their case before a neutral decision maker, the judge or jury.

Aggravating factors. Factors surrounding a crime that heighten its seriousness for purposes of sentencing. In death penalty cases, such factors are weighed before determining the sentence.

ALI/Brawner rule. A standard for evaluating the insanity defense. It recognizes that there must be a condition that *substantially* (a) affects mental or emotional processes or (b) impairs behavioral controls.

All-suspect lineup. A lineup condition where there are no distractors or foils who are known to be innocent. All members in the lineup observed by the witness are potential suspects. See also Foils.

Alternative dispute resolution. Programs that offer nonadversarial means to resolve relational conflicts in divorce and other civil proceedings.

Americans with Disabilities Act (ADA). Federal law passed in 1990 that was intended to correct long-standing discrimination in the areas of employment, housing, public accommodations, and education.

Amicus curiae brief. (Latin for "friend of the court") A document submitted to an appellate court by an outside party to call attention to some matter that might otherwise escape its attention.

Anchoring. This refers to giving excessive weight to the initial starting value (the anchor) when decisions are to be made under conditions of uncertainty.

Appellate courts. A higher-level court that hears appeals from trial courts on points of law.

Approximation rule. Rule that, in contested custody cases, the courts presumptively grant custody to the parent that spent the most time performing caretaking functions in the past.

A priori method. Primary approach to obtaining knowledge in the legal system. Logic and systematic reasoning are the means of eliminating doubt.

Arraignment. The court proceeding during which defendants are formally charged with an offense and asked to enter a plea.

Assisted outpatient treatment (AOT). A legal determination that an individual in need of psychological or psychiatric treatment may remain in the community, contingent upon accepting such treatment. Failure to comply may result in hospitalization.

Attachment theory. Theory that emphasizes the dynamics of human relationships, especially those between child and parents or caregivers.

Attraction-leniency bias. The tendency of juries and judges to be favorably impressed by the attractiveness of a defendant and to make decisions in that defendant's favor.

Automatism. Behavior performed in a state of mental unconsciousness or dissociation, without full awareness.

Backfire effect. Occurs when jurors pay great attention to information after it has been ruled inadmissible, such as after being told to ignore a comment by a witness or attorney.

Behavior analysis investigation (BAI). A more scientific term for profiling. BAI considers verbal, paralinguistic, and nonverbal behavior of suspects or unknown or known offenders to aid in the investigation of crimes.

Bench trial. A trial in which the judge, rather than a jury, is the fact finder.

Best interests of the child (BIC) standard. The legal doctrine that the parents' legal rights should be secondary to what is best for the child.

Beyond a reasonable doubt. The standard required for conviction in criminal cases.

Bifurcated trial. When the equivalent of two trials occurs: One decides on guilt, the other on the sentence. Used primarily in death penalty cases.

Blank lineup. A blank lineup comprises only innocent members; it is shown to witnesses before they view a lineup that contains a suspect.

Capital trials. Murder trials in which conviction can result in a life sentence or a sentence of death.

Case-blind consultants. Appointed by the court to provide knowledge about up-to-date research and professional literature pertaining to the family or child development. The case-blind consultant educates the court on a specific relevant issue or topic, such as dealing with children with special needs.

Case law. Also referred to as "judge-made" law. Law based on judicial precedent rather than legislative enactments or statutes.

Case linkage. A method of criminal investigation that seeks similarities between or among different offenses and attempts to tie them to the same offender. See also Profile–crime correspondence.

Categorization. In eyewitness identification, the cognitive process of putting an encountered face into a group category, such as gender, race, and age.

Certiorari. See Writ of certiorari.

Challenge for cause. Dismissal of a would-be juror when it can be demonstrated that he or she does not satisfy the requirements for jury duty.

Civil capacity. The ability to make decisions in legal matters, such as executing a will. Sometimes called civil competency, though the term capacity is preferred in the literature.

Civil law. That part of the law concerned with noncriminal matters pertaining to the rights and duties of citizens.

Clear and convincing evidence. A standard of proof that is more demanding than preponderance of the evidence but not as stringent as beyond a reasonable doubt. It is required in some civil cases, and it may apply in some criminal matters, but not for finding guilt.

Clinically produced profiles. Profiles of suspects based on the profiler's training, experience, knowledge, and intuition or "gut feelings" rather than on actuarial data.

Clinical measures and assessment techniques. Developed for the assessment, diagnosis, or treatment planning of clinical, school, or other populations.

Coerced-compliant false confession. Coerced confession that results from skillful manipulation and police deception under stressful conditions.

Coerced-internalized confession. Confession made by an innocent person who comes to believe he or she is guilty of a crime.

Coercion errors. Errors leading to false confessions that are made when interrogators apply psychological tactics to manipulate the innocent suspect.

Cognitive behavioral viewpoint. With respect to hypnosis, a perspective that maintains that a hypnotized person is not in a special state of consciousness. Rather, hypnosis is a product of certain attitudes, motivations, and expectancies toward the "hypnotic state."

Cognitive biases. Term for the group of decision errors sometimes made by individuals, including judges and other agents of the legal system.

Cognitive interview (CI). A set of rules and guidelines for interviewing eyewitnesses that encourages free recall of what they observed.

Cognitive load. Refers to the idea that interviewers of suspects should try to increase the "work" of answering questions, such as by asking unanticipated questions. More specifically, the interviewer should create conditions that substantially increase the cognitive difficulty of lying compared with truth telling.

Collaborative divorce. Alternative divorce process in which both lawyers and mental health professionals use a problem-solving approach to find a solution that will be satisfactory to both sides. Both parties agree to continue to work toward this outcome.

Combination method of profiling. Method that includes features of both clinical and scientific approaches.

Commitment bias. A phenomenon that once people commit to a certain viewpoint or identification of a face, they are less willing to change their minds.

Common law. Law based on judicial decisions that emerged from customs in a community. The principles of this type of law are often determined by the social needs of the community.

Commonsense justice. What ordinary people (usually a jury) think is just and fair.

Comparison Question Test. See Control Question Test (CQT).

Compensatory damages. Financial compensation intended to make up for the harm suffered by the plaintiff, sometimes also referred to as a way of making the person whole.

Competency to stand trial (CST). Refers to the legal question of whether an individual has the capacity, at the time of the trial preparation and the trial itself, to understand the charges and legal proceedings, and to be able to help his or her attorney in the preparation of a defense.

Composition bias. When too few people in a police lineup resemble the suspect.

Concealed information test. See Guilty Knowledge Test.

Conciliation court. Courts originally designed to assist couples in reconciling and preserving their marriage. Their services became broader over time.

Concurrent jurisdiction. Situation where two or more courts may have the authority to hear a case. For example, a particular law violation may have the potential of involving both federal and state courts.

Conditional release. Applied to mental patients, this refers to release into the community under court or clinical supervision.

Confirmation bias. The natural human tendency to look for information that will confirm our previously held beliefs.

Confrontation. In the legal system, the constitutional right of criminal defendants to face and challenge their accusers, including the victims of their alleged crimes.

Constitutional law. Law based on the U.S. Constitution and the constitutions of individual states. It provides the guidelines for the organization of national, state, and local government, and places limits on the exercise of government power (e.g., through a Bill of Rights).

Contamination errors. Misinformation fed to a suspect or a witness that can be woven into his or her admission to a crime or description of an event.

Control Question Test (CQT). A procedure used by professional polygraphers in which subjects are asked (1) irrelevant or neutral questions, (2) relevant questions, and (3) control questions.

Court-appointed neutral evaluators. Mental health professionals appointed by court to help with decisions about child custodial arrangements. Both parties must agree on the evaluator chosen. The primary goal of the neutral evaluator is to evaluate the family functioning, parenting styles, and relationships as objectively as possible.

Court trial. Also called a bench trial. Trial in which the verdict is rendered only by a judge.

Crime scene profiling. The process of identifying behavioral patterns, motivations, and demographic variables of an unknown offender based on characteristics and evidence gathered at the scene of the crime.

Criminal law. Law that concerns definitions of crime and its punishments as well as associated procedures.

Criminal responsibility (CR). The extent a person is held personally responsible for a criminal act he or she committed.

Criminalization of the mentally ill. Charging mentally disordered individuals with minor crimes such as disorderly conduct or unlawful trespassing in order to justify detaining them in jail, arguably for their own protection.

Criminological needs. The aspects of a person's life that make him or her vulnerable to crime, such as criminal thinking styles or substance abuse.

CSI **effect.** The presumed effect on jurors of television and cable shows depicting sophisticated technology and methods of investigation. Jurors are believed to expect similar sophistication and perfection in actual cases.

Cue utilization theory. The hypothesis that highly anxious or tense individuals will not scan or notice things in their environments as broadly as less anxious individuals.

Cult of curability. Refers to a time period when it was believed individuals could be cured of their mental disorders by untested techniques, many primitive in nature.

Cult of the asylum. Refers to a time period in the 19th and early 20th century when individuals with presumed mental illness were placed in institutions, usually without effective treatment.

Curative instructions. Judicial instructions to the jury that are presumed to correct or "cure" potential errors in the trial process.

Cured-error doctrine. Judicial assumption that warnings to disregard evidence are effective, or at least partially effective, on the thinking process and prejudice of the jury.

Custodial interrogation. Questioning of suspect once it shifts from an investigatory to an accusatory function.

Custody and isolation. The part of the accusatorial approach to interrogation in which the suspect is detained in a small room and left to experience the stress, uncertainty, and insecurity associated with police custody and interrogation.

Damages. Financial compensation in a civil suit. See also Compensatory damages and Punitive damages.

Daubert standard. A widely applied legal standard for determining whether expert evidence has scientific integrity and should be admitted into a court proceeding. It advises judges to consider the relevance, legal sufficiency, and reliability of the evidence.

Death qualification. The process by which potential jurors are deemed eligible to try a case in which a death sentence is a possible outcome.

Death-qualified jurors. Jurors who are not so against the death penalty that they are believed unable to find guilt and recommend a sentence of death.

Decision rule. The proportion of the total number of jurors required to reach a verdict.

Defendant (civil cases). Person or entity that allegedly harmed the plaintiff, the person filing the suit. The defendant in a civil case may also be called the respondent.

Defendant (criminal cases). The person or party against whom prosecution is brought.

Dementia. Refers to a pervasive loss of cognitive function beyond what might be expected from normal aging.

Depositions. Proceedings during which potential witnesses, including expert witnesses, are questioned by attorneys for the opposing side, under oath and in the presence of a court reporter, although typically away from the courtroom.

Differential experience hypothesis. The argument that the frequency of meaningful and positive contacts one has with other races or ethnic groups engenders perceptual skill in accurate facial discrimination.

Diminished capacity or diminished responsibility. This consideration allows the judge to reduce the punishment or severity of the offense, even though the impairment does not qualify as insanity under the prevailing test.

Discovery process. An important component of the pretrial process in both criminal and civil cases. It is the legal requirement that each side must make available some information to the other side in the preparation of its case.

Disposition. In criminal and juvenile law, the sentence a defendant or juvenile offender receives.

Divided custody. Court decision where each parent is afforded legal and physical decision-making powers, but on an alternating basis.

Divorce mediation. Efforts to resolve divorce disputes with the help of a professional mediator. A primary objective of the process is to reduce the adversarial relations between the divorcing parties.

Donative capacity. A person's capacity to give appropriate gifts to charity, organizations, friends, or relatives.

Double-blind lineup. Lineup in which both the witness and the administrator do not know if the suspect is even in the lineup.

Dual-purpose evaluation. In the competency/insanity context, a simultaneous evaluation of both the defendant's competency to stand trial and mental state at the time of the offense.

Dual relationship. Describes ethically questionable dual professional roles, such as when a trial consultant to a legal team provides treatment services to a witness.

Dual system. Refers to the court system in the United States. It consists of federal and state courts, which are interrelated yet independent of one another.

Durable power of attorney (POA). Document in which the individual appoints an agent or agents to manage financial affairs, make health care decisions, and conduct other business. It may be in effect immediately or in the event the person becomes incapacitated.

Durham rule. (Also known as the product rule) A legal standard of insanity where the accused is not held criminally responsible if his or her unlawful act was the product of a mental disease or mental defect.

Dynamite charge. (Also known as the shotgun instruction, the third degree instruction, the nitroglycerin charge, or the hammer instruction) Refers to situations where judges confronted with the possibility of a hung jury implore the jury to reach a verdict by being open to persuasion by the opinions of others.

Ecological validity. The degree of practical or useful application of a theory or idea to the "real world."

Egocentric biases. A common human belief that we or those close to us are above average in abilities or other positive characteristics.

Employment compensation claims. Civil claims by workers, which primarily involve physical injuries that occurred on the job, but psychological injury or emotional distress may be asserted as well.

Equivocal death analysis (EDA). Another term for the psychological autopsy or reconstructive psychological investigation. See Psychological autopsy.

Error rate. The percentage of mistakes or errors that are estimated to occur.

Estimator variables. In eyewitness research, the influences on human perception and memory that can lead to mistakes in identification. Examples are limited exposure time, speed of the event, and a perpetrator's disguise.

Evidence-based psychological practice. Integration of best research with clinical expertise in the areas of patient characteristics, culture, and preferences.

Evidence-driven deliberation style. A jury deliberation style where the jurors decide to delay the vote until after considerable discussion focusing on evaluations of the evidence in the case.

Excessive impairment. The tendency of individuals who are faking cognitive impairment to perform much lower or differently on various tests than expected for cognitively impaired populations.

Expert testimony. Evidence provided by someone with special skill or knowledge to assist the trier of fact in a court proceeding.

Expert witness. One who testifies to facts observed directly, to tests he or she may have conducted, and to the research evidence in the person's field. These witnesses also provide opinions based on their expertise.

Extralegal factors. Factors not relevant to the legal issue at hand, which jurors are expected not to consider.

Falsifiability. The possibility of showing something not to be true. Falsifiability requires that any statement must be so clearly stated that it can be found to be incorrect by systematic observation or careful scientific testing.

Feigned cognitive impairment. A professional conclusion by a mental health professional following neuropsychological assessment that a person is faking symptoms of cognitive dysfunction.

Feigned mental disorders. A professional conclusion by a mental health professional following psychological assessment that a person is faking symptoms of a mental disorder.

Feigning. Deliberate fabrication or gross exaggeration of psychological and physical symptoms without any assumption about why one is doing this.

Foils. Those persons in a lineup who are not thought to be responsible for the crime.

Forced-compliant confession. A confession, usually a false one, that is produced as a result of skillful manipulation and police deception under stressful conditions.

Forensic assessment instruments (FAIs). Measures relevant to a particular legal standard. Examples include measures of competence to stand trial; capacity to understand *Miranda* warnings; or an older person's ability to manage legal, financial, and health care matters.

Forensically relevant instruments (FRIs). Those measures that assess clinical constructs that are often pertinent to evaluating persons in the legal system. Examples include instruments and techniques to assess psychopathy, malingering, neuropsychological issues, and violence risk potential.

Forensic psychology. The acquisition and application of psychological knowledge to the legal system, broadly defined. A narrow definition of forensic psychology restricts this term to clinical work performed for or presented to the courts.

Friendly parent doctrine. Refers to the idea that sole custody is granted to the parent most likely to facilitate the noncustodial parent's involvement with the children.

Frye **standard.** Commonly referred to as the "general acceptance" standard, whereby expert evidence is admitted if it is generally accepted by the scientific community.

Functional size. The number of lineup members who resemble the suspect in physically relevant features.

Gender harassment. Behavior directed at individuals who appear to violate gender ideals, such as women working in a previously all-male environment. Unlike a more narrow conception of sexual harassment, it does not involve unwanted sexual attention and an implication that the victim must be cooperative.

General acceptance standard. See *Frye* standard.

General jurisdiction. Refers to those trial courts that have broad authority to deal with a wide range of issues.

Geographical profiling. Concerned with analyzing the geographical location movements of a single serial offender.

Grand juries. A body of people (usually 23 in number) that is directed by the prosecutor to weigh evidence and decide whether there is enough to charge a person with a criminal offense.

Grave disability. Legal term indicating one cannot take care of oneself. This is a standard for involuntary civil commitment in many states.

Group-polarization hypothesis. The hypothesis that group interaction tends to draw the average individual pregroup decision more clearly in the direction in which it was already leaning.

Guardianship. A relationship created by state law in which a court provides one person (the guardian) with the duty and power to make personal or property decisions for the incapacitated person.

Guilty but mentally ill (GBMI). An option intended to be an alternative to, not a substitute for, the verdict NGRI. It allows jurors a "middle ground" verdict in the case of allegedly insane defendants.

Guilty Knowledge Test (GKT). A method of polygraphy requiring knowledge about a crime or incident not known by the public.

Hindsight bias. Biased judgments of past events after the outcome is known.

HUMINT interrogation. Government interrogation of individuals believed to have knowledge of terrorist activities or other matters that are a threat to national security.

Hypnotic age regression. A hypnotic process where the hypnotized individual is asked to relive an experience from childhood.

Hypnotic hypermnesia. The enhancement or revival of memory through hypnosis.

Hypnotic trance theory. The perspective that hypnosis represents a special state of consciousness that promotes a high level of responsiveness to suggestions and changes in bodily feelings.

Idiographic approach. Emphasizes the intensive study of one individual.

Indictment. A grand jury's formal written statement of the reasons why an individual should be charged with an offense.

Individualized education program (IEP). Typically prepared by an interdisciplinary team that may include psychologists of various specialties in addition to educators and medical personnel. The program must address whether the child has a qualifying disability and, if so, what methods and resources are necessary to ensure that he or she will be educated. The least restrictive setting must also be considered.

Individuation. Extracting individual identity out of a social group.

Information-gathering approach. A gentler form of interrogation than the accusatorial approach. It is designed for investigators to take a more neutral role by probing the suspect's knowledge and information through open-ended questions and a more informal conversational style. Unlike the accusatorial procedure, the information-gathering approach avoids trickery and deceit.

Informed consent. In mental health situations, it is the concept that treatment decisions can be made only by adults who are not under duress or coercion, are told of risks involved, and are told of consequences of not accepting the proposed treatment.

Initial appearance. The appearance of a detained suspect before a court officer that must occur, usually within 24 hours, to assure that there are legal grounds to hold the individual.

Injunctions. Court orders directing someone to do something or refrain from some activity.

Insanity. The mental state that absolves one of criminal responsibility for his or her actions. It must be determined that the person was insane at the time the crime was committed.

Insanity Defense Reform Act of 1984 (IDRA). A law passed by Congress that is designed to make it more difficult for defendants using the insanity defense in the federal courts to be acquitted.

Intimate knowledge. Information about the crime that only the offender and police investigators could know.

Inventories. Term used for personality measures that are based on a self-report format.

Irresistible impulse test. A rarely applied insanity standard that recognizes that, in some instances, an impulse or desire is uncontrollable.

Joint custody. An arrangement where both parents share legal authority, though the children live predominantly with one parent who will have the authority to make the day-to-day decisions.

Judgment. The final decision made by the court. In the civil process, when a verdict favors the plaintiff, the judgment specifies the remedy to be borne by the respondent or defendant.

Jurisdiction. Refers to the authority given to a particular court in resolving a dispute. Jurisdiction is best understood as the geographic area, subject matter, or persons over which a court can exercise authority.

Jury nullification. The power of a criminal trial jury to disregard the evidence or judicial instructions because they believe the law is wrong, nonsensical, or misapplied to a particular case.

Jury simulation research. See Simulation studies.

Least restrictive alternative. The concept, applied particularly in mental health and juvenile law, that people should be held in the least restrictive setting possible, such as a community setting rather than an institution or detention center.

Legal parental authority. Refers to the decision-making authority regarding the child's long-term welfare, education, medical care, religious upbringing, and other issues significantly affecting the child's life.

Leniency bias. A tendency for juries to be more lenient than judges in rendering verdicts.

Limited joint custody. An arrangement where both parents share legal authority, but one parent is given exclusive physical authority and the other parent is awarded liberal visitation rights.

Limited jurisdiction. Refers to entry-level courts, which usually cannot conduct felony trials, although judges in those courts can hold preliminary hearings, issue search warrants, and conduct a variety of pretrial proceedings.

Limiting instructions. Judicial instructions that warn jurors not to use evidence to evaluate or decide on a certain issue, although the evidence may be used for another issue.

Linkage analysis. See Case linkage.

Lost enjoyment of life (LEL). Also called "hedonic damages," LEL damages are intended to compensate for limitations on one's life brought about by injury.

Malingering. Deliberate fabrication or gross exaggeration of psychological or physical symptoms. It differs from feigning because it is done to fulfill an external goal, such as to avoid criminal prosecution.

Mens rea. The "guilty mind" required by an offender if he or she is to be convicted of a crime.

Mental state at the time of the offense (MSO). The term applied to psychological or psychiatric evaluations conducted to determine whether an insanity defense could be supported. Also called insanity evaluations.

Method of authority. A method for eliminating doubt and gaining knowledge that relies on the information provided by experts in the field.

Method of science. Obtaining knowledge by testing statements through systematic research and observation.

Method of tenacity. A method for eliminating doubt that relies heavily on stereotypes, prejudices, and one's prior beliefs.

Minimization. Strategy used by interrogators that includes sympathizing with the suspect about his or her predicament and morally justifying the crime in order to get a confession.

Misclassification errors. These occur when police mistakenly come to believe an individual is guilty of a crime and thereby "misclassify" the individual as guilty rather than innocent.

Misinformation effect. The phenomenon that when people see an event and are later exposed to new and misleading information about it, their recollections often become distorted.

Mitigating factors. In criminal cases, aspects of a person's life which may reduce the penalty (e.g., a childhood marred by extensive abuse). Mitigating factors must be taken into account at the sentencing phase of death penalty cases.

M'Naghten rule. Also known as the right/wrong rule, this insanity standard absolves an individual of criminal responsibility if it is determined that he did not know the nature and quality of his actions or did not know they were wrong.

Mode of death. Refers to the manner in which death occurs, as opposed to the cause of death. The mode generally falls into one of five categories: suicide, homicide, accidental, natural, or undetermined.

Modus operandi. The methods used and behaviors displayed by offenders in committing a crime.

Motivational analysis. Term used in profiling, it refers to seeking the psychological reasons a person may have committed a crime.

Multiple-transition perspective. The idea that it is the number of transitions experienced by children that influences their sense of well-being and adjustment patterns.

Neuropsychology. Deals with studying and assessing the functioning and dysfunctioning of the human nervous system, particularly the brain. In general, forensic neuropsychology is concerned with the diagnosis and consequence of brain damage within a legal context.

No-fault divorce. Allows a divorce to take place if there are "irreconcilable differences," with no one party bearing the brunt of the blame.

Nominal size. The actual number of members within the lineup, which theoretically may include some very dissimilar foils.

Nomothetic approach. A research approach that concentrates on finding general principles, relationships, and patterns that transcend the single individual and combine data from many individuals.

Nonchoosers. Witnesses who do not identify an offender in a lineup or other identification situation.

Nonhypnotic hypermnesia. Enhancement or recovery of memory through non-hypnotic methods, such as free association, fantasy, and recall techniques.

Not guilty by reason of insanity (NGRI). The judicial determination that a criminal defendant is absolved of criminal responsibility because of a mental disorder that significantly affected his behavior.

Objective assessment measures. See Objective tests.

Objective tests. Basically, a test or measure is objective to the extent that scorers can apply a scoring key and agree about the result.

Own-age bias. The phenomenon that witnesses are much more skillful at identifying faces of their own age than they are at identifying faces of other age-groups. Although this bias appears to be particularly relevant to older witnesses, it may apply to other ages as well.

Own-race bias (ORB). The finding that people are better able to discriminate between faces of their own race or ethnic group in comparison with the faces of other races or ethnic groups.

Paper court. Refers to when a case is disposed of by means of paperwork submitted by the respective attorneys or petitions by individuals on their own behalf.

Parasomnias. Sleep disorders that include somnambulism, confusional arousals, sleep sex (known as sexsomnia), and night terrors.

Parens patriae. (Literally, "parent of the country") The doctrine in law that establishes the right of the state to substitute its presumably benevolent decision making for that of individuals who are said to be unable or unwilling to make their own decisions.

Parental alienation syndrome (PAS). Although this syndrome is not widely accepted in the psychological literature, it refers to one parent's strong effort to make the other parent look bad, thereby encouraging the children to become alienated from the other parent.

Parenting coordination (PC). A form of dispute resolution for parents engaged in high levels of conflict following a divorce.

Parenting plan evaluations. Another term for child custody evaluations.

Parenting plans. An important component of custody decision making; they include not only custody arrangements, but also visitation rights for the noncustodial parent and for close relatives to the child.

Pattern instructions. Standard or uniform jury instructions that can be applied across different jurisdictions.

Peer review. Process by which researchers or academicians review one another's theories, research methods, and findings. Generally achieved through the publication process.

Per se admissibility. The presumption that evidence will be admitted into court absent a judicial finding that it cannot be admitted. For example, in some jurisdictions, evidence obtained under hypnosis is per se admitted, although this is not the norm.

Per se exclusion. The presumption that evidence will be excluded from a court proceeding, absent a judicial decision to override that presumption. For example, numerous jurisdictions have per se exclusion of evidence obtained from polygraphs or from hypnotic sessions.

Perceptions. A person's own interpretations of what he or she sees or otherwise senses at any particular moment.

Peremptory challenge. A rule that allows a lawyer to request the removal of a prospective juror without giving reasons.

Performance-based assessment measures. Often combining the best of projective and objective assessments, these measures bring out the individual characteristics of relevant behavior, association, perceptions, emotions, and interpersonal aspects of personality that can be observed, measured, and documented.

Personal injury. Refers to civil suits in which plaintiffs claim they have been physically harmed by the actions of others.

Personality. The combination of individual differences on which a person can be distinguished from others.

Personality inventory. Psychological measures of an individual's personality based on self-reported answers to questions.

Physical authority. A judicial determination that allows a parent to make decisions affecting the child's daily activities, such as deciding whether the child can stay overnight at a friend's house, attend a party, or have access to the parent's car.

Plaintiff. The person or party that initially brings a legal suit.

Polling the jury. A practice whereby jurors are asked individually by the judge, after the verdict is read in the courtroom, whether they assented, and still assent, to the verdict.

Postidentification-feedback effect. Refers to the increase in eyewitness confidence of the person's identification of a suspect after he or she has been reinforced for the information, such as by being told other witnesses have also identified the same person.

Post-traumatic stress disorder (PTSD). The general term for a variety of disorders that can occur after experiencing a highly traumatic event, such as combat, spousal abuse, or sexual victimization.

Preliminary hearing. A pretrial hearing to determine whether there is probable cause to continue with prosecution or, in some jurisdictions, to refer the case to a grand jury.

Preliminary instructions. Instructions given to jurors at the beginning of the trial, before opening arguments. For example, a judge will routinely warn nonsequestered jurors in high-profile cases not to expose themselves to media accounts of the case and not to discuss the case with others or among themselves until it is time for deliberation.

Preponderance of the evidence. The standard of proof applied in most civil cases.

Presentence investigation (PSI). The investigation and subsequent report, typically prepared by probation officers, that provide information to judges that helps them in making a sentencing decision.

Preventive commitment. Committing a mentally disordered individual before he or she meets stringent standards of civil commitment. This is presumably done in the patient's best interest, to prevent further psychological deterioration.

Preventive detention. Denial of bail on the basis that an individual is a high risk for flight or is dangerous to society.

Principle of nonmaleficence. The ethical requirement and understanding among the medical profession that its members do no harm. Evaluations of competency to be executed are believed by some to violate this principle.

Procedural instructions. Those instructions that enlighten jurors about the various rules that apply across a wide variety of cases. For example, the judge informs jurors whether their decision must be unanimous.

Profile–crime correspondence (P-CC). Profilers report the similarity between two or more crimes, which would suggest that the same individual has committed them. See also Case linkage.

Profile–defendant correspondence (P-DC). When profilers report that a defendant fits the psychological profile that is associated with that crime.

Profiling. The general term for identifying personality traits, behavioral tendencies, cognitive and emotional characteristics, and demographic variables of an offender. It includes categories of crime scene profiling, suspect-based profiling, geographical profiling, psychological profiling, and the psychological autopsy.

Projective assessment measures. A variety of measures, including tests, designed under the assumption that personality attributes are best revealed when a person responds to ambiguous stimuli.

Projective tests. See Projective assessment measures.

Psychiatric diagnoses. The labels used to classify various mental disorders, under either the DSM-5 or other classification manuals.

Psychoactive drugs. Drugs that exert their primary effect on the brain, thus altering mood or behavior.

Psychological assessment. Refers to *all* the techniques used to measure and evaluate an individual's past, present, or future psychological status. It usually includes interviews, observations, and various measuring procedures that may or may not include psychological tests and inventories. Also called psychological evaluation.

Psychological autopsy. A procedure that attempts to ascertain the motivations and state of mind of a deceased individual by interviewing, examining documents, or accessing any information that would yield clues to the reasons for the individual's death.

Psychological coercion. Applied to confessions, it refers to any confession that was elicited by illegal methods that promote psychological harm, such as deprivation of food or sleep.

Psychological evaluation. See Psychological assessment.

Psychological profiling. A form of profiling that attempts to predict future behavioral patterns of a known, and sometimes unknown, individual. Threat assessment and risk assessment are two commonly used approaches.

Psychological testing. One component of the psychological assessment process, it is the use of specific measuring devices that include measures of intelligence, aptitude, attitudes, interest, and personality.

Psychology and the law. The relationship identified by Haney in which psychology enjoys its most independent status, conducting basic and applied research into issues faced by the legal system.

Psychology in the law. The relationship identified by Haney in which psychologists provide services to the courts.

Psychology of the law. The most abstract of the three psychology–law relationships identified by Haney. In this relationship, psychologists try to understand ways in which law seeks to control behavior as well as ways in which individuals react to the legal system.

Psychopath. Term used to describe a person who exhibits a collection of psychological, interpersonal, and neuropsychological characteristics that distinguish him or her from the general population, particularly on such factors as callousness and sensation seeking.

Punitive damages. Damages assessed when the harm done is so grave that the judge or jury believes the defendant needs extra punishment. Punitive damages are also intended to deter the defendant and others from committing similar harmful acts in the future.

Quorum jury. One that does not require a unanimous vote to convict.

Racial profiling. Refers to action that relies primarily on the race, ethnicity, or national origin of a person rather than the suspicious actions of that individual. Although usually discussed in the context of police activity, it may also be initiated outside of a law enforcement context.

Reactance. A motive to protect or restore one's sense of freedom. For example, telling jurors to disregard certain evidence is likely to highlight the material in their minds even more, and consequently they are apt to do just the opposite.

Reality monitoring. In the context of child victimizations, this refers to the child's ability to distinguish actual from imagined events.

Reconstructive theory of memory. The position that believes memory is a reconstructive, integrative process, developing with the flow of new experiences and thoughts.

Reid method. Predominant method of interviewing and interrogation used by police in the United States.

Relative judgment error. A process in which the eyewitness mistakenly selects the person in the lineup who most resembles the culprit, relative to the other people in the lineup.

Relocation request. When the noncustodial parent or the joint custody parent opposes the relocation of the custodial parent, and the parent wishing to move must request permission from the family court.

Respondent. Another word for defendant in a civil trial.

Retention. Also called the storage stage. The second stage of memory, when information becomes "resident" in the brain.

Retrieval. Stage of memory in which the brain searches for the pertinent information, retrieves it, and communicates it.

Risk assessment. An effort to determine the likelihood that an individual will be dangerous, based on psychological assessment.

Risky-shift effect. The phenomenon that when people get together in a group to arrive at a decision, they are more daring or "risky" than when they make decisions as individuals.

Scientific jury selection. Refers to the use of behavioral and social scientists by lawyers to find the type of juror who would be most sympathetic to their side of a case.

Sequential lineup. A lineup condition where the eyewitness is presented with one lineup member at a time in sequence.

Sexual harassment. Broadly defined as unwelcome sexual advances, requests for sexual favors, and other unwanted verbal or physical conduct of a sexual nature. See also Gender harassment.

Sexually violent predator (SVP). Someone who (1) has been convicted of committing a sexually violent crime, (2) is determined under the law to have some mental abnormality, and (3) is considered a danger to the public because of the likelihood that he will commit more sexual offenses.

Show-up. An identification procedure in which police present a single suspect to the eyewitness to see if he or she will identify that person as the perpetrator.

Signature. Evidence left at the crime scene that indicates the crime is the work of a specific serial offender.

Simulation studies. Research conducted in a laboratory that is designed to mimic as closely as possible the "real world." Often used in jury research.

Simultaneous lineup. A lineup in which the eyewitness views everyone (commonly six to nine persons) at one time, either live, on videotape, on computer images, or in a photospread.

Single-suspect lineup. A lineup condition where there is one suspect and the other lineup members are known innocents serving as distractors, foils, or fillers.

Sole custody. A judicial ruling where one parent receives both legal and physical custody of the child, although the noncustodial parent usually retains visitation rights.

Souvenir. In profiling terminology, a meaningful item taken by the offender to remember the incident.

Specialized courts. Courts that focus or specialize on particular cases or points of law. Examples in the federal system are bankruptcy courts and patent courts. Examples in state systems are mental health courts and domestic violence courts.

Split custody. A custodial arrangement where the legal and physical authority over one or more children is awarded to one parent, and the legal and physical authority over the remaining children is awarded to the other.

Stare decisis. (Latin for "to stand by past decisions") A doctrine that encourages courts to be slow and cautious about interfering with or overriding principles announced in former decisions.

Statistical, researched-based profiling. Profiling of suspects based on an empirical and systematic analysis of offenders who have previously committed crimes that are considered similar to those being investigated.

Statutory law. Written rules drafted and approved by a federal, state, or local lawmaking body.

Stipulated polygraph test. In this situation, a suspect *against whom evidence is questionable* agrees to take the polygraph test with the understanding that, if he passes, charges will be dropped. However, if he fails the test and does not wish to plead guilty, evidence of the failed test will be admitted at trial.

Story model. The theory that jurors construct in their minds a story of how events—testified to at the trial—took place, even before hearing all the evidence. They then modify their story as more evidence is obtained.

Strict liability offenses. Unlawful acts whose elements do not contain the need for criminal intent, or mens rea. See also Mens rea.

Structured clinical judgment. A trained clinician's judgment that combines his or her own knowledge and experience with relevant knowledge obtained from actuarial data.

Substantive law. Law that defines the rights and responsibilities of members of a given society as well as the prohibitions on socially sanctioned behavior.

Substantive law instructions. Instructions given during or at the end of the trial process on aspects of the law as applied to a particular case. For example, if a defendant is charged with embezzlement, the judge instructs the jury on the elements of that crime and on what must be proved by the prosecution beyond a reasonable doubt.

Support person. An adult designated by the court who provides emotional and informational support, usually for a child, during judicial proceedings.

Suspect-based profiling. A form of profiling in which data are gathered about individuals likely to commit certain types of crimes, such as drug trafficking, terrorist activities, or a school shooting.

System variables. Refers to those variables that can be controlled by people in the criminal justice system when gathering information from eyewitnesses. For example, police officers can control the number of people in the lineup and how closely they resemble the suspect.

Systems theory. Psychological theory that holds that individuals are nested into numerous contexts, such as families, peer groups, schools, and community, and that all of these contexts must be taken into account in explaining their behavior.

Tender years doctrine. A legal assumption derived from the traditional belief that the mother is the parent ideally and inherently suited to care for children of a "tender age."

Termination of parental rights. When a court decides that a parent is unfit to care for the child or children in his or her custody and places the child in the custody of the state or other party.

Testamentary capacity. The cognitive ability to make a will.

Testator. The person who has written and executed a last will and testament that is in effect at the time of death.

Torts. Civil wrongs; harms perpetrated by one person or entity against another or others, but that may not rise to the level of criminal actions. Examples are invasion of privacy, libel, or damage to property.

Totality of circumstances approach. Allows judges to rule on the merits of any claim by focusing on a variety of factors. In the context of hypnosis, this approach would require the judge to consider its reliability, the qualifications of the hypnotist, the purpose of the hypnosis, and the presence of a permanent record of the hypnotic session.

Traumatic brain injury (TBI). TBI is caused by a bump, blow, or jolt to the head or a penetrating head injury that disrupts normal functioning of the brain.

Trial consultation. Often called litigation consultation. Trial consultants (often psychologists) help attorneys prepare witnesses and determine effective strategies for presenting evidence and persuading jurors.

Trial courts. Judicial bodies with primarily original jurisdiction in civil and criminal cases.

Trial jury. Also called the petit jury; the jury that hears facts and arguments and determines whether a defendant is guilty (in a criminal case) or finds for the defendant or respondent (in a civil case).

Ultimate issue. The final question that must be decided by a court, such as which parent should obtain custody of a child.

Unlikely presentations. Response patterns that are unusual and rare for patients with genuine cognitive impairment.

Unstructured clinical judgment. Judgments made by clinicians that are based on experience and knowledge about dealing with a certain clientele, but without reference to actuarial data. Such clinical judgment is controversial, particularly when used to predict dangerousness.

Venire. The pool of prospective jurors drawn from an eligible population presumed to be representative of a local geographical area.

Verdict-driven deliberation style. Refers to a jury deliberation style where the ultimate goal is to reach a verdict as soon as possible.

Viable minorities. In the jury context, defined as at least two members not in agreement with the majority.

Voir dire. A process that allows the judge and attorneys to question the prospective jurors and possibly disqualify them from jury duty.

Voluntary false confession. A false admission to a crime made without external pressure from law enforcement.

Weapon focus. The concentration of some victims' or witnesses' attention on a threatening weapon, paying less attention to other details and events of a crime, resulting in poor recall of some important aspects of the crime.

Work-product evaluator. One who may be called in to perform an objective appraisal of a child custody report and formulate opinions about the strengths and weakness of the report.

Writ of certiorari. An order issued by an appellate court for the purpose of obtaining from a lower court the record of its proceedings in a particular case.

Writ of habeas corpus. A court order that a detainee or prisoner be produced so the legality of the detention or imprisonment can be determined.

Index

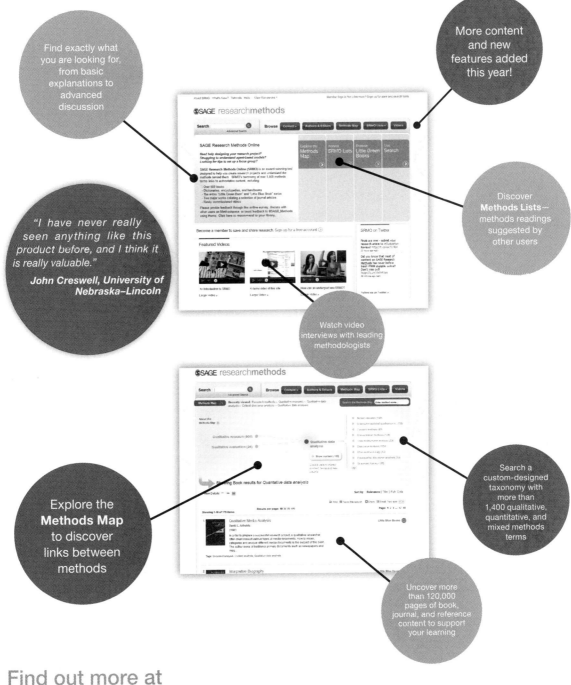